U.S. Policy in
International Institutions

Other Titles in This Series

Presidents, Secretaries of State, and Crises in U.S. Foreign Relations: A Model and Predictive Analysis, Lawrence Falkowski

Congress and Arms Control, edited by Alan Platt and Lawrence D. Weiler

Arms Transfers to the Third World: Problems and Policies, Uri Ra'anan, Robert Pfaltzgraff, Jr., and Geoffrey Kemp

Crisis Resolution: Presidential Decision Making in the Mayaguez and Korean Confrontations, Richard Head, Frisco Short, and Robert C. McFarlane

U.S.-Japan Relations and the Security of East Asia: The Next Decade, edited by Franklin B. Weinstein

Communist Indochina and U.S. Foreign Policy: Postwar Realities, Joseph J. Zasloff and MacAlister Brown

National Interests and Presidential Leadership: The Setting of Priorities, Donald E. Nuechterlein

Political Leadership in NATO: A Study in Multinational Diplomacy, Robert S. Jordan

Foreign Investments and the Management of Political Risk, Dan Haendel

Westview Special Studies in International Relations

*U.S. Policy in International Institutions:
Defining Reasonable Options in an Unreasonable World*
edited by Seymour Maxwell Finger and Joseph R. Harbert

In the immediate postwar period the United States was predominant economically and could command a majority in the U.N. General Assembly; it now faces an increasingly interdependent world economy and an assembly dominated by the third world. The essays in this book analyze the U.N. system as it functions today. Contributors stress the economic issues that constitute most of the agenda—the New International Economic Order, the role of transnational corporations, energy, natural resources, and the new international monetary regimes that are replacing the Bretton Woods system—and the reasonable U.S. initiatives and responses in these areas. They also address the role of the United Nations in peacekeeping and disarmament. The final section realistically examines current institutional structures in the U.N. system and favors active U.S. participation—for lack of a sound alternative—and initiatives to effect institutional improvements.

Seymour Maxwell Finger is professor of political science at the Graduate School and the College of Staten Island, CUNY, and director of CUNY's Ralph Bunche Institute on the United Nations. His service as a career diplomat includes fifteen years at the U.S. Mission to the United Nations where he served as ambassador for four years.

Joseph R. Harbert is currently serving as associate director of the Ralph Bunche Institute on the United Nations. He was formerly assistant director of the Commission to Study the Organization of Peace.

U.S. Policy in International Institutions: Defining Reasonable Options in an Unreasonable World

edited by Seymour Maxwell Finger
and Joseph R. Harbert

with a Foreword by Cyrus R. Vance

Westview Press / Boulder, Colorado

52624

Editors' Note: Westview Press' house style for capitalization was followed throughout this book. We would have preferred upper case usage for all U.N. references, but deferred to the publisher's style for the sake of editorial consistency.

Westview Special Studies in International Relations

All rights reserved. No part of this publication may be reproduced or transmitted in any form or by any means, electronic or mechanical, including photocopy, recording, or any information storage and retrieval system, without permission in writing from the publisher.

Copyright © 1978 by Westview Press, Inc.

Published in 1978 in the United States of America by
  Westview Press, Inc.
  5500 Central Avenue
  Boulder, Colorado 80301
  Frederick A. Praeger, Publisher

Library of Congress Cataloging in Publication Data
Main entry under title:
U.S. policy in international institutions.
  (Westview special studies in international relations)
  Bibliography: p.
  Includes index.
  1. United States—Foreign relations—1945- —Addresses, essays, lectures. 2. United Nations—Addresses, essays, lectures. 3. International agencies—Addresses, essays, lectures. 4. International economic relations—Addresses, essays, lectures.
I. Finger, Seymour Maxwell, 1915- II. Harbert, Joseph R.
JX1417.U57 1978   327.73   78-4335
ISBN 0-89158-077-8
ISBN 0-89158-078-6 pbk.

Printed and bound in the United States of America

To my parents
J. R. H.

To Helen
S. M. F.

Contents

Foreword, *Cyrus R. Vance* xiii
Acknowledgments xvii
The Contributors xix

The U.S. Role in International Institutions: A Redefinition,
Joseph R. Harbert 1

Part One: The United Nations and U.S. Political and Security Objectives

Introduction, *Seymour Maxwell Finger* 9

Disarmament and Arms Control
1. Measures Necessary to Curb Nuclear Proliferation,
   William Epstein 15
2. Nuclear Arms Control: A New U.S. Strategy at the
   United Nations, *Abraham Bargman* 28
3. Approaches to Arms Control and Disarmament,
   Commission to Study the Organization of Peace 40

Peacekeeping
4. The U.N. Peacekeeping Role, *Ruth B. Russell* 57
5. Breaking the Deadlock on U.N. Peacekeeping,
   Seymour Maxwell Finger 62
6. U.N. Peacekeeping and the U.S. National Interest,
   Seymour Maxwell Finger 71

Southern Africa

7. America and Southern Africa, *Julius K. Nyerere* 79
8. U.S. Policy Toward Africa, *Cyrus R. Vance* 93
9. The United States, the United Nations, and Southern Africa, *Wentworth B. Ofuatey-Kodjoe* 100

Part Two: The United States in a Changing International Economic Order

Introduction, *Myer Cohen* 123

The New International Economic Order

10. The New International Economic Order: Toward Structural Changes or a More Tolerable Status Quo?, *Karl P. Sauvant* 125
11. Interdependence and the Reform of International Institutions, *C. Fred Bergsten* 147
12. A Western View of UNCTAD IV, *Paxton T. Dunn* 161

Multinational Corporations

13. Economics, Politics, and the Multinational Corporation, *Robert Gilpin* 167
14. Multinational Corporations in World Politics, *Joseph S. Nye, Jr.* 173
15. The Multinational Corporation: A Corporate View, *Walter B. Wriston* 195
16. The United Nations and Transnational Corporations, *Klaus A. Sahlgren* 203

Monetary and Trade Policies

17. A Monetary Regime for the 1980s, *Edward L. Morse* 211
18. Monetary Reform at Jamaica, *Richard N. Cooper* 224
19. The Institutionalization of Exchange Rates, *Robert Roosa* 230

Part Three: Global Resources and U.S. Interests

Introduction, *Joseph R. Harbert* 241

20. Some Current Problems of Global Cooperation, *Philippe de Seynes* 245
21. American Objectives and the Law of the Sea, *Daniel S. Cheever* 255

22. Ship Aground: U.S. Law of the Sea Policy at the
    United Nations, *John J. Logue* 265
23. The United States in Search of an International
    Energy Policy: Global/Regional Tradeoffs,
    Richard E. Bissell 275
24. Energy Independence—Is It Feasible and
    Desirable?, *Joseph Barnea* 286
25. U.S. Raw Materials Policy: The Pros and Cons of
    Self-Sufficiency, *Bension Varon* 291

Part Four: The U.S. Role in a Changing United Nations

Introduction, *Leland M. Goodrich* 309

U.N. Structures and Procedures
26. Decision Making on Economic and Social Questions
    in the United Nations, *James Frederick Green* 313
27. The Structuring of International Cooperation,
    Robert S. Jordan 327
28. International Law and Majority Rule: The Case
    for Conservatism, *Alice B. Haemmerli* 338
29. Security Council Function and Membership,
    Lawrence S. Finkelstein 363
30. Voting in the Security Council and the PLO,
    Leo Gross 388

The U.S. Role in the U.N. System
31. American Policies in the United Nations,
    Charles William Maynes 403
32. U.S. Policy Toward International Institutions,
    Seymour Maxwell Finger 419
33. U.S. Foreign Policy and the United Nations,
    Abraham Yeselson and Anthony Gaglione 435
34. A New U.S. Policy Toward the United Nations,
    *Ad Hoc Group on United States Policy Toward the
    United Nations* 449
35. American Goals in a Changing United Nations,
    Philip M. Klutznick 464

Selected Bibliography..................................... 473
Index 485

Foreword

Cyrus R. Vance

The United Nations was born into a world ravaged and wearied by war. In 1945 there was much to hope for, but also much to fear. How could peace, achieved at such terrible cost, be secured? It was not surprising that the opening words of the United Nations Charter spoke of the determination of our peoples "to save succeeding generations from the scourge of war, which twice in our lifetime has brought untold sorrow to mankind."

But the charter and the United Nations were meant to stand the tests of time. The charter's opening statement also speaks of concerns we share now in an interdependent world; a world recovered from the devastation of war, though still far from reaching a state of universal well-being. Today food, resources, the human condition, and economic development are recognized as matters of life and death. What we do about them, unilaterally and multilaterally, has come to be as important as what we do about the danger of great powers' use of arms. Thus, the U.N. Charter is as relevant today as it was thirty-two years ago in its statement of our determination not only to advance international law and justice, but also "to reaffirm faith in fundamental human rights," and "to promote social progress and better standards of life in larger freedom."

Now, even more than in 1945, we face global issues that transcend great power diplomacy: issues of need and want, of resources and access to them. Unless we learn how to deal with such issues through the family of organizations that has grown up around the United Nations, we are in danger of falling back into a modern version of tribal feuding: strategically based large states unwilling to take their international obligations seriously; countries joining in powerful factions or numerical majorities to press arbitrary demands. And everywhere forces challenge our mastery of our own destinies: the proliferation of nuclear and conventional arms, and the menace of political terrorism haunt us in all their ugly forms.

A family is composed of members, each strong and each vulnerable in their own ways. The U.N. family of nations has grown from 50 in 1945 to nearly 150 today. And as the issues that concern the U.N. family have multiplied and changed, so have our methods of dealing with those issues, and with each other. The pattern is away from domination of world affairs by the few, toward interdependence among the many.

The reasons are clear. So long as the dominant issues on the international agenda had to do with military matters and world security, the great powers, with their overwhelming military capabilities, led the way. Today, those issues are rivaled in importance by economic and social issues that do not automatically fall into "great power"-"lesser power" patterns. All nations—large and small, rich and poor—face common social and economic problems such as inflation, population control, and threats to the environment. Other fields of international relations such as economic development, management of resources, and control of real or potential instruments of destruction no longer merely mark old divisions between have and have-not nations. Today they are the issues of interdependence. They are the issues on which haves and have-nots must find common ground if mankind is to know a better, safer, and more worthwhile way of life.

The relative positions of great and lesser nations have not stood still. India is now one of the world's ten most important industrial powers. Nigeria is now a larger trading partner of Great Britain's than South Africa. Countries like Mexico and Brazil have achieved an industrial prominence that is astonishing when compared to twenty-five years ago.

We can more readily see the effects of such changes in comparisons like these: In 1950, the United States represented 60 percent of the world's manufacturing capacity; today the figure is 30 percent. In 1950, the United States accounted for 50 percent of the world's military spending; today the figure is half that. In 1950, the United States possessed 50 percent of the world's monetary reserves; today only 7 percent. This has happened not because we have fallen back, but because others (often with our help) have finally begun to make their way. The new prosperity of other nations is a major achievement of the postwar era.

These trends have inevitably affected the way international

institutions work. When we were the predominant force in both economic and military affairs—when, as in the late 1940s and early 1950s, we contributed close to half of the U.N.'s budget—there was no question from whom the United Nations and associated international organizations took their lead. The U.N. system had, in effect, a built-in mechanism of leadership. The mere announcement of a policy by the United States immediately drew support from other countries. Today no power has comparable attractive force for others.

We have worked toward the end of colonialism, new-found power for countries that formerly took a back seat in world affairs, and the growth of democracy in relations among nations, but there is no denying that the consequences for the United Nations and other international organizations have not always been happy. In particular, since no nation's power in the U.N. system is so overwhelming that leadership flows automatically to it, the effectiveness, force, and direction the United Nations can muster is in danger of erosion. And there is nothing we alone can do about it.

A major goal for the United Nations in years to come will be to encourage partnerships and coalitions of nations that share concerns about critical regional and global issues. We cannot escape these issues, and we cannot deal with them in unilateral fashion if we hope to be effective. Seventeen years ago, one of the drafters of the U.N. Charter, Benjamin V. Cohen, spoke of the United Nations in terms that apply today: "The more affirmative the tasks of the United Nations may be, the greater the need for developing a consensus of thinking that will make active cooperation possible and meaningful. . . . In this quest for consensus there is no role for dogmatism and self-righteousness. I would close no doors. In the United Nations, as 'in my Father's house,' there 'are many mansions.'"

Gathered here is a remarkable and timely collection of viewpoints about the world as it is in this fourth decade of the United Nations. The contributors share the perception that we face hard choices in working together through the U.N. family of international institutions, but that there will be worse choices to make if we fail in that joint endeavor. The intention of this volume is to chart a realistic course for that embodiment of idealism, international organization, in full light of how the world has evolved since the birth of the United Nations. It succeeds admirably.

Acknowledgments

We would like to express our thanks to a number of people and organizations whose help was invaluable. First and foremost, we owe a debt of gratitude to the Graduate School of the City University of New York, to its president, Harold M. Proshansky, and to Benjamin Rivlin, Dean for University and Special Programs, for the financial and spiritual assistance they provided to the Ralph Bunche Institute on the United Nations over the past two years. In particular, a CUNY Summer Institute grant supported the Conference on U.S. Objectives in the U.N. System and served as the catalyst for this volume.

A number of people who worked hard for the conference itself deserve our special thanks as well: Myer Cohen, Leon Gordenker, David A. Kay, and James F. Leonard chaired and guided the conference working groups; Leland M. Goodrich provided wise counsel in planning the conference; and Cleveland DaCosta, Mark Donnelly, Ilya Levkov, Elan Steinberg, and especially Phyllis R. Craig served as conference rapporteurs.

We would also like to thank the contributors to this volume for their patience and support. We are grateful to the publishers and journals that granted us reprint rights for some of the articles. Others who were helpful during various stages of our work include Margaret Novicki, who provided valuable assistance on the index; Jacques Fomerand, who supplied the bibliography; Marilyn Stevens, who assisted with typing and editing; Michaela Weininger-Richter, who did highly creative and professional editorial work on a number of the articles; and Nancy Okada, whose good cheer and good sense have kept the Ralph Bunche Institute intact these last two years.

Seymour Maxwell Finger
Joseph R. Harbert

The Contributors

Abraham Bargman, formerly of the Disarmament Affairs Division of the U.N. Secretariat. Currently professor of political science at Brooklyn College, City University of New York

Joseph Barnea, research fellow, UNITAR

C. Fred Bergsten, assistant secretary of the treasury for international affairs

Richard E. Bissell, managing editor, *ORBIS*

Daniel S. Cheever, professor, Graduate School of Public and International Affairs, University of Pittsburgh

Myer Cohen, senior consultant, International Development Research Center

Commission to Study the Organization of Peace, a New York nongovernmental organization which does research on current issues before the United Nations

Richard N. Cooper, under secretary of state for economic affairs

John De Gara, special fellow, UNITAR

Philippe de Seynes, director, Special Project on the Future, UNITAR. Formerly U.N. under secretary-general for economic and social affairs

Paxton T. Dunn, chief economist, United States Council of the International Chamber of Commerce

William Epstein, special fellow, UNITAR, and university visiting professor, University of Victoria

Seymour M. Finger, director, Ralph Bunche Institute on the United Nations, and professor of political science, Graduate School, City University of New York and College of Staten Island

Lawrence S. Finkelstein, professor, Political Science Department, University of Northern Illinois

Anthony Gaglione, professor, East Stroudsberg State College

Robert Gilpin, professor, Princeton University

Leland M. Goodrich, Shotwell Professor Emeritus, Columbia University

James Frederick Green, executive director, Commission to Study the Organization of Peace

Leo Gross, professor, Fletcher School of Law and Diplomacy

Alice B. Haemmerli, director, Conference Program, Chase World Information Corporation

Joseph R. Harbert, associate director, Ralph Bunche Institute on the United Nations, City University of New York

Robert S. Jordan, director of research, UNITAR

Philip M. Klutznick, formerly U.S. representative to the U.N. Economic and Social Council

John J. Logue, director, World Order Research Institute, Villanova University

Charles William Maynes, former secretary of the Carnegie Endowment for International Peace

Edward L. Morse, senior fellow, Council on Foreign Relations

Joseph S. Nye, former professor, Harvard University. Presently deputy to the under secretary of state for security assistance

Julius K. Nyerere, president of the United Republic of Tanzania

Wentworth B. Ofuatey-Kodjoe, associate professor of political science, Queens College, City University of New York

The Contributors

Robert Roosa, partner, Brown Brothers, Harriman. Formerly under secretary of the treasury

Ruth Russell, author, former research associate, Brookings Institution and Columbia University

Klaus A. Sahlgren, director, U.N. Center on Transnational Corporations

Karl P. Sauvant, transnational corporations affairs officer, Centre on Transnational Corporations, United Nations

Cyrus R. Vance, U.S. secretary of state

Bension Varon, former assistant director, Policies and Projections, United Nations Centre on National Resources. Currently senior economist at the World Bank

Walter B. Wriston, chairman, Citibank, N.A.

Abraham Yeselson, chairman, Political Science Department, Rutgers University

The U.S. Role in International Institutions: A Redefinition
Joseph R. Harbert

Roots

In recent years both the composition of the U.N. system and the focus on its activity have changed dramatically. In the United Nations proper a new majority of third world countries has come to dominate the agenda and challenge the views and policies promulgated by the United States and the West over the last thirty years. Quite naturally the actions of this new majority have created doubts in this country about the value of the United Nations for the United States. Indeed, there has developed a new school of thought about U.S. participation in the traditional multilateral fora.

This popular realist view stems from several sources. First, there has always been a segment of American public opinion which has opposed U.S. participation in the United Nations. Second, as United Nations membership has expanded and its character has changed, the issues discussed have been those of concern to the less-developed countries. In most cases the United States has found itself increasingly in the minority, isolated—a somewhat humbled giant. Moreover, the increasingly offensive rhetoric and actions in the General Assembly against Israel have alienated many Americans. In addition, much of this has taken place during the Nixon-Ford-Kissinger administrations which stressed bilateral foreign relations rather than the use of multilateral institutions to promote American interests. Finally, it seems to have taken many Americans over thirty years to lose the hope that the United Nations would deal effectively with problems of peace and security. The 1970s, therefore, have been our real years of disenchantment with the United Nations.

Given these roots of the emerging popular realist view it is not surprising to see academic scholarship begin to catch up with public concern. While much of the literature on the U.N. system during its first decade of existence rested comfortably on certain normative assumptions, i.e., that the United Nations was a positive force in international politics and that there was basic congruence between U.S. goals and U.N. activities, changes in the realities have led to other types of studies. Thus, the second decade or so of U.N.-related literature dealt more scientifically and empirically with U.N. questions and included many fair, objective treatments of emerging issues and institutional developments. In more recent years, in response to dramatic changes in the world political system itself, normative concerns have come to the fore again. Once again two key questions are being asked: (1) What is the proper role of international institutions in the relations among states?; and (2) What is, and should be, the role that the United States plays in these institutions?

This volume reflects a number of emerging patterns of thought and action. It is an effort to bring together in one collection essays that reflect the changes in international relations (e.g., the rise of the non-state actor, the proliferation of nation states, the new primacy of economic issues), the effect these changes have had on the functioning of international institutions (defined here as the U.N. system or family of organizations plus any other multilateral fora used for international decision making), and the impact these have had on U.S. interests. In our view, efforts to redefine or reassess U.S. policy in international institutions cannot be meaningful without examining the changing international and institutional contexts themselves. Thus, with the exception of the concluding section, most of the essays deal with questions of the changing international order and international institutional development rather than merely with U.S. policy as it is or should be.

The length of this volume and its range (from U.S.-southern Africa policy to law of the sea, disarmament, monetary reform, and international norm creation), are indicative of the increased complexity of the international political system itself. This complexity is evident in the ways nations and others have come to use international institutions, and in the proliferation of agencies and institutional arrangements for international decision making and conflict management. The often bewildering panoply of interconnected international institutions reflects, in large measure, the needs of an international system with many actors of varying capabilities and conflicting needs, but no single, centralized decision-making structure.

Although many of us have at times been painfully aware of the limitations of international institutions, it has taken over thirty years for the majority of us to accept that the U.N. system, as constructed in 1945 and operating in a world of nations, is far too fragile an institution to keep the peace. Hence, in the field of peacemaking and peacekeeping, nations have coped—albeit badly at times and with much suffering—by often solving problems outside the U.N. system. As other issues besides conflict management have developed, other institutional patterns have been established. Indeed, one might argue that the international system has been resourceful and adaptive, responding to change by building functional, if necessarily limited, international institutional networks.

Despite this flexibility it is clear that in an interdependent era world problems outnumber the palatable solutions. We may have reached a point, in fact, where the assumptions, policies, and institutions that have formed the web of international relations during the past thirty years have become inadequate. Subsequent adaptation of institutions and behavior has become necessary and has already begun. In a world where arms have become more sophisticated and widespread, where seemingly infinite appetites press on finite resources, where the rich and poor grow further apart in an environment degraded by man-made pollution, it is of great, if not grave, concern whether the issues will be approached by nations and others on the basis of international cooperation or confrontation. Since humanity cannot escape interdependence, the survival of civilization may well depend on our capacity to fashion a new international order, including appropriate changes in international institutions and the behavior of nation-states and individuals.

Yet, notably absent from this collection of articles are any preachy, overly idealistic assumptions about the value of the United Nations itself or the need for world government. Indeed, it appears that the rose-colored glasses have finally been shattered. We view this as a positive step: (1) because it promotes a realistic view of the world and of the limits of the U.S. power; and (2) because U.S. participation in multilateral fora is just that: one aspect of a larger and increasingly complex foreign policy, carried out in an evolving international system. We believe that there are and should be no givens about the American approach to international institutions.

For example, it should not be assumed that all issues are suitable for discussion in the U.N. framework any more than it should be assumed that no issues should be handled at the United Nations or in other multilateral fora. The real question for the United States is where to find the middle ground. On what issues and in which places can the United States best pursue its goals? Indeed, in view of the changing international political environment, what are U.S. goals and what should they be? This calls for an increasingly sophisticated U.S. policy that weighs issues carefully and coordinates policy effectively through different domestic and international agencies.

In dealing with the problems of interdependence—energy, raw material supplies, inflation, economic instability, food, the maintenance of peace and security—the United States has a variety of institutions to choose from. Some issues may be dealt with entirely among the developed nations through the Organization for Economic Cooperation and Development (OECD). Others may require a universal approach, and on some issues there may be options for using the U.N. system or other consortia of cooperative nations. Whatever the forum, U.S. policy must be based on a realistic evaluation of the new forces in world politics.

Organization

Based on the foregoing assessment of the problems involved and the growing need for a reevaluation of U.S. participation in international institutions, the Ralph Bunche Institute on the United Nations (Graduate School and University Center, City University of New York) sponsored a conference on "United States Objectives in the United Nations System" on June 15-17, 1976. The principal objectives of the conference were: (1) to examine the validity of current American goals and policies in the U.N. system; and (2) to consider the usefulness of this system as compared with alternate vehicles for furthering American interests. One hundred participants from the academic world, the U.S. government, the United Nations, business, and various other nongovernmental organizations met in four working groups to consider: (1) U.S. political and security objectives in the areas of peacekeeping, peaceful settlement of disputes, disarmament, human rights, and self determination; (2) economic and social questions, including the development of a new international economic order, the growth of multinational corporations, trade, aid, and international monetary reform; (3) natural resources and the global environment—such issues as food, population, the oceans, and natural resources; and (4) questions of international institutional development and the appropriate U.S. posture and role.

This volume stems from the papers presented and the discussions held at that conference. The majority of the essays in the book are original, although a number of them have been published in the interim in various scholarly journals. In several instances essays already available have been included to give balance or provide a different perspective on a particular issue. We have done this in most cases in order to give the broadest perspective possible; e.g., in the section on multinationals we have essays by the chairman of one of the world's largest banks, the head of the recently established U.N. Centre on Transnational Corporations, and two prominent professors. It is this mixture, and the attempt to involve people with practical experience and responsibility in each subject area, that we think make this volume valuable.

There are four parts to the volume, which largely parallel the conference subdivisions. Part one, "The United Nations and U.S. Political and Security Objectives," deals with disarmament, peacekeeping, and U.S. policy toward southern Africa. Although disarmament and arms control have for many years been thought of as matters for the superpowers to work out, the widespread sale of more sophisticated weaponry to other states and the dangers of nuclear proliferation have made this a subject requiring both national and international action. In the field of peacekeeping the U.N. system has shown some success, hence the essays on the U.N. role and U.S. interests. Although the essays on southern Africa may appear to be anomalous in a section with disarmament and peacekeeping, it is obvious that it is one of the primary political issues facing the United States in the United Nations. Human rights, the Middle East, and decolonization might also have been covered in this section, but progress on human rights issues has been negligible, decolonization is virtually complete, and the Middle East has a vast literature already available; therefore, essays on these topics were omitted.

Part two, "The United States in a Changing International Economic Order," focuses on the predominance of economic issues on the international agenda. Indeed the "new international economic order" has become a top priority issue in North-South relations, both within and outside existing international institutions. The value of this section lies, therefore, in its attempt to give coverage in a collected form to a number of economic issues which have growing importance in international politics. Thus, there is an opening section on the emerging world economic order and more specific discussions of current problems involving: (1) the adjustments of the international monetary system to the realities of interdependence; and (2) the developing role of multinational corporations in world politics.

In part three, "Global Resources and U.S. Interests," a general article places in context the emerging problems of global cooperation: food, population, the environment, the oceans, and natural resources. Five more specific essays deal with U.S. policies in two different but related areas: (1) the law of the sea in its many facets; and (2) the use of natural resources and energy. The absence of essays on the other global problems noted should not be interpreted as open neglect. Indeed, the very fact that international conferences were held under U.N. auspices on food, population, and the human environment is testimony to the importance which the world community has attached to these problems. Yet, to treat them fairly would have required an entire volume.

Part four deals with "The U.S. Role in a Changing U.N. System." Nine essays appear here in two general categories. In the first group are essays which explore changes in structures and procedures in international institutions with special reference to the United Nations. The final group of essays deals most directly with the questions of American participation in international institutions. The authors here attempt to evaluate current American goals and outline various strategies which the United States might pursue in world institutions in order to achieve its goals.

The authors hope that this book serves a number of purposes. First, we hope that it successfully updates earlier collections of essays, which have tended to be too U.N.-oriented. Second, we have attempted to provide coverage of the economic and global resource issues that have become more significant in world politics and in international institutions. Third, we have tried to make available in a single volume current research by scholars and current analyses by practitioners. And finally, we have endeavored to provide a meaningful context for evaluation of U.S. goals and policies in multilateral fora.

We hope that the volume will help fill a gap in the field and that it will contribute to serious thinking on these issues among thoughtful students of American foreign policy and international organization, both in and out of government. We hope further that it will find its way into the college classroom as a book of readings for courses on international relations, international organization, and American foreign policy.

As we move further into the last quarter of the twentieth century, the American reply to the challenges of interdependence will help to shape the face of the future. Sober reflection on the nature of these challenges and the appropriate American responses is what we hope this volume will promote.

PART ONE: THE UNITED NATIONS AND U.S. POLITICAL AND SECURITY OBJECTIVES

Introduction
Seymour Maxwell Finger

An idealist looking at the United Nations Charter in 1945 would no doubt have stressed three international peace and security goals: (1) renunciation of the use of a force as an instrument of national policy, with disputes being settled by peaceful means; (2) collective security based on the last-resort use of U.N. forces to deter or punish any aggressor; and (3) the regulation and reduction of armaments.

Clearly the world has not developed that way. Although war between the major powers has been averted, force has continued to be used as an instrument of national policy. Some disputes have been settled peacefully, with the help of U.N. mechanisms and officials; however, in too many cases nations have decided to rely on the use of force. As Ruth Russell observes in her essay, this has been "a highly revolutionary period of violent change" when "governments are not particularly interested in peaceful settlement per se." The U.N. force envisaged in the charter has never materialized. Collective action by the United Nations to enforce peace has been extremely rare, mainly because the great powers who must provide the backbone and major resources have been divided among themselves. Instead of disarmament, there has been an accelerating arms race, mitigated only slightly by arms control agreements.

Understandably these developments have led many to condemn the United Nations as useless or worse. This makes as much sense as breaking the thermometer when the weather gets too hot. For the United Nations is a stage rather than an actor; its achievements are determined by the degree to which the sovereign states, in which the real power resides, are induced to live up to their charter obligations.

Arms Control and Disarmament

The experts writing in this section review the dismal record to date but also see the possibility of real progress if governments make the most of their opportunities. William Epstein addresses the threat of growing nuclear proliferation and outlines a program of effective technical safeguards buttressed by important political measures to be undertaken by the present nuclear powers in order to reduce the incentives for proliferation. Reaching agreement on the elements of such a program will not be easy, for the impact on important vested interests is bound to provoke a powerful reaction, but failure to act could be disastrous.

In "Nuclear Arms Reduction: A Turning Point for U.S. Arms Control Strategy at the U.N.," Abraham Bargman is highly critical of the "arms control qua arms race" tactics pursued by the superpowers. He concedes that: "The arms control agreements of the last fifteen years have no doubt been instrumental in helping the superpowers move from a state of relentless hostility to one of peaceful coexistence without actually retarding the nuclear arms race."[1] He observes, however, that even this advantage has been dissipated by détente's loss of impetus. Perceiving President Carter's emphasis on actual arms reduction as a turning point in American policy, Bargman sees an active U.S. role at the special session of the U.N. General Assembly in 1978 as a logical corollary of the new Carter policy. It could be the occasion to mobilize support for an integrated program for reducing strategic arms, cutting military expenditures, and strengthening safeguards against nuclear proliferation. Clearly this would be a remarkable turning point for both the United States and the United Nations in the field of disarmament. And, by going public at the United Nations, Carter could show that he is indeed serious about arms reduction and thus help to restore the U.S. image as an idealistic force in world politics.

The Commission to Study the Organization of Peace, in its report, "Approaches to Arms Control and Disarmament," also emphasizes the need for reducing strategic arms, cutting military expenditure, and strengthening safeguards against nuclear proliferation. Its report is particularly helpful in enhancing understanding of the complexities of arms control and disarmament, the interest groups involved, and the interrelationships between arms production and trade on the one hand and political, economic, and security considerations on the other. Stressing the real cost of armaments in nonrenewable resources and alternative uses for economic development, the report offers specific recommendations for measuring and monitoring these costs. It also emphasizes the dangers of the *qualitative* arms race and the consequent need for Congressional oversight of the issuance of contracts for research, development, testing, and evaluation of new weapons systems along with approaches to the Soviets and others now engaged in research and development of new and potentially destabilizing weapons systems. Finally, it makes recommendations for unilateral, bilateral and multilateral steps to control and reduce production of both nuclear and conventional arms and trade in conventional arms.

U.N. Peacekeeping

Prevented by the prevailing forces in the world from carrying out the collective military measures envisaged in Chapter VII, the United Nations has developed, by improvisation, useful instruments not specifically provided for in the charter, i.e., peacekeeping forces and observers. Such forces are small and lightly armed and not designed to fight an aggressor; instead, their role is to separate forces and assist the parties involved to maintain a truce or armistice while a peaceful political solution to the dispute is sought.

My article, "Breaking the Deadlock on U.N. Peacekeeping," has been included in this volume because it provides an ex-insider's view of the nature of peacekeeping and of the principal problems involved. In the spring of 1973 I felt that it was worth a serious effort to get an agreement with the Soviet Union on general guidelines for U.N. peacekeeping in order to enable better advance preparation and assure sounder financing. Secretary of State Kissinger expressed a similar view in his address to the U.N. General Assembly in September 1973. But events of the last four years indicate that Ruth Russell was a better prophet. She wrote in 1962:

> All things considered—especially the limitations of UNEF [the U.N. Emergency Force] and ONUC [the U.N. Congo Operation]—it would seem most likely that the near future will see no more than a continuation of the pattern of the past: the gradual, even reluctant, development of principles and procedures for the utilization of international military force through the world organization—crisis-impelled, unsteady, and precarious in growth.

The fact is that the Soviets have been less rigid in the face of an actual emergency than in overall negotiations. They have been willing to acquiesce on an ad hoc basis to more realistic procedures for the establishment, command, control, and financing of the two current U.N. peacekeeping forces in the Middle East established after the October 1973 war than they were prepared to endorse in the form of general guidelines. Consequently, it now appears wiser to accept these operations as a precedent or model rather than try to negotiate formally codified guidelines. Yet the attempt to negotiate guidelines was not wholly in vain. The proposals made and views expressed during the negotiations were carefully considered and used by the secretary-general in preparing the documents that, with Security Council approval, became the basis for the two current Middle East operations. These, in turn, may become precedents which could serve as de facto guidelines.

As Ruth Russell emphasizes, U.N. peacekeeping "is but part of a larger mission—namely to arrive at a peaceful settlement that will resolve the underlying conflict between the parties." Various methods of peaceful settlement are catalogued in Chapter VI of the U.N. Charter and the techniques for promoting settlement, while subject to improvement, are well known. But all too often states have shown a preference for violence rather than negotiation and compromise.

Southern Africa

Recent U.S. emphasis on southern African issues has clouded to some extent the fact that African problems have been matters of concern to the international community and the United Nations for several decades. As the process of decolonization winds down, however, the areas of southern Africa which remain under white, minority domination have become a focal point for third world activity in the U.N. system. The new emphasis in U.S. foreign policy on human rights issues has led this country, albeit belatedly, to attempt to regain some leadership on African questions. Undoubtedly another factor has been Soviet-Cuban involvement in Angola and the emergence of a Marxist regime in Mozambique.

Although the subject is much broader in scope than three essays can cover, the three pieces included here highlight the important issues and frame the options for U.S. policy. The distinguished president of Tanzania, Julius K. Nyerere, outlines the issues from an African perspective and calls on the United States to stop supporting "racialism and unfreedom" in Rhodesia, Namibia, and South Africa. The remarks by U.S. Secretary of State Cyrus Vance are in some ways an answer to the Nyerere piece. Secretary Vance describes the relationship between American interests and African problems, and attempts to show how the Carter administration's human rights policy will shape its approach toward the solution of those problems. He concludes that the future of Africa will be shaped primarily by African hands. Wentworth Ofuatey-Kodjoe's essay rounds out the section by providing a critical analysis of U.S. Africa policy as it has been pursued in the United Nations.

Notes

1. World military expenditures (in current dollars)—$107 billion in 1960 and $202 billion in 1971—are currently running well over $300 billion. In constant dollars (1973), expenditures of the developing nations have risen from $26 billion to $39 billion. From remarks by C. Maxwell Stanley, *Report of the Eighth Annual Conference on United Nations Procedures* (Muscatine, Iowa: Stanley Foundation), p. 40.

DISARMAMENT AND ARMS CONTROL

1. Measures Necessary to Curb Nuclear Proliferation
William Epstein

Background

It is worth recalling that the Three-Power Declaration made by President Harry S. Truman, Prime Minister Clement Attlee, and Prime Minister W. L. Mackenzie King on November 5, 1945, was intended "to prevent the use of atomic energy for destructive purposes (and) to promote . . . the utilization of atomic energy for peaceful and humanitarian ends." The declaration stated that "no system of safeguards that can be devised will of itself provide an effective guarantee against production of atomic weapons by a nation bent on aggression. . . . We are, however, prepared to share, on a reciprocal basis with others of the United Nations, detailed information concerning the practical industrial application of atomic energy *just as soon as effective enforceable safeguards against its use for destructive purposes can be devised* (emphasis added)."

It is somewhat surprising that thirty years later, not only these three countries but also France, West Germany, the Soviet Union, and others are engaged in selling and transferring nuclear materials, equipment, and technology in ways that can facilitate the proliferation of nuclear weapons.

While reactors for power production are large and expensive undertakings that take five or more years for construction and start-up, research reactors of a few megawatts in size are relatively simple and easy to build. In fact, once any relatively advanced country has a power or research reactor, it is not difficult for it to build a small reactor by itself as India has done. Such reactors can be utilized or programmed to produce the maximum amount of plutonium-239 if their operation for generating power at the lowest possible cost is not the object. A small research experimental reactor using natural uranium as a fuel, which produces more plutonium than one using enriched uranium, can be built at a relatively low cost. And since low-grade uranium resources are present in many countries, these reactors can be used to produce plutonium in sufficient quantities to make one or two bombs a year from indigenous sources.

As far back as 1966, Dr. Glenn Seaborg, then chairman of the U.S. Atomic Energy Commission, stated with regard to the process of separating weapons-grade plutonium from the plutonium produced in civil power reactors, "It is perfectly feasible to build a clandestine chemical processing plant using readily available technology and equipment." Ten years later, it is even more feasible to do so. It has been estimated that a separation plant capable of producing 15 to 20 kg of plutonium-239 a year (enough for two or three explosive devices) could be built in a year or two by any reasonably advanced country at a cost of $1 to 3 million. Even if the cost has been grossly underestimated, it is clear that the amount of money involved is not large.

If French and West German companies continue to sell complete plutonium reprocessing plants, albeit under international safeguards, to any country that promises not to use the plutonium to explode a nuclear device for either military or peaceful purposes, the danger of the spread of nuclear weapons will be greatly increased.

Among the near and potential nuclear powers that are not parties to the Non-Proliferation Treaty (NPT)—India, Pakistan, Israel, South Africa, Argentina, and Brazil—all but South Africa has, or is reputed to have, or has arranged to acquire some type of reprocessing plant. South Africa, of course, having a uranium enrichment process, has no need for a plutonium reprocessing facility.

There is at the present time no need whatsoever to reprocess spent fuel into plutonium. In fact it is not at all clear when a commercial need will arise for plutonium either as a fuel for power reactors or for peaceful nuclear explosions. For the foreseeable future it seems likely that uranium can meet all requirements. Nor are the economic advantages of plutonium recycling and breeder reactors very clear in themselves or in the light of the potentialities of uranium enrichment by some laser process or of developing some alternative energy source.

One can only speculate as to the reasons which now motivate countries to acquire or retain their own national reprocessing capabilities. It seems reasonable to conclude that some of these countries wish to have their own reprocessing facilities in order to acquire a real nuclear weapon option.

Even before the Indian nuclear explosion in May 1974 there was a very marked erosion of faith in the NPT. Many non-nuclear countries, in particular the "have-not" countries, have become disillusioned by the failure of the nuclear powers to live up to their obligations under the NPT. The nuclear powers have not halted tests of nuclear weapons or the nuclear arms race, nor have they agreed to any measures of nuclear disarmament—as they are committed to do by the NPT. In fact, many countries regard the Strategic Arms Limitation Talks (SALT) agreements as mere blueprints for the continuation of the nuclear arms race by the two superpowers under agreed rules and conditions.

The nuclear powers have likewise done very little to fulfill their obligations under the NPT (Article IV) to facilitate the peaceful uses of nuclear energy "especially in the territories of non-nuclear-weapon states party to the Treaty, with due consideration for the needs of the developing areas of the world." They have done practically nothing to make the potential benefits of peaceful explosions available to non-nuclear states. Although Article V provides that "negotiations on this subject shall commence as soon as possible after the Treaty enters into force," no negotiations whatsoever have taken place, except perhaps in the context of the Threshold Test Ban Treaty of July 1974. That treaty and the follow-up treaty signed on May 28, 1976, permitting the United States and the USSR to conduct both military and peaceful nuclear explosions up to 150 kilotons in yield, can only serve to create further doubts about the sincerity of the two superpowers.

The disappointment and frustrations of the developing countries at what they regard as clear breaches of the solemn obligations undertaken by the nuclear powers have greatly weakened the NPT. Its ratification on the eve of the NPT Review Conference by five Euratom countries (West Germany, Italy, the Netherlands, Belgium, and Luxembourg) and by South Korea in April 1975, helped to restore some of the vitality of the treaty. Most third world countries, however, do not regard these accessions as important since they concern mainly developed countries that are allies of the United States and are therefore under the American nuclear umbrella.

In the ultimate analysis, whether a country decides to "go nuclear" and acquire nuclear explosives depends on how it views its needs and interests in the context of the military, political, economic, and moral climate of the world. A country will evaluate its position on this issue not only by what the nuclear powers do or do not do to implement their commitments under the NPT but, more importantly, by what it regards as threats or potential threats to its security from its neighbors or other countries in its region of the world. Thus, Pakistan is obviously much more concerned about what India may or may not do than it is about what the nuclear powers may or may not do in living up to their obligations under the NPT. This also applies to Israel and the Arab states, South Africa and the other African states, Argentina and Brazil, and others. Public opinion in these countries will respond more to the actions of neighboring countries than to policies of the nuclear powers.

What these and other great powers do, however, determines not merely the military, but also the political and moral climate of the world. Their actions can be used as arguments or pretexts by either the doves or hawks in any country. Thus the failure of the nuclear powers to abide by their obligations under the NPT fosters a more acceptable climate and provides a more facile excuse for any country to acquire nuclear weapons, or at least obtain or retain that nuclear option.

Apart from the failure of the two superpowers to implement their commitments, we have witnessed the sale of a reprocessing plant by France to Pakistan and of a complete nuclear fuel cycle (including uranium enrichment and plutonium reprocessing facilities) by West Germany to Brazil. In addition, the announcement in March 1976 that Canada had negotiated an agreement to resume nuclear aid to India was greeted with incredulity and dismay by many people. In view of the strong stand taken by Canada in condemning the Indian nuclear explosion and in immediately cutting off all further nuclear assistance to India, it was argued that the resumption of nuclear cooperation would represent a form of Canadian condonation of the Indian explosion. Fortunately, wiser counsels prevailed, and Canada reversed itself. On May 18, 1976, the Canadian government announced that it had decided against any further nuclear cooperation with India, since India had refused to agree that Canadian supplies of nuclear technology, equipment or materials, past or future, would not be used to manufacture any nuclear explosive device, and that all nuclear facilities involving Canadian technology be placed under safeguards. This Canadian decision not to resume nuclear aid to India was one of the more hopeful developments in an otherwise unencouraging scene.

It is in the light of these developments and circumstances that we must view and assess the credibility and viability of any proposed international arrangements for nuclear fuel cycle facilities as a measure to curb the proliferation of nuclear weapons.

How Good are International Safeguards?

The primary purpose of the International Atomic Energy Agency (IAEA) is to promote and facilitate the peaceful uses of atomic energy for the welfare of mankind. International safeguards were intended not as an end in themselves but only as a means to ensure that the nuclear assistance provided by or through the IAEA would not be misused for military purposes.

The IAEA Statute and its safeguards system do not prevent or prohibit states from acquiring nuclear weapons or material and the equipment to make them. France and India, for example, were members in good standing when they first exploded nuclear devices, as are the United States, the Soviet Union, and the United Kingdom, all of which have continued to conduct explosions. The statute and safeguard system are intended to ensure only that the specific projects, facilities, and nuclear equipment which a *country has agreed to place under agency safeguards* are not diverted to military purposes.

The IAEA actually has two safeguards systems in operation. The first, which is contained in the agency's document INFCIRC/66 and revisions thereto and was adopted in 1965, is referred to as the "agency's safeguards system." The second is the agency's safeguards system under the NPT that was worked out and adopted in 1971 known as the "IAEA/NPT safeguards."

The agency's safeguards under the NPT, unlike the 1965 safeguards under the IAEA Statute, are designed to apply to all nuclear materials in *all* peaceful nuclear activities within a state, as required by Article III (1) of the NPT, to ensure that such material is not diverted to nuclear weapons or other nuclear explosive devices.

Neither of the IAEA safeguards systems can prevent diversion of fissionable material; at best they can only serve to detect any diversion sometime after it has occurred and, thus, have only a deterrent effect. Any nation, however, that is interested in doing so will find it relatively easy to delay, hinder, and evade the effective operation of the safeguards system.

IAEA safeguards do not provide for any physical control or managerial supervision of nuclear material. The IAEA/NPT safeguards system is a system for keeping track of nuclear material primarily on the basis of auditing the accounts of a national government or of its nuclear facilities, supplemented by automatic instrumental checks and by periodic inspections. In some ways, the process is similar to that of the auditors of a bank, but the IAEA inspectors have much less authority than bank auditors, and their task is much more difficult. In a bank, the flow of dollars and securities in and out of the system can be more readily checked (though even under those circumstances banks make mistakes or are victims of theft by outsiders or embezzlement by insiders).

The IAEA/NPT safeguards system can only be as effective as the accounting and security safeguard techniques of each state permit and to the extent each state is willing to cooperate with the agency. If a state regards the safeguards as contrary to its national interest at any time, it is very doubtful that it would enforce them or accept, for example, international surveillance or inspections. If any state should decide at any time that it wished to divert nuclear materials to the manufacture of weapons or nuclear explosive devices, it would not be very difficult to circumvent the safeguards without going to the extent of actually falsifying its records.

There are no real measures of sanction or enforcement in case of noncompliance or violation by any state. The only recourse is under the provisions of Article XII C of the agency's statute. This provides merely that the Board of Governors can give publicity to the violation by reporting it to the members of the agency and to the Security Council and General Assembly of the United Nations. In addition, the board may direct the curtailment or suspension of any assistance being provided by the agency, and the agency may suspend any noncomplying member from membership. It should be noted that there is nothing in the NPT or the IAEA safeguards systems to prevent or make illegal the possession of weapon-grade uranium or plutonium. It is only their diversion to weapons or explosive devices by non-nuclear states that is banned.

In any case, a state wishing to free itself from its commitments need not engage in any clandestine or prohibited activities or even go into the black market to acquire nuclear materials and equipment. It can, if it chooses to do so, openly withdraw from the NPT on three months' notice and be free to do what it wishes. It may risk the suspension or termination of further nuclear aid (as India did), but it is not easy to visualize more drastic sanctions.

As indicated, the IAEA/NPT safeguards system is a system which seeks to deter diversion only by the risk of early detection. The continuing usefulness of such a system of safeguards depends on the moral climate and on the strength of the entire nonproliferation regime. In the final analysis, even domestic law, which is much more effective since it can be enforced by police power and a system of penalties, depends for its observance on the prevailing climate of opinion and on the respect with which the laws are upheld. The same applies, to a large extent, to the NPT and its safeguards. The respect accorded the treaty, and the observance of its obligations by the parties to it, may have more to do with the effectiveness of its safeguards system than the actual measures and procedures themselves. Unfortunately, many of the provisions of the NPT have been honored more in their breach than in their observance.

Restrictions on Exports and the "London Suppliers Club"

As a result of its unfortunate experience with India, Canada unilaterally announced the imposition of what it describes as the strictest export regulations of any nuclear supplier country. On December 20, 1974, Canada announced that it would in the future require that international safeguards to ensure against the development of any nuclear explosive device cover: (1) all nuclear facilities and equipment supplied by Canada; (2) all nuclear facilities and equipment using Canadian-supplied technology; (3) all nuclear material—uranium, thorium, plutonium, and heavy water—supplied by Canada and all fissionable material produced from or with these materials; and (4) all nuclear materials, whatever their origin—produced or processed, in facilities supplied by Canada.

But even these strict regulations can be evaded. A country (such as India or Argentina) that is not a party to the NPT, that has obtained a research or power reactor using natural uranium can build its own reactor and can operate it with its own natural uranium ore or access to foreign sources.

If it buys or builds a small reprocessing plant, it can acquire its own stockpile of plutonium. Thus a country subject to the Canadian safeguards and abiding strictly by them can still manufacture its own nuclear explosive devices. Only the NPT requires that all nuclear activities of a country be placed under international safeguards. Anything short of that can inhibit or delay but not prevent a country from going nuclear.

Unless export regulations require that all of a recipient's nuclear materials and activities be put under IAEA safeguards, they permit the continuation of the invidious discriminatory situation wherein countries that are not parties to the NPT can obtain nuclear materials, equipment, and technology on more favorable terms (i.e., under less strict conditions) than parties.

Thus the Canadian export regulations, and those of other countries (even if they are as strict as the Canadian), are not good enough to prevent a country from acquiring a nuclear explosive device. And if they are not good enough, they are simply inadequate.

In all fairness, it must be said that in the IAEA, in the United Nations and other international bodies, and in the London Suppliers Club, Canada and several other countries should go all the way and refuse to supply nuclear material, equipment, and technology unless the recipient country agrees to put all its nuclear material and facilities under IAEA safeguards. Mainly because of opposition from France and West Germany, the other members of the London Suppliers Club (the

United States, USSR, the United Kingdom, Canada, and Japan) have not been able to agree on such strict export regulations.

While some progress has been made, the measures that have been agreed on are only partial ones and are not sufficient to prevent the proliferation of nuclear weapons.

The meetings of the London Suppliers Club are conducted in the utmost secrecy (a procedure not conducive to great or early progress) and even the provisions of the consensus thus far achieved have not been made public and are not fully known. But enough has been announced or leaked out to make it clear that they are still inadequate. The sale of reprocessing plants is not barred and safeguards do not extend to the full nuclear program of the recipient countries (including indigenous sources), nor do they cover all aspects of nuclear technology.

There are serious grounds for doubting even whether safeguards over the entire nuclear fuel cycle would by themselves be adequate to prevent the further spread of nuclear weapons. But one would have thought that insistence on such broad safeguards would be the minimum required. Such, unfortunately, is not the case.

Although the export regulations imposed by Canada, France, West Germany, and other suppliers provide that the nuclear *technology* transferred cannot be used for any purpose other than that specified in the agreement of sale—which presumably means that the facilities and equipment supplied cannot be copied by the purchaser—there is no way to enforce the restriction. It would be extremely difficult to prove that a specific technique or technology had been copied. And even if a violation could be proved, there would be no remedy or recourse other than cancelling future nuclear assistance.

While the seven members of the London Suppliers Club have been joined by a number of other countries, including the Netherlands, Italy, East Germany, and Sweden, several supplier or potential supplier countries such as India, South Africa, Australia, Argentina, Brazil, and China (although China has not up until now been a supplier or given any indication of becoming one) are not members.

Vast loopholes still exist and the danger of the further proliferation will remain unless all supplier and potential supplier countries join the club and adopt adequate measures to ensure that additional countries will not go nuclear.

Nuclear Fuel Cycle Centers

Various proposals have been put forward for the establishment of regional, multinational, or international fuel cycle centers for uranium enrichment, fuel fabrication, reprocessing, spent-fuel storage, and waste management. While such centers might help to prevent the acquisition of fissionable material for explosive devices by any individual national government, the problems involved in their establishment and operation are immense. The economic, financial, and administrative problems that would have to be solved are outside of the scope of this paper. Assuming they were all capable of solution, however, the overriding political problems might still pose an insuperable obstacle.

The very reasons that motivated a country to remain outside of the NPT would probably also be decisive in keeping it from participating in any international and perhaps even bilateral venture. Apart from any loss from closing down its own national plant, and irrespective of the economic benefits it might gain from participating in a large-scale multinational project, these financial considerations would be relatively insignificant for any state that believed it was important for its national security to go nuclear or to retain the option to do so.

The establishment of nuclear fuel cycle centers might be a useful undertaking as one of a number of measures to help to contain the risks of nuclear proliferation, but it would not alone add a great deal to the present nonproliferation regime.

Additional Measures for Effective Safeguards

If the nuclear supplier states are really serious about trying to prevent the further proliferation of nuclear weapons, they should be willing to take all the necessary measures to do so. A program of measures that would minimize the risks of further proliferation to as near zero as is possible in a world of sovereign states is simple to prepare. The measures themselves are also technically simple and easy to supervise and control. Only the political will is needed to adopt and implement them.

Such a program to be effective and adequate should include the following measures:

1. The nuclear-weapon states that are parties to the NPT (the United States, the USSR, and the United Kingdom) should agree to accept IAEA safeguards over all their peaceful nuclear activities. This would remove the discriminatory features which apply only to the non-nuclear parties to the NPT and which the latter resent. Since the nuclear parties already have more than enough weapons grade U-235 and Pu-239 for any conceivable military use, there should logically be no obstacle to their halting the production of any further fissionable material for military purposes and agreeing to place the entire fuel cycle of their

plants and facilities under safeguards.
2. The nuclear-weapons states and supplier states should agree to make no sales and provide no nuclear material or equipment to any nuclear or non-nuclear country unless that country agrees either to become a party to the NPT or to accept equivalent restraints and to place *all* of its nuclear material and facilities, including re-exports, under IAEA safeguards.
3. The supplier states should make a public declaration (and not conceal it by a consensus declaration in the London club) and have it adopted by the Board of Governors and the General Conference of the IAEA, and by the U.N. General Assembly, that peaceful nuclear explosions under national control are incompatible with the peaceful utilization of nuclear energy.
4. All spent fuel should be returned to the supplier country for storing until such time as reprocessing is required.
5. All spent fuel should be reprocessed by the original supplier at such time when reprocessing is required and becomes commercially feasible, or be sent to some internationally operated and safeguarded plant for reprocessing at cost, and thereafter returned as fuel only for identified peaceful purposes to the country from which it originated. If reprocessing is done at cost, or better still is subsidized, it would provide a substantial inducement to countries not to acquire or use their own reprocessing plants.
6. Nuclear-supplier countries should not export any chemical separation plant for plutonium reprocessing which might come under national control. Nor should they export any nuclear material, equipment, or technology to any non-nuclear country that has or that acquires any reprocessing plant under national control. Those countries that already have reprocessing plants of any kind should be required to place them under international management and operation.
7. The supplier countries should work towards the adoption of physical security systems, both national and international, which woul prevent the theft of nuclear material by terrorists and criminal elements, either at nuclear facilities or during transport of nuclear materials.
8. The nuclear-supplier countries should adopt effective sanctions providing for the immediate withholding of *all* nuclear assistance by *all* suppliers, not only for future contracts but also under previous or existing contracts, from countries that violate any of the above measures.

David E. Lilienthal, former chairman of the Tennessee Valley Authority and the first chairman of the U.S. Atomic Energy Commission, stated in evidence to the Government Operations Committee of the U.S. Senate in January 1976:

> The tragic fact is that the atomic arms race is today proceeding at a more furious and more insane pace than ever. Proliferation of capabilities to produce nuclear weapons of mass destruction is reaching terrifying proportions. We have to decide now what we can do, now, within our own capabilities, to prevent a very bad situation from becoming a disastrous and inevitable one. I therefore propose as a private citizen that this committee with its great prestige, call upon the Congress and the President to order a complete embargo to the export of all nuclear devices and all nuclear material, that it be done now, and done unilaterally. Further, unilaterally, the United States should without delay proceed by lawful means to revoke existing American licenses and put an end to the future or pending licensing to foreign firms and governments of American know-how and facilities paid for and created by American taxpayers' funds and American brains.

In March 1976 the Chairman of the Senate Committee on Government Operations, Senator Abraham Ribicoff, proposed that the United States enter into a cooperative arrangement with the other suppliers, including France and West Germany, that would guarantee each supplier a minimum number of reactor sales a year, in a sort of cartel arrangement to eliminate harmful cut-throat competition. If agreement on strict export controls and market sharing arrangements could not be reached, the United States should unilaterally stop supplying reactor fuel to France, West Germany, and any other countries that failed to meet the American requirements. Domestic pressures might be generated in France and West Germany that would cause their governments to change their policies.

Such actions are obviously very drastic and very serious in their import and could not be lightly undertaken. Their mere public venting and discussion, however, might produce the desired result. In such matters, open publicity rather than secrecy would seem to be indicated.

All countries including France and West Germany and supplier or potential supplier states such as South Africa and India, neither of which is a party to the NPT, ought to regard the prevention of the further spread of nuclear weapons as in their interest. Hence it is possible that even nonparties to the NPT might be willing to support and subscribe to measures such as those listed above that are not dependent on or related to adherence to the NPT.

While the above suggestions for technical measures to strengthen the safeguards system are far-reaching in nature, they are no more radical than is the concept of nonproliferation itself, or for that matter, the Non-Proliferation Treaty. If the nuclear-weapon states and the other supplier states would agree to accept and implement them, the non-nuclear states might be persuaded to do likewise. And if the two superpowers were to lead the way in this regard, they could help to create a momentum and community of interest in favor of the adoption of such a strengthened and expanded safeguards system similar to that which they succeeded in achieving when they worked out the provisions of the Non-Proliferation Treaty and obtained the commendation of the United Nations by an overwhelming majority.

While the foregoing list of safeguards measures would reduce the possibilities of nuclear weapon proliferation to the maximum degree that is technically possible by such means of control, they would not and could not ensure that all further proliferation was stopped. As the three heads of government foresaw in their remarkably prescient declaration in 1945, no system of safeguards could of itself provide an effective guarantee against the production of atomic weapons by a nation bent on acquiring them.

Political Measures

As previously indicated, of even greater importance in preventing the spread of nuclear weapons is the removal of the incentives that motivate countries to acquire these instruments of destruction. That will require a series of political measures that are not only more important but also more difficult to implement than the technical safeguards outlined above. These political actions would be aimed at the "psychological denuclearization" of nations and peoples and be designed to achieve a more secure world.

The most important political measures are the following:

1. A declaration by all nuclear powers not to use or threaten to use nuclear weapons against any non-nuclear state that has no nuclear weapons in its territory. China and France have already announced their support for such a declaration, and in 1966 the Soviet Union submitted a similar proposal under the "Kosygin Formula." The United States and United Kingdom have also given a somewhat similar pledge to the countries that are members of the Latin American Nuclear Free Zone under the Treaty of Tlatelolco. Hence it should not be beyond the ingenuity of diplomats to work out some agreed formula for such

a declaration. If each of the nuclear powers also undertook to give some positive security assurances that it would, subject to the U.N. Charter obligations, come to the aid of any such state attacked or threatened with nuclear weapons, this would help to strengthen the feelings of confidence and security of non-nuclear states.

2. A declaration of non-first-use of nuclear weapons by each of the nuclear powers. This would at a single stroke reduce nuclear weapons to a similar legal status as that of chemical and biological weapons under the Geneva Protocol.

3. An immediate moratorium by the United States and the Soviet Union suspending all underground nuclear tests for five years and the commencement of negotiations to achieve agreement on a permanent ban of such tests.

4. A joint declaration by the United States and the Soviet Union that they would undertake to conduct underground nuclear explosions for peaceful purposes, either for themselves or for non-nuclear states, only when authorized to do so by some competent international authority to be established for that purpose, and that they would begin immediate consultations to convene a conference for the creation of a nondiscriminating and equitable special international regime for peaceful nuclear explosions, as required by Article V of the NPT.

5. A declaration by the two superpowers of a qualitative freeze on the production of new nuclear weapon systems for a fixed period of years pending the negotiation of a treaty to that effect. This declaration would entail the suspension of all flight testing of new delivery vehicles and weapons systems.

6. The immediate commencement of negotiations at SALT and elsewhere for visible progress towards substantial reductions of existing nuclear weapons systems, far below the inflated levels set by the Vladivostok accord.

The above list of political measures to help achieve psychological denuclearization and reduce the incentives for proliferation is not exhaustive but is illustrative of the kinds of political actions that would create the right climate for nonproliferation in a more secure world. Only a combination of both political and technical measures can succeed in providing the required credibility and viability for an effective nonproliferation regime.

2. Nuclear Arms Control: A New U.S. Strategy at the United Nations
Abraham Bargman

Once again American internationalism is exhibiting its hopeful countenance to the world by rejecting the timid and cynical version of political realism. Despite the legacy of previous erratic policies, the Carter administration has launched an energetic drive to sustain and strengthen the nonproliferation regime. Simultaneously, the new president has redefined this country's goal in the Strategic Arms Limitation Talks (SALT) in terms of the reduction of nuclear arms and the curbing of weapons technology. Suddenly the wealth and power of the United States are once again mobilized in the service of international solutions which require us to strengthen international institutions to cope with the diffusion of nuclear capabilities. A stronger International Atomic Energy Agency (IAEA), for example, is an indispensable part of the new nonproliferation policy and there is talk of new international institutions for the reprocessing and storage of spent nuclear fuel.

The premise of this paper is that the United States will wish to seek political support at the United Nations for its new policies. It has been a long time since an American president could argue sincerely for elimination of nuclear weapons and make concrete proposals for arms reduction. The specific task of the paper is to analyze some of the obstacles in the way of an effective U.S. strategy at the United Nations. These are: (1) the American legacy of arms control defined in terms of nuclear superiority; (2) the habit of Soviet-American parallelism with its emphasis on bilateral diplomacy outside the United Nations; (3) the conservative influence of major allies; and, finally, (4) the understandable skepticism of the third world—the new U.N. majority.

The American Legacy

The U.N. Charter's prescription for preventing another world war includes disarmament as one "possible," but by no means the most desirable, way of achieving international peace and security. This is understandable since the lesson of appeasement and military weakness was fresh in the minds of the charter's American drafters. The possible reduction of armed forces, for example, was subject to the caveat that the victorious great powers should command sufficient force to deter breaches of the peace. Peace through military strength was thus an American premise when the cold was and the tensions created by nuclear weapons began to emerge.

Just as the containment of Soviet power has been the overriding goal of U.S. foreign policy, so the prevention of a surprise nuclear attack has been the flywheel of its military decisions. Because of these objectives, the credibility of American threats to use force in retaliation has been a major concern of every administration. In addition, deterrence was extended to some forty countries through military assistance pacts. Given the new military realism, containment and extended guarantees, it is not surprising that the United States has been at war for more than one-third of the postwar period. Prior to Vietnam, periodic wars were the surest means of establishing the credibility of nuclear deterrence. Nor is it surprising that the unilateral attempt to guarantee international security should have taken place under the umbrella of American nuclear superiority.

It is against this background of tough-minded political behavior that the American delegations to the United Nations simultaneously proposed improbable disarmament plans and reflexively rejected Soviet ones. As long as disarmament conferences were ritualistic, what was discussed, proposed, and disposed of was of little concern to those who made national security policy. But when, by some mysterious interaction between ritual, belief, and expediency, the other side accepted an American plan—as occurred in 1955 when the Soviet delegation said "Yes, but" instead of the customary "No, but"—the U.S. representative at the United Nations was forced to withdraw from all previous disarmament positions. At the same time, cabinet officials proclaimed the news that thenceforth the American objectives would be not disarmament but arms control.

The logic of arms control doctrine was inherently incompatible with the ideal of security through the reduction of armaments. It was thought that nuclear war could be prevented only if each adversary had nuclear weapons invulnerable to a surprise attack; talk of disarmament—even at the United Nations— was therefore not only useless but even dangerous. It might weaken the public's resolve to support the ever-increasing expenditures necessary to maintain security through arms competition. The competition was inevitable because nuclear deterrence could be no more static than the nuclear technology on which it was based. Translated into arms policies, mutual assured destruction meant higher levels of nuclear forces and endless investment in research and development. Implicit in the new science of deterrence planning was, of course, the determination to maintain America's technological superiority.

Whereas for Americans the arms control approach meant nuclear deterrence at a high level, for U.N. members who broadly endorsed the new principle of partial measures in 1955, the hope was that step-by-step arms control, or partial agreements between the cold war adversaries would serve as a basis for general disarmament. After some twenty years, however, serious doubts are being expressed about the step-by-step approach. Although many agreements have been concluded, starting with the Antarctic Treaty in 1959, there is little conviction that the process is leading toward disarmament. The reason one hears harsh criticism of the "hoax" or "game" designed to legitimize a well choreographed arms competition is that arms control logic has induced a simultaneous ratchet-like competition in the quantity and quality of nuclear and conventional weapons. This has occurred, in part, because even limited measures of arms control were opposed by the military establishment whose agreement could be obtained only at the price of permitting the development and deployment of new weapons systems.

Doctrines which were innovative in the late fifties, therefore, no longer project an acceptable vision of future policies. Yet to go from disarmament plans to expedient but achievable partial measures is a much easier journey to make than one in the opposite direction. Nevertheless, the advent of the Carter administration, the disenchantment with the legacy of arms control qua arms race and, finally, the political inducements of a Special Session on Disarmament—which would be the natural place to bury the old and articulate new policies and goals—suggest that 1978 presents a unique opportunity for the United States to redefine the legacy of the past two decades. Still working within realistic limits of what is possible, the United States might now point the world in the direction of arms reduction. That may indeed be the only way in which détente and the United Nations might once again garner the respect of world opinion.

Soviet-American Relations

In the early days of the cold war, when the United Nations was the only forum for disarmament debates, the tactical objective of the United States and the USSR was to place the blame for the arms race on the opponent. Votes were demanded on proposals clearly unacceptable to the other side. But even in an atmosphere of total negativism, U.N. debates nevertheless proved useful as a means of communicating mutual fears through the language of disarmament proposals. The fear of a preventive nuclear war was thus expressed by the Soviet Union through its ban-the-bomb proposals; and the American fear of the closed Soviet society was reflected in its insistence that control be given priority.

Now the superpowers have many means of communicating; thus, the United Nations is not as prominent as it once was in their disarmament diplomacy. Indeed, both have applied damage-limitation tactics designed to protect their bilateral negotiations, such as SALT and the Mutual and Balanced Force Reduction (MBFR) in Central Europe, from "mischievous" interference by U.N. members. Even the Conference of the Committee on Disarmament (CCD), which numbers thirty-one participants and is widely perceived to be an organ of the United Nations, reflects their penchant for joint choreography; American and Soviet representatives serve as the CCD's permanent cochairmen. This has given them a strategic position from which to manage the agenda to maximize the conference's potential for parallel or joint initiatives with respect to measures (e.g., the seabed treaty, environmental modification) which are only peripherally related to the arms race. Finally, the two most militarily powerful states have many other channels of communication ranging from expert working groups to periodic summit meetings. As a consequence, American positions at the United Nations have often been developed with the intention of protecting their parallel interests.

The recent parallel phase of their relations in U.N. disarmament deliberations can be seen in voting statistics for the years 1969 (24th General Assembly) through 1975 (30th General Assembly). The votes of the two superpowers were identical in 68 percent of the 95 roll calls on disarmament items. Moreover, they had almost identical patterns of voting:

	Votes in Favor	Votes Against	Abstentions
U.S.	38%	4%	48%
USSR	38%	2%	46%

This parallelism reflects the importance of arms control in Soviet-American détente diplomacy.

The main characteristic of détente, one that has benefited arms control perhaps more than any other issue, has been the search for areas of agreement which, although strong enough to withstand the inevitable buffeting by long-lived tensions, would be weak enough to permit each side to hold up its end of the protracted conflict. The arms control agreements of the last fifteen years have no doubt been instrumental in helping the superpowers move from a state of relentless hostility to one of peaceful coexistence but they have not retarded the nuclear arms race. While in the past, the United States has been useful as a source of approval or legitimacy, détente is no longer automatically popular.

In any event, for the Russians parallelism did not mean that they could not introduce proposals (such as on the prohibition of the use of nuclear weapons) which would isolate the United States from the U.N. majority. Rather, the evidence suggests that the Soviets view U.N. disarmament deliberations as part of the Soviet-American ideological struggle. Since détente and the ideological struggle are complementary in Soviet thinking, there is no contradiction in their Janus-like strategy toward the United States at the United Nations. The Soviet Union has also used the United Nations to further its political objectives in relation to China by attempting to isolate it from the third world.

For Americans, however, General Assembly disarmament resolutions are meaningless rituals which influence no one. As Charles William Maynes notes, "Everyone understands the U.N. debates have little leverage in the 'real world' of disarmament talks. No one, therefore, gets terribly excited about 'irresponsible' resolutions or debates in the General Assembly."[1] Americans thus tend to suffer from a propaganda disability in this field. This super-realist attitude made sense so long as arms control qua arms race was America's underlying philosophy. But if we are indeed moving toward a conception of arms control consonant with the actual reduction of armaments, not to say the elimination of nuclear armaments, a new American appreciation of the ideological function of the United Nations is required.

Moreover, the United States is in a favorable position to take the initiative at the United Nations now that President Carter has articulated what has been the majority position on disarmament. He argues, for instance, that the superpowers must disarm first because they have the largest stockpiles of nuclear arms and therefore can safely reduce before others need join in the process. This view is not shared by the Soviet Union which seems to make the adherence of China a condition for any real progress. By initiating negotiations and public discussion of nuclear reductions, President Carter is responding to the often cited commitment of the two powers in Article VI of the NPT "to pursue negotiations in good faith on effective measures relating to the cessation of the nuclear arms race at an early date and to nuclear disarmament." In addition, the new administration has been responsive to previous demands for the complete cessation of nuclear tests.

Translating these new impulses into items for presentation to the members of the United Nations might not be a significant move when compared with the stakes in SALT and the MBFR negotiations. But it would signal to others that the United States is willing to test the adequacy of its new positions against the demands of other states, large or small. Additionally, this approach should not antagonize the Russians nor prevent progress in SALT. Indeed, its main utility might lie in the message sent to the reluctant part of the American Congress and bureaucracy. By resorting to multilateral, public diplomacy in search of both support and criticism, the administration would be committing itself to the principle of arms reduction in a way press conference declarations cannot. For experts, this approach would constitute a signal that President Carter is indeed reintegrating disarmament into U.S. national security policy and that the Soviet Union, our allies, and the third world can therefore assume that the United States is serious.

Since concrete achievements in SALT are necessarily based on complicated evaluations of relative military advantages, this U.N. strategy and the ensuing deliberations on principles and guidelines for future reductions are not likely to have any immediate effect on SALT. Surely, the Soviet Union will not be reluctant to continue with SALT II or SALT III if the United States simultaneously pursues a U.N. strategy of ideological diplomacy. Finally, U.N. debates on possible nuclear arms reductions should strengthen the dovish forces in both the Soviet Union and the United States, because in both countries a declaration of good intentions has many hurdles to surmount before becoming government policy.

U.S. Relations with Major Allies

One reason the United States has often ignored the United Nations in this field is that initiatives can easily lead to differences with important allies. When, for instance, the U.S. representative to the 1957 U.N. Five Power Subcommittee, Harold Stassen, developed a businesslike relationship with the Soviet representative and discussed with him a new proposal without the consent of the three NATO allies, the uproar of criticism was dampened only when he was prohibited from making any further bilateral approaches. Fears that the Soviet Union might separate the United States from its allies were mitigated once the parity principle was adopted and negotiations moved outside the U.N. framework (as in SALT and the MBFR). Today it is the allies of the United States who believe in direct negotiations with the Russians, and hence may be reluctant to support U.S. initiatives at the United Nations out of an exaggerated concern for Soviet sensibilities. They eschew polemics at the United Nations which might aggravate their relations with the Soviet Union.

Any American initiative at the United Nations to mobilize support for arms control qua arms reduction, in the face of Soviet opposition is, therefore, likely to encounter resistance from U.S. allies. Furthermore, U.S. allies are reluctant to have other states discuss principles which can affect the military balance on which their security system rests. Then again, a reduction of Soviet and American strategic weapons might conjure up the specter of greater American reliance on tactical nuclear warfare in Europe. In short, one reason why American officials have been happy with the conservative arms control qua arms race philosophy is that it has been consistent with the conservative diplomacy of our NATO allies.

Nevertheless, one possible advantage of a more active American disarmament strategy at the United Nations is that it might induce France to take a more active part. Since Soviet-American parallelism first developed, France has dissociated itself to a certain degree from NATO, e.g., it has not taken its seat at the CCD or in the MBFR talks, contending that the superpowers must reduce their strategic armaments before calling upon other countries to make their contribution. In this connection, the United States might go as far as to propose the elimination of the CCD cochairmen positions in favor of an alternative favorable to France.

It will be much more difficult to resolve contradictions on the issue of nonproliferation, and in particular on the question of nuclear export policies. On this issue, France and West Germany may have more in common with the third world than with the United States. But the absence of American initiatives at the United Nations on proliferation has not prevented discord, as the London Suppliers Conference and the editorial comments on both sides of the Atlantic convincingly demonstrate. The fact that these matters have been discussed secretly has not led to the kind of accommodation the Carter administration has rightfully been seeking. Provided the United States is willing to make sacrifices proportional to its existing advantages, and the allies are consulted in advance, differences with leading allies on proliferation need not prevent the United States from also seeking a reaffirmation of Non-Proliferation Treaty (NPT) objectives at the United Nations.

It is plain that the new administration is pursuing nuclear policies at home which are consistent with its new international objectives.[2]

Therefore, the United States might seek U.N. endorsement of measures to strengthen IAEA safeguards (with the United States perhaps putting up most of the additional funds), of multinational or international fuel storage and reprocessing centers (with the United States willing to internationalize its future nuclear activities), and, in general, of new approaches discussed but side-tracked at the 1975 NPT Review Conference. Since there is a broad and deep political consensus in the United States on nonproliferation, a public initiative at the United Nations along these lines might even mobilize public opinion in France and West Germany in favor of greater cooperation with the United States. This is one case where the United States cannot be accused of having failed to try private talks before appealing to world opinion.

Finally, the combination of the forceful championing of arms reduction (with or without Soviet concurrence) and nonproliferation (with or without allied support) might favorably impress the third world countries, enough to take some of the automaticity out of reflexive anti-Americanism. Developing countries tend to turn every problem into a North-South issue, but in this instance that might be a useful development. For only a serious turn toward disarmament and nonproliferation can create the kind of atmosphere and resources necessary for the resolution of the economic and psychological issues that comprise the North-South agenda.

The United States and the Third World

The fact that a U.N. majority which represents only one percent of the world's GNP or military power can adopt resolutions supports the view of those who wish to place a buffer between the United Nations and serious arms negotiations. Yet it was a third world country— India—which tested a nuclear device and thereby challenged the basic premise of the NPT. And all indicators—e.g., arms sales and military expenditure—point to the growing participation of the third world in what have become interconnected regional arms races throughout the world. Finally, the demands of the third world for a more just international economic order are adversely affected by the continued high level of military expenditures by industrialized countries. Thus, even if the third world at the United Nations is not in a position to match sentiment with power, these countries nonetheless constitute a political constituency whose leaders can obstruct American disarmament initiatives.

The specific political concerns of the third world are not as easily translated into the language of disarmament as were the détente objectives of the superpowers. It will be recalled that the underlying purpose of détente through arms control was to reach agreements not for their impact on the arms race but rather because they reflected the absence of relentless hostility and symbolized a mutual desire for wary cooperation. Perhaps the message of nuclear arms reduction is that the United States recognizes the legitimacy of criticism directed toward the discriminatory consequences of the current superpower arms race.

The fundamental problem is indeed one of discrimination as reflected, for example, in the NPT. For some years now, the United States has not given the ideas of the nonaligned (even when they were based on sound advice) the kind of consideration the active delegations among them felt was justified. The notion that the United States can ignore the third world with impunity still reigns in the disarmament field (e.g., the article by Maynes), whereas on economic matters a radical change has taken place—symbolized by the active U.S. role at the U.N.'s Seventh Special Session. Nevertheless, just as this session launched concrete, system-wide negotiations on trade and associated economic questions, so preparations for the forthcoming special session on disarmament can serve to promote a dialogue between the United States and the nonaligned leaders on a program of measures reflecting the chief concerns of the third world. The United States and its allies, as major participants in the redistribution process demanded by the third world, could offer to translate this into disarmament terms. The act of serious consultation might in itself relax tensions with the third world and restore America's image as an idealistic force in world politics.

The much talked-about issue of linking a reduction in military budgets to economic development funds can serve as an umbrella subject for this purpose, especially inasmuch as the Russians have recently proposed something similiar at the United Nations. At present, military expenditures of the most developed countries are thirty times greater than their official development assistance. This is a symbolic linkage, for military expenditures do not stand in the way of more development aid nor do they prevent third world governments from putting their own houses in order. Nevertheless, military expenditure is a subject on which the Group of 77 might be consulted to develop proposals in North-South negotiations.

However, on the issue of nonproliferation, important third world countries, e.g., Brazil, are likely to join some U.S. allies in resisting measures which impede their sovereign right to develop nuclear energy including the implicit option for weapons. While they seem willing to accept IAEA safeguards, and perhaps even to strengthen them if the measures are not increasingly burdensome, they reject the perpetuation of discrimination through a nonproliferation strategy. Nevertheless, if the United States has constructive alternatives and is prepared to encourage cooperation on nonproliferation by making economic and political sacrifices, the United Nations would be the logical agency through which to legitimize such systemic bargaining. By systemic bargaining I mean negotiations in which benefits in one area are exchanged for sacrifices in another. The linkage in this case might take the form of U.S. concessions in the North-South economic negotiations in exchange for third world concessions on proliferation. It also means a negotiation in which the United States would try to form different coalitions with the Soviet Union, its allies, and the third world depending on the subject of the initiative. Ideally, all elements of a new progressive American position would be integrated in a comprehensive program of new measures which would be the core of the U.S. position at the special session.

More than symbolism or propaganda is required to influence third world or non-nuclear states. The rule of thumb is that for a disarmament proposal to be more than symbolic the strongest power must be prepared to make asymmetrical sacrifices. Thus, President Carter's first press conference was encouraging but by no means conclusive. He acknowledged the principle of reciprocity if not asymmetrical contributions:

> We would like to have this (reprocessing) put under international control, subject ourselves to the restraint along with those who have been processing this material for a number of years, and prohibit completely, within the bounds of our capability, the expansion of the reprocessing plants in the countries that don't have it.[3]

The internationalist solutions for nuclear energy—this time in regard to multinational storage and reprocessing centers—have time and again been proposed by the United States only to have domestic and international opposition weaken them (e.g., IAEA) or defeat them entirely (e.g., the Baruch Plan).

Moreover, internationalism of any kind is finding it increasingly difficult to survive in this era of rampant nationalism. Is there any contemporary internationalist movement that has not been splintered by the strong currents of nationalism? In addition to nationalism there exists a tendency toward interest group formation which encourages a return to ad hoc international conferences. Thus, the U.S.-sponsored London Suppliers Conference of about fifteen states meets secretly while the nuclear consumers organize their counterparts. The internationalist mechanisms of nonproliferation, whose importance could stand a ringing reaffirmation by NPT parties at the United Nations, is thus being buffeted by centrifugal tendencies. In this situation, the Carter administration would be well advised to try to introduce an integrated or comprehensive approach for which open diplomacy at the United Nations, particularly at the special session, seems appropriate. Only a forum in which all the groups are represented can accommodate the permutations of national interests and redefine the conditions under which the nonproliferation regime might be strengthened. In this field, there is a great degree of parallel interest with the Soviet Union, except when it comes to the creation of new international institutions with authority to own or manage nuclear processes. The United States must, therefore, be prepared to raise the issue at the United Nations, with or without Soviet support. Alternative attempts to deal with this bilaterally on a case-by-case or group-by-group basis can only result in fragmentation of the nonproliferation regime.

Conclusions

International security against nuclear war among great powers is the supreme interest of all nations. It is ironic that some twenty years after defense experts made the nuclear arms race the core of security policy the fear of surprise nuclear attack has reemerged as a result of intensive competition in new systems of mass destruction. Simultaneously, the world is entering another phase of nuclear proliferation. The insecurity created by nuclear deterrence at high levels has been assuaged somewhat by détente, which has facilitated the transition from relentless hostility to a mixed-motive protracted conflict. However, even this advantage has been increasingly negated by détente's loss of impetus. If détente is still important to the superpowers, it will have to be maintained by more than the cosmetic-type arms control agreements of recent years; it must lead instead to significant arms reductions.

The new adminstration seems to have an integrated approach to armaments. Based on the premise that "it is never too late," it seems to be inclined toward comprehensive solutions. Although this administration has injected some idealism and internationalism into American diplomacy, it has not yet made effective use of the propaganda or ideological functions of the United Nations. Nevertheless, it is only by taking an active role at the United Nations, especially at the Special Session on Disarmament, that the United States can mobilize support for an integrated program of strategic arms reduction, the reduction of military expenditures, and the strengthening of the nonproliferation regime. It is only through the United Nations that the United States can successfully harmonize its new policies with its allies, the Soviet Union, and members of the third world who are still wedded to the theories and assumptions that we have so earnestly diffused for the past twenty years.

Notes

1. Charles William Maynes, "A U.N. Policy for the Next Administration," *Foreign Affairs* (July 1976), pp. 804-819 (appears also in this volume under a new title).

2. See the "Nuclear Non-Proliferation Policy Act of 1977," 95th Congress, 1st sess., S.1432 or H.R. 6910, introduced May 4, 1977.

3. *New York Times,* January 25, 1977.

3. Approaches to Arms Control and Disarmament
Commission to Study the Organization of Peace

Introduction

The subject of arms control and disarmament is full of complexities. Many factors are responsible—the number and kind of weapons systems; the momentum of new technological developments; the competition between the United States and the Soviet Union to increase the sophistication and destructiveness of their weaponry; the policies of major weapons-manufacturing countries to earn foreign exchange, reap political influence, and assist their own armaments development through expanding arms sales and transfers; the view of many states that having armaments provides status and independence from foreign influence; the changing concepts of national security in an interdependent world; the diverse forums in which arms control and disarmament negotiations take place; and the undiminished yearning of a vast majority of the world's peoples to be rid of the weapons of warfare and indeed of war itself, so that pursuit of human betterment can be accelerated and substantial results realized.

Disarmament and arms control are defined in this report as encompassing the following measures: freeze, control, limitation, reduction, or elimination of armed forces, as well as of conventional or nuclear weapons and their delivery systems, including their development, testing, production, or deployment. Also included in the definition are constraints on or reduction in military expenditures

This chapter is excerpted from the Twenty-Fourth Report of the Commission; (Louis B. Sohn, Chairman, Betty Goetz Lall, Chairman, Working Group on Disarmament). A copy of the full report may be obtained from the commission (866 U.N. Plaza, New York, N.Y. 10017).

and the trade in armaments. Arms control and disarmament are envisaged as being achieved through bilateral or multilateral negotiations among states, or in some degree by the unilateral initiatives of individual states which could also serve as catalysts for negotiations. All arms control measures are to be taken under effective verification arrangements.

Interconnections

The complexity of the subject of disarmament is increased by the interrelationships between disarmament and other aspects of international relations and national security policy. In the days of the League of Nations, disarmament was linked to collective security and effective machinery for settling disputes.[1] Today, efforts to limit or eliminate weapons and forces purport to be connected with attempts to resolve political tensions and to maintain international peace and security. Effective arms control can influence international politics and create a better climate for further agreements. This improvement was achieved by the partial test ban in 1963, and, to some extent, by the first round of the Strategic Arms Limitation Talks (SALT I), particularly the recognition of the futility of anti-ballistic missiles (ABMs).

Despite the lessening of tensions and improved relations between the Western non-Communist and the Communist countries over the past decade and a half, no real progress has been made toward reducing and controlling armaments. On the contrary, the arms race seems to increase, especially between the United States and the USSR. Each side still lacks confidence in the peaceful intentions of the other.

It is essential, therefore, to link disarmament and arms control efforts with the current international political situation. When tension is high, arms control and disarmament prospects tend to diminish. In the aftermath of a crisis, however, there are often unique opportunities for arms control and disarmament measures. The domestic situation, nevertheless, also has a particular influence.

In the United States, the continuation of the arms race is primarily due to a perceived threat from the USSR but also to the preeminence in the government power structure of military authorities, civilians with an ideological bias toward heavy and sophisticated arms, defense contractors, and some members of the Congress who hold the view that defense contracts are the best means to help maintain employment in their states or districts. There appears to be a common misconception among the general public that armaments are needed to provide employment—a view the commission believes to be incorrect.

There are probably comparable influences in Moscow, which make an arms race difficult to stop except through international negotiations or unilateral action that is reciprocated. One problem is to ascertain how the public positions relate to actual policy objectives and decisions. For example, the Soviet political leaders and press have publicly advocated disarmament for several years, while U.S. military officials have taken a tough line, especially when their budget is before the Congress. The need for civilian control combined with moderation and balance in the political leadership in both capitals cannot be overemphasized.

Because of the complex interrelationships in the disarmament field, the method of approach becomes paramount. Should the major powers, especially the United States and the Soviet Union, try to take a quantum leap toward comprehensive disarmament? Or should they try to take small steps toward that eventual goal? In other words, the major powers can start with the big issues and work through the details or start with minor issues and work toward the larger ones. Would there be optimum progress by determined pursuit of both approaches?

Several methods of approach are practicable. The major powers can: (1) have a general plan, negotiate each element in it but put no element into effect until the whole plan is complete; (2) have a general plan, negotiate a series of specific elements and put each into effect when agreement is reached; or (3) have no general plan, merely negotiate whatever element seems feasible at a particular moment, and put it into effect when agreement is reached.

On balance, the second method is preferable assuming that a set of priorities and a sufficiently large package of interrelated measures can be agreed upon. This approach might be defined as a policy of barracuda bites, rather than gentle nibbles, in the broad field of arms control leading eventually to the ultimate goal of comprehensive disarmament. That goal,[2] which was accepted by the United States and the Soviet Union in the McCloy-Zorin Agreement of September 20, 1961, and approved unanimously by the U.N. General Assembly, should always be kept in the foreground. Indeed, a new express commitment to that goal in 1978 by the administration in Washington and a reiteration of the objective by the administration in Moscow would seem highly important.

Since the early negotiation in 1962 and 1963 at the Geneva Conference of the Committee on Disarmament, there have not been clearly stated disarmament goals by the United States and Soviet Union. Such clarification is needed; and the commission suggests that the goal of comprehensive disarmament be once again adopted, recognizing that the means to achieve it may be through a series of specific arms control and disarmament treaties, agreements, and arms policy decisions by national governments.

One important factor deserves emphasis: the need to impose both quantitative and qualitative controls in order to achieve a true reduction. To date, most of the emphasis in SALT, for example, has been on quantitative controls. Even worse, the quantitative ceilings on weapons, as in the Vladivostok agreement, are placed high above existing levels—an invitation to build up rather than to scale down. In other words, there is a need for quantitative agreements that make the situation better rather than worse, and for curtailment of the technological arms race, which is the most dangerous. Therefore, much more stress needs to be given to qualitative controls. Whenever a quantitative agreement can be effected, with respect to specific weapons, it should also deal with qualitative improvements in those weapons.

Impact of Arms Production on Economic Resources

All nations are becoming aware that many of the world's physical resources are being consumed at an increasingly rapid rate. As the material well-being of people improves, particularly in the developing world, and as the elimination of poverty everywhere is accepted as a major world-wide priority, people look critically at military programs with their enormous use of resources—physical, manpower, and capital. The waste that armaments entail, however, has not yet substantially affected the efforts to reduce and control these weapons of warfare.

The production and acquisition of arms need to be given a lower priority in all states, in order to be able to transfer to more important endeavors the human and physical resources used to produce them. Both national and international institutions can adopt means to voice the world's consciousness in this regard. At the international level, the United Nations can contribute toward this objective. At the national level in the United States, several possibilities exist within the executive and legislative branches. In the Congress, the Budget Committee and the Congressional Budget Office are especially well-equipped to deal with this task.

A first step toward bringing greater rationality to decisions on military affairs would be to have the public receive data on the extent of the consumption of resources in so-called national defense. Publication of these data alone will, of course, not bring about comprehensive disarmament and the dismantling of military establishments, but it might begin to raise the consciousness of people to what wasteful and often harmful policies their own and other national governments are pursuing.

Recommendations

1. The U.N. General Assembly should call on the governments of the principal arms-manufacturing countries to publish annual reports on the amount of nonrenewable resources consumed in the production of arms and the amount of capital and manpower devoted to producing arms and conducting arms-related research and development.
2. The U.N. Secretariat should publish an annual report showing: (a) the amount of total world production of nonrenewable resources—petroleum, iron ore, copper, nickel, manganese, bauxite, and other key minerals—that are consumed in arms production; and (b) the amount of total world capital and manpower, including scientific and technical resources, that are devoted to arms production and research and development.
3. The U.S. Congress should enact a law requiring that every military budget request contain a report by the Council of Economic Advisers and the Council on Environmental Quality on the amount of resources—manpower, capital and physical— consumed in arms production during the previous fiscal year and to be consumed as a result of the proposed budget. Analysis of these reports should be undertaken by the General Accounting Office and the Congressional Budget Office.

Essential Elements of Control

Controlling the Rate of Research and Development

Perhaps the most difficult and challenging aspect of arms control is how to control the development and introduction of new weapons systems. Thus far, it has proved impossible to design and establish effective control measures over the qualitative arms race. Yet such limitations may prove to be prerequisites for significant progress in other areas of arms control and disarmament.

The problem is compounded by the heavy vested interests of U.S. industry. In fiscal year 1977, the proposed budget for research, development, test, and evaluation (R, D, T&E) work totalled $11 billion in the United States. Most of the contracts involved aircraft, missiles, and electronic programs. While the leading 500 prime contractors in recent years have been located in over 40 states, the District of Columbia, Canada, the Bahamas, and the Trust Territory of the Pacific

Islands, the largest number have been awarded to firms in California, Massachusetts, Michigan, New York, New Jersey, Ohio, and Texas. Thus, enterprises throughout most of the country have a vital stake in these contracts, and bring pressure on both the Pentagon and the Congress to continue and even to increase them. More important, many R, D, T&E contractors expect to win large contracts for production of weapons systems for which they have invested substantially at the R, D, T&E level.

Qualitative advances in weapons technology may fuel the arms race in several ways. First of all, they may exacerbate tensions between adversaries and foster misperceptions concerning a potential opponent's capabilities and intentions, producing an action-reaction phenomenon. Secondly, major research and development programs are expensive and divert valuable technological and human resources from more socially productive tasks. Thirdly, large outlays for research and development projects may create bureaucratic and congressional pressures to procure and deploy a new weapons system in large quantities, even though the national security rationales may not be convincing. Fourthly, some new weapons systems have destabilizing arms control implications in that they either are more destructive than the weapons they replace or increase incentives for a preemptive strike. Finally, new technological developments seem to maintain the momentum of the arms race as each major military power deems it necessary to catch up with developments introduced by others.

Not all new weapons systems decrease military stability and increase costs. Some new systems further arms control objectives by reducing chances of a first strike. For instance, several technological advances in strategic systems—solid fuel, hardened silos, improved command and control, Polaris submarines—have reduced the risk of nuclear war. It has been suggested that the new generation of relatively inexpensive precision-guided munitions (PGMs) may favor the defense over the offense and provide a disincentive to the procurement of expensive tanks and tactical aircraft.

Thus, it is crucial to distinguish between those new weapons which enhance and those which detract from arms control objectives. The basic goals of arms control and disarmament are: (1) to increase military stability and make war less likely; (2) to decrease the probable destruction should war occur; and (3) to reduce the expenditure of scarce resources for military purposes. In general, qualitative constraints should seek to produce a force posture better suited for defensive than offensive operations. But this general principle is very difficult to apply to specific systems since states can employ almost any weapon in an offensive mode. Moreover, the acquisition of a defensive system may also give rise to overconfidence and tempt its possessor to strike first.

Yet these distinctions are important, and policymakers should assign them a high priority in making arms control impact assessments of new weapons systems. It must be borne in mind that qualitative limitations are particularly important in shaping the military balance of the future, since they concern new generations of weapons systems more than current force postures.

Recommendations

1. The Congress should exercise oversight over the issuance of contracts of research, development, test, and evaluation of new weapons systems, especially potentially destabilizing ones, and should pay special attention to and provide maximum publicity for the arms control and disarmament impact statements now required by law.
2. Governmental and nongovernmental approaches should be made to officials and scientists in the Soviet Union and other countries, requesting discussion and negotiation about how best to treat the control of military research and development in the context of the Soviet system, as well as in the United States and other countries.

Arms Control through Unilateral Policy Decisions
Compared with Bilateral and Multilateral Negotiation

The security afforded by a nation's weapons arsenal is diminished if the growth of that arsenal provokes adversaries to increase their arsenals or causes an increase in international tensions. National security is also threatened if defense expenditures divert resources from services essential to the maintenance of an acceptable standard and quality of life and thus foster political instability. In the end, what a nation can afford to spend for armaments depends not only on the amount of its resources, but also on the condition of its economy and the well-being of its society. Determining the proper balance between military and peaceful and domestic needs, accordingly, is the essence of a wise national security policy.

Unilateral Action. The United States can no longer pursue the myth of spending "whatever is necessary" to maintain military superiority— our national budget has begun to reflect that reality. Consequently, the country needs to make national, i.e., unilateral, decisions designed to enhance its national security and to encourage successful multilateral and bilateral negotiations. The commission strongly believes that our national security would not be threatened in the short term by substantial reductions in defense expenditures. The risk to our security from selected unilateral reductions in our defense budget is surely no greater than that we are running by inadequately funding so many vital needs of our people. The commission further believes that the needs of the Soviet people are such that a substantial reduction in U.S. military expenditures might encourage their government to follow suit—if not immediately, then very likely before the military balance could shift dangerously in their favor.

Accordingly, the commission believes that the United States should encourage defense reductions by the Soviet Union and other nations, by itself reducing expenditures for both strategic nuclear and certain conventional weapons systems.[3] Such reductions should be achieved as much as possible by eliminating obsolete weapons categories and unnecessary new weapons programs and not merely by cutting back on funds for authorized programs, the costs of which will have to be met in the future and at a higher level because of inflation.

Finally, the commission believes that savings can be made by avoiding authorizations for so-called bargaining chips. The use of funds to continue obsolete or ineffective weapons simply for the purpose of having something extra to bargain with is not only extraordinarily wasteful of the people's money, but can also lead to further expenditures. Development, production, and deployment of these weapons are frequently taken seriously by Defense Department personnel and some in Congress, and so what was originally found to be unnecessary is subsequently regarded as important, even essential, to national defense; and negotiations with the USSR and other nations suffer as a result.

A period of two or three years of reduced expenditures through the postponement of decisions on new weapons systems and the elimination of obsolete weapons, should enable the United States to test the validity of this national decision taken on its own merits without incurring an irreparable military risk. The United States should also, however, utilize unilateral examples in bilateral and multilateral negotiations as a means of eliciting a parallel response from the Soviet Union, whose military expenditures continue to rise. U.S. reductions in military expenditures should be proclaimed as a major national policy intended to test the interest of the USSR to move détente into the military sphere. To make certain that it is clearly understood as such by world public opinion and by the Soviet public in particular, the United States should propose that both sides divert a significant percentage of the amount of the reductions to established programs of multilateral assistance for those poor nations which are not themselves wasting resources on excessive armaments.[4]

Bilateral Negotiations. While unilateral actions by states can, the commission believes, be used as a deliberate means to induce reciprocity and lead eventually to formal treaty commitments to limit and control arms, in the long run bilateral and multilateral negotiations become essential.

Because of the preeminence of the two superpowers, it was perhaps inevitable that bilateral negotiations regarding their nuclear weapons should take place. After a long series of preliminary consultations, the United States and the Soviet Union initiated the Strategic Arms Limitation Talks, the first session extending from November 1969 to May 1972. Negotiations at this session produced the Treaty on the Limitation of Anti-Ballistic Missile Systems and the Interim Agreement on Certain Measures with Respect to the Limitation of Strategic Offensive Arms, signed by President Nixon and Chairman Brezhnev on May 26, 1972.

The second session (SALT II) began in November 1972 and has continued intermittently to the present time. These bilateral negotiations resulted in a protocol to the Treaty on the Limitation of Anti-Ballistic Missile Systems and a Treaty on the Limitation of Underground Nuclear Weapon Tests, both signed by President Nixon and Chairman Brezhnev on July 3, 1974; and an agreement on the maximum number of strategic nuclear delivery vehicles allowed to each side, signed by President Ford and Chairman Brezhnev at Vladivostok on November 24, 1974.

The bilateral negotiations, however essential they have appeared to the two superpowers, have at least two disadvantages. First, the almost total secrecy surrounding years of talks has restricted knowledge of issues of paramount importance for all mankind to a handful of officials in Washington and Moscow. Most of the executive branch, the Congress, and the American public have been wholly in the dark until the final communiqué is issued, as have presumably been most of the Soviet government and public.

It is vital to strengthen both the national and international constituencies for arms control and disarmament measures. Involving as they do complex and sensitive technical, political, and security issues, arms control and disarmament negotiations tend to be prolonged and difficult for both the public and government officials to comprehend. When, in addition, they are conducted in great secrecy, even experts are hard put to make an informed judgment about the merits of rival

Approaches to Arms Control and Disarmament 49

positions and strategies.

The issue of secret versus open diplomacy is not a new one. In any kind of negotiation—state to state, politician to politician, banker to businessman, management to labor—some secrecy is essential until the outcome is made public. Never, however, have the stakes of diplomatic negotiations been as high. Some formula is needed by which the American and Soviet people, and the rest of the world, are made aware of the progress or non-progress of SALT and other major negotiations— "open covenants, more openly arrived at." Some compromise between total secrecy and total publicity would seem necessary.[5]

A second disadvantage of exclusively bilateral negotiations is the misleading impression they give that only the two superpowers are involved in the need for control of nuclear weapons. Other nuclear powers and potential powers are also affected, and need to be included in negotiations for limiting nuclear weapons. Even though both superpowers strongly oppose efforts to enlarge the negotiating forum in any way that might dilute their hegemonic position and invite pressure upon them, consideration must be given to this issue.

Accordingly, it should be U.S. policy to report more fully and candidly on bilateral and multilateral arms control talks and to utilize congressional hearings as a means of giving further impetus to negotiations. A better informed public and Congress will give greater consideration to promising proposals which one side or the other hesitates to endorse. Fuller disclosures would enable the Congress to deal more effectively with the national military budget. For its part, the Congress should see to it that the principal U.S. negotiators, as well as qualified private experts, receive a full opportunity to testify at open hearings alongside the administration's senior witnesses.

Both the United States and the Soviet Union should publish more complete and systematic reports on the results achieved at each session, reasons for lack of progress, issues in dispute, and each side's negotiating position. The reports should be made available for discussion by the United Nations. The outcome of these talks will affect the lives of people everywhere and both sides should recognize their accountability to the international community.

Recommendations

1. The United States, for a period of two or three years, in order to encourage reciprocal reductions by the Soviet Union and other countries, should: (a) initiate reductions in expenditures for both strategic weapons, particularly land-based nuclear missiles, and conventional forces; (b) postpone decisions on production of

new weapons systems; and (c) propose that states making such reductions devote a substantial part of the amount of the reductions to economic and social assistance, especially multilateral, to those poor nations that are not wasting resources on excessive armaments.
2. The United States should forego authorization for development, production, and deployment of weapons for use as bargaining chips in future negotiations.
3. In order adequately to inform Congress and the public the executive branch should report more fully to them on bilateral and multilateral arms control talks, and together with the Soviet government should issue frequent joint reports during sessions of SALT and other bilateral negotiations, and transmit them to the United Nations.

Controlling and Reducing Conventional Weapons

Introduction

Controlling and limiting conventional weapons requires the consideration of three interrelated components. One component is the development and production of conventional weapons. The second is the trade in armaments, especially by the major powers—and to a much lesser extent by the smaller powers—to states all over the world, particularly to areas where interstate hostility exists. The third area covers the deployment of conventional weapons in areas beyond or near the borders of states possessing these weapons.

This report discusses the trade in armaments and an aspect of their deployment, but it does not cover development and production.[6] The commission recognizes that it would be discriminatory in the long run toward states not possessing a major arms industry if the trade in arms to them were curtailed, while states producing and supplying weapons refused to accept controls and limitations on their own weapons acquisition. Consequently, the commission believes that reductions in conventional weapons stockpiles and curtailment of conventional weapons development and production are necessary aspects of efforts to achieve constraints on the arms trade and deployment of these weapons beyond the boundaries of the states producing them. All of the wars in the post–World War II period have been fought with conventional weapons. Thousands of lives have been lost and billions of dollars of destruction and waste of resources have occurred. Conventional weapons disarmament in terms of moving toward the peaceful resolution of conflict is as urgent as nuclear disarmament.

Conventional weapons reductions have not been the subject of

Approaches to Arms Control and Disarmament

post-World War II international negotiations, except in the early U.N. discussions in the Commission on Conventional Armaments and the first Disarmament Commission, and in the context of negotiations on general and complete disarmament in the early 1960s. Then the issue was how much to cut back in each stage of disarmament and whether the reductions should be by percentage or actual numbers. The negotiations for mutual and balanced force reductions in Europe, still underway, are not about reductions in conventional weapons possessed by the two sides, but are instead primarily concerned with their deployment. Of course, it can be argued that once forces are withdrawn from lines of confrontation it is questionable whether they are needed in similar numbers back home or in the areas to which they are withdrawn, i.e., neighboring countries. In other words, agreements to deploy arms back from points of tension should result eventually in less need for the weapons themselves.

Control of the International Arms Trade

The value of the world arms trade, according to U.S. government estimates, issued by the Arms Control and Disarmament Agency (ACDA), rose from $2.4 billion in 1961 to $9.2 billion in 1974. Because of problems in assembling the data, the ACDA statistics probably understate the total. But even on the ACDA basis, it would appear that we are talking about a current international trade flow of $10-12 billion annually, with inflation accounting for only part of the increase. However, some weapons are sold at a discount. The expansion of this trade in recent years has exceeded even the rapid rise in the rate in military spending.

While the total value of the arms trade represents not more than 4 percent of world military expenditures, its significance to security and peace is much greater than its relative value suggests. The trade stimulates regional arms competition, accelerates the arms race generally, and escalates the destructive effects of wars.

Aside from the extremely rapid expansion of the trade in recent years, it has characteristics which underline both the necessity and the difficulty of limiting it.

1. Over thirty countries are currently arms exporters. About one-third of these are in the big league, accounting for $100 million or more in transfers in a year. France and the United Kingdom are near the top in this group, each representing annual transfers of $500 million or more. But the United States and the USSR dwarf the rest of the competition. Soviet exports are believed to be in the $2-3 billion range, U.S. exports about $5 billion in 1973 and perhaps nearer $8 billion in 1974.

In short, although there are many arms suppliers, just two countries currently account for 80 percent of the trade and four for over 90 percent of it.

2. There are many more importing than exporting countries, one hundred at least. The great bulk of arms transfers goes to the developing countries. In 1961 these countries accounted for about 50 percent of the arms imports, but more recently they have accounted for three-fourths of world arms imports. In 1974, six major importing countries (Iran, Iraq, Saudi Arabia, Syria, and South Vietnam) imported half the arms by value that moved into the developing world.

3. The weapons moving in trade are significantly more advanced and costly than they used to be. A substantial portion of the trade is in major military equipment. In the 5-year period (1967-1971) covered by published ACDA figures, jet aircraft and missiles represented more than 40 percent of the total, and large land armaments, such as tanks and artillery, and naval vessels another 20 percent. Because of the widespread demand for sophisticated equipment, these proportions are probably higher now.

4. The bulk of arms transfers today is believed to be government-to-government controlled. This is in contrast to the large private trade earlier in the century. There has been a shift in the trade from an aid to a sales basis—a trend which both reflects and reinforces sellers' economic motivations.

5. With government control, there has been increasing government activity to promote sales. High officials as well as military attachés act as middlemen and salesmen for arms dealers and manufacturers.

Political-Economic Factors

A review of the economic and political arguments often cited in favor of the arms trade fails to yield convincing evidence that it has provided a new political or economic advantage to supplier nations (as opposed to supplier industries or companies) sufficient to offset its destabilizing effects. The history of arms transfers indicates that they involve diplomatic and military risks without ensuring useful political influence for suppliers. Both the India-Pakistan and Middle East wars illustrated how powerless suppliers are to prevent weapons supplied by them from being used once hostilities start. There are other cases that can be cited.

In the case of Israel, only two countries can meet Israel's military requirements on short notice: the United States and the USSR. Since the latter is excluded from such a role for political reasons, Israel can turn only to the United States. Similarly, only the United States can furnish Israel with the extensive credit she requires. Moreover, the United

States is also not nearly as vulnerable to Arab economic pressures as Britain and France. But Israel is a case of vulnerability to the political influence of the arms "fix" supplier. There is some doubt whether such influence has invariably been successful.

Iran's extensive purchases of American arms and its subsequent dependence on the United States to train its forces has not at the same time led Iran to hold down the price of oil. While Iran's foreign policy is Western-oriented, it is also geared, understandably, toward obtaining maximum economic and political benefits from its current position as a major oil supplier. Iran's gains often appear to have been made at the expense of the developed countries, several of which are major arms suppliers for its armed forces.

Perhaps the most striking example of the failure of large-scale arms transfers to secure lasting political influence is the recent case of the USSR and Egypt. Not only has the Soviet Union's political influence in Egypt markedly declined since 1971, but the Soviet Union has apparently been left with a substantial unpaid bill for earlier arms shipments to Egypt. The Egyptians are now turning to the United Kingdom, France, and China for assistance in modernizing their Soviet-made military equipment.

The arms trade policy of the United Kingdom and France (to the extent that any state has such a policy) is primarily determined by economic factors, largely because these two countries cannot hope to compete militarily with the United States or the USSR, but also because arms exports are so much more crucial to their economies. The sale of French arms to South Africa is a clear example of how an economic rationale for arms sales has prevailed over the danger of alienating much of black Africa from France. The fact that they have not is something of an anomaly, although President Giscard d'Estaing's pronouncement of a limited French embargo on arms to South Africa last year would appear to represent French acknowledgement that such alienation is possible.

Arms trade competition can sour relations among allies and can force the losers to seek markets for their armaments in areas of political and military instability. For example, the victory of the F-16 over the Dassault entry in the recent NATO fighter competition may force the French to seek buyers in volatile areas, merely to preserve their aircraft industry. Fierce competition for arms contracts has also led to bribery and other corrupt practices.

On the economic side, serious disadvantages offset what may be quite temporary employment and balance of payments gains for supplying nations. In a boomerang effect, inflation is stimulated as arms purchasers raise prices for oil and other raw materials in order to pay for weapons. Most important over the longer term, the build-up of weapons-producing capacity provides less employment than the many civilian industries which are more labor-intensive. Capital expansion in the volatile arms industry often occurs at the expense of lagging sectors in civilian industry, diminishing an economy's overall rate of growth in socially useful sectors.

Arms-importing nations in the non-oil producing developing areas of the world in particular are hard hit economically. Not only do they forfeit foreign exchange, they also divert scarce resources (skilled manpower especially) needed for their economic development and for the improvement of living conditions of impoverished populations.

Relying on arms exports to improve or maintain a country's balance of payments position can result in serious dislocations should the market for arms dry up or succumb to foreign competition. The time and capital required for converting from military to civilian-oriented production may be greater than that required for corresponding shifts within the civilian sphere. These extended lags may result in greater losses in overall production as well as more extensive and longer-term unemployment. Nevertheless, maintaining high employment levels and a strong balance of payments position are politically important domestic priorities, particularly in times of recession and high petroleum prices.

Recommendations

1. The United Nations should undertake to publish a yearbook on arms trade, including licensing agreements, arms production, and military expenditures. One objective of such a yearbook should be to develop uniform standards for accounts and categories of military trade, production, and expenditures. All nations should move as rapidly as possible to adopt these standards, recognizing their importance for arms control. Sources for the yearbook should include official reports from governments and reputable nongovernmental research organizations.
2. The United States should proceed immediately to convene a suppliers' conference among the NATO nations, with the objective of scheduling a full international conference in 1978 under United Nations auspices for the purpose of restricting arms sales. The conference should address the question of the need to provide more security to buyer states through regional arms control measures.
3. The President, for a limited period of time, should enunciate U.S.

arms trade policy, in the form of a request for a law or by an executive order, setting an overall dollar limit on all licenses for the export of arms, with a view to inducing other arms suppliers to adopt similar policies.
4. The United States should enlist the cooperation of other arms suppliers in a joint proposal to the United Nations requiring the notification to that body of the nature, amount, and destination of all arms transfers and the registration with it of all licenses for exports of arms technology.
5. All proposed arms transactions by the United States should be accompanied by a presidential finding, on the public record, detailing the considerations on the U.S. side which make the transfer desirable.
6. Licensing of exports of arms technology should be put under controls as strict as those for the export of arms.
7. The United States should seek in the United Nations the convening of negotiating conferences in the various geographic regions, including all interested parties, with a view to resolving disputes and achieving control of armaments in the area.

Notes

1. For example, France would not consent to reduce arms unless the United States and the United Kingdom guaranteed her frontiers.

2. The goal of comprehensive disarmament was first enunciated by the United States in 1952 and was revived by the Soviet Union in 1959.

3. Candidates for such reductions include particularly land-based nuclear intercontinental ballistic missiles and U.S. conventional forces withdrawn from Asia as a result of the end of the Vietnam War.

4. Unilateral reductions with regard to arms transfers are discussed below.

5. The General Assembly in 1975 reiterated its two previous invitations to the USSR and the United States "to keep the General Assembly informed in good time of the progress of their negotiations" concerning nuclear weapons. G.A. res. 3814A(XXVIII), December 18, 1973; 3261C(XXIX), December 9, 1974; 3484C(XXX), December 12, 1975.

6. It was mentioned above that conventional weapons development, production, and deployment are the focus of a report by the United Nations Association of the United States of America, on *Controlling the Conventional Arms Race* (November 1976).

PEACEKEEPING

4. The U.N. Peacekeeping Role
Ruth B. Russell

This paper examines, in general terms, the United Nation's peacekeeping role. It first seeks to clear up the definitional confusion that has developed around the concept of peacekeeping. For purposes of clarification, a distinction is made between peacekeeping activities and peace maintaining or enforcing operations. The focus of the discussion then shifts to the difficulties that have prevented the emergence of an effective peacekeeping system, both in the immediate post-war decades as well as in more recent years. This problem is analyzed in the broader context of international politics.

A recent instance of a peacekeeping mission, as it is generally understood, was the attempted intervention by the Arab League in the Lebanese civil war. As may be recalled, the proposal submitted by a number of its members was the creation of an all-Arab force that would enforce a ceasefire while the parties involved would attempt to resolve their conflict through peaceful negotiations. This plan (which was ultimately rejected) was strongly reminiscent of the peacekeeping machinery established in Vietnam. In both cases the parties to the conflict were included in the peacekeeping operations. This, of course, is in strong contrast to peacekeeping operations conducted under U.N. auspices.

This Lebanese example helps to illustrate the distinct nature of the U.N.'s peacekeeping role. The use of the term *peacekeeping* to cover a wide variety of international military operations such as NATO, the U.S. intervention in Lebanon in 1958, and in Vietnam as of 1965, has over the years obscured the proper meaning of this concept. International peacekeeping in the U.N. sense is, to begin with, fundamentally a political activity. From the perspective of the United Nations, the control of international violence is but part of a larger mission—namely to arrive at a peaceful settlement that will resolve the underlying conflict between the parties. Seen in this context, the creation of a military force to separate the contestants has a purely political function. In view of this, it is not surprising that the degree to which nations, including the United States, maintain an interest in peacekeeping operations of this kind is determined by their views about world politics and the U.N.'s role therein.

In addition to this functional distinction, there is an organizational one as well. U.N. peacekeeping forces are clearly third-party agencies. Thus, unlike the proposed Arab force or the Vietnam operation, a U.N. peacekeeping force excludes the participants to the conflict. For the purpose of clarity, therefore, it would be best to reserve the term peacekeeping only to U.N. operations and to classify international military endeavors to end conflicts outside the United Nations as "peace-maintaining" or "peace-enforcing" activities.

Dag Hammarskjöld once suggested that international organization machinery may be of two kinds. It may either assume the form of a "static conference machinery," such as the League of Nations had been. Or, alternatively, it may become the dynamic instrument of governments," through which they would be able to act collectively.[1] Which of these two would ultimately become the norm, in turn, would depend on what the members wished the United Nations to be: a repetition of the League of Nations or a more advanced and active international body. Over the past thirty years, the United Nations and its peacekeeping operations have fallen somewhere between these two alternatives.

Generally speaking, the development of peacekeeping and other phases of peaceful-settlement machinery and operations in the post-war period has been handicapped by the nature of the contemporary international political scene. This has been, on the whole, a highly revolutionary period of violent change. At such times, governments are not particularly interested in peaceful settlement per se; they may all subscribe to the charter, but they frequently ignore the commitments that the charter entails. Nowadays violence seems to be the mode of settling disputes most frequently favored by individuals and small, terroristic groups, as well as by governments. In theory, the purpose of U.N. peacekeeping has been to stop the fighting between the parties to a conflict so that a peaceful settlement could be arranged that would resolve the problems that had led to the eruption of violence in the first place. This is a very nice theory, which unfortunately fails to work in practice. The major reason for this is that violence itself has become so deepseated.

U.N. peacekeeping groups have been used primarily to bring violent conflicts to a halt. There have been exceptions to this rule, such as the case of West Irian where fighting had already ceased and where the U.N. peacekeeping force was a part of the peaceful settlement agreement. This operation was a highly successful one precisely because the underlying political problem had, for all practical purposes, been resolved before the U.N. force was sent out. Other U.N. peacekeeping operations, however, have been a response to more dangerous and volatile situations. These had frequently reached a point where the governments directly and indirectly involved (which usually included the two superpowers) had become more fearful of developments outside the United Nations than they were of using the international machinery to end the violence.

On the whole, most governments remain highly reluctant to use international machinery of a third party nature, as the current Lebanon situation certainly illustrated. Yet, they have reluctantly accepted the limitations and requirements of U.N. peacekeeping when the situation appeared about to get out of control. This was particularly the case in the short period after the mid-1950s. At that time many came to the mistaken conclusion that U.N. peacekeeping would not only become more frequent and larger in scale, but that such operations would become the pattern for the future. What was not realized, however, was that the United Nations' growing involvement in conflict during this period apparently reflected the fact that the two superpowers had not yet achieved confidence that they could control their own nuclear forces. Consequently, they worried sufficiently about what might happen *outside* the United Nations, in situations such as that of Suez in 1956, that they managed to agree on a holding action *through* the United Nations, even when they were unable to agree on anything else. The same political forces that have precluded any significant achievements in the arms control field also prevented the development of U.N. peacekeeping along the lines that one might have logically expected to emerge had the member governments been really committed to the principles of the charter.

What then is the situation today? Has there been any change in the nature, function, or direction of U.N. peacekeeping? If we look at recent international events, especially from the perspective of American policy positions, the preeminence of political considerations is very clear. In 1973, when Secretary of State Kissinger spoke at the United Nations, he strongly supported international peacekeeping—as the United States usually does. He declared:

We should delay no longer. The time has come to agree on peacekeeping guidelines so that this Organization can act swiftly, confidently, and effectively in future crises to break the deadlock. The United States is prepared to consider how the Security Council can play a more central role in the conduct of peacekeeping operations. If all countries concerned approach this problem with the desire to achieve a cooperative solution, the United Nations can achieve a major step forward during this session.

Between then and now, however, little has changed. Mr. Kissinger's hope that he could prod the Special Committee on Peacekeeping Operations into a more active role has come to naught. It continues to meet regularly, but its achievements remain minimal.

If all countries were to approach the problem of halting violence with a genuine desire for a cooperative solution on which all sides to a dispute could agree, then progress toward a more effective peacekeeping system would be possible. But the period since 1973 has made it clear that the fundamental elements that have traditionally blocked such a system still exist. It is interesting to note that the special committee itself has been unable to agree to a single approach. Hence over the past few years it has repeatedly shifted its emphases and positions on the issue of peacekeeping.

It began with attempts to reach an agreement on observation groups rather than on peacekeeping forces as such. After a long period of little progress, it decided to concentrate on the principles of peacekeeping; on which, however, it also failed to agree. It then turned its attention to the role of the Security Council; Mr. Kissinger's 1973 statement made it sound at that time as though some progress might be made. There actually was agreement within a working group of the special committee on some twelve peacekeeping functions that the Security Council had performed and might continue to perform in the future. But the group did not agree on the most critical functions of command and control through the United Nations; and since it was unable to agree on all the functions under consideration, the partial list of funtions so agreed was never officially accepted by the whole committee.

After this debacle the special committee turned again to the *principles* of peacekeeping. In 1974, it devised a set of principles, most of which, however, were drafted in at least two, if not three, possible versions. But final agreement eluded the committee once again, and the points on which no agreement could be reached were basically the same points in dispute all along. In 1975, however, the committee tried once more to take those alternative statements of principle and work out single agreed ones. By the end of the 1975 General Assembly, it had only debated points one through six, but without agreeing even on those. At that point, Canada suggested that it might be best if the committee temporarily stopped meeting; but that did not succeed either. The net result, therefore, was one more year in which the peacekeeping committee proposed, and the assembly agreed, that it continue its effort. There has been only one new development since that vote, which is the result of the latest peacekeeping operations in the Middle East (UNEF [U.N. Emergency Force] II and UNDOF [U.N. Disengagement Observer Force]). The special committee is not only to continue its effort to agree on principles of peacekeeping, but it should also begin studying the problem of arriving at more permanent peaceful settlement of disputes.

At this point, that is a problem to which no one has the proper solution. That is why the inefficient, but often politically effective, procedure of a U.N. peacekeeping operation can at least halt the violence when a dispute has reached that stage, even if it can do little more than that. Yet this is at best a tentative halt, without assurance that the conflict itself will cease unless and until the parties involved are prepared to compromise on an agreement. In conclusion, I would like to quote from my own first paper on U.N. peacekeeping, which was written in 1962:

> All things considered—especially the limitations of UNEF and ONUC [U.N. Congo Operation]—it would seem most likely that the near future will see no more than a continuation of the pattern of the past: the gradual, even reluctant, development of principles and procedures for the utilization of international military force through the world Organization—crisis-impelled, unsteady, and precarious in growth.

I endorse that in 1977, without change.

Notes

1. *Introduction to the Annual Report of the Secretary-General on the Work of the Organization*, 16 June 1960-15 June 1961 (A/4800/Add. 1), p. 1.

5. Breaking the Deadlock on U.N. Peacekeeping
Seymour Maxwell Finger

The framers of the United Nations Charter worked in an atmosphere strongly influenced by the 1930s and World War II, particularly in writing Chapter VII. It was natural, therefore, that the kind of action most precisely detailed in the charter was enforcement action as set out in Article 42 and subsequent articles of Chapter VII. The threat then uppermost in the minds of the five major wartime allies constituting the five permanent members of the Security Council—China, France, the United Kingdom, the USSR, and the United States—was the resurgence of German or Japanese militarism. An indication of this frame of mind can be found in the "transitional articles," numbers 106 and 107 of the charter.

But the situation has changed radically since 1945. First of all, there was an open split in the allied coalition, thus removing a precondition of effective coercive action against outlaw nations. And the Germans and Japanese have directed their great energy and competence to economic growth, rather than militarism. Second, rapid decolonization, desirable as it has been, has resulted in a proliferation of small new nations and has brought with it a degree of instability in what is loosely called the Third World. Third, both of these developments have taken place in the setting of nuclear stalemate, which has deterred big wars but has not prevented small wars. Thus, the threat of small wars getting out of hand became a major concern of the international community, particularly as represented at the United Nations.

This chapter is excerpted with permission from ORBIS 17, no. 2 (summer 1973):385-394. ORBIS is a journal of world affairs, published by the Foreign Policy Research Institute.

With a few exceptions, notably Korea and Viet Nam on the one hand, and Hungary and Czechoslovakia on the other, the kind of peace-threatening situations the world has encountered and will continue to encounter are local conflicts, not directly involving the forces of major powers. U.N. peacekeeping actions in such situations have been of three types: (1) In quarrels and border disputes between small states, as in the Arab-Israeli conflict, a U.N. mission could supervise a cease-fire and serve as a buffer. (2) In situations like the Congo and Cyprus, where internal strife threatened to draw in outsiders, the United Nations has helped to restore order and stabilize the situation. (3) In situations such as in Greece at the end of the 1940s and Lebanon in 1958, the United Nations helped to spotlight subversion and infiltration.

In more than a dozen such situations since World War II, the United Nations has helped to prevent or end fighting and maintain a truce. But except for Korea, it has not undertaken the more ambitious task of stopping aggression or enforcing the peace. It was unable to take such action, for example, in Hungary, Viet Nam, Laos, or Czechoslovakia. In no case has it ordered any forces into coercive action under Article 42, nor have any forces for this purpose been put at its disposal under Article 43 agreements.

This does not imply that U.N. peacekeeping in disputes involving the superpowers is out of the question. On the contrary, during the Cuban missile crisis of 1962 the secretary-general was prepared, if requested by the Soviet Union and the United States, to observe compliance with the agreement on missiles. This was an important matter to the United States, and Khrushchev indicated a willingness to agree. However, Cuba refused to go along, and other methods of verification were used.

The record of these U.N. actions over the past two decades shows that United Nations peacekeeping, as distinct from enforcement actions, has been primarily an *auxiliary to political measures*—an extension of political action to contain conflict and set the stage for peaceful settlement. The purpose has not been to apply military force in the classic sense of coercing the parties to submit to the United Nation's will. It has rather been to install a political presence which carries out certain ancillary police duties. The late Adlai Stevenson put it in a nutshell in an article for *McCall's* in October 1964, entitled "No Mission But Peace; No Enemy But War."

The essential function of U.N. peacekeeping is far more political than military. From this fact, a number of consequences follow. First, the mandate of a peacekeeping force must be compatible with the national security interests of the countries concerned, including the troop-contributing countries. Second, the consent of the host government or governments, on whose soil the force is to be stationed, is deemed necessary for entry of the force. Third, the force should not resort to violence beyond what may be essential to defend itself and to carry out its primarily political mission. Finally, all principal parties to the conflict must be willing to cooperate with the force.

Peacekeeping operations cannot stop the parties from fighting if they are absolutely determined to fight, but where there is a willingness to observe a cease-fire, U.N. forces or observers can give each side reassurance that the other side is also being observed for honest performance.

Among the major powers, the United States has been the most consistent supporter of U.N. peacekeeping. But though U.S. support has usually been crucial, it is equally true that these operations were made possible only through the support of middle powers that were prepared to provide personnel and financing—such countries as Canada, Brazil, Ethiopia, India, Yugoslavia, Ireland, and the Scandinavian states, to name a few.

For more than twenty years the Soviet Union asserted that there was no such thing as voluntary peacekeeping. Its expressed doctrine held that the only legitimate role for U.N. forces under the charter was the enforcement action governed by Article 42.[1] In practice, the Soviets have been more realistic. They have supported or acquiesced in virtually all peacekeeping operations, although they refused to pay the assessments for the Congo and the U.N. Emergency Force (UNEF)—thus bringing on the Article 19 crisis of 1964-1965[2]—and have insisted, along with France, that the Cyprus operation be financed by voluntary contributions.

Soviet-U.S. Negotiations

In recent years there have been signs that the Soviets might be prepared to bring their position into line with the realities of today's world. They have shown some willingness to negotiate guidelines for future peacekeeping operations. This has been the basis of negotiations in a working group of eight (now enlarged to thirteen)[3] at the United Nations as well as for informal discussions between Soviet and U.S. representatives. Since some question has been raised by other countries concerning American discussions with the Soviets, these should be seen in their proper context.

Our first efforts after the Article 19 crisis in 1964 and 1965 were to work with the smaller and medium-sized countries on behalf of peacekeeping principles supported by a majority of U.N. members but strongly opposed by the Soviets: for example, (1) that the financing of peacekeeping is a collective responsibility, with the costs to be apportioned among the members by the General Assembly in accordance with Article 17 of the charter; (2) that, while the Security Council has primary responsibility for the maintenance of international peace and security, the General Assembly may initiate cooperative action if the council is stymied by a veto; and (3) that, while authorization of peacekeeping operations is the responsibility of the Security Council of the General Assembly, the secretary-general should—in the interest of efficiency—be responsible for day-to-day control of operations.

However, the smaller and medium-sized countries displayed little will to bring the issue to a head against the strong opposition of the Soviets. More and more they signaled that the United States should attempt to work out some sort of understanding with the Soviet Union, without sacrificing the principles the majority considered essential. It was with this background and the hints of some flexibility in the Soviet attitude that we began, early in 1970, discussions aimed at breaking the deadlock.

Both in the Committee on Peacekeeping (the Committee of 33) and in informal discussions with the Soviets, we tried to set aside any disputes over charter interpretation whose solution was not essential to progress. For example, although the United States continues to believe in the residual authority of the General Assembly to authorize voluntary peacekeeping operations in situations where the Security Council is unable to act, the USSR still does not accept this principle; so we agreed to begin discussions on guidelines for operations authorized by the Security Council. The United States has always held to the charter principle (Article 24) that the Security Council has primary responsibility for maintaining peace and security. Moreover, it is obviously a less unwieldy body than the General Assembly of 132 members. Nevertheless, the United States would not foreclose completely a new resort to the General Assembly—as in the Middle East crisis in 1956—if in a dangerous situation the Security Council were again stalemated by a veto.

The Soviet-U.S. discussions concentrated on three essential areas:

1. *Financing.* While the observers in Kashmir and the Middle East are financed on a basis of collective responsibilty in the U.N. budget, the larger operation on Cyprus depends on voluntary contributions—a system which is inequitable and undependable. Although fifty-two countries, including two nonmembers of the United Nations, have contributed to the U.N. Force in Cyprus (UNFICYP) since its inception, currently such contributions are being made by only nineteen

countries out of a total membership of 132. Among the larger members, the most notable omissions are France and the Soviet Union. This is obviously not in accord with the principle of collective responsibility of members. Moreover, it is hardly dignified for the secretary-general to have to go hat in hand to governments in order to carry out an operation to keep the peace.

2. *Preparation.* A second essential is to assure that personnel and facilities for any peacekeeping force are available and ready on short notice. To this end member countries should be encouraged to earmark in advance military personnel and facilities for use in United Nations peacekeeping operations.

3. *Establishment, Command and Control.* Third, there must be agreement on procedures which are politically realistic and operationally practical for the establishment and direction of U.N. operations after they are authorized.

The first two of these three main problems presented no major persistent obstacles. On financing, the United States made it clear at the beginning of the bilateral talks that a *sine qua non* must be a commitment that, if guidelines were agreed, all permanent members of the Security Council must pay their fair share of all future peacekeeping operations carried out in accordance with those guidelines. The Soviets objected to specific emphasis on the permanent members but were willing to include a paragraph requiring *all* members to pay unless the Security Council decided on some other method of financing. There were other differences on the respective authority of the Security Council and the General Assembly in apportioning expenses, but these did not appear to constitute a major obstacle.

On preparations, agreement was reached on the desirability of having member states earmark in advance military personnel and units for potential U.N. service, and maintaining an up-to-date roster of available personnel and equipment. There was some disagreement on who would request the information from member states and who would maintain the roster, but these problems were largely overcome. It was tentatively agreed that the Security Council would request the secretary-general to inquire of member states what personnel, supplies, and equipment they might be prepared to make available for operations authorized by the Security Council, and that he would maintain the roster on behalf of the council. During meetings in 1971 I urged that we recommend such a step in our report to the Twenty-sixth Session of the General Assembly, and most members of the Working Group agreed. But the Soviets strongly opposed the idea of moving ahead on one aspect of the guidelines until agreement was reached on all aspects. Since we were working by consensus, this step could not be taken.

The real stumbling block was the matter of setting guidelines on how peacekeeping operations, once authorized by the Security Council, would be established, commanded, and controlled. Such procedures must be both politically realistic and operationally practical. They must take account of the interest of all parties concerned, must be impartial in both intent and application, and must be calculated to induce the cooperation of contending parties as well as those states on which the operation depends for manpower and funds.

This meant, in the U.S. view, an acceptable and workable balance of responsibilities between the Security Council and the secretary-general. The Security Council has ultimate authority over such operations. It should have the power to authorize the operation, determine the key provisions of its mandate, and exercise broad political supervision over it. The Soviets, however, have advocated extending the authority of the Security Council to encompass *operational* decisions—for example, regarding size and composition of the force and designation of the commander—as well as determination of the method of financing.

The discussions have thus focused on where to draw the line of operational responsibility so as to take account of both political and operational necessities. As the United States sees it, the Security Council has a legitimate interest in assuring political responsiveness, but effective management requires that the executive authority of the Secretary-General not be impaired. The Soviets, on the other hand, urged application of Articles 43-48 of the U.N. Charter, giving command and control to the Security Council and its Military Staff Committee or a special committee of the council. Problems arose because the charter provisions in Articles 43-48 were designed for enforcement action rather than peacekeeping.

Despite this fundamental difference in doctrine, bilateral negotiations were carried on intensively over many months, in a good working atmosphere with a minimum of doctrinaire statements and no bombast. Gradually differences were narrowed, and it began to appear that agreement might be reached on an acceptable delegation of operational responsibilities by the Security Council to a special committee and the secretary-general.

The high point of the negotiations came in June 1970. Ambassador Lev Mendelevich, my Soviet counterpart, was then leaving New York for a new assignment in Moscow. To sum up the results of five months of intensive discussions the U.S. delegation drew up a working paper incorporating points of agreement as well as certain suggestions for resolving remaining issues. It was not an agreed paper; however, it represented a serious U.S. effort to meet Soviet concerns expressed during the negotiations. Mendelevich, while clearly unable to commit the USSR at that point, was sufficiently interested in our paper to request five separate meetings with me for clarification during his final week in New York.

We hoped then that a Soviet response would be forthcoming by August or September. Unfortunately it did not come for thirteen months, too late for progress at either the Twenty-fifth or the Twenty-sixth Session of the General Assembly. But the documents submitted in the spring of 1972 to the secretary-general by the USSR and the United States[4] show some of the progress made during the first half of 1970. Though important and substantial differences remain, I believe a further effort to close the gap is in order.

The Soviet document, which is a response to the U.S. working paper and incorporates many parts of it, represents a step forward in the following ways:

1. It acknowledges something the Soviets long denied, i.e., that *voluntary* U.N. peacekeeping operations are a legitimate enterprise under the charter and are something quite different from the enforcement actions envisaged in Article 42 of the charter.

2. While urging prompt resumption of negotiations on agreements for the provision of military contingents under Article 43 of the charter, the Soviet document would give signatory countries the right to decide on the occasion of each operation whether or not such contingents may be used, instead of being obliged to make contingents available to the Security Council "on its call," as provided in Article 43. Thus the agreements would not differ in essence from those made by the secretary-general since 1956; the difference would be the participation of the Military Staff Committee in negotiating them. In paragraph IV (4), the document stipulates that contingents may also come from member states of the United Nations that have *not* concluded Article 43 agreements.

3. There is no rigid insistence on a "troika" composition of U.N. forces. Instead paragraph IV (5) states,

> it is necessary to make all efforts to reach an equitable balance in the composition of the participants in the operation so that no State Member of the United Nations is excluded from participation because of its political, social and economic system or because of its belonging to a certain geographical region. At the same time, the following considerations should be taken into account: the necessity to receive the

consent of the host-country, the state of readiness and fitness for the conditions of the situation of furnished contingents, military personnel and facilities, and the necessity to ensure good working relations of the participating personnel with other parties concerned and among themselves.

The acknowledgement that contingents and the commander must be acceptable to the host country—a major advance—resulted in part from the fact that the special committee has an Egyptian rapporteur who made this point emphatically during working group discussions.

The United States, on its side, took certain steps forward to meet the Soviets:

1. As noted earlier, despite its position that the General Assembly has residual authority to recommend peacekeeping operations when the Security Council is blocked by a veto, the United States agreed to begin the search for guidelines by discussing operations authorized by the council.

2. The U.S. proposal[5] acknowledges the ultimate authority of the Security Council over all aspects of a peacekeeping operation, an important point for the Soviets. It also proposes the establishment, in accordance with Article 29 of the charter, of a council committee to be consulted by the secretary-general on important operational matters; e.g., the choice of a commander, the provision of military observers and contingents, and the preparation of directives for the operation. This would give member states, and notably the Soviet Union, a significantly greater involvement in the conduct of U.N. operations than in the past, and corresponds to an earlier Soviet proposal.

On many significant points the two documents are parallel; for instance, the establishment of a special committee, the establishment and maintenance of a roster of available military observers and contingents, the role of the host country, and the ultimate authority of the Security Council. These parallel points are, in substantial part, the product of the negotiations. Yet the remaining gaps will not be easy to close.

The most serious problem is Soviet insistence that decisions in the committee may be taken only if *all* permanent members of the Security Council agree to them. This extends the veto, which can now be applied to the council's authorization of an operation, to *all aspects* of its establishment, direction, and control. Indeed, under paragraph VI (3) of the Soviet document, if any member objects to any activity by the field commander, he must suspend such activity unless or until it is approved by the committee or by the council—in both of which the veto would apply. Under such conditions one would have a peacekeeping vehicle with a weak motor, powerful brakes, and many hands on the steering wheel, as in Viet Nam.

The U.S. proposal would allow any member who disagrees with the way the secretary-general or the commander is carrying out an operation to raise the matter in the committee or in the council. The obvious difference is that, under the U.S. proposal, a majority would be needed to *stop* the action, not to sustain it.

Thus, one side fears arbitrary or unjust action by the commander or the secretary-general contrary to its interests; the other fears paralysis of an operation after its launch. Both fears can be supported by rational argument, but that leads nowhere. Can the differences be reconciled?

Notes

1. U.N. General Assembly (UNGA), statements by P. Morozov (USSR) to Special Committee on Peacekeeping Operations, March 6, 1968.

2. Adlai E. Stevenson, "The UN Financial Crisis," *Department of State Bulletin,* November 9, 1964, pp. 681 ff.

3. The original eight members of the working group were France, the United Kingdom, the Soviet Union, the United States, Canada, Czechoslovakia, Egypt, and Mexico. In 1972 Argentina, Brazil, India, Japan, Nigeria, and Pakistan were added, while Mexico withdrew.

4. UNGA documents A/8669, March 30, 1972, and A/8676, April 3, 1972.

5. Annex to UNGA document A/8676, part II, April 3, 1972. The working paper given to the Soviets in June 1970 contained everything in this document plus certain additional concessions offered on a quid pro quo package deal basis. That working paper is still classified, as the Soviets have not yet accepted the package.

6. U.N. Peacekeeping and the U.S. National Interest
Seymour Maxwell Finger

Given the lack of clear charter provisions for U.N. peacekeeping and the serious problems—particularly financial—that have arisen with past operations, I have been among those who argued that agreement on guidelines for peacekeeping should be vigorously sought, particularly through negotiations with the Soviet Union.[1]

The establishment of the U.N. Emergency Force (UNEF II) in October 1973 has, to my mind, changed the situation. This force, with a current strength of 4,300, supervises the truce and disengagement between Egyptian and Israeli forces in the Sinai desert. Its operation is based on a report by the secretary-general which sets out its terms of reference, general considerations, a proposed plan of action, estimated costs, and the method of financing (document S/11052/Rev. 1, October 27, 1973). I have been informed by highly reliable sources in the Secretariat that this document was drafted in light of proposals and statements made in the Committee on Peacekeeping Operations over many years. Consequently, the committee's work has not been in vain. The beauty of the secretary-general's document lies in the fact that it has been careful not to offend any major power seriously, that it has incorporated all agreed elements and that it has drawn up a *modus operandi* in which all powers can acquiesce even though they would not specifically endorse some of its features. This technique has been particularly important with regard to the establishment, command, and control of the operations. For that reason, I believe the future of peacekeeping would be better served by using UNEF II as a model or precedent, as in common law, rather than to attempt to codify guidelines.

First, the secretary-general's document concerning the establishment of UNEF states, "that the force will be under the command of the

United Nations, vested in the Secretary-General, under the authority of the Security Council. The command in the field will be exercised by a Force Commander appointed by the Secretary-General with the consent of the Security Council. The Commander will be responsible to the Secretary-General." This brief paragraph skillfully overcomes some of the main problems encountered in the working group of the committee on peacekeeping. It clearly gives the secretary-general a mandate to run the operations on a day-to-day basis and to appoint a Force Commander, both of which were resisted by the Soviets in negotiations on general guidelines.

Second, paragraph 3 (c) of the secretary-general's document states: "The Force will be composed of a number of contingents to be provided by selected countries, *upon the request of the Secretary-General.*" (Emphasis added.) The Soviets have argued that the Security Council should make the request. The paragraph continues: "The contingents will be selected in consultation with the Security Council and with the parties concerned, bearing in mind the accepted principle of equitable geographic representation." Although equitable geographic representation is mentioned here, "bearing in mind" is less rigid than the preferred Soviet version: "it is important to *base it* on the accepted principle of equitable geographic distribution." (Emphasis added.)

Third, this document, in its proposed plan of action, indicates that the secretary-general will appoint the commander of the emergency force as soon as possible, with the consent of the Security Council. Meanwhile, he had already apppointed Chief of UNTSO (U.N. Truce Supervision Organization), Major General Siilasvuo, as interim commander of the force. I can recall months of inconclusive negotiations with the Soviets in 1970 over this question of what should be done in an emergency before the secretary-general can consult the Security Council about the commander. Here the problem is resolved in one brief paragraph. Similarly, the secretary-general, after consultation with the president of the Security Council, began negotiations with Austria, Finland, and Sweden on the sending of contingents which would proceed immediately to Egypt.

Fourth, the final paragraph of the secretary-general's document stipulates, "The costs of the Force shall be considered as expenses of the Organization to be borne by the Members in accordance with Article 17, paragraph 2, of the Charter." The Soviets were long reluctant to agree that the General Assembly could decide on assessments for peacekeeping, as set out in Article 17 (2).

In these important respects the secretary-general's document represents a practical answer to the real problems of running a peacekeeping force. It is apparently easier for the Soviets to acquiesce in these provisions in a particular case rather than to endorse them as general principles or guidelines—hence my view that a "common law" precedent approach is better than an attempt at codification. The subsequent establishment of the U.N. Disengagement Observer Force (UNDOF) on the same general criteria as UNEF II reinforces the precedent.[2] (A force of 1,250, UNDOF supervises the disengagement agreement between Syrian and Israeli forces on the Golan Heights.)

It should be noted, however, that the Soviet viewpoint has also gained some ground in the UNEF II precedent. First, the operation was authorized by the Security Council, whose overall authority is recognized. Second, a Polish contingent is included, representing the first time a Warsaw Pact country has provided troops for a U.N. force. Third, at Soviet insistence, the USSR has 36 observers with UNEF, as has the United States.

This is not, in any case, a zero-sum game. The Polish contingent has by all accounts performed very well and its inclusion represents no loss to the United States. Nor is there any reason why, in current circumstances the United States should object to a model in which authorization comes from the Security Council, rather than the General Assembly. The assembly has an overwhelming third world majority whose views are often contrary to American policy. It is also large and relatively unwieldy. In the entire history of the United Nations only one major peacekeeping operations has even been initiated by the assembly, i.e., UNEF I. Thus, it is possible that a peacekeeping operation could be launched by the General Assembly if Security Council action is blocked by a veto, provided that such an operation has the support, or at least the acquiescence, of the two superpowers and a substantial majority of the assembly. But it would be a rare situation indeed (though not inconceivable) in which this same degree of support could not result in Security Council action.

It would appear, therefore, that neither the USSR nor the United States has sacrificed anything of substance in accepting the secretary-general's proposals for UNEF II. Moreover, their acceptance provided a sounder political and financial basis than was true for earlier U.N. peacekeeping forces.

As for coercive enforcement action, where participation by the members is binding, it is clear that only the Security Council is authorized by the charter (Articles 25, 39, 41, and 42) to take such decisions. Enforcement action can be blocked by the negative vote of any of the five permanent members of the Security Council, but this is the clear intent of the charter; it accords with practical realities; and it should reassure those who fear that United States security interests could be threatened by U.N. action.

Financing

The most serious problem hanging over the future of U.N. peacekeeping is the large and growing U.N. deficit. There is first of all the substantial deficit left from the earlier operations in the Middle East (1956-1967) and the Congo, for which short-term deficits of over $60 million remain. As a result, countries which provided contingents for the Congo and the Middle East operations have not been reimbursed for very substantial services provided and the Working Capital Fund of $40 million has been depleted.

UNEF II and UNDOF appeared at the outset to be on a sounder financial basis. Both are financed by assessments on the members, determined by the General Assembly each year in accordance with Article 17 (2) of the charter. Costs for 1976-1977 are estimated at $76,276,000. In contrast to UNEF I and the Congo operation, the Soviets and their allies have agreed to pay their share; however, China, Albania, Iraq, Libya, and Syria have refused to pay. Chinese arrears for UNEF II and UNDOF will amount to $22.7 million by November 1977. Moreover, starting in September 1975, the Soviet Union has refused to pay that part of its assessment which it attributes to additional UNEF costs involved in carrying out the disengagement agreement between Egypt and Israel negotiated by Henry Kissinger in that month. As a result, the USSR withheld $10.4 million for the year ending October 24, 1976, and $11.8 million for the current year. Since UNEF is now actually smaller than it was in September 1975, it is difficult to see how the USSR could attribute such huge sums to the alleged additional costs. A more probable explanation is a combination of political pique at being left out of the negotiations and habitual Soviet reluctance to contribute money to operations run by international organizations. In any event, the growing deficit for these two operations, coming on top of large deficits for past operations, is a matter for serious concern.

The third major current peacekeeping operation, the U.N. Force in Cyprus (UNFICYP), has had chronic financial problems since its inception in 1964. Financing is entirely voluntary, with about ten countries (out of 147 members) providing virtually all the funds. There has been a chronic and growing deficit. Costs borne by the United Nations have totaled about $250 million for the 12-year period ending December 1976, with cumulative receipts amounting to $187.6 million and anticipated receipts of $17.3 million, leaving a deficit of some $45 million—proportionately much greater than for UNDOF or UNEF II.

This means a serious delay in reimbursing countries which have responded generously to the secretary-general's call for contingents. Moreover, these countries already absorb costs at the rate of about $6 millon per year. Thus, these "good peacekeepers" are making a substantial sacrifice on behalf of world peace, which benefits all members; yet the great majority of member states make no contribution at all.

Taking into account both categories of contributions—direct contributions to the U.N. fund and costs absorbed by those providing military and police personnel—the U.S. pays about one third of the total UNFICYP costs. The USSR, France, and China do not contribute at all. This is manifestly unfair, but compared to the importance to the United States of avoiding conflict between Greece and Turkey, two NATO allies, our contribution of about $9.6 million per year should not be begrudged.

Despite meetings of various committees and other efforts to negotiate a solution to the financial crisis and generous contributions by some member states, the problem remains; in fact, it is getting worse. In my view the importance of peacekeeping to the United States and to world peace is such that greater efforts to find a solution are warranted.

One proposal advanced some years ago by a panel of the United Nations Association of the United States of America was to establish a United Nations Peacekeeping Fund designed to finance intitial costs of an operation where there is a shortage and to make up for unavoidable withholding, such as the Chinese and Soviets now pratice with regard to the Middle East operations. The obvious problem with such a fund is that it appears to accept noncontribution by some members and thus might encourage them not to pay. Nevertheless, I believe the United States should support the establishment of such a fund at a substantial level.

The sums now involved in peacekeeping operations are very small compared either to U.S. defense costs or total contributions to the U.N. budget. The total costs of U.N. peacekeeping to the United States this year will be about $42 million, which is about a tenth of our contribution for all U.N. programs. Compared to a defense budget of over $120,000 million this year, it appears to be a drop in the bucket.

The most costly U.N. peacekeeping operation to the United States was in the Congo, 1960-1964, where we paid about one half of a total cost of $400 million. This sum of $200 million might have paid for four or five days of the Viet Nam war. While Mobutu's government in Zaire may not be ideal, it is obviously considerably better from the U.S. viewpoint than the situation in Viet Nam after the expenditure of tens of thousands of lives and over $150 billion.

If other powers would agree, a formula could be devised under which a small fraction of military budgets (for example, one hundredth of 1 percent) could be set aside annually for U.N. peacekeeping as a supplement to other sources of income. In setting up such a peacekeeping fund, or seeking other solutions to the financial problems of peacekeeping, we should negotiate with all substantial contributors to the U.N. budget, including the Soviet Union. We should make every effort to enlist Soviet cooperation, but we should not emulate their ruble-pinching attitude toward U.N. peacekeeping. After all, the United States contributes about forty times as much as the Soviets to voluntary programs, including the U.N. Development Program (UNDP), where our national interest is less directly involved. Why be penurious only with respect to peacekeeping?

Standby Forces

Another important problem is that of having earmarked and trained contingents available for service. To date only the Scandinavian countries, the Netherlands, Austria, the United Kingdom, Italy, Iran, and New Zealand have taken steps to provide standby forces on call to the United Nations. The Scandinavians have also undertaken practical and helpful training exercises and the International Peace Academy has initiated useful seminars for similar purposes. Yet these countries represent only a tiny fraction of the membership. If there is to be "equitable geographic distribution" in future peacekeeping forces, the United Nations should have a roster of potential available contingents from all over the world. Discussion in the U.N. Peacekeeping Committee revealed no opposition to establishing such a roster; however, the Soviets were reluctant to have the General Assembly endorse the concept separately from agreement on the rest of the guidelines and principles under negotiation. No further progress has been made.

At various times a permanent force has been suggested, most recently by Colombia. Aside from the major problem of paying for such a permanent force, which Colombia would assign to the great powers, there is some doubt as to its usefulness. Since peacekeeping contingents must be accepted by the host country where they operate, many elements of such a permanent force might not be usable in a particular situation.

Conclusion

It may be true that the United Nations as now constituted can deal with only a fraction of the security problems facing the United States. Yet experience has demonstrated that U.N. peacekeeping activities are in the U.S. interest in those areas where they can be used; consequently, we should use them wherever possible and strengthen the United Nations's capacity to act effectively when required. Building on the precedents of UNEF II and UNDOF, we should work together with other U.N. members—including the Soviets wherever possible— toward the establishment of a roster of potential available contingents from countries of the world, improved training of contingents, and the provision of adequate financing for peacekeeping. U.N. peacekeeping is too valuable an instrument to be neglected.

Notes

1. See S. M. Finger, "Breaking the Deadlock on U.N. Peacekeeping," ORBIS (summer 1973), p. 385.

2. For a more detailed analysis of the UNEF and UNDOF operations, see N. A. Pelcovits, "U.N. Peacekeeping and the 1973 Arab-Israeli Conflict," ORBIS (spring 1975), pp. 146-165.

SOUTHERN AFRICA

7. America and Southern Africa
Julius K. Nyerere

Introduction

The dominant element in American foreign policy since 1946 has been opposition to communism and to the Communist powers. As far as Africa was concerned, responsibility for pursuing these objectives was delegated to America's trusted allies—Britain, France, Belgium, and even Portugal—whose policies in the area were therefore broadly supported despite minor disagreements which arose as American business became interested in Africa's potential. Inevitably this placed America in opposition to an Africa which was trying to win its independence from those same powers; but when political freedom could be achieved peacefully, America was able to appear to Africa like a bystander. It was therefore able to adjust its policies and accept the new status quo of African sovereign states without any difficulty. Notwithstanding these adjustments, however, America has continued to look at African affairs largely through anti-Communist spectacles and to disregard Africa's different concerns and priorities.

And in southern Africa events did not force any readjustments of American policies during the 1960s; so none were made. Practical support for the status quo continued unabated until after the Portuguese revolution in April 1974. Thus, despite America's verbal criticism of Portuguese colonialism, American arms and equipment were used by Portugal in its military operations in Angola, Guinea-Bissau, and Mozambique. Despite the verbal opposition to apartheid, American trade and investment in South Africa were expanded, and America

---

Reprinted with the author's permission for *Foreign Affairs* (July 1977), pp. 671-684. Copyright 1977 by the Council on Foreign Relations, Inc.

opposed any effective U.N. demonstration of hostility toward the apartheid state. The United States has also fought a hard, and largely successful, rearguard action against the demands for international intervention against South Africa's occupation of Namibia. And on Rhodesia, America has trailed behind British policies, emasculated the sanctions policies it had endorsed at the United Nations, and criticized Africa for the vehemence of its opposition to the minority Smith regime.

This general approach to African questions, and particularly to southern Africa, culminated in the American government's support for the National Front for the Liberation of Angola–National Union for the total Independence of Angola (FNLA/UNITA) forces in the dispute between the Angolan nationalist movements.

Throughout the anticolonial war in Angola, that is from 1960 to 1974, America had supported Portugal, not any of the nationalist forces. Supplies to the FNLA of money and military and other equipment while decolonization was taking place were thus a rather blatant attempt to place "friends" in political power in the new state. Not surprisingly, it was the least effective of the contending nationalist groups which was open to this kind of purchase; success therefore depended upon the quick collapse of the Popular Movement for the Liberation of Angola (MPLA) under assault. But the MPLA did not collapse. Instead it asked for and received more arms from those who had been helping it for the ten years of its anticolonial war; to meet the simultaneous south African invasion of Angola, the MPLA also welcomed Cuban troops. And when the FNLA demanded more help than the American administration alone could give it, the U.S. Congress—with the lessons of Vietnam still fresh in its mind—refused finance.

It is not cynicism which attributes the beginnings of the "Kissinger initiative" in April 1976 partly to this experience. Nations, like people, sometimes need to be shaken out of habitual modes of thought. Nor was the Angolan debacle the only factor leading toward a reassessment of traditional U.S. policies in southern Africa. Some Americans had for long been urging support for the antiracialist and anticolonial struggle, and American blacks were beginning to take a greater interest in these matters. Further, trade with independent Africa has been growing, and now includes oil from Nigeria. The possibility that this trade might be jeopardized by pro-South African actions is no longer of merely academic interest to the United States. And the guerrilla war in Rhodesia has been intensified since mid-1975, arousing fears of a repetition of the Angolan experience.

Africa welcomed the Lusaka statement by Dr. Kissinger that

majority rule must precede independence in Rhodesia, and that America would give no material or diplomatic support to the Smith regime in its conflict with the African states or the African liberation movements. With some hesitation, Africa also cooperated with the Kissinger "shuttle diplomacy" later in the year. For Africa hoped that, even at that late stage, the use of American power in support of majority rule could enable this to be attained in Rhodesia without further bloodshed.

The "Kissinger initiative" did force Ian Smith to shift his ground, but it did not succeed in its declared objective. Neither did it remove Africa's uncertainty about the depth and geographical limitations of America's new commitment to change in southern Africa. For decades of history cannot be wiped out by one speech and a few months of highly individualistic one-man diplomacy. They cannot even be eradicated by the clear sincerity of a new president's commitment to supporting human rights, and the sympathetic understanding shown by the ambassador he has appointed to the United Nations.

The United States of America is the most powerful nation on earth. Africa is weak, economically and militarily; its unity in action is still fragile. Africa does therefore naturally desire the friendship and cooperation of the United States; it does need trade and economic assistance.

But overwhelming everything else in Africa is the sense of nationalism, and the determination of all African peoples that the whole of this continent shall be free and relieved from the humiliation of organized white racialism. Within Rhodesia, Namibia, and South Africa, and within the nations immediately bordering them, the commitment to the struggle against minority or colonial rule overrides all other matters.

This basic fact is important to America, as it is to the rest of the world. For power is not all-powerful. Nationalism cannot be overcome by it. Nationalist wars have no end except victory, however long that takes to achieve, whatever the cost and the inevitable setbacks. All that can be affected by the actions of its opponents is the character of the nationalist state and society after victory. The harder and longer the struggle for freedom, the more austere and radicalized the new state is likely to be. It may also be more intolerant. For wars are liable to destroy everything except hatred and mutual suspicion—which they nurture.

The United States, like other nations of the world, has a legitimate interest in the future as well as the present societies of southern Africa. It must be concerned about America's continued ability to buy the goods it needs, and its ability to sell sufficient goods to pay for its imports. America must be interested in whether or not these states will determine their own foreign policies according to their own interests after winning their freedom, or whether they will be dominated in these matters by states hostile to the United States. And America, like the rest of the world, will continue to have a legitimate interest in the status of human rights in southern Africa as well as elsewhere. None of these things will it be able to control in a state which is really independent—that is the meaning of independence. But one would expect that current American policies toward the nationalist struggles in southern Africa would be determined with these long-term interests in mind. And it does not seem to Africa that these factors have determined American policies in the past. At least they have not done so on any intelligent assessment of the paramountcy of nationalism in shaping the future.

One thing is quite certain. The status of human rights could not be worse in the independent states of southern Africa than it is now. The very idea of there being "human rights" presupposes the basic acceptance of human equality. Yet colonialism is in principle a denial of equality. It means that the interests of the colonized are subordinate to the interests of the colonizers, or at the very least are interpreted and judged by the colonizers. Support for human rights therefore involves opposition to colonialism, regardless of how gentle, well-intentioned, or selfless the colonial government may be. Greater urgency in ending this status is imparted to the situation when, as in Namibia and Rhodesia, colonialism has none of these virtues. Two hundred years after Americans fought their own kith and kin to end colonialism it should not be necessary for Africa to try to convince America that Africans find colonialism intolerable.

Human rights are also inconsistent with the practice of racialism. They are denied by any law or practice which distinguishes the rights and duties of men and women according to their racial origin. And in South Africa there is hardly a law which does not make this distinction; the entire state machinery is directed at organizing and upholding the domination of one racial group over all others. This would be inconsistent with human rights if the majority racial group were using racial discrimination as a means of controlling a dissident minority. It is not made more consistent when 83 percent of the south African population is denied elementary political, economic, and social justice by legislation and economic power used by and in the interests of the whites.

Every aspect of the South African state organization is thus inconsistent with the American philosophy of human equality and freedom. But this is not simply an internal South African matter. Without the kind of practical support which the South African government and society have been receiving—and are still receiving—from their relations with America and its allies, the present apartheid structure could not be sustained for very long. And therefore minority rule in Rhodesia and Namibia could not continue.

Thus, for example, South Africa has a continuing and large deficit in its foreign trade, which is financed by capital imports, both long and short term. American investment in South Africa has more than tripled since 1966 and now stands at more than $1,600 million. All these investors profit from apartheid and the discriminatory wage structure—and thus have an interest in sustaining it.

Further, until now America has continued to act in the United Nations and elsewhere as if South Africa were a bastion against Soviet infiltration into southern Africa, and against the spread of communism in Africa. This image is carefully fostered by the apartheid regime, which prides itself on its anti-communism, and had defined a Communist as "anyone who supports any of the aims of communism"—including the declared aim of human equality!

Yet by identifying itself in practice with the apartheid regime and its satellites, America is liable to bring about the very things it most fears—the growth of Communist influence, the radicalization of the opposition to apartheid and colonialism, and the damage to its own economic interests. For opposition to the regimes in southern Africa is inevitable. Men will not indefinitely accept humiliation, exploitation, and tyranny. Sooner or later, by one means or another, the dominant minority will lose its ability to control the country and run the economy in its own interests. It is natural that Africa should seek American help in ending its humiliation. Americans should not find it natural when their country aids the oppressor instead of the oppressed.

The organizational and material weakness of the nationalist forces in southern Africa which results from decades of ruthless oppression, does, however, have two consequences of international relevance. First, nationalists cannot be particular about the means through which they carry on the struggle; they have to take advantage of any opportunities which they can find. Secondly, they have to accept help from wherever they can get it. The stronger apartheid and minority rule become, and the more supporters those forces enlist, the greater becomes the nationalists' need for outside help.

When seeking external support for their struggles, it is natural that African nationalists should look first to the African countries which have already secured their own freedom. And it is equally natural that free African states should give that support. No independent African state can rest secure while colonialism continues in Africa, for colonialism is a denial of its own right to exist. Further, the human dignity of all Africans is denied when Africans anywhere are humiliated because of their race. On the principle of giving assistance to the freedom movements in southern Africa, therefore, the whole of free Africa is united. But in comparison with South Africa, free Africa is weak. All African states are poor, some are almost overwhelmed by the task of trying to make independence economically meaningful and beneficial to their people. Further, no African state has an armaments industry of its own. The nationalist movements of southern Africa therefore need more help than Africa alone can give them.

Outside Africa, however, experience has shown that Communist countries are almost the only ones which are both able and willing to assist the nationalist movements of southern Africa. The major countries of the Western bloc urge patience and nonviolence as if these had not been tried for the past thirty years; simultaneously they continue to bolster South Africa's economic and military strength by trade, investment, and political cooperation. Some of the Nordic countries give humanitarian assistance to the freedom fighters. Only the Communist countries are willing to make arms and other military help available when an armed struggle becomes the only way forward.

Why the Communist states are willing to assist the freedom movements is for them to say. Africa knows why it needs that assistance, and what it will be used for if it can be obtained. Anything else is, at this stage, irrelevant to us. If the West decides to give us similar aid, I for one would not question its motives. Africa is concerned with existing oppression, not with hypothetical dangers in the future. Any new threats to freedom will be dealt with after it has been won—not before! In the war against Nazism the United States and the Soviet Union were allies.

But the peoples of southern Africa are not asking others to fight their liberation battles for them. They know that a people can only free themselves; they cannot import freedom. The peoples of these countries are asking only for appropriate support for the freedom struggle they are themselves conducting. Whether that support needs to be political, economic, or military—or all three— depends upon the type of struggle which has to be waged before victory is achieved. It is in this respect that the differences in the political and economic situations of Rhodesia, Namibia, and South Africa become relevant to current policies for other nations of the world.

Yet although the three countries do present different problems, and opportunites, it is pointless to try to treat each one in isolation. The objective is freedom for the whole of southern Africa. This means independence on the basis of majority rule in Rhodesia; independence on the basis of majority rule for Namibia as a single political unit; and an end to apartheid and minority struggle in South Africa itself. So it is one struggle, with three geographical areas.

Therefore, South Africa cannot be regarded as an ally in the fight for majority rule in Rhodesia, any more than Rhodesia could be expected to support the anticolonial movement in Namibia. Rhodesia and South Africa are natural allies to each other. The most which could be achieved is for South Africa to recognize the differences between it own position and that of the Smith regime, and therefore to buy time for itself by refraining from direct assistance to minority rule in the British colony.

Rhodesia

In Rhodesia, or Zimbabwe—to use its African name—we now have to face the fact that this is 1977, not 1965. A liberation war has started. Government "reforms," or reductions in the intensity of racial discrimination, which would have given hope of change fifteen or even ten years ago and thus prevented war, are now irrelevant. Options which existed at the time of Rhodesia's unilateral declaration of independence (UDI) no longer exist.

This should not be strange to Americans who know their own history. Very few inhabitants of the American colonies were calling for independence when the dispute with the British government arose in the 1760s. According to John Adams, one third of the colonists remained opposed to the rebellion even during the War of Independence. Yet concessions made by the British government in 1770 were already too late to avert conflict. And once the war had begun it could have only one end. So it is in Rhodesia now. Ian Smith's unilateral "package of reforms" announced in March of this year will now not even buy him time.

The only question which remains open is whether independence on the basis of majority rule will be achieved by a fight to the finish, or whether that same end can be achieved by a minimum of bloodshed leading to negotiations.

Therefore negotiation cannot now be about the principle of majority rule before independence. Nor can it be about the establishment of an "interim government" under white control. The nationalists are insisting tht the 270,000 whites cannot be allowed to continue governing 5,800,000 Africans, whatever promises the former make about organizing an "orderly transfer of power," or anything else. For the argument now is about power, not about promises; the fighting which has started will not end until a transfer of power from the minority to the majority has actually taken place. A ceasefire without such a transfer of power was tried in December 1974; it led to a strengthening of the minority regime.

What was possible until the collapse of the Geneva Conference in December 1976 was a delay in independence. For in accordance with the British tradition of decolonization, the nationalists had separated independence from internal self-government under majority rule. The latter they were demanding immediately, with some minority representation in an interim nationalist government. But they had agreed on a delay of twelve months before independence, in the hope that effective British sovereignty during that period would allow members of the minority community either to adapt to majority rule, or to leave the country. For in this connection it is relevant to remember that more than one third of the 270,000 whites at present in Rhodesia have immigrated during the past eleven years—they can hardly be regarded as committed to the country.

These demands were rejected by Smith, as were the British government proposals. The British government then abandoned the conference, showing that despite their legal responsibility for decolonization in Rhodesia, they regarded themselves merely as umpires between Smith and the nationalists, not as participants in a struggle against the Smith regime.

That opportunity for a negotiated settlement has therefore been lost. The attempt of the new British foreign secretary to organize talks on another basis has thus to overcome still more suspicion. And even if agreement between the British and the nationalists is reached at new talks, the removal of Smith and the dismantling of his power structure still have to be achieved before any political agreement can be converted into the reality of majority rule.

The world in general, and Africa in particular, does, however, still have an interest in bringing the Rhodesian war to a rapid end. Ian Smith and his supporters have no such interest. On the contrary, their objective is the continuation of the war until South Africa, and possibly even the United States, come to their support.

Ian Smith recognizes that, on a long-headed assessment of South Africa's own interest, Prime Minister Vorster does not want to get directly involved in the Rhodesian conflict. But in any guerrilla war, civilian casualties are likely to occur; they are already happening in Zimbabwe. If the dead women and children begin to include large numbers of whites, then Smith knows, because Vorster has admitted it, that the Pretoria government will be under pressure from its own electorate to increase South African material support for the Smith regime. And as the casualties begin to include South African citizens who live in or visit Rhodesia, Smith believes that his armed forces will be strengthened by direct South African military intervention.

Direct South African military involvement would make a great change in the balance of forces in Rhodesia. It would not defeat nationalism. But it would greatly increase the difficulties of the freedom fighters. The nationalists would therefore be forced to seek increased external help; and it is only Communist states which are likely to give whatever assistance is required. Even if an intelligent American government is then able to withstand the consequent pressure to intervene "against communism" and to maintain its opposition to Smith, the conflict would have been internationalized. Smith desires this. Africa does not. Whether the internationalization of a limited war of independence is in America's interests is for America to judge.

But America is not a helpless bystander to events in Rhodesia. It is a powerful nation and influences developments there. It can frustrate Smith's attempts to escalate the war, and can even help to get the war ended.

First, it has to make it quite clear that the United States will give no support of any kind to the minority regime of Rhodesia, at any time, and regardless of the progress or possible escalation of the war.

Second, as evidence of this determination, it has to follow up the rescission of the Byrd Amendment by active steps against all sanctions-breaking (whether by American firms or others), and by greater efforts to prevent the Rhodesian recruitment of American citizens into the regime's army.

And third, the United States has to put pressure on the South African government to desist from further help to the Smith regime. It is not realistic to expect Vorster to act against Rhodesian minority rule; but he can be prevented from propping it up—at least more than he is already doing. The United States has sufficient leverage to do this without treating South Africa as if it is an ally in the struggle for justice in southern Africa.

No one is suggesting that there are quick or painless solutions to the problems in Rhodesia. In the eleven years which have passed since UDI, many opportunities have been lost, and new forces have arisen which now have to be taken into account. Thus, it is true that the Zimbabwe nationalists do not control all the forces which will influence Rhodesian events in the near and far future. But no settlement of this problem can now be reached without their participation in drawing it up, and their active support in its implementation. In 1977 it is in that context, and only in that context, that America or Britain—or Tanzania—can work for an end to war in Rhodesia.

Namibia

Namibia is politically different from Rhodesia in two major respects. First, if Prime Minister Vorster really accepted the principle of majority rule outside South Africa, as he has sometimes claimed, it is within his power to introduce it in Namibia. And if he really wants Namibia "off his back," as he once asserted, he has the power to make the necessary arrangements. Namibia is not a client state like Rhodesia; it is completely under the de facto control of the South African government and armed forces.

Secondly, Namibia is de jure a trusteeship territory. The United Nations has, by General Assembly and Security Council decision, withdrawn the authority of South Africa over Namibia. It has established the U.N. Council for Namibia, and appointed a full-time commissioner, whose task is to arrange for an orderly transition to Namibian independence on the basis of political unity and majority rule, and periodically to report progress to the United Nations. Also the General Assembly has recognized the South West African People's Organization (SWAPO) as the sole representative nationalist movement of Namibia.

Apart from these two respects, however, the situations in Rhodesia and Namibia are becoming increasingly similar. A united nationalist party now exists, and cannot be ignored. An armed struggle has started in Namibia, although it is not as yet very intense.

South Africa is still trying to evade the necessity of negotiating the form of Namibian independence with SWAPO under the auspices of the United Nations. In response to a threat of action by the United Nations if its resolutions were not observed, South Africa organized the Turnhalle Constitution Conference in 1975. Representation was by "ethnic group" (*i.e.,* South African–designated racial and tribal groups), and political parties were barred. The outcome of Turnhalle, not surprisingly, is a set of proposals which basically maintain the structure of "tribal homelands" and "white areas," and would leave intact the existing racialist domination by the 99,000 whites among the 850,000 population. The South African government is proposing to present the result to the United Nations as an act of decolonization.

Proposals such as these will not solve the problem in South West Africa. Nationalism in Namibia cannot be overcome by establishing another independent apartheid state. The choice for the world, and for South Africa, remains unaffected by such maneuvers. The choice is: either a transfer of de facto power by South Africa to the United

Nations, which can then negotiate an independence constitution with SWAPO; or negotiations between South Africa and SWAPO under U.N. auspices; or an intensified war, with all the dangers to world peace which that will bring.

Once again, America cannot control these events. But it could use its considerable influence to avert the dangers of a serious war of liberation in Namibia. In order to do this, America would first have to accept that SWAPO is the only Namibian nationalist organization, and that no settlement is possible without its agreement. Then it would apply some pressure on South Africa to negotiate with SWAPO under U.N. auspices. Alternatively it would give active American support to the struggle at the United Nations for a South African withdrawal from Namibia, and the introduction of an effective transitional U.N. administration.

What America must not do, if it aims to prevent a major war in Namibia, is to give any encouragement to the Turnhalle conference, its participants, or South Africa's espousal of its proposals. For time is running out. If the Namibian war has to be intensified—as it will be if there is no progress—the time available for an orderly transition from minority to majority rule will again be exhausted before the work has begun.

South Africa

South Africa is an independent state. It is not a colony of anyone, and within the boundaries of the republic there are no colonies to be granted independence. But its organized denial of human rights to all but 17 percent of its people, on the grounds of their race, make South Africa's internal affairs a matter of world concern. For nations have learned, and mankind has learned, that the hope for world peace and justice precludes indifference in the face of organized racialism.

The official reply to all demands that the world should put South Africa into quarantine has been that apartheid is best countered by diplomatic and other contact with more open societies. Unfortunately, however, the South African whites are correct in saying that their society is unique. Nowhere else has the privileged lifestyle of the dominant minority ever rested so completely and exclusively on racial oppression. Other experiences of gradual desegregation, in the southern states of the United States or elsewhere, will therefore do no more to persuade the whites of South Africa to change their policies than has the polite criticism of Western statesmen since the last world war.

Policies are also based upon the argument that, provided foreign investors pay a living wage to their employees, they will be increasing the pressures against apartheid because economic growth shows up the inefficiency of things like racial job reservation and migrant skilled labor. Quite apart from the fact that these are only a small aspect of apartheid, the evidence of the past 30 years—and longer—should by now have dispelled that illusion also. South Africa has been getting economically stronger and more developed at a rapid rate. Racial oppression has been increasing even faster. For the stronger the economy, the more can be spent upon suppressing the majority without any economic sacrifice being demanded of those who benefit by white supremacy. A strong South African economy strengthens the government, not the victims of its oppression.

The South African economy needs to be weakened, not strengthened, if apartheid is to be overthrown. South Africa therefore needs to be isolated economically, politically, and socially, by the rest of the world until there has been a change in political direction. The sooner that change begins, the less violence and chaos there is likely to be.

No one can doubt the desire of the people of South Africa to end apartheid. Organized opposition by the non-whites has been smashed, but the Soweto and Cape Town riots are only the latest of a long series of spontaneous uprisings. And they will not be the last outburst of frustration. For despite everything which the South African state can and will do, instability is inherent in a situation where the majority of the people are excluded from the benefits of a society which depends upon their work. Change can be delayed by an intensification of oppression and human suffering. But apartheid is doomed. The only question is whether the society subsides into chaos, or whether there is an orderly but speedy movement toward justice.

At present there may still just be time for the republic to avoid ultimate economic and social collapse if the whites can be woken up to their own danger. They would have to begin by setting free, and then entering into a dialogue with, the real leaders of the non-white peoples who are now being held in jails, detention centers, and restriction—people like Nelson Mandela, Robert Sobukwe, and their colleagues. For it is only such people who would have a chance of organizing and channeling the irresistible opposition of the black peoples to their present humiliation.

So far there has been no evidence that the South African white government intends to guide the country in this direction—on the contrary. The whites remain self-confident in their strength and their racial arrogance, and they do this partly because the world continues to talk with them and support them in action. They have not been shocked into a reassessment of their position. They have not yet realized their need to talk with non-white South Africans about their common future. Instead they are able to talk with the rest of the world, and solve their economic problems by new foreign investment, new trade, and new immigration.

Conclusion

Each nation has to decide for itself what will be in its own interests, and these will determine its policies. But no one is asking that America should fight for the freedom of southern Africa. Africa is simply asking that America should stop supporting racialism and unfreedom in that area.

For the penalty, as well as the opportunity, of America's great power relative to that of any other nation, is that every American action, or failure to act, has an effect upon the timing and the nature of developments outside its own borders. This is not to say that America can impose its will on an unwilling world; only that it cannot avoid involvement in events elsewhere. When Tanzania trades or fails to trade, or indicates support or opposition for another government, the world goes on unchanged and unruffled. When America does any of these things it is affecting what will happen elsewhere. One may like this or not; it remains a statement of fact.

Thus, America cannot prevent men from struggling against colonialism and racialism in southern Africa. But American actions will either ease the inevitable triumph of the freedom struggle, or strengthen the resistance to it and thus force the anticolonial and antiracist movements into a hard, ruthless, and hostile mold. There is no way in which powerful America can avoid doing one or the other of these things, as long as it needs to have commercial and state relations with the rest of the world.

Africa is therefore asking that America should recognize the conflict in southern Africa as the nationalist struggle which it is, and that it should refuse to be taken in by the Communist bogey paraded by the racialists. It is asking that America should refrain from profitmaking out of apartheid. South Africa needs the United States; but the United States does not need South Africa. Africa is asking that America should carry its declared support for human equality and dignity into policies which will weaken the forces of racialism and colonialism in southern Africa, so that the peoples of those areas can triumph more quickly and with less bloodshed.

With or without American support during the struggle, freedom in southern Africa will not mean the birth of ideal democracies, where all citizens enjoy human rights, civil liberty, and a consumer society to boot. Popular governments in Rhodesia, Namibia, and later in South Africa, will face immense problems of poverty, disruption, and unrealizable expectation. They will also inherit a legacy of mutual hostility and bitterness. The racial prejudice which has been inculcated by years of deliberate indoctrination, and by bitter experience, will not disappear when majority rule begins.

But it is only after freedom has been won in the states of southern Africa that the positive struggle to build human equality and dignity can begin there. We in Africa hope that the new administration of the United States will fulfill its early promise, and help the peoples of southern Africa to get to the position where they can make a beginning. At the very least, we hope that America will not continue to use its power and prestige to hinder the movement for freedom and humanity in the south of this continent.

8. U.S. Policy Toward Africa
Cyrus R. Vance

We proceed from a basic proposition: that our policies must recognize the unique identity of Africa. We can be neither right nor effective if we treat Africa simply as one part of the third world, or as a testing ground of East-West competition. African reality is incredibly diverse. But out of this diversity comes a general fact of great importance. Africa has an enormous potential—in human talent, in resources to be developed, in energy to be harnessed. Let us consider how this is true in terms of our own national interests. For Africa's potential is tied to our own.

- The success or failure of the search for racial justice and peace in southern Africa will have profound effects among the American people. And our participation in that search is based on the values of our own society.
- The role of the African nations at the United Nations, and in other multilateral bodies, is pivotal. One-third of the U.N. member states are African.
- Africa's mineral and agricultural wealth already provides a substantial portion of our imports of such commodities as copper, cobalt, and manganese for our industries, and cocoa and coffee for our homes. And Africa supplies 38 percent of our crude petroleum imports.

Excerpted from remarks by U.S. Secretary of State Cyrus R. Vance before the Annual Convention of the National Association for the Advancement of Colored People (NAACP) (St. Louis, July 1, 1977).

- Our direct investment in sub-Saharan Africa has increased nearly sixfold over the past 15 years; our trade now is almost twelve times what it was then. And the pattern of our trade with Africa includes an even larger share for black Africa. Trade with South Africa in 1960 was 39 percent of our commerce with Africa; now, our trade with Nigeria alone is double the value of that with South Africa.
- Beyond these political and economic ties that bind our futures, there are the social and cultural links from which we have benefited greatly. Our society and culture are enriched by the heritage so many Americans find in Africa. We experience this enrichment every day—in our literature, our art, our music, and our social values.

During the past few months, as we have considered the specific policies I will discuss today, a number of broad points emerged. They define the general nature of our approach.

First, the most effective policies toward Africa are affirmative policies. They should not be reactive to what other powers do, nor to crises as they arise. Daily headlines should not set our agenda for progress. A negative, reactive American policy that seeks only to oppose Soviet or Cuban involvement in Africa would be both dangerous and futile. Our best course is to help resolve the problems which create opportunities for external intervention.

Second, our objective must be to foster a prosperous and strong Africa that is at peace with itself and at peace with the world. The long-term success of our African policy will depend more on our actual assistance to African development and our ability to help Africans resolve their disputes than on maneuvers for short-term diplomatic advantage.

Third, our policies should recognize and encourage African nationalism. Having won independence, African nations will defend it against challenges from any source. If we try to impose American solutions for African problems, we may sow division among the Africans and undermine their ability to oppose efforts at domination by others. We will not do so.

Fourth, our policies must reflect our national values. Our deep belief in human rights—political, economic, and social—leads us to policies that support their promotion throughout Africa. This means concern for individuals whose rights are threatened—anywhere on the continent. And it means making our best effort peacefully to promote racial justice in southern Africa. In this we join the many African nations who, having won their freedom, are determined that all of Africa shall be free.

Fifth, our ties with Africa are not only political, but cultural and economic as well. It is the latter two that are most enduring.

And finally, we will seek openness in our dealings with African states. We are willing to discuss any issue, African or global; to broaden our dialogue with African nations; and to try to work with them, even when we may not agree.

Only thus can we promote our views without rancor. Our renewed relations with the People's Republic of the Congo, our experience at the conference on southern Africa in Maputo May 16-21, 1977, and our work with African delegations at the United Nations all demonstrate the value of this approach.

In the end, of course, our Africa policy will be judged by results, not intentions.

Promotion of Human Rights

We will be firm in our support of individual human rights. Our concern is not limited to any one region of the continent.

We must understand the diversity of African social and value systems. Gross violations of individual human dignity are no more acceptable in African terms than in ours. One of the most significant events in modern African history—and in the international effort to promote human rights—was the recent decision by Commonwealth countries to condemn the "massive violation of human rights" in Uganda. Many African nations took part in this decision. Their action should be applauded.

Abuse of human rights is wrong on any grounds. It is particularly offensive when it is on the basis of race. In southern Africa, issues of race, of justice, and of self-determination have built to a crisis.

- The conflict in Rhodesia is growing. Rhodesian incursions into neighboring countries exacerbate an already dangerous situation and deserve the condemnation they have received. The choice between negotiated settlement and violent solution must be made now. The same is true for Namibia. Many lives—black and white—hang in the balance.
- The risk of increased foreign involvement is real.
- Violence within South Africa grows. There may be more time there than in Rhodesia and Namibia for people of goodwill to achieve a solution. But progress must soon be made, or goodwill could be lost.
- Crisis within the region has brought pressure for stronger action at the United Nations, and appeals to our responsibilities under its charter.

This is the reality we face. The dangers, our interests, and our values, as well as the desires of the Africans themselves, require our involvement—and our most dedicated and practical efforts.

We cannot impose solutions in southern Africa. We cannot dictate terms to any of the parties; our leverage is limited. But we are among the few governments in the world that can talk to both white and black Africans frankly and yet with a measure of trust. We would lose our ability to be helpful if we lost that trust. It is, therefore, essential that our policies of encouraging justice for people of all races in southern Africa be clear to all.

After careful consideration, this Administration has decided to pursue actively solutions to all three southern African problems—Rhodesia, Namibia, and the situation within South Africa itself. These problems must be addressed together, for they are intertwined.

Some have argued that apartheid in South Africa should be ignored for the time being, in order to concentrate on achieving progress on Rhodesia and Namibia. Such a policy would be wrong and would not work. It would be blind to the reality that the beginning of progress must be made soon within South Africa, if there is to be a possibility of peaceful solutions in the longer run. It could mislead the South Africans about our real concerns. It would prejudice our relations with our African friends. It would do a disservice to our own beliefs. And it would discourage those of all races who are working for peaceful progress within South Africa.

We believe that we can effectively influence South Africa on Rhodesia and Namibia while expressing our concerns about apartheid. Implicit in that belief is the judgment that progress in all three areas is strongly in the interest of the South African government.

We believe that whites as well as blacks must have a future in Namibia, Zimbabwe, and South Africa. We also believe that their security lies in progress. Intransigence will only lead to greater insecurity.

We will welcome and recognize positive action by South Africa on each of these three issues. But the need is real for progress on all of them. Let me review briefly our approach to each.

Rhodesia

We are actively supporting a British initiative to achieve a negotiated settlement of the Rhodesian crisis. In coming weeks, we will be seeking agreement on a constitution that would allow free elections, open to all parties and in which all of voting age could participate equally. These elections would establish the government of an independent Zimbabwe. Our goal is that this be accomplished during 1978.

This constitution should include a justiciable bill of rights and an independent judiciary, so that the rights of all citizens, of all races, are protected.

We also hope to lend greater assistance to the people of neighboring nations whose lives have been disrupted by the crisis in southern Africa.

Namibia

In Namibia a solution leading to independence is being sought through the efforts of the five Western members of the Security Council with South Africa, the United Nations, and other interested parties, including the South West Africa People's Organization. That solution would include free elections in which the United Nations is involved, freedom for political prisoners, repeal of discriminatory laws and regulations, and the withdrawal of instruments of South African authority as the elections are held and independence achieved.

On the basis of our discussions thus far, we are encouraged by the prospects for an independent Namibia—one which will take its rightful place in the African and world community. We welcome the indications of flexiblity on the part of South Africa. We are gratified by the confidence shown by many African governments in the efforts of the United States and Western associates on the Security Council. Differences remain, however, and progress will require a willingness on all sides to be openminded and forthcoming. But we will persevere.

South Africa

While pursuing these efforts for peace and justice in Namibia and Rhodesia, we have also expressed to the South African government our firm belief in the benefits of a progressive transformation of South African society. This would mean an end to racial discrimination and the establishment of a new course toward full political participation by all South Africans.

The specific form of government through which this participation could be expressed is a matter for the people of South Africa to decide. There are many ways in which the individual rights of all citizens within South Africa could be protected. The key to the future is that South African citizens of all races now begin a dialogue on how to achieve this better future.

The South African government's policy of establishing separate homelands for black South Africans was devised without reference to the wishes of the blacks themselves. For this reason, and because we do not believe it constitutes a fair or viable solution to South Africa's problems, we oppose this policy. We did not recognize the Transkei and we will not recognize Bophuthatswana if its independence is proclaimed in December, as scheduled.

We deeply hope that the South African government will play a progressive role on the three issues I have discussed. We will applaud such efforts. If there is no progress, our relations will inevitably suffer. We cannot defend a government that is based on a system of racial domination and remain true to ourselves.

For our policy toward South Africa is reinforced by change in our own society. The activities of the NAACP are a testament to the inseparability of our foreign and domestic goals. It is also entirely fitting that Andrew Young (U.S. Ambassador to the United Nations), who has done so much in the struggle against our divisions at home, should now be contributing so well to the design and effectiveness of our policies abroad.

Support for African Nationalism

I have heard some suggest that we must support the white governments in southern Africa—come what may—since they are anti-Communist. In fact, the continued denial of racial justice in southern Africa encourages the possibilities for outside intervention.

Similarly, when such crises as the recent invasion of Zaire arise, we see no advantage in unilateral responses and emphasizing their East-West implications. We prefer to work with African nations—and with our European allies—in positive efforts to resolve such disputes. As President Carter recently said, it is best to fight fire with water.

The history of the past fifteen years suggests that efforts by outside powers to dominate African nations will fail.

Our challenge is to find ways of being supportive without becoming interventionist or intrusive. We see no benefit if we interject ourselves into regional disputes. We hope that they can be resolved through the diplomatic efforts of the parties themselves in an African setting.

We are aware of the African concern that we have sometimes seemed more interested in the activities of other outside powers in Africa than in Africa itself. They know that some argue we should almost automatically respond in kind to the increase in Soviet arms and Cuban personnel in Africa. We cannot ignore this increase—and we oppose it. All sides should be aware that when outside powers pour substantial quantities of arms and military personnel into Africa, it greatly enhances the danger that disputes will be resolved militarily, rather than through mediation by African states or by the OAU (Organization of African Unity).

This danger is particularly great in the Horn, where there has been an escalation of arms transfers from the outside. The current difficulties in Ethiopia, and the tensions among nations in the area, present complex diplomatic challenges. We seek friendship with all the governments of that region. We have established an embassy in the new nation of Djibouti. Its peaceful accession to independence marks a step toward stability in what remains a troubled area.

We will consider sympathetically appeals for assistance from states which are threatened by a build-up of foreign military equipment and advisors on their borders, in the Horn and elsewhere in Africa. But we hope such local arms races and the consequent dangers of deepening outside involvement can be limited.

In accordance with the policy recently announced by the president, arms transfers to Africa will be an exceptional tool of our policy and will be used only after the most careful consideration. We hope that all the major powers will join us in supporting African nationalism, rather than fragmenting it, and in concentrating on economic assistance, rather than arms.

Our approach is to build positive relations with the Africans primarily through support for their political independence and economic development and through the strengthening of our economic, cultural, and social ties. Our new and positive relationships with nations like Nigeria encourage us in this course. Our efforts to build such relations may not seize the headlines. But this quiet strategy will produce long-term benefits.

Our relations will be closest with those nations whose views and actions are most congruent with ours. We will never forget or take old friends for granted. Their continuing friendship is a fundamental concern; they can rely on our support. When the territorial integrity of a friendly state is threatened, we will continue to respond to requests for appropriate assistance.

We do not insist that there is only one road to economic progress or one way of expressing the political will of a people. In so diverse a continent, we must be prepared to work with peoples and governments of distinctive and differing beliefs.

American representatives in Africa met last May to compare notes and discuss new policy ideas. They agreed that almost everywhere in the continent there is a new feeling about America—a sense of hope, a sense that we have returned to our ideals.

The future of Africa will be built with African hands. Our interests and our ideals will be served as we offer our own support. It will require the understanding and approval of Americans everywhere.

9. The United States, the United Nations, and Southern Africa
Wentworth B. Ofuatey-Kodjoe

This study brings together two issues which are of great significance to the peace and security of the entire world: U.S. participation in the United Nations, and U.S. policy on southern Africa. Separately, these two issues are important enough, but together, they achieve greater significance due to the reciprocal effect they have on each other.

Since the inception of the United Nations, there have been intermittent calls from some Americans for the limitation of U.S. contributions to and participation in the organization.[1] These calls became more strident as the U.S. began to lose its early hegemony over the organization. But as long as these calls did not represent responsible American opinion, there did not seem to be any cause for alarm. However, in the past few years, we have seen occasions, such as the 1975 General Assembly vote on Zionism, on which official U.S. spokesmen have threatened that the U.S. government may have to reassess its participation in the organization because of its dissatisfaction with some of its activities. It is clear that such a development would have a deleterious effect on the already unstable peacekeeping potential of the organization. After the experience of the League of Nations, it became clear that no world organization could hope to function effectively without the participation of the great powers. The recognition of this fact was one of the principal factors in determining the structure of the United Nations. And the subsequent activities of the organization have borne out this reality.[2]

The importance of U.S. policy on southern Africa for international peace and security is also clearly evident. In the past, informed observers of the southern African scene who had warned about the eventual development of serious armed conflict in that area were dismissed as being unnecessarily alarmist. However, recent events have confirmed these prognostications, so that it is now apparent that, in the words of Henry Kissinger, "the risks to world peace of an escalating violence in southern Africa (are) very serious."[3] It is also clear that the crucial factor in the unfolding drama of the conflict in southern Africa is the policy of the United States. Of the two superpowers, it is the United States which has had a long and sustained involvement in that area; an involvement which has been an important influence on the way in which the conflict has evolved.[4]

The interrelatedness of U.S. participation in the United Nations and U.S. policy on southern Africa lies in the fact that the United Nations has been the main forum in which the issues of southern Africa have been debated. Therefore, U.S. participation in that organization has had an important effect on how the issue has been handled in the United Nations. At the same time, the way in which issues of southern Africa have evolved has affected the attitude of the United States to the organization. In fact, one of the latest instances of U.S. displeasure with the United Nations occurred when verbal attacks were directed at the U.S. as a result of its southern African policy. In sum, U.S. policy on southern Africa affects U.S. policy on the United Nations and vice versa; and together they can have a major impact on general international peace.

The key to the relationship between these issues and world peace is the policy on southern Africa that the United States has been pursuing in the United Nations. On the one hand, this policy has tended to generate opposition among the vast majority of the international community, leading to a decrease in the confidence that can be placed in the organization as an instrument of justice and an appropriate forum to which states can bring their grievances. On the other hand, the kind of southern Africa policy that the United States pursues in the United Nations could have an important effect on the probability of reaching a solution to the southern African conflict with a minimum of violence, thus enhancing the organization's potential as a peacekeeping mechanism.[5] What this study attempts to do is to determine the effect of the southern African policies pursued by the United States in the United Nations on the overall foreign policy interests of the United States, the viability of the United Nations system, and general international peace and security. Before such an assessment can be attempted, and because of the considerable confusion that exists on the subject,[6] it is necessary to state as clearly as possible the exact nature and objectives of U.S. policy.

U.S. Policy on Southern Africa

The confusion about the nature of U.S. policy on southern Africa is caused, in large part, by the contradictions between U.S. verbal declarations in support of the principles of self-determination and human rights, and U.S. actions which have seemed to consistently support Portugal and the white minority regimes of South Africa and Rhodesia. These contradictions have been well documented and need not be discussed here at any length.[7] However, some of the attempts by supporters of U.S. policy to explain these contradictions are instructive contributions to a clearer understanding of the real nature of the southern African policy and objectives of the United States.

For instance, one writer has tried to explain the contradictions in U.S. policy towards southern Africa by characterizing U.S. policy as "straddling the fence, with an ear to the ground, and eye on the future, and a finger in the dyke."[8] This characterization is completely contrary to the facts of the case. The United States may, indeed, have its finger in the dyke, but supporting Portugal and South Africa with weapons and material, as it has done,[9] while attempting to mollify African opinion by mere verbal declarations, cannot possibly be described as straddling. According to another apologist, the contradiction between U.S. policy pronouncements and U.S. actions arises because U.S. policy is based on two principles: self-determination and nonviolence, and that "it frequently happens that one principle or guideline comes into conflict with another."[10] There are two problems with this proposition. First, while the attainment of self-determination can be a foreign policy objective, nonviolence is never a foreign policy objective. Therefore, it is illogical to assert that the principles of self-determination and nonviolence conflict. It may be reasonable to say that the United States has a normative preference for nonviolent methods in the quest for self-determination. We have frequently heard U.S. officials say that violence solves nothing. For the United States to take the position that self-determination should only be pursued as a policy objective only if it can be achieved by nonviolent means is merely to admit that the commitment of the United States to the principle of self-determination for blacks in southern Africa is limited. At no time in its own history including its own war of independence and even the Vietnam war, has the United States been willing to accept for itself the proposition that only those policy objectives which can be achieved nonviolently should be pursued. Secondly, in view of the intransigence of the whites in southern Africa and their demonstrated willingness to use violence to maintain their dominant position, the U.S. admonition that the quest for self-determination and human rights for blacks should be pursued with only nonviolent means amounts to a cynical acceptance of the racist and colonial status quo. If we add to this the diplomatic and material support that the United States has given the whites, then it is not difficult to see that the United States has, in fact, become a partner in colonialism and apartheid in southern Africa. As several authorities on civil strife have noted, a refusal to give aid to insurgents, when the incumbents have more power, amounts to tacit support of the incumbents.[11] But to go that additional step of actually giving support to the more powerful incumbents, while expressing verbal sympathy for the cause of the insurgents, is a hypocritical attempt not only to maintain the status quo, but to *guarantee* the failure of the insurgency. U.S. pronouncements which purport to be against the same racist and colonialist status quo must be seen not as an accurate reflection of the policy of the United States, but as a calculated attempt to confuse the issue. Whatever their declared intentions, U.S. officials cannot but be fully aware that their actions have worked "in practice for the maintenance of the existing white-dominated regimes in southern Africa."[12] The simple fact is that U.S. policy has been supportive of the white regimes in southern Africa, as an examination of the actual practice of the United States on southern African issues in the United Nations shows.

U.S. Practice on Southern African Issues

From its inception, much of the attention of the United Nations has been focused on southern Africa. This is due to the fact that the efforts to eradicate colonialism and racism, which have been such a significant part of the work of the organization, have had to concentrate on that area where those problems exist in the particularly intransigent forms of apartheid, South Africa's rule over South West Africa (Namibia), Portuguese colonialism, and latterly, the illegal white supremacist regime of Southern Rhodesia. The United States has taken an active part in the discussion of all these issues and has developed a record on them which should provide some understanding of the nature of U.S. policy towards southern Africa.

Apartheid. During the early years of U.N. consideration of the question of apartheid, the United States consistently supported South Africa's argument that the United Nations had no competence to discuss the issue, on the basis of the claim that it was within the exclusive jurisdiction of the South African government.[13] In 1958, this pattern began to change, and the United States began to adopt a position of expressing "regret" and "concern" over the racial situation in South Africa. After 1960, the United States went as far as a vote with the majority in several resolutions condemning the racial policies of South

Africa.[14] Throughout this period, however, the United States was extremely careful to vote against any resolution which might attempt to translate the verbal condemnations into enforcement action.[15]

Namibia. In the early days of the U.N., the United States supported demands for the transformation of South West Africa into a trust territory. Between 1960 and 1966, the United States stepped up its support for U.N. action on Namibia, voting affirmatively in several General Assembly resolutions calling on the Security Council to recognize continued South African control over Namibia as a threat to international peace and security,[16] and in the General Assembly resolution 2145 (XXI) of 1966 which terminated the South African mandate over Namibia. Characteristically, never did the United States support any resolution calling for enforcement action or sanctions against South Africa.[17] After 1969, the United States retreated from this pattern of mild verbal support for the independence of Namibia towards a more thoroughgoing support of South Africa.[18]

Portuguese Colonialism. From 1961, when the United Nations General Assembly began intensive consideration of the question of Portuguese colonies, until 1966, the United States voted in support of resolutions calling for the granting of self-determination to the colonies and condemning the use of repressive measures by Portugal against the colonial peoples.[19] However, here again, the United States was scrupulous in avoiding any commitments which could lead to enforcement action against Portugal.[20] In 1967, the United States voted with Portugal and South Africa against a Security Council resolution calling for economic sanctions against Portugal. Thereafter, the United States voted consistently against any efforts to condemn Portugal, until the question of the Portuguese territories in Africa was eventually resolved by armed struggle.[21]

Rhodesia. On the issue of Rhodesia, the United States has voted against the Smith regime on two important resolutions. The first was General Assembly Resolution 2024 (XX), November 11, 1965, which condemned the Smith government's unilateral declaration of independence (UDI), and the second was the Security Council Resolution 232, December 12, 1966, which adopted the application of mandatory sanctions against the illegal Smith regime. But, as in the other situations, the United States carefully avoided any commitments to enforcement action. Thus, the United States voted against numerous resolutions which called upon Britain not to transfer power to the illegal regime and to use all available means to stop UDI.[22] Even U.S. support for Security Council Resolution 232 was clearly an attempt to help Britain defeat the majority view in the United Nations, which was demanding even stronger measures. The fact that the United States supporting vote was meant to be nothing more than an empty gesture is clearly demonstrated by the passage in 1971 of section 503 of the Military Procurement Act (the Byrd Amendment) legalizing the importation of Rhodesian chrome into the United States, in blatant defiance of the same Security Council Resolution 232, for which the United States itself had voted.[23]

What this survey of U.S. activity shows is a pattern of consistent support for the white regimes in southern Africa from the early 1950s to the present. During the 1958-1966 period, there seemed to be a slight deviation from this pattern as the United States began to make general statements in support of the principle of self-determination and human rights, and more vociferous condemnations of colonialism and apartheid. However, this was more a change of tactical style than substance. The United States was always very careful not to carry these verbal condemnations into any kind of effective enforcement action. The U.S. voting record identified it as being firmly in the same camp as the colonialist powers. According to one observer:

> It appeared that no sooner had the United States moved to a point where it could . . . vote for a mildly condemnatory resolution, than the majority of world opinion took another long stride ahead, leaving the U.S. again in the minority, along with the 'colonialist' nations.[24]

By 1967, the United States was returning to the pre-1957 policy of straightforward and overt support for the racist and colonialist status quo in southern Africa. And by 1970, this trend had crystallized into a clearly articulated policy, the stated objective of which was to "maintain public opposition to racial oppression but relax political isolation and economic restrictions on the white states."[25] Moreover, this pattern of U.S. diplomatic activity in the United Nations is consistent with the pattern of economic, technological, and defense cooperation between the United States and the white governments.[26] Thus, the only conclusion that the facts will support is that U.S. policy in southern Africa has been one of giving diplomatic and other kinds of support to the white regimes in southern Africa, all the general statements of U.S. support for the principle of self-determination and the equivocation of U.S. officials notwithstanding.

The Sources of United States Policy on Southern Africa

There are two principal factors which account for the U.S. policy of support for the status quo in southern Africa. The first of these factors is the set of objectives which the U.S. officials are attempting to achieve in that region, and the second is the official U.S. perceptions of the conditions which prevail in that region. The nature of U.S. policy has been the result of a combination of these factors, or, to be more precise, it has been the strategy which U.S. officials considered efficacious for achieving their objectives under the prevailing political conditions.

The Objectives of U.S. Policy on Southern Africa

It is generally recognized that foreign policy is derived from a combination of security, economic, and cultural interests, as they are perceived by the officials who have the responsibility for formulating and implementing policy. The foreign policy of the United States is no exception. Thus, the U.S. policy of supporting the white regimes in southern Africa has to be based on official perception of the security, economic, and cultural interests of the United States. As they see it, the security interest of the United States in southern Africa is in denying that region to Communist ideological, political, and military influence, maintaining control over the sea lanes around the Cape of Good Hope, and maintaining preemptive access to important strategic raw materials produced in that region.[27] The economic interest of the United States is associated with the need to safeguard U.S. investments and maintain trade with the region.[28] The cultural interest of the United States in southern Africa is concerned with developing in that region the kind of political and cultural conditions which would be compatible with the survival of "Western culture" and, more specifically, the American way of life.[29]

The strategic and economic aspects of U.S. interests in southern Africa have been discussed at great length, and they need not be dwelt on here.[30] However, the cultural interest of the United States in the region has not received nearly as much attention, and yet, it must be clear that this aspect of national interest is just as important a determinant of foreign policy objectives as the strategic and economic aspects, if we adopt Holsti's formulation of cultural interest as the need to "perpetuate a particular political, social and economic system...."[31] Thus, it is not possible to explain fully the objectives of U.S. foreign policy in southern Africa without taking this cultural interest into serious consideration.[32]

As U.S. policymakers see it, the cultural interest of the United States lies in ensuring that the African territories adopt a political culture conducive to the American way of life; an idea based on the more general notion that "the survival of Western culture is dependent upon its assimilation to a significant degree measure in the modernizing societies of Asia, Africa and Latin America...."[33] Thus, an important reason for the U.S. policy of supporting colonialism in the United Nations has been the official view that, in Africa, this interest could only be served by prolonging colonial rule so that the colonial powers, in cooperation with the United States, could continue to be powerful instruments in "affecting the course of cultural change" in the African territories.[34] In colonial Africa, the logical policy for achieving this cultural interest was simply to continue colonialism as long as possible, and then translate the colonial relationship into a neocolonial relationship where feasible. In southern Africa, the formulation of a policy to achieve the cultural interest has been rendered more complicated, due to the multiracial character of those societies and the increasingly intransigent confrontation of racial nationalism there. In the face of this complication, the view that has been adopted by U.S. officials is that the best way to achieve the cultural interests of the United States is by making sure that southern Africa remains under the control of the whites, since the whites are "Western," natural allies who can be depended upon to preserve Western values and Western "civilization" in that area.[35]

This is not to argue that the United States government has not been in favor of change in southern Africa. The constant claim by the U.S. government that it favors change in South Africa is a credible one. The real question, however, concerns the kind of change the U.S. government is interested in. The official explanation of the Nixon policy of dialogue and communication with the white-dominated regimes is that "friendly persuasion rather than condemnation would be more likely to make them *modify* their policies."[36] The use of the term "modify" is significant. It is an accurate representation of the fact that the objective of the United States in southern Africa is not a fundamental change but a modification. What the United States wants is not a transfer of power to the black majority, but a modification which would leave power and control still effectively in the hands of the whites. What the United States wants is a modification by which South Africa would depart from the infamous rigidity of apartheid and adopt a form similar to the integrationist-assimilationist type of white control practiced in the United States itself.[37]

There are two reasons for this. First, there is a body of opinion in the United States which believes that segregation is inconsistent with the principles of justice and equality on which American society is supposedly built. Sometimes this body has had an effect on U.S. policymakers, although, as the Kerner Commission Report has pointed out, the strength of this body of opinion is much less than is generally believed,[38] and therefore, the extent to which it may affect U.S.

policy towards southern Africa is quite limited.[39] Second, and more important as a determinant of U.S. policy objectives, is the official judgement that a desegragated South Africa will, in fact, be the best guarantee of the maintenance of Western interests and Western culture in Africa. This judgement is based on the belief that such a development would attract the support of conservative South African blacks and nullify any chance of any general black unrest within the area. In addition, such a development would be more likely to receive international acceptance, since it would bring South African domestic policy more in line with contemporary international norms of self-determination and human rights, thus effectively reducing any international support that South African black insurrectionists might receive from the outside.[40] Furthermore, by such a policy, the South African government will be able to escape the intense international disapprobation it is presently receiving, thus, making the U.S.-South African alliance more consistent with the image that the U.S. government would like to project as the leader of the "free world" and the champion of freedom and justice.

The dilemma of the United States government is that, while it finds the policy of apartheid an embarrassment, the whites in southern Africa are committed to the view that nothing short of explicit white domination will "save Western civilization" in that area. The extent to which U.S. administrations have been willing to accept this view has depended, in part, on their commitment to integration as domestic policy. Thus, U.S. administrations that have been less committed to desegregation in the United States have also been more willing to accept apartheid and the South African government's view of its prospects. On the other hand, those U.S. administrators that have had a greater commitment to integration at home have been the ones which have been more vociferous in their condemnation of apartheid. However, even those administrations have never permitted their minor differences with the white minority regimes to interfere with their support for them, because, in their judgement, South Africa with apartheid is preferable to the possibility of a total loss of white control in that region. The development of the Bantustan policy by South Africa is a shrewd attempt to resolve the U.S.-South Africa dilemma. It is the hope of both the South African and the American governments that the creation of these "independent" homelands would accomplish the magic trick of maintaining white superiority while, at the same time, seeming to be consistent with contemporary international norms of self-determination and human rights.

In sum, U.S. policy on southern Africa has consistently been to support the colonial and racist status quo in southern Africa. This policy is not an aberration, an accident, or the unanticipated consequent result of conflicting principles, as some apologists would have us believe. It is a conscious policy that is designed to meet what U.S. officials consider the strategic, economic, and cultural interests of the United States in that region. The objectives of this policy have been the denial of southern Africa to Communist influence, the maintenance of control over the sea lanes around the South African coastline, the advancement of U.S. economic interests, and, most important, the maintenance of the power of the white societies there as a way of stabilizing the region and guaranteeing the survival of Western culture.

The Evolving Political Situation in Southern Africa

As we have pointed out above, U.S. policy in southern Africa is the result of official perceptions of objectives in the region, and the conditions under which the United States must attempt to achieve these objectives. In view of the status quo commitment of U.S. policy, the most important factor in causing tactical shifts in policy has been the increasing potential of African nationalist movements to destabilize or overturn the status quo.

As we have seen, during the early period of its activity in Africa, the United States carried on a policy of outright, unabashed support for colonialism in Africa, because it was widely believed that the Africans lacked the capability to change their political status without the acquiescence of the colonial powers. The tactical change toward the end of the 1950s to a policy of support for the colonial regimes and simultaneous pronouncements of anticolonial rhetoric was due, mainly, to official judgement that the development of African nationalism might have a potentially destabilizing effect on policy objectives. As the African countries began to agitate for independence, it became clear that the role that the colonial empires had played in the chain of containment against international communism might collapse if the new African states were to gravitate towards Communist international connections. Thus, in the event of African nationalist movements becoming successful in their bid for independence, the United States would have to renegotiate its strategic interests with these nationalists. The dilemma facing U.S. officials was how to continue its policy of supporting colonialism without antagonizing the Africans. The way that U.S. policymakers decided to deal with this dilemma was simply to go on supporting colonialism, while simultaneously making general statements in support of the principle of self-determination, thus giving birth to the familiar contradiction between U.S. actions and statements.

As Hans Morgenthau has noted, the United States merely decided to support colonialism without admitting it to the Africans.[41]

U.S. policy on southern Africa during the 1960s was a logical continuation of its African policy in the 1950s. As the African diplomatic offensive against the white regimes in southern Africa gained momentum, there was a growing feeling in the U.S. government that its support for apartheid might become increasingly self-defeating and detrimental to its objectives of maintaining stability in the region, as well as a strain on relations between the United States and the black African states. The U.S. response was not to change the substance of its policy, but to increase the stridency of its antiapartheid rhetoric in the United Nations; a strategy which admittedly was more consistent with the domestic policies of a U.S. administration that was more responsive to Afro-American demands for desegregation.[42]

The return of the United States to a more thoroughgoing support of the white redoubt in 1967 was due to increasing resistance to desegregation at home, together with a calculation that Africans were not as powerful in affecting the situation in southern Africa as had been originally anticipated. By 1966, the African diplomatic offensive in southern Africa had run its course without seriously shaking the resolve of the white minority regimes. At this point, it became increasingly clear that if the Africans were to make any serious headway, it would have to be on the battlefield, and U.S. officials decided that the chances of that happening were negligible, because the whites were "tough, determined, and increasingly self-confident."[43] This prognostication became the basis of the Nixon-Kissinger policy on southern Africa, a policy which was carried out until 1975, when it was overtaken by new realities.

The achievement of independence by Mozambique and Angola through armed struggle changed the situation in southern Africa both objectively and psychologically. Objectively, it showed that the Africans had not only begun to fight in earnest, but that they could win. Psychologically, it dramatically enhanced the determination and self-confidence of the guerrillas operating in southern Africa and destroyed the myth of the invincibility of the white man. Thus, almost overnight, the assumption on which the "tar-baby" option had been based was proved wrong, and the United States was faced with the prospect of another potential threat to the stability of the region.[44] It was in the face of this new reality that Kissinger announced his "new" policy for southern Africa.

It is important to understand that what prompted this new policy was not a change in U.S. objectives. There has been no change in the U.S.

commitment to support the white regimes. What caused the change in policy were the changing conditions in the area, specifically the beginning of actual fighting. It is clear that if the Africans had not started fighting, the United States would have continued with the policy that it had consistently followed over the years. The fact is that the beginning of fighting posed a threat to U.S. policy objectives, and the new policy was activated in order to attempt to save the situation. As discussed above when faced with African diplomatic pressure in the mid-1950s, the U.S. government adopted the tactical ruse of paying lip service to the principles of self-determination and human rights, while continuing with its policy of supporting the white-dominated regimes. The new Kissinger twist of "African solutions to African problems"[45] was another tactical move designed to maintain the integrity of the same fundamental policy objectives of maintaining as much white control as possible. When President Carter was making his famous forthright statements in favor of the international respect for human rights, some thought that a departure from the Nixon-Ford-Kissinger policy might be expected. It now seems clear from continued U.S. rejection of economic sanctions against South Africa, U.S. support for the development of "independent Bantustans," and South African control of political development in Namibia throughout the Turnhalle constitutional talks, that there has not been any substantive departure from the policy of supporting de facto white minority rule in southern Africa.[46]

The Effect of U.S. Policy on Southern Africa

The most readily apparent effect of the U.S. policy on southern Africa is that is has failed to achieve its avowed goal of maintaining the peace in that region. It has led to hostilities which have already involved non-African countries. As such, U.S. policy has paradoxically led to a situation which threatens its interests, since, as a global power, the United States has a definite interest in any situation which can threaten the stability of the international system as a whole.[47] But beyond this, the present situation is detrimental to U.S. interests in more specific ways. First, the longer the conflict continues, the more bitter and openly racist it is likely to become, with the result that it would be more difficult to achieve a compromise which would preserve the legitimate interests of all, including those of the local whites, as well as the United States. Secondly, as the conflict continues, as we have already seen, the Africans have come under increasing pressure to accept aid from wherever they can get it, including the Communist countries. The effect of this development has already been to introduce Communist influence into Africa: precisely the development which American foreign policy was designed to prevent.[48]

Apart from the deleterious effects of U.S. policy on its own interests, it has also had the effect of seriously damaging the viability of the United Nations and its mechanism for the maintenance of international peace.[49] The United Nations has been an effective instrument for clarifying the international norms of self-determination and human rights to the extent that it has established the existence of an impressive international consensus which deplores apartheid and colonialism, and considers the occupation of Namibia, as well as the existence of the Rhodesian government, as contrary to international law, as well as the letter and spirit of the United Nations Charter.[50] The fact that Rhodesia and South Africa have been able to defy the organization with impunity has been a serious blow to the organization and strengthened the hand of those who argue that the only way for the Africans to achieve justice is to "de-escalate the talking and escalate the fighting."

That the policy of the United States has been a major factor in the ability of South Africa and Rhodesia to arrogantly defy the United Nations and international opinion cannot be denied. To be sure, these outlaw states have had even more blatant support from other states: for many years, France has been the biggest arms supplier to South Africa; Japan has substantial trade relations with her; cooperation on various levels between South Africa and Israel and other Western countries has increased in the past few years; even some African countries have surreptitious trade relations with South Africa.[51] However, from the standpoint of international order, the support that the racist regimes have had from these other states has not been anywhere near as significant as the diplomatic and material support they have received from the most powerful country in the world. Therefore, by its action, the United States has not only helped to undermine the already fragile enforcement machinery of the United Nations, but also created a situation in which lack of respect for the United Nations could spill over into other areas of enforcement action. In this regard, U.S. violation of the mandatory sanctions for which it had itself voted was serious enough, but to have violated the sanctions in the most flagrant manner possible could not help but have the most deleterious effect on the already tottering prestige of the organization. As Ralph Zacklin has noted,

> the most damaging consequence of the Byrd Amendment is the moral and psychological encouragement that it provided to the Smith regime and the concomitant undermining of the viability of international sanctions, and, indirectly, the United Nations.[52]

Conclusion: U.S. Responsibility, Opportunity, and Challenge

At the present time, the threat to international peace and security is the most pressing problem. Continued talk of peaceful solution is idle, unless something is done about the fundamental issue which underlies the conflict: the issue of black majority rule. It is certain that the way in which white domination has been maintained is through violence, violence against the dignity and the lives of blacks. It is also certain that the only way white domination can continue is through violence, because the Africans will not submit to it peacefully any longer. In fact, as the events of the past few months have shown, the Africans are settling into what they believe to be a long, protracted conflict against the white-dominated regimes. Whether they win or not is just a matter of time.

In this situation, the first responsibility of the United States is to defuse the conflict. The responsibility of the United States is clear on two grounds: first, the U.S. has a responsibility as a great power with an interest in world security. As Chester Bowles has stated:

> The most powerful country in the world, which asserts that it is leading a global coalition for freedom, cannot declare itself to be nonparticipant in the affairs of a continent boiling with change, without abdicating its position of leadership.[53]

Beyond this, however, the United States has an additional responsibility. The role played by the United States in letting the situation deteriorate to this point is inescapable. It is doubtful that Rhodesia and South Africa can maintain the stubborn hope of eventual victory without the support of the United States.

How can the United States help to defuse the conflict? One suggestion is that the conflict can be defused by giving such forthright support to the whites that the Africans will see that they cannot win. Apart from the fact that this perverted idea shows total disregard for the justice of the African cause, such a policy cannot possibly be successful. The Africans have been remarkably patient under extreme provocation, and they have attempted every possible peaceful means in pursuit of demands which the overwhelming majority of the international community recognizes as being eminently legitimate. At this point, it has to be clearly understood that the minimum that the Africans will accept as a condition for peace is their freedom and dignity. As President Nyerere of Tanzania has put it: "The situation in Southern Africa is one of principle. It does not allow of compromise, because compromise on a matter of human rights is a denial of those rights."[54] To the Africans nothing short of majority rule will be acceptable. For there to be lasting peace in southern Africa, apartheid must go.

On the other hand, it would be unrealistic to suggest that the United States undertake, unilaterally, to coerce the white-dominated regimes in southern Africa. Due to the white-dominated nature of American society itself, it is clear that it would be impossible for the U.S. government to find acceptance among the powerful interest groups which influence U.S. foreign policy for a southern African policy which might seem to be abandoning the interests of the white South Africans.[55] However, there are many measures short of the use of force, such as rigorously enforced arms and trade bans, investment sanctions, and other types of economic and diplomatic pressures, which can be used by the United States in concert with other states. What is being suggested is that the United States take an unequivocal stance, both in word and in deed, of denying moral, diplomatic, economic, military, or any other form of support for the white redoubt.

Beyond the immediate problem, the United States has an opportunity to help establish conditions of lasting peace in southern Africa by strengthening the peacekeeping capacity of the United Nations. In this connection, it is not enough for the United States to take a stance against supporting apartheid in private diplomatic intercourse. It is of crucial importance that this policy be publicly espoused, and pursued in association and coordination with the efforts of the United Nations. By so doing, the United States would be cooperating with the majority of the members of the organization to give strength to the resolutions and enforcement capability of the United Nations. The United Nations has been the forum in which the issues of southern Africa have been discussed and debated, and it still remains one of the hopes of retrieving the situation from its present collision course, if the United States can put its vast resources to the aid of the United Nations.[56] This will be of great importance, not only for the solution of the problem of South Africa in particular, but for strengthening the U.N. machinery as a whole.

Therefore, the challenge of the United States is not to jettison the United Nations because the organization would not accept its support of the states which have consistently defied its fundamental principles, but rather to reexamine its policies and attempt to bring them into harmony with the charter principles which it professes to believe in. The choice facing the United States is clear. On the one hand, it can continue to take the posture of a defender of breachers of international norms and be dragged unwillingly along by international consensus, or it can assert categorically its leadership in the struggle for international order, based on the principles of self-determination and human rights.

In the past few years, the United States government has shown a marked tendency to avoid U.N. mechanisms for conflict resolution. This attitude has been prompted, in part, by the feeling that, in such issues as apartheid and colonialism, the new states have automatic majorities which they have been able to use "irresponsibly." To pick up its isolationist marbles and go home is hardly consistent with the position of the United States as the leader of the free world and the supporter of international order; especially since, until quite recently, the United States itself was able to amass automatic majorities on a whole range of issues. In any case, the rules of international order, and the respect for those rules, cannot be maintained unless the interest of members of the international community in the long-term stability of the rules which sustain this order is greater than their interest in winning on the substance of any particular issue.

In spite of its sometimes justified characterization as "a dangerous place,"[57] there seems little doubt that if the United Nations were to cease to exist, the international community would have to create it all over again.[58] So far, it has been a significant contribution to a more orderly international system, and its future impact might be even more substantial if the United States, with its vast influence, would give higher priority to strengthening bonds of community among the nation members than to pursuing more narrowly defined national priorities.[59]

We must remember that what has caused some of the most tragic conflicts in the history of mankind has not been the people struggling to attain for themselves and others the best humanity has to offer, but rather the unwillingness of dominant peoples to respond in a timely manner to the legitimate aspirations of the oppressed and the deprived. It has been said that, if we must choose between order and justice, we should choose order at the expense of justice. But we must remember that there is a minumum of justice without which order cannot be maintained. In southern Africa, that minimum is the right of the Africans to govern themselves in their own land and be treated as equals in their own land. Finally, we must not forget the great lesson of the League of Nations: that in this finite world we cannot fail to defend the rights of seemingly powerless and remote peoples without at the same time jeopardizing the peace and security of the whole world.

Notes

1. Richard N. Gardner, *In Pursuit of World Order: U.S. Foreign Policy and*

International Organizations, rev. ed. (New York: Praeger, 1967), p. 19.

2. John G. Stoessinger, *The United Nations and the Superpowers*, 2nd ed. (New York: Random House, 1974), p. 24.

3. Bureau of Public Affairs, *Press Conference* (Washington, D.C., September 11, 1976), p. 1.

4. W. Ofuatey-Kodjoe, "Conflicting Political Interests of Africa and the United States," in Frederick S. Arkhurst, ed., *U.S. Policy Toward Africa* (New York: Praeger, 1975), pp. 198 ff.

5. Gardner, *In Pursuit of World Order*, p. xvi.

6. For a partial list of the literature which discusses this confusion, see Bruce Oudes, "Observations on American Foreign Policy in Southern Africa," *Issues* 3, no. 4 (winter 1973); John Marcum, "The Politics of Indifference: Portugal and Africa, A Case Study in America Foreign Policy," *Issues* 2, no. 3 (fall 1972); Herbert Spiro, "The American Response to Africa's Participation in the International System," *Issues* 3, no. 1 (spring 1973); Waldemar Nielsen, *The Great Powers and Africa* (New York: Praeger, 1969).

7. Ibid.

8. Nielsen, *The Great Powers and Africa*, p. 297.

9. For some analyses of patterns of economic, technological, and defense cooperation between the United States and South Africa, see George Hauser, "U.S. Policy and Southern Africa," in Arkhurst, *U.S. Policy Toward Africa*, pp. 88-130; Robert Manning, "The South African Connection," *Encore* (March 22, 1976); Corporate Information Center, National Council of Churches, *Church Investment, Corporations and South Africa* (New York: Friendship Press, 1973); Larry Bowman, "Southern Africa Policy for the Seventies," *Issues* 1, no. 2 (fall 1971): 25-26; Vaughan E. Taplin, "U.S. Support of Rhodesia," *The Black Scholar* (February 1971), pp. 51-55.

10. Herbert Spiro, "The American Response to Africa's Participation in the International System," *Issues* 3, no. 1 (spring 1973): 22.

11. George Modelski, "The International Relations of Internal War," in James N. Rosenau, ed., *International Aspects of Civil Strife* (Princeton: Princeton University Press, 1964), pp. 23-24.

12. Clinton Knox, "Comment," in Arkhurst, *U.S. Policy Toward Africa*, p. 227.

13. See U.N. General Assembly resolutions 616 (VII), December 5, 1952; 721 (VIII), December 8, 1953; 820 (XI), December 14, 1954; 917 (X), December 6, 1955; 1518 (XII), November 26, 1957.

14. U.N. General Assembly resolutions 1598 (XV), April 13, 1961; 1663 (XVI), November 28, 1961; 1881 (XVIII), October 11, 1963.

15. See for instance U.N. General Assembly resolutions 1761 (XVII), November 6, 1962; 2054 (XX), December 5, 1965; U.N. document A/4968, November 28, 1961.

16. U.N. General Assembly resolutions 1568 (XV), December 18, 1960; 1596 (XV), April 7, 1961; 1979 (XVIII), December 17, 1973.
17. U.N. General Assembly Resolution 1899 (XVIII), November 13, 1963.
18. U.N. General Assembly resolutions 2248 (S-V), May 17, 1967; 2325 (XXII), December 16, 1967; and Security Council resolutions 264 (1969), March 20, 1969; 269 (1969), August 12, 1969.
19. U.N. General Assembly resolutions 1699 (XVI), December 9, 1961; 1742 (XVI), January 30, 1962.
20. U.N. General Assembly resolutions 1807 (XVII), December 14, 1962; 1819 (XVII), December 18, 1962; 1913 (XVIII), December 3, 1963; 2107 (XX), December 1965; 2184 (XXI), December 12, 1966.
21. U.N. General Assembly resolutions 2908 (XXVII), November 4, 1972; 2918 (XXVII), November 4, 1972.
22. U.N. General Assembly resolutions 1760 (XVII), October 31, 1962; 1883 (XVIII), October 14, 1963; 1889 (XVIII), November 6, 1963; 2022 (XX), November 6, 1965.
23. For a discussion of the role of the Nixon administration in the adoption of the Byrd Amendment see Mohamed A. El-Khawas and Barry Cohen, eds., *The Kissinger Study of Southern Africa: National Security Study Memorandum 39* (Westport, Conn.: Laurence Hill, 1976), pp. 42-44.
24. Quoted in Rupert Emerson, *Africa and United States Policy* (Englewood Cliffs, N.J.: Prentice-Hall, 1962), p. 90.
25. See Mohamed A. El-Khawas and Barry Cohen, *Op. Cit.,* p. 106.
26. See note 9 above.
27. Hans Morgenthau, "United States Policy Toward Africa," in Calvin W. Stillman, ed., *Africa in the Modern World* (Chicago: Chicago University Press, 1955), p.318.
28. John Marcum, "Southern Africa and United States Policy: A Consideration of Alternatives," in George W. Shepherd, Jr., *Racial Influences on American Foreign Policy* (New York: Basic Books, 1970), pp. 200-204.
29. See W. Ofuatey-Kodjoe, "Conflicting Political Interests of Africa and the United States," in Arkhurst, *U.S. Policy Toward Africa*, p. 203.
30. For an extensive listing of titles dealing with economic relations between the United States and Africa, see Frederick S. Arkhurst, ed., *Africa in the Seventies and Eighties: Issues in Development* (New York: Praeger, 1970). See also Andrew Karmack, "The African Economy and International Trade," in Walter Goldschmidt, ed., *The United States and Africa* (New York: Praeger, 1965), pp. 157-58; and Nielsen, *The Great Powers and Africa*.
31. K. J. Holsti, *International Politics: A Framework for Analysis,* 2nd ed. (Englewood Cliffs, N.J.: Prentice-Hall, 1972), p. 137. See also Morton A. Kaplan, *System and Process in International Politics* (New York: John Wiley and Sons, 1957), pp. 164-165.

32. George Shepherd, Jr., and Tilden LeMelle, eds., *Race Among Nations* (Lexington: D.C. Heath & Co., 1970), P. 2; George Shepherd, Jr., ed., *Racial Influences on American Foreign Policy* (New York: Praeger, 1970), pp. 182-185, 204-206.

33. Gabriel Almond, *The American People and Foreign Policy* (New York: Praeger, 1960), p. 30.

34. *Ibid.,* p. 30.

35. For further elaboration of this point, see Ofuatey-Kodjoe, "Conflicting Political Interests of Africa and the United States," pp. 207-208.

36. Mohamed A. El-Khawas and Barry Cohen, *Op. Cit.,* pp. 105-106. My italics.

37. On the white-dominated character of the United States, see the *Report of the National Advisory Commission on Civil Disorders* (New York: Bantam Books, 1968), especially p. 203.

38. For a comparison of the relative potency of racial constituencies in U.S. policy towards Southern Africa, see Ofuatey-Kodjoe, "Conflicting Political Interests of Africa and the United States," p. 221; Vernon McKay, "Southern Africa and Its Implications for American Policy," in William A. Hance, ed., *Southern Africa and the United States* (New York: Columbia University Press, 1968), pp. 19-25.

39. James N. Rosenau, "Foreign Policy as an Issue Area," in James Rosenau, ed., *Domestic Sources of Foreign Policy* (New York: Free Press, 1967), p. 36. For a full discussion on the influence of race on international politics see James Rosenau, "Race in International Politics: A Dialogue in Five Parts," in Shepherd and LeMelle, eds., *Race Among Nations,* pp. 61-122.

40. For a discussion of the evolution of the principle of self-determination in United Nations and contemporary international practice, see W. Ofuatey-Kodjoe, *The Principle of Self-Determination in International Law* (New York: Nellen Publishing Co., 1977), pp. 97-147.

41. Morgenthau, "United States Policy Toward Africa," p. 322.

42. John A. Davis, "Black Americans and United States Policy Toward Africa," *Journal of International Affairs* 23, no. 2 (summer 1969): 236-249.

43. *National Security Study Memorandum 39,* p. 117.

44. For a general discussion of the "tar-baby" policy, see Anthony Lake, *The "Tar-Baby" Option: American Policy Toward Southern Rhodesia* (New York: Columbia University Press, 1976). Also, Mohamed A. El-Khawas and Barry Cohen, *Op. Cit.*

45. Bureau of Public Affairs, *Secretary Henry A. Kissinger before the Senate Foreign Relations Committee* (May 13, 1976).

46. George W. Shepherd, Jr., "The Struggle to a New Southern African Policy: The Carter Task," *Journal of Southern African Affairs* 2, no. 1 (January 1977): 116.

47. Robert E. Riggs, *U.S./U.N.: Foreign Policy and International Organization*

(New York: Appleton-Century-Crofts, 1971), p. 152.

48. George W. Shepherd, Jr., *Non-Aligned Black Africa* (Lexington: D. C. Heath, 1970), p. 74.

49. Riggs, *U.S./U.N.*, p. 152.

50. W. Ofuatey-Kodjoe, *The Principle of Self-Determination in International Law*, p. 146-147.

51. See Robert Manning, "The South African Connection," *Encore* (March 22, 1976); also Harris Schoenberg, "South Africa's Silent Partners" (unpublished paper, Office for U.N. Affairs, B'nai B'rith International Council, 1976).

52. Ralph Zacklin, *The United Nations and Rhodesia: A Study in International Law* (New York: Praeger, 1974), p. 84.

53. Chester Bowles, *Africa's Challenge to the United States* (Berkeley: University of California Press, 1956), pp. 96-°7.

54. Julius Nyerere, "South Africa: Peace of War," *Pan-African Journal* 4, no. 1 (winter 1971): 54.

55. Shepherd, "The Struggle to a New Southern African Policy: The Carter Task," p, 116. Also Ofuatey-Kodjoe, "Conflicting Political Interests of Africa and the United States," p. 221 ff.

56. Riggs, *U.S./U.N.*, p. 155.

57. See Abraham Yeselson and Anthony Cagliano, *A Dangerous Place: The United Nations as a Weapon in World Politics* (New York: Grossman Publishers, 1974).

58. Ralph Stuart Smith, *The United States and the United Nations* (Dept. of State Publication 8875, September 1976), p. 10. See also Richard N. Gardner, *In Pursuit of World Order* (New York: Praeger, 1967), p. 45.

59. Robert E. Riggs, *U.S./U.N.*, p. 307.

PART TWO: THE UNITED STATES IN A CHANGING INTERNATIONAL ECONOMIC ORDER

Introduction
Myer Cohen

The most striking thought to emerge from the series of presentations in this section is one of awe at the scope, magnitude, and potential implications of the New International Economic Order (NIEO). Vistas are opened up, for example, in Karl Sauvant's presentation of a new international economic order which goes far beyond what he describes as reformist or liberal thinking. Whereas there is much preoccupation with putting the developing countries in a position to benefit from the international economic mechanisms and system, it may be necessary to think of entirely new relationships, rather than fitting newcomers (the developing countries), into a relationship (assumed to be somewhat static) with the countries of the industrialized world. For example, is it sufficient to admit new groups to share in the management of the International Monetary Fund (IMF) without examining the underlying financial structures? Or with respect to science and technology, how can the transfer of technology and a code of conduct avoid codifying the technological dependency of the third world, rather than establishing indigenous science and technology capacities and infrastructures?

Questions such as these illustrate the range of conceptual possibilities which open up when the New International Economic Order is considered. The basic theme is applicable whether one is discussing transnational corporations, monetary problems, or trade policies.

Robern Gilpin sees the transnational corporation not so much as an economic institution, but as a means of pursuing U.S. economic objectives through direct investment, which has shifted from extractive industries to manufacturing. He raises questions as to whether American corporate expansionism is in the larger interest of the United States; in particular, whether, as U.S. influence declines and as foreign governments force American corporations to serve their interests,

Americans, will find that corporate and national interests coincide. A new international economic order may encompass this type of issue.

In the area of monetary policy, Robert Roosa emphasizes the possible emergence of a new type of monetary system. This new system involves the broadening of the exchange rate system by basing it on a clustering around several key currencies—i.e., the Deutschemark in Europe, and the yen in the Far East—rather than limiting it to the dollar as has been done in the past. Both Roosa and Edward Morse agree that at present the monetary system is guided by only the loosest of rules—following the example of British common law in eschewing precise definitions while adhering to general principles. This in fact may be a prescient approach in a period when a NIEO is in the making.

Morse emphasizes the change in the locus and fundamental meaning of economic power. While it would be inaccurate to maintain that economic and political power had shifted from the United States to other parts of the industrialized world (as fleetingly appeared to have been the case at the beginning of the 1970s), it is true now that important economic decisions are being made *outside* the industrialized world—in oil exporting countries, and in commodity-rich countries of the less-developed world. One sign of this has been the unity of the less-developed countries in various international forums.

Throughout all of the papers there appears the recognition—sometimes explicit, other times more hidden—that the United States (and *mutatis mutandis*, other industrialized nations) will have to face for the first time an international order in which their economic power, while perhaps superior to that of others, will have to be tempered by the aspirations, needs, and political power of the third world. Perhaps the true meaning of the NIEO is its genuine global implications, and a recognition that value judgments have a place in decision making alongside economic and financial power.

THE NEW INTERNATIONAL ECONOMIC ORDER

10. The New International Economic Order: Toward Structural Changes or a More Tolerable Status Quo?
Karl P. Sauvant

Since the 1974 Sixth Special Session of the United Nations General Assembly the establishment of the New International Economic Order (NIEO) is the priority item on the international agenda. After briefly introducing the main proposals of the NIEO program (in relation to the main problems they are meant to deal with), the question is asked whether the implementation of these proposals could indeed be expected to lead to a change of the structures of the present system. It will be argued that this cannot be expected and that, in fact, a number of the key elements of the NIEO program have stabilizing effects for the existing system, or amend it in a reformistic way, in the interest of alleviating the most pressing current problems of the developing countries. Important as such stopgap measures are, permanent relief can only be obtained through a change of the underlying structures of the system and the establishment of an order that serves the needs of all its members. Structural changes, it will be suggested, can be obtained through an international program of affirmative action for development and the pursuance of individual and collective self-reliance on the part of the third world.

On May 1, 1974, the United Nations General Assembly, at the end of its Sixth Special Session, adopted by consensus two resolutions entitled "Declaration on the Establishment of a New International Economic Order" and "Programme of Action on the Establishment of a New

The views expressed in this chapter do not necessarily reflect those of the institution with which the author is currently affiliated (U.N. Centre on Transnational Corporations). A somewhat revised version of this piece appears in *Dissent* (winter 1978).

International Economic Order."[1] With the adoption of these two resolutions, the developing countries (DCs) had succeeded in making development the priority item on the international agenda.

The program for the establishment of the NIEO consists of the proposals and measures contained in the resolutions adopted at the Sixth Special Session and contained in the "Charter of Economic Rights and Duties of States" and the resolution on "Development and International Economic Co-operation." The key components of this program have been discussed elsewhere in great detail.[2] The following brief outline of the main elements of the program in the crucial areas of North-South relations—trade and commodities, financial matters, science and technology, and industrialization—is merely intended to serve as an immediate reference point for the remainder of this article.

In the area of trade—the motor of development—the main problem of the DCs concerns their declining share in world trade. This deterioration is largely a result of the primary-products structure of the DCs' exports, especially the long-term worsening of their terms of trade and their insufficient access to the markets of the industrialized countries. In the NIEO program, therefore, trade and primary-product questions receive detailed attention. The centerpiece is an integrated program for commodities whose principal purposes are to improve the DCs' terms of trade and to develop a more orderly management of commodity supplies. The key measures proposed to achieve these objectives are: (1) the establishment of international buffer stocks for a number of commodities and (2) the creation of a common fund for the financing of these stocks. The main function of these buffer stocks is to absorb market fluctuations, to balance supply and demand, by stabilizing the prices of the products covered between negotiated lower and upper price margins. Obviously, in a world in which 5-10 percent inflation is the rule, these price margins have to be periodically adjusted in order to protect the real prices originally negotiated. The adjustment mechanism preferred by the DCs is indexation. Thus the initially negotiated price could, for instance, be linked to a basket of prices of goods imported by DCs.[3]

While commodity agreements deal with the basic supply of raw materials, as well as the receipts for them, the NIEO program also supports increased processing in developing countries and the expansion and diversification of the exports of these countries. The achievement of this objective requires improved access to the markets of the industrialized nations. Consequently, the removal or restriction of tariff and nontariff barriers receives great attention. Special attention is given to an improvement of the nonreciprocal, nondiscriminatory Generalized System of Preferences (GSP) and the elimination of restrictive business practices that adversely affect the trade of DCs.

One of the main functions of trade is to generate the foreign-exchange earnings necessary to finance the import of capital goods required for industrialization. Partially because of the conditions outlined above, however, exports alone are not able to provide the necessary resources. Other mechanisms must be utilized. One of these mechanisms is official development assistance (ODA), i.e., official bilateral and multilateral capital flows with a minimum grant element. These flows, however, have failed to increase in real terms since the middle of the 1960s and, in fact, have dropped sharply as a percentage of the industrialized countries GNP; from 0.52 percent in 1961-1962 to 0.33 percent in 1974. The improvement of the ODA performance is therefore a key plank of the NIEO program and the developed market economies (DMEs) are reminded that their ODA should reach (at the latest by 1980) the target of 0.7 percent of GNP, a target they had already agreed to earlier (without a time limit, however). Moreover, since one important reason for the decline of ODA has been its voluntary character—making it dependent on the prevailing political situation in donor countries—the DCs want an element of automaticity to be introduced into concessional flows in order to make them predictable, assured, and continuous.

The decrease of ODA made it necessary for the third world to obtain the required resources under less favorable conditions from private capital markets. As a result, the external indebtedness of over 80 non-OPEC (Organization of Petroleum Exporting Countries) DCs has risen dramatically from $9 billion in 1956 to over $170 billion in 1976 (of which about $70 billion are owed to commercial banks), and annual debt payments (of about $12 billion in 1974) already more than cancel the annual inflow of ODA. In this situation, the debt issue has become a priority problem for the DCs and a number of measures have been suggested to alleviate it. Foremost among them are an international conference of major donor, creditor, and debtor countries that would devise principles and guidelines governing the renegotiation of debts, leading to the multilateralization of measures aimed at bringing relief to debt repayments and servicing pressures.

The question of financial resources for development is also at the basis of a set of third-world proposals aimed at bolstering the capital of the World Bank group as well as other development institutions and at increasing the third world's credit line with the IMF. With respect to the latter, proposals have been made: (1) to increase the quotas, which govern the availability of IMF finance; (2) to enlarge the first (automatic) credit tranche and to derestrict drawings under the other tranches; (3) to liberalize, enlarge, and review the various existing balance of payments mechanisms and, if necessary, to create new ones; and (4) to liberalize drawings under the buffer stock financing facility.

Another approach—particularly attractive because of its automaticity—is to link the distribution of special drawing rights (SDRs) to development assistance. Such a link would be especially promising if SDRs would become the central reserve asset of the international monetary system and, consequently, the role of gold and national reserve currencies (which give privileged credit to a few countries) would be reduced—a key plank of the NIEO program. Since all these changes are unlikely to be achieved under the present voting system of the IMF, DCs are pressing for a greater voice in the fund and in the management of the international monetary system in general—a system, after all, that constitutes the framework for their trade transactions and their development efforts.

In no other area is the asymmetry of relations between North and South so pronounced as in the area of science and technology. Virtually all R&D is conducted in developed countries (including the socialist countries) and, as a consequence, nationals or institutions of the same countries hold virtually all patents in the world. Recognizing that in this situation the transfer of technology is the only way through which DCs can obtain the technology required for their development, the main emphasis of the NIEO program in this area is the regulation of the transfer processes and their conditions. Specifically, the adoption of a legally binding code of conduct for the transfer of technology is urged to deal with such matters as relations among suppliers, restrictive business practices, access to technology, and pricing. Changes are also envisaged for the international patent system and efforts are encouraged to formulate policies and build institutions that will improve scientific and technological infrastructure of DCs.

The purpose of restructuring the international mechanisms and structures in the areas of trade, finance, and science and technology is to serve industrialization—the basic objective of most DCs. At the present time, the manufacturing output of the entire third world is about as high as that of the Federal Republic of Germany—approximately $108 billion. It is the goal of the DCs, to increase this output more than tenfold before the end of this century—an objective that will require a substantial mobilization of resources and major adaptations of the world's industrial structures. The structural adaptations envisaged by the NIEO program amount essentially to a clearer international division of labor: the DMEs are asked to encourage the redeployment of their less competitive industries (i.e., usually labor-intensive, low-technology industries) to developing countries. In fact, the establishment of a "system of consultations" is urged to facilitate this process.

In market economies, the primary agents of any redeployment of industries are, of course, private business firms and especially transnational enterprises (TNEs). TNEs are in fact expected to play an important role (especially under conditions of decreasing ODA) in the industrialization process by mobilizing the capital and technology resources required and by providing the markets for the expanding economies of the third world. TNEs are explicitly encouraged to participate in third world investment projects. At the same time, however, and similar to the situation in the area of transfer of technology, the conditions under which foreign direct investment is made available, the purposes it is supposed to serve, is a critical matter for DCs. Consequently, the elaboration of an effective code of conduct for TNEs is an important aspect of the NIEO program.

Toward Implementation

For most developing countries, the NIEO program represents an effort to restructure the present international economic system—which is primarily geared to the interests of the DMEs who created this system—to make it also responsive to the interests and special conditions of the DCs—who inherited it. It represents an effort to free themselves from their all-encompassing dependence on the DMEs, to move toward a more equitable and equal participation in international economic transactions, and to be able to pursue independent development. The need for changes in the present system has been widely acknowledged, even by the DMEs, and development has been accepted as a purpose that should be among those served by the system.

The Sixth Special Session had achieved this basic objective, the seventh consolidated it. This success is, of course, based on a number of factors, most notably among them: (1) the politicization of the development issue since the beginning of the 1970s; (2) the remarkable unity achieved by the DCs whose political organization—the nonaligned movement—had transformed itself in the early years of the 1970s into a highly organized international pressure group for the reorganization of the international economic system; and (3) the new assertiveness of the DCs, an assertiveness that expresses itself, inter alia, in the formation of producers' associations.[4] These factors are also largely responsible for the shift of the discussion toward the translation of principles into concrete actions, i.e., toward the implementation of the NIEO program.

These discussions have been pursued in various regional and international economic negotiations, all of which have received considerable impetus from the élan created by the Sixth Special Session. Thus, for instance, within three months after the end of this session, the forty-six developing countries negotiating the Lomé Convention with the European Economic Community (EEC) presented the Kingston memorandum to their European interlocutors.

In the spirit of the NIEO, this suddenly revitalized the negotiations and led to their relatively rapid conclusion (February 28, 1975)—along the lines outlined by the 46. The convention pioneers a number of progressive mechanisms, including an export-earnings stabilization fund and free access (as far as formal tariffs are concerned), without reciprocity, to the EEC's market for virtually all export goods of the associates.[5] Third world countries also lobbied for support and acceptance of the NIEO program in another interregional context, in the framework of a Conference of the Commonwealth Heads of Government (April/May 1975).

On the international level, a number of major U.N. conferences, held subsequent to the Sixth Special Session, were infused with the spirit of the NIEO. Although these conferences had originally been conceived of as dealing with more specialized topics, they were now geared to the overall objective of development. Less than two months after the end of the sixth session, the initial substantive session of the Third Conference of the United Nations on the Law of the Sea offered the first opportunity to implement part of the NIEO program. The opportunity was indeed seized. In fact, the preceding experience of the special session probably played an important role in the rapid attainment of a common third world bargaining position.[6] A number of other major conferences followed which also experienced the new assertiveness of the DCs and their attempts to integrate them into the NIEO framework: the World Population Conference (August 1974); the World Food Conference (November 1974); the World Conference of the International Women's Year in Mexico (June/July 1975); Habitat: United Nations Conference on Human Settlements (May/June 1976); and the Tripartite World Conference on Employment, Income Distribution and Social Progress and the International Division of Labour (June 1976).

Other meetings had, in the interim, further refined the NIEO program in the areas of industrialization and raw materials. Industrialization had been the topic of the second conference of the U.N. Industrial Development Organization (UNIDO) (March 1975) whose final document, the Lima Declaration and Plan of Action on Industrial Development and Co-operation, presented for the first time a detailed program for industrialization. This declaration and plan of action is almost identical with the resolution adopted by a ministerial meeting of the Group of 77 that was held in preparation for the UNIDO conference. Raw materials had been discussed two months earlier in Dakar at a Conference of Developing Countries on Raw Materials, during which economic development had been examined for the first time with particular reference to the role of raw materials. The Dakar conference had been called on the initiative of the non-aligned countries whose meetings had multiplied since their 1973 summit in Algiers.[7] Most important among them were their 1975 conference of ministers of foreign affairs—which took a number of decisions aimed at strengthening the third world's action capacity in the field of raw materials (e.g., it decided to establish a council of producers' associations)—and their 1976 summit in Colombo, which refined the economic program of the third world.

Within the United Nations framework, the NIEO program was further consolidated with the adoption, in December 1974, of the Charter of Economic Rights and Duties of States, and, in September 1975, of a resolution on "Development and International Economic Cooperation" (by the Seventh Special Session).[8] The fourth U.N. Conference on Trade and Development (UNCTAD IV—May 1976, prepared by a ministerial meeting of the Group of 77 in Manila, January/February 1976), finally, took some very cautious steps toward negotiations about the implementation of the integrated commodity program (including the modalities of a common fund for the financing of buffer stocks) and negotiations concerning a code of conduct on transfer of technology (although a decision on the legal character of the code—voluntary vs. mandatory—could not be reached). No progress was made with respect to debts. The implementation of the NIEO program is also being pursued by the third world in the General Agreement on Tariffs and Trade's (GATT's) Multilateral Trade Negotiations (the "Tokyo Round") and the (Paris) Conference on International Economic Co-operation.

The most concrete results, however, have been reached so far in the World Bank (with the establishment of the Third Window) and in the IMF, which after a series of meetings culminating in a session in Jamaica, reached agreement on: (1) the increase of quotas by nearly SDR $10 billion, to a total of SDR $39 billion; (2) the doubling of the shares of the major oil producers; (3) the establishment of the oil facility and its temporary continuation on an enlarged basis (including an interest-subsidy account for the most seriously affected countries); (4) the sale of one-sixth of the IMF's gold for the benefit of DCs, to be distributed over the next four years through a trust fund (the first sales of gold have already taken place); (5) an improvement of access to drawing under the buffer stock financing and the compensatory financing facilities; and (6) the enlargement (until the effective date of the quota increase) of the size of each credit tranche by 45 percent.[9] Together, the trust fund, the liberalized compensatory financing facility, and the credit tranche could yield up to $3.5 billion for the DCs for 1976. However, if the loss of IMF financing due to a discontinuation of the enlarged oil facility after April 1976 is subtracted from this amount, the financial gain for the third world for 1976 is reduced to about $2.5 billion—which does not even approach the financial needs of the third world.[10]

This unprecedented set of conferences clearly shows that development has become the priority item on the international agenda. Unquestionably, these conferences have contributed to a further acceptance of the NIEO program; they have created support for it and have led to some first steps toward its implementation. However, except for the Lomé Convention—some of whose features may indicate that the associates are "inching toward interdependence"—no major breakthrough has been achieved in changing the mechanisms of the international economic system. No agreement has been reached on any of the main points of the program reviewed in the preceding section. This includes the World Bank and the IMF. While the appropriation of additional funds for the third world signals some progress, the allocation of these funds remains solidly under the control of the industrial states, thus forestalling the automaticity of development finance that is a key element of the NIEO program.

The NIEO Program: A Liberal Holding Operation

This leads to another question. Could a change of the mechanisms of the international economic system, in full accord with a complete implementation of the NIEO program, be expected to alter the structure of the system and the distribution of benefits associated with them? What, in other words, would happen to these structures if all concrete measures—including the entire integrated program for commodities, unrestricted access to the markets of the DMEs (including the full implementation of the GSP), higher financial flows, better access to IMF finance, the link, a greater voice in the management of the IMF, a binding code for technology transfer and TNEs, and the redeployment of industries—contained in the main economic documents of the last few years were implemented?

The answer is, I submit, that the structures of the international economic system would not be changed appreciably. The underlying philosophy of the NIEO program seems to be essentially reformistic.

Its main objective appears to be to put the DCs—within the framework of the existing system—in a better position to pursue their goals, especially to engage in free trade and to participate in a "rational" international division of labor. The emphasis is on "to put in position."[11] As such, the program basically reflects—not surprisingly, one may add, in view of the training of many third world leaders and experts in the academic centers of the DMEs—a liberal economic approach to the solution of the problems of the developing nations, taking into account their special situation (in a variation of the infant-industry argument) by proving for a number of exceptions to the free play of international market forces, e.g., commodity agreements and preferential and nonreciprocal treatment for developing countries in a number of areas. But such exceptions are by no means unfamiliar to liberal practices as is demonstrated, for instance, by the negotiation of "voluntary" trade restriction agreements, the long-term purchasing agreements between the United States on the one hand and Japan and the Soviet Union on the other, the management of the agricultural market, and the organization of the raw material market through transnational enterprises. In fact, the Lomé Convention, and especially the sugar agreement attached to it, represents a recognition on the part of some DMEs that free market mechanisms do not work properly when the participating parties are unequal.

Thus it is almost surprising that countries subscribing to liberal economic norms, and especially proponents of the existing structures, should have great difficulties in agreeing with the NIEO program. To be sure, the implementation of the program requires a number of adjustments, but the program itself should be acceptable. In fact, a number of the key elements of the NIEO program have clear stabilizing effects for the existing international economic system and their implementation may possibly even represent a kiss of death for long-term restructuring objectives—especially for those governments whose time perspective is short. At the very least, the implementation of the NIEO program may give a new lease on life to the existing structures.

The integrated commodity program, for instance, has stabilizing effects for the conjunctural management of the economies of the industrialized countries and the development process of third world countries. At the present time, the prices of most raw materials are characterized by heavy fluctuations.[12] Given the dependency of many DCs on their raw-material exports as their primary source of foreign exchange earnings, these price fluctuations translate themselves immediately into similar fluctuations in the availability of funds for the import (from DMEs) of capital goods for development purposes. These short-term earnings fluctuations frequently follow the conjunctural movements (i.e., the business cycles) in DMEs. During periods of economic boom, the demand for primary commodities usually rises, and so do their prices; in periods of recession, demand and prices usually fall. Commodity-price movements are therefore largely procyclical in nature. In the first case, they add to inflation—directly (through higher commodity prices) as well as indirectly (through increased purchases by developing countries in industrialized ones). In the second case, the reduction of export earnings affects the import ability of the third world, i.e., demand in DMEs is further reduced. Several fluctuations in commodity prices—fluctuations that could be largely stabilized through buffer stocks—complicate, therefore, the management of the world economy, regardless of whether the aim is development or conjunctural stability.

Beyond this stablizing effect, there is a real danger that the relief gained from commodity agreements may tempt DCs to relax their efforts to change the composition of their exports, to ease their dependence on primary-product exports, and to end their status as raw-material suppliers of the North. Under these conditions, even the move into processing facilities may be neglected. If governments succumb to these temptations, commodity agreements would tend to perpetuate existing structures with their inherent inequalities and inequities. Indexation could further support this tendency by assuring the maintenance of short- and long-term purchasing power and by removing pressures for diversification. Indexation is also an example of the essentially conservative character of the NIEO program. If the DCs wished to use trade and primary products as mechanisms for development, they would first insist on a substantial increase of the price of their exports before discussing indexation. (This is, of course, exactly what the OPEC countries have obtained; not surprisingly, they are interested in the indexation of petroleum). Without such an increase, the third world merely ratifies the deterioration of their terms of trade and institutionalizes the existing gap.[13]

In the area of finance and the international monetary system, the implementation of the NIEO program would lead to easier and more plentiful finance as well as a sharing in (but not control of) the management of the IMF. The danger is, however, that the developing nations could be satisfied with such improvements, with the result that the underlying financial structures remain unchanged. Besides, such participation would be of questionable value for the management of the system as a whole since the countries of the Group of 10 (or even smaller groupings) would not—could not—relinquish the power which the facts of the existing structures give them, regardless of the formal rights of other groupings.

Similar considerations apply to science and technology. The current preoccupation with transfer of technology and a code of conduct for it places the emphasis on the wrong issue. All a code would do is to codify the technological dependency of the third world. Even worse: if the DMEs actually implement the proposals of the program (most of which are likely to be incorporated in a code) and encourage more third world relevant R&D and adaptation of technology in their countries, provide more information about the availability of alternative technologies, ease access to them, and improve the terms and conditions under which they are made available,[14] technological dependence may well become more tolerable and easier to live with for many DCs. The result could be that the establishment of indigenous science-and-technology capacities and infrastructures and the diffusion (rather than transfer) of technology within the third world are neglected or that efforts directed toward the realization of the local potential are impeded.[15] The emphasis on transfer of technology tends to obscure the fact that only indigenous capacities[16] can break the dependent position of the third world and that, therefore, they should receive primary attention.[17] The fear that this is not occurring is not entirely unfounded: the relevant sections of the resolutions adopted at the Sixth and Seventh Special Sessions are very general when it comes to the establishment of scientific and technological capacities—in marked contrast to the much more elaborate and concrete provisions concerning transfer of technology.

Finally, much the same is true regarding industrialization. As already mentioned, a key element is the redeployment of industries to DCs. In strict application of liberal economic theories, the NIEO program recommends a strategy for an international division of labor, in which DCs would concentrate on labor-intensive, low-technology industries on the basis of their comparative advantage, while "the industrial structures of the developed countries themselves evolve in a complementary fashion,"[18] i.e., would evolve in the direction of future-oriented, high-technology industries. This creates the real danger that the DCs remain locked into the present international division of labor whose division of benefits and other more general spin-off effects[19] is highly unfavorable to them. Furthermore, where this redeployment is effected by TNEs (and, as discussed above, they can be expected to play the crucial role[20]), it would be *vertical* redeployment, i.e., certain production processes would be moved to the third world within the framework of the entire TNE system. This would leave the foreign affiliate dependent on the parent enterprise for its R&D, transportation facilities, marketing and distribution channels, etc. (whose local development, conversely, would be discouraged). By extension, therefore, host countries would remain dependent on the parent enterprises involved and also, by extension, on the main DMEs, to the extent that their industrial sectors consist of foreign affiliates. At the same time, horizontal links to other DCs would be difficult to develop.

None of the present efforts at controlling TNEs can be expected to change very much in this situation since none of them aims at the internal decisionmaking mechanisms of TNEs, i.e., at the actual locus of control over decisions relevant to redeployment and, more generally speaking, the allocation of private resources to DCs. Thus, the redeployment of industries may not only further solidify the existing international division of labor but may also, where it is effected through TNEs, extend and further consolidate the dependence of the developing on the developed countries. All that a code of conduct for TNEs is likely to accomplish is to take off some of the edges of the existing situation (especially as far as the distribution of short-term benefits associated with the activities of TNEs is concerned), and to make dependence more tolerable.

This is not to say that the NIEO program is misdirected or that the measures suggested by it should not be taken. Far from that. It is clear that the implementation of the program would in many ways smooth the functioning of the present system, create better opportunities for DCs to pursue their objectives and, in general, would lead to improvements in their economic situations. It is a necessary step toward the immediate alleviation of the most pressing problems of the DCs, ranging from the prevention of a further deterioration of their purchasing power to a stabilization of their export earnings, to a diversification of their exports, to improved access to markets, to increased finance for balance-of-payments deficits and development, to better terms and conditions for technology transfer, to more control over the conditions and purposes of foreign direct investment, and, ultimately, to the containment of acute poverty, chronic unemployment, and endemic undernourishment prevalent in developing countries. Given the urgency of these problems, it is not surprising at all that the NIEO program is most concrete with respect to measures that bring immediate relief and that it pays special attention to the two major issues most conspicuously neglected in the present international economic system: the management of natural resources and the establishment of an international framework for foreign direct investment. But, by the same token, this stress on short-term measures and immediate needs gives the NIEO program more the character of a holding operation than that of a restructuring operation.

It is the intent of the preceding observations to emphasize the continued need for change in the underlying structures of the system; only such a change can bring permanent relief, can achieve the objective of development, and can turn the system into one that serves all its members according to their needs. It appears that as a result of the pressures of the immediate situation and the need to develop stopgap measures, the long-term objectives have not received sufficient attention in the NIEO program. Elaborate measures have been proposed to deal with the symptoms of the problems—but the strategies aimed at their causes are still vague. What is more, such strategies may require another approach than the one characterizing the NIEO program.

Changing Structures: Other Approaches

The NIEO program relies essentially on a reformistic, liberal economic approach. Its key objective is to give third world nations equality of opportunity of pursue their objectives. But the imbalances between developed and developing countries (as well as the imbalances among the latter themselves) are so great, the structural institutionalization of dependence is so strong—encompassing, as it does, all areas of interaction between North and South—that merely providing equal opportunities may not be sufficient to bring about the fundamental changes required for the establishment of a more equitable order.

The achievement of fundamental structural changes requires, first, a change in philosophy. Opportunities would not only have to be provided, but every effort would have to be made to ensure that they are taken. Thus, what might be necessary is the complementation of the liberal economic approach by a massive international program of "affirmative action," coupled with a maximum of international cooperative development efforts and some international development planning. The basis of such an approach would be the recognition that the creation of equal opportunities alone is not sufficient to help the third world overcome its historically determined disadvantageous position, a position in which it remains largely for the mere reason that it is already in it. Going beyond the basic orientation of the NIEO program, the essence of such an approach would therefore be for the developed countries to take positive, affirmative steps to break down the structures created in the past in order to terminate the underprivileged status of the DCs and to integrate them equally and equitably into the world economic system.

The concrete mechanisms of an international affirmative action program for development would, of course, have to be elaborated with great care. To give a few examples of the kind of action that such an approach could include, one should consider the introduction of reverse quotas; thus, governments of developed countries could agree to ensure that a minimum quota of certain manufactured, semimanufactured, or processed goods produced by developing countries would be sold in their countries. Another such method to support the transformation of the DCs from primary-producing suppliers to industrialized countries is to create incentives for the location of processing facilities in the raw material-producing countries, e.g., by virtually reversing the present tariff structure through a decrease of tariffs on manufactured, semimanufactured, and processed goods exported by DCs while possibly even levelling some tariffs on raw materials imported from them. DMEs could also resolve, as part of their public procurement policy, to obtain a certain percentage of their goods and services from the third world, and they could decide to subsidize loans to DCs. It is unimportant whether or not some of the elements that could be incorporated into an international affirmative action program for development are already in existence in one form or another; what is important is that they be utilized in a different context and with a different purpose. Moreover, a change in philosophy could also open new avenues for imaginative thinking that could help to remedy a situation which everybody agrees has to be changed.

In this context, special attention has to be given to TNEs since the allocative decisions of these enterprises—allocations involving human, financial, technological, and physical resources as well as attitudinal and behavioral patterns (including consumption patterns)—play a very important role in all major areas of economic interaction between developed and developing countries. It is therefore important for the developing countries to gain some influence over the allocative decisions of TNEs. The characteristic of current control efforts—including the code of conduct elaborated under the auspices of the United Nations—is that they all focus on possible *external* frameworks that could constrain TNEs. As such, they are mainly reactive and corrective in nature and only indirectly influence the allocation process—assuming that these frameworks are comprehensive and that they are effectively implemented and enforced, an assumption that does not even hold for developed countries. Consequently, if host countries desire to directly influence allocative decisions affecting and even shaping their economies, they have to participate in the *internal* decision making of these enterprises. One way of achieving this objective is to establish host country councils at TNE headquarters.[21] Through these councils, host countries could gain immediate influence on the decision making process of the main enterprises operating in their territories, thus supplementing policies aimed at setting up external control mechanisms. Together, these external and internal control mechanisms would enable host countries to gain greater control over decisions that affect both their short- and long-term economic development.

Self-reliance

It would be ignoring the experience of the past twenty-five years to expect too much from international development efforts—be they in the form of the implementation of the NIEO program or an international affirmative action program directed at the structures of the international economic system. This is not to say that one should abandon them. Rather, it is to say that third world countries must also search for alternatives that are independent of the decisions of the international community as a whole. The developing countries are beginning to explore one such alternative with their turn to the concept of individual and collective self-reliance.[22]

Toward the end of the 1960s, DCs began to realize that if they wanted to break out from the reproduction process of international inequality, they would have to reduce their dependency on inputs from abroad and mobilize their own resources. This realization required a change in the basic development model because the traditional model is based on capital inputs—inputs that (in the quantities necessary) can only be obtained from abroad. In this approach, the mass of people was regarded as a liability, viewed mainly as consumers who needed to be fed and clothed, i.e., who absorbed already scarce capital. However, questions began to be asked whether one could not regard the mass of people as an asset whose creative potential, when released and combined with other local resources and appropriate technology, could be the basis of autonomous development, aimed at the satisfaction of the minimum needs of the entire population. At the same time, a capacity for autonomous goal setting, decision making and decision implementation would be built up. Thus, a model had to be developed that reduced the role of foreign inputs and put greater emphasis on the utilization of the resources in plentiful supply in the third world.

These thoughts are captured in the concept of self-reliance, a concept enunciated at the 1970 summit of the non-aligned countries in Lusaka, and increasingly (even if slowly) gaining acceptance in the third world.[23] Self-reliance is not an attempt to replace capital by labor, but rather an attempt to change the balance between the two factors by a margin that would make development more independent of financial-assistance flows (i.e., aid flows) from abroad. This does not necessarily imply the refusal of foreign aid or even autarchy. But international economic transactions are seen in a different perspective: the motor of development is no longer trade and transfers from abroad, but rather the mobilization of indigenous resources. Improvements in the terms and conditions of international transactions remain, of course, desirable and helpful and have therefore to be pursued (e.g., through UNCTAD, whose dominant approach to development continues to be trade-oriented); however, one does not pin one's hopes on them.

This change in the approach to development is also important because it represents an act of sociocultural emancipation. This is a dimension of development (and also of self-reliance) that has so far been largely neglected. During the colonial period, the countries of the third world were not only subjected to political and economic but also to sociocultural colonization. The values and behavioral patterns of important segments of third world societies had gradually been transformed to reflect those of the metropolitan countries. After independence had been achieved, these patterns have been maintained and reinforced through a variety of mechanisms. Increasingly important among them have been TNEs (whose investment package consists not only of capital and technology but also of such sociocultural investments as values and behavioral patterns) and advertising agencies (which directly appeal to and manipulate a society's values, especially its consumption values).

In addition, the choice of production for foreign affiliates in DCs (and for local enterprises imitating them) is largely a combination of the production and R&D experiences of parent enterprises, on the one hand, and the foreign-induced wants of the small elites and middle classes in host countries on the other. The problem is that both factors reflect the relative abundance of developed countries and not the absolute poverty of developing ones, the wants of consumers in developed countries and not the needs of large proportions of the population in developing countries. At least for the time being, therefore, these wants can only be satisfied through continued inputs from abroad. Consequently, economic dependence on countries and institutions that can help to fulfill these foreign-oriented wants continues and is reinforced. Self-reliance, thus, requires sociocultural emancipation. If this emancipation does not take place, if industrialization continues to model itself on the demand and supply situation of the developed market economies, the economic development of the third world will tend to remain dependent development.[24]

The achievement of self-reliance, and through it economic

development, demands fundamental internal and external changes. In its internal dimension, the implementation of the concept of (individual) self-reliance requires that conditions for the mobilization of the population and the realization of its potential for development be created. This requires a substantial raising of mass consciousness through greater participation which, in turn, is not very likely to occur without drastic changes in the class structure of the individual countries. Only through the mobilization and organization of the masses can the "spirit of self-reliance"[25] be cultivated and reliance on foreign capital decreased. This focus on the population as a whole is not only a function of the need to mobilize indigenously available resources, but is also an expression of the fundamental aim of this approach, which is to satisfy the basic needs of all classes and not only of the wants of the elites and small middle classes. The concept of individual self-reliance, therefore, draws attention to the internal conditions in DCs, the need for change in them, and their importance for the development process. Partly, this attention follows from the realization that whatever benefits had been reaped with the traditional model (and probably including those to be secured by the NIEO program), they rarely trickled down to the masses but tended rather to be absorbed by the elites.

In its external dimension, the implementation of (collective) self-reliance necessitates a change in the structures of vertical interaction (between developing and developed countries) and in the direction of structures of horizontal interaction (among developing countries). As the patterns outlined previously indicate, this requires a reorientation of interactions in literally all major areas. Trade with other DCs, for instance, accounts for only one-fifth of total trade of the third world—and this share has been declining.

Increased cooperation among third world countries[26] demands, first of all, measures aimed at facilitating interactions among them. Among these are various measures to provide preferential treatment to imports from other DCs[27]; the expansion and strengthening of existing clearing arrangements and the creation of a broad multilateral payments scheme (including clearing arrangements as well as arrangements for the settling of balances); the facilitation and encouragement of flows of financial resources (especially from OPEC countries); and the encouragement and further strengthening of regional integration schemes and cooperation projects. The last measure involves direct collaboration efforts among developing nations and their institutions. This type of effort has to be expanded to a wide variety of activities, including the establishment of multinational marketing and other enterprises, as well as collaboration in producer's associations.

For many of these schemes, concrete proposals have already been elaborated[28] and several sets of activities are under way to bring them closer to implementation. Thus, the Group of 77 decided, during its 1976 Manila ministerial meeting, to establish an intergovernmental working group for the purpose of preparing the details of a comprehensive program for economic cooperation. Similarly, the non-aligned countries decided at their 1972 Georgetown foreign ministers conference to designate a number of coordinating countries to be responsible for the implementation of the four main areas of self-reliance covered in the action program; some progress in fulfilling this mandate has been made.[29] The Group of 77 and the non-aligned countries, furthermore, institutionalized and deepened their consultations for the cooperation during every major international economic conference.

The third world's efforts to implement individual and collective self-reliance are still in a very embryonic state. They will take some time to evolve since they require a complete reorientation of existing models and structures. Some of these efforts are likely to lead to a certain "decoupling"[30] of the third world from the developed market world—and the dependence on this world. Such a decoupling may even be necessary, if not desirable, until the third world is strong enough to reintegrate itself into the international economic system on the basis of interdependence.

International affirmative action and self-reliance both aim at the restructuring of the international economic system and at the creation of a system that serves the needs of all its members. The two approaches are not mutually exclusive. On the contrary, through an international affirmative action program, the international community could greatly facilitate and serve the task of self-reliance and decrease the time required to implement it. The two approaches also do not exclude a vigorous implementation of the NIEO program in order to alleviate most pressing immediate problems. And all three approaches can be expected to benefit from the politicization of the development issue, the new assertiveness of the third world, and the transformation of the nonaligned movement into a highly organized international pressure group for the reorganization of the international economic system. However, in playing the checkers game of immediate improvements, one should not forget that the chess game of structures is played on the same board. Since the two games are played simultaneously (and in the real world interact), one has to ensure that the moves in checkers do not divert attention from the moves in chess—or even prejudice the outcome of the chess game.

Notes

1. For a discussion of the origin of the Sixth Special Session, see: Branislav Gosovic and John Gerard Ruggie, "On the Creation of a New International Economic Order: Issue Linkage and the Seventh Special Session of the UN General Assembly," *International Organization* (spring 1976), especially pp. 309-319; and Odette Jankowitsch and Karl P. Sauvant, "The Evolution of the Non-Aligned Movement into a Pressure Group for the Establishment of the New International Economic Order." Paper presented at the XVII Annual Convention of the International Studies Association, Toronto, February 1976.

2. Gosovic and Ruggie, "On the Creation of a New International Economic Order," especially pp. 323-345. See also: Mahbub ul Haq, *The Poverty Curtain: Choices for the Third World* (New York: Columbia University Press, 1976); and Jan Tinbergen, coordinator, *Reshaping the International Order: A Report of the Club of Rome* (New York: Dutton, 1976). A collection of relevant articles and documents on all aspects of the NIEO is contained in Karl P. Sauvant and Hajo Hasenpflug, eds., *The New International Economic Order: Conflict or Cooperation between North and South?* (Boulder: Westview Press, 1977). The following discussion of the NIEO program draws on these materials and especially the resolutions cited in the previous footnotes.

3. In cases where the long-term equilibrium trend of the real market price of a commodity is deteriorating and the capacity of a buffer stock has been reached, the negotiated real price has to be supported by the management of supply, i.e., excessive production has to be discouraged (e.g., through export quotas).

4. For an elaboration of these factors, see Karl P. Sauvant, "Toward the New International Economic Order," in Sauvant and Hasenpflug, eds., *The New International Economic Order*.

5. For a discussion of the convention, see Isebill v. Gruhn, "The Lomé Convention: Inching toward Interdependence," *International Organization* (spring 1976), pp. 241-262; see also Steven J. Warnecke, "The Lomé Convention and Industrial Cooperation: A New Relationship Between the European Community and the ACP States," in Sauvant and Hasenpflug, eds., *The New International Economic Order*.

6. See Michael Morris, "The New International Economic Order and the New Law of the Sea," in Sauvant and Hasenpflug, eds., *The New International Economic Order*.

7. For further details regarding the activities of the non-aligned countries, see Jankowitsch and Sauvant, "The Evolution of the Non-Aligned Movement."

8. For an analysis of changes in tactics by the LDGs and developed countries, see Catherine B. Gwin, "The Seventh Special Session: Toward a New Phase of Relations between the Developed and the Developing States?" in Sauvant

and Hasenpflug, eds., *The New International Economic Order*; for an analysis of the outcome of the Seventh Special Session, see Gosovic and Ruggie, "On the Creation of a New International Economic Order."

9. The communiqué (January 8, 1976) of the interim committee is contained in UNCTAD, "Money and Finance and Transfer of Real Resources for Development: International Monetary Issues. Problems of Reform. Report by the UNCTAD Secretariat" (TD/189), March 11, 1976.

10. UNCTAD, "International Monetary Issues," p. 20. This compares with the expected deficit (for 1976) of about $30 billion for the non-oil-exporting DCs.

11. To quote Mahbub ul Haq: "The basic objective of the emerging trade union of the poor nations is to negotiate a new deal with the rich nations through the instrument of collective bargaining. The essence of this new deal lies in the objective of the developing countries to obtain greater equality of opportunity and to secure the right to sit as equals around the bargaining tables of the world"; see his "Negotiating a New Bargain with the Rich Countries," in Guy F. Erb and Valerina Kallab, eds., *Beyond Dependency: The Developing World Speaks Out* (Washington: Overseas Development Council, 1975), p. 158.

12. During the period of 1953-1972, for instance, market prices for sugar fluctuated at an average rate of 33 percent, those for cocoa by 23 percent, those for copper by 21 percent, and those for sisal by 18 percent; see UNCTAD, "Commodities: Action on Commodities, Including Decisions on Integrated Programme, in the Light of the Need for Change in the World Commodity Economy. Report by the UNCTAD Secretariat" (TD/184), March 4, 1976, p. 8. Needless to say, such fluctuations make economic planning for development exceedingly difficult for the DCs concerned.

13. Another problem concerns the final beneficiaries of a direct indexation scheme. Under such a system, enterprises are the final beneficiaries since the prices of the raw materials produced by them would be maintained at a certain level. Considering that TNEs have an important position in many primary-product industries in DCs, the main beneficiaries of a direct indexation scheme may therefore well be the foreign affiliates of these TNEs.

14. See the section on science and technology of the resolution adopted at the Seventh Special Session.

15. One wonders here about the resistance of developed countries and TNEs to a binding code of conduct for the transfer of technology.

16. Indigenous capacity, however, does not necessarily include R&D by foreign affiliates of TNEs. Although such R&D—as well as the transfer of technology—may have important externalities, it usually has a different (i.e., global) reference point and is therefore not automatically relevant to the host country. Greater research efforts by TNEs may merely create the illusion that an indigenous scientific and technological infrastructure has been established

and that dependence has been decreased, when all that has been achieved is an improvement in the royalty balance.

17. This observation is also immediately relevant to the patents questions. As long as the indigenous capacity to utilize patents is lacking, the liberalization of the international property system can only have a limited effect and may, moreover, divert attention from the real issues.

18. See UNCTAD, "New Directions and New Structures for Trade and Development: Report by the Secretary-General of UNCTAD to the Conference" (TD/183), April 14, 1976, p. 38.

19. For a discussion of spin-off effects, see, Johan Galtung, "A Structural Theory of Imperialism," *Journal of Peace Research* 8 (1971): 81-118.

20. This is also indicated by the current discussion concerning the implementation of the industrial cooperation title of the Lomé Convention; see Warnecke, "The Lomé Convention and Industrial Cooperation."

21. For a further discussion of this approach, as well as for a discussion of the purposes of control, a review of host-country efforts at the national, regional and international levels, and the role of labor unions, see Karl P. Sauvant, "Controlling Transnational Enterprises: A Review and Some Further Thoughts," in Sauvant and Hasenpflug, eds., *The International Economic Order*.

22. The basic documents of self-reliance are: Third Conference of Heads of State or Government of Non-Aligned Countries, "Declaration on Non-Alignment and Economic Progress," in Guyana, Ministry of Foreign Affairs, ed., *Main Documents Relating to Conferences of Non-Aligned Countries* (Georgetown: Ministry of Foreign Affairs, 1972); and Third Conference of Ministers of Foreign Affairs of Non-Aligned Countries, "The Action Programme for Economic Co-operation," in ibid. See also: Samuel L. Parmar, "Self-reliant Development in an 'Interdependent' World," in Erb and Kallab, eds., *Beyond Dependency*; "Twenty-fourth Pugwash Symposium, "The Role of Self-reliance in Alternative Strategies for Development," *Pugwash Newsletter* 13 (October 1975): 57-77; Julius K. Nyerere, *Ujamaa: Essays on Socialism* (London: Oxford University Press, 1968); and Dieter Senghaas, "Essays ueber autozentrierte Entwicklung" (Frankfurt: Hessische Stiftung Friedens-und Konfliktforschung, 1976), mimeo.

23. Obviously the example of China, which had succeeded in eradicating mass undernourishment and mass unemployment, played an important role in the formulation and popularization of this concept, especially after China had begun to become more accessible to foreigners from the beginning of the 1970s.

24. On the importance of sociocultural emancipation and the mechanisms of sociocultural domination, see Karl P. Sauvant, "His Master's Voice," *Ceres: FAO Review on Agriculture and Development* 9 (September-October 1976): 27-32; for a further elaboration and some data (especially on advertising), see Karl P. Sauvant, "The Potential of Multinational Enterprises as Vehicles for the

Transmission of Business Culture," in Karl P. Sauvant and Farid G. Lavipour, eds., *Controlling Multinational Enterprises: Problems, Strategies, Counterstrategies* (Boulder: Westview Press, 1976). Relevant data are also contained in Heinz Hartmann, *Amerikanische Firmen in Deutschland* (Köln and Oplanden: Westdeutscher Verlag, 1963) and Bernard Mennis and Karl P. Sauvant, *Emerging Forms of Transnational Community: Transnational Business Enterprises and Regional Integration* (Lexington, Mass.: Lexington Books, 1976), chapter 5. For a review of the role of communication in this area, see: Rita Cruise O'Brien, "Domination and Dependence in Mass Communications: Implications for the Use of Broadcasting in Developing Countries," *Institute of Development Studies Bulletin* 6 (March 1975): 85-99; Tapio Varis, "The Impact of Transnational Corporations on Communication" (Tampere: Tampere Research Institute, 1975), mimeo.; as well as his *International Inventory of Television Programme Structure and the Flow of TV Programmes between Nations* (Tampere: University of Tampere, Research Institute and the Institute of Journalism and Mass Communication, 1973); and the no. 2, 1976, issue of *Development Dialogue* on "Information and the New International Order."

25. Third Conference of Heads of State or Government of Non-Aligned Countries, "Declaration on Non-Alignment and Economic Progress," p. 82.

26. See especially UNCTAD, "Economic Co-operation among Developing Countries: Report of the UNCTAD Secretariat" (TD/192), December 22, 1975, and UNCTAD, "Economic Co-operation among Developing Countries: Elements of a Programme of Economic Co-operation among Developing Countries. Report by the UNCTAD Secretariat" (TD/192/Supp.1), March 26, 1976; see also the self-reliance documents of the nonaligned movement cited above and annex 1 of Third Ministerial Meeting of the Group of 77, "Manila Declaration and Programme of Action" (TD/195), February 12, 1976.

27. See especially UNCTAD, "Economic Co-operation among Developing Countries: Elements of a Preferential System in Trade among Developing Countries. Report by the UNCTAD Secretariat" (TD/192/Supp.2), January 14, 1976.

28. See especially UNCTAD, "Elements of Economic Co-operation."

29. These countries had been designated in December 1972 during a meeting of the Co-ordinating Committee of Non-Aligned Countries in New York. Guyana was given the responsibility for implementing cooperation in trade, industry, and transport; Yugoslavia and Algeria for technology, know-how, and technical assistance; India and Indonesia for financial and monetary cooperation; and Egypt and Nigeria for international cooperation for economic development.

30. Johan Galtung, "Decision-making: Appraisal," in *Symposium on a New International Economic Order: Report* (The Hague: Ministry of Foreign Affairs, n.d.), p. 47.

11. Interdependence and the Reform of International Institutions
C. Fred Bergsten

The Historical Context

The world has entered its third postwar wave of institution building. The first wave came immediately after 1945, with the creation of the United Nations system including its economic components—the International Monetary Fund (IMF), the World Bank, and subsequently the General Agreement on Tariffs and Trade (GATT). The second came around 1960 and included the Common Market, the Organization for Economic Cooperation and Development (OECD), the regional development banks and—though it was barely noticed at the time—the Organization of Petroleum Exporting Countries (OPEC).

The third wave began around 1973, and continues to this day. It has witnessed creation of a United Nations Environment Program, a World Food Council, and International Energy Agency (IEA), a series of producers' associations of exporters of primary products, and most recently a Conference on International Economic Cooperation (CIEC) with its four standing commissions.

Two functional and two political themes characterized each of these waves of international institution building. The functional aim of each was to provide an international framework within which to manage issues where national management had become inadequate, or to handle better those issues where earlier international arrangements had failed. The need for new international arrangements spawned institutions to cover international money and trade in the early postwar years, the beginnings of macroeconomic policy coordination and decentralized

This chapter is reprinted with permission from *International Organization* (spring 1976), pp. 361-372.

development financing around 1960, and a series of newly globalized issues (such as environment, food, and energy) most recently. To do an old job better, the United Nations was created to supplant the League of Nations and later the World Food Council sought to perform the most critical responsibilities previously entrusted to the Food and Agriculture Organization (FAO).

The two political objectives of each phase of institution building were (1) the ratification and legitimization of the power structure underlying international relationships at the time and (2) the integration of newcomers into those relationships. In 1945, this largely meant codifying U.S. hegemony and involving the rest of the independent nation-states of the day (except the Communists, who dropped out). Around 1960, it meant an increased role for the now-recovered economies of Western Europe and Japan, and incorporation of the newly independent developing countries of Asia and Africa. Now it requires new modes of collective leadership and sharing the rights and responsibilities of leadership across the entire spectrum of nations, including the third world, on many important issues.

A number of guidelines for future institutional steps derive from our experience with the creation and evolution of international institutions, most of which encompass both sets of rules and procedural arrangements for implementing them, over the past thirty years.

First, international institutions help restrain member countries from resorting to unilateral beggar-thy-neighbor policies, through which they might otherwise seek to export their internal problems to other countries. This is partly due to the legal prohibitions against such measures and their mechanisms for implementing those agreements. For example, the United States may pause before erecting a particular import barrier because it would then have to reduce other import barriers to compensate the rest of the world or face retaliation against its exports.

But less tangible effects of international institutional arrangements are probably more important. The very existence of such cooperative structures, more than the specific rules themselves, inspires confidence in both private sectors and government circles around the world that economic progress will not be disrupted by conflict among nations. International agreements strengthen the hand of outward-looking forces within each government. And they promote transnational coalitions among those forces, which often prove importantly reinforcing in pursuing internationalist initiatives.

Second, functionally specific international organizations succeed far better than multipurpose organizations in accomplishing concrete tasks. This is clearest for essentially nonpolitical issues, such as those handled

Interdependence and Reform 149

by the International Postal Union and World Health Organization. But it is also true for the functionally specific economic institutions, such as the IMF and GATT (and OPEC) when compared with the U.N. agencies. Within the U.N. system itself. the functionally specific agencies accomplish more than the multipurpose bodies. The broader groups may play a useful role, as for consultation and debate, but the record spreads doubt about their capacity to achieve clearly defined tasks.

Functional specificity works better for a variety of reasons. The issues are smaller and better defined, and hence more manageable. Like-minded officials are thrown together. There can be less blackmail over setting agendas. Perhaps most important, issue-area linkage and politicization—both of which usually deter functional progress—are better avoided.

A third lesson is that all important actors must be involved. The classic case is the League of Nations, which the United States never joined and where several other key powers were absent at key times. At present, there can be no satisfactory solution to the energy problem as long as OPEC and the IEA stand apart; indeed, the CIEC arose from an effort to bring them together. The complaints about international trading arrangements from the third world stem at least partly from the absence of many developing countries from the GATT, and the U.N. Conference on Trade and Development (UNCTAD) was created largely to provide an alternative forum for structuring international trade.

A fourth lesson is that strong secretaries-general and international staffs can make a big difference in implementing international economic agreements. The histories of the United Nations, GATT, and IMF all reveal the importance of strong, impartial leadership from the institutions themselves. Such leaders can propose solutions when no country is able or willing to do so, help galvanize support in individual countries, and implement decisions when everyone else goes on to the next issue. The willingness of governments to entrust responsibility to an international institution often depends, quite rightly, on the competence of those who staff it.

These lessons from the past suggest several steps which should *not* be taken in any reform of international institutional arrangements. There should be no "dusting off" of the International Trade Organization (ITO), in an effort to bring all international economic issues under a single roof. Those issues should not be moved into the United Nations. Even amalgamation across functional lines, such as merger of the IMF and GATT, would violate the precepts for effective institutions. The creation of new institutions limited to the industrialized countries would generally be a mistake, since one of the major objectives of the current period of institutional reform must be to integrate at least some of the developing countries.

The Problems of Today

What positive reforms of international institutional arrangements should be contemplated today?

The basic issue of international relationships for the foreseeable future is the tension between the imperatives of international interdependence and the quest to retain adequate degrees of national autonomy. There is some optimum level of international rules and institutions for reconciling this tension in a politically feasible manner, to provide collective economic security for nations whose real sovereignty has already declined much faster than their nominal sovereignty may ever fall.

The search for that optimum will pervade the evolution of international arrangements. The overriding goal is to make the world safe for interdependence, by protecting the benefits which it provides for each country against the external and internal threats to those benefits which will constantly emerge from those willing to pay the price of more autonomy for individual nations.[1] This may sometimes require slowing the pace at which interdependence proceeds, and checking some aspects of it. More frequently, however, it calls for checking national intrusions into the international exchange of both economic and noneconomic goods.

A second contemporary need is integration of the newcomers and dropouts. As Japan was integrated in the early 1960s, by joining the OECD and adopting Article VIII status in the IMF, the new "international middle class"—most notably the members of OPEC, but also many other countries with rapidly growing economic or military strength—must be integrated today.

Indeed, history has shown that the greatest dangers to international stability often arise from those actors whose real power is inadequately reflected in both real involvement in the relevant sets of international arrangements and symbols of status therein. Such actors can challenge the legitimacy of the system with actions as well as rhetoric. And much of the current call for a new international economic order flows directly from such concerns. Indeed, only through integration in the management of international arrangements are such countries likely to acquire the systemic interests necessary for the constructive formulation of their own foreign economic policies.

Similar considerations argue for restoring participation by the dropouts. Most notable are the Communist countries, several of which (including the USSR) participated in creating the postwar international economic system but left before it began to function. They are now reentering the world economy, particularly in such key individual markets as food (especially the Soviet Union) and energy (especially China). France has also been an important dropout, in both the security area (NATO) and economic arrangements (the old gold pool, IEA). Ways must be found to reintegrate these countries in order to meet the criterion of participation by all those who count.

The third current problem of international institutional arrangements is the absence of leadership.[2] History shows that an effective international system requires a custodian which is willing to internalize systemic costs. In the economic area, such a role was played by Britain in the second half of the nineteenth century and America in the first generation after the Second World War. During the interwar years, there was no leader and the system collapsed.[3]

America must still play a major role in managing the international economic system. However, both its internal politics and the unwillingness of other countries to follow its lead rule out the same degree of American dominance which existed in the recent past.

There are two alternatives. One is leadership by another individual country. However, no country now seems equipped to play such a role. The other is collective leadership, such as exists at the highest levels of the security system between the United States and the Soviet Union as they seek jointly to prevent nuclear war. Japan, Germany, and perhaps one or two other countries of Western Europe, and one or two OPEC countries on some issues, would seem the likely partners of the United States in any such collective arrangement. Strong management and staff in the international institutions themselves can help, but individual countries will continue for some time to bear the primary responsibilities—especially in structuring the system within which the process of international economic cooperation can proceed.[4]

Indeed, there have already been steps toward such collective leadership through the informal meetings of the "Group of Five" to discuss international monetary matters, the economic summit at Rambouillet in November 1975 to discuss the whole range of international economic issues, and the meetings of ten industrial, OPEC, and nonoil countries to organize the CIEC in late 1975. These beginning steps confirm that the collective leadership which is needed can be exercised only through international institutions, be they formal (à la CIEC) or informal (like Rambouillet). They also represent efforts to get Japan, the countries of Western Europe, and OPEC to take systemic concerns into account in formulating their own national policies.

To be sure, there is a difference between leadership and systemic concern. Smaller countries (such as Switzerland and the Netherlands) frequently adopt policies geared to systemic as well as purely national objectives. Larger countries (such as France) often ignore systemic effects, though they both aspire to leadership and must play such a role if the system is to work. It is desirable for all countries to exercise systemic concern: the scope for "free riders" has been sharply reduced with the dispersion of economic wealth and power throughout the world. But it is imperative at this point in history for the more important countries to join together to exercise systemic leadership.

A fourth problem which challenges today's international institutional arrangements is the increased interdependence among the whole array of functional issues. The energy crisis has epitomized the tight relationship among trade, monetary, resources, development, and security issues—and led to the CIEC, with its four functional commissions and high degree of politicization. The world inflation of 1973-1974 and world recession of 1974-1975 further confirmed the pervasiveness of these linkages.

So it is impossible to keep separate the major international economic, and even security, issues. A return to the earlier postwar situation, in which each was handled largely within its functionally narrow framework, appears most unlikely.[5] Indeed, skillful linkage by OPEC— between oil and Middle East politics, and then between other commodities and oil—was the proximate trigger for the dramatic reversal of U.S. policies toward the third world whose beginnings were presented to the special session of the General Assembly in September 1975. But excessive linkage makes issues harder to manage technically and so politicized that progress becomes much more difficult. And weaker countries will inevitably seek to link, to maximize their more limited bargaining leverage. Hence a major requirement for any new systemic custodians is to suppress their own temptations to link in the interest of achieving substantive progress.

Specific Proposals

International institutional reform must therefore focus on five issues: the creation of new institutions to deal with topics where they are now needed to protect international interdependence, the reform of some existing institutions to deal better with the problems they are already addressing, more effective mobilization of both sets of institutions, better coordination across issue-areas, and progress toward resolving the leadership issue. Several proposed approaches have already been ruled out. What positive steps should be taken?

New Institutions

New institutions are needed where an issue-area is of profound importance to relationships among nations and no existing institution exists. These two criteria are met for specific issue-areas within three broad aspects of international interdependence: the "commons" of mankind, security relationships, and international economic relations.

Among the "commons," the most urgent requirement is the creation of an international regime for the oceans to cover a host of related issues including fishing, shipping, mining from the deep seabeds, and ocean pollution. Other "commons" which may need new regimes include Antarctica, outer space, and the weather and climate of our planet. A new agency to centralize and improve world population programs is often proposed. Global environmental problems are already covered in the new United Nations Environment Program.

The most important security issue which needs new institutional arrangements is probably terrorism. A new institution might also be needed to check nuclear proliferation, although more vigorous effort through the International Atomic Energy Agency (IAEA) is an obvious alternative.

There is one economic issue where new institutional arrangements are needed: foreign direct investment and multinational enterprises. The value of international production by multinationals now approximates the value of world trade, and transactions within such firms indeed account for a sizable share of that trade. A highly articulated set of international rules and institutions has governed world trade, with outstanding success, for a generation. Yet there are no rules or institutions whatsoever to govern international investment. The codes of conduct now being discussed in several forums would scarcely begin to deal with the issues. This anomaly, along with that concerning the oceans, is perhaps the major institutional gap in international relations today.

Two kinds of rules and institutional arrangements are needed. One would seek to safeguard the benefits generated by foreign direct investment by checking the widespread and increasing efforts of home and host governments alike to export their internal problems and policies to each other through the firms. The other would set international standards to govern those aspects of the behavior of multinational enterprises (such as transfer pricing and antitrust) which transcend the national jurisdictions of individual governments.[6]

Reforming Existing Institutions

Many existing international institutions need reform if they are to deal effectively with new aspects of their traditional domains.[7] Reform of the IAEA has already been mentioned as a possible response to the critical threat of nuclear proliferation.

The central economic issue which requires institutional change is access to supplies. The traditional GATT arrangements have protected access to markets for producers. However, its rules governing access to supplies for consumers were weak from the outset and have been totally useless in practice. New arrangements are needed to govern export controls, like the rules which have for a generation governed import controls.[8] It may also be desirable to institute generalized rules governing international commodity agreements, to assure their conformity with overall international trading relationships.

The international monetary rules need revision in two major areas. The Bretton Woods system was based on fixed exchange rates to achieve balance-of-payments adjustment, and the dollar to expand world liquidity. Neither is suitable for the future, and much de facto reform has already occurred. The need here is for formal amendment of the rules to provide effective multilateral surveillance over the operation of the systm of flexible exchange rates, and to arrest the disturbing trend toward the proliferation of monetary assets.[9]

A third need is for more effective coordination of domestic economic policies, at least among the major industrialized nations. As with the problem of access to supplies, it might be desirable to create a wholly new international institution. But reform of the OECD seems a more cost-effective means to proceed, at least at this early stage in the process.

An issue which has triggered much of the demands of the developing countries for a new international economic order is the distribution of income and wealth among countries. A number of changes are needed in the international trading, investment, monetary, and other rules to promote a more equitable distribution, and all of the proposals made above for new or modified arrangements in economic institutions should incorporate such changes.[10] There is no need for a new international institution aimed specifically at the distributional issue, however, and efforts to create one would almost certainly slow or even derail the substantive progress which is needed and appears possible.

Mobilization of International Institutions

Both the existing and proposed new international institutions need to be mobilized much more effectively than has been the case in recent years. This of course requires a greater willingness by national governments to use the institutions. But there are many things which the institutions can do largely on their own to foster progress.

The institutions, through their top management and staffs, should seek actively to promote their constitutional objectives.[11] These efforts should seek to engage actively officials in national governments concerned with the relevant functional issue, at both the political and senior bureaucratic levels. They should also involve the private sector in countries where it can be influential. Indeed, unofficial groups can often be mobilized formally to help catalyze international action; the Rey Committee of the OECD helped lay the basis for the current Multilateral Trade Negotiations, and the U.N. Group of Eminent Persons paved the way for its new Commission on Transnational Enterprises.

The institutions should also seek to galvanize, and provide a forum for, earlier external input to national policy decisions. The goal should be formal consultation prior to such decisions, as is in fact required by the Articles of Agreement of the IMF regarding exchange-rate changes. But even without such formality, which is extremely difficult in terms of domestic politics in most countries, a major function of international institutions should be substantive discussions early in the decision-making process.

The deepening of transnational networks suggested above would of course contribute greatly to this process. Expansion of the consultative process would help create such transnational networks. So the relationship between international consultation and institutional evolution could become a self-reinforcing process.

Both steps require strong, active, and effective management of the international institutions themselves, at both the director-general and staff levels. Again there is a self-reinforcing process: if the institutions take a more active and initiatory approach to problems, they will attract better management and staff.

Finally, effective mobilization of international institutions requires stronger support for them within national governments. Few governments are in fact organized effectively to backstop the international organizations of which they are members; most often there is a wide gap between the people responsible for relations with the institutions and those responsible for the substance of the issues. The same government officials who are responsible for national decisions must participate directly in the international institutional process if that process is to succeed.

Coordination across Issue-areas

History has demonstrated that it is unwise to pursue coordination by locating functionally separate issues under a single institutional roof. But this leaves unanswered the question of how to achieve the increased degree of coordination required by the increased interrelationships among issues.

Informal collaboration among the leading countries is probably the best route to effective coordination. Indeed, such coordination as has occurred in the past came through such devices. In the 1971 monetary crisis triggered by the U.S. suspension of dollar convertibility and imposition of an import surcharge, for example, the Group of Ten was forced to relate trade to monetary measures. The institution of the CIEC and the economic summit meeting in late 1975 are steps toward such an approach.

The only issue is the means through which such coordinating efforts will take place. Formalization, either through ad hoc public meetings of a few key countries or institutionalization thereof, raises major problems of legitimacy and internal political difficulties for those left outside. It also reduces the flexibility needed to alter the composition of the steering group as the importance of different issues waxes and wanes; for example, Switzerland is important to many international monetary matters while Saudi Arabia is an essential participant in energy discussions.

One can envisage a series of concentric circles of decisionmaking through which international progress can be made. A very small number of key countries, perhaps as few as two or three on some issues, could decide on a common course of action through completely informal discussions. Next, each could seek to broaden the agreement through discussions with its own closest associates; for example, individual European countries would consult with the rest of the Common Market. Finally, implementation would come through the existing (or newly created) institutions where all relevant countries would become involved. This process could of course encompass prior consultations between members of each circle with members of the more outside circles, as an input to their own thinking and sense of subsequent saleability.

Leadership

The issue of coordination raises directly the question of leadership, which of course arises as well within individual issue-areas as well. Who stands in the innermost circles? Who, within that group, takes the initiative? Who tries to assure follow-up? In short, who is the custodian of the custodians, both for individual pieces of the international system and its overall integrity?

As already noted, history raises doubts about the feasibility of collective management of the international economic system. And there is a risk that no one will lead if several are expected to do so. Nevertheless, there is no alternative:

- The United States is the largest single economy, the home country of one half the world's foreign direct investment, and the least dependent of the industrialized countries on foreign energy. But its days of dominance are gone, both because other countries are now strong enough to reject a hegemonial world and because its internal politics make extremely difficult the unilateral internalization of systemic costs.
- Germany has become the second economic superpower with monetary reserves double the American, the world's second key currency (and the center of a major currency area), higher exports of manufactured goods, and the world's strongest trade balance and lowest rate of inflation.[12] But it fears that a bid for unilateral leadership, even on economic issues, would jeopardize both European unity and détente and even revive memories of the Nazi period.
- The Common Market as a group dominates would trade, and its monetary reserves dwarf those of anyone else. But it has shown an inability to act together on issues outside trade. In addition, it has great trouble even finding a common stand when the economic going is rough and hence world leadership is needed most intensely.[13]
- Japan has the second largest non-Communist economy. But it stands culturally outside the rest of the industrialized world, has no tradition of world involvement let alone leadership, and is contained both by its internal decision-making process and its extreme vulnerability (and hence sensitivity) to OPEC and other suppliers of raw materials.
- OPEC is of course a critical factor in the energy markets, and important financially as well. It comprises the most important set of newcomers which must be integrated into the system and hopefully imbued with systemic concerns, but it is too much to ask it to leap into leadership so quickly.

Hence collective leadership is indispensable. Within that framework, there are numerous tactical approaches depending on the issue involved and the nature of the problem. As already noted, the management of international institutions themselves can play a critical role in such a milieu by taking intitiatives—after consultation with the key countries—when no individual country feels able to do so. American initiatives are often undesirable, because they trigger negative reactions by virtue of being American. European initiatives appear to be particularly well received by the developing countries, and may thus be the most effective route on issues concerning North-South relationships. The issue of who takes the lead on specific issues, and how it should be done, would indeed be one of the key issues for discussions among the collective management.

Epilogue

The objective of these proposals is to bring all issues of international interdependence under the governance of effective international rules and institutional arrangements. This requires the creation of a few new institutions and the reform of several existing institutions, each to pursue functionally specific tasks. It requires engaging all relevant actors in the decision-making process, while at the same time developing collective leadership of the system through joint management by a small group of the most powerful countries. It requires both more national willingness to submit important issues to international institutional determination, and more effective management in the institution to spur the process.

History has shown that effective international institutions can defuse conflicts among nations and promote positive-sum outcomes, and that such conflicts are not only possible but probable in the absence of such institutions. International interdependence is expanding rapidly in a whole range of issue-areas.[14] So is its antithesis, nationalist opposition to international approaches. Hence a high priority must be attached to the further evolution of international institutional arrangements.

The first and second postwar waves of international institution building made the world safe for the explosion of interdependence of the last generation, which has been a central element in the explosion of prosperity and the maintenance of peace. Imaginative conclusion of the third wave, which has already begun, is a necessary element in ensuring such results for the next generation. It must thus rank high on the foreign policy agendas of all countries in the years ahead.

Notes

1. The several criteria against which to judge international economic

arrangements, including the several trade-offs between economic and political objectives, are analyzed in C. Fred Bergsten, Robert O. Keohane, and Joseph S. Nye, "International Economics and International Politics: A Framework for Analysis" in Bergsten and Lawrence B. Krause, eds., *World Politics and International Economics* (Washington: The Brookings Institution, 1975), pp. 22-36.

2. "Leadership" and "management" can of course be exercised through market forces as well as overt governmental action. But governmental action will always be necessary to establish a market-oriented system in the first place, hold at bay those forces which perennially seek to reduce the scope for market forces, and make the market work better by countervailing distortions to it (such as the monopoly power of some individual firms). A recent example is the active U.S. lead in maintaining maximum scope for market forces to determine international exchange rates.

3. This point is stressed by Charles P. Kindleberger, most recently in *The World in Depression 1929-1939* (London: Allen Lane, The Penguin Press, 1973).

4. The useful distinction between structure and process levels is developed in Robert O. Keohane and Joseph S. Nye, "World Politics and the International Economic System," in C. Fred Bergsten, *The Future of the International Economic Order: An Agenda for Research* (Lexington, Mass.: D.C. Heath and Co., 1973), especially pp. 117-26.

5. This was characterized as a "two-track" (security and economic) or "multi-track" (security, monetary, trade, etc.) system in Richard N. Cooper, "Trade Policy is Foreign Policy," *Foreign Policy* (winter 1972-1973).

6. These proposals are detailed in C. Fred Bergsten, Thomas O. Horst and Theodore H. Moran, *American Multinationals and American Interests* (Washington: The Brookings Institution, 1977). The need for institutional reform is featured in C. Fred Bergsten, "Coming Investment Wars?," *Foreign Affairs* (October 1974).

7. See also the views expressed by Lawrence B. Krause and Joseph S. Nye, "Reflections on the Economics and Politics of International Economic Organization," in C. Fred Bergsten and Lawrence B. Krause, eds., *World Politics and International Economics* (Washington: The Brookings Institution, 1975).

8. For detailed proposals see C. Fred Bergsten, *Completing the GATT: Toward New International Rules to Govern Export Controls* (Washington: British-North American Committee, October 1974).

9. Detailed proposals are in C. Fred Bergsten, *The Dilemmas of the Dollar: The Economics and Politics of United States International Monetary Policy* (New York: New York University Press, for the Council on Foreign Relations, 1976). A shorter analysis of the liquidity problem is in C. Fred Bergsten, "New Urgency for Monetary Reform," *Foreign Policy* (summer 1975).

10. One set of proposals can be found in C. Fred Bergsten, "The Response to the Third World," *Foreign Policy* (winter 1974-1975). A series of official U.S. proposals were announced at the Seventh Special Session of the U.N. General Assembly on September 1, 1975.

11. On this issue see Robert O. Keohane and Joseph S. Nye, "Transgovernmental Relations and International Organization," *World Politics* (October 1974).

12. See "The United States and Germany: The Imperative of Economic Bigemony," in *Toward a New International Economic Order: Selected Papers of C. Fred Bergsten, 1972-1974* (Lexington, Mass.: D.C. Heath and Co., 1975).

13. See "U.S. Foreign Economic Policy and Europe: The Ascendance of Germany and the Stagnation of the Common Market" in work cited above.

14. Peter J. Katzenstein, "International Interdependence: Some Long-Term Trends and Recent Changes," *International Organization* (Autumn 1975).

12. A Western View of UNCTAD IV
Paxton T. Dunn

Introduction

The United Nations Conference on Trade and Development (UNCTAD IV), held in Nairobi, Kenya, May 3-31, 1976, was the fourth in a series of quadrennial conferences held since 1964 on the problems of international trade and development of the developing countries. UNCTAD was established in 1964 as an integral part of the economic sector of the United Nations with headquarters in Geneva. In addition to the full conference of 154 member states which meets every four years, UNCTAD is governed by a 68-member Trade and Development Board (TDB) which meets annually in regular session and in special sessions as required.[1]

UNCTAD IV was held in the wake of the Seventh Special Session of the General Assembly held in New York in September 1975, and following the first few sessions of the 27-member Conference on International Economic Cooperation (CIEC) being held in Paris to discuss North-South economic issues. Previous sessions of UNCTAD had concentrated on improving the terms of trade of less-developed countries (LDCs) and in accelerating their development process through the establishment of new principles of international trade (notably the generalized system of tariff preferences) and a series of measures aimed at increasing the flows of financial resources from developed to developing countries. It was decided that the Nairobi session would place its major emphasis on stabilizing and improving prices of basic commodities of export interest to developing countries

Excerpted from *Report on UNCTAD IV: The Business Point of View*, published by the U.S. Council of the International Chamber of Commerce, New York, July 1976.

in an effort to improve their terms of trade. Other key issues concerned relief measures for debt-servicing problems of LDCs, and a series of provisions to facilitate the transfer of technology from industrialized countries to the LDCs. In addition, the standard questions of international trade and finance, special treatment for the least-developed countries and other disadvantaged countries, relations between the socialist countries of Eastern Europe and the LDCs, cooperation among developing countries, and institutional arrangements were on the agenda.

The conference was held in a spirit of conciliation and cooperation, a legacy held over from the Seventh Special Session. Only near the end of the conference when it appeared that no compromise would be reached between the "North" and the "South" on the integrated program of commodities, was there a hint that a return to confrontation tactics would prevail. In the end, except for the brusque defeat of the U.S. proposal for further consideration of an international resources bank, there was a remarkable spirit of consensus displayed among the participants of the conference.

The major innovative idea presented during the general debate was Secretary Kissinger's proposal for an international resources bank (IRB) to stimulate private investment in natural resources in developing countries. Relatively few countries commented on the proposal, and the majority of those that did saw it as a diversionary tactic to thwart the adoption of the commodity program. Many saw the IRB as a subterfuge to increase the alleged domination of LDC economies by transnational corporations. This added fuel to one of the favorite themes of many LDCs—that transnational corporations are the cause of most of the ills of underdevelopment of the LDCs. Private enterprise was either ignored or criticized by the representatives of the developing countries who spoke. The only defenders were a handful of industrialized countries, such as the United States and Germany; the Organization for Economic Cooperation and Development (OECD) and the International al Chamber of Commerce (ICC).

The Agenda

Major attention was focused on the proposal of the Group of 77 for an integrated program for commodities. Major features of the program included the formation of buffer stocks for at least eighteen key commodities, the establishment of a common fund for the financing of international commodity stocks, provisions for supply management measures and the indexation of prices, promotion of increased local processing of raw materials and for the diversification of production, and the improvement of compensatory financing arrangements to stabilize export earnings of LDCs. The major industrialized countries, led by the United States, Germany, the United Kingdom, and Japan, opposed the establishment of a common fund and had misgivings on several other aspects of the integrated program. Agreement in this crucial area was slow in coming, but all sides persisted, knowing that some sort of compromise was essential to avert a breakdown in the conference.

The resolution that was finally adopted did not really satisfy anyone, but enough elements of the Manila Declaration were retained for the Group of 77 to claim victory. The concept of a common fund was retained, but the only certain element was agreement to hold preliminary meetings for the purpose of elaborating objectives and determining financing needs, sources of finance, mode of operations, and decision-making machinery. The United States, in its statement of reservations on the commodity program, made it clear that its participation in a later negotiating stage for the common fund was dependent on the results of the preliminary sessions.

A second key issue before the conference related to monetary and financial problems, with particular reference to the debt-servicing problems of the developing countries. The compromise achieved in the commodity field made it possible for the Group of 77 to accept a resolution on debt considerably weaker than they had been seeking. They had been insisting on the convening of a conference of major developed creditor and interested debtor countries for the implementation of principles and guidelines on the renegotiation of official and commercial debts. The compromise resolution adopted merely notes that governments of developed countries pledge themselves to respond in a multilateral framework by quick and constructive consideration of individual requests for debt relief by LDCs. No compromise was possible on the other resolutions in the monetary field relating to the transfer of real resources to LDCs and on international monetary reform.

The third major issue of the conference involved the transfer of technology from industrialized to developing countries. Three resolutions were adopted in this area. The one on the strengthening of the technological capacity of the LDCs called for the establishment of national, subregional, and regional centers for the development and transfer of technology to formulate technology plans and to coordinate government policies regarding licensing arrangements, industrial property laws, foreign investments, and research and development. A noncontroversial resolution on industrial property was also approved.

The third aspect was on the code of conduct for the transfer of technology. The Group of 77 had been holding out for a decision at Nairobi that would make any code to be negotiated binding on the parties involved. Under the terms of the compromise reached, an intergovernmental group of experts would be established to elaborate a draft code of conduct with the aim of completing its work by mid-1977. The General Assembly would be asked to convene a U.N. conference under the auspices of UNCTAD by the end of 1977 to negotiate on the draft elaborated by the group of experts and to decide on the legal character of the code.

Conclusions

Evaluations on the success of UNCTAD IV will differ according to the political persuasion and bias of the evaluator. As to whether the industrial North or the poor South won more points at the conference, we would call the contest a draw. The South won a qualified victory in the integrated program for commodities and got much less than they wanted on debt and monetary problems. The issues of the transfer of technology and institutional arrangements had positive and negative aspects for both the North and the South. Clearly, the UNCTAD Secretariat and in particular, Secretary General Gamani Corea, was the winner as the consensus achieved in the field of commodities, manufactures and trade, the transfer of technology, cooperation among developing countries, special treatment for the least developed countries, and institutional arrangements all called for increased activity by the UNCTAD Secretariat. The financial implications paper submitted at the end of the conference, reflecting the increased staff required to implement the resolutions adopted, totalled $2,415,000.

For the international business community, the results were not too positive. Clearly, private enterprise cannot ignore the aspirations of the third world for a better life and a more equitable distribution of wealth. The constant shrinking of the globe and the increasing interdependence of nations is a fact of life. Private enterprise, however, can also not remain oblivious to the doctrinaire approach and anti-free market bias of UNCTAD and its third world adherents. The hostile atmosphere vis-à-vis transnational enterprises and private investment was fanned by the vast majority of nongovernmental organizations (NGOs) and press following the proceedings. Among the NGOs, the ICC was unique in its forthright defense of the free market economy.

What are the implications for international business of the results of the Nairobi session?

1). Although it is dubious that the ambitious timetable set forth for the implementation of the integrated program for commodities can be maintained, or that anything resembling the program can be achieved, the whole process can only mean a permanently higher price level for raw materials. It would also mean increased state control and intervention in production and trade of commodities.

2). The irreversible process of negotiating a code of conduct for the transfer of technology can only culminate in increased prices for technology to the LDCs and a drying up of its transfer, if the third world persists in its present line of action.

3). The resolution on increasing the industrial potential of developing countries by the relocation of production centers from developed to developing countries could have adverse effects for industrial production in general and should be watched very carefully.

Action Program

What actions should the international business community take to meet the challenge of UNCTAD IV?

1). It should not turn its back on UNCTAD and the legitimate development problems under consideration, although the temptation to do so is very strong.

2). On the contrary, the business community, through the ICC and other like-minded organizations, should be more actively involved in specific aspects of the UNCTAD agenda that affect it most intimately and where practical business expertise can be of help. These areas would include, at a minimum, the transfer of technology and the commodity program.

3). With respect to the integrated program for commodities, the ICC should press the UNCTAD Secretariat to set up a panel of experts, consisting of private traders, producers, and consumers of commodities to provide advice on the negotiations. National committees should be in contact with their foreign ministries to ensure that business experts are included in the official delegations for the negotiations of specific commodity arrangements.

4). Regarding the code of conduct for the transfer of technology, the same technique should be used so that practical business experience can be brought to bear on all aspects of the problem. There is also ample room for input by the private sector in relation to the establishment of national and regional technological centers.

Notes

1. The member states of UNCTAD are divided into four distinct groups for negotiating purposes as follows:

    Group A: Afro-Asian countries with the exception of Japan, and including Yugoslavia.
    Group B: Western industrialized market economy countries, including Japan.
    Group C: Latin America and the Caribbean.
    Group D: The Soviet Union and the socialist countries of Eastern Europe.

Groups A and C are also known as the Group of 77 developing countries. This combined group comprises more than 110 developing countries.

MULTINATIONAL CORPORATIONS

13. Economics, Politics, and the Multinational Corporation
Robert Gilpin

The necessary condition for the rapid growth of multinational corporations over the past several decades has been the steady emergence of the United States as the world's dominant power. This process began in the latter part of the nineteenth century, when American industry began to supersede its European rivals. As American power grew, the United States created an increasingly large sphere of influence. This expansionism reached its zenith in the decades after World War II: following its victory in the war and in response to the Soviet challenge, the United States created in its own security interests the pattern of relations among the non-Communist countries within which American multinational corporations have flourished.

The sufficient conditions for the rise of the multinational corporation have been economic and technical. That is to say, the reasons why American corporations took advantage of the pattern of relationships created by the United States and expanded overseas are to be found in the evolving nature of the American economy itself and in the contemporary revolution in communications and transportation. The steady growth of American industrial corporations and shrinkage of the globe underlie this process of corporate expansionism.

The term "multinational corporation" (MNC) is used in this study to designate any business corporation in which ownership, management, production, and marketing extend over several national jurisdictions. The term is, of course, a misnomer in that these corporations are seldom multinational in either ownership or control; however, it is the one in general usage. Though there exist more technical definitions, an MNC

Excerpted with permission from *United States Power and the Multinational Corporation* (New York: Basic Books, 1975), pp. 8-18.

is essentially a corporation that invests in other countries for a variety of reasons: to have access to a foreign market, to secure foreign sources of supply, or to have the benefit of lower-cost production or lower taxes, for example. Market-oriented investment accounts for nearly 90 percent of foreign direct investment in manufacturing.[1] There also are a number of American and foreign corporations that invest abroad, especially in places like Hong Kong, Taiwan, and Mexico, in order to cut costs; the destination of the goods produced by such "offshore production" is usually the American market itself. Increasingly, however, this latter type of investment is becoming integrated into a corporate strategy of global production of components and semiprocessed goods.

Certain general characteristics of multinational corporations may be noted. In the first place, they make direct investments in a foreign country.[2] In contrast to portfolio investment, which involves the purchase of noncontrolling equities in a firm or debt instrumentalities of any kind, direct investment implies the establishment of a foreign branch or subsidiary or the takeover of a foreign firm. The underlying motive behind portfolio investment is largely financial; managerial control continues to rest with the borrower, and the liabilities incurred by debt borrowing can be liquidated through repayment. The motivation behind direct investment and the possession of foreign branches or subsidiaries, on the other hand, is primarily the acquisition of managerial control over a production unit in a foreign country. Direct investments are intended to establish a permanent source of income or supply in the foreign economy; consequently, they create economic and political relationships of a lasting and significant character.

Second, the MNCs of greatest interest to this study are characterized by a parent firm (usually American) and a cluster of subsidiaries or branches (owned wholly or partially by American corporations) in several countries. There is a common pool of managerial, financial, and technical resources, and, most importantly, the parent operates the whole in terms of a coordinated global strategy. Purchasing, production, marketing, research, and so forth, are organized and managed by the parent in order to achieve its long-term goal of corporate growth. Through vertical integration and centralization of decision making, the multinational corporation seeks to perpetuate its predominant position with respect to technology, access to capital, sources of supply, or whatever else gives it competitive advantage and market power.

Traditionally, British and European capitalism have practiced

TABLE 1

British and American Foreign Investment

	BRITISH, NINETEENTH CENTURY	UNITED STATES, TWENTIETH CENTURY
Investors	Banks Individuals Bond Market	Corporations
Type of Investment	Portfolio Loans	Direct
Activity	Raw Materials Agriculture Utilities (railroads and seaports)	Manufacturing Raw Materials (especially petroleum Marketing
Primary Motivation	Local opportunity for immediate profit	Global corporate strategy
Location of Investment (bulk of investment)	Europe United States Lands of recent settlement (Australia, Canada)	Europe Latin America Canada Middle East (petroleum)
Migration	Stimulated mass migration	Corporate management

portfolio investment, loans, and similar forms of capital export. Although Great Britain and other countries did make direct investments in the nineteenth century, these investments were invariably infrastructure investments (utilities, port facilities, and railroads).[3] In the twentieth century, American and other direct investment has been largely in manufacturing, particularly in the growth sectors of advanced or rapidly developing economies (e. g., Europe, Canada, South Africa, Brazil). Another major area for foreign direct investment has been petroleum.

Although Table 1 undoubtedly oversimplifies the contrast between British investment in the nineteenth century and American investment today, it does serve to point out the differing emphases of these two important capital-exporting nations. The table speaks for itself, but one point ought to be made. Whereas British investment was accompanied by mass migration of labor, American investment has been accompanied by the flow of corporate management. Management, capital, and technology have gone as a package to foreign lands in search of labor, markets, and resources.[4] In the nineteenth century, at least in the so-called lands of recent settlement (Canada, Australia, the United States, and South Africa), management and operating control usually remained in local hands. The essence of American direct investment has been the shift of managerial control over substantial sectors of foreign economies to American nationals. In character, therefore, these direct investors in other countries are more similar to the trading companies of the mercantilistic era than to the free traders and finance capitalists that dominated Britain in the nineteenth century.[5]

Some Facts and Figures

Although the corporations of other industrial powers are among the oldest multinationals (Royal Dutch Shell, Unilever, Nestlé), the multinational corporation today is most frequently American. Eleven of the fifteen largest multinationals are American.[6]

In 1971, American corporations held 52 percent of the total world stock of foreign direct investment. Great Britain held 14.5 percent, followed by France (5 percent) and the Federal Republic of Germany (4.4 percent). Japan held only 2.7 percent. Although European direct investment had increased substantially by the mid-1970s, American direct investment in Europe was still three times that of European direct investment in the United States in 1973. Japanese direct investment had also increased by 1973, but it still lagged far behind that of the United States and the major West European powers (Great Britain, France, and West Germany). At the end of 1972, total foreign investment in the United States was $14.4 billion, or less than one-sixth of the $94 billion in direct investment abroad held by American corporations. This situation is rapidly changing. Yet, foreign direct investment in the United States remains small compared to American direct investment abroad.

Foreign corporations and investors tend to prefer portfolio to direct investment. Moreover, if one examines the international production of major countries as against their exports, it is seen that foreign countries greatly prefer exporting whereas American corporations prefer foreign production. For all these reasons, therefore, the term "multinational corporation" is still largely a euphemism for the outward expansion of America's giant oligopolistic corporations. Corporate control has remained in America's hands. As a British friend remarked to me, "The multinational corporation is about as 'multinational' as the Indian army was 'Indian' under the British raj. While the troops were Indian, the officers were British."

Although American firms expanded abroad as early as the 1850s, it was only after World War I that American investment abroad began to increase rapidly.[7] At the same time that Britain had to liquidate billions of dollars in overseas investment, the United States emerged from the war as a creditor nation. Throughout the interwar period, American corporations expanded their holdings in both Latin America and Canada. Then, following World War II, and particularly after the founding of the European Economic Community or Common Market in 1958, the magnitude, direction, and character of American direct investment abroad changed rapidly.

From an initial accumulated investment of only $7 billion in 1946, by 1973 the book value of American direct investment had increased to over $100 billion, with an annual output estimated at over $200 billion.[8] Furthermore, whereas prior to World War II, Latin America accounted for most of this investment, after the war Canada, Western Europe, and other industrial areas absorbed the great bulk of it. Investment in the production of raw materials and in traditional manufacturing industries has remained strong; however, a large fraction of postwar investment (40 percent) has gone into advanced manufacturing industries, where it is heavily concentrated in the so-called commanding heights of the modern industrial economy (automobiles, chemicals, and electronics). The other large segment of U.S. foreign direct investment is in petroleum (30 percent). This $20 billion investment accounts for about 40 percent of American direct investment in the less-developed countries. (See Table 2.)[9]

TABLE 2

Sectoral Distribution of U.S. Foreign Direct Investment in Developed and Developing Countries, Yearend 1972

Developed Countries:	
Manufacturing	51.2%
Petroleum	22.1
Mining and Smelting	6.9
Other	19.8
Developing Countries:	
Manufacturing	26.4%
Petroleum	39.2
Mining and Smelting	10.8
Other	23.6

By the early 1970s, the United States had become more of a foreign investor than an exporter of domestically manufactured goods. International production by MNCs had surpassed trade as the main component of international economic exchange. Foreign production by the affiliates of American corporations was over four times as great as American exports abroad. Moreover, a substantial proportion of American exports of manufactured goods were really transfers from an American branch of an MNC to an overseas branch. In 1969, the American multinationals alone produced approximately $140 billion worth of goods, more than any national economy except those of the United States and the Soviet Union, and in 1971 the MNCs accounted for 15 percent of total world output. Moreover, by the early 1970s, the financial resources held by multinational corporations were nearly $300 billion. Thus there can be little doubt of the significance of multinational corporations; they loom large as a factor in contemporary world affairs.

Notes

1. Robert Keohane and Joseph Nye, "World Politics and the International Economic System," in *The Future of the International Economic Order: An Agenda for Research,* C. Fred Bergsten, ed. (Lexington, Mass.: D. C. Heath, 1973), p. 116.

2. Ibid.

3. Ibid.

4. Paul Samuelson, *Economics: An Introductory Analysis* (New York: McGraw-Hill, 1967), p. 5.

5. Harold Lasswell and Abraham Kaplan, *Power and Society: A Framework for Political Inquiry* (New Haven: Yale University Press, 1950), p. 75.

6. The top fifteen in 1971 were: G.M., Exxon, Ford, Royal Dutch Shell*, G.E., IBM, Mohl, Chrysler, Texaco, Unilever*, ITT, Gulf Oil, British Petroleum*, Philips, and Standard Oil of California. (Asterisks signify companies that are not of the United States.)

7. Hans Morgenthau, *Politics Among Nations* (New York: Afred A. Knopf), p. 26. For a more complex but essentially identical view, see Robert Dahl, *Modern Political Analysis* (Englewood Cliffs, N.J.: Prentice-Hall, 1963).

8. Charles P. Kindleberger, *Power and Money* (New York: Basic Books, 1970), p. 227.

9. U.S. Department of Commerce, Bureau of Economic Analysis, *Survey of Current Business* (1973), pp. 26-27.

14. Multinational Corporations in World Politics
Joseph S. Nye, Jr.

I

As dramatic as the rise of the multinational corporation has been its increased political prominence. The very term implies a political visibility not associated with the words "direct investment" that were used a decade ago. In the past two years the role of these spreading enterprises has been debated in the International Labour Organisation, the Organization for Economic Cooperation and Development, the European Community, the U.S. Senate, and the U.N. General Assembly. During 1973 a "Group of Eminent Persons" met under the auspices of the U.N. Economic and Social Council to study the role of multinational corporations in international relations and the process of development.[1]

To the common (and oversimplified) question of whether multinational corporations are likely to render the sovereignty of the nation-state obsolete, the answer surely is a qualified "no." The multinationals are undoubtedly a large force to be reckoned with. There are currently some 200 large multinational enterprises or clusters of corporations which operate simultaneously in 20 or more different nations and are joined together by common ownership and management strategy.[2] The three billion dollars of value added annually by each of the top ten multinationals is already greater than the gross national product of some 80 member-states of the United Nations, and some observers are predicting that by the end of the century 300 giant corporations will account for a large majority of world industrial production. Yet even weak states can and sometimes have nationalized the local affiliate

Reprinted with permission from *Foreign Affairs* (October 1974), pp. 153-175. Copyright 1974 by Council on Foreign Relations, Inc.

of a multinational corporation. For the foreseeable future, the two kinds of entities will continue to coexist, in uneasy tension.

Why do multinational corporations now seem to many nations to represent an important threat? What in fact are the intended or unintended political roles they play? What can one now say about the longer-term impact of multinational corporations? And, the most acute subject of present controversy, what can be done to cushion or regulate the conflict that many now see between multinational corporations and the less-developed countries?

Apart from their sheer size, the significance of multinational corporations has acquired an additional dimension in consequence of the growing prominence of economic and welfare-oriented objectives in the national security equation. Nuclear technology and changing domestic values have made the use of military force a more costly option for the governments of the advanced industrial societies. While in extreme situations force is indeed necessary to guarantee national suvival, much of international politics is not extreme and not about survival, and in these areas military force is far too blunt and costly an instrument to be useful. (A threat of bombardment may have helped the United States to induce Japan to trade a century ago, but it was not a useful instrument in the recent struggle over the value of the yen.[3]) Most national security policies in today's world are designed not merely to insure the physical survival of individuals within national boundaries, but to assure some minimal expected level of economic welfare, a certain political and social autonomy for the nation, and a degree of national political status. Indeed, some national security policies actually increase the risks to physical survival in order to insure greater certainty in the enjoyment of economic welfare, political status, and national autonomy.

For many states, the strongest sense of threat has shifted from the military area and territorial integrity to the economic area. Often such threats are unconventional and unintentional. As the distinguished Canadian John Holmes has described Canada's relations with the United States, "it isn't Washington we have to fear. It is Houston and Pittsburgh and Hollywood. . . . Our fear is not that the U.S. army will destroy Toronto a second time, but that Toronto will be programmed out of existence by a Texas computer."

Thus it becomes quickly apparent why multinational corporations have become important in world politics whether they wish it or not. Shifts away from the use of force are shifts away from the area of corporate weakness, and shifts toward greater prominence of economic welfare objectives are shifts in the direction of corporate strength.

Beyond this, generalizing about the political roles of multinationals becomes rather complicated. Corporations invest abroad for a variety of reasons. Firms in service industries differ considerably in size and mobility from those in extractive industries or in manufacturing. Even within manufacturing there are important differences in the bargaining positions at home and abroad of firms whose investments are oriented more or less toward access to local markets, inexpensive labor, or exploitation of a technological advantage. Moreover, the same firm may have a very different impact on a country with a weak economy and fragmented society than on a country with a balanced economy and stable government.

Nonetheless, in general terms, multinational corporations can be seen to play at least three important roles in the day-to-day processes of world politics.

The Direct Role: Private Foreign Policy

Here lie some of the most dramatic examples—notably the case of the International Telephone and Telegraph Company (ITT) in Chile, which helped stimulate both the U.S. Senate hearings and the creation of the special U.N. group. This sort of case becomes particularly notorious because it contravenes the traditional assumption of world politics that governments deal with governments and that citizens or corporations affect governments of other countries indirectly through policies they press upon their own government. But here citizens and corporations are also affecting the governments and politics of other countries by dealing with them directly, quite apart from the activities of their home governments.

It is true that the widespread publicity attendant on such dramatic cases may lend them a disproportionate significance. The Chilean disclosures are informative in that ITT was notably unsuccessful in persuading other multinational corporations to join in direct political intervention. While evidence about this type of direct role is almost impossible to assemble scientifically, present evidence suggests that cases of major direct political involvement such as United Fruit in Guatemala in the 1950s, Union Minière in Katanga in the 1960s, or ITT in Chile in the 1970s, are a small portion of state-corporation interactions. Indeed, one careful case study that documents the political roles of American corporations in Peru indicates a trend away from such blatant direct political involvement.[4] If we conceive of a scale of direct political actions by corporations ranging in descending order from the hiring of private armies through the bribery of host country soldiers or politicians, campaign contributions to political parties, legitimate lobbying of host government legislators, and so on down to advertising in order to influence the climate of ideas,[5] we would undoubtedly find most direct political activities clustered at the lower end of the scale.

Nonetheless, direct transnational political behavior can be of crucial importance to particular states. Beyond the rather routinely used battery of lower-level political activities, corporations may also use economic means (both inducements such as the promises of new investment, and deprivations such as threats of withdrawal) in direct bargaining with host governments for favorable policies.

When one considers the direct political role of the corporation in world politics, it is useful to drop another traditional assumption, that states always act as coherent entities. If one recognizes that different groups in societies have different interests and that governments are sometimes alliances of competing bureaucracies pulling in different directions, one can conceive of policy coalitions composed of parts of different governments and corporations.

Private foreign policies toward host countries thus may work on internal differences within a country or may try to bring outside pressure to bear. Faced with the prospect of Chilean copper nationalization in the late 1960s, Anaconda relied on the local political defense of forming an alliance with the conservative elite in the host country—to no avail. Kennecott, on the other hand, worked out a sophisticated external defense based on transnational market and credit networks, so that when nationalization occurred the Chilean government would jeopardize its standing with credit institutions on several continents if it failed to provide adequate compensation. In situations of rising nationalism, the latter strategy may be the safer for a corporation. In retrospect, Harold Geneen, president of ITT, has argued that

> the answer may be a multinational approach. By this I mean the Germans, the Swiss, the World Bank, and others share in the investment. Then six countries are involved, not one. If something goes wrong, the countries can get tough and do things. You don't go to war, but maybe everybody refuses to give the offending country credits.

Finally, it is important to make clear that transnational coalitions do not always direct their influence toward host-country governments. The radical critique of multinationals, focusing on their penetration of weak states, or on alliances between corporations and central sectors in peripheral states, sometimes ignores the fact that these enterprises can also affect the coherence of home governments and societies. A prime example is the international lobbying that has taken place over a new seabed regime. There one could find oil companies (and some elements of the U.S. government) allied with some relatively cohesive poor states and against the official U.S. government position.

The Unintended Direct Role: Instruments of Influence

Apart from any political initiative of their own, the existence of corporations with decision domains crossing several national boundaries has provided an additional instrument that governments may attempt to use in their relations with each other. For example, the United States has attempted through extraterritorial control of the trading relations of affiliates of U.S.-based corporations to extend its foreign policy embargoes into the jurisdiction of other states. Similarly, in the 1960s, the United States used guidelines on capital transfers by multinationals to strengthen its international monetary position. And there can be little doubt that the U.S. government has on occasion been able to use, wittingly and unwittingly, the information-gathering capacities of global corporations domiciled in America for intelligence purposes.

Examples of political problems arising from such instrumental use are not hard to find. Of sixteen conflicts cited by J. N. Behrman as arising from corporate activities among the Atlantic nations in the mid-1960s, twelve involved the American Trading with the Enemy Act, one involved computer technology related to nuclear weapons, and three involved enforcement of U.N. sanctions. In none of these cases did a corporation directly or deliberately provoke or profit from the conflict. And in the data assembled by David Leyton-Brown on sixty-one public conflicts in Britain, Canada, and France arising as the result of the activities of multinational corporations, interstate conflicts arose primarily from extraterritorial assertions of jurisdiction. In only two cases did a multinational enterprise seek the diplomatic support of its parent government.[6]

Manipulation of transnational corporations, however, is an instrument available to the host as well as the home government (an aspect to which the U.N. report gave little attention). The most dramatic recent example was the 1973 oil embargo. While the companies exerted some independence in diverting non-Arab oil to the Netherlands and the United States, the Arab countries were able to obtain almost total company compliance in regard to Arab oil. Even a small country like the Philippines was able to use a threat to nationalize American corporations in the 1960s to induce the U.S. government to extend trade preferences.[7]

Canada, with a third of its corporations foreign-owned (58 percent by value in manufacturing), is sometimes cited as a victim of the home government's ability to manipulate its corporations. Yet in a recent study of thirty-one non-trivial conflicts between the United States and Canada that reached the presidential level in the 1950s and 1960s,[8] corporations were used as instruments as often by the Canadian government as by the U.S. government. Altogether nine of the thirty-one cases involved activities of transnational corporations; in five of the nine, corporations played an active lobbying role, but in four others, they were used (successfully) as instruments by governments—twice by the United States and twice by Canada. In the auto pact of 1965, the Canadian government achieved its objectives by obtaining letters of intent from the American auto companies, and on the Arctic sovereignty issue it got a de facto acceptance of its jurisdiction from Humble Oil. In general, Canada did no worse in government bargaining in cases involving foreign corporations than in those in which corporations were not involved. As Americans found out in the auto pact or in the oil negotiations at Tehran in 1971, multinational corporations have their own interests; when they are pressed in different directions by different governments, they cannot automatically be expected to be hard bargainers on behalf of the U.S. government's interests.

Fixed investments can be hostages as well as outposts—not only for governments but also for non-state groups. The corporation as hostage has provided a particularly valuable instrument for terrorist groups, both as a source of finance and as a means of destroying a government's credibility. In 1974, in Argentina alone, guerrillas kidnapped more than twelve foreign corporate officials and raised over $36 million in ransom.

Political suasion, rather than force, is also used against the corporations by non-state groups. Pressure from black workers in the United States, for example, led Polaroid to adopt policies in South Africa that were designed to improve the social position of the South African blacks.

The important point is that direct investment creates a transnational interdependence which groups or governments may try to manipulate for their own political purposes. Governments and interest groups in both developed and developing countries frequently employ this instrument, even as they may deplore its use at other junctures. A double standard is widely applied in this area.[9]

Indirect Roles: Setting the Agenda

Why some issues rather than others absorb the attention of statesmen is a question of considerable political importance that has received too little attention. Even if they had no other effect, the intentional and unintentional roles of multinational corporations in helping to set the agenda of interstate politics have been significant. Their lobbying for particular actions by their home government toward the host country is familiar but nonetheless important, often taking the form of appeals for intervention in support of claims against host governments. As a classic example, in the 1960s the dispute between the International Petroleum Corporation and Peru became a tail that for years wagged the dog of American policy there.

In other cases, such as the lobbying of Congress by executives of multinational corporations in favor of more liberal tariff treatment of the host country by the home country, the lines of policy influence run in the other direction. Canada has benefited from such allies in a number of instances. Perhaps most intriguing, in light of supposed ideological differences, has been the recent lobbying by business executives on behalf of more liberal trade arangements with the Soviet Union. (Nor, one might add, is there much evidence for the charge that multinational corporations form a powerful lobby for a militaristic foreign policy. With a few exceptions, American multinational—as distinct from merely large—corporations do not have a particularly strong stake in military-oriented production or activities.)

Where multinational corporations have created conflicts among states, they have more often done so unintentionally than intentionally. One can identify three major unintended effects on the political agenda. First, in the past decade, the transnational activities of such enterprises have given rise to conflicts of jurisdiction and problems of extraterritoriality in such matters as antitrust, capital controls, trade restrictions, and taxation policy.

Second, multinationals have had major effects on the flow of trade and money. It may startle the uninitiated that production by subsidiaries of corporations outside their home countries has now grown to over twice the total value of trade among the developed countries. Moreover, a significant portion of international trade (more than a quarter of U.S. exports by some estimates) has been transformed from "arms length" to intra-enterprise transactions, between one arm of a multinational corporation and another. The result is that a variety of new trade policy questions have been put on the intergovernmental agenda and become intertwined with a broader range of industrial policy questions. Similarly, the ability of a few score corporate treasurers, thinking globally and acting rationally, to transfer vast sums with extraordinary rapidity was one of the factors that contributed to the inability of countries to maintain an international monetary system based on fixed exchange rates.

Third, multinational corporations have unintentionally affected the agenda of interstate relations by stimulating other social groups to press for particular governmental policies. Groups such as banks, advertising agencies, and some labor groups have been stimulated to press for policies of liberalization that would permit them to emulate the transnational strategy of the multinational corporation. Other groups, particularly most of labor, which are less transnationally mobile and feel themselves threatened or disadvantaged by the activities of the corporations, have pressed their governments for protective or nationalist policies. An apt example was the recent struggle between transnationally mobile corporations and the relatively immobile labor unions over the Burke-Hartke bill, which would have sharply affected the trade and investment policies of the United States.

II

It is easier to identify the various roles of multinational corporations in the day-to-day processes of world politics than to assess their likely long-term effects on its structure. Will they become more important as actors or instruments in world politics or have they passed their period of prime political importance? If they continue or grow in importance, will they have beneficial or malign effects on the creation of a peaceful and just world order? Will they redistribute power, wealth, and status or lead to their increasing concentration?

It is sometimes argued that the political importance of the multinational corporation is a product of a unique confluence of factors in world politics in the decades following World War II. A major aspect of this situation was American military strength and a geographically broad definition of security that resulted in what has been called a Pax Americana. According to this line of thought, the multinational corporation is largely a creature of American political preponderance in the period following World War II, and will recede in economic and political importance as the American government defines its security interests in less expansive terms in the aftermath of Vietnam.

While there is certainly some relationship between the Pax Americana and the transnational activity of multinational corporations, it is not as simple as this "military-security determinism" implies. First, it is sometimes forgotten that the American multinational corporation arose in the nineteenth century when the United States was a net debtor; that it was not (then or later) located primarily in the Caribbean and Latin America; and that it had already created fear of a *défi américain* in Europe at the turn of the century. In fact, U.S. direct foreign investment was a large a percentage of GNP (seven percent) in 1914 as in 1966.[10]

Second, the causes of growth and the causes of continued existence are not necessarily the same. Sorcerers' apprentices have been known to take on lives of their own. While the United States was the primary source of the rapid growth of multinational corporations in the postwar period, there is a current trend toward the development of European- and Japanese-based multinationals. American preponderance as a source of direct foreign investment (some 60 percent of book value in the mid-1960s) is slowly being eroded by the more rapid growth rates of European and Japanese direct investment. Moreover, the past and future relations of Swiss and Swedish multinationals to a Pax Americana is at best uncertain and indirect.

Third, some 70 percent of U.S. direct investment is located in other advanced industrial societies, not in the less-developed countries. Yet it is the latter which are the most likely areas to be left out of a more narrowly defined conception of national military security.

In other words, the erosion of bipolarity and the decline of American hegemony need not diminish the role of multinational corporations unless it should be accompanied by a shift toward greater use of force and away from economic welfare goals. While it is true that multinational corporations exist within, and are affected by, the structure of political-military relations in world politics, it does not follow that the postwar Pax Americana is the only such structure under which they could prosper.

A somewhat different case for projecting a decline in the political importance of multinational corporations might be based on the continued importance of nationalism and on long-term trends toward government intervention in economic affairs. Protectionism is not a temporary aberration. Governments are unlikely to give free rein to organizations that powerfully affect their economies, and that threaten feelings of national autonomy and national status. The trend toward politicization of issues of direct foreign investment is likely to continue. Indeed, the process is prompted by the rapid growth and large scale of multinational corporations as they stimulate domestic groups to emulation and opposition.

Such politicization, however, need not imply a decline in political importance. If multinational corporations were merely a nuisance or an inconvenience, states could simply curtail them by resorting to restrictive economic policies or their police powers. Multinationals, however, present opportunities as well as problems. Governments are faced with trade-offs between their objectives of welfare and autonomy. Even when government controls constrain and diminish the direct corporate role in world politics, they may simultaneously increase the indirect importance of multinational coporations as an instrument or agenda item in intergovernmental politics.

Thus, the odds are that both the size and political impact of multinationals will continue to grow. On the other hand, predictions that 300 giant corporations will run the world economy tend to be based on simple projections of past ten-percent annual growth rates, and fail to take into account some of the disadvantages that appear with large size, particularly in manufacturing, when temporary monopoly advantages have been competed away. The challenge to governments will come more from global scope and mobility than from corporate size. Even smaller multinationals can make crucial allocative decisions that challenge the welfare goals of governments.

Corporate mobility (which is greater in service and some manufacturing than in extractive industries) is not only a challenge to small states, but also to large states like the United States (and particularly to groups like labor which influence the foreign policy of large states). If there is increased movement of some corporate headquarters and major divisions, whether to remote and pleasant tropical islands as some foresee, or simply in the form of shopping among developed states, the process of separating or differentiating corporate and home government interests will be speeded along.

Today most multinational corporations can be identified with a single home country. They are multinational in operation, but rarely in ownership or top staff. Home governments tend to have jurisdiction over a major portion of the corporate empire's assets, and to have close informal ties with top management. Nonetheless, because corporate profits and growth come to depend on economic and political jurisdictions other than that of their home government, corporations gradually develop a view of their short-term interests coinciding with different governments at different times, and of their long-term interests as different from the interests of any particular state. The point was put rather dramatically by Carl Gerstacker, chairman of Dow Chemical, when he admitted to dreaming of buying a neutral island for Dow's headquarters, "beholden to no nation or society."

This trend toward corporate differentiation from both home and host countries has not yet gone very far. Of some 193 manufacturing firms that operate transnationally and for which data was available, the U.N. Secretariat found only 9 percent had more than 50 percent foreign content in employment; seven percent derived half or more of their earnings from abroad; and some 14 percent had half or more of their sales abroad. Nonetheless, some corporate developments do seem to point toward increased multinationality and autonomy of staff. Technological improvements are continuing to reduce the costs of communication and to enhance the corporate capacity to develop global strategies divorced from identification with the interests of any particular country.

This trend is complemented and to some extent reinforced by political attitudes toward multinational corporations in their home countries. A decade or more ago, multinationals were much less an object of domestic controversy, and it was widely assumed that the interests of American-based multinationals were roughly similar to the national interest. Today the range of domestic attitudes is more diverse. The AFL-CIO has called for limits on direct foreign investment, and Senator Jackson has accused oil companies of disloyalty for obeying the embargo of Saudi Arabia even on deliveries to the U.S. Navy. While such criticism may force some firms to a closer identification with their home government, it is at least equally likely that the experience will encourage other firms to move activities out from under their original home jurisdiction. It is said that some American-based corporations, with nearly half their operations abroad, planned in the event of congressional passage of the Burke-Hartke legislation to establish binational structures, with European headquarters handling operations outside the United States.[11]

If the trends toward growth and differentiation of multinational corporate interests from national interests continue, would the effects on world order be benign or malign? Not surprisingly, there is a good genie and a bad genie theory of whatever may be escaping from the national bottles.

The enthusiasts, or optimists, endorse the growth of corporate autonomy as having a profound potential for transforming world politics and creating a better world order. Increasingly autonomous corporations, in this view, can even transform world politics from a contest among states into a broader game with more actors who focus primarily on welfare-oriented goals. Multinationals will become a vehicle by which mankind transcends the nation-state, our dominant international institution of the past four centuries. States will not cease to exist, but transnational production units will take over a large part of their role in providing for the citizens' welfare—and will even claim a proportionate share of their loyalties. These broadened economic domains will call forth new political institutions that go beyond the nation-state.

The optimists thus see the multinational corporation tying the world together in a meaningful way. It shifts industrial production toward the poorer parts of the globe. It transfers technology and managerial resources from advanced to less-developed countries. It promotes both regional and global economic integration. *The Economist* has predicted, for example, that by the end of the century most automobile and machinery production will be carried out in less-developed countries. As it becomes politically difficult to bring workers from poor countries to jobs in rich countries, multinational corporations will promote global economic integration by taking the jobs to the workers.

The multinational corporation may also help to erode the great ideological cleavage that divides the world. Already there are more than a thousand agreements between Western corporations and Communist countries. Many of these are simple arrangements for "turn-key" plants. (A multinational corporation builds a plant, turns it over to the Communist government, and is paid out of future production.) But a number of Communist countries in Eastern Europe have found that long-term managerial involvement by the multinational corporation is a better way to insure continuous inputs of managerial and technological resources. Now some East European governments, particularly Yugoslavia, have followed this logic a step further, and to insure full access to the latest generation of technology, have invested abroad, often in joint ventures with multinationals. Should this trend continue, it would require ideologists to reinterpret their view of imperialism as the transfer of labor's surplus value across national borders and raise questions about the simple equation of multinational corporations, capitalism, and imperialism.

Looking further ahead toward the end of the century, it is possible that the multinational corporation will itself evolve into a new and flexible form of functional international organization. Not only will East European (and other) governments participate, but with increasing politicization of the question of control of multinationals in their former home countries, demands may increase for government, labor, or consumer group representation on their management boards. Large segments of world industrial production will be managed by large public and quasi-public multinational corporations as well as a host of smaller private ones. Autonomous management (regardless of ownership) will provide flexibility and efficiency in the organization of global production. Questions of public versus private ownership will have been transcended. Only questions of managerial autonomy versus democratic control will remain.

Pessimists share with the optimists many of these projections about the future of multinational corporations—but see the malign effects prevailing over the benign. The economic benefits of global integration, they feel, wll be unevenly spread and some areas will gain very little, so that the resulting inequality is likely to breed conflict. Moreover, even if multinational corporations distribute industrial production more evenly about the globe than is now the case, they will tend to centralize strategic decisions in regional coordinating centers and at global corporate headquarters. Technologies and areas to develop will be determined from a few key cities in the advanced countries, surrounded by regional subcapitals, while the rest of the world is confined "to lower levels of activity and income, i.e., to the status of towns and villages in a new Imperial System."[12]

This might not matter if economic welfare were the only goal that peoples seek. But middle classes seek high status occupations that are associated with managerial and research functions. In addition, people often desire status for their nations, and some sense of autonomy, of helping to shape decisions rather than always feeling shaped by them. Such people fear that the transnational systems of production organized by multinational corporations will perpetuate and even accentuate an international economic structure that leaves them dependent on the advanced countries. Slogans of global interdependence frequently gloss over the reality that it makes an important political difference if one party is continually more dependent than the other.

As multinational corporations become more autonomous, this sense of dependence, threatened status, and lost autonomy may not be confined to poor countries. Social groups and regions within advanced countries may experience the same feelings. Autonomous corporations are a challenge to governments and politically important groups in large states as well as small.

According to this view, the diminution of the role of the nation-state would signal a new feudalism rather than healthy progress. Kings and corporate barons will engage in conflicts and coalitions, but the serfs of the world will suffer. The real global divisions will not be among nations, but between a world city knit together by transnational elites and the diverse but intense parochialisms of the world countryside. The decline of the nation-state would not be a sign of health but a sign of disaster: "a sound international order cannot be built on the wreckage of nation-states."[13] The nation-state provides the internal order and sense of political community that underlie democratic institutions, and there is little prospect that our political norms can be adapted to keep pace with the evolution of powerful and autonomous transnational corporations playing increasingly political roles.

III

At the extremes, neither the optimistic nor the pessimistic view of the future seems likely to come to pass. Indeed it is unlikely that there are any prognoses that represent reality as it will be at the end of the century. What is clear, however, is that the evolution of multinational corporations has tremendously important implications for current and future world order. Apart from the direct and indirect political roles they already play, their effects on the long-term structure of world politics amply justify the attention of a United Nations charged by its charter to achieve cooperation and harmonization of the actions of nations.

On any reading the most likely intermediate prospect is that the relations between multinational corporations and nation-states will continue to be mixed. To a certain extent they are complementary institutions: one, the corporation, pursues (with a few notorious exceptions) a relatively specific set of economic objectives; the other, the territorial community of the nation-state, seeks a broad range of goals. Each institution can profit from the activities of the other.

But it is also amply clear that conflict is endemic in the relationship. As nonterritorial entities without military force, corporations are not a threat to the physical survival of a nation, but their economic power can be used to threaten particular political parties or ruling regimes. Second, while multinational corporations may bring in the technological and managerial resources that enhance national autonomy vis-à-vis other states (and vis-à-vis the corporations themselves in the long run), there may be high costs in terms of autonomy in the short term, and possibly over the long run as well, if a structure of dependent relationships becomes firmly established with strong local roots. Third, although corporate contributions to development may in one sense enhance national status, a too-powerful foreign ownership (particularly if high-status managerial and research jobs are concentrated abroad) may be seen as a threat to national status in another sense. This is the contrast, and dilemma, that seems to have developed in Canada in the course of the past decade.

Even in regard to economic welfare, where corporate benefits are likely to be greatest, a certain amount of conflict is unavoidable. What distinguishes the modern multinational enterprise from the large international corporations of earlier centuries is its global management strategy, made possible by the technology of modern communications. The most honest corporate manager allocating resources rationally within a transnational perspective is bound to have conflicts of interest with the most reasonable of statesmen whose rationality (and democratic responsibility) is bounded by national frontiers. For example, Chrysler resisted British government pressures in 1971 and granted an inflationary wage increase to its British workers, not because it wished to thwart the government but because the increased wage costs were less important, from a global point of view, than avoiding disruption of production for the American small car market.

Given the complex pattern of potential threats and benefits that multinational corporations present in relation to a variety of national values, it is sensible to expect conflictual relationships. It is equally likely, however, that the conflicts will frequently be of the type that have solutions from which both parties can benefit. In many instances, the enlarged size of the pie can be more important than the size of the slices. A basic principle for an international economic order will be to enhance situations in which joint gains are perceived and shared by states and corporations. This will help to diminish the intensity of conflicts.

However, since many national values are involved, and their intensity may vary among nations and over time, a second and equally important principle must underlie a just international economic order. National communities must be allowed to decide for themselves what degree of interdependence with corporations they find optimal and what they are willing to pay for it. If the benefits of multinational corporations are as great as proponents claim they are, then there should be no objection to letting host countries choose freely. If the economic, social, and political costs are as great as the critics charge, then host countries should be free to reject the transnational organization.

IV

These two principles—that all parties should seek to enhance actual and perceived net economic gain, and that in the end individual nations must be free to decide—help to illuminate the most difficult area of present and potential conflict, that involving the relationship of multinational corporations to the less-developed countries.

This is the area which received greatest attention both in the deliberations and in the report of the U.N. Group of Eminent Persons. As the International Chamber of Commerce has correctly pointed out, the report thus does not focus on the two-thirds of investment that is among the developed countries. Nonetheless, the focus of the group was politically justified. Multinational corporations do pose greater political problems for less-developed countries, because of the difference in scale (General Motors' annual profits exceed the annual income of most African states), the sensitivity of postcolonial states to situations of dependence, and the internal cleavages that often make their politics both penetrable and fragile. Moreover, poor countries have generally found themselves as hosts, but rarely as homes of multinational corporations.

There has been no shortage of arguments recently about the economic costs and benefits of multinationals to less-developed host countries. Proponents contend that transferring technology and relocating industrial production from the richer to the poorer parts of the globe can only be done through transnational organization, to overcome what for many states is the economic irrationality of narrowly bounded political sovereignty. Unlike portfolio investment, the contribution of the multinational corporation is not so much the movement of capital as the organization of capital, management, technology, and access to rich country markets into an economic package which is greater than the sum of its parts.

Critics, on the other hand, argue that the four parts of the package are often obtainable separately, and that the costs of "packaging" are too great. Among the costs sometimes charged to the corporation are inappropriate technology; creation of inefficient oligopoly patterns in small national markets; discouragement of local entrepreneurship; erosion of local economic policy and controls; stimulation of inappropriate consumer tastes; and illegitimate meddling in the local political process.

Evidence can be marshalled on both sides of the economic argument, and the facts vary from case to case. From a practical point of view, proponents and critics who focus on the system as a whole often fail to ask the crucial question: "What are the realistic alternatives in a given situation?" In some cases a critical factor such as advanced technology can be obtained by licensing; in other cases, it may be unobtainable except as part of a corporate package. In some cases, access to markets is a simple matter; in others, protected markets in rich countries can only be reached through the sales network or political clout of a multinational corporation.

Less-developed countries can follow a wide range of strategies vis-à-vis multinational corporations. At the two extremes are the strategies of laissez-faire and complete exclusion. (The benefits or costs of exclusion look somewhat different depending on whether one thinks of it as the "Chinese" or "Burmese" example.) Another approach is to let multinationals enter on generous terms and renegotiate these terms as the factors that the corporations bring in become less scarce. This situation of "let them in and squeeze them later" has characterized many raw material investments, where the terms of the original bargain tend to become politically obsolete over time.

A quite different approach is the "high threshold." The Andean Group of countries, for example, permit entry only on quite stringent conditions (including eventual divestment), which are agreed to by the corporation at the outset. Other countries permit entry only if corporations agree to joint ventures with local capital or the local government. A further variant of this approach is to disassemble the four-part package of direct investment and allow corporations entry on contractual terms to provide a specific service.

These various strategies are discussed at some length in the U.N. report. A recurrent theme in the dissenting comments is the fear that any restrictive strategies will discourage corporate investment in less-developed countries and inhibit the beneficial relocation of industrial production in the southern part of the globe. A common-sense conclusion, however, might be that each of these strategies promises different costs and benefits for different countries, and for different economic sectors at different times. No single strategy or legal regime is likely to satisfy all countries, or even the same country over time. For this reason alone, agreements on international legal regimes are distasteful to many less-developed countries.

As we saw earlier, multinational corporations can also follow a number of political strategies in their bargaining with host states: (1) they can appeal to their home governments for support; (2) they can use their economic power to participate in the local political process, legally or illegally; (3) they can organize external boycotts and restrictions of credit. Alternatively, the corporations can restrict themselves to economic agreements, attempting to convice host states that the corporation brings in resources from which there is a joint gain. In other words, they can seek to prove that the goose roasted is worth less than the goose laying golden eggs. As Charles Robinson, president of Marcona Corporation, has put it, "the only thing that counts is whether you [the corporation] are worth more alive or dead."

If one is concerned with an international order that involves global equity and freedom of choice—or indeed if one seeks merely to avoid unbearable strain and conflict—it is clearly preferable that corporations eschew the more extreme forms of action and pursue the "golden egg strategy." A process of realistic discussions and bargaining with individual host countries is what is needed, and what a U.N. commission charged with developing international codes of conduct should attempt to promote—rather than rigid rules that cannot hope to cover the great variety of cases and political attitudes involved.

In line with the principle of free choice (and, one might add, with political realism), host countries must be free to disassemble the package of direct investment, to accept or reject all or part of any proposed investment project. But it is essential that the bargains be freely struck, and free choices require meaningful alternatives and accurate information. Particularly with regard to the less-developed countries, international institutions should help enhance the conditions and opportunities for free political choice on such matters as how much aggregate growth a people are willing to sacrifice for autonomy and experimentation (and vice versa). This requires dispelling the fear and mistrust that frequently block clear appraisal of self-interest by poor, weak countries. It also means discouraging the use of home government influence that goes much beyond normal diplomatic representation, or corporate political activities that prevent free choice by the indigenous political processes of the host state. As a number of comments in the U.N. report indicate, it is unrealistic to expect governments to refrain completely from support of their corporations. Nonetheless, the basic diplomatic norms should reflect the principle of free choice.

V

It is sometimes suggested that the only international institutions needed are those which would establish a legal order to facilitate the corporation's work. This view, however, fails to take into account the political roles of the corporation that we have described above. Even while pursuing economic goals, their involvement in the political process is too untidy and changeable to be contained within a static legal order.

Given deep-seated differences among countries, moreover, it is unrealistic at this stage to expect, for example, a strong supranational organization to oversee the activities of multinationals, or the global chartering of corporations as suggested by George Ball, or Charles Kindleberger and Paul Goldberg's "GATT for direct investment."[14] A global charter would formally denationalize corporate origin, but would remove none of the real conflicts stemming from the central dilemma of differing decision domains. As for a specific legal convention, the broader the agreement in numbers of countries or scope of subject matter the less likely the prospects for success.

The problem is not only one of organizing collective action among large numbers of states. It also stems from the basic political reality that underlies corporation-state bargaining, particularly between rich and poor. As Raymond Vernon has pointed out, when the basic bargain is political and may be obsolescing over time, poor countries consider it unwise to institutionalize a set of norms or adjudication procedures that represent a stage in which they are relatively less favored.[15] (This is one of the reasons why a number of countries have refused to join the

International Center for the Settlement of Investment Disputes that has been established by the World Bank.)

The U.N. report recommended the creation of an expert commission which would, among other things, work out codes of conduct for multinationals. This sort of continuing discussion and negotiation of codes of conduct is a more realistic approach to the task of creating and adjudicating norms than the more elegant solutions would be. As L. K. Jha, former governor of the Bank of India and chairman of the group, commented in the report, developing countries need not feel disappointed with the recommendations if they look upon the report as the beginning rather than the end of an exercise in the creation of norms.

The U.N. group also recommended the creation of an information and research center on multinationals as part of the Secretariat, and a number of specific steps, including technical assistance, designed to strengthen the bargaining position of the less-developed countries vis-à-vis the multinationals. Access to information, variable identity and mobility of resources are key assets of multinational corporations in their bargaining with states. Information that improves governments' knowledge about global corporate activities and about mutual alternatives can affect the terms of the bargain. Much of the information will be difficult to obtain and equally difficult to assess. Since knowledge is power, it will not be easily parted with, either by corporations or by governments. Many countries have weak rules for disclosure of corporate information, and sometimes governments find it to their advantage, on tax incentives for example, not to disclose information they have. Even the Commission of the European Community has had to compile inadequate data on corporate mergers from public sources because some member-governments refused to share the information that they collected nationally.

Nonetheless, the collation and sharing of information from public sources can be useful to many governments. Moreover, the amount of information in the public domain may increase as national demands grow for corporations to demonstrate their contribution to the local economy. Comparison of such company national reports by an international staff can identify discrepancies and raise important questions. The usefulness of the international institution will be greater the more the staff develops a reputation for fair-mindedness. This last point is essential, since the only sanction which a U.N. Commission on Multinationals would have is publicity. This is not an insignificant sanction against corporations dealing with the public, but it would be quickly dissipated by biased work.

Not all governments have the ability to make full use of the information already available to them. Providing experts in this area can be an important function. Technical assistance cannot remove all conflicts from the interaction of weak states and foreign corporations, but at least it can help to dispel the mistrust that stems from fear of the unknown, and allow the parties to bargain on the basis of more clearly perceived self-interest. The experience of Harvard's Development Advisory Service in helping countries such as Liberia and Indonesia to improve the terms of their contracts with foreign corporations is an instructive example. Again, while controversy cannot (and should not) be completely avoided, a reputation for fair-mindedness is essential.

The obstacles to any larger role for the United Nations here are several. Specifically, there are the problems and pitfalls of "geographic distribution," extraneous politicization, and occasional bias that beset the U.N. system. Steering clear of these will be essential. More generally, one cannot be too optimistic about states reaching agreement on international institutions in the short run, because, as we saw earlier, states have conflicting as well as complementary objectives vis-à-vis multinational corporations.

On the other hand, there are several trends that increase the elements of common challenge which corporations present to governments. With Europe and Japan growing rapidly as sources of direct investment, more of the crucial governments—and particularly the United States—will feel the divided interest of being both home and host rather than merely home to multinational corporations. Second, as we have seen, many corporations are moving toward differentiation of their corporate interests from the interests of either their home or host countries. Third, corporations are more and more caught up in politics, whether they will or no.

The initial response to these challenges is likely to be unilateral national efforts, rather than international cooperation. But conflicting unilateral policies can be self-defeating unless there are some international rules and mechanisms for coordination. Moreover, multinational corporations may find themselves so hindered by contradictory national regulations that they may press various governments to initiate efforts to achieve greater international uniformity. At this point the prospects for international economic organization improve. Whether the United Nations or another institution will acquire a sufficiently strong mandate to deal with the problem, the political challenge of the multinational corporation seems to be gradually leading to a concerted response. The role of the multinational corporation today cannot be understood merely in economic terms, but must be seen in terms of this larger political challenge and response.

Notes

1. Of the twenty persons appointed, eight came from less-developed countries, two from Communist countries, and ten from the "rich" countries, including two Americans, Senator Jacob Javits of New York and J. Irwin Miller, chairman of the Cummins Engine Company. During 1973 the group heard testimony from corporate presidents, professors, trade unionists, and general social critics, and in the summer of 1974 presented its report. U.N. ECOSOC, *The Impact of Multinational Corporations on Development and on International Relations* (E/5500/Rev. 1), 1974.

2. In a document prepared for the Group of Eminent Persons, the U.N. Secretariat discussed problems of alternative definitions, and pointed out that the number of multinationals can be set as high as 7,300 if one foreign affiliate is set as the criterion. *Multinational Corporations in World Development* (ST/ECA/190), 1973. While the term *enterprise* is more strictly accurate, *multinational corporations* remains the more popular term.

3. The relationship between politics and economics is developed in "World Politics and the International Economic System," by Robert O. Keohane and Joseph S. Nye, Jr., in C. Fred Bergsten, ed., *The Future of the International Economic Order* (Lexington, Mass.: D. C. Heath, 1973).

4. Charles T. Goodsell, *American Corporations and Peruvian Politics* (Cambridge: Harvard University Press, 1974).

5. Or not advertising. In 1972, some U.S. companies in Mexico organized an advertising boycott of the "anti-American" newspaper *Excelsior*. *The New York Times,* June 23, 1974.

6. J. N. Berhman, *National Interests and the Multinational Enterprise* (Englewood Cliffs, N.J.: Prentice-Hall, 1970); David Leyton-Brown, "Government of Developed Countries as Hosts to Multinational Enterprises: The Canadian, British and French Policy Experience," unpublished Ph.D. dissertation, Department of Government, Harvard University, 1973, p. 423.

7. J. N. Behrman, "The Multinational Enterprise and Nation States: The Shifting Balance of Power," in A. Kapoor and Phillip D. Grub, eds., *The Multinational Enterprise in Transition* (Princeton: Darwin Press, 1972), p. 420.

8. J. S. Nye, "Transnational Relations and Interstate Conflicts: An Empirical Analysis," *International Organization* (autumn 1974), pp. 961-999.

9. The recent U.N. report is no exception, seeming to deplore multinationals' pressure on host governments at some points, while inviting

home governments to influence corporations to further positive social objectives within host countries in others.

10. Contrast Robert Gilpin, "The Politics of Transnational Economic Relations," in Robert O. Keohane and J. S. Nye, eds., *Transnational Relations and World Politics* (Cambridge: Harvard University Press, 1972) with Mira Wilkins, *The Emergence of Multinational Enterprise* (Cambridge: Harvard University Press, 1970).

11. I am indebted to Howard Perlmutter of the Wharton School for this point.

12. Stephen Hymer, "The Multinational Corporation and Uneven Development," in Kapoor and Grub, *The Multinational Enterprise in Transition*, p. 441.

13. David Calleo and Benjamin Rowland, *America and the World Political Economy* (Bloomington: Indiana University Press, 1973).

14. "Toward a GATT for Investment: A Proposal for Supervision of the International Corporation," *Law and Policy in International Business* 2 (summer 1970).

15. Raymond Vernon, *Sovereignty at Bay* (New York: Basic Books, 1971), p. 46.

15. The Multinational Corporation: A Corporate View
Walter B. Wriston

Much has been said and written about the fate of all of us who live on this planet. In this era of almost instantaneous communication, any new intellectual fashion that catches the attention of the media is repeated endlessly throughout the world. In recent years, these fashions have ranged from the desirability of unlimited growth all the way to the Club of Rome's no-growth formula. Intellectual tides have moved from predictions that the world will soon run out of food and natural resources to a blind faith that new technology will provide for us all. The common denominator of most predictions of doom and gloom is a simplistic belief in straight-line projections combined with an unwillingness to consider that man is capable of innovation to meet his own needs. Like most things in this world, history would suggest that trends, no matter how strong, are not irreversible and can be changed by the concerted actions of mankind.

Today, as always, there is both good and bad news. The bad news is that more and more human resources are diverted from productive work into government bureaucracies. The good news is that more and more people all over the world have reached the same conclusion. Guido Carli recently wrote, "In the last five years public expenditure has more than doubled with no noticeable improvement in the quantity or quality of service, and with more and more funds going to replenish the coffers of the countless public bodies that dot the Italian landscape."[1]

In the same vein, Norman Macrae has stated that "the marginal productivity of new employees in the government sector has for some time been negative."[2] The point is easily documented. Mr. Macrae asks simple questions about productivity, such as: "By how much have crime rates gone down? How far has the legal system become more expeditious? To what extent is the urban environment more beautiful and its infrastructure better fitted to meet changing demands?" You can make your own list of questions, but the answers will always be the same. If in fact we have a negative marginal productivity in government, it is clear that if we are to feed ourselves in the future, we cannot do so through government action.

In contrast to declining productivity of the public sector is the increasing productivity of the great global corporations of the world. They are even now the principal agents for the peaceable transfer of technology and ideas from one part of the world to the other. Since no country has a monopoly on industrial and agricultural skills, the transfer of men, money, and ideas is crucial if we are to raise the world's living standards. The perceptions of the needs of mankind are not uniform in the public and private sectors. As a general rule, the politicians have been engaged in fragmenting the world, while the multinational corporations have been viewing the planet as one marketplace. The clash of these perceptions has understandably created a great deal of intellectual friction, which has been manifest in great outpourings of scholarly and not-so-scholarly attempts to clarify the issues between the public and the private sectors. We have witnessed lengthy United Nations debates about such weighty details as whether we should call a company multinational, transnational, international, supranational, or perhaps some other term in some other language. None of this rhetoric has really been useful. It is the kind of clarification that consists of filling in the background with so many details that the foreground sinks out of sight.

What has tended to be pushed from sight in the current debates is the real nature of the choice confronting us. The arguments that focus on the world corporation are only a proxy for the real issue. The present struggle for control of the future is not between national vs. international companies nor European vs. American or Japanese companies, nor even the currently fashionable theme of the developed vs. the developing countries. The debate is really the continuation and intensification of the battle between two historic ideas about economic and social behavior. One idea, associated with words like "free trade," "free enterprise," and "laissez-faire," holds that business is politically neutral, existing only to satisfy the economic desires of the world's people. The other, older idea holds that business is—or should be—the chosen instrument of the state, or, what amounts to the same thing, that the state should be the chosen instrument of business.

Today's global corporation is the modern heir to the tradition whose seeds were planted in the United Kingdom by the industrial revolution and harvested most abundantly in the singularly free economy of the early United States. Despite the enormous success of the world corporation in supplying the world's needs, the state-dominated system that it displaced not only dies hard, but in some areas is expanding. That system, once known as mercantilism, remained dormant for a period, but it has already been resurrected twice, first as nineteenth-century imperialism and then as twentieth-century totalitarianism.

Today, much of the criticism of the global company is really the disquieting voice of neomercantilism. In this larger historical context, the themes being repeated today are distressingly familiar. Protectionist movements are becoming prominent, and governments are manifesting desires to restrict and control the freedom of the world corporation to conduct its business. It has all been heard before; the challenge comes again from sovereign authority and from affected interest groups using that authority to resist the market allocation of capital, labor, and purchasing power to areas of greater productivity.

Sometimes it seems that the more successful the enterprise is in supplying the real needs of the world's people, the louder become the voices of protest. Often, nationalism is used as the stick to beat a world corporation. At the beginning of the 1960s, when more than 60 percent of the large multinationals were based in the United States, bestselling books all over Europe were sounding the alarm over what Servan-Schreiber called, "This strange phenomenon, dangerous and massive in its size and power . . . so hypnotizing and overwhelming, that it threatens to plunge us from our present ignorance into total despair."[3] This inflammatory rhetoric never had any connection with reality, but it served a political purpose. Ten years later, only slightly more than half of the world's multinationals were headquartered in America, and books were published in New York with titles like *The Infiltrators*, warning Americans about the impending takeover of their factories by Volkswagen and the Rothschilds.[4]

All such controversies overlook a fundamental point. In the tough, competitive global marketplace, it does not matter where a multinational corporation's headquarters are located. Any global company, whether based in America, Europe, Japan, or somewhere else, will sooner or later have to operate under the same economic and political rules that govern its international competitors. In order to stay in business, any company will be compelled to get its materials for production from wherever they are available most cheaply, conduct its processing activities wherever they are most efficient, and market its goods wherever there is a demand. And all of this has to be done in compliance with a bewildering variety of laws and value systems which have been constructed by our nation-states.

It is precisely this economic necessity that makes the multinational enterprise our best instrument for assuring the most efficient, most thrifty use of the world's resources. In an era when many people express concern that those resources might be squandered, the need to make them go as far as possible and to avoid waste is an economic and human necessity. Yet, efficient use of the world's resources does not generate much applause for the world corporations.

The neomercantilistic ideas never died. Today they furnish ammunition for critics of multinationals both at home and abroad. These familiar themes are articulated by some in developing countries who accuse multinational companies of "milking" the economies of their host countries by taking more out of them than they put in. At the same time these charges are leveled at the world's corporations abroad, labor leaders at home are averring that multinationals are exporting capital, technology, and jobs that might otherwise be used to build the domestic economy.

It has become a two-front war. If the international managers prove to a host country that they are creating more wealth for it than they are taking out, this very evidence will be used against them at home. If they prove to the labor unions at home that, on balance, they are creating more jobs at home than they export, or prove to their governments that the repatriated foreign earnings are good for the country's balance of payments, that evidence fuels the arguments of their foreign critics.

Because of their intellectual training, many of the critics are quite sincere in believing that international managers are lying when they say that everybody profits from their operations, home and host countries alike. The critics cannot accept this simple truth because they have been taught to believe that business is what twentieth-century mathematicians call a zero-sum game. They believe that a profit for one must mean a loss for someone else. But business is not a poker game that transfers a static pot of money from one player to another. It is a creator of wealth. The zero-sum game concept of business is the modern reincarnation of pure mercantilism. It belongs to the age of Louis XIV and the economic philosophy of Colbert, who said of French prosperity, "This state is flourishing not only in itself but also by the deprivation which it has inflicted on all the neighboring states."[5]

The dead hand of Colbert is easy enough to see when one country after another hoists the flag of protectionism. But there is another, less familiar ingredient in his unhappy legacy with which we are also burdened. Adam Smith described Colbert as "a man of probity . . . and of abilities . . . every way fitted for introducing method and good order into the collection and expenditure of the public revenue." Smith went on to say that because Colbert was "accustomed to regulate the different departments of public offices, and to establish the necessary checks and controls for confining each to its proper sphere . . . he endeavored to regulate the industry and commerce of a great country upon the same model as the departments of a public office."[6]

The economic consequences of Colbert's policies were, of course, disastrous. Business can no more be run like a government than a government can be run at a profit. But there are still people of "probity and ability" who do not understand the difference and who, with what they believe to be the best of intentions, may wind up doing for the global economy what Colbert did for Europe.

Free enterprise, as preached by Adam Smith and his band of disciples, has never meant license to conduct business without limitations imposed by government. It is the acknowledged function of government to formulate and enforce laws designed to insure, so far as possible, equality, liberty, and justice for its citizens. Free enterprise asks only that, within those guidelines, no commercial enterprise should enjoy extraordinary privileges, and none should be laid under extraordinary restraints. This is all the modern global company requires to become a highly effective institution for making optimum use of the world's resources.

The concept of global efficiency, however, places a great strain on even the most liberal of modern nation-states. Each ruling government is primarily concerned with optimizing conditions within its own boundaries. All countries today participate to some degree in international specialization, contributing to the world economy what they can do best, and therefore most profitably. But every country at some point subordinates its possible economic advantages to considerations of military security, domestic stability, the protection of home industries or economic groups, and even to national pride. Many of the developing countries struggling to feed and educate their people deem it more prestigious to build a steel mill than a fertilizer plant or public schools.

National governments often assert their dominance over business enterprises not only in pursuit of competitive advantage abroad, but also in furtherance of domestic political policies. No country completely permits free enterprise, but controls in today's world tend to come from one of two diametrically opposed political extremes, with the freer countries positioned somewhere in the middle of the spectrum. One type of government tends to organize its economy to favor public ownership of enterprise. It adopts policies of income redistribution, regulates consumption, maximizes central planning and government allocation of resources. At the authoritarian extreme of this system are countries like the People's Republic of China, the USSR, the nations of Eastern Europe, North Korea, Vietnam, Cambodia, and the socialist countries of Africa. The fruits of this system are written plain in history. The medium-term economic consequences of such policies always involve depressed internal growth rates and can lead to extreme economic degeneration, as we saw in Nasser's Egypt, Sukarno's Indonesia, and Allende's Chile.

At the other end of the political spectrum, another group of countries pursues policies that favor private business ownership, deliberately depress current consumption in favor of capital accumulation, permit market mechanisms rather than fiat to allocate resources, tightly control their labor unions, and generally practice social regimentation. These states tend to take a positive view of the world economy and favor policies that foster global interdependence. They usually also experience relatively strong growth rates. But very often these societies produce an increasing maldistribution of income which may ultimately create an explosive social situation. If the situation deteriorates, it is not unusual to see what one economist euphemistically calls "a strong military infrastructure" take over the government.

All the other national economies are strung out somewhere along the spectrum between these extremes. The most comfortable location is somewhere as close as possible to the middle, but it takes an effort to stay there. Every economic crisis creates pressure on governments to flirt with one extreme or the other, sometimes with both at the same time. There is always the temptation to solve short-term problems by exchanging them for long-term instability.

In the long run, both types of controlled economies are unstable. The progressive ruination of the economy in the one case and the social regimentation and inequitable income distribution in the other cause internal pressure that will press for radical change. Such countries can either change rather slowly, or they can abruptly flip from one kind of economy to the other. When internal pressures become irresistible, the regimes in charge may either give ground gradually or be quickly replaced. The transfers of leadership from Sukarno to Suharto, Nasser to Sadat, Allende to Pinochet, and Spinola to Soares are but very recent examples of how rapidly events occur.

No matter where a government is positioned on the political spectrum, the public and private sectors are often in conflict. This natural interplay has generated a great deal of nonsense about the relative power of multinationals and governments. The facts are clear and simple.

A multinational corporation, no matter how large, is essentially helpless in the hands of a nation-state, no matter how small. Despite the overwhelming evidence of this truism, investigations abound. The Group of Eminent Persons appointed by the United Nations Economic and Social Council in 1972, at the instigation of the then Communist government of Chile, started an investigation of the relative powers of multinational companies and the sovereign states. It is not now, nor has it ever been, a contest. I can give them one example that occurs daily right next door to the U.N. headquarters in New York, where I live.

New York is a difficult place to park an automobile. Members of missions assigned to the United Nations enjoy diplomatic immunity. They can ignore the No Parking signs—which many of them do, to the constant irritation of less-privileged New Yorkers. If I park my own car in the neighborhood, the police department tows it away. And the head of every global company is in the same fix.

There you see the true difference between sovereignty and the lack of it. If the example I chose seems a little absurd, it is no more so than books with titles like *Sovereignty at Bay*. Or for that matter, some of the reports that were turned out by the Group of Eminent Persons who parked their cars outside the U.N. building, in clear defiance of local laws.

The same may be said of the accusations of neocolonialism. Paolo Rogers of Olivetti put it well when he asked: "What kind of colonialism could it be when taxes are paid to the colonized country? Multinational corporations, whether U.S.- or Europe-based, when investing abroad, have no power to infringe on the sovereignty of host governments, and like it or not, they are bound to abide by local laws, rules and regulations."[7]

As a last resort, all the multinational company can do in its relations with a sovereign state is to make an appeal to reason. If this fails, capital, both human and material, will leave for countries where it is more welcome. Whether or not there is a shortage of capital is the subject of debate, but no one asserts there is a surplus. Since men and money will in the long run go where they are wanted and stay where they are well treated, capital can be attracted but not driven.

In the long run the future of the global company in any one area will be determined by the degree to which a particular government is willing and able to sacrifice the material well-being of its citizens to noneconomic factors. Everything we have discussed thus far will be resolved almost automatically when our nation-states make up their minds about this one basic question.

The reality of a global marketplace has been the driving force pushing us along the path of developing a rational world economy. The progress that has been made owes almost nothing to political imagination. It has been the managers of the multinational corporations who have moved to supply mankind's needs as efficiently as politics would allow. The thousands of products that have helped raise the living standards of manking have made this economic process highly visible to millions of people. Far too many of the world's people have now seen what the global shopping center holds in store for them. They will not easily accept having the doors slammed shut by nationalism. The reason for optimism about the future of the world corporation rests on the solid base that it is the best way that has yet been found to organize our society to give it the optimum chance of supplying the needs of mankind in an increasingly crowded world.

Notes

1. Guido Carli, "Italy's Malaise," *Foreign Affairs* (July 1976).
2. Norman Macrae, "Multinational Corporations: A European View." Remarks at the American Academy of Political and Social Science, Philadelphia.
3. J.-J. Servan-Schreiber, *The American Challenge* (New York: Atheneum, 1968), p. xiv.
4. Nicholas Faith, *The Infiltrators: The European Business Invasion of America* (New York: E. P. Dutton & Co., 1972).
5. Jean Baptiste Colbert, *Lettres, Instructions et Memoires,* ed. by Pierre Clement, 1859-82, vol. VII, p. 230.
6. Adam Smith, *An Inquiry into the Nature and Causes of the Wealth of Nations,* 1776.
7. Paolo Rogers, in a private conversation with the author.

16. The United Nations and Transnational Corporations
Klaus A. Sahlgren

Within the last thirty years, the international community has perceived the need to establish some kind of framework for the conduct of international commercial and monetary relations. The attempts that have been made in this regard have not always been successful, as the abortive Havana charter of 1948 demonstrated. Such failures have, at least, revealed the dimensions of the challenge that must be faced. But where the efforts have resulted in the successful elaboration of internationally agreed upon instruments, although they may have fallen far short of what is necessary, the international community has been the beneficiary. However, the field of transnational corporations (TNCs), which cuts across many areas including international commercial, monetary, development, and environmental concerns, has so far not been brought within the ambit of any international instruments.

In an attempt to fill this gap, individual countries and groups of states initiated legislation and rules designed to protect their own particular interests. A legal climate composed of a wide variety of disparate national legislation supplemented by differing regional proclamations is a sure source of jurisdictional and, ultimately, political conflicts. This situation is certainly undesirable from the point of view of host countries and home countries, as well as the transnational corporations themselves.

To this must be added another consideration: the changing perception of the relationship between transnational corporations and the states with which their operations bring them into contact. This, more than any other factor today, underlies current efforts at international regula-

Adapted from *Proceedings of the 70th Annual Meeting, American Society of International Law*, Washington, D.C., April 22-24, 1976.

tion. Early in the game, transnational corporations were recognized as dynamic generators of technology, entrepreneurship, and capital and as efficient organizers of production and distribution systems. These distinct capabilities, facilitated to a large extent by centralized decision making and a global network, were appreciated by both developed and developing countries which counted heavily on the contribution of the TNCs to their development effort.

However, these same capabilities gave rise to apprehension when it became apparent that global strategies did not necessarily take into account the national objectives of host countries. Consequently, many governments, especially those of the developing countries, felt frustrated in their efforts to integrate the foreign affiliates of transnational corporations into their economic objectives. The possibility that these affiliates might escape national policies, control essential resources, and transfer funds in not readily apparent ways troubled host countries. In the recent past, revelations of incidents of political interference and of corrupt practices certainly have not contributed to an atmosphere of trust.

The first efforts to elaborate a code of conduct at the United Nations arose in July 1972. While the specific event which triggered the U.N. involvement was the complaint on the part of a host country regarding political interference by a powerful TNC, it is safe to say that the U.N. involvement was inevitable, given the importance of the subject to international economic relations. The majority of countries had come to the conclusion that some generally acceptable rules of the game would be preferable to unilateral state action which, at times, could assume arbitrary overtones. Thus, in 1972 the Economic and Social Council (ECOSOC), by a unanimous resolution, requested the secretary-general to appoint a group of twenty eminent persons from developing and developed countries and from various backgrounds to study the impact of transnational corporations on world development and on international relations. The group invited about fifty personalities from business, labor unions, universities, and consumer organizations to hearings. It had at its disposal work done by the United Nations and other bodies on the subject. Their report, "The Impact of Multinational Corporations on Development and on International Relations," dealt with the nature of the impact of TNCs and with such specific issues as ownership and control, financial flows and balance of payments, technology, competition and market structure, employment, consumer protection, taxation, and transfer pricing. The group recommended the establishment of a permanent body within the United Nations; a commission to deal comprehensively with the issue on a continuous basis and a center within the U.N. Secretariat to collect and disseminate information, conduct research, provide technical assistance to developing countries, and generally support the commission in its work. ECOSOC accepted these recommendations and, again unanimously, established both a Commission on Transnational Corporations and an autonomous body within the Secretariat, of which I have the privilege to be the executive director.

The objectives of the commission and the center are the following:

(1) To further understanding of the nature and the political, legal, economic, and social effects of the activities of transnational corporations in home countries and host countries and in international relations, particularly between developed and developing countries;
(2) To secure effective international arrangements for the operation of transnational corporations designed to promote their contribution to national and developmental goals and world economic growth while controlling and eliminating their negative effects; and
(3) To strengthen the negotiating capacity of host countries, in particular the developing countries, in their dealings with transnational corporations.

The commission decided to give the highest priority to the formulation of a code of conduct. The Group of Eminent Persons had considered the varying interpretations that may be attached to this term and had made it clear that what it had in mind was "a consistent set of recommendations which are gradually evolved and which may be revised as experience or circumstances require. Although they are not compulsory in character, they act as an instrument of moral persuasion, strengthened by the authority of international organizations and the support of public opinion." Furthermore, the group considered that a code should go beyond general recommendations by adding that it should be "attuned to particular sectors or categories." It implied that the code should take into account the variety of issues involved, the idiosyncrasies of particular economic sectors, the different levels of development of countries, and the nonuniform character of transnational corporations.

Closely related to the foregoing issue is a whole series of questions relating to the juridical nature and effects which the code of conduct should ultimately bear. Should the code be mandatory in nature, or should it take the form of a simple declaration of principles? In either case, should it also contain some international machinery to ensure or monitor compliance with the norms it spells out? Should it be addressed only to transnational corporations, or states, or both? Although these questions were left unresolved the commission reached agreement and made significant decisions in other respects. For instance, it was agreed that work on the drafting of the code should proceed without delay, and that, whatever its nature, the code of conduct when completed should be effective.

The commission is the body with primary responsibilities for the drafting of the code. At its second session, held in Lima, March 1-12, 1976, the commission adopted and recommended to ECOSOC a procedure for the formulation of the code, the sources to be consulted, the framework in which such consultation should take place, and the time limits within which to accomplish the task. An intergovernmental working group of the whole on the code of conduct was established. This group will meet intersessionally and will carry out its task with the help of a number of important inputs.

At the governmental level it will be necessary to articulate more precisely respective views and proposals on a code. Toward this end two procedures are envisaged. First, individual governments will be invited to submit their views and proposals. Second, and perhaps more important, regional meetings were organized during the second half of 1976 which were intended to bring together representatives of developing countries in Africa, Asia, and Latin America respectively, with a view to defining proposals for a code in the light of the particular conditions and needs in each of the regions.

The center has been requested to prepare two important documents. One deals with the various substantive issues related to the scope and content of the code. Hopefully, this study will be of some help to governments in defining their own views and proposals. The second document, which will be completed late in 1976, will focus on issues related to the actual formulation of the code, particularly the possible structural alternatives and their implications, including possible institutional arrangements.

Of course, the working group has been requested also to take into account the relevant work done elsewhere, both within the U.N. system by organizations such as the U.N. Conference on Trade and Development (UNCTAD), and outside the U.N. system such as in the Organization for Economic Cooperation and Development (OECD), the European Economic Community (EEC), and the Organization of American States (OAS). The commission recognized the necessity of receiving inputs from nongovernmental interested parties, in particular from business, trade unions, and consumer groups. In the first instance, the center has been requested to solicit the views of these groups and to incorporate them into a document to be submitted to the working group. This will be done during the coming months.[1] Provision has also been made for direct assistance to the working group by individuals with experience in business, trade unions, and other groups.

This decision actually goes beyond the work on the code of conduct. When establishing the commission, ECOSOC called upon it to select persons with extensive practical experience in the areas just mentioned and to associate them in its work in a manner that it deems appropriate. The commission was unable to take a decision on this matter at its first session. A decision has now been made. The commission has requested that we, after consultations with all its members, propose to the commission some time during the second or third quarter of 1976 the names of twelve to fifteen persons. These persons would thus be available to assist the working group as well as the commission when it meets again in 1977. At the same time, we in the center will, of course, remain in touch with all interested parties.[2]

It is envisaged that the working group should have ready: (1) an annotated outline of the code by the time of the third session of the commission; and (2) a final draft of the code by the fourth session of the commission, namely by the spring of 1978.

While stressing that the formulation of a code of conduct receive the highest priority, the commission recognized the importance of moving ahead concurrently in a number of other areas. The commission requested the center to move ahead speedily with the collection of publicly available information of a general or specific nature, including the preparation of profiles on individual transnational corporations. The commission recognized the magnitude of this task and urged that the necessary computer facilities be made available to the center.

Without wishing to minimize the importance of publicly available information, the commission is anxious that the information collected by the center go beyond that which may be publicly available. The commission was, of course, aware of the constraints imposed by existing national legislation and of the requirements of business confidentiality, which may present obstacles to the collection of information that is normally not publicly available. It therefore requested the center to undertake a feasibility study in order to identify more clearly what the problems are and what measures should be considered to overcome them.

As mandated by the commission, the center is now in the process of establishing the group of experts on international standards of accounting and reporting, which will hold its first meeting in late August of 1976. This group will review existing reporting practices and will propose a minimum number of items and their definitions which should be included in corporate reports.[3]

In the equally important area of research, the commission, on the basis of a survey carried out by the center, concluded that while considerable work is being done, it is not sufficiently problem-oriented and does not focus adequately on the impact of transnational corporations in developing countries. The commission therefore decided that a considerable body of work was to be carried out or promoted by the center, ranging from a comprehensive, integrated study which will be a sequel to the study carried out by the U.N. Secretariat in 1973, to in-depth studies covering such vital issues as the impact of transnational corporations on the balance of payments, particularly of developing countries; the effects of investments by transnational corporations on investment and production by domestic enterprises; and the effects of transnational corporations on employment. In addition, the center has been requested to examine the role and impact of transnational corporations in a number of sectors, notably banking, insurance, shipping, tourism, and the extractive, food, and phamaceutical industries.

The commission also attached great importance and urgency to the center's technical cooperation program, which is aimed at strengthening the negotiating capability of the developing countries. It endorsed the proposals contained in one of the documents the center prepared for Lima. This assistance will take a variety of forms. Advisers will be made available to requesting governments to assist them on matters which could range from national investment policies and legislation and their application to specific investment proposals. We will also continue to organize training workshops for government officials, and we will respond to inquiries from governments for specific information. I am convinced that effective and informed negotiators on both sides of the table can reduce significantly the areas of contention and are therefore in the interest of all concerned.

The General Assembly unanimously adopted a resolution on corrupt practices in December 1975. It requested the Commission on Transnational Corporations to include this problem in its program of work. An initial discussion therefore took place in Lima. The commission took two specific measures. First, it requested the center to undertake studies on the subject of corrupt practices with a view to assisting the commission in making recommendations on ways and means of effectively preventing them. Second, it received a proposal by the United States which called for the establishment of a working group to prepare an international agreement on the subject. This initiative was generally appreciated and welcomed. However, some delegations felt that more time was needed to study the matter. For this reason, and because the scope of the U.S. proposal covered not only foreign direct investment but also trade, it was recommended the ECOSOC consider this issue and take appropriate action at its July 1976 session.[4]

As you can see, a good deal of activity is under way. The accomplishments so far are not minimal. Of course, many serious problems remain to be solved and much work, debate, and negotiating still need to take place. But the process has been launched and that, in itself, is a significant demonstration of the responsiveness of the international system to contemporary problems.

Notes

1. (Editor's note.) Views and proposals of states and of nongovernmental interests on a code of conduct are summarized in U.N. documents E/C.10/19, and E/C.10/20 and Add. 1, respectively.

2. (Editor's note.) The Commission on Transnational Corporations met in early March 1977 and selected sixteen persons to assist it in its work.

3. (Editor's note.) The first meeting of the Group of Experts on International Standards of Accounting and Reporting met in August 1976.

4. (Editor's note.) The Council adopted resolution 2041 (LXI) on August 5, 1976, in which it decided to establish an ad hoc intergovernmental working group to conduct an examination of the problem of corrupt practices.

MONETARY AND TRADE POLICIES

17. A Monetary Regime for the 1980s
Edward L. Morse

The Jamaica agreements to formally modify the basic rules that govern the international monetary system have given rise to two general conclusions, neither of which should be warranted except perhaps in the very short run. One conclusion is that there is nothing very new happening in the international financial arena that should lead a scholar or policymaker to redefine or reexamine his or her assumptions about the way that arena operates. The other conclusion is that those who pessimistically argued that the management of the international economy was in the process of possibly irreversible breakdown, with the dispersal and decentralization of economic power, were wrong. Optimism rather than pessimism has now become a prevailing mood among those concerned with governing not simply the international monetary system, but, more generally, the world economy.

When one tries to examine recent events and trends in the international economy and to focus upon a longer time frame, one should pause on both counts. A great deal that is new and even unprecedented seems to be happening in the international economy, which makes it decreasingly plausible to rely on time-tested assumptions. Whether one looks at recent trends in debtor-creditor relationships, or at attempts to deal with price stability and employment, or at the effectiveness of older, more comfortable patterns of relations among central banks and finance ministries, the same general conclusion seems to be borne out: things do not work the way textbook analysis would dictate. And the extrapolation of trends like the politicization of issues in the international economy—at East-West, North-South, or even West-West levels of interaction—can only bring discomfort once one's vision moves from the immediate future to the next decade.

Events and shifts occuring during the past five to ten years in patterns of economic and political relations among societies might well be described as far more momentous and fundamental than one often prefers to believe. Indeed, they have been described as revolutionary, in the sense that they represent a shift from an older system—the fixed rate Bretton Woods system—to something which is not only new, but in the minds of some people, untried—a managed floating rate arrangement. To be sure, elements of what is now being tried can be found in the past in efforts to manage a floating rate system in the 1930s. But the present, highly interdependent context is vastly different from previous efforts to manage floating.

One clear difference between what is now happening and the way the international monetary system was governed during the 1950s and 1960s is that, while formerly governments agreed to adjust their economies to one another to provide new liquidity, or to intervene in private financial markets according to more or less explicit rules, now the system is guided only by the loosest of rules. To be sure, an optimist might argue that this shift from the Bretton Woods system of both implicit and explicit rules to a floating rate system with only the loosest of agreement on guiding principles is quite a fortunate development. The older arrangements, after all, reflected a world that was dominated economically and politically by the United States, whose government played the key role in managing the world economy as well as in providing general security for an enormous number of other societies. Today's world has become increasingly pluralistic and in such a world it would be unrealistic to expect that the rules of the earlier system would now be relevant.

Moreover, if there were one fundamental characteristic of the international political economy during the past five to ten years it would be change—change in the locus and fundamental meaning of economic power. A decade ago it still seemed to those who observed such things that the twentieth century was an era of American technological, military, and economic prowess. By the beginning of the 1970s, after the devaluation of the dollar, inflation in the United States—and indeed the world economy—brought on by deficit expenditures in paying the costs of the Vietnam war and the flourishing of economies in Western Europe, it appeared as though economic and political power had shifted from the United States to other parts of the industrialized world. But soon thereafter the Organization of Petroleum Exporting Countries (OPEC) cartel price increases, calls for a new international economic order, and the selective levelling of embargoes in oil as well as soybeans made it appear that Europe and Japan's ascendance would be short lived.

With oil import payments made in dollars, the American economy regained some of its lost economic power. But, more significantly, economic decisions that counted were now being made outside the industrialized world—in oil exporting countries, especially in the Middle East, and in commodity rich countries of the less-developed world. The unity of less-developed countries in a variety of international forums and the forcefulness and stridency of demands to protect national economic sovereignty made the dispersion of economic power all the more striking.

Changes in the location and nature of economic power were accompanied by other interrelated shifts, which were by no means inconsequential. Double-digit and seemingly unmanageable inflation in the industrial world, together with paralysis in governmental decision making and the reemergence of class consciousness in many richer democracies called into question (in a recessionary environment) the very stability of industrial society as we have known it since World War II. Defensive actions, including impulses toward trade restrictionism for the first time since the establishment of the liberalizing General Agreement on Tariffs and Trade (GATT) trading rules, provoked the danger that a spiral of unilateral abrogations of commercial rules would tear apart the trade and payments system. Another relatively new phenomenon—the synchronization of cycles within the world economy—demonstrated, furthermore, that the economy had indeed become global for the first time in history. And, there were simply no political instruments available to governments to manage this global economy, if only because there was no international consensus on the goals to be sought or the tools to be used.

Some optimists who accept the ineluctable nature of change in the world economy would argue that the flexible exchange rate system, which succeeded Bretton Woods has in fact provided new instruments for managing the international economy. And their argument would be buttressed theoretically by the logic that dictates that flexible rates permit governments to achieve autonomy—lost during the Bretton Woods era—in domestic demand management. As well, flexible rates, for a while at least, seem to defuse the heady politics of adjustment and trade friction associated with the fixed rate regime. Most importantly, an optimist would regard the events of the last half decade as demonstrating that the major governments in the international economy have, in confronting unprecedented change, been able to cooperate remarkably with one another. Indeed, as some of the optimists would argue, the basic characteristic of international negotiations leading up to Jamaica is that of cooperative and incremental change associated with the working out of something new: rules for managing a flexible rate system. Some would go further and argue that in the face of crisis, the major participants in the world economy have committed themselves to their long-term goal of fostering a relatively free international market based on relatively free trade. And, they would argue, the only way to do this today is not by institution building along the lines of 1945, but rather through the development of a common law tradition in the international monetary system, similar to the development of the British common law system. This, they assert, can be done only with experimentation and a long-term process of norm generation and rule making at the international level.

Pessimistic reactions to these recent events and apparent shifts in the structure of international financial flows and its management would emphasize rather different factors. Here, the argument would be put forward that the Bretton Woods rules have been irremediably broken, and they are being replaced not by a new system of rules, but rather by an anarchical system. A system without rules is no system at all. The lack of international guidelines has two principal repercussions, each of which is to be feared. Internally, the lack of guidelines creates a loss of discipline required for effective demand management. When trade-offs exist in choices governments make in dealing with price stability, balance-of-payments equilibrium, growth, and employment, governments will more likely select options whose repercussions are far more inflationary than would otherwise be the case. In terms of foreign economic policy, the lack of international rules facilitates unilateral governmental actions associated less with international cooperation than with "damage limitation." Such unilateral actions are guided almost entirely by domestic considerations. Their international effect is not simply to distort trade and the benefits of relatively efficient international markets, but to reinforce a climate in which unilateral trade measures serve, in a spiral effect of actions and reactions by other governments, to break down even further the norms and goals of a liberal world economic order. Unilateral foreign economic policy measures, in short, politicize those very economic issues that the International Monetary Fund (IMF)–GATT system was designed to defuse. And, as economic issues become politicized the potential is increased for anarchy in the international economy and the breakdown of the whole trade and payments system from which all participants have benefited.

It would be difficult for any sensible observer of the international economy to argue that either the pessimistic or optimistic view is necessarily wrong. A number of elements in the current situation give verisimilitude to both. And, it is difficult to develop guidelines for determining how to evaluate which argument has the greater validity, whether it is the optimistic account (which is based on the need for and likelihood of international cooperation) or, the pessimistic position (which stresses the lack of discipline currently manifested in the international economy). However, it seems clear that whichever position one is inclined to accept or to emphasize, it is impossible to escape the conclusion that a great deal of fundamental change has been taking place in the trade and payments system. And, therefore, it is essential to ask whether recent changes and transformations in the international economy require a form of management different from anything attempted in the past.

When one focuses upon questions of managing the international economy it is obviously essential first to ask whether any past experience in governing the international economy will be relevant for the next decade and beyond. Is there anything, for example, in the experience of managed floating in the 1930s or in the fixed-rate Bretton Woods system of the 1950s and 1960s which provide lessons for the future? Or, have recent changes been so great as to force us to rethink how the rules might be developed for the collective management of the international economy generally, and the international monetary system more specifically? This, in turn, leads one to question the stability of the Jamaica solution: Will the Jamaica agreements have a built-in stability, or will they generate instability not only in the middle run but in the long run as well?

It seems that fundamental changes in the international economy in the recent past, if projected into the near and mid-term future, provide a context within which judgments on this series of questions might be formulated. Two types of change, in particular, warrant further thought. One has to do with the growth in the horizontal scope of the international economy during the past few decades. The other has to do with the integration of markets—financial and otherwise—within the system and beyond anything which has hitherto existed.

The growth in the international economy—from one that effectively circumscribed only the advanced, market-based societies (roughly the Organization for Economic Cooperation and Development [OECD] area) to one of global proportions—has been surprising and difficult to manage. For the first time, elements of a global economy exist, especially through financial mechanisms: "business cycles" or more general cyclical fluctuations now involve or significantly affect virtually all societies simultaneously. The synchronization of cycles within the OECD area has certainly been clear and has spawned such new and highly political efforts as summit meetings to cope with their effects.

But the synchronization of cycles goes far beyond the OECD area and touches the economies of the less-developed and socialist worlds. If the globalization of the world economy is to continue, efforts at managing cyclical fluctuations will become extraordinarily difficult to implement. Conflicting political objectives pursued by the governments of the Federal Republic of Germany, France, and Britain have made such efforts difficult within the European communities. The same sorts of conflicts impede even modest coordination among Japan, the United States, and Germany within the OECD area. If the precedents set by these efforts are valid, there is no clear way that politically reliable solutions will be found when they need to involve such less-developed country governments as Brazil, Mexico, or Iran, let alone such Eastern governments as the Soviet Union, Hungary, or Poland.

The second apparently inexorable trend—the growth in interdependence through the integration of various markets—poses more difficult intellectual and policy problems than the horizontal extension of the international economy. For within the global economy, some parts have achieved much higher levels of interdependence than others. In monetary terms, these more interdependent areas generally form "optimal currency areas." All other things being equal, this would provide a natural basis for forming discrete, probably regional, monetary systems. Yet, none of these highly interdependent areas form a closed universe and they cannot become encapsulated. Together with other well-known features of an interdependent world, those of differential levels of financial integration and openness pose almost insuperable problems of management.

It appears that if these trends involving the globalization of economic relations, on the one hand, and market integration and interdependence, on the other hand, continue, the management of the international monetary system will look radically different in the future from what it has been in the past. As well, it means that appropriate planning might enable governments to avoid some major problems and to steer the structural development of the international economy in ways in which most, if not all, societies benefit. But, constitutional planning for the international monetary system, itself, poses some rather general questions. These might be summarized under two headings.

First, how might we expect governments to behave in this world toward which we appear to be moving? Upon what sorts of monetary and trade instruments are they likely to want to rely? How will governments try to manage a global economy that will reflect processes and activities not simply of governments, but of private individuals and institutions as well? What appropriate management areas might emerge? Will a central management area be constructed around the Group of Ten, which successfully, if informally, has provided liquidity and confidence in the international economy? Will a new group of five, six, or seven governments emerge as the central management arena and involve the United States, Britain, France, Germany, Japan, Italy, and Canada? Will additional governments currently outside the central network—like Iran, Mexico, Brazil, or Saudi Arabia—be brought centrally into an informal club that manages the system? Might some Eastern economies be co-opted, if only for management of debt burdens? Will governments be willing to allow informal arrangements to emerge or will more formal, constitutional arrangements be required?

Whatever the answers might be to these and related questions, it is clear that effective planning for the management of the international monetary system will require an accurate assessment of likely behavioral patterns on the parts of governments and large-scale private actors.

A second set of questions relates to normative approaches in the construction of monetary regimes. They relate less to what governments are likely to want than to what they should want. What is the range of plausible monetary regimes that we might imagine as being relevant for major monetary problems of the next ten to twenty years? In what ways would each such regime usefully describe how management areas should be developed? What sorts of organizational patterns can we conceptualize that will deal with an increasingly global and interdependent system? What trade-offs exist among these patterns in terms of who is likely to benefit most from each?

Neither set of questions readily provides or suggests immediate answers. I do believe, however, that we can sketch out a variety of ways that we can expect these questions to be answered, and that it is important to do this now if we want to maintain stability in the international monetary system, and if we are to assure the maximization of a variety of forms of equity and efficiency within that system.[1]

Governmental behavior in foreign economic policy is likely to be characterized increasingly by defensive attitudes and actions. The desire to ward off the most perverse consequences of international interdependence will likely predominate over other motivations. Having found themselves vulnerable to a host of "imported" phenomena, including inflation, unemployment, and monetary speculation, governments' major aims will be to reduce the vulnerability of their economies to those external interruptions that are induced largely by economic openness.

The assumption that governmental motivation will be based on the rather negative desire to avoid vulnerability and disruptions induced from abroad contrasts markedly with two alternative assumptions that are usually made about what governments primarily want. On the one hand, there are those who argue that, in economic affairs as in security affairs, governments seek essentially to increase their power or wealth, and, when necessary, to do this at the expense of others. This assumption runs through analyses that focus primarily on so-called political as opposed to economic factors. On the other hand, there are those who argue that foreign economic policy will be motivated primarily by the selection of the most efficient way to optimalize welfare gains from trade, investment, or short-term capital flows. This assumption predominates in analyses that focus on putatively economic factors. Neither the traditional political nor economic focus seems to reflect accurately the way governments act in an interdependent environment, although the rationales that underlie them remain plausible. For reasons too complex to put forward here, it appears that the assumption concerning defensive orientation will be far more realistic as a key to understanding foreign economic policy in an interdependent world.[2]

Defensive actions will consist largely of attempts by governments to close off their economies to those aspects of interdependence, like integrated international financial markets, that make it more difficult to carry out internal distribution of wealth. Governments will also be conscious of ways to reduce the "importation" of recession and inflation. This will not necessarily mean that one should necessarily expect an increase in the use of such border controls as tariffs, capital controls, or quotas. Rather, governments can be expected to take a series of internal measures, including manipulation of interest rates or fiscal policies, which will have effects similar to border controls.

In general the major governments with which we are concerned can be expected to follow one of two overall defensive strategies in their foreign economic policies. One strategy is to reduce interdependence with others through direct measures. The other is to try to institutionalize to one degree or another their policy interdependence with other economies to create new patterns of joint international management and control. That is to say, governments are likely to try to move out of the system to some degree, or to integrate their policies more fully with other governments. In both instances, governments will aim to increase their control over the international economic environment. Whether they try to reduce vulnerability through new forms of national encapsulation or to institutionalize interdependence will depend largely upon economic size and openness. As well, the strategy will be affected in part by noneconomic goals that a government might pursue in its foreign policy, including international security concerns and preferences for creating regional institutions (especially in the case of European governments).

In addition to being defensive, foreign economic policy is likely to be motivated by—and oriented toward—domestic concerns and interests rather than toward external targets. Several factors will push governments in this direction, including pressures from different constituencies to maintain price stability or bolster employment levels. Additionally, electoral politics will play a role, as will the more general desire of governments to enhance their own authority and autonomy in managing the domestic economy. Indeed, since the majority of the governments centrally involved in managing the international economy will continue to be OECD area countries with democratic political systems, the role of electoral politics should not be minimized. The point, however, is that foreign economic policy will be designed less as a means of bolstering foreign policy objectives (as for example was the case of Gaullist foreign economic policy in France in the 1960s) than of bolstering the domestic socioeconomic objectives of governments.

In summary, the major motivations of foreign economic policy in the years ahead will be dual: on the one hand, foreign economic policy will aim to reduce the vulnerability of economies and societies to the unmanageable consequences of international interdependence; on the other hand, it will be oriented primarily toward the achievement of domestic rather than foreign objectives.

An analysis of governmental motivations alone will not enable us to sketch out viable institutional patterns through which international monetary relations might be managed over the next five to fifteen years. As well, we should add the premise that governments will be willing to accept greater regulation of their monetary relations with others if such regulation will maximize potential benefits from both market interdependence and policy interdependence, and if governments will be able through new international regulatory mechanisms to preserve— or enhance—national control over domestic demand management. If we then add a set of broadly distinguishable notions about other sorts of goals, four types of management systems can be defined as reasonably realistic for the next decade or so.

1. The most obvious type of international monetary regime that comes up continually in discussions is highly centralized and based on the principle of "global efficiency" in fostering liberalized trade, with minimization of financial market upheaval, the defusion of politics associated with the adjustment process, and the facilitation of economic

development. This sort of regime has often been recommended as the only viable long-range approach to global monetary order. In recent years it has been discussed in the context of providing necessary credits to deal with the over-all structural imbalance in the international economy that results from the "permanent" surpluses that certain oil-exporting countries are expected to maintain. A centralized regime could be created by the advanced market-based societies through a deliberate process of long-term planning. It could also come about as a means of coping with a severe liquidity crisis associated with efforts by oil-exporting countries to draw down petromoney investments to pay for eventual trade deficits. Another scenario sees the creation of new central banking facilities as part of a global bargain between the West and less-developed countries in dealing with debt burdens in the North-South dialogue. Still another scenario sees a high degree of centralization resulting from efforts to reinstitute fixed-exchange rates. However it might come about, it would likely be supported by less-developed countries since it would provide mechanisms to assure both credit and fixed-exchange rates, which those nations want in order to facilitate their development goals.

2. The logical inverse of a centralized regime is one based on narrowly defined national economic interests. It could come about through the continued fragmentation of the international monetary system in particular, and the international economy more generally. Elements of fragmentation include the gradual elimination—or delimitation—of the multiple roles of the dollar (reserve currency, interventionary currency, medium of exchange, store of value, etc.), the bringing under national control of the Eurodollar and other parallel international financial markets, and the desire evidenced by most governments to reduce significantly the exposure of their domestic economies to external interruptions. Many observers of the international economy would regard such a regime as a deterioration of the interdependent monetary system that has emerged since World War II. Yet, it is not at all clear that a fragmented system would necessarily reduce the gains from—or the desirability of preserving—a system of free trade. But, free trade conditions would not likely be regarded highly by even most of the major participants in a fragmented system and would be difficult to preserve. Such a regime would more clearly be oriented to the preservation of national economic controls and to the reduction of asymmetries that describe the current regime.

3. More plausible, perhaps, than a fully fragmented system would be a regime based on regional (or otherwise limited) economic areas, each of which would work out its own relations with other regional areas.

As under the fragmented regime, governments would be motivated in this instance primarily by the desire to reduce the vulnerability of their economies to external forces. But, they would also find it in their interest to associate themselves with other governments in order to preserve many of the benefits of economic openness. Such associated arrangements would likely be regional because of strong political ties between countries within different geographical areas who, acting together, would be able to assure a more equitable distribution of power in the world. Regional associations would in some instances be based on key currencies (e.g., the dollar, yen, or Deutschemark), or, under other scenarios, would be based on internationally created assets or units of account (e.g., Europa or petromoney).

4. A fourth and much more plausible arrangement would be a regime based primarily on efforts of the governments of the West collectively to manage market and policy interdependences, to preserve traditional liberal values, and to manage jointly their mutual vulnerabilities. The regime would be created in part by the greater need these governments have to coordinate domestic demand management policies, but also by the need to manage long-term debts likely to arise in some parts of the industrial world (e.g., Britain, France, or Italy). The creation of this regime would be predicated upon the recognition that obstacles to creating a fully centralized system cannot be overcome at this juncture. The regime would be characterized, then, by incremental departures from the existing system, but it would make far more explicit the responsibility of the major OECD countries for managing the system for their own good as well as on behalf of other societies.

It should be noted that the four regimes ought not to be thought of as mutually exclusive efforts with respect to the objectives that governments would want to enhance or to the treatment of such issues as potential adjustment mechanisms, reserve assets, or desired level of currency convertibility. Each is, rather, based on a discrete managerial principle. Insofar as each has its roots well within the present international monetary area, it represents a plausible direction that the system might take if pressures moving it in one direction became sufficiently powerful. It is likely that the future system will—just as the current one does—embody aspects of each of these regimes, but it will stress certain elements and relationships and minimize others.

For a variety of reasons I find the fourth regime to be both the most likely one to emerge in the future, and the most desirable. As I argue more fully elsewhere,[3] I feel that the binding cement of such a regime will be the development of explicit rules for managing exchange-rate relationships. Whether these rules are called rules for managed floating or rules for fixing exchange rates will make little difference, since in practice I do not think the two will look very different from one another.

This regime would be tiered and centered around the five or six major Western economies whose international trade and financial levels would give them a special role. Special arrangements would have to be made for governments of the South and for the East, including arrangements for market access, commodities, efforts to postpone or otherwise relieve debt burdens, and efforts to stabilize private financial markets. But, the system would, in sum, be differently interdependent and pluralistic. It would, therefore, reflect the messy crosscutting and contradictory factors that are likely to characterize the international economy over the next decade or so—but it would also be ordered and promote stability.

However desirable such a system might be, four major obstacles stand in its way. First, nonparticipants would attack it as inequitable. They would demand participation in decision making by others when those decisions have an impact on them. Second, the regime would work only if members of the central club were willing to work out an economic truce among themselves. If the United States or some other government felt its interests would be better served through unilateral action and decision making, the system would not work. Nor would it work if the core countries did not develop a systemwide frame of reference for managing their domestic economies—a special burden on the governments of Europe or Japan. Third, the regime might be viewed as impeding the achievement of such other high priority goals as European integration, so that governments would be unwilling to support it. Finally, the regime's long-run success would depend on its acceptability to the less-developed countries outside the inner club.

There are, however, sufficient incentives and sweeteners to overcome these obstacles. The major open questions are whether the market-based advanced nations will be willing to constitutionalize their relationships rather than leave them to evolve on an informal basis, and whether non-Western governments will perceive the system to be sufficiently in their interest so that they would cooperate in its development.

Notes

1. For a more complete treatment of these themes, see my essay, "Political Choice and Alternative Monetary Regimes," in Fred Hirsch, Michael Doyle, and Edward L. Morse, *Alternatives to Monetary Disorder* (New York: McGraw-

Hill for the 1980s Project/Council on Foreign Relations, 1977), pp. 65-139.
2. This case is argued at greater length in Edward L. Morse, *Modernization and the Transformation of International Relations* (New York: The Free Press, 1976), chapters 4 and 5.
3. See source listed in note 1, above.

18. Monetary Reform at Jamaica
Richard N. Cooper

The last year has seen numerous high-level conferences on the functioning of the world economy. A special session of the United Nations General Assembly was devoted to it in September 1975. The heads of state of six leading nations met at the Château de Rambouillet in November 1975. The Paris meeting between oil-producing and oil-consuming nations met in December, with an agenda that went way beyond oil. And, in January 1976, the Interim Committee of the International Monetary Fund (IMF) met in Jamaica. The frequency and the high-level participation at such meetings testify to the turmoil prevailing on the world economic scene. At issue are the international monetary system, resource scarcity and prices, transfers of resources to the poorest nations, and the short-run performance of the world economy. The Rambouillet meeting was ostensibly concerned primarily with the last of these issues, while the Jamaica meeting was concerned with the first. But, in fact, each issue intruded strongly on the others.

The Jamaica meeting was distinguished among these conferences by having led to concrete, substantive decisions. It addressed the regime of exchange rates among countries, the disposition of gold in the international system, and the enlargement of lines of credit to developing nations.

A New Regime for Exchange Rates

The Jamaica agreement legitimized flexible exchange rates. Once ratified, the new Article IV of the Articles of Agreement of the

From *Reflections on Jamaica*, Edward M. Bernstein et al. (eds.). Essays in International Finance, No. 115, April 1976. Reprinted by permission of the International Finance Section, Department of Economics, Princeton University, Princeton, N.J.

International Monetary Fund will make "legal" prevailing practices that are not permissible under the original Bretton Woods agreements, still formally in force though in fact in abeyance.

The new Article IV pays obeisance to exchange-rate stability and even envisages a time when fixed parities can be reestablished "on the basis of the underlying stability of the world economy" and with an 85 percent majority of the total voting power of the IMF. (This percentage was chosen to permit either the United States or the European Community [EEC] to block such a restoration.) But the language is carefully chosen. Countries pledge themselves "to promote a stable system of exchange rates," not a system of stable exchange rates. And they are to "seek to promote stability by fostering orderly underlying economic and financial conditions and a monetary system that does not tend to produce erratic disruptions," thus implying that "unstable" exchange rates are a consequence of unstable underlying conditions rather than a failure to fix the rates. The new article in effect allows each country to have any regime of exchange rates that it wants, subject only to the conditions (1) that it notify the IMF of its arrangements and (2) that it "avoid manipulating exchange rates or the international monetary system in order to prevent effective balance of payments adjustment or to gain an unfair competitive advantage over other members."

Having legitimized a system of flexible rates, the Jamaica conferees left open all the difficult problems of actually managing a system of flexible rates. I take for granted that governments will intervene from time to time in the foreign-exchange markets. All major governments are now held responsible for managing their economies, and this can hardly encompass total abstention from directly influencing an economic variable as important for most countries as the exchange rate. We therefore need supplementary provisions for coordinating both the objectives of intervention and the actual practice of intervention, so that two countries do not find themselves working at cross-purposes on the same exchange rate.

For most countries formal coordination will not be necessary, since they can rely on their small size relative to the world economy and can frame their intervention policies against some major currency or bundle of currencies (such as the sixteen-currency special drawing rights [SDR]). For the sake of overall economic stability, however, there must be some mechanism for calling into account countries that either strongly undervalue or strongly overvalue their currencies, in accordance with the limited stricture on exchange-rate regimes noted above.

For major countries, coordination of exchange-rate policies needs to be more explicitly cooperative, since stability of the world economy can be aided by avoiding erratic movements in exchange rates among major currencies. Guidance for intervention should involve two components, in my judgment: (1) avoiding rapid rates of change in exchange rates, except when they are manifestly necessary owing to rapid and unexpected changes in underlying conditions, i.e., assuring orderly markets, as we try to do with money and bond markets and in a more limited way with commodity markets; and (2) linking intervention policies to national levels of international reserves to assure that exchange rates are not allowed to deviate very far from the rates that would clear the market without intervention over a period of time, i.e., requiring that if reserves are built up or run down relative to desired levels (which would have to be established) as a result of intervention designed to smooth movements in exchange rates, the direction of intervention should be reversed when market conditions permit so as to move reserves back to the desired levels. Reserve management, in other words, should be similar in character to ideal buffer-stock management or to monetary management, which involve short-term price targets and long-term volume targets.

The Jamaica agreement leaves all these important operating details to be worked out. No doubt they will be worked out on the basis of practical experience in the next few years.

Disposition of Gold

Amending the IMF articles to permit exchange-rate flexibility is a good step. But it merely legitimizes the status quo and represents no real innovation. Currencies must of necessity float for some time to come. The agreement on gold, in contrast, introduces an important innovation. In an arrangement that is a variant of one that Professor Kaji, Dr. Segré, and I proposed to the Trilateral Commission in Tokyo in 1973 (Motoo Kaji, Richard N. Cooper, and Claudio Segré, *Towards a Renovated World Monetary System*, The Triangle Papers No. 1, New York, The Trilateral Commission, 1973), the IMF will sell one-sixth (25 million ounces) of its substantial gold holdings on the private market and will devote the capital gains from such sales (the difference between the price it fetches on the market and the official price of $42.22 an ounce) to helping the poorest countries of the world, especially those that have been hit hardest by the increase in oil prices and the current world recession. Estimates differ on how large the gains will be, but if the average price of these sales is $100 an ounce (compared with a current market price of around $140 an ounce), then the total gains will be about $1.5 billion, spread over the four years of the projected sales. This is not a huge amount, but it will help significantly, particularly if it can be used as leverage for larger amounts of private or official funds, for example by subsidizing the interest rates on World Bank loans.

The agreement on gold is deficient in two respects. First, although the new draft Article IV does specifically exclude the use of gold as a basis to which monetary values are tied, the agreement does not settle the issue of monetary gold for the future; further understandings will be necessary, particularly on the extent to which central banks may buy or sell gold. In addition to the one-sixth of the IMF gold to be sold on the market, for instance, a further sixth is to be redistributed to member countries. What are they to do with it? That is not settled. Provision is made, however, for a procedure to decide on the disposition of the remaining IMF gold.

Second, the agreement to sell one-sixth of the gold is marred by a side understanding that, in one fashion or another, all developing countries will get their prorated share of that gold, at market prices. Thus the capital gains available for distribution to the poorest countries will arise only from the share (about two-thirds) that was originally subscribed to the IMF by developed countries. In effect, moderately wealthy countries such as Argentina and Venezuela have refused to aid in this fashion such desperately poor countries as Chad and Bangladesh, even though the arrangement would have involved no direct cost to them. There is, of course, an opportunity cost, in the language of economists, but that exists for developed countries as well. The precedent is a bad one and has not been missed in the developed countries. France in the end abandoned its position that all the IMF's gold should be returned to its original subscribers. But Australian officials have been heard to mutter that perhaps they should withdraw from the IMF to get their gold, and two American senators have introduced a bill in Congress that would insist on distribution to original subscribers (fortunately, the bill has little chance of passing).

Earlier suggestions by developing countries that major central banks should buy the gold to prevent the market price from falling (and hence to increase the capital gains) happily were overtaken by sounder judgement at Jamaica, when it was realized that in the long run such an action would probably kill the special drawing rights of the IMF, which are more important to developing countries.

Financing World Economic Recovery

The central concern of the Jamaica meetings, however, was the state of the world economy, and rightly so. Economic recovery seems to be taking place, but it is limping rather than leaping ahead.... The weak recovery means that the earnings of primary producing countries—

many less-developed countries plus countries such as Australia and Finland—will remain low. And it means also that sectoral protectionist pressures in the industrialized economies will remain high. Protectionist moves, such as Britain's recent restrictions on imports of textiles, will reduce the earnings of those developing countries that have been successful in selling manufactured goods on the world market.

Moreover, many countries of the world, including the smaller industrial countries as well as non-OPEC (Organization of Petroleum Exporting Countries) developing countries, have experienced an alarming growth in external debt. Indeed, these countries have been supporting world economic activity, particularly the production of equipment, by their heavy borrowing—an example, to paraphrase Keynes, of national vice being international virtue. But the outstanding debt has now reached staggering proportions—probably $160 billion for the non-OPEC developing countries alone, nearly twice the level of late 1972. . . . (While world inflation has eroded the real burden of debt outstanding before 1973, the rise in interest rates and in outstanding debt far outstripped world inflation in 1974 and 1975.) This magnitude of borrowing is not likely to continue, for both borrowers and lenders have become extremely uneasy about it. If developing countries are not to cut back their imports significantly, and thereby set back world economic recovery, the receipts of these countries must be greatly increased. The best way to do this is through a more vigorous world recovery.

Faster recovery could take place in most industrial countries without threatening faster inflation. Unemployment is at a postwar high in all the major industrial countries, and capacity-utilization rates are low. Faster recovery would raise primary-product prices, but it would not raise the prices of finished goods appreciably faster than they will rise anyway, for cyclical productivity increases would result in lower average costs despite higher materials prices.

The economic summit meeting at Rambouillet paid lip service to faster recovery, but in fact most of the corridor talk reflected a preoccupation with inflation. President Ford's veto of a bill to extend 1975 tax cuts into 1976—although later reversed—reflected the same preoccupation. Inflation unquestionably is a serious problem, but it is not susceptible to easy remedy. . . . The recovery could be nearly twice as fast as its current projection in the United States and still not have much effect on the rate of inflation, for unemployment would remain above 6 per cent of the labor force into 1977. To be sure, such a rapid recovery would require a significant deceleration in 1977. Faster recovery would both raise the volume of exports from developing countries and improve the terms of trade of primary producing countries.

The alternative, if cutbacks are to be avoided, is more loans. But whence? A key decision at Jamaica, taken at the behest of developing countries, was to extend temporarily the credit tranches of the IMF by 45 percent, pending the coming into force of an increase in total IMF quotas to $49 billion, also agreed at Jamaica. Each member country would be able to borrow that much more than it can now. The total amounts are not large—some $4 billion for all less-developed countries—and to some extent merely replace the expiring oil facility. But they presumably will also permit somewhat greater borrowing from the private sector.

In the absence of faster recovery and/or additional loans, world recovery will be delayed by declines in sales to developing countries; more serious, the liberalization of trade that has been so painstakingly accomplished in many less developed countries over the past decade will receive a grievous setback, as one country after another feels forced to restrict imports for balance-of-payments reasons. Korea and Brazil have already started in that direction. If deliberalization becomes widespread, it will take another decade to undo it. Domestic political resistance to trade liberalization is high, and because trade negotiations now exempt developing countries from reciprocity in trade liberalization, there are few offsetting domestic pressures.

Conclusion

The Jamaica meeting accomplished some important long-term objectives. It ignored other questions, such as the long-run role of the SDR and of reserve currencies, and the Eurocurrency market. But its most remarkable achievement was that finance ministers not only discussed the world economic scene together but actually took some action, in the form of gold sales and credit liberalization, to do something about it. If a crude analogy to national central banking may be made, IMF gold sales mark the beginning of international open-market operations (though in the present instance motivated by the prospect of usable capital gains rather than a desire to reduce currency holdings in the hands of the public), and liberalization of the IMF credit tranches represents the beginning of international rediscount policy. Jamaica may mark the introduction of a more coordinated approach to global economic policy.

19. The Institutionalization of Exchange Rates
Robert Roosa

In recent years, we have witnessed renewed attempts to develop an effective and equitable system of international exchange rates. To one acquainted with similar endeavors in the past, however, it would appear that the capacity for creating disorder is as striking under a regime of floating exchange as it is in a system characterized by fixed exchange rates. In the course of these experiences, we have had to relearn some lessons that had already been evident back in the 1930s. One of the successes of the Jamaica conference is that it validated a monetary system which had already been in existence for some time, and under which there would for the present be no implied commitment for any country to maintain a fixed par value of its currency. Second, the Jamaica agreements made a renewed commitment to many of the conditions that have traditionally been associated with a fixed parity system. The agreements even provided for a possible return to the fixed parity system for any country that desired to take that step. Thus, should conditions warrant it, the IMF would provide the structure through which this return could be accomplished.

The Jamaica meetings, therefore, legitimatized a world of floating or fluctuating exchange rates, within the framework of the International Monetary Fund. Second, it recognized that exchange rates, whether floating or fixed, must always serve two kinds of purposes: (1) to assure the transferability of goods and capital among countries through a medium of exchange that can actually be converted in the marketplace, and (2) to maintain through each country's exchange rate a norm that ideally reflects its potential for the export or import of goods or of capital in relation to the rest of the world. The participants recognized also that if a country wished to maintain a viable position in the world economy, that norm must reflect those conditions which define the limits within which any country's domestic economic policy ought to be formulated.

The agreements concerning the interconvertibility among currencies were one of the principal achievements of the Jamaica conference. They echo in part arrangements that had previously been agreed to at Rambouillet. Together these agreements have all of the technical conditions necessary for the continued conversion of one currency into another. Moreover, they have achieved this within a framework that will be relatively free of disorder. On the whole, the Jamaica design sought to avoid provisions designed to maintain order. They did, however, try to avoid disorder—and there is a meaningful difference between these two objectives. That is to say, these agreements intended to reduce undue management of the rates they move. Their aim was not to limit all movement but, rather, to check cumulative movements.

To assure the role of each exchange rate as a guideline toward balancing a country's domestic policies and its external economic relations was the second key concern of the Jamaica meetings. On this issue the negotiators promptly found themselves locked into the same conflicts that have bedevilled international monetary negotiations since time began. Such troubles certainly marked the early sixties, after that brief period following the war of rather exhilarated revival of fixed exchange rates. The culmination of that situation came in 1958 with the acceptance of the full convertibility of most currencies of the developed countries. In most of the more developed countries these established parities provided a reasonable guarantee of stability which lasted until 1967.

During that interval much more attention was given to the way in which the "discipline"—and I use the word carefully in view of its ominous implications—of a fixed rate system functioned as a constraint on individual country's efforts to develop their own domestic economic policies. In this period, a principal complaint was that the dollar, as the reserve currency against which all other parities were determined, enabled the United States to be the only country that was unrestrained and not limited by the design of the system. To many observers it became clear that such an arrangement would eventually become intolerable to the other partners. With President Nixon's dramatic announcement on August 15, 1971, in which he took the United States off the gold standard, these submerged tensions and resentment broke into the open.

There were many ways in which the United States could have resolved that impasse and a number of them have actually been considered. Unfortunately, the approach to the problem of parity, which evolved during the Jamaica meetings, fails to come to grips with the need for a set of principles that would help determine what is called the "adjustment process." Many of the participants had, on previous occasions, struggled to revise and reform the postwar system. Such efforts were made right up to the August 15, 1971, announcement, and they continued thereafter until March of 1973 when the United States and other developed countries agreed to a twice-revised parity system. These experiences left many negotiators so conscious of the dilemmas of asymmetry that they knew no formulation could be agreed in one high-level conference. Those earlier attempts to develop standards for a meaningful pattern of currency adjustment among countries recognized that viable relationships require adjustments from both surplus and deficit countries.

In principle, most participants at the Jamaica conference had come to recognize the need for a global system in which surplus countries would be subjected to the same pressure to harmonize currency movements as had been inherently the case for the deficit countries. Yet on all previous occasions, efforts to define criteria that would govern this system had become so embroiled in immediate issues and immediate tradeoffs that they ended in complete frustration. This frustration was still in the minds of many of the participants by the time they reached Jamaica.

The result was that they did not even try to arrive at an agreement establishing criteria for an adjustment process that would be reasonably symmetrical for both the surplus and deficit countries. Instead, they were content with getting an acknowledgment of the principle that all countries ought to accept some discipline regarding their balance-of-payments position whatever the prevailing arrangement, whether it be one of floating rates or of fixed parities. The failure to agree on an acceptable adjustment process in effect left it to each individual economy to sustain by itself a pattern of relations with other countries that would optimize both the movement of goods and the shipment of capital. Such a relationship would continue to be reflected through its exchange rate. As for any guide to action, all countries would have to rely either on a variable rate or on a movement of reserves. Yet, the problem of reconciling domestic and foreign economic policies is an old one, and one that is likely to persist as long as the relations among countries are not characterized by total autarky.

At the same time, the participants at Jamaica recognized that there was some value in following a course analagous to the principles of the British common law. That is, they would avoid immediate defeat, or even the failure of the conference, that would have occurred if they had tried to clarify a system of agreed guidelines which might possibly be administered by a neutral force such as the International Monetary Fund. Instead, they concentrated on procedures. In effect, they ended up by refurbishing procedures rather than by redefining principles. In the process, they chose to go beyond arrangements that had already evolved in a rather striking manner since 1960. These involved an ever-expanding circle of direct communication, the exchange of both information and judgments among the industrial countries, and even the beginnings of some relations between them and the developing countries.

Under the Jamaica approach, this whole complex of interrelations will emphasize consultations to a much greater degree. The facilities of the International Monetary Fund will be utilized, but, recognizing the cumbersomeness of that body and its larger membership, the participants at Jamaica created in the proposed permanent council a body which will be the counterpart of the twenty members of the executive board. It will consist of the twenty governors selected by that same cluster of countries that selects each of the twenty executives on the fund board. The agreements reached at Jamaica provide permanent arrangements for frequent, if not precisely regular, meetings. At these meetings the ministerial group as a whole, with the assistance of the IMF staff, will review the ways in which the system is functioning. They will also point out those countries which need most clearly further adjustments of domestic policy to international requirements.

But the hope that the arrangements of Jamaica, based as they were on flexible rates, would free us from the spasms of recurrent financial crisis was certainly premature. Thus, the striking change in the economic positions of Italy and the United Kingdom have demonstrated that flexible rates alone cannot obviate the need for adjustment, nor can they fully assure symmetry in the adjustment process. In practice it is natural, and in fact essential, for firms engaged in international trade or the movement of capital always to try to minimize losses or to maximize speculative gains whenever an exchange rate seems likely to move. In a system of flexible exchange rates, whenever a country and its currency fall out of line, this natural precautionary urge, which previously took the form of a massive loss of reserves, now turns into a flight from that country's currency. This, in turn, creates a rapid decline in the exchange rate. Such a decline may go so far as to create unbearable strains for the economy affected.

This certainly occurred in the British case. Changes in the British economy dramatically affected the value of the pound. The pound's decline was not only evident in relation to the dollar, against which it fell to a low of $1.67, but also in relation to comparable cross rates with all other leading currencies. The British entered this precarious situation in part because they had been unable to control their own inflation. They now found that the rapid as well as extensive depreciation of their currency caused the cost of imports expressed in sterling to rise even more. This further accelerated the domestic inflation. It became clear that the British were either going to have to impose massive restrictions, such as direct controls on their trade, or the international community would have to demonstrate its support to give time to take the internal steps necessary to limit their inflation. That is why an agreement was reached to support sterling. Whether the problem was resolved in the right way or with the right techniques, and whether the approach to rebuilding confidence in the pound was appropriate is of course debatable. Undoubtedly, some might have preferred alternative courses of action.

Yet both the evident readiness to act within the Jamaica framework and the apparent willingness to take steps that were reminiscent of those taken during the old parity days constituted a further reminder that the basics of a floating rate system or a par value system are the same. In both instances, the need for achieving a degree of harmony between the performance of an individual economy and the rest of the world has persisted. Similarly, both systems produce the same disturbance and annoyance among the political forces of an individual country. Both systems ultimately force them to realize that the only alternative is simply to cut themselves off by means of direct controls over trade as well as over capital movements and thus to push themselves back into a fortress type of economy.

The problems that we are facing are really those inherent in a world of relatively free trade and relatively free capital movement, in economies that are on balance relatively biased toward dependence on a market system rather than upon autarkic controls. These problems are the price we must pay for enjoying a world that gives us the kind of fruits we like. These problems are likely to remain with us forever. Undoubtedly, we shall have to continue to improvise compromise solutions to them.

Jamaica was an important step toward closer international collaboration. It may help assure that as successive governments participate in international conferences they will develop a perspective on the world economy as a whole and thus accept more easily the lessons of the past. Above all, the Jamaica conference may help develop a greater awareness among politically responsible people in most countries of the need to keep domestic economic policy in line with external exigencies. Ultimately, it may make a greater degree of discipline more acceptable to those who participate in today's global, interdependent economy.

Despite occasional setbacks, the Jamaica arrangement will contribute to a more orderly and effective system of exchange rates. But there have been promising developments in addition to the Jamaica agreements. One is an approach which originated in the proposals that sought to provide an alternative to the IMF when that body was first being considered back in 1940. It is the notion that, whether or not an IMF system exists, the world requires the steadying influence that may ensue from a clustering of many countries around a few key currencies.

Such clusterings have, in fact, already occurred, generally around one currency. This is certainly taking place in Europe, mostly around the Deutschemark. In the Far East, the Japanese yen is assuming a leading position much like that of the Deutschemark in Europe. Recently, after fifteen years of discussion, the Japanese government has officially committed itself to the principle of creating such a clustering around the yen. They have adopted six measures to liberalize access to their own market and they are trying to establish greater freedom in the flows of capital in and out of Japan, as in the financing of their exports and imports. Japan seems genuinely to be trying to develop a yen market but of course this will work only if and when other countries can use the yen as currency.

As of now, the Japanese claim that they finance roughly 20 percent of their exports and 1 percent of their imports in yen, the rest is still financed in dollars, but they hope to increase the share of their imports and exports to be financed by the yen. Thus, it appears that Japan is clearly going to begin to assume some of the obligations of a key currency. It can do so completely only if the yen is usable, if it can be readily exchanged, and only if it is less severely restricted than it has been. These steps, nevertheless, constitute another inch of progress.

Despite all of these developments the dollar will continue unavoidably, as the principal transactions currency. If, however, the clustering develops around the two other key currencies, it may become possible to focus on the relations among those three currencies as a sort of central hard structure of the whole system. That will, I think, eventually prove to be a promising route, especially if the Japanese react not as the Swiss have done, but more like the Germans who are at least beginning to accept their obligations within the "snake."

Summary

The need for a sound as well as equitable system of international exchange rates has been recognized since the 1930s. Yet past attempts to establish such a system have proven to be either ineffectual or subject to the same disorders as the arrangements that preceded them. Thus, the shift to floating exchange rates failed to correct substantially the strains that had plagued the previous system of fixed parities.

The most recent endeavor to establish a rational and efficient exchange-rate system, namely the Jamaica conference, although not entirely successful, proved to be at least encouraging. The participants validated the existing floating rates but, at the same time, reaffirmed their commitment to a set of conditions generally associated with fixed rate arrangements. More importantly, the participating nations recognized that whatever monetary system would ultimately emerge, it would have to meet two conditions. It would be required not only to facilitate the interconvertability of currency but also to establish an adjustment process under which each country's currency would reflect both its overall economic potential and its actual external trade position.

What the Jamaica conference failed to do, however, was to agree on the nature of the principles that are to guide the adjustment process. Nor did the negotiators agree on the criteria for the standard in terms of which national currencies could be evaluated. The conference also left unresolved the problem of how the discipline that is inherent in any monetary system can be imposed equitably on both deficit and surplus countries.

These of course are issues that, in an asymmetrical world, virtually defy solutions. The approach finally taken at Jamaica—namely to follow the example of British common law in eschewing precise definitions while adhering to general principles—may be short of what is needed. It is, however, a step in the right direction. Perhaps the most significant outcome was the agreement on the need for regular meetings and the establishment of an executive board to handle the consultative machinery.

None of these steps are likely to eliminate the financial disorders that have remained as endemic to the floating rate system as they were to the fixed parity arrangement. Nevertheless, as the case of Great Britain has shown, the lessons of recent experiences have not entirely been lost. Thus, in the wake of Jamaica, a genuine collaborative spirit emerged that made it possible to contain the British economic crisis. Equally encouraging are the signs that a new type of monetary system may be emerging. The clustering around the Deutschemark in Europe and the yen in the Far East points to the possibility of an exchange-rate system based on several key currencies rather than on the dollar alone as was the case in the past. This system may prove to be the most stable one, provided those countries whose currencies would form the central structure of this system acknowledge their new obligations.

PART THREE:
GLOBAL RESOURCES
AND U.S. INTERESTS

Introduction
Joseph R. Harbert

The 1970s have witnessed a relatively new development in international institutional patterns—the increased use of ad hoc international conferences under U.N. auspices to deal with issues of global concern. Major conferences on food, water, population, human settlements, law of the sea, the human environment, and deserts have been held, and others are planned. One of the themes which ties these conferences together is the somewhat belated recognition that contemporary world problems are interrelated. This rise of global consciousness has stimulated the creation of a new world agenda, one which stresses common interests, interdependence, and human survival.

Clearly, this agenda has not and cannot displace our attention from traditional politico-military concerns which continue to affect our well-being. But the realization that there is general world predicament—what the Club of Rome has called the *problematique*—has raised a number of critical questions. Perhaps the central issue as it concerns this volume is whether our social and political institutional systems can handle the weight and complexity of interrelated contemporary problems.

In a comprehensive essay which examines issues of human survival and the implications of a more just international economic order, Philippe de Seynes calls for a global design and a refined set of international rules or codes of conduct. Unlike the Club of Rome, de Seynes stresses the dialectical tension between rich and poor and analyzes its impact on current global problems. While stressing the faults in social organization rather than physical or technological limits, de Seynes evinces some optimism about the evolution of a pluralistic international system of institutions and mechanisms for global problem solving.

One of the most critical areas on which global attention has been focused is the fate of the oceans. Since its introduction on the U.N. agenda in 1967, the question of revising the law of the sea has embroiled the nations of the world in continuing conflict. Dramatic advances in marine technology, and a greater awareness of the vast economic potential of seabed mineral resources, have changed the parameters of interaction, making it clear that the existing Geneva Conventions needed to be supplemented. The U.N. Law of the Sea Conference has been the international community's response.

In the early 1970s much optimism was aroused within the U.N. community itself over the prospects that the resources of the deep sea would be declared "the common heritage of mankind" to be developed by an international instrument under U.N. auspices. It was the hope of many that such an international agency, operating under a new treaty which would prohibit military uses of the seabed, would not only strengthen the U.N. system financially but serve also as an aid to the developing countries. Moreover, it was hoped that a strong international authority might limit further ocean pollution and, in general, curtail or manage controversy among nations arising from conflicting claims to, and uses of, the sea and seabed.

As we write, little of this has come to pass. Indeed, the fight is far from over and there appears to be little hope that a strong international sea regime will emerge. Two articles in this section of the volume explore the current state of law of the sea negotiations from two somewhat different perspectives. Both John Logue and Daniel S. Cheever deal primarily with United States goals and policies at the conference. Professor Cheever emphasizes, however, the political conflict between North and South as it has developed regarding seabed minerals and transit rights issues. He concludes that a new public order of the oceans is emerging, treaty or not. Professor Logue's piece, in contrast, argues that the United States has failed to take an imaginative approach to the law of the sea negotiations and concludes that less narrowly nationalistic policies would benefit the world community.

An equally critical if more immediate concern of U.S. foreign policy in the 1970s has been the role of energy and other raw materials. The OPEC oil boycott of 1973 was testimony to the impact that interdependence has had on U.S. interests. As on the law of the sea issues, however, a key element of the public discussion has been in defining precisely what U.S. interests are. This step necessarily precedes the development of new instrumentalities, national, regional, or global, for achieving U.S. objectives. Hence, the United States continues to grope for a new energy policy—one that reflects domestic

Introduction

considerations as well as those of international politics.

Two key questions regarding U.S. energy policy are examined in this volume. Joseph Barnea explores the problems of the desirability and feasibility of energy self-sufficiency for the United States and contends that the prospects are good for energy independence. Richard Bissell's article explores the international institutional aspects of U.S. energy policy, and argues that, because it has treated energy as an economic rather than political problem, the United States has taken a stand which emphasizes national damage limitation rather than global institutional development.

The final essay in this section explores the larger question of raw materials and U.S. policy. Bension Varon traces the history of U.S. raw materials policy from the 1950s when stockpiling was done for military security reasons to the present harsh realization of economic interdependence. As economic issues have assumed greater prominence in foreign affairs, the dependence of the United States on outside supplies has become a matter of serious concern. Varon argues persuasively, however, that this is more a result of the changing U.S. perception of its own vulnerability than of objective conditions. Besides offering a realistic assessment of the pros and cons of self-sufficiency, the Varon piece is valuable in demonstrating the degree to which natural resource management remains in the domain of national rather than international institutions.

20. Some Current Problems of Global Cooperation
Philippe de Seynes

With more problems being viewed as international, with interdependence as a central (if as yet ill-documented) theme of international life, and with a seemingly narrower margin of freedom between aspirations and constraints, it is clear that the time of international pragmatism has gone. Not that the multiple ways in which international society has more or less spontaneously or empirically developed, through public and private initiatives, should be discouraged or that it should have lost its usefulness. But more is needed. Governments have clearly indicated that they want a global design and an increasingly refined set of rules. International pragmatism was hardly a tenable proposition even at the time when continuing linear progress was postulated, when "trickle-down" economics were hardly questioned, and when faith in the overall benign effects of technology had not been seriously shaken. Such propositions have now been generally discarded, if not discredited, and the effort toward developing designs and sets of rules has been significantly intensified.

Rules, or codes of conduct, not legally binding but endowed with a moral authority derived from their universal or quasi-universal acceptance are becoming a substitute for international law, which is inevitably slow in its development. They have been drafted or are being drafted in such diverse fields as shipping (liners' conferences), transnational enterprises, transfer of technology, environment, and others. The most significant and comprehensive is the Charter of Rights and Obligations of States developed over the last two years. Rules and codes are more ambiguous and at a higher level of generality than law can afford to be, since there are not courts to adjudicate right or wrong. The procedure of their acceptance conceals divergencies, and for that reason it is sometimes the subject of heated controversy. The trend, however, is a most important one in the progress toward a New International Economic Order (NIEO).

Rules and codes are also useful elements in the building of a conceptual framework in which the design must evolve. The need for designs has expressed itself most powerfully in recent years, first, through the International Development Strategy in 1970 and then through the Programme and Plan of Action for a New International Economic Order. Less comprehensive documents have also been elaborated in such fields as environment, population, food, women's rights and participation in society. All these documents have one powerful feature in common: their overall objective is change. They rule out a notion of interdependence which would not be geared to change and, for that matter, rapid change. They are not concerned with the management of the status quo. This is why the negotiations in the economic field today differ from those which affect the preservation of peace, or economic negotiations of earlier times. Designs worked out in the United Nations postulate faults in social organization which can be corrected through the process of political will and international concertation. In this light, they proceed from goals, based on human improvement, to strategies, policies, and programs. They have evolved from early recognition of asymmetries adversely affecting third world countries and expressed in the crucial "gaps": the trade gap and the saving gap, and in the theory of the inevitable deterioration of the terms of trade.

Whether demonstrable or not, these propositions continue, as a conceptual instrument, to exercise a considerable influence on the minds of politicians and on the actions of the international community. The designs recognize, as any economic document should, certain limiting factors affecting the development of resources and the implementation of corrective measures. These factors are reflected in the choice of the quantitative targets and of the time span for their attainment. They do not, however, include a recognition of ultimate physical limits. Nor do they as yet integrate such emerging but ill-documented concepts as the carrying capacity of the biosphere or absolute scarcities in nonrenewable natural resources. One important feature of these designs is that they view respect for national sovereignty as an imperative and the search for national identity as a positive factor in the process of change. They do not take the leap toward supranational institutions and provide for only a limited number of centrally managed programs, mostly in the more technical fields.

Newly emancipated countries still see their independence threatened in many devious and subtle ways, and in any suggestions of central management they fear manipulation by the rich and the powerful. But the industrial countries have not shown a greater propensity toward the sacrifice of a portion of their sovereignty. For instance, they have resisted progress toward a true monetary reform which would inevitably involve a much greater managerial role for the International Monetary Fund as a central authority. This state of affairs must be seen in a context where a very vast area of potential cooperation—without surrendering of sovereignty—is still unattended. And it may be surmised that even with the law of the sea the likely agreements—so remote from the great hopes raised only a few years ago—would not foreclose real cooperation in the major areas of environment, scientific research, and exploration and exploitation of resources.

Most pervasive—and increasingly so—is the ever-present, if not always expressed, feeling of intolerable inequalities, and of enormous concentration of power. This seems to create insurmountable inhibitions even in fields where risks are great, such as the proliferation of nuclear technology. In areas such as the exploitation and exploration of natural resources, so closely related to the management of the environment, the present concentration of power must be viewed as an obstacle to the development of international policies and programs. To mitigate the effects of such concentration should be viewed as an objective per se not to be dismissed, as so often, as purely ideological, and as a condition of progress in crucial fields of international cooperation. Measures aiming at more equal sharing of power by whatever means, however modest (e.g., in the form of restraining actions by powerful nations or of changes in decisionmaking mechanisms in international institutions), will be more intensely explored from now on.

All this may help to explain why the school of thought so dramatically exemplified by the Club of Rome has not found ready and general acceptance in the United Nations. Their early world models emphasize physical and technological limits rather than faults in social organization; they do not integrate (even though they recognize) the conflict inherent in the world today, the dialectical tensions between the rich and the poor. They appear to underestimate the role of nations, and to subsume their early demise into worldwise problem-solving institutions. This important work, therefore, proves difficult to fit into the conceptual framework which conditions the International Development Strategy or the New International Economic Order.

It is clear, nevertheless, that at least the questions posed by the Club of Rome are beginning to permeate the arenas in which U.N. policies are elaborated. But considerable ambivalence is shown in regard to the answers. At times they are evoked as an additional argument for redistribution of resources. But, perhaps, more frequently, they are perceived as a factor retarding an already slow development, on the basis of a precarious methodology and with motives which are suspected. Since the feeling of limits, however vague, may be already influencing some policy decisions and investment actions, and may therefore affect the equilibrium and coherence of the designs, it would be important to work toward a consensus in that respect, however difficult it may prove. This would certainly require a rapid development of positive and specific knowledge which seems to have limped behind the emergence of overall philosophies and value systems.

The global vision has nevertheless made considerable advances during the last few years. Turbulent events and newly perceived problems have produced a greater sense of urgency, broadening and stepping up the pace of cooperation even in the absence of a conceptual consensus. The state of cooperation on a global level differs greatly in its intensity and manifestations from one field to another.

Food. The greatest advance is to be found in the field of food as a result of the preparation and unfolding of the Rome conference in November 1974. A comprehensive set of institutions and arrangements has been established, which brings the international community closer to a measure of central management than it has ever been. Increase in investment for food production and infrastructure in the less-developed countries, intensification of technological research, constitution of security reserves, continuation and improvement of food aid as a necessary transitional measure, and establishment of a council with an overall coordinating mandate are the main features of a remarkably coherent enterprise which enlists greater commitment than has been witnessed previously. On the basis of the evidence available to the conference from national and international institutions, the plan does not foresee shortage of land or of production capacity within the next 25 years. Even in the context of the population projections of the United Nations, it implies substantial improvement in nutritional standards.

Population. At the other end of the spectrum, in the field of population, whatever cooperation exists is of a pragmatic, ad hoc type, not supported by any formalized consensus. At the conference in Bucharest, the discussion of population as a factor in development strategies destroyed some of the more simplistic ideas which had led some to overestimate the efficiency of population programs. Here again the lack of positive knowledge in regard to such important problems as the determinants of fertility, made it very difficult to oppose convincingly those who did not consider population stabilization or control as an element of the New International Economic Order and who at times were even tempted to dismiss demography as irrelevant to development. The clarification, however, was useful as a reminder that population programs had little chance of succeeding except in the context of a change in social and economic conditions and that their indiscriminate advocacy was not necessarily a positive element in the promotion of international cooperation.

Environment. In the field of environment, important programs, some of them involving global cooperation under the United Nations Environment Programme, have been set forth as a consequence of the Stockholm conference of 1972. However, the conceptual problems relating to the place of environment protection in the complex set of objectives of the international and national societies have not been significantly elucidated. Previous decisions, sometimes hard fought, have been reversed almost overnight, illustrating the lack of reliable methodology for rational decision making. A global model commissioned by the United Nations, under the direction of Professor Leontief and recently released, has given useful indications in regard to costs. Particularly preoccupying, however, is the difficulty encountered in reducing the uncertainties affecting such matters as climate modifications, genetic engineering, or new nuclear technology. There are serious risks involved even if they cannot be convincingly documented. The notion of risk is easier to identify and perceive than that of limits, and as long as great uncertainties becloud certain areas, restraining policies, arrived at internationally, should commend themselves even in the absence of scientific proof, particularly if alternative approaches can be discovered.

Natural Resources. This lends particular importance to the work undertaken in the United Nations on natural resources. Planning and concentration have been slow to come, even though they seemed to be called for, long before the notion of physical limits invaded our thinking. This is an area of large and slow-maturing investments. Natural resources are wealth, the latent richness of many of the poor countries. They are linked with the complex power problem created by the multinational companies and their grip on innovative technology. The failure to develop a reliable inventory, to embark in time on exploration on the right scale and to outline long-term international policies, has resulted in the present disquieting rush into nuclear technology. The fashionable notion of scarcities is not well understood. There is considerable confusion about reserves or costs. Programs for organizing the existing knowledge and developing additional knowledge through exploration, forecasting, and technological assessment are now recognized as among the most immediate tasks of the U.N. system.

It is implied (and sometimes very explicitly) in models emphasizing global constraints that a drastic change in the value system of contemporary society should take place, and given the stringent time span of the "overshoot and collapse" process of the first Club of Rome report, that this change should take place rapidly. Values are not very specifically stated in either the International Development Strategy or the Program of Action of the NIEO. Those which are subsumed in these documents include the improvement in the material conditions of the people—particularly the poorest; the general advocacy of economic and social rights; and a desire for more equality, both between nations and within nations. The values in the early documents have been made somewhat more specific as efforts were undertaken to refine targets and indicators in a new emphasis on employment creation, distribution of income, and eradication of mass poverty. However, the process of specification has not gone very far. The attempt made in a Secretariat document to suggest social indicators, as well as new objectives pertaining to some of the important parameters of social progress, was not pursued, even though it was only suggested that such targets should be set by governments themselves, and not established as collective norms.

The reason for this failure may lie in the fear of interference or in the suspicion that obeisance to new imperatives might in some way stifle growth, or in the mistrust of untested models of growth which postulate that, under certain circumstances, an early emphasis on social improvement might lay the groundwork for more rapid growth in the longer term period. In fact the debate on the content and conditions of development—which had been one of the original expressions of interdependence as a concern for the difficulties of others—is not easy to pursue very much further in the United Nations. Our greater understanding of the development process requires now that its sociological and political content—including the existing structures of power—be explored, as these factors were ignored in the optimistic hypotheses of former years. However, social experimentation and innovation are pursued in developing countries themselves, and may be assisted by programs of cooperative action such as the rural development program of the World Bank (IBRD) and the employment program of the International Labor Organization (ILO). New models based on different values may be developed in peripheral organs such as regional institutes or in such new institutional arrangements as the Third World Forum where research and debate on highly controversial

matters can more easily reach out toward new frontiers. In this context
it becomes natural for the U.N. organization to be more and more open
to the outside world and to remain cognizant of trends, in thinking and
action, toward new styles of development which command the
allegiance of a number of its member governments.

A greater diversity of paradigms may be observed today in third
world countries than was the case when the International Development
Strategy was adopted. Some are directly inspired by shifts in the value
system. They emphasize *dependencia,* and postulate the need to overcome
it as an objective in itself and the condition of healthy development.
Others simply aspire to a more egalitarian society, with emphasis on the
satisfaction of basic human needs. Both types converge in the advocacy
of more self-reliance, of a greater degree of insulation from certain
world currents (especially consumption patterns so widely disseminated
by the mass media), and of modification of traditional arrangements of
international intercourse.

Great hope is attached to the realization of collective self-reliance, as
an expression of solidarity between third world countries, which today
has acquired a new and concrete operational meaning. This is one of the
most significant trends to emerge in the recent past, and, in spite of some
scattered resistance, it is more and more seen by all as a positive element,
to be encouraged and supported by the international community.
However far the goal of self-reliance may be pursued, given the size and
factor endowment of the large majority of third world countries and
their links with international markets, the problems of relationship with
the industrial world through trade, and capital and technological
transfers remain crucial.

These have been the subject of debate and negotiation over twenty-
five years, with very slow progress recorded. It is important to
recognize that the perspective of a more rapid advance may, in the light
of the more recent circumstances, appear in a brighter light. The
implications of the OPEC countries' strategy, the discontinuity created
by the sharp increases in the oil prices and the jolt imparted to the
international community by such action, may in fact mark a turning
point for the history of international cooperation. The difficulties raised
have been duly analyzed, recorded, and lamented. As it turned out, they
proved not quite as stringent as had been assumed. Balance-of-payment
deficits of major importing countries were less forbidding than
anticipated. Oil surpluses were spent in the import of goods, in
productive investments, and—most significantly—in outflows of aid to
developing countries particularly affected by the oil price increases.
There was no rush toward protectionism and "beggar thy neighbour"

policies on the part of industrial countries. Quite to the contrary, they cooperated rather effectively to cope with prolonged balance-of-payment deficits, and they also contributed through flows of capital to mitigate the effects of the increase in food and oil prices on less-developed countries.

Each country will draw for itself the detailed balance sheet; and it is, unfortunately, true that many situations remain highly difficult and precarious. However, in the context of international cooperation—for so long stagnant or languishing—the most useful view of the developments of the winter of 1973, is to recognize them as a transforming event which may stimulate the international community to new and constructive actions—including, of course, the mitigation of its adverse effects. If some would doubt the reality of the transforming event, they should only look at the changes and innovations which have taken place at an accelerated pace since the decisions of the Organization of Petroleum Exporting Countries (OPEC).

Several factors deriving from these decisions have been instrumental: (1) an important pool of capital has become available, less conditioned by Pavlovian reflexes than the savings of industrial countries, and freer to move in certain desirable directions; (2) the change in one of the more important parameters of the world economy has improved the cost-benefit ratios of a number of projects in industry, natural resources, and even agriculture, which previously were regarded as nonprofitable; (3) finally, the transfer of economic power to OPEC countries and their declared solidarity with the whole of the third world have improved the context in which global negotiations are taking place.

The list of positive actions and developments recorded since the winter of 1973 is impressive. Some are the result of spontaneous forces and the resilience of the market; some have been brought about by concerted action of governments. Most have been in directions which had been defined as desirable in the last ten or even twenty years of history of the United Nations. They include: (1) an incipient redistribution of industries toward countries of the third world, mostly, but not exclusively, those rich in energy sources; (2) new investments in agricultural infrastructure for subsistence as well as export crops; (3) the diversification and refinement of the international financing system; (4) more consultation between financial authorities of the industrial countries to protect and safeguard a highly vulnerable financial system; (5) more attention to the poorest countries, more thorough analysis of their situation and new systematic channeling of aid flows in their direction; (6) important agreements such as those of the world food conference, the signing of the Lomé Convention with the first attempt at income guarantee for forty-six of the poorest countries; (7) the reemergence, at Kingston, of the Commonwealth as an instrument for consultation on worldwide policies; (8) the softening of positions held to be immutable in regard to such matters as commodity arrangements; (9) a much greater awareness of the need for conservation of natural resources and energy; and (10) the awakening of a solicitude for the requirements of future generations.

It is, therefore, not unreasonable to assume that ongoing and forthcoming negotiations have a better chance of progress than they had in the past. This is because conditions have been made somewhat less unequal by the new power of the oil countries and their operational solidarity with the rest of the third world. In fact, at the Sixth Special Session of the General Assembly in April 1974, the first such session devoted entirely to economic matters, this change in context was very clear. It is interesting to note that the declaration of principles and the program of action contained very few elements which were not previously recorded, notably in the International Development Strategy and that even the changes in emphasis did not appear far-reaching if taken in their literal expression.

Yet, the new circumstances gave these documents a new coloration and significance. In them is implicit the notion, not previously expressed, that interdependence can only be achieved and organized within a less unequal sharing of power, that the mechanisms whereby certain decisions, notably relating to capital movements, should reflect a truer partnership between poor and rich countries as well as between old-rich and newly rich countries. The changes in the context are perhaps not of revolutionary proportions, yet it is important to capitalize on them in the period ahead, as was done at the Seventh Special Session of the General Assembly and at the fourth U.N. Conference on Trade and Development (UNCTAD IV).

For years negotiations have taken place in a context where the area of joint benefits (the positive-sum game) was seen to lie in the future, with a more stable and prosperous world based on a more rational division of labor, whereas the process leading to it seemed compounded by a series of zero-sum games in which one of the partners inevitably lost what the other gained. Only moral imperatives or acute political foresight could lead to the acceptance of the desirable concessions. Now more opportunities of joint gains may be discovered in the present or the near future. A situation may exist, in which security and regularity of supplies of essential raw materials could be perceived and negotiated within a broad context of measures affecting trade, aid, investment, and technology. The agenda and even the format of the negotiations must remain very broad, not only because the economic factors involved are inherently interrelated, but because areas of joint gains can only be discovered in multiple negotiations and in a package of quid pro quos.

Reflection on the adequacy of the only universal institution—the United Nations system—has also been highly stimulated by recent events. Adjustments or reform are felt to be needed in the management of international gatherings in order to maximize the potentialities of negotiation. It is also important to explore how the administrative and technical instances may help to smooth the inevitable frictions and distortions of a rapid industrialization program, to develop international policies in the field of natural resources, to facilitate and improve the process of transfer and acquisition of technology which are an important ingredient of the desirable changes in the structure of the world economy, to normalize the relationship of governments with transnational enterprises through a process of dialogue as well as regulation, and to develop the data base and analytical capacity which will be needed if worldwide arrangements on commodity prices, income guarantee, and indexation are to be seriously discussed as part of the negotiation for the NIEO.

These would appear to be some of the major elements which should guide the restructuring of the U.N. system of institutions, rather than the ever present temptation to simplify, hierarchise, and centralize. The system is made up of number of loosely coordinated units but it has the advantage of pluralism. When one unit fails to respond to a challenge, another may succeed. Most elements of the system are still weak, but they have a potential for creativity and innovation which might vanish in the process of sweeping changes. Traditions, routine, and acquired reflexes do not easily yield to legislative fiat. Reformers should keep in mind that the system, over the past few years, has shown considerable vitality. Through the conferences on global problems, it has progressed in its work of conceptualization. Its message has been widely disseminated. It has proved capable of opening its door to the participation of other transnational agents who may exercise significant influence on the world economy, and of listening to the voice of outsiders through a more effective use of the consultative status of nongovernmental organizations, which was one of the boldest innovations of the charter. Combining the measure of streamlining which is needed with the preservation and enhancement of the creative forces inherent in the system is a difficult and even speculative task. But at this stage, when the management of interdependence is gradually being accepted as an imperative, the evolution of the only universal institution is rightly seen in the United Nations as one of the important keys to success.

21. American Objectives and the Law of the Sea
Daniel S. Cheever

The United States' overarching concern in three U.N. conferences on the law of the sea has been to legitimate its power as an industrialized maritime state. The developing countries, on the other hand, seek to limit the extent to which the United States and other industrialized states use their marine or maritime capabilities. They do so to realize the aims they have propounded in their proposals for a new international economic order. The Third U.N. Law of the Sea Conference (LOS III), in particular, has been a testing ground for these conflicting objectives. Thus the members of the Group of 77 seek to deny the United States and the other countries of the industrialized North the right to exploit seabed minerals as they wish. Rather, the Group of 77 or the South seek a seabed minerals regime beyond national jurisdiction that will regulate "activities for the benefit of mankind as a whole, irrespective of the geographical location of States, . . . and taking into particular consideration the interests and needs of the developing countries. . . ."[1] The Group of 77 also seek to regulate the ways in which maritime powers utilize certain straits which some of them claim as coastal areas falling within their jurisdiction. The Northern countries challenge this position as an unacceptable limitation on the exercise of their military power.

Sometimes North and South agree on specific policies. Thus both sides seem to agree that coastal states have exclusive rights to regulate resource exploitation in economic zones extending two hundred miles off their coasts. Despite this congruency in policy, however, the underlying objective of each side is to lessen the influence of the other. The United States seeks exclusive ownership and control over the living and energy resources on and under its long and, to a considerable extent, broad continental shelf. It has a particular need for these resources

255

to meet its energy requirements, and it has the requisite technology and financial strength to exploit them. While the developing countries, in contrast, have neither the financial strength nor the industrial capability in many cases to exploit their own coastal resources, they have at least been able to establish proprietary rights over them. In so doing they have succeeded in curbing the exploitive capabilities of the industrially advanced countries which might otherwise have laid exclusive claim to resources on and under their coastal shelves. As matters now stand, multinational corporations exploit energy resources on and off foreign shores only on conditions set by the coastal states concerned.

My thesis may be summarized as follows: While the North and South often agree on specific policies, as evidenced by their mutual acceptance of the bulk of the articles of the Single Composite Negotiating Text at LOS III, their disagreement on objectives appears so sharp as to preclude the coming into force of a single, comprehensive ocean treaty. The disagreement on objectives needs further analysis and definition. This can be done by examining two of the major unresolved issues in LOS III: the control over seabed minerals and transit rights through international straits.

On these issues the United States, generally speaking, finds itself in company with the Common Market countries, other Western European countries, Japan, Australia, New Zealand, and usually, but not always, Canada. The Soviet Union as an industrialized maritime state, and its Eastern European allies, take a similar line. The Group of 77, actually more than a hundred developing states mostly in the southern hemisphere, includes African, Latin American, Pacific, and Asian countries, which oppose the North both on mineral rights and on transit rights. With these two blocs on a collision course the LOS III has thus far failed to produce an acceptable treaty to regulate the exploitation of ocean resources.

The United States is concerned to gain access to the mineral riches of the seabed, minerals essential for modern industry. It desires access not only for reasons of military security but also to support its free-market economy. The United States pursues a policy of unimpeded transit through straits lest control over transit rights by coastal states interfere with the clandestine movement of submarines (the sea-based deterrent) and the free movement of tankers on the way to oil-thirsty industrialized countries. The United States fears its national security will be threatened unless it has its way on both counts. It seeks assured sources of energy and mineral resources so as to be as independent as possible of foreign imports. Ocean resources on both the shelf and the deep seabed offer a welcome opportunity to achieve this objective.

The developing countries, on the other hand, see the availability of ocean resources as a chance for them to gain revenue and technology to enable them to be independent of foreign economic control. They seek a comprehensive ocean regulatory regime that will help them shed their dreaded economic dependence on the industrialized Northern countries. In the seabed regime they advocate to regulate mineral mining they see a way to turn the industrial prowess of the North to their economic advantage. In seeking to control the rights of passage through straits and archipelagoes by insisting on "innocent passage" rather than "transit rights" many of them seek to exploit the resources of location to lessen their dependence on the military, industrial might that passes daily along their shores. In American eyes, coastal state control over straits and over the coastal waters near the mouths of straits would inhibit the movement of U.S. submarines, would lessen the opportunity to install listening devices to track enemy submarines, and would jeopardize the transport of goods and raw materials, particularly oil.

American policies at LOS III, in sum, are perceived by the Group of 77 as attempts to perpetuate in treaty law the economic and military predominance of the industrialized North. The group's policies are perceived in turn by the United States as efforts to challenge this predominance. The doctrine of the new international economic order is designed, in effect, to reorganize the world economy for the "benefit of developing countries" (a phrase included in a U.N. resolution of 1970 designating the resources of the deep seabed beyond national jurisdiction as the "common heritage of mankind" and declaring a moratorium on their exploitation pending agreement on a seabed treaty).[2] With the American point of view in the minority, the outcome of LOS III is problematic at best. Although the conference has sought to conduct its deliberations by consensus (without votes) it must finally muster a two-thirds majority in support of an agreed text to replace the Informal Composite Negotiating Text of July 1977 with an oceans treaty open to signature and ratification by the 156 nations participating in the conference. At global ocean treaty must run the gauntlet of the one-state-one-vote rule.

The principal reason LOS III is seen by the Group of 77 as an obvious chance to redress their economic dependency is that ocean resources outside the traditional three-mile territorial sea heretofore have been *res communis*, resources available to any one able to exploit them. This arrangement pleased the industrialized maritime powers which were able to use ocean space pretty much as they wished. In cases where these resources, including navigational routes, lay within territorial limits, the rule of innocent passage protected the interests of sea-going states to a generally satisfactory degree. Ocean resources in the high seas to a large extent were free public goods or collective goods, requiring little in the way of regulation or management beyond generally accepted rights to navigate, to fish, to conduct naval operations, to engage in research, and to punish pirates. Such a laissez-faire ocean regime enforced by customary high-seas freedoms admirably served U.S. interests. Submarines and overflying aircraft transiting international straits, tankers taking economical routes, and fishermen pursuing tuna in foreign coastal water benefited from it. The status quo was not to continue, however, owing to new developments in ocean politics that were in large degree the consequences of achievements in ocean engineering, fishing technology, and marine science.

As important fish stocks became scarce from overutilization, the customary laissez-faire regime yielded first to contiguous zones and fisheries zones in the Geneva Conventions of 1958. In the Informal Composite Negotiating Text of LOS III, high-seas freedoms retreated still further before exclusive economic zones of 200 miles. In addition, territorial waters have expanded in practice from three miles to twelve miles, and this now customary limit is challenged by broader claims, many from Latin America. On the seabed, national jurisdiction has extended since the United States propounded the Truman Doctrine of 1945 to regulate the exploitation of resources on and under the continental shelf. A major difficulty in seabed resources management is that the extent of the shelf has not been defined in any formal, general treaty, so that no one can be entirely sure where national jurisdiction ends and international jurisdiction begins.

Beyond territorial waters and exclusive economic jurisdiction lies all that remains of the common heritage of mankind, a term used by Ambassador Pardo in 1967 in the First Committee of the U.N. General Assembly when narrow national waters and wide high seas were still the general rule. In deciding what the common heritage is to mean in practice the voting power of the geographically disadvantaged states at LOS III is particularly striking. These states include the landlocked states, those with short coastlines and those fearful of being denied access to high seas because their coasts and territorial waters are locked in by other states' continental shelves and exclusive economic zones. These states can wield a blocking third of the conference votes. They may do so because, with the exception of the European landlocked states, they are generally united in their efforts to change the economic order which they feel the United States seeks to perpetuate in its oceans policy.

The general thrust of the United States to establish an ocean regime to serve its economic and military interests does not mean, however, that the United States favors the traditional high-seas, laissez-faire tradition at all times on all issues. There are almost as many American interests involved in the LOS III negotiations as there are uses of the sea. Nor do all uses pit the United States against all the Group of 77. Sometimes American interests parallel those of the nonindustrialized coastal states. This proved to be the case in the management of coastal fisheries. When U.S. coastal fisheries interests finally persuaded Congress to pass the Fisheries Management and Conservation Act of 1976, the president, with the State Department opposed, signed the bill with apparent reluctance lest a unilateral move by the United States stimulate similar moves by other states to diminish high-seas freedoms by extending coastal management regimes. Indeed, the majority of coastal states, rich and poor, have done just this. They have restricted freedom of movement on the world ocean by claiming limited jurisdiction for limited purposes such as fisheries management, pollution control, and oil exploitation on the continental shelf to a distance from shore of at least 200 miles.

While this unilateral move by the United States to protect its coastal fisheries was significant because it seemed to foreclose bargaining opportunities in a multilateral forum called to agree on a multilateral treaty, it was inevitable. There was no question that American coastal fisheries stocks were being depleted in large part because of overexploitation by offshore fishermen from abroad. The voluntary, and for this reason uncertain, constraints of fisheries commissions were unequal to the tasks of fisheries conservation. Regulation by some public authority in someone's public interest was essential. Under the circumstances, national interests and national administration provided the most available means for fisheries conservation. Prior to this action high seas freedoms were in fact leading to a repeat performance of the "tragedy of the commons."[3] In this instance United States fisheries legislation was used to curb the fishing power of other industrialized states such as the Soviet Union, Japan, and the German Democratic Republic, among others. In fact, with the passage of the fish bill the United States found itself seemingly in more agreement with Ecuador and Peru than with its industrial bedfellows. This irony does not negate the proposition advanced here that the United States objective at LOS is generally to enhance its influence and control over the marine resources it needs. Only occasionally does this objective lead it to side with the Group of 77 and to oppose the industrialized North. Indeed, the latter, notably the Common Market countries, soon followed suit to adopt for themselves the 200-mile fishing rule.

The fisheries experience invites reflection on the work of the U.N. Law of the Sea Conferences. Failure or delay in agreeing on, and signing, a treaty does not mean the LOS III is failing to produce results. In the case of fisheries there has begun to emerge a fairly consistent global pattern of fisheries management. It consists of national regulation in coastal areas of increasingly uniform widths. This particular resource regime, though national in character and unilaterally or regionally arrived at, conforms in some degree to international norms and standards. It is, therefore, an international regime. The international norms enforced by national authorities include the proprietary rights of coastal states over coastal stocks with opportunities for other states to share in harvesting these stocks within limits allowed by the principle of maximum sustainable yield. Noncoastal (anadromous) species such as salmon now have an improved chance of survival owing to the growing adherence of coastal states to management principles suitable for that particular species and specified in the Informal Composite Text. The continuing process of international negotiating in major treaty-making conferences in the nearly twenty years since LOS I would appear to have had some influence in shaping this emerging global pattern of fisheries management. If the pattern is deficient in some respects and if no comprehensive ocean treaty emerges from LOS III, bilateral and regional treaties can do someting to fill the gaps. Certainly countries and their officials that until recently knew little and cared less about fisheries management are now relatively well-informed as a consequence of intense negotiations over a long period of time.

It can be argued also that fisheries conflicts have subsided as the breadth of coastal jurisdiction has increased. The cod war off Iceland is over. American tuna boats are not longer under fire, and the United States government for the moment at least is not paying fines to Ecuadorian authorities. In this case, of course, not every fisherman is satisfied. The American tuna fleet, based primarily at San Diego, was soon reported to be up for sale since the federal government no longer claimed it had a right to fish in foreign coastal waters as close to shore as the twelve miles allowed by the traditional fisheries zones. Another restriction, however, may have contributed more to the dissatisfaction of the San Diego fishermen. The tuna boat owners claim that restrictions on the number of porpoises that can be legally killed during netting operations have reduced the economic viability of the tuna industry—at least that part of it engaged in fishing.

What has happened in essence is that the negotiating process at LOS III has contributed to an abatement of fisheries conflicts by forcing governments participating in the conference to set priorities. In the tuna case, the United States decided in favor of American environmental protectionists and coastal fishermen who sought national protection in American coastal waters. The United States could not protect both coastal and offshore fishermen at the same time. If it had decided in favor of the offshore fishing interests (tuna men) it would have sacrificed coastal fishing interests because highly mechanized foreign fishing fleets under the 1958 Geneva Fisheries Convention would have continued to overexploit coastal stocks on both sides of the American continent. This is not to argue that the only trade-off leading to the fisheries legislation was between coastal and offshore fishing interests. The drama of the American unilateral action to protect coastal fisheries was played against a broader backdrop of domestic politics and economic concerns. The United States needed to be sure its claim to other resources in its coastal zone was secure. This was notably true in the case of petroleum as the amount and the price of oil imported from abroad rose dramatically in the years following the embargo of 1973. Therefore, the United States has joined in the general support of an exclusive economic zone of 200 miles which will provide for the regulation of many activities besides fisheries. When resources become scarce, the need for resources management increases. Under these circumstances limited national jurisdiction, if not territorial jurisdiction, is bound to expand to regulate the exploitation of such resources. International management by international authorities seems inadequate for the task. A pattern of mutually supporting national management regimes constitutes, in effect, an international regime. U.N. conference machinery, like LOS III, contributes to the establishment of such a regime by influencing the behavior of the participating national governments.

Other issues at LOS III besides mining, straits, and fishing present problems for the United States but not to such an extent as to preclude international agreement. One of these is marine science. The preeminence or at least the high performance of American marine science in the twentieth century has been due in part to the same laissez-faire high-seas regime that served commercial interests. That regime also facilitated marine scientific investigation because it could be undertaken on the high seas with little or no regulation by public authorities. Now the marine scientist faces a new world of regulations and constraints. He must have the consent of coastal authorities not only for investigations in internal and territorial waters and on continental shelves, as has been the case since the 1958 Geneva Conventions came into effect, but also for scientific research in the exclusive economic zone specified in the Informal Composite Text. In effect, this means that much if not most marine science research must come under the supervision of national authorities because the most inviting research opportunities, especially fisheries research, lie in coastal waters. That is why jurisdiction over Antarctica is increasing in importance as krill becomes important in maintaining the food chain.

The freedom of the seas has been largely obliterated for the marine scientist who is now faced with restrictions and delays, both of which are costly. The reasons for this state of affairs are easy to find and hard to improve. The most important is that scientific activity is not clearly distinct from resource exploration which is intended to pave the way for commercial exploitation. Once again developing coastal states seek to turn to their advantage the capabilities of the scientifically sophisticated maritime states. They have sought to do this by specifying in the proposed treaty the conditions under which research will be allowed to take place in "their" coastal waters. These conditions are principally the right of participation by coastal state nationals in scientific activities conducted by foreigners and the right of access to information disclosed by the investigation. While scientific investigation is another factor in the tug of war between rich and poor for influence in ocean governance, it does not jeopardize the outcome of LOS III nearly so much as do the issues of transit rights through states and access to seabed minerals.

Another point at issue between North and South is pollution control. The extension of national jurisdiction for pollution control imposes national constraints over activities formerly sanctioned on the high seas and in international waterways. The action of Canada, though not a member of the Group of 77, to extend unilaterally its authority over its Arctic coastal waters despite protests from the United States illustrates the problem. The Canadian action is relevant for this discussion because it was an effort to regulate the behavior of maritime states, notably the United States. By limiting navigational right in a pollution control zone Canada acted much like the "77" who seek to harness the industrial power of the North for their benefit by establishing an International Seabed Authority to control seabed mineral production. In the case of Canada's pollution control zone it is fair to say, however, that the United States objected to the means, unilateralism, rather than the end, pollution control. Indeed the United States seeks by multilateral means to accomplish the same result—an obligation on coastal states to proscribe activities that cause pollution in their coastal waters. In doing so, along with other industrially advanced states, generally speaking, it finds itself opposed in some degree by the Group of 77, many of whom are unwilling to limit opportunities for economic growth by adhering to restrictive and costly pollution controls. Many of these countries, for example, have not signed treaties to lessen ocean pollution prepared under the auspices of the Intergovernmental Maritime Consultative Organization (IMCO). In any event, efforts to control pollution afford another example of a disagreement between the industrially advanced and industrially disadvantaged coastal states. The United States wants to control ocean pollution because it knows firsthand the threat pollution poses to the global ecology (and therefore, to the global economy). As a developed state it can afford to worry and take remedial action. Members of the Group of 77 are in many cases unaware of the dangers and unable or unwilling economically to take remedial action. Once again, each side at LOS III seeks to lessen the influence of the other. Fortunately, this issue, like the issue of scientific research, does not of itself threaten the conference's outcome.

The preceding pages by no means exhaust the list of U.S. objectives at LOS III. Nor do they do justice to the politics of ocean resources management. They are intended rather to suggest that two issues, transit rights through straits and access to seabed minerals, provoke such differences between the North and the South that agreement on a comprehensive global ocean treaty seems unlikely. Even if such a treaty were to be signed by a two-thirds majority, it might well fail to come into force because of an insufficient number of ratifications. This result does not mean failure, however. There is reason to believe that a new comprehensive public order of the oceans is emerging, treaty or not. There will be ample rights for most navigational purposes through straits even though submarines may be legally required to follow the rules of innocent (surface) passage (with the ensign flying). If the United States really needs minerals from the seabed, which is not the case at the moment, it is hard to imagine anyone interfering. It is even more difficult to imagine that a new global authority will be able to impose price and production controls and to conduct mining operations. Disagreement is simply too intense for international authorities to regulate the exploitation of ocean resources and the distribution of benefits in ways demanded by the proponents of the New International Economic Order.

Notes

1. Article 7 of U.N. document A/CONT.62/WP.8/Re.1/Part I, Revised Single Negotiating Text. The three U.N. law of the sea conferences referred to are:

1. 1958 Geneva—It produced the four Geneva Law of the Sea Coventions now in force;
2. 1960 Geneva—It failed to specify exact limits to territorial jurisdiction;
3. 1973 present—It began its first session in New York, held a second session at Caracas in 1974, a third session in Geneva in 1975, and sessions four through six in New York. The Sixth Special Session of the U.N. General Assembly in May 1974 resolved the establishment of a New International Economic Order in resolution 3201 of May 9. See *UN Monthly Chronicle,* XI, May 5, 1974.

I am indebted to Penelope Mahon and Hizkias Assefa of GSPIA at the University of Pittsburgh for helpful criticism.

    2. U.N. General Assembly Resolution 2749, December 17, 1970, in the Twenty-fifth Session.

    3. Richard Falk explains the "tragedy of the commons" in *This Endangered Planet* (New York: Random House, 1971), pp. 48-49.

22. Ship Aground: U.S. Law of the Sea Policy at the United Nations
John J. Logue

My central thesis is that U.S. law of the sea policy has been too private and far too unimaginative. This was true under the Nixon and Ford administrations, and there is reason to believe it will be true of the Carter administration as well. This lack of imagination is a major reason why the giant United Nations Conference on the Law of the Sea is in such sad straits. A bolder approach would mean a more worthwhile treaty—and a more worthwhile treaty would get more votes—not only in the United Nations, but very importantly, in the United States Senate.

Part of the problem is that the Law of the Sea Conference is misnamed. It should be called "The Politics-of-the-Sea Conference" or "The Constitutional Convention for the Oceans." If it had either of those names, many more people would be following its discussions; they might even begin to care about it. And public understanding and support is what the faltering conference desperately needs particularly in the United States. With such support, U.S. law of the sea policy could be much bolder and much better. Public support for a more imaginative law of the sea policy might have made a major difference in the direction and tone of the conference, making it not only a milestone in the fight to preserve the marine environment and marine species, but also a major influence on the struggle to build peace and economic and social justice.

One thing is clear. The Law of the Sea Conference is undertaking an immense job that will have a great influence, whether positive or negative, in the years ahead. Its task is the reconstruction of the basic legal system for 70 percent of the earth's surface. That "freedom of the seas system" lasted for more than three centuries. But in the last thirty years a revolution in ocean technology has undercut the two assumptions on which the old law of the sea was based. The first assumption of the old Grotian system was that the wealth of the oceans is inexhaustible. The second assumption was that there is nothing we can do to the oceans that will harm them. Neither of these things is true any longer. We can exhaust and are exhausting the marine and mineral resources of the oceans. Overfishing has resulted in the almost complete disappearance of certain species of fish and the threatened disappearance of others. And there is no way we can replace the seabed oil and gas which we began to exploit only a very short time ago and are now exploiting at a suicidal rate. Moreover, we pollute the oceans to such an extent that 40 percent of ocean life may already be dead. This pollution has many sources and takes many forms. And though oil spills have received much publicity, it is important to stress that some 90 percent of ocean pollution comes from the land. Unfortunately the treaty text on which the conference is now working—the Informal Composite Negotiating Text—does virtually nothing about land-based pollution.

For some 350 years we have had a system of *negative* laissez-faire law with respect to the oceans. Although this system was biased to some degree in the direction of the "haves" and against the "have nots," it has served the world rather well. But, like the wonderful "one horse shay," that freedom of the seas system "went to pieces all at once." What we need now is a *positive* law of the sea, law which protects the oceans and the marine species within them and orders the many different uses of oceans space. It seems clear that we are going to get positive ocean law. But that does not mean the new system will be better than the old. Indeed, the cure may be worse than the disease. It appears that we shall be getting not one, but rather one hundred systems of positive sea law made by one hundred coastal states. And because of the disputes and conflicts that will inevitably follow from this jurisdictional morass, we may eventually conclude that the new law of the sea is even worse than the old. For with all its faults the old system had the very important virtue of uniformity and thus of predictability.

U.S. law of the sea policy thus far at the Law of the Sea Conference has been very clever and very capable. The American delegation has probably been the hardest working delegation at the conference; it has probably taken more positions—and usually very responsible positions —on agenda items than any other country. But, in my view, U.S. policy has been too responsive to the views of U.S. interest groups professionally involved with the oceans and to the legislators sympathetic to those groups, in particular the petroleum, fishing, and hard minerals industries and such legislators as Muskie of Maine, Metcalf of Montana, and Magnuson of Washington. The latter have been responsive to what they believe to be the interests of their constituents. But what is good for the fishermen of Maine may not be good for the United States as a whole, not to speak of the world as a whole.

The U.S. delegation has not been—or has ceased to be—bold and imaginative when it comes to the law of the sea. It has not seen the tremendous potential of the oceans for building peace and security, promoting economic justice, and protecting the human environment. Or, if it has seen these things, it has not had very much to say about them. A bold approach to the law of the sea might even be better politics than the timid approach of the last three administrations.

In recent times there have been few important public policy areas in which strong and wise presidential leadership was more needed—and less evident—than in the law of the sea. Long ago President Theodore Roosevelt taught us that the White House is a "bully pulpit," i.e., that an effective chief executive has a tremendous opportunity to teach and preach. But Presidents Ford and Nixon had very little to say about the law of the sea, and Secretary Kissinger's performance was spasmodic, improvised, and usually crisis-related.

Indeed, under Ford, presidential leadership was so weak that an almost incredible thing happened. Veteran internationalist senators from midwestern and Rocky Mountain states voted for a bill which was a torpedo aimed at the Law of the Sea Conference. I am, of course, referring to the bill with which the United States unilaterally declared its sovereignty over marine species out to 200 miles. That bill was opposed by the State and Defense Departments. It was a clear violation of international law and a grave threat to the future of the conference. Yet Senators McGovern of South Dakota, Mansfield of Montana, and Symington of Missouri cast key votes in favor of the 200-mile bill!

Surely in the Rocky Mountains, on the Great Plains, and in the state of Missouri, there was no great constituent pressure on senators to vote for a bill to protect ocean fishermen. Then why did those senators vote for the bill? Probably in order to do a favor for very influential colleagues from the coastal states, e.g., Senators Magnuson and Muskie. It would not have been difficult for the president and the secretary of state to win the votes of these Democratic internationalists. But, apparently Messrs. Ford and Kissinger did not even try.

In December of 1975, I wrote that the conventional wisdom with respect to the 200-mile fishing bill was that both houses would pass the bill, the president would then veto it and there would not be enough votes to override his veto.[1] Thus, internationalists need not worry about the bill undercutting the Law of the Sea Conference. I argued instead that it was quite possible that President Ford would sign the bill and that is just what happened, acting more as candidate Ford than as a national leader. In response to Ronald Reagan's challenge, Ford evidently felt he could not afford to alienate the fishermen, whether sport or commercial, who might vote in the Republican primaries. Thus, when the 200-mile bill reached the president's desk in the middle of the spring primaries, he caved in and signed it on April 13, 1976.

My point is not so much that Mr. Ford should not have signed the bill, but rather that he should have used his influence to prevent its passage by the Congress. If he had anticipated the problem, if he had educated the country about the ocean crisis and if he had backed alternative legislation, the bill need not have passed. But since he had not educated the electorate, Ford faced a terrible dilemma—to veto the bill and risk losing his party's nomination or to sign the bill even though it would have a very bad effect on the law of the sea negotiations.

I have purposely dwelt at length on the 200-mile bill. In the long history of the law of the sea, April 13, 1976, may be at least as famous as September 20, 1945, when President Truman unilaterally declared that the United States owned the resources of the seabed out to the end of the continental shelf. The Truman Proclamation was perhaps the most important law of the sea development since Grotius wrote his *Mare Liberum*.

Truman's unilateralism was quickly imitated, first by Latin American states and later by others. However, the Latins did not stop at the 200-meter depth line as Truman did. They stated their claim by distance rather than by depth—claiming *all* the resources, whether marine or mineral, as their own out to a 200-mile limit. Meanwhile, other states began to claim extended jurisdiction over pollution or research or both. Some, the "territorialists," even claimed a 200-mile territorial sea.

The Truman Proclamation was a body blow at the traditional system of freedom of the seas. Similarly, the 1976 200-mile bill was a body blow at the Law of the Sea Conference and its valiant effort to modernize the law of the sea by international agreement rather than by the unilateral actions of coastal states. Before the 200-mile bill passed, only about twenty nations had unilaterally proclaimed fishing jurisdiction out to 200 miles. By July 1, 1977, scarcely a year after the U.S. bill became law, fifty-six nations had joined the ranks of the unilateral 200-milers. The irony is that the most important purpose of the bill, the preservation of marine species, could have been achieved by another bill, H.R. 1070, which would not have violated international law. But President Ford evidently could not wait. And the wave of unilateralism which he triggered has been a major force in undercutting the conference.

I will give two further examples of the negative results of such American timidity and the essentially private way in which U.S. law of the sea diplomacy has been carried on. The first has to do with the important negotiations with respect to the structure and powers of the international seabed authority. It should have been clear from the start that the third world would insist that the proposed authority have its own "exploiting arm." Instead of welcoming such a development as a means of strengthening international institutions, the United States has fought against it. We have wasted precious time, making it appear that if we could not revive Grotius, we could at least resurrect Adam Smith! In turn our intransigence has encouraged intransigence and extremism on the other side. Fortunately, however, the United States has accepted the idea of a dual system for exploiting the deep ocean—partly private or national, and partly international. The international effort will be carried out by the "Enterprise," the exploiting arm of the proposed international seabed authority. The May-July 1977 session of the conference reflected the great division of opinion on this question. Nevertheless, by the end of the session a compromise seemed probable. However, the relevant articles of the composite text were labelled as completely unacceptable by Ambassador Elliot Richardson, the head of the U.S. delegation.

My second example of timidity in U.S. law of the sea policy has to do with the immensely important question of ownership of offshore mineral resources, more specifically, mineral resources within 200 miles of shore. This question can and should be separated from the question of the ownership of marine species. The key questions are: should all, or a substantial part, of these mineral resources continue to be regarded as *res communis,* the common property of the human family (the "common heritage of mankind"), or should these resources become the property of the coastal states? These questions are critical because the overwhelming proportion of exploitable mineral resources is within 200 miles of shore. And those resources are immensely valuable. Indeed, a recent U.N. study indicated that oil resources alone are worth $24 trillion, i.e., $24 thousand billion![2]

Unfortunately, the United States delegation is now supporting a proposal that all these trillions of dollars of mineral resources should become the property of the coastal states, each nation having complete control of the resources in a 200-mile exclusive economic zone (EEZ) off its shores. The EEZ is a radical departure from the central idea in the 1970 U.S. draft treaty, i.e., the idea that a substantial share of the revenue from that area should go to the international community to be used especially to assist developing nations. The "trusteeship zone" proposal in the draft treaty provided that 50 to 66 percent of the mineral revenues from the continental slope and the continental rise would go to an international seabed resources authority for the above-mentioned purposes. But the trusteeship zone idea had hardly been broached before the State Department began to back away from it in a retreat that rivals Napoleon's retreat from Moscow. Needless to say, U.S. oil companies encouraged that retreat.

In four short years the United States moved from the generous sharing proposal of the draft treaty to the endorsement of the 200-mile EEZ, a concept which would give the United States title to 2,222,000 square nautical miles of ocean resource, a larger area than any other country would get. A General Accounting Office (GAO) study says that at least 20 percent of all the world's fish are within 200 miles of the United States and there is, of course, a tremendous amount of oil and gas within this same area. The U.S. has justified its decision to support the exercise in self-enrichment with the arguments that the third world had not welcomed our trusteeship zone proposal. But we abandoned this trusteeship zone proposal at a time when the landlocked and geographically disadvantaged states had barely begun to understand the implications of the issue, much less arrive at a common strategy with respect to it. The landlocked countries had their work cut out for them as they tried to develop positions on law of the sea. Some of their fellow third world countries, countries for which they had real affection and respect, knew a great deal more about the law of the sea than these young countries did. What is more, they knew exactly what they wanted. Countries with long histories—and even longer maritime traditions—knew the law, the politics, the economics of the law of the sea. They knew how to urge their own law of the sea views in third world rhetoric. It is not difficult to imagine the blow it was to them when the U.S. and the USSR, two of the most powerful opponents of the EEZ, suddenly embraced the concept at the beginning of the Caracas session. The delegates had, it was implied, only two choices: to warmly embrace the EEZ; or to agree that, whether desirable or not, its realization was inevitable. It was a long time before the "landlocked and geographically disadvantaged states"—as they would later call themselves—recovered from the Sunday punch they received at Caracas.

Superficially, U.S. diplomacy has been brilliant on this question of the EEZ, for our initial opposition to the concept was of immense help to those promoting it. This paradox reflects the sad truth that in the United Nations overt U.S. support for a proposal can be a real liability, and overt U.S. opposition a real asset. Key third world states—states with much to gain from the EEZ—tried with considerable success to make the EEZ a test of loyalty to the third world. Then, in June 1974, the United States suddenly indicated it could live with the EEZ. It was a fateful decision and one which, like the trusteeship zone proposal, was taken without consulting the Congress or the general public.

If, as seems probable, it is endorsed by the conference, the 200-mile EEZ will give our very rich nation title to a tremendous amount of ocean wealth, much more than any other nation will get. But it will also insure that the idea that inspired the conference—the very promising idea of the oceans as the common heritage of mankind—will be a mere shadow.

Conclusions

If there is a law of the sea treaty, U.S. policymakers will probably get what they want with respect to the three major issues before the conference. Through the mechanism of the EEZ they will get the largest share of the $30 trillion worth of offshore mineral wealth. Second, they will probably get the *substance* of freedom of navigation if not the exact treaty language they prefer. So many nations, including third world nations, have such a strong interest in that freedom that it is not likely to fall victim to the so-called territorialists, i.e., the handful of nations calling for a 200-mile territorial sea.

The third part of the "probable treaty" will be the establishment of a powerful but poor seabed authority with the power to organize exploitation of hard minerals in the deep seabed. If there is agreement (and it is a big "if"), it will almost certainly result in a system for exploiting the deep seabed: partly private or national, and partly international. The modalities of that system are the most controversial part of the proposed treaty. Indeed the dispute about the authority is so heated that it may well doom the treaty.

A deep seabed authority would be a very desirable influence on building sentiments of world community. But its importance—and the possibility of its success—can easily be exaggerated. Because it is limited to the deep seabed the authority will produce very little revenue for the international community, i.e., for developing nations. Indeed, launching it will require a great deal of money. It is quite possible that there will be enough national nodules, i.e., nodules within 200 miles of the baselines of certain island states, that it will not be possible to have the effective price and production controls which the third world so ardently desires. It is unfortunate that the passionate dispute over the nature and powers of the seabed authority has served to divert attention from the tremendous grab of the real ocean treasure, the offshore oil and gas, through the device of the EEZ.

What about the other major conference issues, e.g., pollution, scientific research, dispute settlement, etc? The final treaty articles on each of these subjects will probably be ambiguous and contradictory. Operative systems for each of them will evolve slowly by state practice and by uneasy bargaining between coastal states, flag states, and other categories of states. One thing is clear though. The composite text favors the coastal states.

I have stressed the timidity and lack of imagination in U.S. law of the sea policy. This obliges me to suggest what bolder, more imaginative policy I think we should have pursued and to indicate why I think such a policy would have been more successful. The present ocean crisis offers a major opportunity for the international community not only to protect the ocean environment and living species within it, but also to build third world development, to strengthen international organization, and thus to strengthen peace. The ocean crisis is an opportunity not only to deal with specifically ocean problems but also to build habits of cooperation and trust. An integrated ocean strategy thus offers mankind a major alternative to the present drift toward heightened political and economic confrontation and an ever more dangerous arms race.

The great ocean crisis may be compared in some ways to the great crisis which threatened Europe after World War II. The nations of Western Europe responded so brilliantly to that crisis that no one believes that those traditional enemies, France and Germany, will make war against each other again. There are other reasons for the historic rapprochement but surely one of the most important is that Jean Monnet and Robert Schuman saw that the "German problem" was a European opportunity, an opportunity to intregrate these economies of Europe and in that way to undercut the destructive nationalisms of the past.

I think we should take the same kind of imaginative and broad-gauge approach to the Law of the Sea Conference. We should see the law of the sea question not just as a sea problem, or a means for enrichment from the sea; we should also see it as a precious opportunity to reconcile nations East and West, and North and South.

There have been some imaginative proposals from critics of U.S. policy and of the probable treaty toward which that policy has been working. However those critiques have had little if any effect on the American policy. Probably the most interesting proposal was that made by the Trilateral Commission in early 1976.[3] It suggested that wealthy states contribute as much as fifty percent of the mineral revenues from their 12- to 200-mile economic zones to help poorer nations. The commission's proposal takes on special interest when one realizes that when their report was issued the U.S. members of the commission included five men who would be the top foreign policy people in the Carter administration: President Carter, Vice President Mondale, Secretary of State Vance, Secretary of Defense Harold Brown, and National Security Council Director Zbigniew Brzezinski. Other members included William Scranton, then U.S. ambassador to the United Nations, David Rockefeller, chairman of the Chase Manhattan Bank, and Elliot Richardson, soon to be head of the U.S. delegation to the Law of the Sea Conference.

Another interesting proposal, known as "the *Barba Negra* Appeal," was adopted on August 22, 1976, by the U.N. delegates and other prominent persons who sailed the square-rigger *Barba Negra* from the United Nations to Manasquan, New Jersey. The onboard signers and later endorsers included anthopologist Thor Heyerdahl, political scientist Hans Morgenthau, Nobel Prize-winning economist Jan Tibergen, and many others. The key proposal in the appeal was that coastal states would be required to contribute between 20 percent of their revenues from within the zone to a world common fund. The fund would be used to promote third world development, to fund the fight against ocean pollution and to support the work of the United Nations and its specialized agencies. Contributions would be graduated to the per capita income of the coastal state, thus insuring that the burden on almost all third world coastal states would be very light, i.e., approximately 1 percent. According to a recent study of the Center for War/Peace Studies[4] the *Barba Negra* formula would provide approximately $3 billion a year for its stated purposes and provide it at once. By contrast, "deep seabed—only" sharing would, a recent U.N. study suggests, provide no more than $300 million a year—and that figure would not be reached until 1987.

The Trilateral and *Barba Negra* proposals address themselves to a central problem of the negotiations: how to give real substance to the dream of the common heritage. It has become increasingly clear that the deep seabed will furnish only a very small income to the international community. The real wealth, trillions and trillions of dollars, will go to a very few states, many of them developed states. Indeed, six of the seven nations which get the most ocean real estate from the EEZ are developed states—the United States, Australia, New Zealand, Canada, the USSR, and Japan. In my view, the radical nature of the third world's proposals for the international authority is closely related to the realization that the EEZ dooms any meaningful common heritage funding. If they cannot get ocean wealth perhaps these states can at least make point idologically by insisting on a radical seabed authority.

And many of them are willing to risk having no treaty at all rather than give in on this point. Meaningful sharing would probably cause them to be less doctrinaire on the question of the authority.

Substantial common heritage funding is thus essential to the achievement of a worthwhile and durable treaty. Such funding must include some of the mineral revenues within 200 miles of shore. More importantly, such a treaty could be a turning point in international politics, signifying growing realization of the need for common action on common problems, self-generated funding to deal with those problems and strong institutions to work on them. T. S. Eliot once said that there is only one thing worse in life than not to realize your dreams—and that is to realize them! The chances are good that our law of the policymakers will realize their dreams. With or without a treaty the United States will probably gain a fantastic amount of ocean wealth. And—how beautiful!—we shall be able to blame the third world for enriching us. How clever! But sooner or later we shall realize that our dream of enrichment was utterly inconsistent with other and more important American dreams—dreams of peace, of reconciling the "haves" and the "have nots," or protecting the human environment. American law of the sea policy is making each of these goals much harder to reach.

Notes

1. Logue, John J., "The Coming Showdown with Ocean Nationalism," *America* (December 27, 1975).

2. Trilateral Commission, "A New Regime for the Oceans" (New York: 1976).

3. Ibid.

4. Hudson, Richard, *Three Scenarios: The Law of the Sea, Ocean Mining and the New International Economic Order* (New York: Center for War/Peace Studies, 1977).

23. The United States in Search of an International Energy Policy: Global/Regional Tradeoffs
Richard E. Bissell

International politics is taking on an increasingly sophisticated air. Behavior of new nations considered random ten or twenty years ago is admired now as relatively shrewd judgment by managers of national power on the international stage. The choice of forums for the pursuit of national aims in a world of multiplying institutions has been so purposive—the proliferation of international institutions has been so rapid as to give the modern foreign minister a veritable supermarket of organizations from which to choose a diplomatic arena in which to press his case. In international economic policy coordination, in place of the few organizations founded after World War II, we now have dozens. They range from global to subregional in the scope of their membership, and in their issue coverage they may simply regulate one commodity or attempt to integrate all of modern man's economic woes in one basket.[1]

Few would deny the proposition that the structure of international relations is related to the organization of institutions established to service transactions and resolve disputes over proceedings. Yet, there has been little testing of hypotheses regarding the choice exercised by national governments when confronted by several institutions that address similar problems. Such decisions may appear to be arbitrary, or even instinctive, but when one is considering the case of the United States, whose diplomacy is subject to as much anticipatory analysis as that of any country in the world, one can assume a more deliberative approach. Interviews with government officials, indeed, confirm the notion that a great deal, though perhaps not enough, of man-hour effort goes into the trade-offs between the utility of using different organizations on specific problems.

The specific hypothesis to be considered in this essay is that countries aim for consensus on the most extensive level, using global organizations such as the United Nations if it is felt that a decision amenable to the interests of all the countries can be reached. Such a hypothesis might be accepted intuitively, based upon the difference between the United Nations authorizing issuance of postage stamps and the North Atlantic Treaty Organization authorizing nuclear attack contingency plans. But the case of energy suggests certain corollaries to the hypothesis with fairly wide-ranging implications. One is that the degree of consensus demanded on an issue in any organization is related to the centrality of the issue in a nation's society and economy. The second corollary is more specifically rooted in the historical experience of the last three years, namely that nations, such as the United States, with a lowered expectation of their international capabilities (i.e., in perceiving a generally hostile environment after Vietnam and other foreign policy setbacks) will frequently underestimate the consensus available, and thus reach out diplomatically to only a limited audience. Proof of such hypotheses may not be forthcoming, but the questions deserve consideration as emerging economic issues move into the diplomatic forefront.

As with most international organizations, history has played a decisive role in the present "structure." Control by present nation-state actors over the energy environment is thus diminished. At the same time, the United States suffers from the fact that many powerful institutions have been created and are controlled outside this country. In each aspect, the United States has lost a measure of economic sovereignty.

The principal historical development in institutional terms was the international growth of the enegy trade at a time when liberal capitalism and colonial empires gave a privileged position to certain corporations.[2] Those companies, five out of seven being American, worked to create an aura of apolitical, free-market forces at work, in order to discourage the possible intervention of governments against the economic sovereignties of the multinational oil companies. Those in the U.S. government interested in petroleum matters knew that various government agencies did provide support for the companies (as in the 1953 coup overthrowing Mossadeqh in Iran and in the transfer of military aid to those governments with the most friendly attitudes toward American oil companies). Thus, to a degree, the American government is constrained in its ability to respond to the present environment by past policy patterns, which would dictate leaving day-to-day policy initiative to the oil companies.

The second major development to remove control from the U.S. government has been the formation and strengthening of the

Organization of Petroleum Exporting Countries (OPEC) and its Arab sister organization, the Organization of Arab Petroleum Exporting Countries (OAPEC).[3] Formed in 1960, OPEC remained largely powerless until the early 1970s, when the United States became a significant net importer of petroleum and thus lost control over the marginal barrels of oil. Marginal goods tend to determine the price, and the United States was no longer producing them in the petroleum fields of East Texas.

Even as OPEC emerged into visibility in the early 1970s, however, the public continued to believe that the energy issue was primarily an economic issue. For example, in the *Statesman's Year-Book* of 1974/1975, there was still no entry for OPEC, and yet there were entries for SEATO, the Andean Group, and the Danube Convention.[4] OPEC was apparently perceived as an organization offsetting the western oil companies, upon which the industrialized nations could rely to demand the best bargain available. Widespread doubt appeared only when the oil companies were unable to deliver all of their commitments in the aftermath of the Yom Kippur War of 1973. It appeared that OPEC had not only matched the oil companies in demonstrating the ability of the producers to determine price, but was able to use petroleum as a political tool to affect developments, at least in the Mideast region.

The events that could simply be recorded to that date would appear to lend substantial support to the theories of Robert Gilpin and Edward Morse.[5] Their views bear recounting here, since they shed some light upon the probable institutional structures faced by the United States in the near future. Briefly, Gilpin has maintained that the power of the multinationals in the international system, and thus the previous energy structure, existed only at the sufferance of the governing political authorities, i.e., governments friendly to the West. With the global transition to economic nationalism, natural political forces have retaken control over what has always been considered a basic and strategic commodity—energy. The role of energy in the industrialized societies, especially their capacity to wage war, cannot be overstated, and thus it is logical that energy would be treated as a political commodity. Historical parallels could be drawn with the roles of gold and salt in earlier civilizations, but there is no denying the present central role of energy.[6]

The United States has yet to admit the essentially political nature of the energy problem. Despite well-documented studies that rebut any significant role for economic logic in meeting the core of the energy problem,[7] the American government has persistently treated the problem as an economic problem with a political twist. The distinction between an economic and political issue may appear to be a semantic game. In the institutional context, however, it has great operational significance. The course of policy formation within the U.S. government will reflect the distinction, mitigated only to the degree that the Federal Energy Administration (FEA) centralizes and harmonizes the differing points of view. Even within the FEA, however, there exist differences (more pronounced at certain times than others) between policy planners prone to trust the oil companies and those inclined toward state intervention.

On the international level, the projection of U.S. policy thus reflects an emphasis in an economic or political direction. It should be made clear, though, that the issue here is not economic as opposed to military security considerations.[8] Rather, I am focusing on the degree to which energy transactions involve centralized, politicized actions by the government rather than the traditional autonomous decision making of individuals and companies operating under economic "laws."

In the aftermath of the oil boycott and price rises of 1973-1974, the rhetoric and actions of the U.S. government developed in a mixed pattern. Proposals for more active government intervention, ranging from establishment of a government-operated oil trading company to a military invasion of the Persian Gulf fields, were rapidly rejected by potent forces in the American political scene. The petroleum multinationals were among those deploring possible overt political intervention, feeling that they would lose their reason for existence. The concern over their own survival was justified in the extreme circumstances of 1973-1974, and their influence has contributed to the evolution of a basically nonpolitical response by the United States to OPEC.

In response to the oil boycott and the Yom Kippur War price rises, the United States was initially obligated to no reply at all. If it was receiving no oil, the price rise had no impact, and the military supplies to Israel (the immediate political target of the Arab producers) could still be shipped on the basis of American stockpiles. However, as it quickly became clear that serious economic damage was being done to the West European economies, causing the American allies to disengage from American Mideast policies, the United States began to act. Talks with the European states yielded nothing, as those hard-pressed governments scrambled to sign bilateral contracts with various Arab producers. The United States, having lost control, persisted in its view that the situation simply required some economic adjustments, mostly in domestic conservation, diversification of foreign and domestic energy sources, and the efficient recycling of Arab payments surpluses.[9] Indeed, as the 1974 International Economic Report of the President optimistically suggested, "U.S. exports of energy-related equipment will ultimately be a major component of U.S. sales abroad."[10] Aside from the political sacrifices implicit in Project Independence, the president seemed unwilling to go out on a limb. He called a conference in Washington in February 1974 for the major industrialized nations "to discuss the problems of ensuring adequate energy supplies at reasonable cost." Few were likely to disagree with that goal.

With the failure of the United States to muster the political will for a successful Project Independence, the government was left with essentially no choice except to address in some manner the challenge of interdependence, or in this case, the dependence of the United States on foreign-produced energy. The brief surge of economic nationalism engendered no enthusiasm, and so equally difficult issues had to be faced. From this point onwards, government policy followed two tracks simultaneously: bilateral political ties to major producers of oil for political and military security, and the maintenance of the multinational oil companies as window-dressing middlemen in petroleum importing, so long as they would accept a steadily diminishing role in the international energy system.

The diplomatic events of 1974 did little to dispel this impression. The formation of the International Energy Agency (IEA) meshed in a somewhat more elaborate arrangement the existing Oil Committee of the Organization for Economic Cooperation and Development (OECD) and emergency allocation bureaucracies of the national governments, with the oil companies designated as the executors of the policies in the event of another boycott. It is fortunate that the standby arrangements of the IEA have not been tested since their formation, since their value was meant to be largely deterrent and on that basis can be considered as successful as any alliance that has not experienced a war. The far more meaningful stipulations of the IEA were those covering oil stockpile levels and energy conservation measures, both presumably accomplished only by government action and therefore making their implementation in the United States somewhat problematic.

The willingness of the United States to acquiesce in the creation of a regional energy organization, based on the trilateral cooperation of Japan, North America, and Western Europe, might initially suggest the abandonment of the global approach by the American government. One might readily accept the notion that the structural rules of the energy war had been established by OPEC, and the United States was obtaining all that was possible in institutional terms in 1974. A closer examination, however, suggests that the U.S. government had little interest in the regional dimension; the IEA was intended only as a holding action, and remains such.

The American administration was not relying upon the IEA or the oil companies to maintain the oil supply to the United States and its major allies. Far more important transactions were occurring with the Iranian and Saudi allies of the United States that were designed to undercut any possible future embargo based on a Mideast war. The Iranians provided assurances that the oil supply to Israel would continue after a pullout from occupied territory, and the Saudis agreed to dampen subsequent militancy within OPEC, a promise they have managed to keep with the aid of suppressed world consumption. The basic political problems, in so far as they could be settled for the short term, were thus dealt with bilaterally.

At the same time, the State Department has tested the international environment repeatedly in efforts to raise the rhetorical war to the global level, and thus form a multiregional alliance against OPEC. Diplomacy among the oil-importing third world attempted to convey the message that their best interests would be served by denouncing the regional, beggar-thy-neighbor pricing policies of OPEC. Few responded, at least publicly. In this environment, the U.S. government saw little use in carrying the dispute to a global body such as the United Nations.

A few states (particularly in Western Europe), however, retained the vision of global cooperation on the energy question. To them the formation of a regional IEA represented a building block for a subsequent global organization.[11] The splits within the IEA give the observer some sense of where support lies for the building block theory. It has been said by one knowledgeable insider that "underlying tensions have existed in the IEA since its inception both in terms of strategies to be followed vis-à-vis OPEC and measures to be adopted at the national level among the member states themselves. While there appears to be some change, American policy has inclined more toward confrontation with OPEC while other members have leaned toward a more cooperative posture."[12] Thus there have been efforts on the part of the French, in particular, to encourage global discussions in a forum free of historical constraints—in this case, the Conference on International Economic Cooperation (CIEC). The Paris talks have encountered serious problems, partially because of the initial American response, which was to oppose diplomatic proceedings that might grant legitimacy to commodity producers' cartels. Thus, the United States once again attempted to keep the historical structure alive (in the multinationals' control of the oil trade) at a time when the exporting countries and the third world had moved in the direction of political control of energy flows.

The above interpretation of events is not given to condemn the policy directions of the U.S. government, but to explain some of the constraints on the American response to the energy problem. Since the maximalist goals of different sectors of the U.S. government differ, it is safe to say only that the American view simply favors the emergence of some global consensus—all of which offers no conclusion about the desired substantive outcome. Far more important is the challenge of determining the change in conditions required for a transfer of interest by the U.S. government to the global level.

The first hurdle is the gap between the U.S. tendency to consider energy as an *economic* problem, and the insistence of the OPEC states that petroleum be considered in relation to many other, frequently political, issues. Even if the minimal demand of the third world was that petroleum be considered in relation to other commodities, the issue as perceived by the West would be one of principle of free trade. Just as the introduction of domestic price controls sparks vicious ideological debate in the United States, the concession of such a point of principle at the international level would bring to the surface of American society many deep-rooted conflicts. Some Western governments support the American position. Many governments take a compromise position, and much of the third world, due in part to de facto state control of the petroleum trade, sides with OPEC.[13]

The possibilities of changes in the international environment and American attitudes that might lead to a broad-scale treatment of the energy issue in a global forum can be reduced to four.

1. *New Technologies* could have a significant impact on the nature of the energy issue, in displacing oil's role as the primary energy source, or in dispersing the control over oil production to other producers. The use of technology in nonpetroleum energy to further U.S. independence from OPEC political pressure is feasible primarily through nuclear power or solar energy. The use of new technology to permit conservation on a significant scale, particularly in the industrial processes of the United States and Western Europe, would help reduce the centrality of the petroleum trade as a factor in international life. The process envisioned here would mean a change in the role of oil to that of a commodity like coffee or copper, where substitutability actually exists as the price reaches undesirable levels. There would need to be either substitute sources of energy, or people would need to be willing to forego energy supplies altogether for periods of time. The likelihood

of either scenario occurring in the near future, thus reducing the political pressure on maintaining current levels of petroleum flows, is nil. In the long run, of course, new forms of energy are very probable, but if no actions are taken on the global level in the meantime, the political environment is likely to get much worse before it gets better.

2. An *ideological reversion* to free-trade capitalism in the international system would create a climate in which the United States could participate more comfortably. A decision by the major petroleum exporters to reverse the trend toward state-dominated energy decisions would allow the return to the "brokered" market dominated by the oil companies. This viewpoint is defended by working people in the field, such as Ulf Lantzke, executive director of the IEA since November 1974. In a recent article, he maintained that

> governments, for their part, should be prepared to accept that the "international oil business"—in the broadest sense of the term—still provides the most efficient logistical apparatus for performing the extraordinarily complex task of matching world energy supplies with ever changing patterns of demand. . . . On the other hand, private business, including, above all, the international oil companies, will have to recognize that theirs is not a private economic world, but that it remains very much at the center of public and political attention.[14]

A conscious OPEC decision to move in this direction can be dismissed out of hand, but somewhat more likely would be such a trend imposed by the breakdown of the international economy. In a severe depression, in which the production capabilities would far outstrip world-wide demand, one can foresee the resurgence of independent brokers who might be able to place spot sales of petroleum more advantageously than national governments. Such an environment, however, would still fail to encourage intergovernmental organizations to assume a governing role in international energy affairs. Indeed, it could be safely posited that there would be no interest in the United States for referring energy and other "economic" affairs to international organizations.

3. *Acceptance of energy's political status* by all states would establish a base of common assumptions on which to negotiate a new system for petroleum or other energy transfers. The breakdown of the united IEA front against state-to-state deals can already be seen. Recent negotiations between the Iranian prime minister and the French government involved bypassing the oil companies in a large sales transaction.[15] A useful parallell can be seen in the formation of the International Atomic Energy Agency (IAEA), based upon a common

viewpoint toward atomic energy—useful, but so politically charged as to need control by governments rather than private interests. There exists an analogous potential for damage by conventional forms of energy, not just to power conventional war machines, but also damage to industrial economies by its withdrawal.

It has become commonplace to remark upon the increasing fragility of industrial civilization as it become more complex, and yet there is a reluctance to ensure supplies of those material elements basic to its day-to-day survival. Energy (and presently petroleum) is one of those elements, and has not been treated with due respect because of its previous abundance. Just as the potential impact of wanton use of atomic energy was eventually recognized (perhaps too belatedly to control its proliferation), it resulted in the formal mechanisms of the IAEA, recognized as one of the most effective international organizations today. Even when formal organizations proved unwieldy, we have witnessed the emergence of informal groupings such as the Group of Seven (now expanded to include Italy, Sweden, Belgium, East Germany, and the Netherlands in addition to the original United States, USSR, Britain, France, West Germany, Canada, and Japan). Their efforts to establish guidelines in the export of nuclear power equipment could establish precedents in the area of trade in politically sensitive goods.

Establishing an intergovernmental organization to deal with a functional problem raises its own peculiar hazards. What, for instance, would such an organization do to enforce its system if a new Mideast war were to break out? Is it possible that recognizing the basic political role of energy in fact precludes the international regulation of the commodity until a more stable international order emerges? Is energy too important to be regulated by a relatively immature international system? These are difficult questions, not raised for the first time as a result of the energy problem, and their answers will probably not emerge as a result of dealing with the energy problem.

4. *Abandonment of economic nationalism* by the major nations involved in energy transactions would eventually allow for a cooperative approach to energy allocations in place of the present competition. The nationalist influences on the energy market place introduce a contentiousness conducive to imposed solutions (OPEC price rises) and the introduction of force (political as well as military) as the only recourse. Much has been said about interdependence, but few actions have emerged on the global level as a result. The internalization of the interdependent spirit in nations would presumably result in a cooperative outlook, driving out the present zero-sum-game approach where our gain is our neighbor's

loss, and thus looking to the most efficient use of energy that results in global economic health. The strength of economic nationalism today can be seen in the paucity of critical economic activities undertaken by global organizations. The United States has generally reaffirmed its economic sovereignty in its actions on energy to date, whether out of conviction or in response to the international environment. The attempt to maintain the international oil companies' role has undoubtedly involved political and economic costs, even though the exact calculations are obscure. The testing of the alliance structure of the Atlantic community to obtain the cooperation of other nations has spent political capital. The commitment of private and public funds as loans to Western Europe and the third world to finance deficits has also been costly economically.

The obstacles to global cooperation are thus of a systemic nature, and the possibility of any one of the four options outlined in the previous section coming to pass must be considered remote. The pressure to maintain ideologies in the West, in OPEC, and in the developing countries appears to be sufficient to continue bending the objective economic and political realities into continuing distortions. Thus, until the economic costs of the present policy courses force an admission of the bankruptcy of one of the ideologies, one can assume that energy planning will continue on its current regional course.

Notes

1. To offer a regional example, Nazli Choucri lists the following "major institutional developments in Arab states" along with dates of establishment: Abu Dhabi Fund for Arab Economic Development (1971), Arab Bank for Industrial and Agricultural Development in Africa (1974), Arab Company for Shipping and Repair (1974), Arab Energy Institute (1974), Arab Financial Company (1974), Arab Fund for Economic and Social Development (1968), Arab Investment Guarantee Organization (1974), Arab Petroleum Investment Company (1974), Islamic Development Bank (1973), Kuwait Fund for Arab Economic Development (1961), Iraq Foreign Development Fund (1974), Saudi Development Fund (1974), Special OAPEC Fund for Arab Nonoil Producers (1974), and Special Arab Fund for Africa (1974). See *International Politics of Energy Interdependence* (Lexington: D. C. Heath, 1976), pp. 140-142.

2. The development of the Seven Sisters as the dominant structure is chronicled in Marian Kent, *Oil and Empire* (New York: Barnes and Noble, 1976); Christopher T. Rand, *Making Democracy Safe for Oil* (Boston: Little Brown, 1975); Neil Jacoby, *Multinational Oil* (New York: Macmillan, 1974).

3. See: Fuad Rouhani, *A History of OPEC* (New York: Praeger, 1971);

Zuhayr Mikdashi, *The Community of Oil Exporting Countries* (Ithaca: Cornell University Press, 1972); and Mana Saeed al-Otaiba, *OPEC and the Petroleum Industry* (New York: John Wiley, 1975).

4. John Paxton, ed., *The Statesman's Year-Book 1974/1975* (New York: St. Martins Press, 1974).

5. See Robert Gilpin, "The Politics of Transnational Economic Relations," *International Organization* 25 (summer 1971): 398–419, and Edward L. Morse, *Modernization and the Transformation of International Relations* (New York: Free Press, 1976), pp. 18-20.

6. Dramatic proof is indicated by the U.S. government's calculation of the "tolerable" cut in energy consumption before "serious domestic unrest" would result: 7 percent or one million barrels per day.

7. See Nazli Choucri, *International Politics of Energy Interdependence*.

8. On this topic, see the *Proceedings, National Security Affairs Conference, July 14-15, 1975* (National War College, Washington, D.C.), especially Panel V, where participants discussed the "importance of protecting the national security label from misuse in support of parochial concerns of particular interest groups" (p. 8).

9. *International Economic Report of the President,* transmitted to the Congress, February 1974, pp. 44-50.

10. Ibid., p. 51.

11. The theoretical validity of such a notion is described by Inis L. Claude, *Swords Into Plowshares,* 3rd ed. (New York: Random House, 1964), pp. 97-100.

12. Lawrence Scheinman, "Energy and Cooperation Among Consumer Countries," draft paper presented at Conference on the Changing Faces of the Energy Problem, New Orleans, February 1976, p. 8.

13. For the OPEC point of view, which emphasizes the removal of the concessionary system to permit "direct contacts between the producers and consumers of oil," see Ali Ahmad Attiga (secretary-general of OAPEC), "New Possibilities for Oil Producer-Consumer Relations," *Oil and Arab Cooperation* 2 (1976): 12-24.

14. Ulf Lantzke, "International Co-operation on Energy—Problems and Prospects," *The World Today* 32 (March 1976): 88.

15. Bart Collins, "State-to-State Oil Deals," *Oil and Gas Journal* (June 7, 1976), p. 71.

24. Energy Independence—
Is It Feasible and Desirable?
Joseph Barnea

There appears to be little doubt that energy independence has become desirable. The last five years have seen the world pricing of oil being taken over by a group of governments, with world prices of oil determined primarily by political considerations and not by demand and supply factors. Secondly, the oil boycott we witnessed showed that the reliability of depending on foreign supplies of oil is now questionable. Finally, the high cost of imported oil in terms of prices and foreign exchange makes local development of energy resources in many cases economically attractive.

Energy independence is not only desirable for economic reasons but also for strategic and political reasons because energy is the lifeblood of a modern economy, the lifeblood of any army, and the one group of products which is as vital for each country as is the supply of water. Indeed, energy and water are the two groups of commodities which a country should possess in order to be economically strong and not subject to serious economic disturbances beyond its control.

It is comparatively easy to argue that energy independence is desirable for every country in the world, great and small, developed or developing. However, the question of whether it is feasible is much more complex. The question of the feasibility of a country to achieve energy independence depends on a series of factors, the most important of which is the energy resource potential of a country. Further, there is the question of whether the country has the technology and the capital to explore and develop its local energy resource potential. Among the other factors is the capability of a country to replace the demand for oil and gas to some extent by coal and other energy resources. There is the factor of increasing the efficient use of the country's energy by investment in house insulation, better equipment, etc. Finally, there must be the political will for a consistent energy policy to achieve energy independence.

As a model, we will discuss the energy resource potential of the United States. A country like the United States has the resource potential, the technical capacity, and the capital to achieve energy independence within a given period of time. It has large oil, gas, coal, as well as geothermal, hydro, wood, and other renewable resources, including agricultural and municipal wastes, wind and sun, ocean thermal resources, microbiological, and many others.

It is common belief that the United States will soon be running out of oil and gas. And although this view is held also by many policymakers, it is not entirely true. The published estimates by practically every organization in the United States for oil and gas are based on very narrow definitions which, at a price of $13.00 for imported oil, simply do not make sense. The U.S. Geological Survey employs for its estimates of its reserves the following definition: "Crude oil is a natural mixture of hydrocarbons occurring underground in a liquid state as it flows from a well at atmospheric pressure." This definition restricts the reserves from a conventional oil field to oil coming out by its own pressure, or what is called in technical terms primary recovery, which may be only 15 to 25 percent of the oil in place. This definition excludes almost all oil which needs to be pumped, all oil from secondary and tertiary recovery, as well as oil in plastic form, such as heavy crude and tar sand, oil in solid form such as oil shales, and so on. The oil estimate therefore probably includes only a fraction of 1 percent of the oil in place underground in the United States. A similar definition is applied to natural gas based exclusively on two types: associated gas from conventional oil fields and dry gas from natural gas fields. But we know today of twelve sources of nature-made natural gas, and ten of them are disregarded in the resource and reserve figures which are published in this country. The U.S. Geological Survey estimates also exclude oil beyond 200 meters depth offshore, even though offshore leases have been issued, offshore exploration takes place in far deeper water, and oil fields have been discovered in deeper water.

What this means is that our resource definitions and reserve definitions are old-fashioned and reflect price and cost relationships before the oil crisis. With the new oil price, much of the oil not included in the present definition is economical to extract. Perhaps half of all oil was produced in 1976 by secondary recovery in the United States. The price and cost relationship is crucial. It is often not realized that with a sudden jump of the world oil prices from $2-$3 to $11, $12, and $13 (depending on whether one considers posted prices or delivered prices), the energy resource base has sharply expanded and the more costly oil resources, which were uneconomic to extract at $2 or $3 per barrel, are now attractive, provided the technology has been developed to extract it. The United Nations Institute for Training and Research (UNITAR) is organizing jointly with the International Institute for Systems Analysis (IIASA), a conference in Vienna on "The Future Supply of Nature-Made Oil and Gas." In this conference experts on all the variety of types of oil and gas will meet together in order to discuss the present status of extraction technology and the outlook for the future of better extraction technology, the necessary manpower, etc. Underlying this conference, as well as many other studies on the future supply of oil, is the assumption that, because the government producers group exists, the oil prices will not decline.

There are valid economic reasons for this assumption. Looking into the future, it is not decisive what the cost of extraction will be, provided that the extraction technology will be developed. If certain types of oil shale, for example, would require a price of $15.00 to $18.00 per barrel for the extraction of oil, we know that at present world market prices this will be uneconomical, but it may be economical in 10 to 15 years. If such oil shale resources are explored in the meantime, they will come in, at that future price level, as a new and additional source of energy. Consequently, as prices in the future increase, the resource base expands, and more oil supplies as well as natural gas supplies will become available. However, this strategy of expanding higher-cost oil resources works only if there is a government policy which encourages local production.

In the United States, natural gas prices were kept low by a high court decision of 1954, and this price control is still in effect. Similarly, the Energy and Conservation Act passed by Congress in December of 1975 keeps oil prices in this country considerably below world market prices, while at the present time there is no price control over imported oil nor any control over the quantities of oil imported. The local oil price for certain categories of oil is kept at $7.00, which prevents the local production of oil costing between $7.00 and $13.00 per barrel (unless it is newly discovered oil) and it also discourages the exploration for higher cost oil and the development of the extraction technology. Thus, an energy policy is also a vital element in the strategy of achieving energy independence.

Another aspect of any energy policy in the United States is the ability of environmentalists and other citizens' groups to delay exploration and other energy developments by using the courts. Such environmental opposition has delayed the construction of the Alaska pipeline for

Energy Independence

several vital years and has delayed a number of offshore exploration projects such as development projects, especially in the West. There is no doubt that no long-term policy can be effective if private groups of citizens have the right through the courts to delay or to oppose projects and policies which have been approved by Congress and the executive.

Only a very small percentage of the offshore potential of the United States has been opened for exploration and, in spite of the hundred years of oil exploration in this country, there is still much exploration to be done for conventional oil and gas. Moreover, the coal resources of the United States are vast, measured in trillions of tons. The proved reserves are very much smaller, however, because the artificially low prices of natural gas since 1954 brought a decline in U.S. coal production—coal in the sixties was a declining industry. Circumstances have changed now, but there are still environmental and other obstacles to the opening up of a number of coal areas, including the low sulphur and low-cost coal in the West. There is little doubt, however, that coal could easily take over as boiler fuel in power stations and the use of coal could be expanded in a number of other areas. Slowly this process is under way, but it lacks a strong government policy encouraging such development.

I will not analyze here all the other energy resources in the United States. Let me mention only geothermal energy, of which the United States has a vast potential. Most of it is on federal land, but federal land was opened only in 1973 to geothermal exploration. A number of other factors have delayed the development of this low cost and attractive source of energy.

This short and abbreviated analysis of some of the energy resources of the United States is perhaps sufficient to indicate that it has the resource potential for energy independence, and I believe it also has a potential to become a significant supplier of energy to other parts of the world.[1] The position is significantly different in energy-importing developing countries, because we know far less about their energy resource potential and very often they do not have the capital and the technology to both explore and develop their energy resources. For such developing countries there is no easy solution to the energy problems because most of them do not have the foreign exchange to pay for increasing quantities of high-cost petroleum. Thus, the effect of their energy situation is often a reduction in the rate of growth and sometimes even a decline in their standard of living. There is no doubt, however, that energy independence is also desirable for such energy-importing developing countries even though it may not be feasible in the near future for financial reasons.

Notes

1. A recent report by the Department of the Interior, "Energy Perspectives," (June 1976) shows on page 10 that 49 percent of the measured world recoverable energy reserves in 1974 were in North America. Though the composition of energy resources and other details may be open to criticism, the figures nevertheless demonstrate the predominant role of North America in energy resources.

25. U.S. Raw Materials Policy: The Pros and Cons of Self-Sufficiency
Bension Varon

Origins of the Renewed Debate

The origins of the current debate about self-sufficiency in the developed countries, like so many others, can be traced to the by-now classic MIT study, *Limits to Growth,* and the landmark success of the Organization of Petroleum Exporting Countries (OPEC). The MIT study dealt with the problem of global sufficiency. Initially it embodied no political controversies, but this did not last. It was, after all, conceptually but a step from world sufficiency to national sufficiency—from "is there enough for everybody?" to "is there enough for us?" By posing the question of the distribution of benefits from the consumption of nonrenewable resources among generations, the study drew attention to the distribution of benefits among nations in the form of consumers and producers.

Concern over the scarcity and control of natural resources intensified with the four-fold increase in the price of oil by the members of OPEC. The OPEC action was ushered in with an embargo; it involved a truly critical material; it affected nearly all countries; it coincided with one of the sharpest commodity cycles in the post-war era; it created fear about physical or politically induced scarcities of other raw materials; it exposed the vulnerabilities of the industrial giants; it changed the constellation of power; it reduced the financial maneuverability of nations to allocate resources to the production or acquisition of food and

The views expressed in this chapter are the author's and do not necessarily represent those of the United Nations or the World Bank with which he has been affiliated. The author gratefully acknowledges the assistance and useful comments of Mr. Jerry J. Gumpel.

raw materials; and it made self-sufficiency through conservation or domestic resource development a universally attractive goal, which, by the way, is advocated in the strongest terms by the OPEC countries themselves for nations who have the potential. If ever there was a strong package, this was it, given that there has always been a dormant view that self-sufficiency is synonymous with national strength and freedom of action.

In response, most industrialized countries rushed to examine their demand-supply balances, prospects, and choices in the whole range of raw materials, with special attention to their sources of supply of nonrenewable commodities. While the United States is in the most advantageous position in this respect among developed market-economy countries (with the possible exception of Canada), the concern was also most explicit here largely for two reasons: (1) the United States has the greatest flexibility in terms of unexploited reserves, capital, and technology, and (2) it has the kind of political commitments and objectives which lead it to believe that it is a prime target for disruptive action.

Perceptions of Threat and Stockpile Policy: Past and Present

United States dependence on foreign supplies of "strategic and critical" materials is not a new phenomenon, nor is the concern over it. What is new are the perceptions of the dangers that may flow from such dependence. The first indication of official concern with the problem of supply of materials can be found in 1939 when the Strategic Materials Act (Public Law 117, 76th Congress) established stockpiling of strategic materials as a public policy. Few earlier indications of government concern can be found because as late as 1900 the United States produced more raw materials than it consumed. By 1939 the situation had changed, and the United States, fearing that the coming war would interrupt supplies of necessary materials, began to build stockpiles. After World War II, Congress again enacted a stockpiling law, the Strategic and Critical Materials Stockpiling Act of 1946 (Public Law 529, 79th Congress). Nonetheless, by the time the Korean War broke out, the country was quite unprepared. President Truman, alarmed at the implications of materials shortages in times of war, on January 22, 1951, created The President's Materials Policy Commission, known as the Paley Commission after William S. Paley, its chairman. This commission's report[1] can be regarded as the first major attempt by a government body to study "the materials problem of the United States."

Both the creation of the commission and its pronouncements underlined the indispensability of materials to economic strength and the close link between economic strength and national security. The basic concern of the commission was that of approximately one hundred materials surveyed, the United States imported all or part of its requirements in more than two-thirds. Although the criteria used in drawing up the list of "strategic and critical" materials are not explicitly stated in its report, the commission was clearly concerned with those materials necessary to keep the war machine functioning in times of armed conflict.[2]

Why did the commission find U.S. dependence on imports of critical materials so disturbing? The answer is political; the report was written at the height of the cold war and reflected the fear that it might escalate into a hot war. (The report actually uses this terminology.) The commission feared that if an all-out war broke out, the supply of critical materials to the United States would be interrupted. It is important to stress that the commission did not foresee any politically motivated interruptions of supply, and not once did it doubt that the other countries of the free world would continue to supply the United States. What it did fear was that such countries could be invaded by the enemy and would hence no longer be able to ship materials to the United States. The commission also feared that the sea lanes of communication would come under enemy control, thus interrupting the supply of critical materials.[3]

The Paley Commission recommended ten main steps to prepare for matching wartime requirements of materials with supplies. Of those steps, five were aimed at reducing demand, five at increasing supply. The recommendations, in retrospect, are remarkable. Rather than becoming outmoded, many of them are on the current list of options for extending the availability of scarce resources, nationally or globally.[4] I shall discuss below only one of these recommendations, namely that calling for the stockpiling of strategic and critical materials.

The basic assumptions behind the recommended stockpile policy were: (1) in case of a new war, unlike previous wars, the United States would not have a long period to achieve the necessary buildup; (2) as much as 50 percent of total U.S. output would be needed by the military; and (3) the war would last for "a number of years," perhaps as many as four or five. An implicit assumption was that the United States could not rely entirely on civilian consumption cutbacks to supply the military. When the commission's recommendation became enacted policy, the assumptions behind the stockpiling program were: (1) a three-year conflict; (2) material supplies from North America and the Caribbean would be available throughout the conflict; and (3) various selected countries would be accessible in the second and third years of conflict.[5]

The 1952 notion of the purpose of stockpiles can be reconstructed from the Paley Commission's report. It held that stockpiling is not a device to ensure self-sufficiency in wartime, but that stockpiles are to be seen, rather, as "strength-in-being for the first surge of demand if total war breaks out, and are planned to further supplement supplies for an all-out war of considerable duration."[6] It is interesting to note that the commission's definition of stockpiles included domestic products.[7]

Moving on to the late 1970s, the first thing to observe is that with the notable exception of petroleum, the dependence of the United States on imports of critical materials has not changed significantly.[8] Yet, U.S. dependence is being fully reevaluated. This time, however, the perception of the problem is different. No longer are the raw material contingencies of war at the root of the concern. Indeed, when the stockpiling policy was changed in 1973, the basic assumptions were that the stockpile must cover U.S. needs for only the first year of conflict (in contrast to the earlier provision of three years) and that access to certain suppliers could be assured for three years. Furthermore, the revised policy explicitly relied on increased austerity and substitution as means of reducing vulnerability, should the conflict last longer than assumed.[9] In accordance with this change, the quantitative objectives of various stockpiles were reduced and disposal authorizations were signed into law for six materials. When in April 1973 the administration proposed to authorize sales from stockpiles, most reports on this proposal claimed the reason for it to be the desire of the administration to combat inflation and to balance the budget. If so, it indicates a changed perception of threat, and a subordination of military considerations to economic considerations in stockpile policy.

More solid indications of the changed perception appeared in the aftermath of the OPEC embargo, when recession followed inflation and culminated in "stagflation." The extraordinary events of 1973-1974 (commodity boom, oil embargo) triggered a series of reviews of the commonly held assumptions on the strength and weaknesses of—and the dangers faced by—the developed market-economy nations. To most, the threat of economic collapse seemed more real than the threat of armed conflict. Soon, many policymakers, economists, and political scientists posed these questions: What is the possibility of cartel-like action in other critical materials for which the United States, Western Europe, and Japan depend on imports, and what is the possibility of price-gouging by the suppliers of such materials?[10] Despite the fact that a number of studies showed that neither action was likely—that in all probability the OPEC experience cannot be duplicated with equal success in other raw materials[11]—many policymakers remained skeptical. The rapidity with which such investigations mushroomed and the lingering skepticism of the validity of their conclusions underscored the changed perception of threat and the prevailing sense of beleaguerment.

Of the two new dangers to consumers, embargo and price-gouging, the latter was considered the more real and also more acute.[12] Many feared that if the prices of all commodities were raised simultaneously through unilateral action by the producers, the developed-market economies would not be able to withstand the resulting inflationary pressure and that the threat eloquently articulated by Bergsten[13] would become reality. Associated developments affecting policymakers were the decline in exploration expenditures in the developing countries, the worsening financial crunch of the mining industry, and the impediments to the flow of venture capital to the developing countries, which have a large share of the world's unexploited resource potential.[14] These raised visions of serious and extended shortages in the future, and of associated power-play opportunities for the producing countries.

Again, the altered perception was reflected in the making of U.S. stockpile policy. The report of the Sub-Committee on the Domestic and International Monetary Effects and Other Natural Resource Pricing of the House Committee on Banking, in November 1974, recommended the creation of an "economic stockpile." Two years later, the report of the National Commission on Supplies and Shortages made a similar recommendation. The policy was changed officially in this direction in October 1976. According to the new policy, stockpile objectives are to be determined on the basis of the first three years of a conflict of infinite duration. For the first time, civilian needs will be considered separately from military needs. Hence, there will be two separate estimates of stockpile requirements, one for the civilian population, the other for the military.[15] With the announced changes, it is clear that the military stockpile is becoming increasingly an economic stockpile. Stockpile objectives have been renamed and redefined. The new term is "goals"—flexible targets which are subject to change with, inter alia, economic conditions. An important aspect of the new policy is explicit concern with the materials market and industry. Implicit in the role assigned to stockpiles in peacetime is withstanding or discouraging collusive action by producers for economic or political gain. This is a far cry from the purpose of stockpiles at the time of the Paley Commission.

Self-sufficiency and Interdependence

Whereas stockpiling policy, even in its latest version, is a tool for minimizing emergency dependence, self-sufficiency is an economic and political goal with long-term implications because it involves decisions on production. The Paley Commission realized that in many instances it was cheaper to import materials than to produce them domestically, and it therefore rejected self-sufficiency categorically:

> This Commission is convinced that... the U.S. and other free nations... must coordinate their resources to the ends of common growth, common safety, and common welfare. In turn, this means that the U.S. must reject self-sufficiency as a policy and instead adopt the policy of the lowest cost acquisition of materials wherever secure supplies may be found: self-sufficiency, when closely viewed, amounts to self-imposed blockade and nothing more.[16]

In recommending that the United States reject self-sufficiency, the commission laid the basis for one of the most important criteria in U.S. materials policy of the past twenty-five years, namely, that economics—prices—should be the overriding consideration in the determination of the sources of supply of materials.[17] In 1973, the National Commission on Materials Policy endorsed the traditional U.S. policy of "relying upon market forces as a prime determinant of the mix of imports and domestic production, subject to considerations of public policy involving the national security, health and viability of domestic materials industries, and fair competition."[18] In 1976, the National Commission on Supplies and Scarcities—a modern counterpart of the Paley Commission—also rejected self-sufficiency for reasons similar to those advanced in 1952 and 1973.[19]

The above brief chronology may give the impression that not much has changed since the days of the Paley Commission. This is not the case because, as argued earlier, the perception of the danger of dependence has changed and, with it, the notion of interdependence and its concomitant policy implications. Although the Paley Commission did not deal with the question of interdependence explicitly, a careful reading of its report reveals that the commission did have a very specific view of interdependence and its manifestatioin in U.S. policy. It reflected: (1) a perception of the United States as an almost invulnerable world power and as the unchallenged leader of the free world; (2) an assumption of communality of interest among allies, developed and developing, to resist communism; and (3) an almost paternalistic attitude in perceiving its responsibility to help the nations of the non-Communist bloc to develop economically. Although this sense of responsibility had moral underpinnings, it was based in large measure on self-interest. On balance, U.S. economic dependence on the rest of the world was neither strong nor obvious. By contrast, the reverse dependence was rather glaring, considering that Western Europe was still the beneficiary of concentrated assistance at that time. The aim of economic assistance was to create an institutionally and militarily strong anti-Communist bloc. United States dominance was such that there could not be a concept of an interdependent world as there is today.

Today's realities have made the issues of interdependence and self-sufficiency more complex and more difficult to isolate. Interdependence, as currently perceived, has important implications both for relations among nations of the free world and for relations with Communist countries. The somewhat simplistic notion of common strategic goals among large groups of nations has fallen into disuse with the increased number of players and their more autonomously defined interests and goals. The overwhelming concern now is with levels of well-being. The unprecedented rise in standards of living experienced in the postwar era by the industrialized nations, especially the market economies, has raised material aspirations almost universally. This has increased current and potential interdependence through trade and aid. Ironically interdependence has produced doubts about internationalism and has created new and shifting alliances. It has created an artificially rigid categorization of the players into producers and consumers, created broad pressures and counterpressures, and caused general uncertainty about the future economic order, exacerbating the difficulty of planning.

In sum, the world's political geography and economy, international relations, and the position of the United States are vastly different from the time of the Paley Commission. Although the United States is still the world's leading economic power, its margin of clear-cut superiority has been substantially reduced, and the strength it retains is intimately linked—economically, politically, strategically—with the strength as well as weaknesses of others. Its strength can be severely tested if any part of the larger fabric comes under stress. The United States depends much more than before on the industrialized market economies—for markets, employment, and the stability of the monetary system in which it operates. Also, for the first time it is dependent for the lifeline of its economy on a specific group of "developing countries"—OPEC—a group whose demands are not only economic but also political and who lends enormous strength to the more comprehensive demands of the third world. The seriousness of the situation is accentuated because while OPEC's new economic and political power is utterly visible, the parameters for the adjustment (resource availability, conservation, political will, reordering of priorities) are not. Nor has there yet emerged a clear-cut commitment to deal seriously with the demands of the third world.

Thus, while the Paley Commission was concerned primarily with military interruptions of supplies, the focus is now on the economics. Together with a reassessment of self-sufficiency, this change has led to highly selective transfers of arms, capital goods, and technology in order to: (1) counteract the U.S. dependence on others, especially OPEC; (2) preempt adverse unilateral action by its suppliers (supply curtailment, price-gouging, expropriations, etc.) by increasing their dependence on the United States; and (3) weaken the solidarity of the third world by accentuating differences in self-interest among the countries of the group. Increasingly, the moral and humanitarian aspects of aid have been overshadowed by the notion of using aid as a tool to futher the self-interest of the giver, whether the new rich or the old rich. This is a regrettable regression at a time when we are more skilled than before at quantifying need and have a tradition of development economics that acknowledges the indispensability of aid.

Problems of Measurement and Credibility

While no public body has categorically advocated self-sufficiency in materials as a policy, self-sufficiency is an indispensable concept. It provides a yardstick for measuring where a country stands at any given time—a necessary first step in formulating policy on external economic relations. Because of this basic role, it is important that self-sufficiency be assessed objectively and comprehensively, with due recognition and communication of the problems of measurement and interpretation.

Import dependence in a material is usually measured as the ratio of net imports (imports minus exports) to apparent consumption (domestic production plus imports minus exports). Though straightforward in definition, this measure suffers from the same ambiguities in interpretation attaching to the ratio of aggregate imports to GNP. A low import ratio at this level of aggregation, for example, can mean that a country is either already developed and resource-rich in the broadest sense and therefore does not require vast imports, or too underdeveloped to absorb or pay for additional imports. Similarly, in the case of a specific material, a low ratio of net imports to consumption can be the result of policies designed to curtail consumption (e.g., through excise or import taxes) rather than a reflection of a large and healthy production base. Furthermore, regardless of the level of disaggregation, this measure provides no indication of the interdependence between exports and imports (either in terms of ability to pay for imports or of the indispensability of imported inputs to the production of exportable goods), nor of the volume and internal distribution of the economic and social benefits of imports.

Recognition of these shortcomings, plus the growing complexity of international economic relations have led to increasingly sophisticated attempts to measure and evaluate dependence. An indication of this trend is the greater pains taken these days to evaluate *critical* dependence as a basis for decisions on self-sufficiency. For example, the criteria adopted for this purpose by the International Economic Policy Association include: (1) criticality of the resource for industrial production; (2) vulnerability to cutoff and effects of national security; (3) the economic costs of self-sufficiency; (4) time needed to bring reserves into production; (5) balance of payments implications; and (6) foreign policy objectives involved.[20] Even these do not cover all the relevant considerations; they are difficult to apply without subjective judgement and as measures of changing dependence over time; and they run against the conceptualization of materials production and consumption as a *system*. For the sake of brevity we shall illustrate these points with reference to the first two criteria: criticality to industrial production and vulnerability to cutoff.

With few exceptions, information on the end-use patterns of minerals is imperfect.[21] We know for certain, though, that the end uses of most minerals are so varied that it is extremely difficult, even with expanded knowledge, to develop reliable and meaningful technical coefficients of their criticality as inputs into the production of specific goods. The problem is exacerbated by the fact that many of the products made with minerals are semimanufactured, intermediary goods. It is therefore difficult to determine uniformly when consumption takes place: is the end use of nickel stainless steel, bumpers, cars, or transportation? If nickel is critical to the making of stainless steel, is it, by inference, critical to the provision of transportation? In addition, how do we assess criticality, distinguishing for example, between raw materials with declining intensities of use and those with rapidly rising levels of consumption? If consumption has been declining in either absolute or relative terms, does it mean that the material is in the process of being phased out entirely or that, at the lower level of consumption, it has become more essential because it has retained those end uses in which it is indispensible? If consumption is rising rapidly, is it because it is being stimulated artificially? Is an increase in import dependence from 90 to 95 percent the same thing as an increase from 20 to 25 percent?

What degree of dependence is critical? And can one use the same criterion for Bangladesh and the United States? Most of these questions do not have simple answers; yet, estimates of critical dependence continue to adorn the pages of congressional reports without caveats.

Another problem is that the criticality of a material cannot be assessed in isolation, especially if one subscribes to the dynamic view of resources. Self-sufficiency is a time-bound concept rather than a mode-bound concept, and its utility depends on the objective pursued. To illustrate, if, as at the time of the Paley Commission, the objective is to supply the military and "to keep the economy going" in times of war, it is proper and feasible to begin with an assessment of self-sufficiency in the materials required for that specific purpose. If, on the other hand, the objective is to determine the optimum strategies for indefinite continued growth, that approach is inadequate, for it would not absorb the dynamics of growth in terms of changes in tastes, technology, and combination of inputs.

The criterion of vulnerability to cutoff is intimately linked to the problem of sources of supply and is inherently political. Although a number of studies have included in their assessment the possibility of cutoffs by Canada, Australia, the Republic of South Africa, and Rhodesia, the "danger" of cutoffs in the United States is associated mainly with the developing countries. Yet experience demonstrates that, with the exception of the OPEC action of 1973, interruptions of production of vital industries in peacetime have been due largely to internal actions such as strikes by dock, rail, mine, or factory workers, rather than to the withholding of supplies by the developing countries.[22] In fact, it might even be argued that developed-country exporters have been somewhat guilty in this regard as well—as illustrated by the soybean export embargo of the United States.[23]

One reason for the sensitivity of the United States to the danger of the supply cutoffs is the absence of a concept of basic needs. The standard of living is so high and expectations that it will be maintained are so deeply rooted in the American system that the reaction to any cutback in the supply of mass-consumption items is strong. A case in point is the speed with which a congressional investigation followed the increase in coffee prices and the reluctance in some quarters to accept that a frost in Brazil is no more political than a frost in Florida. A double standard permeates all assessments of supply cutoffs—their possibility, motives, and impact, and the measures designed to neutralize or avert them, for example through self-sufficiency, stockpiles, or control over the suppliers. If the commitment to help the developing countries develop is real, and if trade is one of the best vehicles for development (as indeed it has been in the case of Japan and Taiwan), why deny the developing countries this chance to help themselves? If, furthermore, trade is seen as a valuable agent for cementing political relations, why should we use this view to justify increased trade with China while dramatizing the degree of import dependence on nickel and cobalt produced by Canada and Zaire—an argument that has often been made in support of more rapid exploitation of the ocean's manganese nodules?

For a large and rich nation with an outward-oriented foreign and economic policy, the goal of self-sufficiency simply does not make sense. In a dynamic society, the very ideas of needs and levels of needs change all the time, as do the sources of vulnerability. Furthermore, the economic and political fate of the industrialized nations is so interwoven that individual levels of sufficiency do not mean much. There is simply no such thing as total security. The foundation of interdependence was built for the benefit of all and the structure cannot be completed effectively if it is given a conditional commitment.

No one can gainsay each country's right to make decisions on its national interest. But all have responsibilities toward preserving global stability, which in the case of developing countries means a climate in which continued growth is possible. It is naive to assume, however, that the roles in this are equally apportioned. Because of its strength, the United States, rather that erecting more defenses, should try, as a matter of policy, to express good faith in the common enterprise of sustaining well-being and achieving development on a global basis and trust that its strength makes it not more vulnerable than others but rather more capable of exercising greater responsibility. For while all players have a responsibility in working toward a practical consensus about the rules, some are more handicapped than others because of overwhelming need or overwhelming problems. Those with the broadest range of options and greatest capabilities can not be excused when they take the narrowest approach.

It is difficult to summarize the evolution of policy in Western Europe because it continues to be fragmented. In recent years there have been clear signs of a growing desire to emulate Japan in materials procurement, with the European Economic Community (EEC) Secretariat advocating a speedier change in this direction than some governments or industries; concern over excessive dependence on the United States; and reexamination of the social justification for maintaining uncompetitive industries. The greater willingness to curtail consumption, when necessary, and the system of historical, cultural, and economic ties with the developing nations (including the association arrangements with the European Community and the Lomé Convention) are factors which distinguish the Western European perspective from that of the United States or Japan. Although some national policy reevaluations have been undertaken, the direction of new policies (if any) is not clear, in view of the unsettled political situation in several countries. One outcome of new reevaluations is likely to be the strengthening of integration.

In the developing countries the cry is not for self-sufficiency but for self-reliance, a concept which has gained a pejorative meaning in the West because of its association with the call for a new international economic order. It calls not for goods but for opportunity: *access* to capital, *access* to technology, *access* to markets. It asserts that developing countries are eager to achieve self-sustaining growth, capable of setting their own targets, determined to choose the mode, willing to do the work and, above all, accept responsibility.

It is inevitable to conclude from this brief review that no country is as spoiled as the United States. The greatest perception of threat is, ironically, in the one country economically and institutionally best equipped to advance modes of adjustment to the shift in dependence.

Concluding Observations

1. While the oversensitivity of the United States at present to possible supply cutoffs by producers seems unjustified, it must be understood that extreme threats of manipulating supplies for economic and political gain are bound to elicit extreme responses in the future. Similarly, precipitous claims of the ability and disposition to go it alone as a countermeasure to perceived threat, forces the claimant into a corner and builds domestic pressure to follow through irrespective of cost and broader interests.

2. Returning to the original juxtaposition of "Is there enough for everybody?" and "Is there enough for us?" we find that our argument against the pursuit of self-sufficiency ultimately rests on the fallaciousness of the "us." The nationally defined "us" does not take into account the reality and complexity of interdependence among allies and even adversaries, nor provide for dealing with the unfinished business between the rich and the poor.

3. Any narrow definition of "us" does not bode well for the future of aid and expanded opportunities for developing nations. The tempting notion of "sufficiency for us," a concept whose time has passed, must give way to the more demanding ideal of "sufficiency for all" which requires a commitment to aid trade, and interdependence. After we strip from aid its manipulative aspects and layers of self-interest on the part of the giver, there remains a moral core to the idea of aid. That core is irreduceable and absolute. Philosophically, no commitment to an absolute can be conditional.

Notes

1. *Resources for Freedom,* a report to the president by the President's Materials Policy Commission, 5 vols. (Washington, D.C.: U.S. Government Printing Office, 1952).

2. This conclusion is based on the fact that in the example selected to illustrate the growing importance of the materials problem, the commission compared the amount of certain materials needed to build a fighter plane in 1944 with those required for 1951 jet fighters (*Resources for Freedom*, vol. 1, p. 155). With regard to criteria of criticality, it is interesting to note that the commission stated that among the various materials listed, there was no difference in terms of essentiality—that all materials were equally critical and important to national security (ibid., p. 147), the only differentiation made with respect to the quantities of each material deemed to be necessary.

3. It is interesting to note that the Chiefs of Staff, who gave strategic guidance to the Munitions Board—the body charged with accumulating stockpiles of material—not only made assumptions as to the probable duration and general scope of future wars, but also assessed the military accessibility of various areas in the world and the extent of transit losses (*Resources for Freedom*, vol. 5, p. 143).

4. For example, on the demand side, the recommendations emphasize, albeit with respect to meeting military demand, the need to focus on using abundant rather than scarce materials; to reduce the intensity of use (the unit of materials per unit of product); to prepare "stand by" designs utilizing available substitute materials to improve care, maintenance, conservation, and scrap recovery. On the supply side, the recommendations call for, inter alia, promoting the discovery and development of reserves "by the use of long term contracts" and for steps to increase supplies from "unconventional sources, such as oil shales, aluminum clays, and process recovery of manganese" (*Resources for Freedom*, vol. 1, p. 156).

5. *Raw Materials and Foreign Policy* (Washington, D.C.: International Economic Studies Institute, 1976), p. 281.

6. *Resources for Freedom,* vol. 1, p. 162.

7. "When materials are stockpiled, other economic resources such as manpower, energy and transportation are stored with them. . . . The release of reserve material in an emergency thus can lighten somewhat the pressure on the whole industrial machine. Stockpiling is as prudent for materials that are domestic as for imports if wartime demand for them would expand faster than the country's capacity to produce them (ibid., p. 163).

8. I will argue against such generalizations, in principle, later. Nevertheless, there is considerable agreement among analysts on this point and attempts to refine the measure of dependence or to change the periods of comparison do not

materially affect this conclusion. See *Materials Needs and the Environment Today and Tommorrow*, final report of the National Commission on Materials Policy, June 1973, p. 8-9; and *Government and the Nation's Resoruces*, report of the National Commission on Spplies and Shortages, December 1976, p. 27.

9. Interim report of the study on *U.S. Natural Resource Requirements and Foreign Economic Policy* by The International Economic Policy Association and the IEPA Advisory Committee on Natural Resources, July 18, 1974, p. 11. See also *Raw Materials and Foreign Policy,* p. 261.

10. See, for example, the *Special Report on Critical Imported Materials* by the Council on International Economic Policy, December 1974, p. 16-21.

11. See: Raymond F. Mikesell, "More Third World Cartels?" *Challenge* (November-December 1974); Stephen D. Krasner, "Oil Is the Exception," *Foreign Policy* (spring 1974); and Bension Varon and Kenji Takeuchi, "Developing Countries and Non-Fuel Minerals," *Foreign Affairs* (April 1974). For articles holding the opposite point of view, see: C. Fred Bergsten, "The Threat from the Third World," *Foreign Policy* (summer 1973), "The Threat is Real," *Foreign Policy* (spring 1974); and "The New Era in Commodity Cartels," *Challenge* (September-October 1974).

12. The two terms are defined in *Critical Imported Materials,* Special Report of the Council on International Economic Policy, December 1974, as follows: *"Price-gouging:* an exorbitant administered price increase by one or more producers, exploiting a tight supply situation, to a level that can be maintained over the long term only by restricting supply; *cartel-like action:* an exorbitant adminstered price increase by one or more key producers supported by actual restriction of supply" (p. 18). The difference between the two terms seems to lie in the source (or means) of the price increase: whether it is a natural shortage or an artificial, contrived shortage. Otherwise there is no real difference; actually the former terms eventually become the latter for, if price-gouging continues beyond the natural shortage, it must become cartel-like action. Both imply concerted action by suppliers in products for which demand is price inelastic.

13. See note 11.

14. See *Minerals: Salient issues, Report of the Secretary-General* (E/C. 7/68), March 29, 1977.

15. *Mining Journal,* October 8, 1976, pp. 92 and 276; and *Raw Materials and Foreign Policy,* pp. 261-262.

16. *Resources for Freedom,* Vol. 1, p. 3.

17. In so doing, the commission underlined that there were varying economic as well as political costs associated with different degrees of self-sufficiency.

18. *Material Needs and the Environment Today and Tomorrow,* final report of the National Commission on Materials Policy, June 3, 1973, p. 1-6.

19. *Government and the Nation's Resources,* p. 30-31.
20. IEPA, *U.S. Natural Resource Requirements and Foreign Economic Policy,* p. 5.
21. Analysts have been aware of this for some time, but only recently have they realized the enormous impact that greater knowledge of consumption patterns can have on the formulation of policy. Resources for the Future, Inc., (Washington, D.C.) is carrying out an intensive investigation of the end use patterns of minerals on the basis of four country studies.
22. A dramatic example is provided by the British coal mining industry. When the industry substituted a system of measure day work for an incentive-based system of wage determination, the pattern of industrial disputes changed: although the number of local disputes fell dramatically, the concept of national strikes was introduced, resulting in two such strikes in 1972 and 1974. The coal losses from each of these disputes amounted to about 26 million metric tons, or approximately 22 percent of average annual output in 1970-1975. This was greater than the cumulative losses from all of the local strikes since the nationalization of the industry in 1945. See David Gidwell, "Wage Payment Systems in the British Coal Mining Industry: An Appraisal," *Industrial Relations Journal* (summer 1977). It is interesting to note that some Japanese raw material importers have a policy of diversifying their suppliers in the United States with a view to reducing their dependence on unions with a history of strikes.
23. A short-lived embargo on exports in the summer of 1973 was followed by a "partial embargo," restricting the quantities of soybean which could be exported (50 percent of the orders on hand, for soybean, by June 15, and 40 percent of the orders for soybean meal). This "partial embargo" lasted until September 8, 1973, when a new U.S. soybean crop was harvested. On October 10, 1974, "export curbs" were introduced. This new policy required that exporters get permission from the government for any exports to any single buyer, on any single day or week, if the quantity to be exported exceeded 50,000 and 100,000 tons, respectively. Thus, implicit in the new policy was the possibility of future export cuts. The export curbs were eased on January 29, 1975, when the quantities that could be exported without prior government approval were doubled. Finally, on March 6, 1975, all export curbs were ended.

PART FOUR:
THE U.S. ROLE IN A CHANGING UNITED NATIONS

Introduction
Leland M. Goodrich

Political, economic, social, and technological developments of the years since World War II have not only radically changed the nature of the world in which we live, but also have led to important changes in the international institutions initially created during or immediately following the war to deal with common problems of peace and well-being. The United Nations, in particular, conceived as an organization responsible for dealing with the whole range of problems of common concern, has been no exception. It has, in fact, experienced the most radical change in the course of adjusting to new conditions and demands. Indeed, the principal reason why U.S. policy toward the United Nations is in the process of being reexamined is not change in the basic objectives and purposes of U.S. foreign policy, but rather changes that have taken place in the nature of the United Nations and its manner of operation which raise questions as to the suitability of the organization for furthering the larger purposes of U.S. policy.

The United Nations was originally conceived as an organization with the primary purpose of maintaining international peace and security. This was to be achieved in the first instance through the cooperation of the major military powers whose concerted action had been responsible for victory in World War II. It soon became clear that this cooperation would not take place to the extent necessary to make the United Nations effective. The "cold war" became a dominant influence, and many members, with the United States taking the lead, sought security instead in self-defense arrangements. Even when the spirit of "détente" emerged to weaken, if not to eliminate, the spirit of cold war confrontation, the new spirit manifested itself not so much in cooperation within the United Nations as in limited and cautious collaboration outside. Détente has restored only to a limited extent the originally hoped-for primacy of the United Nations in the peace and security field. Nor is it likely that greater United Nations effectiveness in the maintenance of peace and security will be achieved by any change in the composition of voting procedures in the Security Council. Lawrence Finkelstein concludes that no mechanical improvements in election criteria or procedures are likely to improve the functioning of that organ. Leo Gross, on the basis of a detailed analysis of Security Council voting on the Palestine question, comes to the conclusion that the voting rules of Article 27 of the charter were, and continue to be, an essential condition for the existence and continued functioning of the United Nations in the maintenance of peace and security.

Initially the United Nations, like the League of Nations before it, was predominantly European and Western Hemisphere in membership. Except for the Soviet Union and other members of the Communist bloc who constituted a small minority within the organization, members of the United Nations accepted the values and policy assumptions of the West, which the charter incorporated. The United States found it relatively easy to pursue its national objectives within this framework, assuming a role of leadership with the great majority of other members willing to accept it. Following the initial membership deadlock which was finally broken in 1955, the membership of the United Nations quickly changed in size and character. Under the impact of the rapid liquidation of colonialism, membership not only more than doubled within two decades, but newly independent states, formerly colonies, and predominantly Asian and African, acquired majority status. This new majority, which found that it had many common interests, challenged the original assumptions of the charter regarding the relation of power to responsibility by seeking to build up the power and influence of the General Assembly and by using their voting strength in that organization to achieve results not always acceptable to the United States and other older members. This development has threatened the special interests of the major powers who originally believed that their special interests would be sufficiently protected by voting privilege in the Security Council and the fact that on most questions the General Assembly could only recommend.

Accompanying the creation of a new majority in the General Assembly has been an insistence by that majority on something close to legislative power for the General Assembly and a willingness to use this power contrary to the plain provisions of the charter. While the charter states that on important issues of substance the assembly only has powers of discussion and recommendation, the new majority has sought in effect to give these recommendations, particularly when adopted by large majorities, the force of binding law. Their claim goes considerably beyond the view of many jurists that assembly recommendations, when generally supported, have evidential value of what states accept as binding law in their international relations. It brings into question the very character of the General Assembly as an international organ: Is it a standing international conference or a quasi-legislative body?

James F. Green, in his analysis of decision making, emphasizes the importance of distinguishing among the various kinds of decisions which the General Assembly takes. He also stresses the need, in connection with the enunciation of principles and policies and the adoption of programs requiring wide participation by members, that restraint be shown and that decisions be taken on the basis of wide consultation and consensus. Green calls attention to the recent development and use of promising techniques for achieving consensus in place of majority decisions which may lack support necessary to their implementation. Alice B. Haemmerli, concluding that the time for majority lawmaking has not come, argues that there is no present substitute for consensus based on negotiation, consultation, and compromise within a framework which includes those states "whose agreement is essential to implementation."

Another consequence of the expanded membership of the United Nations, and more particularly the nature of the new membership, has been a change in the principal concerns of the organization. An added contributing cause to this change, however, has been modern technology which has created new problems and provided new means of dealing with old ones. This change in U.N. concerns has been reflected particularly in the General Assembly since this is the organ with the widest competence and in which all members of the organization have an equal right and opportunity to express their concerns and desires. The initial preoccupation with questions of peace and security has been to a large extent replaced by concern for the particular human rights of black majorities in white-ruled countries in Africa and of Arabs in Israeli-occupied territories, and the economic needs of new, developing countries. It is significant that not all human rights, or violations of human rights, have received equal attention, but only those of political interest to the majority. Nor has equal attention been given to achieving conditions of economic prosperity and well-being throughout the world. Rather, the emphasis has been on improving the conditions of the poorer countries.

The new concerns of the United Nations have not been limited, however, to matters for which the new majority in the assembly has been responsible. Other questions of a broader nature, relating in some instances to the plight of the poorer countries but also of concern to all countries, have come to occupy prominent places on the United Nations's agenda. Population, food, energy, housing, and the environment are among the questions modern technology and the complexities and interdependencies of modern life have brought to the forefront of international concern.

In dealing with the problems of the modern world, the United States must determine the role that the United Nations is to have in the complex structure of international cooperation that must be developed and used, and within the United Nations what its own role will be. The changes that have taken place in the original model, which we persuaded our friends and allies in the Second World War to accept, may provide grounds for modifying our original acceptance of the United Nations as a chosen instrument of international cooperation. Yeselson and Gaglione, for example, favor less reliance than in the past on the United Nations for the advancement of our national purposes, believing that the organization has become a forum often hostile to their achievement.

Nevertheless, we need to look to ourselves to determine whether we have not been responsible, by neglect or shortsighted action, for some of the developments which we now condemn. It is entirely possible that for achieving certain purposes, other forms of organization, regional or narrowly functional, will be more effective. It is also possible that more active and constructive participation in U.N. activities than we have shown at times in the recent past will produce results more in line with our desires and interests. This is the view of Philip Klutznick, who, on the basis of his long U.N. experience, is convinced that the answer to our discontents with the United Nations is to put our best talents in its service and to present and support creative programs and positions.

The United Nations has shown thus far a great capacity for adaptation to new needs and circumstances. Robert Jordan believes that the hope for building a future structure of peace in the world lies in the continuing development of the United Nations and its adaptation to new conditions and needs. Such development and adaptation clearly requires strong leadership on the part of the United States. No other member, least of all any of the major powers, has shown a willingness or capacity to assume that responsibility. To perform this role the United States must adopt an approach to the organization and a strategy in making use of it that reflect confidence in its continuing vitality and usefulness. Charles Maynes, Seymour M. Finger, and the Ad Hoc Group on U.S. Policy Toward the United Nations devote their contributions to outlining what that approach and strategy should be.

U.N. STRUCTURES AND PROCEDURES

26. Decision Making on Economic and Social Questions in the United Nations
James Frederick Green

The differing views of the developed countries, the Communist countries, and the third world are reflected whenever a vote is taken in the General Assembly, the Economic and Social Council (ECOSOC), and other bodies. During the first ten years of the United Nations, when the membership ranged from 51 to 76, the Western group had little difficulty in commanding a majority vote, even a two-thirds vote, on all political questions and on most economic, social, and human rights questions. As the membership increased, however, to 99 in 1965 and 147 in 1977, the Western group declined proportionately to a small minority. Their position became critical in 1974, when the third world, supported by the Communist countries, mobilized massive majorities for the adoption of the New International Economic Order, at the Sixth Special Session, and the Charter of Economic Rights and Duties of States at the Twenty-ninth Regular Session.

As a result of being continually defeated on issues that they regarded as of major importance to their interests, the developed countries initiated the "great debate" in the General Assembly in December 1974. After criticizing the developing countries for their "sterile pursuit of empty majorities," and for forcing through resolutions that could not be implemented except with the support of the developed countries, Ambassador John Scali warned that U.S. support for the United Nations might be jeopardized by what were regarded as unwise, unjust, and sometimes illegal actions. The third world replied in kind, protesting that the West was merely resentful over the loss of its former influence

---

This paper will serve as a working paper for the Commission to Study the Organization of Peace's forthcoming report on global economic problems.

in the United Nations and unwilling to acknowledge that the present voting pattern reflected the distribution of population throughout the world.

The decision-making process in the General Assembly, ECOSOC, and elsewhere have thus become a crucial aspect of international cooperation for economic development. Continuation of this confrontation between the "haves" and the "have nots" and the overwhelming defeat of the former on major economic issues could only lead to an even more serious crisis in the organization. For this reason, consideration needs to be given not only to *what* decision the United Nations should reach on substantive issues, but *how* the General Assembly and other bodies should make these decisions. It should be noted that this paper is limited to economic and social questions, and that security, political, human rights, and budgetary matters, where recorded votes are often regarded as essential by specially concerned members, lie outside its scope.

The essence of the matter is the principle of one state–one vote prescribed in the charter. Under articles 18 and 67, respectively, each member of the General Assembly and the Economic and Social Council has one vote. Decisions in the General Assembly on "important questions" are taken by a two-thirds majority; and on other questions, by an ordianry majority. All decisions in the council are by ordinary majority vote. This rule accords with the principle of "sovereign equality" of all members, enshrined in Article 2 (1), and was initially regarded as a reflection of democratic principles.[1]

Ever since the San Francisco conference, the one state–one vote procedure has been criticized (as has the veto procedure, in the Security Council, for opposite reasons).[2] Many proposals have been made for often ingenious ways to reflect the economic weight and interests of the industrialized countries: (1) a bicameral assembly, in which a second house would be constituted on the basis of population, as in the American House of Representatives, or gross national product, or contribution to the U.N. budget, or some combination of these or other factors; or (2) some form of weighted voting to balance the one state–one vote rule on the one hand with power and responsibility on the other.[3] Any proposal to amend the charter or even to revise the rules of procedure in favor of the richer would certainly be unacceptable to poorer members. Whatever the logic of some kind of balancing of the dual principles of sovereign equality and of proportional representation, the 100 or more developing countries can hardly be expected to give up one of the most valuable prerogatives of sovereign equality—i.e., voting rights. Indeed, that prerogative of the small, poor, and weak member is regarded as the equivalent of the veto enjoyed by the permanent members of the Security Council.[4]

At least five techniques, or some combination of them, are feasible alternatives to a vote that divides the organization and embitters its membership. None of these techniques would deny any member the right to call for a vote, but would help make a vote unnecessary. The objective should be to reach a meaningful agreement—one that will enhance, not damage, the prestige of the United Nations.[5]

Consensus

In the League of Nations, the principle of unanimity was prescribed for both the Security Council and the General Assembly; hence every member enjoyed the right of veto.[6] Although any representative in one of these bodies could demand a vote and by voting negatively thwart the will of the others, in practice, wisdom prevailed. On many occasions, the president asked whether any members had observations to make on a proposal. In the absence of such observations, the president declared the proposal adopted; the lack of objection, made possible by the rapporteur system discussed below, was held to denote tacit consent.

Within recent years various bodies of the United Nations have similarly avoided the public revelation of disagreement that results from a recorded vote by the adoption of a motion or draft resolution by consensus. After debate and private consultations, usually initiated by the sponsors of a draft resolution, the presiding officer asks if there are any objections. In the absence of an objection, arranged in advance, the presiding officer then declares the text adopted.[7]

Adoption of a resolution by consensus does not imply that all members present in the U.N. body fully or unanimously support the entire contents, merely that none opposes the contents strongly enough to insist upon the right to vote against the text. A resolution adopted by consensus in the General Assembly, giving the impression of a vote of 147-0-0, obviously carries more prestige than one adopted with even a small number of negative votes and abstentions. The impression is thus given of unity and harmony, rather than of division and dissension.

The consensus procedure is widely used in the Plenary and Main Committees of the General Assembly and in the Economic and Social Council and its commissions. For example, the Seventh Special Session, convened in early September 1975 to consider "development and international cooperation," adopted a comprehensive and constructive resolution by consensus—thanks to the leadership of the United States on the one hand and the moderates among the developing countries on the other. Of the 256 resolutions, parts of resolutions, and decisions approved in plenary by the General Assembly at its Thirty-first Session in 1976, 89, or 35 percent, were adopted by roll call or recorded votes; and 167, or 65 percent, were adopted without a vote, i.e., by acclamation, without objection, or by consensus. Many other bodies have functioned successfully without taking votes—e.g., the North Atlantic Council of NATO, the U.N. outer space committee and seabed committee, and the conferences on environment at Stockholm, population at Bucharest, and food at Rome.

The new practice of nonvoting has both advantages and disadvantages. On the one hand, the practice avoids forcing the minority into obvious isolation in a public vote. Just as in the cold war period the Soviet bloc must have resented being isolated year after year by the overwhelming majorities mobilized by the Western delegations, so today the Western delegations resent being isolated by the massive votes of the third world, often supported by the Communist delegations. Except on issues that one group or another regards as highly important, the consensus procedure permits a U.N. body to fulfill one of the purposes set forth in the charter: "to be a center for harmonizing the actions of nations in the attainment of these common ends."[8]

On the other hand, adoption of a resolution without vote sometimes papers over a division of opinion and provides a false sense of harmony. The minority, usually the developed countries at present, merely decides that it does not feel strongly enough about the question, or the fact that a U.N. body is taking a position on it, to demand a vote; but the minority by no means concurs in the decision. The minority thus has the unpleasant choice of either abandoning its position and conceding to the majority for the sake of superficial unity, or fighting for its position to the point of demanding a vote and suffering a public defeat. Alternatively, one or more members of the minority may enter formal resolutions or "explanations of vote" after adoption of the resolution, thus in effect nullifying the effect of the consensus. The more the technique of reservations is employed, the less meaningful the use of the consensus procedure becomes.

Although consensus and unanimity when possible should be the goal, other techniques are needed to ensure that the consensus is a genuine one, and not a superficial show of agreement where agreement on important issues does not exist.

Rapporteurs

The principle of state sovereignty and unanimity in voting enshrined in the Covenant of the League of Nations required, if any meaningful decisions were to be taken in the council and assembly, that extensive consultations be undertaken before a vote or before the president, as indicated above, declared a proposal adopted without objection. The need to find some means of reaching this agreement was, therefore, imperative. The league's council, at its second session, established a system that was common in Western European but not Anglo-Saxon legislatures—the appointment of a rapporteur for a specific subject. The task of the rapporteur was to assemble and analyze the relevant facts about a subject, develop possible solutions, consult his colleagues, and prepare a report, with a recommendation, to the full council.

The league system was followed in the San Francisco conference in 1945, but it has rarely been used in major bodies of the United Nations. In the Security Council, however, the president in recent years has assumed the consultative function of rapporteur, conferring privately with other members, individually or in small groups, until he has achieved agreement on a draft resolution. The broader functions of the league rapporteur, assembling the facts as well as negotiating an agreement, might well be tried in the Security Council on political matters and in the General Assembly and Economic and Social Council on all important matters.[9]

Another use of this technique is in the Commission on Human Rights and the Sub-Commission on Prevention of Discrimination and Protection of Minorities. A special rapporteur is frequently appointed, with the approval of the Economic and Social Council, to prepare a study of one particular right or freedom and to draft principles upon which action should be taken. The special rapporteur thus fulfills, with the assistance of the Secretariat, the study function but not the negotiating function of the league rapporteur. Broader variants of the rapporteur system have also been practiced occasionally in the United Nations, for instance through the "Committee of Neutrals," which, with strong Secretariat support, negotiated the complex and detailed basis for the agreement lifting the Berlin blockade.

A variation of the rapporteur system occurs when officers of the Secretariat in an assembly committee or elsewhere take the initiative in consulting interested delegates and helping develop an agreed text of a resolution. Although the sponsor or cosponsors retain responsibility for the draft, the Secretariat officers, maintaining an attitude of strict neutrality, undertake the necessary footwork. This very useful procedure succeeds only if a Secretariat officer is willing and able to exercise initiative and if the field has not been preempted by the Group of 77 or others. Much of the success of the group of experts on restructuring the United Nations, mentioned below, is credited to its secretary, Uner Kirdar.

Group of Experts

Another technique frequently used in the United Nations is the appointment of a group of experts, usually by the secretary-general at the request of an organ or subsidiary body. Although nominated by member states or selected in consultation with them, these experts serve in their personal capacity and do not represent their governments or commit them to the findings and recommendations.

Groups of experts have been widely used to produce basic documents on technical subjects, such as geographic names, travel and tourism, transportation of explosives, water resources, energy, crime prevention, and the like. More important, such groups have been established to explore political and economic issues where the U.N. membership is obviously divided. In the field of disarmament, for example, groups of experts have studied such controversial matters as the economic and social consequences of disarmament, napalm and other incendiary weapons, the effects of the possible use of nuclear weapons, and the security and economic implications for states of acquisition and further development of these weapons.

More relevant to this study are two recent examples relating to two highly important and controversial issues in the economic field. In 1974, the secretary-general, at the request of the Economic and Social Council, appointed a Group of Eminent Persons to study the relatively new and delicate problem of the multinational corporations and the possible need for some kind of international supervision of them. The twenty eminent persons produced a report that contained both unanimous recommendations and divergent interpretations, but it has served as the basis for further debate and action.[10] In 1975, the secretary-general, at the request of the General Assembly, appointed a Group of Experts to study the structural changes needed for economic development. The unanimous report of these twenty-five experts, to which this study is addressed, served as a major document in the Seventh Special Session of the General Assembly, and is currently under consideration by the assembly's Ad Hoc Committee.[11]

The use of groups of experts thus warrants consideration as a valuable method of clarifying issues, exploring differences, reconciling those differences where possible, and developing recommendations for further action—all without any prior commitment by governments. This approach could be used, as in the case of multinational corporations and the U.N. structure, as a preliminary step toward a debate in the assembly or the council and then for further exploration by other groups on the governmental level.

Negotiating Groups

As an integral part of its recommendations for restructuring the General Assembly and the Economic and Social Council, the Group of Experts proposed some novel consultative procedures. Under these arrangements, either the assembly or the council would appoint negotiating groups on specific subjects—no more than three in the first two experimental years. Each group would consist of ten to thirty members, under a full-time chairman, to work for one or two years until unanimous agreement was attained. The agreement would then be submitted to the assembly or the council, as the case might be, which would then adopt the agreement, or refer the matter back to the negotiating group for further consideration, or take some other action.

The Group of Experts drew upon the conciliation procedure prescribed for the U.N. Conference on Trade and Development (UNCTAD), but omitted the provision for postponement of a vote for a fixed period of time. In recommending a full-time chairman to lead the search for an agreed solution, this proposal incorporates, in effect, the rapporteur system used by the council of the League of Nations. The chairman might well be paid an honorarium or at least expenses by the United Nations, to emphasize his special status.[12] The proposal limits the number of groups initially but embodies a maximum degree of flexibility in the selection of subjects for negotiation, the size of the negotiating group, and the time allotted for its work. The experience of U.N. bodies suggests that, to be successful, a negotiating group should have a hard core of delegates from every region who agree in advance to participate actively, but should be open to any other interested delegation.

Utilization of negotiating groups would give effect to the concept underlying the procedures for conciliation devised for UNCTAD bodies, though not used, i.e., postponement of a final vote until all possibilities of achieving agreement, preferably unanimous agreement, are exhausted. This procedure was used over a period of seven years of negotiation in two different U.N. bodies: the Special Committee on Principles of International Law concerning Friendly Relations and Cooperation among States, 1964-1970; and the Special Committee on the Question of Defining Aggression, 1968-1974.[13]

The use of negotiating groups has been perfected in the Third Law of the Sea Conference, which convened in its sixth session in May 1977. The conference has developed a variety of informal working groups, workshops, and ad hoc consultative groups, all designed to reach agreement and to eliminate the need for a vote in committee or plenary. The negotiating groups, open-ended in membership, vary in size and duration, depending upon the question under discussion. The core delegates are those whose interests are primarily at stake in a particular text; others participate whenever they feel their interests may be affected. The convenor of the group ensures that all regions and viewpoints are represented.

Most of these meetings take place in small rooms, where relatively few delegates sit at a table, while others observe the proceedings from the sidelines. In the First Committee, this procedure was aptly called the "arena approach." The essence of this technique is two-fold: informal and private. The meetings are closed to the press and public and no records are kept. Indeed, most of the meetings of the three committees have been of this character, in order to expedite agreement.

Another aid to these informal negotiations has been the preparation, by the president of the conference and the chairmen of the three committees, of draft portions of the hoped-for Convention. Toward the end of the Geneva session in May 1975, and again at the end of the New York session in May 1976, the president asked the three chairmen to prepare consolidated texts of the negotiations to date, for further consultation before the next session. These informal texts, binding upon no one, combined portions that were already acceptable and others that required further negotiation. Through the use of this Single Negotiating Text, as it was called in the summer of 1976, progress toward a consensus, article by article, was promoted.

These ingenious and flexible techniques have given effect, in an informal fashion, to the formal Rules of Procedure of the Conference. These rules carry out a "gentleman's agreement" adopted by the General Assembly in 1973, which expressed "the view that the Conference should make every effort to reach agreement on substantive matters by way of consensus; that there should be no voting on such matters until all efforts at consensus have been exhausted. . . ." The rules provide accordingly: (1) When a matter of substance comes up for voting the first time, the president may propose, or 15 representatives may request, deferment of the vote for a period not exceeding ten days. (2) At any time, on a proposal by the president or on a motion of a representative, the conference may decide, by a majority of representatives present and voting, to defer the vote for a specified period. (3) During any period of deferment, the president shall make every effort to achieve agreement and report to the session before the end of the period. (4) If at the end of a specified period of deferment the conference has not reached agreement, a decision shall be taken by a two-thirds majority of those present and voting, provided that the vote includes a majority of states represented in the conference."[14]

Conciliation

One of the innovative features of UNCTAD is provision for conciliation in event of disagreement over certain subjects. Because of a bitter division between the "haves" and the "have nots" at the first conference in 1964 over voting procedures, a new procedure was devised to give some protection to the former.[15]

A small group of states can move to postpone a vote on a subject that affects their economic or financial interests (but not on matters of procedure, general principles, or establishment of subsidiary bodies). Postponement to the next session of the body concerned is automatic. The motion for postponement needs to support of only 10 members of the conference, 5 of the 55 members of the Trade and Development Board, or 3 in the 4 permanent committees—commodities (55 members), manufacturers (45), invisibles and financing (45), and shipping (45).

Each conciliation group must include representatives of countries especially interested in the subject matter. If the group can reach agreement during the same session, a new text can then be voted. If not, the group continues to work toward an agreement. When the group reports an agreed text to the next session, it can be voted on. When the group reports failure, a decision can be taken to continue the conciliation procedure, or the original text or some variant can be voted on. In the event that a conciliation group reports failure to reach agreement, its report will contain the majority and minority views and the votes of each member.

The conciliation procedure proved useful at the outset as a compromise device to set UNCTAD in motion. It has never been actually used, however, during the past ten years. The procedure remains in readiness as "a 'cooling off' period, usually about six months, during which agreed solutions can be sought through quiet diplomacy." In practice, the conciliation process has taken place through informal consultations, often on the initiative of the Secretariat. This process has narrowed the gap between the developed and developing countries on numerous issues, but it has not prevented a final vote on many resolutions wherein the developed countries are isolated in a negative minority.

Conclusions

Decision making is thus the heart of the matter in the current confrontation between the developed and the developing countries. The developing states can continue, as in recent years, to push through resolutions by massive majorities over the objections and negative votes of the developed states, whose cooperation is necessary for implementing the resolutions. The developed states can continue to protest, vote negatively and threaten to withdraw their support from the United Nations. The cirsis that has arisen will benefit no members, however, especially the weaker and poorer members. Some way out of this confrontation and possible impasse must be found. Otherwise, any other reform of the United Nations system will be jeopardized.

A distinction must be made between the debating process and the decision-making process, even though both often involve bitter and divisive controversy. The General Assembly has become, as predicted by Senator Vandenberg, the "town meeting of the world." As in national legislatures, the oratory and frequent bombast have served to air the issues, to reveal the points of agreement and disagreement, to express hopes and ambitions and to expose failures and violations of trust. The security, well-being, and freedom of the world community, have been fostered by the debates about forced labor, prisoners of war, and infringement of human rights in the Communist countries during the early years; by the continuing campaign against imperialism, racial discrimination, and apartheid; and by the more recent demands of the developing countries for a redress of the economic imbalance. Indeed, the constant agitation and landslide votes of the developing countries have done much to pressure the developed countries into some measure of accommodation.

What is needed today is not a limitation of debate, or elimination of votes where major interests are at stake, but a limitation of decisions that do not genuinely reflect the will of the whole world community. No decision is often better than a decision that isolates, humiliates, and angers a minority, especially if that minority happens to comprise the members upon whose political and economic support the whole United Nations system depends. Every effort must be made in the future to blunt the sharp edge of controversy, to avoid public confrontations, to defer divisive votes, and to labor persistently for an agreement satisfactory to all or at least not totally unacceptable to any. Such an approach will require the utmost self-restraint, patience, and understanding on the part of each of the 147 members, as well as continuing consultation among governments before a meeting and among delegates during a meeting.

Equally important is the recognition, in U.N. organs and in the member states, that the General Assembly is not an international parliament capable, with certain exceptions, of making binding decisions. It is essential to distinguish among the various kinds of decisions taken by the General Assembly. Some quasi-legislative decisions are binding upon all members: election of individuals to the international court or other offices, election of states to membership in other organs, adoption of the budget, establishment of subsidiary bodies, initiation of action programs, and procedural decisions. All other actions, especially the enunciation of principles and policies, are nonlegislative in character—i. e., recommendatory and advisory only. It is these nonlegislative actions that cause most of the controversy; and it is they that require restraint on the part of all members and continuing consultation before any consensus is reached.

If it is understood by all concerned that a resolution of the General Assembly on some substantive issue contains not a law imposing obligations on the member of the organization but rather a declaration of principle or a recommedation of action, then the need for recorded votes becomes less necessary and a consensus becomes more appropriate.[16] The increasing resort to the consensus technique, in addition to the various preliminary forms of consultation and negotiation discussed above, offers much hope that cooperation rather than confrontation will prevail in the future.

Notes

1. Mahdi Elmandjra, *The United Nations System: An Analysis* (London: Faber & Faber, and Hamden, Conn.: Archon Books, 1973); Martin Hill, *Towards Greater Order, Coherence and Coordination in the United Nations System* (New York: UNITAR Research Reports, no. 20, 1974); J. G. Hadwen and Johan Kaufmann, *How United Nations Decisions Are Made* (Leyden: Sijthoff, 1960); Johan Kaufmann, *Conference Diplomacy* (Leyden, Sijthoff, and Dobbs Ferry, N.Y., 1968); A. J. P. Tammes, "Decisions of International Organs as a Source of International Law," *Recueil des Cours of the Academy of International Law* (The Hague, 1958-II, Leyden, Sijthoff, 1959); *A Study of the Capacity of the United Nations Development System*, 2 vols. (E/ 70.I.10), 1969; and Ninth Conference on the United Nations of the Next Decade, *Decision-Making Processes of the United Nations* (Vail, Colorado, June 9-16, 1974), sponsored by The Stanley Foundation, Muscatine, Iowa. Henry G. Schermers, *International Institutional Law*, vol. II (Leyden, Sijthoff, 1972), pp. 305-375.

2. The need for reviewing the system of decision making in the General Assembly was recognized by the Commission to Study the Organization of Peace in its Tenth Report, February 1958, p. 35: "The present one state—one vote is clearly unrealistic, and has become a serious impediment to the development of the Assembly's prestige as the collective spokesman of a global viewpoint. *We urge the United Nations to continue its examination of possible changes designed to produce a more equitable system of representation and voting in the General*

Assembly." See: Inis L. Claude, Jr., *Swords Into Plowshares: The Problems and Progress of International Organization,* 4th ed. (New York: Random House, 1971), pp. 112-140; and Louis B. Sohn, "United Nations Decision-Making: Confrontation or Consensus?" *Harvard International Law Journal* 15 (June 1974): 438-445.

3. See: Commission to Study the Organization of Peace, "Reconciling Power with the Sovereign Equality of States," in Seventeenth Report, May 1966, pp. 13-20 and 63-82; C. Wilfred Jenks, "Unanimity, the Veto, Weighted Voting, Special and Simple Majorities and Consensus as Modes of Decisions in International Organizations," in *Cambridge Essays in International Law: Essays in Honour of Lord McNair* (London: Stevens & Sons, Dobbs Ferry, Oceana, 1965), pp. 48-63; Catherine Senf Manno, "Selective Weighted Voting in the U.N. General Assembly," *International Organization* (winter 1966), pp. 37-62, which contains a long bibliographic note; Louis B. Sohn, ed., *Cases on United Nations Law,* 2nd ed. (Brooklyn: Foundation Press, 1967), pp. 248-267; Francis O. Wilcox and Carl M. Marcy, *Proposals for Change in the United Nations* (Washington, D.C.: Brookings Institution, 1955), pp. 344-373; and Richard N. Gardner, "The Hard Road to World Order," *Foreign Affairs* (April 1974), pp. 570-571. The Commission to Study the Organization of Peace has offered proposals for weighted voting in its Ninth Report, 1955, pp. 77-129; Tenth Report, 1957, pp. 47, 52, 227-232; Eleventh Report, 1959, p. 10; and Seventeenth Report, 1966, cited above. In the Twentieth Report, 1969, the possibility of weighted voting in the General Assembly was mentioned on p. 57, and in a supporting paper, pp. 119-121.

4. The relationship of the two kinds of voting, as seen by the major powers, was early appraised by a Chinese scholar: "The great powers have been willing to assent to this equality in the voting procedure in the General Assembly. Such unusual influence as they may be able to exact through the promotion of blocs, or when voting collectively, will naturally play an important part in the decisions of that body. But these are not prerogatives which can be included in an international instrument. On paper, the great powers have consented to equality in the Assembly because, in the final analysis, they are not committed to the responsibilities of action through the decisions of that organ, and because acceptance of voting equality in the Assembly makes it easier for them to defend their special prerogatives in the Security Council." Wellington Koo, Jr., *Voting Procedures in International Political Organizations* (New York: Columbia, 1947), p. 257.

This relationship was noted more recently by a group of ten specialists of different nationalities: "The existence in the United Nations of a 'power minority' as well as of a 'voting majority' was noted, and it was considered that the same ethics of conduct should apply to both in terms of restraint and dialogue, if efforts to modify or abolish the veto were not actively to be pursued. . . . Another participant expressed the opinion that the one State–one vote provision in the General Assembly was a *quid pro quo* for the veto. . . . A further suggestion was made that a possible *quid pro quo* existed between limitations in the use of the veto and restraint in the formulation, introduction and adoption of resolutions by large majorities." *Report of the Sixth Annual Conference on United Nations Procedures* (New Paltz, New York, May 30–June 2, 1975), sponsored by The Stanley Foundation, Muscatine, Iowa.

5. Cf. Harlan Cleveland, "The U.S. vs. the U.N.," *The New York Times Magazine,* May 4, 1975, pp. 26ff.

6. Cf.: John Spenser Bassett, *The League of Nations: A Chapter in World Politics* (New York: Longmans Green, 1928), pp. 36-37; Felix Morley, *The Society of Nations: Its Organizational and Constitutional Development* (Washington, D.C.: Brookings Institution, 1932), pp. 408-413; and F. P. Walters, *A History of the United Nations,* 2 vols. (London: Oxford University Press, 1952).

7. Halina Okularczyk, "Consensus in the Decision-Making Process of the United Nations Organs," *Studies on International Relations,* no. 1, 1973, p. 145; Louis B. Sohn, "United Nations Decision-Making; Confrontation or Consensus?" *Harvard International Law Journal* 15 (summer 1974): 438-445.

8. Anne Winslow, "Benchmarks for Newcomers," *UNITAR NEWS* 4, no. 3 (1972): 12.

9. Commission to Study the Organization of Peace, *Strengthening the United Nations,* Tenth Report, 1957, pp. 5-6, states: "We suggest that the United Nations develop the practice of dealing with a dispute or situation, either before or after preliminary debate, by referring it to private negotiation under the auspices of a *rapporteur* to be appointed by the Secretary-General in consultation with the President either of the General Assembly or of the Security Council. If the process of a quiet consultation does not produce agreement, we recommend that a resolution proposed by the *rapporteur* should be given priority over any other draft resolution in the public debating and voting process."

10. *The Impact of Multinational Corporations on Development and on International Relations: Report of the Group of Eminent Persons* (E/5500/Rev. 1), 1974.

11. *A New United Nations Structure for Global Economic Co-Operation: Report of the Group of Experts on the Structure of the United Nations System* (E/AC.62/9), May 28, 1975.

12. The General Assembly has established the principle that no fee or other remuneration in addition to travel expenses and subsistence allowances should be paid to members of organs and subsidiary bodies. Nevertheless, honorariums are being paid to officers and members of the International Law Commission, International Narcotics Control Board, and the United Nations Administrative Tribunal. See U.N. document A/C.5/1677, August 20, 1975.

13. Despite the fact that the group of experts proposed no change in voting procedures, their recommendation concerning negotiating groups aroused suspicions recently in the minds of thirteen specialists of different nationalities: "Doubts were expressed lest the creation of negotiating groups might limit the right of the majority, even though voting procedures would remain." *Report of*

the Sixth Annual Conference on United Nations Procedures, p. 25.

14. Decision of the General Assembly, 28th Session, taken on November 16, 1973; Third United Nations Conference on the Law of the Sea, Rule of Procedure, A/CONF. 62/30/Rev.1, chapter VI. See also Louis B. Sohn, "Voting Procedures in United Nations Conferences for the Codification of International Law," *American Journal of International Law* (April 1975), pp. 333-352.

15. Sidney Dell, "An Appraisal of UNCTAD III," *World Development* (May 1973); Richard N. Gardner, "The United Nations Conference on Trade and Development," *International Organization* (winter 1968), pp. 99-130; Branislaw Gosovic, "UNCTAD: North-South Encounter," *International Conciliation* (May 1968); Joseph S. Nye, "UNCTAD: Poor Nations Pressure Group," in Robert W. Cox and Harold K. Jacobson, eds., *The Anatomy of Influence: Decision-Making in International Organization* (New Haven: Yale, 1973); and Oscar Schachter, "Conciliation Procedures in the United Nations Conference on Trade and Development," in Pieter Sanders et al., *International Arbitration: Liber Amicorum for Martin Domke* (The Hague: Nijhoff, 1967), pp. 268-274.

16. See Leland M. Goodrich, *The United Nations in a Changing World* (New York: Columbia University Press, 1974), pp. 80-81. The author is indebted to Professor Goodrich and many other members of the Commission to Study the Organization of Peace—especially Clarence A. Berdahl, Roy Blough, Samuel DePalma, Louis B. Sohn, Ruth B. Russell, and Richard R. Wood—for their many helpful comments on earlier versions of this paper. Thanks are also due the late W. Martin Hill (United Nations Secretariat), Oscar Schachter and Aida Luisa Levin (United Nations Institute for Training and Research), and Sidney Dell (United National Development Program). All of these individuals bear no responsibility, however, for the accuracy of facts and wisdom of interpretations in the paper.

27. The Structuring of International Cooperation
Robert S. Jordan

Introduction

U.N. Secretary-General Kurt Waldheim has said that in looking at the United Nations and other international bodies, it is important to realize that their weaknesses in modern conditions stem from the same misconceptions that often exist at the national level.[1] In a similar vein, Daniel Bell has noted that the adaptive tasks of American society in the last 150 years have been the creation of new institutions to reconcile political power, adding that the problems the nation faces in the coming decades will be in mediating the multiple conflicting demands that are upon us now and that will multiply since the "social" and the "political" are now so inextricably joined.[2] Perhaps enlightened self-interest, one of the cornerstones of American political and economic practice (as well as principle), will encourage the industrialized states to participate in a new international economic order with the so-called third world. However, interdependence is not yet reflected in a set of established policies. Even though the North and the South need each other, their problems are still to be solved at the global level. In the future, global norms and principles will have to be established to ensure greater justice and equity between, as well as within, factions. Development can no longer be considered a process restricted to one part of the world. It is, in fact, a universal phenomenon, embracing both the industrialized

---

The views expressed in this chapter are solely the responsibility of the author and not of the U.N. Institute for Training and Research (UNITAR). The author is grateful to Margaret M. Croke, assistant to the director of research at UNITAR, in connection with research for and drafting of the chapter.

and the developing countries and is no longer a purely economic issue, but one with social, cultural, and environmental dimensions.

For example, the resolution adopted by the U.N. General Assembly at its Seventh Special Session in 1975 dealt with expansion and diversification of the trade of developing countries; improvement of the terms of trade of developing countries to eliminate the imbalance with industrialized countries; transfer of real resources for financing development, and related international monetary reforms; development of the scientific and technological infrastructure of developing countries; industrialization; and changes in world food production and trade to increase food production rapidly in the developing countries. These and other related questions are frequently referred to as the problems of development, but they are much more than that. As Michel Jobert of France pointed out at the Sixth Special Session,[3] a fair and stable international economic order presupposes that the radical changes that have been proposed in the relationship between developing and industrialized countries should benefit both. Equity involves not merely transfer of resources; it also involves the fairer distribution of resources, industry, and the capacity to produce.

The community of nations is mediating multiple conflicting demands (with regard to food, population, health, education, housing, and the environment) that cannot be resolved separately. Each is a component part of the complex of factors that together constitute a global human society, and the institutional methods and framework will perforce continue to evolve. Multipurpose goals will need pluralistic approaches. The United Nations's normative function has been carried forward by the resolutions of the Seventh Special Session,[4] which are all parts of the process on the substantive side, accompanied by the establishment of the Ad Hoc Committee of the Restructuring of the Economic and Social Sectors of the U.N. System, and the International Civil Service Commission, which are part of the process on the organizational and administrative side.

The Complexity of Facilitating Change

The United Nations is frequently criticized for its inability to adapt to changing circumstances and, like any other human institution, the U.N. system has its weaknesses. It is interesting to reflect on the use of the word *system*. The requirements of a living system are different from those of a machine. It seems that change in the U.N. system is frequently discussed in terms of adjustment of a machine rather than adaptation of a living organism. Not only is it much easier but it is also quicker to adjust a machine; it takes time for a living organism to adapt.

In addition to the vast increase in membership, the range of organs available for dealing with international problems is appreciably greater in number than three decades ago when the United Nations was founded. To name just a few of the more recent additions, there is the International Agricultural Development Fund that is about to be established as a specialized agency; the International Civil Service Commission that began its work last year; the Commission on Transnational Corporations and the United Nations Information and Research Centre on Transnational Corporations; and after years of discussions on disarmament and arms control in different forums within and outside the United Nations, an Ad Hoc Committee on the World Disarmament Conference has been established. The Ad Hoc Committee on the Restructuring of the Economic and Social Sectors of the United Nations System is also evidence of the organization striving for change.

It is of interest to note that the current debate on restructuring of the system is focusing on three questions in particular: (1) the strengthening of the Economic and Social Council by finding some means of increasing the political input; (2) the role of the U.N. Conference on Trade and Development (UNCTAD) in development and long-range commodity planning; and (3) the use of special sessions of the General Assembly rather than ad hoc conferences to deal with global problems. The use of special sessions would ensure that the full range of political opinions are considered and accommodated. Because of the multiplicity of views that must be harmonized in a special session, the task is not easy—it calls for statesmanship and innovative thinking, and it takes time. However, the results may be more likely to be satisfactory than those of the more "efficient" ad hoc conferences where the results may tend to mirror the views of some states but not balance out conflicting political views. In other words, the general thinking in the United Nations at the present time is toward finding ways for all shades of political opinion to be heard, to be considered, and if possible, to be harmonized.

While the pace of change in the United Nations is subject to criticism, decision making within individual governments on important policy issues is also rarely instantaneous. As E. F. Schumacher has said, "Organization does not jump; it must gradually evolve to fit changing circumstances."[5] When one considers the number of sovereign states that take part in the decision process in any U.N. organ—let alone the 147 in today's assembly—and the number of individuals who participate in policymaking and negotiation, it is perhaps surprising that the process of change in the United Nations is not slower than it is. This should not be interpreted as implying that sufficient change has taken place or that attempts should not be made to accelerate the pace of change. It is simply a reflection, in the light of counsels of perfection, on the nature of change as it affects the U.N. system.

It is a fact that the more nation-states there are taking part in the process, the greater is the number of interactions required to reach a decision, and the longer the process. There are a greater number of individuals who participate in the policymaking and negotiation, a greater diversity of views to be accommodated, and a greater variety of ideas as to possible lines of approach to problem resolution. Because of this increased complexity, attempts have been made to negotiate in smaller groups, such as the Paris Conference on International Economic Cooperation, while at the same time endeavoring to retain a representative political balance.

The process of negotiation differs in different instances; usually it moves incrementally, although sometimes there are quantum jumps when, at a particular time, a synthesis of views takes place. In the minds of some, the Seventh Special Session represents a quantum jump. Among factors involved in such negotiation are: (1) the reaching of agreed policy within governments; (2) the coordination of that policy with other governments in a given region or with like-minded states, including the necessity of revising and adapting some original positions; (3) negotiation in U.N. organs on decisions to be taken, again including adjustment and return to original national policy sources to obtain agreement on a policy that can be supported by many nations; (4) requests to certain governments to carry out certain actions or to provide certain information; (5) requests to one or more U.N.-system or other intergovernmental organs; (6) requests to nongovernmental organizations; (7) and/or requests to secretariats of organs within the U.N. system.

With the exception of certain decisions of the Security Council, and some budgetary procedures, all U.N. decisions are recommendatory to governments and other international organizations. Thus, after a decision has been reached and a resolution adopted, it is up to one or more of the entities just mentioned to decide on the way in which it will, or can, give effect to the decision. With the best will in the world, these entities may be faced with constraints of personnel, finance, organizational infrastructure, and so on. If the goal at which the initial resolution was aimed is not attained within a reasonable time, then the organ that adopted the resolution may try another approach—renewed requests, exhortation, continued program review, establishment of a committee or committees to deal with one or more aspects of the methods by which the desired goal is being achieved, etc. The process is, of necessity, time consuming and protracted. It is, however, an equitable process in that it permits every sovereign nation to make its voice heard. It can, of course, be argued that there are inherent inequities inasmuch as the economic size, or strength of bloc political coherence, may affect the nature and rate of international response to the mandate of a U.N. political decision-making body. While these are not necessarily determinants of influence, it has been said, both, that "he who pays the piper calls the tune," or alternatively, "he who speaks most is listened to most."

One cannot say that the process is either simple or is likely to be speeded up significantly—although there is always the possibility of new ways being found to increase the pace of change in the U.N. system. Dr. Davidson Nicol, the executive director of the U.N. Institute for Training and Research (UNITAR), has stated than any coordination of the U.N. system must also involve more effective coordination within the individual member states.[6] Questions pertaining to the United Nations should perhaps be considered at cabinet level by each government instead of being left for a final decision to the ministry or department concerned with that particular question. The delegates to the committees of the General Assembly or to the Economic and Social Council would then arrive aware of governmental-wide decisions that had been made and so be able to contribute more meaningfully and decisively in the debates. This internal coordination, resulting in a more uniform external approach by a member state, could then be reflected in coordination among the agencies themselves and the U.N. Secretariat.

The structure and functions of the U.N. Secretariat have been the object of numerous studies.[7] The interchange of views among persons from nations of different size and administrative structure is valuable in this context, as it tends to balance out what may be an overemphasis in some quarters on administrative efficiency. The performance of an international secretariat cannot be judged in the same terms as that of a national bureaucracy, tempting as this may be. In international bureaucracy, a multiplicity of nations and viewpoints must be represented and the process of harmonization of views will necessarily be a different process from that in a more homogeneous national setting.

The test of efficiency, however, is whether, given the tools of finance and personnel, the international secretariat performs the functions required. The membership of the United Nations sets multiple goals that it wishes the organization to achieve, requiring multiple institutional responses within the system, possibly even with some overlap. While this may sometimes be criticized as inefficient and a less than optimum use of resources, by some national standards, it also, and I believe more importantly, can bring about healthy competition and cross-fertilization of ideas.

A recent report by the American Council on Education,[8] speaking of the United States, made a point that applies also to the United Nations, namely, that the values and perceptions of reality of two kinds of publics—the general citizenry and specialized political and economic interests—can substantially affect the capacity to cope with global interrelationships and, both directly and indirectly, set effective limits to the direction of policy. In this connection, by analogy, one of the problems of the United Nations may be that it is constantly subjected to searching political criticism in the news media and in many other forums, with only limited and unequal means to counter such criticism. More positively, however, using the United Nations as a "whipping post" may help to ameliorate tensions and political competition among the member states that otherwise could be even more damaging to the purposes for which the organization was established.

The Importance of Facilitating Change

Professor Stanley Hoffmann has contrasted "the old-type military alliances against a well-defined enemy" with "the new fluid functional bargaining coalitions" and has emphasized that there is today no substitute for global bargaining, issue by issue, for a "colossal expansion of diplomacy, resembling the constant maneuvering and coalition building of domestic politics."[9] Yet, while there are calls for the U.N. system to change, to reform, to accept new responsibilities, there are few calls for increasing the financial resources of the system. As was noted in the *Report of the Group of Experts on the Structure of the United Nations System*,[10] the total budget of the system, throughout its first thirty years, was equal to less than half of one percent (0.4 percent) of the combined GNP of the member states in one year (1974). Yet, the need for bargaining on a global scale, as a means not only of achieving equity among nations but also of avoiding war, seems to be fairly well accepted. Anything on the scale suggested by Hoffman would certainly require a substantial financial underpinning.

In a sense, that "colossal expansion" is already beginning to take place, but unofficially. While there continue to be informal negotiations between various nations and groups of nations in the corridors of the United Nations, in the offices of the permanent missions, and in non-U.N. intergovernmental organizations, there are an increasing number of structured gatherings that take place at the United Nations. While unofficial, they are listed as "Other Meetings" in the daily U.N. journal. Several such meetings may take place each day, but behind closed doors with no records of the discussions being given general circulation. They also have attracted little scholarly notice. Reference to a few of the groups will illustrate their range: The Non-Aligned Group's Working Group on Transnational Corporations; the Group of 77's Working Group on the Restructuring of the Economic and Social Sectors of the U.N. System; the African Group of the Members of the Economic and Social Council; the Meeting of Permanent Representatives of the Commonwealth Countries; the Meeting of Members of the Islamic Conference; the Bureau of the Group of 77 meeting in connection with the Third United Nations Conference on the Law of the Sea. Other such meetings in connection with the Law of the Sea Conference include the "territorialist" group; the Group of Landlocked and Geographically Disadvantaged States; Working Group on Third Committee Matters (marine scientific research); the African Group on Peaceful Settlement of Disputes; and the Group of 77's Group on Peaceful Settlement of Disputes. In addition, five regional groups—African states, Asian states, Eastern European states, Latin American states, and Western European and other states—appoint chairmen each month whose names are announced in the U.N. journal.

Bargaining is an important way of dealing with conflicts, especially in North/South relations. Can international law, and international organization in general, be utilized to facilitate conditions of collective bargaining? The Declaration on the Establishment of a New International Economic Order calls for "the broadest cooperation of all the States members of the international community, based on equity, whereby the prevailing disparities in the world may be banished and prosperity secured for all."[11]

However, Zbigniew Brzezinski has pointed to some of the constraints inherent in the new bargaining conditions.[12] A greater concern with the promotion of global development will require assumption of new responsibilities by the system vis-à-vis its participants that is bound to involve limitations on national sovereignty. Indeed, this has already happened in a number of instances. There is also the possibility that social advantages may have to be purchased at the cost of economic efficiency.

The question is sometimes raised as to whether the future of international bargaining lies within or outside the United Nations. It seems to me that the answer is both within and outside. The United Nations, as the only extant virtually universal international organization, will play a significant role in global bargaining. As it establishes new machinery it establishes "presences" and forums that did not exist before, which provide a potential for aiding in problem-solving and in bringing about further change. On the other hand, given the magnitude, variety, and complexity of world problems, the United Nations cannot work in isolation. For example, at its 30th Session, in its resolution dealing with the Paris Conference on International Economic Cooperation, the General Assembly recognized that the work and results of the conference will, directly or indirectly, have a bearing on the ongoing work on international economic cooperation and development within the U.N. system.[13]

The history of man has been one of increasingly larger units of mutual cooperation. It is evident that there is need for a universal organization and this need is likely to be more apparent, rather than less, in the future. In a sense, the existence of today's United Nations is only the reflection of this need. As Hoffmann has argued, neither nations nor individuals can be totally enmeshed with one another without breakdown—physical or mental.[14] Therefore, one objective in world economic affairs should be to ensure that as many nations and regions as possible have a considerable degree of self-reliance and self-identity, even while creating new means for global interaction.

Parts of the global bargaining process are being carried out and will continue to be carried out in many forums and at various levels—local, intranational, national, regional, and international. Discussion of and action on world problems move into and out of the United Nations. There are many examples. Monetary talks led to the Smithsonian agreement, which was followed by the Rambouillet pact, which laid the basis for the International Monetary Fund (IMF) conference in Jamaica. Disarmament negotiations began in the United Nations, then there were phases of talks between the two superpowers, between the five permanent members of the Security Council and Canada, and subsequently between increasingly large numbers of states, the discussions on this, as on other subjects, always being interwoven into General Assembly debates. Now there is an Ad Hoc Committee on the World Disarmament Conference and a Center for Disarmament Studies.

Similarly, the debates on energy, raw materials, and other questions relevant to the establishment of a new international economic order have taken place both within and outside the United Nations. The proceedings of the Paris Conference on International Economic Cooperation in December 1975 were influenced by developments at the Seventh Special Session. The conference reconvened later in 1976 to receive the reports of the four commissions it established to deal with energy, raw materials, development, and financial questions. The secretary-general reported to the 31st General Assembly on his participation in the conference.

The process of global bargaining aimed at equity among nations is thus a step-by-step process, each set of discussions being influenced by previous discussions and, in turn, affecting subsequent discussions—positions are clarified, facts are gathered, ideas exchanged—with the United Nations as the pivotal global forum in which past action is reviewed and future action recommended. The United Nations acts not only as a catalyst of change but also as a gyroscope during the course of change.

Conclusions

The willingness with which nations approach the task of harmonizing their views, both on the role of the U.N. system and on the solution of global problems, and the continuing ingenuity they bring to devising the requisite institutional mechanisms—the ability to resolve their conflicting views of global reality—seem likely to be the determinants of how much "conflict resolution" in the traditional sense will be needed in the future. They are the main parameters in dealing with the problem of peace.

In an era of interdependence, zero-sum activities (where the gain of one nation is achieved at the expense of another) will decline.[15] With the recognition of the "spaceship Earth" concept, brought about in part by increased speed of travel and communication, and realization of interdependence on such questions as human survival in the face of environmental pollution, international policy today must be based on the certainty that unless all win, all will surely lose. The art of statesmanship is required to transform seemingly intractable conflicts into situations that are more amenable to negotiated settlement. This is always difficult, sometimes in the short run impossible, and requires changes in attitudes, beliefs, dispositions, values, and interests that may take a long time to achieve.

The ability of the U.N. system to change, and to respond to change, has been proven and augurs well for the future. The system has shown over the past thirty years that it can change—that the differing views of numerous states with differing national interests and priorities can be harmonized. There is a continuing need and demand for change. Changes of the magnitude required are not easily made and they cannot be given a precise definition in advance; they will involve inconsistencies and paradoxes. But given political will to reach accommodation of interest, the system will continue to change to meet global needs. It will prove capable of resolving conflicting ideas and approaches and of defining and addressing itself to the problems of peace.[16]

Notes

1. Kurt Waldheim, United Nations secretary-general, keynote speech at a conference on New Structures for Economic Interdependence, May 1975. In the proceedings of the conference published by the Institute on Man and Science, Rensselaerville, N.Y., p. 2.

2. Daniel Bell, "The End of American Exceptionalism," *The Public Interest* (fall 1975), as quoted in "For the Record," *The Washington Post,* January 16, 1976.

3. Michel Jobert, then minister of foreign affairs of France, in a statement to the United Nations General Assembly at its Sixth Special Session, April 10, 1974. U.N. document A/PV.2209.

4. It is worth noting that provisions to ensure institutional adaptation—provisions for systematic and comprehensive program review, appraisal, and evaluation—are being included in more and more of the resolutions adopted by the General Assembly. That is to say, built-in provisions for change are increasingly being used. These reviews, etc., are reported back to the assembly, which can then make further recommendations based on progress.

5. E. F. Schumacher, *Small is Beautiful: Economics as if People Mattered* (New York: Harper and Row, 1973), p. 159.

6. Statement of Dr. Davidson Nicol, executive director, UNITAR, to the Ad Hoc Committee on the Restructuring of the Economic and Social Sectors of the United Nations System (New York: UNITAR, February 25, 1976), mimeo.

7. See for example, "Reports of the Committee of Experts on the Review of the Activities and Organization of the Secretariat" (A/4776), June 14, 1961; "The Reorganization of the Secretariat at the Higher Level" (A/7359) 1968; "Report of the Joint Inspection Unit on Personnel Problems in the United Nations" (A/8454) 1971; and "Report of the Economic and Social Sectors of the United Nations System" (A/31/35), United Nations Official Records of the Thirty-first Session of the General Assembly, supplement no. 34.

8. "Education for Global Interdependence," September 1975, American Council on Education, Occasional Paper no. 3, chapter II, as quoted in "ACE Looks at Research in International Studies" in *FAR Horizons* (autumn 1975), p. 6.

9. Stanley Hoffmann, "Groping Toward a New World Order," in "The Week in Review," *The New York Times,* January 11, 1976.

10. Report of the Group of Experts, "A New United Nations Structure for Global Economic Cooperation" (E/AC.62/9), May 28, 1975.

11. "Declaration on the Establishment of a New International Economic Order," resolution adopted by the General Assembly at its Sixth Special Session (A/RES/3201 [S-VI]). U.N. Official Records of the Sixth Special

Session of the General Assembly, supplement no. 1.

12. Zbigniew Brzezinski, "The Changing International System and America's Role," *The New York Times,* October 15, 1975.

13. "Conference on International Economic Cooperation," resolution adopted by the General Assembly at its Thirtieth Session (A/RES/3515 [XXX]). United Nations Official Records of the Thirtieth Session, supplement no. 34.

14. Stanley Hoffmann, "Groping Toward a New World Order."

15. Daniel Bell, "The Management of Information and Knowledge," paper prepared for the eleventh meeting of the Panel on Science and Technology, Committee on Science and Astronautics, United States House of Representatives, 1970, quoted from John McHale, "The Changing Information Environment: Selective Topography" in *Information Technology: Some Critical Implications for Decision Makers 1971-1990* (New York: The Conference Board, 1971).

16. This paper has drawn on a number of sources not identified in the footnotes, among them Stuart Hampshire, "Thinking About Social Costs," *The New York Times,* March 24, 1976.

28. International Law and Majority Rule: The Case for Conservatism
Alice B. Haemmerli

The concept of interdependence—both sectoral and international—has become a leitmotif of contemporary political discussion. One can hardly consider the energy crisis, environmental problems, world population growth, or the future of the seabed without acknowledging the notion's suitability. Yet, despite recent emphasis on the global management of problems posed by interdependence, a universal political commonwealth remains an elusive ideal. If an international society exists, it is one polarized between an industrialized minority and a less developed majority, and the gap between them is profound and persistent. Given a divided world and the need to regulate its most pressing problems, two important questions arise. How can new rules of international law be most expeditiously generated? Have new forms of authoritative norm-creation evolved to keep pace with the universalization of socioeconomic issues?

The dichotomy in the world society has extended not only to specified problems but to the means of dealing with them, including international law and organization. The United Nations itself has been viewed for some twenty years from incompatible perspectives: by the second, third, and fourth worlds as a means of righting the injustices of earlier epochs and their contemporary vestiges; and by the Western minority as a conservative agency of political/legal regulation. International law has been the object of intense discord. Both its rules and its means of generation have been questioned by majority

This chapter is adapted, with permission, from ORBIS 20, no. 2 (summer 1976): 315-341, a Journal of World Affairs, published by the Foreign Policy Research Institute, where it appeared as "International Norm-Creation for a Divided Society: A Reappraisal of Some Perennial Problems."

spokesmen. . . . Majority-made law has often been acclaimed as the "new international law," expressed in certain General Assembly resolutions, particularly those believed "law-declaring." The U.N. majority has frequently emphasized the importance of voting in these cases as a valid means of expressing legal rules and as alleged proof of such rules' legitimacy. The West, meanwhile, has clung to the notion of consensus, in the sense of quasi-universal agreement including member states of opposing sides. . . . The basic issue is whether the new majority, by virtue of its size (representing the vast majority of the human population), can transform the international system into what Echeverría calls an "international democracy," or whether the old requirement of consensus—that pluralistic system stressed by Moynihan —remains a sine qua non of international norm-creation. . . .

Many current problems are being approached as objects of parliamentary diplomacy and multilateral conferences. . . . Such conferences may well, like the General Assembly, adopt resolutions that purport to be crystallizations of international public morality, or even of law. Resemblances to the assembly are heightened when such conferences are universal in membership and when their agendas are . . . multipurpose and generalized. The questions posed here may therefore be answered through an examination of conference-style norm-creation as exemplified by General Assembly efforts in that area.

The underlying purpose of our study is clarification. Loose usage of the term *consensus,* for example, has rendered its meaning ambiguous Insistence on voting "if consensus cannot be reached" is a refrain often heard, yet few probe its inherent improbability: if consensus qua agreement general enough to sustain a rule of law cannot be achieved, what can a majority vote—probably omitting one side of the polarized society—signify? And if the claim is made that consensus *has* been reached, what does this mean? Is there a criterion whereby a consensus can be judged to be significant? The issues have been further obscured by appeals to "progressive" international law; assertions that regulation can be dictated by the majority if the minority remains recalcitrant; confusion between consensus and consent; and lack of attention to the value, rather than mere extent, of consensus. In addition, while formal General Assembly competence to enunciate binding rules is almost universally rejected, assertions of a quasi-legislative function need further examination.[1] This is especially important in view of the argument that meaningful consensus can be inferred from majority votes. Thus, the study will attempt to delineate, and to analyze critically, the nature, virtues, and defects of voting and consensus as means whereby the international society can or should make law.

The Problem of Antilegalism

Norm-creating conferences are viewed by most states as diplomatic forums, i. e., as political rather than legal arenas.[2] The preference is not an arbitrary one, but is the result of specific views on international law that merit consideration. By 1960, the notion of international law as a vehicle of domination by an industrial-nations club had been fully elaborated in the United Nations and elsewhere. Advanced by socialist and newly independent member states, the concept was intimately connected with their accompanying view of the United Nations as the appropriate forum in which to reform the legal, as well as the social, system of the international society. Serious to begin with, the conflict between this perception and the West's traditional approach was exacerbated by the fact that, in legal debate, the two sides often used the same terms ("right," "obligation") to mean entirely different things. This led to unprecedented mutual miscomprehension, eventually accompanied by the majority's rejection of classical legal approach for its own sake.

Take the debate on the U.N. convenants on human rights. In the course of a seventeen-year period (1949 to 1966), one of the primary issues was the inclusion of an article affirming the right of peoples to self-determination. The acerbic exchanges occasioned by that controversy were interesting examples of the obstacles to norm-creation for a divided society. For it became clear that the anticolonialist majority deemed traditional considerations (such as the *opinio juris* of responsible or practicing states, technical precision in drafting, definition of terms, and general applicability of the proposed rule) irrelevant or inconsequential compared with the larger political issue of decolonization. In vain did the Western states and their allies (the same states that form today's minority in economic confrontations) make their legal points with logic and vigor. The relevant consideration for the majority was not logic, nor—although the exercise at hand was the drafting of a treaty—was it law. It was instead a combination of ethics, justice, and the redressing of colonial wrongs. In face of those principles, arguments relying on the classical requirements of law were rejected as ephemeral at best; at worst, they were viewed as obscurantist devices employed to divert attention from the real issues.

For the West, on the other hand, a real issue was the corpus of events overtaking the law, for the majority attitude toward specific legal desiderata was rapidly expanded to embrace international law itself. In one sense, the charge that international law had been evolved and designed to serve the interests of a small group of states was unanswerable. Classical international law was indeed a Western product originally intended to serve the needs and interests of its authors. The problem was that attacks on the content and method of the law were not accompanied by generally acceptable alternatives. Rather, proposed reforms often appeared to be just as self-serving as the old system, and just as likely to codify special or transitory interests as "law."[3] Self-determination again provides an apt example. The content of Article 1 of the Universal Covenants was specifically and explicitly directed at colonial peoples. As for method, the 1963-1970 debate on principles of international law concerning friendly relations and cooperation among states (i.e., in the special committee and in the sixth committee) included the majority's heated defense of charter legitimation of colonial wars of liberation and assistance to them.[4] In affirming those principles, the majority called for a "break... from the rules of traditional international law"[5] and its methods of norm-creation, which "entailed excessive rigidity"[6] and encouraged "legalistic arguments."(!)[7] Classical legal method, it was said, "should on occasion be readily abandoned, in the general interest, in order to ensure that provisions in keeping with the charter were made part of international law, by a simple majority. . . ."[8]

More recently, in the Twenty-ninth General Assembly, Western arguments based on legal construction of the U.N. Charter were dismissed, not because they did not make legal sense, but because they were legalistic. In the case of the South African exclusion, legal constraints were given attention by the majority only to the extent that they could be averred irrelevant or inapplicable. "The World Organization [could] act outside the normal restrictions placed by the Charter on interventions [regarding] domestic jurisdiction";[9] South Africa's "moral incapacity" was the salient point,[10] and one state sharply rebuked the West for attempting to "give lectures on law." The same member reminded the errant big powers, after the triple veto, that "the Security Council derives its power from the Members of the Organization" and could not act in accordance with the charter if it acted against the wishes of the majority.[11] A true "dialogue of the deaf" ensued, wherein majority aruguments for an ethically inspired construction of the charter and of credentials committee rules of procedure contrasted dramatically with the conspicuously legalistic points made by France, the United Kingdom, and the United States:

> [We are] either a law-abiding, law-respecting body or we are nothing. . . . If we put aside the Charter whenever its provisions may seem to a majority of us . . . to be inconvenient, then we lose all claim to authority and credence.[12]

To the majority, this attitude reflected... a fixation on rules for their own sake, and under the circumstances legalism could be viewed as... an indulgence in luxurious trivia at the expense of millions of people subjected to colonialist oppression. To the West, the majority attitude represented an indulgence in emotionalized anarchism which, by establishing a precedent for complete chaos[13] was a myopic surrender to political expedience. It is not an evasion to maintain that that side was correct in its own way, if one considers the lifestyle on a Bantu reservation but also believes in a modicum of respect for legal rules as a prerequisite of international sanity. The problem in the General Assembly was that there were no apparent attempts to concede possible validity to opposing arguments as a prelude to dialogue. What is most interesting is the implication for legal interpretation in the idea of the assembly majority as the authoritative interpretative organ of the charter:

> [The Security Council could not] pretend to act in accordance with the Charter if it hinder[ed] prompt and effective action... on a matter of the greatest concern to the overwhelming number of the Membership, on whose behalf it is expected to act.[14]

Given this view of existing rules, it comes as no surprise that the wishes of the majority are often believed to be the legitimate determinant of new rules. The question is whether it makes legal sense. Is this viewpoint definitive of a serious approach to international law whereby binding rules can be determined and generated by majority votes? Or is it a political argument which is occasionally applicable to legal questions?... Has the quantitative expansion of the international society over the last thirty years involved a qualitative change in its means of generating authoritative norms?

Majority Voting as a Means of Norm-Creation

Does any hard evidence exist that the use of majority voting to generate new rules of law is generally acceptable to the international society? The continued emphasis that state sovereignty and sovereign equality receive from the less developed and socialist worlds[15] would seem, prima facie, to discourage an affirmative reply. Yet, ... the conflict between that emphasis and one on majority voting has not impeded appeals to majority-made law. The conclusion dictated by this inconsistency is that sovereign equality is the governing concept of international relations unless the majority finds itself united on an issue, in which case sovereignty (as an attribute of the minority states) is subordinated to the principle of majority rule. This reasoning is somewhat offensive to logic, but it must be confronted, especially since those issues dividing the society into a large majority and a tiny but powerful minority seem to multiply daily. In essence, the question is how seriously to take affirmations that the "international society has changed" and that the body of rules and their means of generation must change in consequence: has the "ought"—the idea that processes of norm-creation should be revolutionized along with societal change—transformed the "is"?

The necessity for flexibility in law, enabling it to adapt to and reflect social change, has been a favorite theme of writers for several decades. . . . [16] Yet to what extent has the "new" international law become a reality or implied any transformation in norm-creation? Jessup wrote explicitly *de lege ferenda*; Friedmann predicated the law of cooperation on the workings of a welfare calculus. Roling has presented a persuasive analogy of the modern international society and the expansion of suffrage within the modern state. But the very aptness of that analogy detracts from its implications of new sources of law. Evolutionary democratization within the state need not (and in a gradual transformation from oligarchy to democracy does not) entail a new basis of legitimacy for rules or for the means of creating them. Their authoritative basis is enlarged rather than transformed.[17]

In the international arena, no new method of norm-creation can be casually assumed. Rather, the basis of traditional sources of law has expanded to include a multitude of new states. The question therefore remains whether that multitude, by its very existence, implies any transformation in the sources of international law. If possibility is insufficient to prove existence, is there empirical evidence of that transfiguration? This query leads to an examination of arguments that General Assembly majority votes in certain cases have a legal or protolegal effect, and that the transformation may now be under way.

The Legal Problem of Majority Voting

According to the view that the General Assembly possesses a protolegal capacity, majority-adopted resolutions can yield cumulative evidence of evolving rules of law. Authors employing this approach usually stop short of attributing to the assembly a legislative competence. Power to bind states by recommendation (aside from internal budgetary matters) is not asserted. Rather, the emphasis is on the United Nations as a forum wherein evidence of state practice and *opinio juris* may be conveniently evaluated by reference to states' public diplomacy and votes. As Rosalyn Higgins, a major proponent of this approach, says, "The body of resolutions as a whole taken as indications of a general customary law, undoubtedly provide a rich source of evidence."[18] Thus, the corpus of resolutions is ostensibly accorded a value more evidentiary than legislative. Even assertions of a "quasi-legislative competence," such as Richard Falk's tend to rely on a preexisting juridical "consensus of the membership" as the prerequisite of such competence.[19] In this case the question "What does the resolution add?" is not answered with an affirmation of legislative power capable of binding a powerful minority. The vital requirement appears to lie instead in the achievement of international "consensus" that may then be expressed in votes.

Yet, in the last fifteen years, it has become fairly commonplace to hear claims that General Assembly resolutions adopted quasi-unanimously have a special protolegal nature, and/or that clusters of resolutions on an identical subject provide cumulative evidence that law has emerged by virtue of its reassertion in those resolutions. In these cases, the line between evidentiary and legislative function becomes blurred. The shift from the former to the latter is usually the result of excessive assumptions regarding the significance of adopting majorities. It can be precipitated by the number of resolutions adopted on a given subject; by presumptions that the U.N. practice necessarily implies state practice; or by the assembly's endowment of legal significance to its own resolutions. All of these factors—the repetition of resolutions, the quality as well as size of the majorities and the implications of their makeup, the relationship between U.N. and state practice, and ostensibly "law-declaring" resolutions—can be analyzed through a case history. Here again, self-determination is an appropriate subject. First, a great many resolutions adopted by the assembly[20] have attributed a legal nature to self-determination. Second, Resolution 1514 (XV), including its repetition of the covenant's article on self-determination, has been assigned a legal significance by the U.N. majority and by some observers outside the United Nations.

On the matter of repeated resolutions, Leo Gross has succinctly pointed out: "If individual resolutions have no binding force for the members, this must be due to the absence of legislative authority. If this is so, then how can it be explained that an accumulation of such nonbinding resolutions results in a binding norm of international law?"[21] The resolutions adopted by the General Assembly on self-determination have been numerous; but this in itself says little about their legal nature or binding force. More important is the fact that the colonial states' rejection of self-determination as a legal right was iterated with monotonous regularity in numerous debates preceding the adoption of those resolutions from 1950 to 1960. This point has been accorded inadequate significance and has been almost overshadowed by the recommendations' numbers and their adoption by large majorities. But it is crucial to a consideration of whether the resolutions as a body possess(ed) any legal value. For the arguments of those who would find law embodied in recurrent resolutions do not rest on numbers alone, but on the allegation that the sizable majorities adopting them have reflected the *opinio juris* of the international society. This idea entails serious problems: (1) U.N. practice is merged with state practice, even when the practice of crucial states may have been contrary to that of the organization;[22] (2) it is assumed that a vote for (or abstention on) a resolution implies *opinio juris* on its content as legally obligatory; (3) there is the presumption that the *opinio juris* of responsible states is included in that majority.

If one uses self-determination as the test and considers the adoption of General Assembly Resolution 1514 (XV), these assumptions emerge with exceptional clarity. Regarding the practice of the United Nations and the practice of states, the supposed value of General Assembly resolutions is as evidence of "state practice, an accepted source of law."[23] Yet what is relied upon is not state practice at all, but U.N. practice. Higgins, for example, finds self-determination law in Resolution 1514 because the declaration "taken together with seventeen years of evolving practice by the U.N. organs, provides ample evidence . . . [for] a legal right."[24] But does it? In the case of self-determination, state practice must have included that of colonial states; and those states rejected self-determination as law. Further, as Gross has mentioned, to attribute to resolutions the value of practice as an element of customary international law "is to confuse the practice of organs with the practice of members. . . . Customary international law is the product along with *opinio juris* of the practice of states and not the practice of organs."[25] Finally, if U.N. organs' practice is to be assimilated with that of states, why not include state speeches in U.N. organs' debates? That, after all, is where it is easiest to find and evaluate how states perceive a proposed rule, whether they intend to follow it, and whether they consider it juridical. In the case at hand, the evidence against a legal right to self-determination is unequivocal once state and U.N. practice are differentiated.

As for assumptions on affirmative or abstaining votes, Resolution 1514 (XV) was adopted without dissent; abstaining were the United Kingdom, the United States, Australia, Belgium, France, Portugal, Spain, the Dominican Republic, and South Africa. It has often been said that the lack of negative votes on the delcaration indicates a universal or quasi-unanimous consensus in the legal sense, including one on its paragraph on self-determination.[26] The resolution is thus believed to possess "a different status from ordinary resolutions,"[27] enabling it to have become "part of our international law."[28] But what does the absence of nay votes signify in legal terms? Does it have to mean that there was a positive *opinio juris* regarding its contents? This is a conversion that requires a leap of faith in view of the facts mentioned above. Moreover, the contents of this resolution, like those of others, were affirmed (or abstained from) in much the same manner as sin is opposed by political candidates.[29] . . . and agreement or abstention can be a priori facilitated by the conviction that a resolution is not legally binding, or is ajuridical in nature.[30] In the case of 1514 and its right to self-determination, any perusal of the debates on the subject (in the Third Committee, the Commission on Human Rights, the Economic and Social Council [ECOSOC] and plenary) shows conclusively that the abstaining states expressly rejected self-determination as a legal right. How, then, can it be said that self-determination was affirmed as such a right via Resolution 1514's adoption without dissent?

How, indeed, unless the negative *opinio juris* of the states expected to practice self-determination is counted for naught? Yet this interpretation involves obvious conceptual shortcomings. For one thing, it assumes acquiescence in a proposition in direct contradiction to the available empirical evidence. Once the abstaining states' rejection of self-determination as a legal rule is admitted, however, the question becomes one of whether an overwhelming majority vote can bind a dissenting minority on the juridical nature of a proposed rule. But the question is even more complex when it happens—as it does here—that the dissenting minority contains virtually all states expected to practice the rule! As a classical example of legislation for others, the case of self-determination presents a peculiarly appropriate paradigm. First, this type of legislation has become a frequent practice of many General Assembly majorities, and it constitutes a considerable obstacle to realistic norm-creation today. Second, political self-determination has been, since 1952, conceptually twinned to economic self-determination, permanent sovereignty, and economic decolonization—the same notions that have resulted in the Charter of Economic Rights and Duties of States, and that lie at the heart of the present confrontation. The *opinio juris* of those states expected to perform is thus a problem of paramount interest. It may clarify matters to consider just what huge majority votes, on purportedly legal rules, really signify in terms of the international consensus they supposedly represent. To do this, superficial unanimity cannot be taken at face value; nor can "organizational practice" suffice as evidence of state practice and *opinio juris*. Rather, the existence of consensus, including the agreement of interested and responsible states, must be ascertained.

Given situations like the passage of Resolution 1514 or the adoption of the economic charter (over two-thirds of whose articles received unanimous votes), wherein responsible states dissent from the legal nature of certain contents,[31] the underlying problem is one of determining, as Rupert Emerson says, "the nature and extent of the evidence required to justify the proposition that a norm has achieved the consensus . . . of the international community."[32] Writers advocating a quasi-legislative competence for the United Nations insist on the fact that consensus, rather than consent, should be the criterion for a new rule's existence.[33] This is reasonable, and few today would demand the unanimous consent of the international society on a given rule. Rather, it is a question of degree, as Emerson says, or as Falk puts it: "[It is] the extent and quality of the consensus" that is important.[34] The key world would seem to be *quality* rather than *extent*. Is an overwhelming numerical majority sufficient to establish or represent consensus? No matter how often asserted, can a rule be regarded as representing law if a group of influential states consistently opposes it? Can a consensus be asserted on the basis of numbers alone? Higgins affirms that the majority should be able to bind a dissenting minority, since the size and nature of a majority create expectations about legally permissible behavior. This consideration is also emphasized by Falk and McDougal (the latter judging it as more important than *opinio juris*).[35] But how can realistic expectations be created if the majority in question does not contain states responsible under the alleged rule? In this respect, it is helpful to recall the International Court of Justice (ICJ) . . . judgment of 1969 on the *North Sea Continental Shelf Cases,* wherein the court held:

> [Allegedly juridical rules determine acts which not only] amount to a settled practice, but . . . must also be such, or be carried out in such a way, as to be evidence of a belief that this practice is rendered obligatory by the existence of a rule requiring it. . . . *The States concerned must* . . . feel that they are conforming to a legal obligation.[36]

Again, "State practice, *including that of states whose interests are especially affected,* should have been both extensive and virtually uniform [in addition to the *opinio juris* accompanying it]."[37]

This opinion lends itself easily to the evaluation of alleged rules of law as adopted by majority vote. If the dissenting minority includes virtually all states expected to act in accordance with the alleged rule, and the majority contains states with no responsibility to perform, how can one maintain that the majority opinion represents consensus on a rule of law to be acted upon? If the ICJ standard here is rigorous, it is also reasonable. International law should reflect the expanded society it governs, including new states; but it would seem self-defeating at best to exclude the old ones if they are the ones with primary responsibility under a proposed rule.

The real question, then, is whether a consensus can be said to exist if responsible states reject the rule in question as law. Higgins seems to think that such rejection should not be decisive, that it "surely does not do to rely so totally on the behavior of the parties directly concerned."[38] This point may appear valid (and desirable) if the dissenting party is one state like South Africa; on the other hand, if the dissenting minority is a group of states like the entire Western alliance, it seems implausible. In the latter case, the viewpoint of other commentators seems closer to reality: "[One must] distinguish . . . the cases where majorities are asserting law which meaningfully applies to all from resolutions in which they purport to declare law which in fact would apply primarily to others.[39]

The temptation to accept majority votes as evidence of juridical consensus on resolutions is heightened when the assembly itself proclaims a resolution legal or protolegal in nature. Resolution 1514 (XV) serves as a good example of this, as does Resolution 2625 (XXV), incorporating the Declaration on Principles of International Law Concerning Friendly Relations and Cooperation Among States. That declaration has often been cited as a determination of existing law. . . .[40] Thus, declarations are sometimes attributed legal significance on the basis of their very nature. Again, caution is necessary: the legal significance of such resolutions depends on the content, rather than form, of the declaration; i.e., the extent to which that content really is based in the practice and *opinio juris* of states. If the resolution's own claim is taken as prima facie proof that its contents are law, one endows the General Assembly with legislative powers.

This ignores the fact that if the General Assembly is not . . . formally competent to legislate, its mere pronouncement of a rule as law is insufficient evidence that the rule is law. That an assembly or conference resolution purports to declare existing law may be significant; but this in turn necessitates an inquiry into the basis of the assertion, i.e., the veritable existence of the law being declared.

In this connection, it is well to remember that states representing opposing interests (as in the case of self-determination or economic rights and duties) may assent to a declaration where they would not agree to a convention, for the very reason that the declaration is not viewed as creating, or necessarily expressing, binding law.[41] Finally, as the United Nations's own Office of Legal Affairs has pointed out:

> ... There is probably no difference between a "recommendation" or a "declaration" in United Nations practice as far as strict legal principle is concerned. A "declaration" or a "recommendation" ... cannot be made binding upon Member States, in the sense that a treaty or convention is binding upon the parties ... purely by the device of terming it a "declaration" rather than a "recommendation." However ... [a] "declaration" ... may be considered to impart, on behalf of the organ adopting it, a strong expectation that Members of the international community will abide by it. Consequently, *in so far as* the expectation *is* gradually justified by State practice, a declaration *may by custom become recognized* as laying down rules binding upon States.[42]

The memorandum cited here was written in 1962; but though the world has changed since then, it still would seem that a burden of proof rests on those disagreeing with its statement, rather than on those who concur with it.

The Political Problem of Majority Voting

As Inis Claude has noted, majority voting is feasible only in the presence of an "appropriately advanced moral consensus" and of minority confidence in the "ultimate reasonableness of the majority."[43] Neither of these conditions is present today. The goal of majority rule is democratic government and effective functioning of the body politic, not one at the expense of the other. One case history, the U.N. expenses crisis, reveals that the attempt to endow the U.N. majority with legislative authority—using, ironically, a functional approach to international organization—may result in a dysfunctional organization. A look at the ICJ advisory opinion on *Certain Expenses of the United Nations* is instructive.... The most conspicuous point raised was that of U.N. *telos:* fulfillment of the organization's purposes provided the ultimate yardstick for the assessment of other questions. A new facet of "institutional effectiveness"[44] was developed as a means of determining whether certain expenses fell within the meaning of Article 17(2) and, secondarily, whether the operational basic resolutions were legal.[45] The majority concluded that, although the basic resolutions were recommendatory in nature, they created obligations to pay for U.N. Emergency Force (UNEF) and U.N. Congo Operation (ONUC) activities because these were consistent with the United Nations's primary purpose of maintaining international peace and security. In a rationale reminiscent of the *Reparation for Injuries* case,[46] the guiding principle was that of institutional function. The court found that, if the first question was "What are U.N. expenses?," the major premise of subsequent reasoning was that expenses were amounts paid to defray the costs of carrying out U.N. purposes; ergo, if General Assembly resolutions were intended to carry out U.N. purposes, they entailed "expenses."

Thus, the opinion was an ends-justify-the-means argument wherein U.N. purpose impelled the logic. Further, the court used the existence of the resolutions as a basis for determining their conformity with U.N. purposes; that is, the ipse dixit of the assembly was depended upon to a large extent at the urging of the United States, the United Kingdom, and other Western states.[47] The teleological argument and this circular reliance on resolutions (if the assembly voted the expenditures, it evidently considered them expenses of the United Nations)[48] are relevant to the problem of U.N. practice as a lawmaking agency.

First, the majority asserted that nonbinding General Assembly resolutions could ultimately give rise to binding obligations to bear the cost of their implementation.[49] Taken to its logical conclusion, this could amount to carte blanche for the assembly. The breadth of U.N. purposes, after all, leaves considerable latitude to any determination of which acts conform to the organizational *telos*. Today it is obvious that the assembly interprets the charter through socioeconomic rather than predominantly politicolegal lenses.[50] Considering that the United Nations is a multipurpose institution, and keeping in mind its total commitment to economic development, any serious *reductio* of this implication could spell financial ruin for the organization. Second, if General Assembly resolutions were considered prima facie proof of consistency with U.N. "purposes," the assembly was, in effect, endowed with authority to interpret the charter in a binding fashion. Again, this is a notion with disturbing implications if one recalls the manner in which the majority has recently advanced it (e. g., the exclusion of a state from participation in its debate).

Third, the idea of a world legislature was approached, wherein the U.N. constitution and functions could be determined by a majority and made binding on a dissenting minority. The idea was enhanced by the concept, advanced by both the Western states and the ICJ majority, that the United Nations had power to act (in the aforementioned sense) in the absence of any prohibition to the contrary. As both Leo Gross and Stanley Hoffmann have pointed out[51] (and as Judges Koretsky and Quintana held), this notion contradicts the principle that whatever power is not conferred explicitly on the institution is retained by the member states. Finally, the opinion implied that majority rule, in the manner outlined, could operate in the absence of a consensus. Had there been a consensus, the need for an opinion would not have arisen. The majority opinion could thus be taken to mean that majority rule was: (1) feasible and (2) necessary to organizational effectiveness, even if no political consensus underlay it.

Some of the inherent problems of the opinion speak for themselves. At the crux of the matter, though, the interrelationship of institutional effectiveness, political consensus, and majority rule merits some elaboration. One may ask how effective an organization can be if it: (1) takes action in the absence of consensus, action that *requires* consensus if its costs—financial and otherwise—are to be assumed by the institution as a whole; and (2) then exacerbates the division by assuming a mantle of supranational authority[52] in direct contradiction to its constitution and to the existing political configuration, which includes a minority that can (and does) refuse to be bound. Yet for institutional effectiveness to exist at all, the institution must first be preserved, a point raised in several judges' dissenting opinions. As Hoffmann relates, they considered that

> the purpose of the Organization cannot be met by *any* means, for the founders intended those purposes to be reached by a certain balance of powers. . . . Indeed . . . the founders preferred to have certain purposes abandoned rather than having this balance sacrificed.[53]

If organizational effectiveness provides one criterion of treaty interpretation, so do clear and evident meaning and, presumably, survival of the organization along the lines prescribed by its constitution![54] Just as the veto in the Security Council can be rationalized as a device preventing action in the absence of a consensus enabling and sustaining effective measures,[55] so the limitations imposed on the General Assembly in the operational sphere were designed for a purpose. Their elimination carries dangers, among them the possibility of arbitrary charter interpretations endowed with "authoritative" status merely by virtue of their repeated appearances in assembly resolutions.[56]

Perhaps the most famous metaphor of the opinion is Judge Fitzmaurice's description of the United Nations as a "club" wherein members pay their dues or resign.[57] The problem is that such a club depends on two factors not present in the United Nations in 1962 or 1976: (1) general consensus on the functions and priorities of the club; and (2) a belief that, on an issue-by-issue basis, today's majority may be tomorrow's minority. To belong to a club in which one is permanently assigned to the minority detracts mightily from the club's attractiveness! But while the majority and the minority have changed in the United Nations, the factors generating and sustaining that change have been temporal rather than issue-determined; and on matters of the United Nations's *raison d'être,* the lines today are fairly static. Further, since a great influx of new states is no longer possible, this situation seems unlikely to change.

The most glaring defect of the expenses opinion is, as Hoffmann put it, the predilection for "wallowing in politics and giving it the name of law."[58] The parallels to the present are striking. The 1962 opinion hardened the opposition of France and the USSR, just as the present majority attitude toward General Assembly powers regarding participation has had the same effect on the United States. A historical irony can therefore be perceived. Judge Koretsky's dissenting opinion could, in its strict construction, serve as a present-day primer for the West; and what, for example, could better buttress the Nigerian view of the General Assembly as the authoritative interpreter of the Charter's division of powers (and of Security Council consistency with the charter) than the American attitude of 1962?

On the issue of political majorities, one should note Judge Bustamente's argument that "a conditional link exists between the states' duty to accept institutional decisions and the conformity of those decisions to the Charter."[59] If the charter is interpreted in opposing fashions, the level of acceptance of institutional decisions reached by majority vote will be erratic at best. Asserting the authoritative or binding nature of such votes reveals an indulgence in wishful thinking at the expense of serious efforts toward compromise.

Consensus and Norm-Creation

One can conclude that majority voting remains severely deficient in the realm of international norm-creation. As a process it suffers from both political and psychological disabilities, foremost among them the possibility of enunciating rules that do not command general agreement essential and sufficient to their implementation. As a phenomenon it is misleading. It entails superficial appearances of unanimity where none exists, and encourages ascriptions of consensus on false premises.

Consensus means, essentially, two things: a description of agreement and a means of reaching agreement. In its first sense, it can be described as quasi-universal or universal agreement *qualitatively* sufficient to sustain a proposition as a general rule of international law or as a new legal norm of behavior, applicable to the society as a whole. As such, *significant* consensus has several prerequisites, which apply equally to determinations of existing law and the elaboration of new rules of law. Those requirements are:

1. *Responsibility.* Any alleged consensus, including one affirmed to underlie a majority vote, must be assessed in terms of the participation of states "whose interests are especially affected." This can determine which states, and how many of them, can be nonparticipants in the "consensus" without endangering its character as representative of the society as a whole. A functional approach is indicated here: the significance of states' agreement to, or rejection of, an alleged rule can be judged on the basis of their importance in terms of the issue at hand.

2. *Clarity.* General agreement or "consensus" can be chimerical if what is agreed to is hyperambiguous. For example, the "consensus" reached on self-determination by the Special Committee produced a principle in the 1970 Declaration on Principles of International Law susceptible of, and subjected to, diametrically opposed interpretations. Or, as a U.N. Institute for Training and Research (UNITAR) study mentions, the "consensus" in the Security Council on Resolution 242 has meant entirely different things to its contributors.[60] In fact, ambiguity may be a device deliberately employed to permit opposing sides to assent to a draft. But one may legitimately question the usefulness of this process, especially in extreme cases, when the objective *after* adoption is action or regulation. What is the value of having an ostensible consensus if (a) action or expectations based on it imply opposite things to its authors, and (b) any attempt to implement it therefore renews controversy? Obviously, clarity can never be more than a relative thing, in law as in other human endeavors. But if law is essentially a regulatory agency intended to enhance predictability and order, the enunciation of norms and the achievement of "consensus" on them must be conducted with an eye to the dangers of extreme ambiguity. Otherwise, confusion may be so extensive as to yield fundamentally divergent expectations regarding legally permissible behavior. The result is dysfunctional law.

3. *Specificity.* As terms become more generalized ambiguities increase, particularly if natural law, subjectively determined, is introduced into the norm-creating exercise. Universal multipurpose conferences are especially vulnerable to this process. The verbiage appears to have universal appeal or signification but its underlying premises are the object of intense discord. The inclination to generalize the issues would seem to exist in inverse relationship to the chances of productive results and genuine consensus on the problems in question.

Consensus as a Method

Consensus is both a result and a means of reaching decisions. Because it does not rely on unanimity, it would seem to be a midpoint between the principle of consent and the goal of majoritarian lawmaking. Due to the confusion surrounding majority voting, however, the consensual method is frequently attacked as though it were indistinguishable from consent. The first of two major complaints aired in this respect charges that consensual methods amount to virtual veto power for certain states.[61] Consensual method is viewed as acceptable only insofar as it does not "serve the interests of a minority."[62] While this appears superficially reasonable, it misses two important points: (a) why should a given method not protect the interests of the minority if the political preconditions of valid, meaningful majority rule are absent? (b) such protection would seem an unavoidable necessity in a world wherein states regularly affirm their sovereign equality. As a Western state remarked in 1966,

> The new States, which did not consider themselves bound by rules laid down before their accession to independence, would understand that other States felt themselves equally unable to consider themselves bound by rules the existence of which they disputed. . . . For the principle of the sovereign equality of States was not a one-way street. That fact, too, implied the necessity of the rule of consensus.[63]

The second complaint regarding consensus usually attacks the method as one tending to result in determinations of lowest-common-denominator value. Again, what is wrong with this, or what makes it worse than determinations that have little basis in reality? As any student of international protection of human rights knows, the complex question of national standards vs. a minimum international standard has been perennially plagued by the dilemma of choosing between lowest common denominators and unrealistic expectations. In fact, were lowest common denominators along the lines of a minimum *or* national standard to be consistently and universally honored as binding obligations, few would complain about them. Given a choice between the pedestrian and the illusory, the former appears more rewarding.

Conclusions

The Western minority in the United Nations cannot afford any form of complacency. Whether it is a question of the organizational mandate, its *raison d'être* or its lawmaking powers, the time has passed when arguments might rest with mere citations of the charter establishing the institution. That treaty has come to mean very different things to its participants, and the organization is viewed from essentially opposed perspectives. For the West, it remains conceptualized as an intergovernmental body constrained to conform to its constitution and to the requirements of juridical consensus in its norm-creating activities. For the great majority, however, it is often seen as a prototype of world majority rule:

> The United Nations is today . . . leaving behind the rule of the minority which characterized it for decades . . . Our Organization must . . . become the contemporary forum of a new majority. . . . That majority is waging a responsible struggle to bring the sovereign will of the peoples of the world to the point of deciding, on the basis of law, to undertake that change of course . . . which must not be decided . . .by the arbitrary imposition of the will of any minority.
>
> We must reinforce the decision-making capacity of the General Assembly. . . . Parliaments established on the basis of the minority power of one or more countries have now yielded pride of place and must henceforth be governed by the historic will of the majority. . . . [64]

The considerations explored in this study lead to the conclusion that the time has *not* arrived for majority lawmaking. Its advocates' continued emphasis on sovereign equality renders it implausible in theory, and the kind of division between majority and minority that exists today constitutes an insuperable practical obstacle to majority rule. But the pressure for such processes may well increase in direct ratio to the growing confidence and self-consciousness of the third and fourth worlds. International conferences, as well as the General Assembly, may thus suffer from a progressively more severe normative dichotomy.

The United States appears to be making an effort to comprehend, and deal with, the ideological perceptions underlying the arguments of the less developed world, judging [from] the speeches made by Secretary of State Kissinger at the Organization for Economic Cooperation and Development (OECD) in May 1975, at the Seventh Special Session of the General Assembly in September 1975, and in Africa in May 1976. . . . On the other hand, it is quite clear that the response in question has coincided with those demands (regarding concessionary loans, raw materials, price stabilization, and transfer of technology) more in broad outline than in plans for implementation—which would obviously have to be consistent with the United States' perceived interests. Most important, any rapprochement on substantive issues can be undermined or destroyed by the normative division regarding implementation and authoritative norm-creation. It is therefore advisable to discover what can be done to alleviate that dichotomy.

... The minority states of the United Nations are apparently in need of normative arguments that possess a basis other than power rationalizations. While the West rejects the arbitrary assumption of power by the majority, it has evidently appeared equally arbitrary in its insistence on consensus. Its calls for consensus have resulted as much in condemnations of minority rule as in appreciations of the value of consensual method. The problem lies partly in the Western states' manner of voicing their desiderata.... Under the circumstances, a vital point seems to be the necessity for their arguments to be based on more *politically* plausible legal considerations.

How can the West better make its point? There is widespread agreement that the speeches made by Mr. Moynihan during his U.N. tenure, particularly as they related to democratic and nondemocratic member states, suffered from a problem of tone. That the West should reply to verbal agression was well and good—and overdue. For the future, however, rather than emphasizing the idea of the majority ganging up on the democracies, why not place more stress on what working democracies can contribute to the normative debate? If international democracy is the ostensible majority goal, states with functioning democratic systems could make certain observations.

First, they could point out that majoritarianism rests on a preexisting sense of a community of interests, and that sense of community, in the form of socioeconomic interdependence, is now embryonic at best. Premature assumptions of its existence, and concurrent affirmations of majoritarian legitimacy unacceptable to crucial participants, can only threaten its continued gestation.

Second, the West could reaffirm the democratic requirement that responsibility be assumed by members who affirm rules. The Echeverría speech cited above repeats the term *repsonsible* and its author also says that the majority must "with full responsibility be ready to take on the transfer of a large part of the rights and obligations ... formerly the domain of a minority."[65] The West could legitimately ask how that responsibility and those obligations are envisaged.

Third, the United States and its allies could emphasize that a vital feature of democratic rule is the protection of minority rights. This characteristic of extant democratic governments can be asserted as a necessary feature of an international society aspiring to majority rule. If minority rights are clearly denied adequate consideration under the present system of sovereign equality, the minority can hardly have confidence in any protection under a majority system. Yet without a clear demonstration of such consideration, the only possible minority attitude is opposition to the majoritarian goal.

Again, these points can be made vigorously, but without shrillness. The essential connection between the responsibility expected and an appropriately proportionate voice in norm-creation should continue to be stressed, but in a politic manner. Perhaps it could be phrased in terms of a *quid pro quo*. What the third and fourth worlds wish to see recognized is the industrialized world's greater responsibility in the creation of a new economic order. The West can afford to acquiesce in that attribution of responsibility. In return, however, for assuming uneven burdens—e. g., in nonreciprocal trade preferences—it can certainly request a direct relationship between responsibility and inclusion in any norm-creating processes. It can, above all, emphasize that its policy in this regard is not arbitrary, but determined by functional necessity. In so doing, it can legitimately continue to argue that there is no viable substitute for consensus based on negotiation, consultation, and compromise, preferably within a context of fairly precise terms, limited subject-matter, and the realistic inclusion of states whose agreement is essential to implementation.

Notes

1. See: Rosalyn Higgins, *The Development of International Law Through the Political Organs of the United Nations* (London: Oxford University Press, 1963) and "The United Nations and Lawmaking: The Political Organs," *Proceedings, American Society of International Law* (1970); and Richard Falk, "The Quasi-Legislative Competence of the General Assembly," *American Journal of International Law* 60 (1966): 782-791.

2. Robert L. Friedheim, "The 'Satisfied' and 'Dissatisfied' States Negotiate International Law: A Case Study," in Richard A. Falk and Wolfram F. Hanrieder, eds., *International Law and Organization* (New York: Lippincott, 1968), pp. 69-77.

3. Representative was the desire expressed during the 1963-1970 debate to codify as law the legitimation of wars of colonial liberation and assistance to them. By 1970, the term *colonial* had been broadened to include various states' policy objectives. Thus, colonial came to mean not only salt-water colonialism but racial discrimination in southern Africa and Rhodesia, present occupation (Palestine), occupation of several hundred years' duration (Gibraltar), and so forth. The legitimation of wars of liberation as the "law of the charter" would have meant the codification as law of specific desiderata while opening the door for an infinite expansion of legitimized use of force: the only requirement would have been the definition of a situation as colonial.

4. See note 5; also drafts A/AC. 125/I. 16, I. 31 and Adds. 1-3, I. 48, L. 74.
5. Tunisia (A/C.6/SR. 1004), November 21, 1967, *GAOR* 22:9, p. 276.
6. Ghana (A/C.6/SR. 998), November 15, 1967, *GAOR* 22:9, p. 225.
7. Hungary (A/C.6/SR. 999), November 16, 1967, *GAOR* 22:9, p. 231.
8. Guinea (A/C.6/SR. 996), November 13, 1967, *GAOR* 22:9, p. 214.
9. Somalia (A/PV. 2248), September 30, 1974, p. 18 ff.
10. Guyana (A/PV. 2248), September 30, 1974, p. 27.
11. Nigeria (A/PV. 2281), November 12, 1974, pp. 60-61.
12. United Kingdom (A/PV. 2281), November 12, 1974, pp. 23-25.
13. Namely, the idea of the Credentials Committee assessing the "representativity" of each member before accepting credentials and permitting participation in the assembly.
14. Nigeria (A/PV. 2281), p. 61. See below on expenses case, and see Leo Gross, "The Development of International Law Through the United Nations," in James Barros, ed., *The United Nations: Past, Present and Future* (New York: The Free Press, 1972), p. 200, on alleged General Assembly power to interpret the charter authoritatively.
15. See, e.g., a statement by Cuba on self-determination as sovereign equality, whereby a "State did not recognize any authority superior to its own" (A/C.6/SR. 995), November 10, 1967, 22:9, p. 206. The general idea of permanent sovereignty, a ruling concept of the new economic order, also reflects this stance. See testimony of Campillo Sainz, undersecretary for industry and commerce of Mexico, before the Group of Eminent Persons to Study the Impact of Multinational Corporations on Development and International Relations (ST/ESA/15), pp. 22-29.
16. See Philip C. Jessup, *A Modern Law of Nations* (New York: Macmillan, 1948); Oliver J. Lissitzyn, "International Law in a Divided World," *International Conciliation,* no. 542 (1963); B. V. A. Roling, *International Law in an Expanded World* (Amsterdam: Djambatan, 1960); Wolfgang Friedmann, *The Changing Structure of International Law* (London: Stevens, 1964).
17. Roling, *International Law in an Expanded World,* pp. 56-71. Lissitzyn, "International Law in a Divided World," p. 61ff., stresses the continuity of the legal system in Roling's thesis.
18. Higgins, *The Development of International Law,* p. 5.
19. Falk, "The Quasi-Legislative Competence of the General Assembly," pp. 786-788.
20. Resolutions 421 (V), 545 (VI), 637 (VII), 738 (VII), 837 (IX), 1188 (XII), and 1514 (XV).
21. Gross, "The Development of International Law Through the United Nations," p. 199.
22. "Crucial" meaning states expected to implement an alleged rule. For recognition of the necessity of such states' inclusion in a "consensus," see Saudi

Arabia's comments on the self-determination article (A/C. 3/R. 653), November 4, 1955, *GAOR* 10:6, p. 148.

23. Higgins, *The Development of International Law*, p. 7.

24. Ibid., p. 104.

25. Gross, "The Development of International Law Through the United Nations," p. 199.

26. See Higgins, "The United Nations and Lawmaking," p. 40. In this paper she attributes a yes vote to the United Kingdom. See also *The Development of International Law*, p. 97 and 100.

27. Louis Sohn, comments in *Proceedings, American Society of International Law* 1970, p. 61.

28. Samuel A. Bleicher, "The Legal Significance of Re-Citation of General Assembly Resolutions," *American Journal of International Law* 63 (1969): 475, cited by Gross, "The Development of International Law Through the United Nations," p. 201.

29. See Benjamin Rivlin, "Self-Determination and Dependent Areas," *International Conciliation*, no. 501 (1955), p. 204; Rupert Emerson, "Self-Determination," *American Journal of International Law* 65 (1971): 466; Leo Gross, "The United Nations and the Rule of Law," *International Organization* 19 (1965): 541.

30. Sir Hersch Lauterpacht, *International Law and Human Rights* (New York: Praeger, 1950), p. 309ff.

31. See statement by Ambassador Clarence C. Ferguson, Jr. to the fourth meeting of the U.N. Committee on Natural Resources, Tokyo, *United States United Nations Documents* 27 (75) (April 2, 1975): 2: "The United States . . . voted against the Charter of Economic Rights and Duties . . . because the Charter included the same unacceptable formulations on permanent sovereignty to which we had persistently and consistently objected since December 14, 1962. . . . The claim of the existence of a United Nations consensus on permanent sovereignty is [thus] demonstratedly false." See also Committee Report on the Charter, Record of the Association of the Bar of the City of New York, vol. 30, no. 5/6 (May-June 1975): 411-415 on controversial provisions.

32. Emerson, "Self-Determination," p. 459.

33. Higgins, "The United Nations and Lawmaking"; Falk, "The Quasi-Legislative Competence of the General Assembly," passim.

34. Falk, "The Quasi-Legislative Competence of the General Assembly," p. 786.

35. Ibid.; Myres McDougal, comments in *Proceedings, American Society of International Law* (1970), p. 56.

36. *ICJ Reports* (1969), *North Sea Continental Shelf Cases*, judgment of February 20, 1969, pp. 43-44. (Emphasis added.)

37. Ibid. (Emphasis added.) As far as self-determination is concerned,

although state practice in the form of decolonization has occurred, this phenomenon can more readily be laid to political expediency than to any *opinio juris* on the subject. See Emerson, citing Gross, p. 461, and "The United Nations and Colonialism," *International Relations* 3 (1970). For a view that decolonization is proof of a legal right to self-determination, see Umozurike Oji Umozurike, *Self-Determination in International Law* (Hamden, Conn.: Archon, 1972).

38. Higgins, "The United Nations and Lawmaking," p. 42.

39. Louis Henkin, *How Nations Behave* (New York: Praeger, 1968), p. 167. See also Jorge Casteñeda, *The Legal Effects of United Nations Resolutions* (New York: Columbia University Press, 1969), pp. 123, 132ff.

40. See Robert Rosenstock, "The Declaration of [sic] Principles of International Law Concerning Friendly Relations: A Survey," *American Journal of International Law* 65 (1971): 714 ff. Rosenstock's comments may also be related to the problem of ambiguity discussed below.

41. See Lauterpacht, *International Law and Human Rights,* pp. 276-426; Casteñeda, *The Legal Effects of United Nations Resolutions,* p. 193 ff.

42. United Nations document E/CN. 4/L. 610, April 2, 1962. (Emphasis added.)

43. Also upon "such conviction of the ultimate community of majority and minority interest that it can afford to respect the right of the majority to rule. . . ." Inis L. Claude, Jr., *Swords into Plowshares,* 3rd ed. (London: University of London, 1966), p. 118.

44. Leo Gross, "Expenses of the United Nations for Peace-Keeping Operations," *International Organization* 27 (1963): 3, 26.

45. See Stanley Hoffmann, "A World Divided and a World Court Confused: The World Court's Advisory Opinion on U.N. Financing," in Lawrence Scheinman and David Wilkinson, eds., *International Law and Political Crisis: An Analytic Casebook* (Boston: Little, Brown, 1968), p. 257.

46. See ICJ *Reports* (1949), *Reparation for Injuries Suffered in the Service of the United Nations,* Advisory Opinion of April 11, 1949. The opinion is excerpted in Sohn, *Cases on United Nations Law.* See p. 39, e. g.: "Under international law, the Organization must be deemed to have those powers which, though not expressly provided in the Charter, are conferred upon it by necessary implication as being essential to the performance of its duties."

47. See Hoffmann, "A World Divided and a World Court Confused," p. 261, and Gross, "Expenses of the United Nations for Peace-Keeping Operations," p. 30.

48. Hoffmann, "A World Divided and a World Court Confused."

49. Ibid., p. 260.

50. This consideration, incidentally, vitiates Judge Fitzmaurice's attempt to distinguish essential and "permissive" activities of the United Nations. See

Sohn, *Cases on United Nations Law*, p. 290; Hoffmann, "A World Divided and a World Court Confused," p. 267; and Gross, "Expenses of the United Nations for Peace-Keeping Operations," pp. 24-26.

51. See Gross, p. 9 ff.; Hoffmann, "Expenses of the United Nations for Peace-Keeping Operations," p. 268.

52. See Hoffmann, "A World Divided and a World Court Confused"; also, Judge Koretsky's dissent, in Sohn, *Cases on United Nations Law*, p. 798.

53. Hoffmann, "A World Divided and a World Court Confused," p. 257. Hoffmann draws a parallel to the Security Council and the veto, citing Claude's *Power and International Relations*.

54. See Separate Opinion of Judge Sir Percy Spender in Sohn, *Cases on United Nations Law*, pp. 17-23. "The cardinal rule of interpretation that this Court and its predecessor has stated. . . is that words are to be read, if they may so be read, in their ordinary and natural sense." He then argued that the use of criteria such as intent and subsequent practice were justifiable only if the former standard led to ambiguous or unreasonable results. Sir Percy's opinion contained several points highly relevant to the problem, discussed earlier, of assimilation of state practice and the practice of U.N. organs, and is worthy of repetition: ". . . Subsequent conduct may only provide a criterion of interpretation when the text is obscure, and even then it is necessary to consider whether that conduct itself permits of only one inference. . . . I find difficulty in accepting the proposition that a practice pursued by an *organ* of the United Nations may be equated with the subsequent conduct of the *parties* . . . and thus afford evidence of intention of the parties to the Charter . . . and in that way . . . provide a criterion of interpretation. . . . The subsequent conduct of one party alone cannot be evidence . . . of a common understanding of the meaning to be given to the text of a treaty. . . . It is not evident on what ground a practice consistently followed by a majority of a Member States not in fact accepted by other Member States could provide any criterion of interpretation. . . . I . . . . entertain considerable doubt whether practice of an organ of the United Nations has any probative value either as providing evidence of the intentions of the original Member States or otherwise. . . . The Charter . . . cannot be altered at the will of the majority . . . no matter how often that will is expressed or asserted against a protesting minority and no matter how large be the majority . . . or how small the minority."

55. See Claude, *Swords into Plowshares*, p. 139, on the Security Council veto as a "safety valve" inhibiting undertakings that the organization will be able to carry through.

56. Hoffmann, "A World Divided and a World Court Confused," p. 273.

57. Judge Fitzmaurice in Sohn, *Cases . . .* , p. 789. Also see Hoffmann, p. 269.

58. Hoffmann, "A World Divided and a World Court Confused," p. 270.

59. Ibid., p. 260.

60. See F. Y. Chai, "Consultation and Consensus in the Security Council," UNITAR (1971), p. 16.

61. Comment of Finland (which later revised its position) (A/C.6/SR..934), November 21, 1966, *GAOR* 21:9, p. 203; also see Chile (A/C.6/SR. 937), November 23, 1966, *GAOR* 21:9, p. 223.

62. Cameroon (A/C.6/SR.1160), November 26, 1969, *GAOR* 24.9, p. 296; also Kenya (A/C.6/SR. 1161), November 28, 1969, *GAOR* 24:9, p. 304.

63. France (A/C.6/SR. 932), November 17, 1966, *GAOR* 21:9, p. 193. See also Shabtai Rosenne's comments following presentation of the Higgins paper in *Proceedings, American Society of International Law* (1970), to the effect that protection of the rights of states with unpopular or minority views was a serious matter.

64. Echeverría address (A/PV 2377), October 7, 1975, pp. 22, 23-25, 26-30.

65. Ibid., p. 7.

29. Security Council Function and Membership
Lawrence S. Finkelstein

Membership of the U.N. Security Council was closely linked in the thinking of the founding fathers with the functions members were to perform. That accounts for the provision of Article 23 of the charter that, in electing nonpermanent members, the General Assembly should "specially" pay "due regard . . . *in the first instance* to the contribution of members of the United Nations to the maintenance of international peace and security and to the other purposes of the organization, and *also* to equitable geographic representation."[1] It also partially explains why Article 23 accorded "a special position to certain states," i.e., the five designated permanent members.[2] They were the states thought to have "the greatest responsibility for the maintenance of peace."[3] That the size of the council was originally fixed at eleven reflected the belief of the sponsoring powers that a small body was essential for effective action.[4] Their proposal prevailed against some resistance at San Francisco.[5]

In fact, the original priorities intended to govern election of nonpermanent members appear to have been reversed in the political history of the Security Council. The emphasis has been on "equitable geographic representation" at the expense of "the contributions of members . . . to the maintenance of international peace and security."

This chapter is a much revised version of a paper originally delivered at the International Studies Association annual conference in Toronto, Canada, on February 28, 1976. The author wishes to acknowledge assistance received from the following graduate students in the Department of Political Science at Northern Illinois University: Robert Cavey, MacArthur Corsino, James Schiller, and Eugene Tadie and also the critical comments of Professors David and Margaret Karnes and Robert O. Keohane.

"Geographical representation" has come to mean representation of regions and the search for "equity" in the distribution of nonpermanent places has come to dominate the politics of Security Council elections. The potent urge to achieve greater equity in regional representation, particularly under the pressure of rapidly growing U.N. membership, inspired the movement to amend the U.N. Charter to permit greater scope for distribution of elected Security Council seats among nonpermanent members on a regional basis. As a result, the Council was enlarged to its present size (of 15) by means of the amendment ratified and given effect in 1965.[6] The record seems clear. The quest for equity has seemed a more potent motive than the belief of the founding fathers that functional considerations should dominate the election of nonpermanent members. Yet, as this paper will show, elections have resulted over the years in disproportionate selection of nonpermanent members which rank relatively high on the scale of indicators of capacity to act effectively, even if that is not quite the same as the charter standard, "contributions of members. . . ."

By focusing on the record of nonpermanent membership, this essay will examine first whether equity has been served in elections to membership. Presumably, equity implies equality of service for individual members based on "the principle of the sovereign equality of all its Members," enshrined in Article 2, paragraph 1, of the charter. A section on individual membership will explore the practice in this respect. Second, it will seek to understand what other considerations seem to have operated in the election process and, particularly, whether such other variables reflect the mandate of Article 23 to attend to "the contribution of Members of the United Nations to the maintenance of international peace and security and to the other purposes of the Organization." Equity also, according to Article 23, involves geographic distribution and a section of the paper will examine the pattern of regional places in the Security Council. A concluding section will speculate about the significance of selection criteria for the effective performance of the Security Council's functions.

Individual Membership in the Security Council

When one looks at Security Council service by individual members, what immediately leaps to the eye is the considerable disparity in the number of years they have served. There is no surprise that only the five permanent members have served for all thirty years the Security Council has been in existence. More surprising is that the next highest cumulative service should total only ten years, and that only one nonpermanent member has served that long—Brazil (1946-1947, 51-52,

54-55, 63-64, 67-68). Three members have served eight years each: Japan (58-59, 66-67, 71-72, 75-76), Argentina (48-49, 59-60, 66-67, 71-72), and Colombia (47-48, 53-54, 57-58, 69-70). Total Security Council participation by other members ranges downward from these highs. Sixty-one U.N. members have never served on the Security Council at all,[7] and, of that number, eight are original members of the organization: South Africa, Luxembourg, Saudi Arabia, and five small countries of the Caribbean–Central America area—Dominican Republic, El Salvador, Guatemala, Haiti, and Honduras. In addition, three countries which were elected to membership in the United Nations's first year have never served in the Security Council: Afghanistan, Iceland, and Thailand. Of the original members, three have served only one year each in the Security Council and twelve have served two years each. Only nine states have served three or more two-year terms.

The raw figures obviously conceal part of the significance of the differences because states have been U.N. members for differing periods of time and thus some have had greater opportunity to be elected to the Security Council than have others. Therefore, a sort of U.N. Security Council tenure "batting average" has been computed for all U.N. members. This involves simply dividing the number of years of Security Council service for each member by the number of years of its U.N. membership. It gives a simple, but revealing, picture of what might be thought of as the propensity of individual members to have been selected for Security Council service.

Table I shows for each nonpermanent member of the Security Council[8] its Security Council batting average in descending order, followed by each member's length of U.N. membership. The numbers will change annually as years of U.N. membership accumulate more than do the number of Security Council places, with more downward effect on the averages for newer members than for older ones. The figures are affected also by aberrations in the membership patterns of some states: Indonesia's withdrawal in the mid-1960s and the temporary merger of Egypt and Syria for example.

Table I clearly suggests that if equity is judged in terms of the principle of "sovereign equality," the allocation of nonpermanent places in the Security Council has not been notably equitable. Some states have clearly done better than have others. Why? Perhaps there are factors at work which are relevant to the injunction of Article 23 that attention should be paid first of all to members' contributions to the organization, especially in the realm of peace and security. To examine such possibilities Table II sets forth the results of some rankings of those

TABLE I

Country	Service Average	Years in the Council	Years in the UN*
Japan	.400	8	20
Brazil	.333	10	30
Italy	.286	6	21
Argentina	.267	8	30
Colombia	.267	8	30
Australia	.200	6	30
Belgium	.200	6	30
Canada	.200	6	30
Guyana	.200	2	10
India	.200	6	30
Pakistan	.172	5	29
Netherlands	.167	5	30
Panama	.167	5	30
Poland	.167	5	30
Turkey	.167	5	30
United Arab Rep.	.167	5	30
Yugoslavia	.167	5	30
Zambia	.167	2	12
Kenya	.154	2	13
Syria	.154	4	26
Algeria	.143	2	14
Burundi	.143	2	14
Chile	.133	4	30
Cuba	.133	4	30
Denmark	.133	4	30
Ecuador	.133	4	30
Iraq	.133	4	30
Mauritania	.133	2	15
Norway	.133	4	30
Peru	.133	4	30
Sierra Leone	.133	2	15
Sweden	.133	4	30
Tanzania	.133	2	15
Cameroon	.125	2	16
Ivory Coast	.125	2	16
Mali	.125	2	16
Nigeria	.125	2	16
Senegal	.125	2	16
Somalia	.125	2	16
Guinea	.111	2	18
Ghana	.105	2	19
Morocco	.100	2	20
New Zealand	.100	3	30
Sudan	.100	2	20
Tunisia	.100	2	20
Austria	.095	2	21

TABLE I (cont.)

Country	Service Average	Years in the Council	Years in the UN*
Bulgaria	.095	2	21
Ceylon	.095	2	21
Finland	.095	2	21
Hungary	.095	2	21
Jordan	.095	2	21
Nepal	.095	2	21
Rumania	.095	2	21
Spain	.095	2	21
Indonesia	.083	2	24
Uganda	.071	1	14
Bolivia	.067	2	30
Byelorussian SSR.	.067	2	30
Costa Rica	.067	2	30
Ethiopia	.067	2	30
Greece	.067	2	30
Iran	.067	2	30
Lebanon	.067	2	30
Nicaragua	.067	2	30
Paraguay	.067	2	30
Philippines	.067	2	30
Ukrainian SSR.	.067	2	30
Uruguay	.067	2	30
Venezuela	.067	2	30
Dahomey	.063	1	16
Malaysia	.053	1	19
Ireland	.048	1	21
Libya	.048	1	21
Czechoslovakia	.033	1	30
Liberia	.033	1	30
Mexico	.033	1	30
61 countries	.000	0	1-30

*Article 23 (2) of the Charter provides that a "retiring member shall not be eligible for immediate reelection." Thus, states that have been members of the Security Council were ineligible for reelection in some years, depending on the number of terms served in the Council. Recalculating the "service averages" in terms of years of eligibility does not change the rank order, although it does evidently change the averages themselves, if only slightly.

states which have been elected to the Security Council. The first column ranks the states by their service averages taken from Table I. The breakdown into twenty-three categories no doubt implies greater discrimination than either the data or the analytical method allow. The breakdown should thus be taken *cum grano salis*. Strictly speaking, the top rank should be occupied by the five permanent members which have been omitted. Attention is given first to indicators of general capacity of states—population, GNP, and power.

Column 2 shows how these states rank by total population. The figures have been taken from the *World Handbook of Political and Social Indicators*[9] and are for 1965. More current figures could be used but the changes seem unlikely to affect the rankings very much. The five permanent members rank as follows: China-1; USSR-3; United States-4; United Kingdom-11; France-13.

Column 3 ranks the nonpermanent Security Council membership by GNP. The source, again, is the *World Handbook*[10] The five permanent members rank as follows: United States-1; USSR-2; United Kingdom-4; France-5; China-7. The third place is occupied by West Germany which has not yet served on the Security Council.

GNP has been used as an overall yardstick of national capabilities, or power, and it has been claimed that there is no better measure.[11] Cox and Jacobson argue that GNP does not adequately take into account what they term "the psychic element in power."[12] They have designed a composite indicator based on five scaled components: GNP, per-capita GNP, population, nuclear capability, and prestige taken as "degree of autonomy or independence of a state's foreign policy." Their indicator seems to assign greater weight to GNP than to the other factors and the way they scale GNP per capita seems to undervalue the discontinuous effects of very high per-capita GNPs. In short, the Cox-Jacobson indicator is ambiguously better than a simple GNP indicator. Their results for 1967 appear in column 4. Since the indicator incorporates both population and GNP, it is by no means totally independent of the ranks in columns 2 and 3. The Cox-Jacobson scale is limited to the top 39 states, including the five permanent members of the Security Council, "the others being all small powers."[13] In the Cox-Jacobson ranking, the five permanent powers fare as follows: United States-1; USSR-2; United Kingdom-3; France-4.5; China-4.5.

Column 5 sets forth the rank order of members' contributions to the U.N. budget. On the face of it, U.N. budget contributions seem relevant both to general capacity, since members' obligations are determined by a scale reflecting capacity to pay, and to actual contributions to the organization in the past. Obviously, budget contributions are not the only measure of states' contributions to the United Nations, but it is hard to doubt that they are relevant. The figures in column 5 are for the most recent budget assessment period, 1974-1976. The data are from the *Statesman's Yearbook* for 1975-1976. The five permanent members rank as follows: United States-1; USSR-2; France-5; China-6; United Kingdom-7. The third and fourth places are occupied by Japan and West Germany respectively.

Service in U.N. peacekeeping missions is evidently an indicator of contribution to the maintenance of international peace and security. Column 6 shows how nonpermanent Security Council members rank on this dimension, with the actual number of missions shown in parentheses following the rank in each case.[14] Because the five permanent members have been largely excluded deliberately from participation in the U.N. peacekeeping operations since the United Nations Emergency Force (UNEF) and since the USSR was politically excluded from earlier operations, there would be no point in giving their rankings.

Rational patterns are not self-evident in these tables. None of the variables clearly dominates the selection process. Countries of large population, high GNP and power, and high U.N. budget contribution concentrate in the upper portions of Table II. At the same time, the deviations are notable—especially Austria, Spain, Indonesia, the Philippines, Czechoslovakia, and Mexico, and, by contrast, Colombia, Guyana, Panama, and Zambia. Within the clusters, variance is more impressive than homogeneity, even taking account of the vagueness and essential permeability of the boundaries among the twenty-three clusters. One conclusion is clear. No state qualifying as a ministate by Blair's standards[15] appears on the list, and only two—Guyana and Mauritania—from her list of states next removed from ministates. Perhaps power and capacity are relevant.

To push the analysis a step further, a comparison was devised with the purpose of showing how high or low scores on the variables employed in Table II affected selection for Security Council service. The analysis compares the cumulative Security Council service of groups of states paired according to the following characteristics in each case:

1. *Power.* States which appear on the Cox-Jacobson list versus those which do not.
2. *General capacity.* On the one hand, states on the Cox-Jacobson power list which also exceed the medians in the Table II population and GNP rankings, and contributed at least one tenth of 1 percent of the U.N. budget versus states which are not on the Cox-Jacobson list, fall below the population and GNP

TABLE II

RANKINGS OF STATES AS NONPERMANENT SECURITY COUNCIL MEMBERS

Average SC Service	1965 Pop.	1965 GNP	1967 "Power"	UN Budget	Peace keeping
1. Japan	7	6	5	3	---
2. Brazil	8	14	15	22	6(5)
3. Italy	12	8	8	8	5(6)
4. Argentina	25	20	21	21	7(4)
Colombia	30	40	40+	40	10(1)
5. Australia	44	12	15	11	6(5)
Belgium	49	21	21	17	6(5)
Canada	26	10	9.5	9	2(9)
Guyana	126	116	40+	65	---
India	2	9	9.5	16	5(6)
6. Pakistan	6	24	21	43	8(3)
7. Netherlands	40	18	15	14	5(6)
Panama	117	93.5	40+	65	---
Poland	17	11	21	13	---
Turkey	18	31	31.5	34	---
UAR	20	43	31.5	46	10(1)
Yugoslavia	27	30	15	29	8(3)
Zambia	85	85	40+	65	---
8. Kenya	51	82	40+	65	---
Syria	68	71	40+	65	---
9. Algeria	42	54	40+	52	---
Burundi	92	125	40+	65	---
10. Chile	54	42	40+	43	6(5)
Cuba	60	49	31.5	47	---
Denmark	74	28	26.5	23	3(8)
Ecuador	71	73	40+	65	8(3)
Iraq	56	59	40+	58	---
Mauritania	121	129	40+	65	---
Norway	84	34	31.5	27	4(7)
Peru	43	44	40+	53	10(1)
Sierra Leone	103	108	40+	65	10(1)
Sweden	59	16	11	12	1(10)
Tanzania	46	86	40+	65	---
11. Cameroon	69	90	40+	65	---
Ivory Coast	82	76	40+	65	---
Mali	76	110	40+	65	10(1)
Nigeria	10	41	36	50	8(3)
Senegal	89	89	40+	65	---
Somalia	101	124	40+	65	---

TABLE II (cont.)

Average SC Service	1965 Pop.	1965 GNP	1967 "Power"	UN Budget	Peace-keeping
12. Guinea	88	111.5	40+	65	10(1)
13. Ghana	58	58	40+	59	9(2)
14. Morocco	38	55	40+	55	10(1)
New Zealand	97	38	36	35	5(6)
Sudan	37	68	40+	65	10(1)
Tunisia	78	78	40+	65	---
15. Austria	62	29	15	24	7(4)
Bulgaria	57	35	40+	43	---
Ceylon	45	62	40+	62	7(4)
Finland	75	32	36	28	4(7)
Hungary	47	25	40+	30	---
Jordan	108	101	40+	65	---
Nepal	48	87	40+	65	9(2)
Rumania	28	22	40+	33	---
Spain	16	19	15	18	---
16. Indonesia	5	27	26.5	38	8(3)
17. Uganda	61	91	40+	65	---
18. Bolivia	86	95	40+	65	---
Byelorussia	NA	NA	?	25	---
Costa Rica	115	96	40+	65	---
Ethiopia	24	75	40+	65	9(2)
Greece	55	37	40+	31	10(1)
Iran	23	36	40+	37	10(1)
Lebanon	99	72	40+	62	---
Nicaragua	112	98	40+	65	---
Paraguay	106	106	40+	65	---
Philippines	15	39	36	39	10(1)
Ukraine	NA	NA	?	10	---
Uruguay	96	65	40+	55	9(2)
Venezuela	53	33	36	31	10(1)
19. Dahomey	102	120	40+	65	---
20. Malaysia	50	51	40+	53	10(1)
21. Libya	114	81	40+	47	---
22. Ireland	95	53	40+	41	4(7)
23. Czechoslovakia	36	13	26.5	19	---
Liberia	120	115	40+	65	10(1)
Mexico	14	17	26.5	20	9(2)

medians and which fall in the lowest category of U.N. contributions, i.e., states which contribute one fiftieth of 1 percent of the U.N. budget.
3. *U.N. peacekeeping roles.* States which participated in three or more U.N. peacekeeping operations versus states which participated in none.
4. *U.N. contribution.* States which both qualified at the high end of the peacekeeping scale as in 3) above and also contributed at least one tenth of 1 percent of the U.N. budget versus states with no peacekeeping service which also fall in the lowest category of budget contributions, i. e., states which contribute one fiftieth of 1 percent of the budget.

Since the criteria used in Table II are not discrete and since the standards employed for this comparison are at best arbitrary, the results cannot be conclusive. But, as is shown in Table III, they are suggestive.

Apparently, the Table II criteria do matter. While, by these measures, nonpermanent members in the lower group equal or outnumber those drawn from the higher group in three of the four categories, the picture changes dramatically when what is compared is not simple membership numbers, but years of Security Council service. The key comparisons are between the percentages in columns 3 and 6

TABLE III

	HIGH				LOW		
1	2	3	4	5	6	7	
Characteristic	No. of members	% of states with nonpermanent SC service (76)	yrs. in SC as % of total years of SC service by nonpermanent members (230)	No. of members	% of states with nonpermanent SC service (76)	yrs. in SC as of total yrs. of SC service by nonpermanent members (230)
1. Power	28	37	52	46	61	46
2. Gen. Cap.	24	32	47	23	30	22
3. UN Peacekeeping	22	29	42	35	46	38
4. UN contribution	20	26	40	20	26	20

and in columns 4 and 7. Pairing columns 3 and 6 compares the ratio between the numbers of states with nonpermanent Security Council service in each of the two groups as a function of the number of all U.N. members with such service. Pairing columns 4 and 7 compares the cumulative length of service of states in the two groups as a function of cumulative service by all states which have been nonpermanent members of the Security Council. The results are shown in Table IIIA.

Table IIIA

	Col. 3-Col. 6	Col. 4-Col. 7
1. Power	-24	+6
2. General Capab.	+2	+25
3. UN Peacekeeping	-17	+4
4. UN Contribution	0	+20

A further word is in order about peacekeeping service. Not too much should be made of the unvarnished numbers. They do not reflect the offers of service which were not accepted for various reasons. They do not reflect onerous service in other U.N. operations not captured in the Fabian analysis employed in Table II, such as Turkey's fighting role in Korea. They do not, for example, reflect the considerable peacekeeping service of Latin American states in operations of the Organization of American States.[16] The figures do reflect political ineligibility, such as has affected South Africa, Israel, and by and large, the Warsaw Pact countries. While disability on this ground is not necessarily a reason to consider a state disqualified for service on the Security Council, Israel and South Africa have also been excluded from Security Council service; the Eastern Europeans have not. Also, there are a number of states with the vocation for service which appear to have served disproportionately little time on the council. Ireland, Finland, New Zealand, Sweden, Norway, and Denmark have all served on more than half of the twelve operations on Fabian's list but their "service averages" fall below the .167 level in Table I, which signifies one year served on the Security Council for six years of U.N. membership.

More generally, a very rough measure of the ratio between

peacekeeping service and time spent on the council is possible. U.N. members other than permanent members of the council have performed a total of 159 units of peacekeeping service based on Fabian's count, considering as a unit the participation by one country in one peacekeeping operation. Nonpermanent members have totalled 230 years of participation in the Security Council. A rough standard to equate peacekeeping and Security Council service—a standard which ignores qualitative differences in peacekeeping performance and which treats all peacekeeping operations as though they were the same, which they were not—might be that each country's years of service in the council divided by 230 should approximate the number of its peacekeeping units divided by 159. This is not a very severe standard. It amounts to a requirement for about two-thirds of a year on the Security Council for each peacekeeping unit. Sweden, thus, should top the list with seven years on the council, or a .233 service average. Countries which by this standard have had a good deal too little time on the Security Council include one which has never been elected to the council, Burma, with five peacekeeping missions. States with disproportionately little Security Council service include Australia, Austria, Belgium, Canada, Ceylon, Chile, Denmark, Ethiopia, Finland, Ghana, Guinea, India, Indonesia, Ireland, Italy, Mexico, Nepal, Netherlands, New Zealand, Nigeria, Norway, and Sweden. States with disproportionately more Security Council than peacekeeping service include: Argentina, Brazil, Colombia, Cuba, Iraq, Japan, Panama, Peru, Poland, Syria, Turkey, and the UAR.

It may be relevant also to introduce some rankings for U.N. members which have not served on the Security Council. The list is selected in order to show countries which rank higher on some of the dimensions than do many states which have served in the council.

It might also be noted that Switzerland, which is not a U.N. member at all, ranks quite high on two of the three indicators: while it is sixty-seventh on the *World Handbook* population list, it ranks twenty-third in GNP and shares fifteenth place in the Cox-Jacobson power ranking.

One possibility not yet explored is that length of U.N. membership may affect the probability of Security Council service. The total U.N. membership was broken down into seven cohorts: the original members, and those which joined the United Nations in each of the six five-year periods of the organization's existence. Data were tabulated, by cohort, for: number of states in each cohort; the percentage of each cohort with no Security Council service; cumulative years of cohort service in the Security Council; cumulative years of cohort membership in the United Nations; average years of Security Council membership

TABLE IV

SOME RANKINGS OF SOME UN MEMBERS
WITH NO SECURITY COUNCIL SERVICE

State	1965 Population	1965 GNP	Cox-Jacobson Power Indicator 1967	UN Budget Contribution	Peacekeeping Participation
W. Germany	9	3	7	4	--
Thailand	19	45	40+	47	10(1)
Burma	22	61	40+	65	6(5)
U. of South Africa	31	26	21	25	--
E. Germany	32	15	26.5	15	--
Zaire	34	69	40+	65	10(1)
Afghanistan	35	70	40+	41	10(1)
Portugal	52	46	40+	41	10(1)
Saudi Arabia	64	66	40+	55	--
Israel	100	47	26.5	36	--
Luxembourg	131	92	39	59	--

for each year of Security Council service. The results are set forth in Table V.

Table V seems to show a very good relationship[17] between length of U.N. membership and service in the Security Council, marred only by the aberrational second cohort, the class of 1946-1950. That deviation from the dominant progression is not surprising, since that relatively small cohort happened to include Israel, a state excluded from the Security Council on political grounds, and three states (Burma, Indonesia, and Thailand) from Southeast Asia, a subregion which has lacked voting power to claim a Security Council seat to which it has not had an assured access.

The evidence that the length of U.N. membership seems to be a strong factor in Security Council membership is paradoxical. It implies that U.N. experience is considered an asset in connection with Security Council membership. Much of the concern about seating equity, however, has focused on the problem of the newer members and it was principally to make additional room to enable them to serve on the Security Council that the amendment to enlarge the council was adopted. The evidence seems clear that the tenure principle works against them.

Altogether, the evidence assembled thus far does not support simple, or terribly clear, conclusions about the election record. If equity is understood to require distribution of places based on the principle of

TABLE V

Security Council Membership in Terms of Length of UN Membership

Member Cohort	No. of Members	No. SC Service %	Total SC Years	Total UN Years	SC Yrs. Per Capita	UN Yrs. Per SC Yrs.
1. Original	46	17	144	1380	3.1	9.6
2. 1946-1950	9	67	11	259	1.2	23.5
3. 1951-1955	16	25	26	336	1.6	12.9
4. 1956-1960	24	42	32	408	1.3	12.8
5. 1961-1965	18	56	15	237	.8	15.8
6. 1966-1970	9	89	2	79	.2	39.5
7. 1971-1975	15	100	0	44	0.0	inf.

sovereign equality, the standard has been poorly met, judging by the large number of U.N. members who have never served in the Security Council and the uneven distribution of periods of service among those who have. The tenure principle results in inequitable distribution of places between older and newer members. If the standard of contribution to the United Nations is past peacekeeping service, the analysis suggests that this factor has some influence on length of service in the Security Council but also that the factor is very unevenly effective in "rewarding" and "punishing" states which have and have not borne the peacekeeping burdens. Seemingly, the indicators of capacity—population, GNP, the Cox-Jacobson indicator, and contribution to the U.N. budget—show up in disproportionate cumulative service in the Security Council. At the same time, it seems clear that these factors work unevenly. Certainly, states of great variety have been nonpermanent members and, except for ministates, no category seems to have been excluded.

Regional Membership in the Security Council

Analyzing seats by regions is confusing because of the ambiguity concerning the regional designation of some states. For simplicity, this analysis follows Leland Goodrich's choices.[18] Thus, Egypt is considered African, despite its close identification with Arab League states across the Suez Canal and the Red Sea. Turkey is considered Asian despite its

TABLE VI

Percentage of Nonpermanent Seats by Regions 1946-1976

	Latin America	W. Europe & Others	W.E. Others	E. Europe	Africa	Asia
1946-65	33.3	17.5	8.3	8.	11.7	20.8
		25.8			32.5	
1966-76	20.0	15.4	4.5	10.0	30.0	20.0
		50.0			50.0	

membership in NATO. States which occupied the "East European seat" are assigned to their geographic regions. There is one not entirely consistent departure from Goodrich's list: Greece is considered a West European state for the purpose of analysis, not an East European one. Goodrich's list is brought up to date for the years after 1972.

Another source of confusion is the shift in regional designations following the General Assembly resolution adopting the charter amendment to increase the size of the Security Council.[19] In that resolution, the General Assembly allocated nonpermanent seats on the following basis: Latin America—2; Western Europe and "other states"—2; Eastern Europe—1; Africa and Asia—5. Until that time, the pattern had been to allocate seats as follows: Latin America—2; Western Europe—1; Eastern Europe—1; the Middle East—1; the Common-

TABLE VI-A

Percentage of Security Council Seats by Region 1946-1976

	Latin America	W. Europe & Others	W.E. Others	E. Europe	Africa	Asia
1946-65	18.2	36.8	4.5	13.6	6.4	20.5
		41.3			26.9	
1966-75	13.3	30.3	3.0	13.3	20.0	20.0
		33.3			40.0	

wealth—1. This analysis will distribute the countries which, until 1965, occupied Middle Eastern seats to either Africa or Asia as appropriate and includes the old Commonwealth states under the heading "Western Europe and others."

Table VI shows how the regions fared in the distribution of nonpermanent council seats by percentage, before and after the amendment went into effect.

If permanent places are included in the calculation, a quite different picture emerges, as is shown in Table VI-A. For the purpose of this calculation, the United States is assigned, somewhat arbitrarily, to the category "Western Europe and others."

Evidently, excluding or including the permanent members in the calculation makes a considerable difference. Latin America's share in the early years shrinks from a third to less than a fifth when permanent members are considered and from a fifth to about a seventh of the total in the recent period. The share of Western Europe doubles in both periods when permanent members are included. Eastern Europe does better in both periods when permanent members are included. Africa's share about triples either way from the earlier period to the later, while Asia's remains stable throughout. With permanent members included, Africa's recent share is a fifth, rather than three-tenths when they are excluded. The combined Afro-Asian total looks a bit less impressive at two-fifths with permanent members included than it does at one-half when they are excluded. Either way, Africa is the big gainer from the amendment and Latin America the big loser, although it should be recalled that the Latin American loss is relative, not an absolute reduction in the number of Latin American places. Since "others" refers in practice to members of the "old Commonwealth," which have carried heavy peacekeeping burdens, it may be a matter of concern that the "others" share has fallen relatively heavily by either calculation.

Table VI-B shows a simple summation.

Tables VI, VI-A, and VI-B tell only a limited part of the story, however. Proportional distribution of seats among regions requires that each region have the same proportion of available seats in the Security Council as its proportion of the total membership of the United Nations. One analyst has noted that the amendment resulted in a "reasonable arrangement" in this connection: "Asian and African members had one representative per eleven states, as compared with one per ten for Latin America and West Europe and others, and one per nine for East Europe."[20] The membership has grown over the years, however. The ratios of regional seats available compared with the number of states per region since the amendment took effect is shown in Table VII.

TABLE VI-B

Gainers and Losers as a Result of the Amendment

	Latin America	W. Euopre & Others	W.E. Others	E. Europe	Africa	Asia
Permanent Members Excluded	−	−	−	+	+	N.C.
			−		+	
Permanent Members Included	−	−	−	N.C.	+	N.C.
			−		+	

In Table VII, column 2 under each region defines the probability of a state which is not a permanent member of the Security Council being elected to a nonpermanent seat allocated to the region. Thus, in 1975, the odds were, for a state in: Latin America—1 in 13; Western Europe and others—1 in 10.5; Eastern Europe—1 in 10; Africa—1 in 15; Asia—1 in 18. When permanent members are taken into account, Europe, both East and West, does much better proportionately than do Latin America, Africa, and Asia.[21]

Table VIII shows the relationship between the percentage of places occupied by each region in the Security Council and each region's percentage of the total U.N. membership at five-year intervals from

TABLE VII

Ratio of Security Council Seats to Regional Membership 1966-1975

	LA*		WE*		Others*		E. Eur.*		Afr.*		Asia*	
	1	2	1	2	1	2	1	2	1	2	1	2
1966	2/24	2/24	4/18	1/15	1/5	1/5	2/10	1/9	3/37	3/37	3/38	2/27
1967	NC	NC	NC	NC	NC	NC	NC	NC	NC	NC	3/29	2/28
1968	NC	NC	NC	NC	NC	NC	NC	NC	3/40	3/40	NC	NC
1969	NC	NC	5/18	2/15	0/5	0/5	NC	NC	NC	NC	NC	NC
1970	NC	NC	NC	NC	NC	NC	NC	NC	NC	NC	3/30	2/29
1971	NC	NC	NC	NC	NC	NC	NC	NC	NC	NC	3/35	2/34
1972	NC	NC	NC	NC	NC	NC	NC	NC	NC	NC	NC	NC
1973	2/25	2/25	4/19	1/16	1/5	1/5	2/11	1/10	NC	NC	NC	NC
1974	2/26	2/26	NC	NC	NC	NC	NC	NC	3/41	3/41	3/36	2/35
1975	NC	NC	NC	NC	NC	NC	NC	NC	3/45	3/45	3/37	2/36

*In each case, column numbered 1 takes account of permanent seats on the Security Council and column 2 excludes permanent seats.

TABLE VIII

Equity Ratios

	LA		WE		Others		E. Eur.		Africa		Asia	
	%SC* 1	%UN 2	%SC* 1	%UN 2	%SC* 1	%UN 2	%SC* 1	%UN 2	%SC* 1	%UN 2	%SC* 1	%UN 2
1946	18 33	36	36 17	20	9 17	7	18 17	11	9 17	5	9 0	20
1951	18 33	33	36 17	18	0 0	8	18 17	10	0 0	5	27 33	25
1956	18 33	25	36 17	21	9 17	6	18 17	13	0 0	8	18 17	28
1961	18 33	19	18 0	16	0 0	5	9 0	10	18 33	26	18 17	24
1966	13 20	20	27 10	15	7 10	4	13 10	8	20 30	30	20 20	23
1971	13 20	18	33 20	14	0 0	4	13 10	8	20 30	30	20 20	27
1976	13 20	18	33 20	13	0 0	4	13 10	8	20 30	31	20 20	26

*Under each regional heading, column 1 takes permanent members of the Security Council into account and column 2 excludes them.

1946 to the present. This relationship can perhaps be thought of as the "equity" or "inequity" ratio.

The main significance of Table VIII is that if permanent members are included in the reckoning (and counting the United States with Western Europe as is done here), Latin America has always been underrepresented in the Security Council, least of all just before the Security Council was enlarged and somewhat more so now. Excluding the permanent members produces a quite different effect and it appears that the Latin American share of the nonpermanent places has been more or less equitable, except for the period before the increase in Security Council membership when Latin America's unchanging number of Security Council seats gave the region a relative advantage in terms of its declining proportion of the whole U.N. membership. Western Europe seems overrepresented when permanent members are counted, especially given the arbitrary attribution of the United States to this region. Without the permanent members, Western Europe still comes out about as it should, especially if it is viewed in conjunction with the "others" group. As for Eastern Europe, it has always fared a bit better than equitably except, discounting the Soviet Union's seat, when the politics of the cold war diverted the nonpermanent Eastern European seat to an occupant from another region. Like Latin America, Africa suffers in equity when permanent members are counted but comes out all right when permanent members are excluded from the count. Asia seems to be the most underrepresented region whichever way the count is made. The odd coincidence of percentages since 1965 when permanent members are counted and when they are not is an artifact of the combination of the region's one permanent seat and the Security Council's size: when China is included, there are three Asian places out of fifteen and, when it is not, there are two out of ten.

The analysis of seat distribution points toward the conclusions that: (1) the existing pattern of nonpermanent seat distribution is somewhat, but not severely, skewed as between regions; (2) such difficulties of interregional distribution as emerge appear to be related to the rigidities resulting from permanent membership (and the arbitrary, perhaps misleading, location of the United States in the West European group) more than from the distribution of the nonpermanent seats among regions; (3) more distortions could arise if future membership increases fatten some regions more than others; and (4) the greatest source of inequity in Security Council seating arises not from the sharing of seats among regions but from the allocation of seats within them.

The Functions of Nonpermanent Membership

What qualities of elected members are important to the Security Council's ability to perform its peace and security functions in the foreseeable future? Does the answer to that question depend a great deal on the role the Security Council is expected to fulfill henceforward? Tentatively, the answer given here to the latter question is no.

The most extreme possibility should be looked at first. It cannot be ruled out altogether, although it seems unlikely, that circumstances will convince all five permanent members that their interests require that a threat to the peace or an act of aggression be suppressed by whatever means are necessary, not excluding "action by air, sea, or land forces."[22] In such a case, the means to achieve the agreed objective would probably be supplied principally by the permanent members themselves, as was the original intention of the charter. It is, of course, conceivable that the permanent members' agreement on what needs to be done could be dependent on its being done by others. Given such great power agreement, it is likely that the necessary means for action against a less than great power could be mobilized among other U.N. members which need not be members of the Security Council. Indeed, Article 44 of the charter specifically provides a procedure for participation by a state which is not a member of the Security Council when its forces are to be employed. Moreover, the proper conclusion to be drawn from the record set forth in Table II above is that members have been willing to bear U.N. burdens when they are not Security Council members. For example, of the thirty-four states listed by Fabian as having participated in the United Nations Operation in the Congo, only thirteen were Security Council members at any time during the four years the operation continued and many of them made their commitments to participate before they were elected to the council. Their decisions were likely made in most, if not all, cases on other grounds than whether they were or were not members of the council. The argument based on Table II really goes in the other direction: that states which do bear U.N. burdens may be more qualified for Security Council contribution than others on the ground of their "contribution . . . to the maintenance of international peace and security," not that membership generates "contribution."

If the Security Council decides that "measures not involving the use of armed force" are necessary "to give effect to its decisions,"[23] as has been the case with respect to Rhodesia,[24] what is essential is that cooperation be forthcoming from all the states whose participation is necessary to make the measures agreed upon effective. Security Council decisions can legally be effective with respect to all U.N. members, whether Security Council members or not.[25] What really matters is that the relevant states be willing and able to make the measures effective, whether voluntarily or under pressure or inducement. It is not necessary that they be on the Council. The same considerations apply to peacekeeping or, to use Dag Hammarskjöld's term, "preventive diplomacy" measures which may require deployment of observation, supervisory, or buffer personnel or units in a tense situation. In short, operations which the Security Council might conduct do not imply material criteria for selecting nonpermanent members.

For the most part, of course, the Security Council has spent its time doing other things than enforcing its decisions or conducting field operations, and this is likely to continue to be the case. The council is a forum for the airing of complaints, often with no action intended or decision called for. It can thus serve as a safety valve. It is also, as Hiscocks has pointed out, an instrument used for the shaping of opinion and the forging of collective policy on important issues.[26] Recent resort to the Security Council with respect to issues of southern Africa and the Middle East suggests that this may be a function of growing importance. It can also serve as an instrument for negotiation with respect to contentious issues which might lead to threats to the peace or which have already resulted in breaches of the peace. In this context, the Security Council performs what a recent analysis terms essentially a "third party" role.[27]

None of the categories of functions the Security Council is likely to perform require special material capacities on the part of nonpermanent members. What is needed is the assurance that the forum not be predisposed against the interests of states which might come before it. In that sense, it is important that the elected members reflect the broad range of outlooks in the U.N. membership. Geographic distribution will not in itself ensure that, because of the cleavages along political, linguistic, religious, and ideological lines which occur within regions. The degree of geographical distribution of places which has been made possible by the amendment enlarging the council is desirable in itself and contributes to the kind of representativeness which is needed. Moreover, with respect to all its functions, it is important that the council contribute to definition of the limits of the feasible and acceptable, not just as those limits may be drawn through the exercise of great power vetoes but also through the ability of the nonpermanent members to reflect accurately and persuasively the interests of the nonmembers whose interests may be involved or whose help may be called upon. The relative importance of consensus procedures in the council in recent years underscores the desirability of thinking of elected members as essentially, although not legally, representing the regional groups by which they are chosen. The well established practice of electing to the council the candidates chosen through regional consultation implies a degree of accountability by the nominee to the constituency, and, it is suggested here, that is probably a good thing.

Indeed, there is much to be said for an approach to membership which would regionalize all Security Council places, both permanent and nonpermanent ones. Such a scheme has been advanced by Ambassador Arthur Lall who has proposed a structure of eight regions, each with both permanent and nonpermanent places in the Security Council.[28] The Lall plan seems optimistic in two important respects. He believes that the size of the council can be limited by resorting to composite representation to fill the permanent seats from some regions, among them Western Europe. Effecting such a plan would depend on the willingness of France and the United Kingdom to relinquish the special status they now enjoy as permanent members in favor of an arrangement under which they would share a place with West Germany and Italy. Such a result can hardly be anticipated confidently, nor can one be sure that Brazil, Argentina, and Mexico could agree on sharing a Latin American seat or, if they did, that Chile, for example, would acquiesce in its own exclusion. Secondly, Lall emphasizes the consensus principle as a response to the seeming undesirability of enlarging from five to eight or more the number of veto-wielding members of the council. The trouble with that is that, along with the increased emphasis on consensus which has been evident in recent years, there has been a parallel trend to employ the council to establish policies by majority votes, giving rise to a substantial recent rise in the number of great power abstentions and vetoes. It hardly seems possible to claim that the principle of consensus is well established enough to convince members with the veto power that they can afford to relinquish it or accede to expectations about its use that would have the effect of constraining it. Thus, the Lall plan as such seems to have major defects. All the same, his regional emphasis seems sound and there is room for much improvement in the degree to which members of the Security Council, both permanent and nonpermanent, regard themselves as obliged to consult with nonmembers from their regions and as having regional responsibilities.

It is evident, but deserves emphasis, that the performance of the council's functions will profit from the election of members which command respect and have leadership qualities and authority among the regional constituencies from which they come. If the elected members are to serve as two-way communication channels to nonmembers, to assist in delimiting the desirable and feasible and to generate support and help for decisions taken in the council, they should have easy access to the nonmembers and have persuasive influence on them. That implies that the founding fathers were correct in calling for regard to the contributions of members "to the maintenance of international peace and security and to the other purposes of the organization." Members which contribute much are more likely to have the desired access and influence than are lesser contributors. Moreover, it suggests that preference should be given to states with prior experience in the Security Council.

It is desirable that states elected have given evidence of ability to view Security Council issues in terms of broad conceptions of the collective interest, rather than more narrowly based perspectives, and in this regard a record of service in peacekeeping functions may be a relevant criterion. Finally, states of at least moderate size and resources seem more likely to command the respect and exert the influence called for than lesser states.[29] In this regard, the practice of excluding ministates from election to the Security Council makes sense. Intangible considerations deserve to be kept in view also and the desirable capacities may be influenced as much by the abilities and experience of the individuals representing members as by the qualities of the states themselves.

No mechanical improvements in the election criteria or procedures are likely to contribute much to improving the functioning of the Security Council. The existing pattern of electing nominees put forward through regional processes implies the kind of relationship between elected members and their constituencies that is called for. Improvement can best come through increasing concern by participants in regional nominating processes that their nominees be chosen with a view to the best feasible performance of the Security Council.

Notes

1. Italics added. The impetus for this provision came from the Canadian delegation. F. H. Soward and Edgar McInnis (with the assistance of Walter O'Hearn), *Canada and the United Nations* (New York: Manhattan Publishing Co. for the Carnegie Endowment for International Peace, 1956), pp. 26-27.

2. Leland M. Goodrich and Edvard Hambro, *Charter of the United Nations: Commentary and Documents,* 2nd and revised ed. (Boston: World Peace Foundation, 1949), p. 199.

3. Ruth B. Russell (assisted by Jeannette E. Muther), *A History of the United Nations Charter: The Role of the United States 1940-1945* (Washington, D.C.: Brookings Institution, 1958), p. 650.

4. Leland M. Goodrich, Edvard Hambro, and Anne Patricia Simons, *Charter of the United Nations: Commentary and Documents,* 3rd and revised ed. (New York: Columbia University Press, 1969), p. 194.

5. Ruth B. Russell, *A History of the United Nations Charter*, pp. 649-650.

6. See for example: Leland M. Goodrich, *The United Nations in a Changing World* (New York: Columbia University Press, 1974), p. 64; Goodrich, Hambro, and Simons, *Charter of the United Nations,* pp. 196-199; Richard Hiscocks, *The Security Council: A Study in Adolescence* (London: Longman, 1973), pp. 315-318; and H. G. Nicholas, "The United Nations as a Political Institution: A Personal Retrospect," *International Journal* (spring 1970), p. 265.

7. Of the sixty-one, ten are states which joined the United Nations in 1973-1975 and might be considered not yet primary candidates for Security Council membership. Except for the original members, no state has been elected to the Security Council upon joining the organization. The shortest interval has been two years in the case of Japan and the usual interval has been longer. See Table V.

8. The five designated permanent members, of course, bat 1,000, counting Chinese service as continuous.

9. Charles Lewis Taylor and Michael C. Hudson, *World Handbook of Political and Social Indicators,* 2nd ed. (New Haven: Yale University Press, 1972), pp. 295-298.

10. Ibid., pp. 306-311.

11. A. F. K. Organski, *World Politics,* 2nd ed. (New York: Knopf, 1968), pp. 209 ff., and A. F. K. Organski and Jacek Kugler, "The Costs of Major Wars: The Phoenix Factor" (prepared for delivery at the 1975 Annual Meeting of the American Political Science Association), p. 9-12.

12. Robert W. Cox, Harold K. Jacobson, et al., *The Anatomy of Influence* (New Haven: Yale University Press, 1973), p. 441.

13. Ibid., pp. 437-443. The rank order is taken from the table on p. 442.

14. See Larry L. Fabian, *Soldiers Without Enemies: Preparing the United Nations for Peacekeeping* (Washington: Brookings Institution, 1971), pp. 266-268. Fabian lists twelve "Peacekeeping Missions":

UNCI:	United Nations Commission for Indonesia
ONUC:	United Nations Congo Operation
UNEF:	United Nations Emergency Force
UNFICYP:	United Nations Force in Cyprus
UNIPOM:	United Nations India-Pakistan Observation Mission
UNMOGIP:	United Nations Military Observer Group in India and Pakistan
UNOGIL:	United Nations Observer Group in Lebanon
UNSCOB:	United Nations Special Commission on the Balkans
UNTEA—UNSF:	United Nations Temporary Executive Authority— United Nations Security Force
UNTSO:	United Nations Truce Supervision Organization (in Palestine)
UNTSO Suez Canal:	United Nations Truce Supervision Organization— Suez Canal
UNYOM:	United Nations Yemen Observation Mission

15. Patricia Wohlgemuth Blair, *The Ministate Dilemma.* Occasional Paper no. 6 (New York: Carnegie Endowment for International Peace, 1967), pp. 97-98.

16. OAS service does not appear to correlate in any discernible fashion with Security Council tenure. The record (compared with 9 participations for the United States): 7 participations—Mexico, Brazil; 5—Argentina; 4—Costa Rica, Paraguay; 3—Bolivia, Uruguay, Ecuador; 2—Panama, Nicaragua, Colombia; 1—Haiti, Dominican Republic, El Salvador, Chile; 0—Haiti, Peru, Venezuela. J. S. Nye, *Peace in Parts* (Boston: Little, Brown, 1971), p. 151.

17. Analyzing by ten-year intervals instead of five does not significantly change the picture.

18. Goodrich, "The UN Security Council," in James Barros, ed. *The United Nations: Past, Present and Future* (New York: Free Press, 1972), pp. 34-36.

19. GA Resolution 1991 (XVII), December 17, 1963.

20. Hiscocks, *The Security Council,* pp. 99 ff., citing Jaskaran J. Teja, "Expansion of the Security Council and its Consensus Procedure," *Netherlands International Law Review* 16, no. 4.

21. It has been vigorously asserted that the permanent members do not represent the regions from which they come. See Arthur Lall, *The Security Council in a Universal United Nations.* Occasional Paper no. 11. (New York: Carnegie Endowment for International Peace, November 1971), pp. 8-11.

22. U.N. Charter, Article 42.

23. Article 41.

24. In the Rhodesian case, armed force was authorized to intercept tankers carrying oil to Rhodesia. See, for example, Hiscocks, *The Security Council,* p. 223.

25. Articles 41 and 25.

26. Hiscocks, *The Security Council,* chapter 6, pp. 249-264.

27. Richard S. Rhone, "What You See Is Not Necessarily What You Get: The Role of the United Nations Security Council," unpublished ms.

28. See Lall, *The Security Council in a Universal United Nations,* pp. 29-39.

29. But see Andrew Boyd's ironic reminder that having a high proportion of "substantial states" as members did not prevent the council's "fateful inactivity" prior to the Middle East blowup in 1967. See Andrew Boyd, *Fifteen Men on a Powder Keg* (New York: Stein and Day, 1971), pp. 188-192.

30. Voting in the Security Council and the PLO
Leo Gross

On November 30, 1975, the Security Council, by a vote of 13 to 0, with China and Iraq not participating in the vote, adopted Resolution 381 (1975),[1] prolonging the mandate of the U.N. Disengagement Observer Force (UNDOF) for six months and linking this third extension with the decision "to reconvene on 12 January 1976, to continue the debate on the Middle East problem including the Palestine question, taking into account all relevant United Nations resolutions."

There is no harm, following the precedent of the council's Resolution 338 (1973), in linking peacekeeping with peacemaking. In the case of Resolution 381 (1975), however, there is a deliberate attempt . . . to introduce into the debate in the council resolutions of the General Assembly which had been opposed by a minority including the United States. As interpreted by the United States, for instance, "all relevant United Nations resolutions" meant "only for Security Council resolutions 242 (1967) and 338 (1973)."[2] The Soviet Union understood the words to include "first and foremost Security Council Resolution 338 (1973) and General Assembly Resolution 3236 (XXIX)."[3] If the debate was to be based on Security Council resolutions alone, the United States and possibly the United Kingdom and France should have voted against the resolutions unless the controversial terms were eliminated. This might . . . have prevented the extension of the mandate of UNDOF, but in the circumstances this might have been the lesser evil. In any event the cease-fire and disengagement of forces do not depend upon the stationing of the force.

Excerpted from an article by the same name which first appeared in the July 1976 issue of *The American Journal of International Law.*

. . .

After the adoption of Resolution 381 (1975), the president of the council, on the basis of informal consultations, read a statement "regarding the agreement of the majority of the Security Council as an opinion of that majority":

> It is the understanding of the majority of the Security Council that when it reconvenes on 12 January 1976 in accordance with paragraph (a) of Resolution 381 (1975) the representatives of the Palestine Liberation Organization will be invited to participate in the debate.[4]

In accordance with the prior agreement, no vote was taken on this statement,[5] although some members of the council declared that they were not part of the majority.[6] France, although not objecting to the president's statement, correctly pointed out that this was "a procedural step which could have been settled, in accordance with normal practice, when the debate planned for January is taken up."[7]

. . .

The next step relating to the participation of the Palestine Liberation Organization (PLO) occurred on December 4, 1975, when the council met pursuant to a letter of December 3, 1975, from Lebanon concerning Israeli attacks directed at Palestinian refugee camps on Lebanese territory. The council had also recieved a letter of the same date from Egypt, requesting the participation of the PLO in the discussion of the Lebanese complaint. At the outset, the president of the council (the representative of the United Kingdom) made the following statement:

> In the course of the informal consultations that have taken place prior to this meeting, the representatives of Guyana, Iraq, Mauritania, the United Republic of Cameroon and the United Republic of Tanzania have put forward the same proposal. I have been asked by those five members of the Council to record that this proposal is not being put forward under rule 37 or rule 39 of the provisional rules of procedure of the Security Council, but, if it is adopted by the Council, the invitation to the Palestine Liberation Organization to participate in this debate will confer on it the same rights of participation as are conferred when a Member State is invited to participate under rule 37.[8]

The strongest statement on the proposal, from the legal point of view, was made by the president of the council speaking as the representative of the United Kingdom:

> That proposal contemplates conferring on the Palestine Liberation Organization a right to participate in the proceedings of the Council in this debate going far beyond what has customarily been accepted as appropriate in such a case. The granting to the PLO of this exceptional status in the Council's proceedings would, in the view of my Government, constitute an undesirable and unnecessary departure from the established practice of the Security Council. The provisional rules of procedure of the Council provide only for Member States of the Organization to enjoy such treatment. We see no sufficient reason to depart from that position. We certainly do not regard it as appropriate to accord such exceptional treatment to a body which does not claim to be a State at all, nor to be the government of a State. The Palestine Liberation Organization has been accorded a certain status by the General Assembly, but it does not, in our view, have the same status as those States which have been recognized as permanent observers to this Organization.[9]

Clearly what was involved was not merely a procedural issue and respect for precedent. What was involved was a constitutional issue of the first magnitude. There was also a political issue, namely the question whether the PLO should be invited at all. The United States representative spoke primarily to the latter issue when he urged "all who share the hope for a just peace in the Middle East to withhold their support from this egregious attempt to use this body to deal with an amorphous, terrorist organization as though it were a concrete entity with the attributes of a sovereign Government."[10]

. . .

The proposal was put to the vote and the result was nine votes in favor, three against (Costa Rica, the United Kingdom, and the United States), with three abstentions (France, Italy, and Japan). And the president declared: "Accordingly, the proposal has been adopted."[11] This was perhaps not unexpected, but the president should have declared that the proposal had not been adopted as two permanent members of the council, the United Kingdom and the United States, had voted against it.

Clearly the proposal presented a procedural and substantive

constitutional issue. The procedural issue was that part of it which accorded an invitation to the PLO. The second part of the proposal, namely that the invitation "will confer upon it [the PLO] the same rights as are conferred when a Member State is invited to participate under rule 37," poses a constitutional question of the first magnitude. Rule 37, along with rule 38, refers exclusively to members of the United Nations as does Article 31 of the charter, and rule 38 refers to Article 32. Both articles of the charter stipulate the conditions under which members of the United Nations which are not members of the Security Council or states which are not members of the United Nations may be invited to participate in the discussion of any question in case of the former and of any dispute to which they are parties in case of the latter. The council never determined whether the item on its agenda was a "question" or a "dispute." As it must have been obvious to all members of the council that the PLO was neither a member nor a state nonmember of the United Nations, and that the PLO itself, as pointed out by the United Kingdom, made no claim to be a state or the government of a state,[12] rule 37 could not be applied.

There is no provision in the charter or in the rules of procedure for "as if" decisions or actions by the council, that is for the treatment of a body as if it were a member state. It follows that the action of the Security Council was *ultra vires* the powers of the council under the charter as well as the procedure laid down in the rules of procedure. The action of the council was, legally speaking, null and void.

It was within the rights and, indeed, the responsibilities of the permanent members to prevent the intrusion into the council of the sheer majoritarianism cultivated in the General Assembly. Even if the argument of *ultra vires* is not accepted, the second part of the proposal would have to be decided in accordance with Article 27 (3) of the charter and not, as the president seems to have assumed, in accordance with paragraph 2 of Article 27. It seems unconscionable that the United States, which so strongly criticized certain actions of the assembly, should have acquiesced in this obvious violation of the charter.

. . .

Finally, a word on the observer status of the PLO, which was strongly emphasized by supporters of the invitation with the rights of a member state.[13] Invitations to organizations to attend General Assembly sessions as observers are nothing new. The Organization of American States (OAS) was so invited by General Assembly Resolution 253 (III) and the

League of Arab States by resolution 477 (V). At the same session at which the PLO was invited as observer, the assembly also invited, by Resolution 3208 (XXIX) the European Economic Community, and by Resolution 3209 (XXIX) the Council for Mutual Economic Assistance (CMEA) "to participate in the sessions and work of the General Assembly in the capacity of observer." As explained long ago by the secretary-general: "Observer status in the General Assembly simply means the right to attend without participation in debate or in voting and, on invitation, to participate in debate."[14] Such invitations are extended to organizations without in any way modifying or enhancing their status. To be sure, in Resolution 3375 (XXX), the General Assembly called on unspecified conferences on the Middle East to invite the PLO "on an equal footing with other parties."[15] Even this language changes nothing in the status of the PLO and it remains to be seen which conferences will heed the call of the assembly. There are conferences and conferences, and some may be more flexible than others in inviting nongovernmental bodies on a footing of equality with states and governments. In any event, the Security Council is not a conference "held under the auspices of the United Nations," and therefore Resolution 3375 (XXX) is inapplicable.

The third stage relating to the participation of the PLO in the Security Council started on January 12, 1976, when the council met to discuss the Middle East problem in conformity with the council's Resolution 381 (1975) of November 30, 1975. In accordance with the president's statement on that occasion, the representatives of the PLO were to be "invited to participate in the debate."[16] However, having recalled the statement, the president of the council (United Republic of Tanzania) proceeded to say:

> This proposal is not being put forward under rule 37 or rule 39 of the provisional rules of procedure of the Security Council, but if it is adopted by the Council, the invitation to the Palestine Liberation Organization to participate on this debate will confer on it the same rights of participation as are conferred when a Member State is invited to participate under rule 37.[17]

. . .

The supporters of the formula could base their arguments this time not merely on the observer status of the PLO but on the "precedent when at one of its previous meetings it [the council] invited the representatives of the Palestine Liberation Organization to participate as full representatives in a debate of the Security Council from beginning to end of that debate."[18] Among the opponents, the United States stressed the need to safeguard "the integrity of Security Council procedures and . . . the future effectiveness of this body," and that if members "take liberties with those procedures and, under the influence of immediate political positions with respect to a given question before this council, establish or reaffirm unwise precedents, this will come back to haunt us." The United States also, correctly, it is believed, argued: "For the most elemental of reasons, only Member States can participate in our proceedings as Member States,"[19] but as on December 4, 1975, it failed to draw the correct consequence from this most elemental reason. The United Kingdom, while recalling its earlier opposition to the "undesirable and unnecessary departure from our established practice" and that its earlier "procedural objections . . . were not shared by the majority" of the council, announced that it did not "think it right to press these procedural objections to the point of voting against the proposal, and therefore we will abstain."[20] The third permanent member of the council, France, insisted after the vote that outside of rule 39 "only representatives of States, whether Members or non-members of the Organization, may be heard by the Security Council" and that its abstention "can be explained by the status which the Council, contradicting its rules of procedure, is attempting to confer upon the PLO in our work."[21] Thus, of three permanent members which were opposed to the proposal, two surrendered to the majority and one—the United States—cast a negative vote without invoking Article 27 (3) of the charter.[22] Thus the unprincipled majoritarianism[23] of the Soviet and third world blocs which all too often has come to prevail in the assembly has found a second home in the Security Council.

Concluding Observations

Could this outcome have been prevented? Obviously no categorical answer is possible. It is possible, however, to indicate briefly alternatives which were open to those permanent members of the council which opposed the objectionable part of the invitation, namely that it would confer upon the PLO "the same rights of participation as are conferred when a Member State is invited to participate under rule 37."

The motion to invite the PLO consisted of two parts: the first part was the invitation, and the second part was the status of the PLO if invited. . . . It seems just possible, though no more than that, that if the motion had been voted in two parts at the December 4, 1975, meeting the first part would have been adopted by more than the requisite majority, but the second part might not have been adopted. Sweden which was in favor of inviting the PLO, might have abstained in the separate vote on the second part, but as it was given no choice Sweden cast the crucial vote with the Soviet and third world bloc in the vote which took place on December 4.

An attempt to separate the vote on the motion was the first possibility which was missed. The second possibility, which was also missed, was to argue the impermissibility of the second part on constitutional or, to adopt the usual language, on substantive grounds. As indicated earlier, to invite a state or an organization to participate in the council debate is one thing, to confer upon such a state or organizaion the rights of a member state is another. No matter how strongly the United States, the United Kingdom, and France deplored a departure from established practice or the erosion of the rules of procedure, they put their arguments on the plane of procedure. This was, in the present submission, a fundamental error. The pretended assimilation of the PLO to a member state of the conferral of rights of a member state raises a question of the constitutional law of the United Nations and not of procedure. There is nothing in the provisional rules of procedure to permit the council to assimilate a state, or still less, an organization to a member state. Nor could there be any such thing in these rules which are solely concerned with the conduct of proceedings in the council. They supplement the applicable articles of the charter and do not and cannot supplant them. This is seen particularly clearly in rule 40 which deals with the delicate question of voting: "Voting in the Security Council shall be in accordance with the relevant Articles of the Charter and of the Statute of the International Court of Justice."[24]

Assuming that the objecting permanent members of the council, or the United States alone, had taken a stand on the constitutional grounds of the law of the charter, what might have been the outcome? On December 4, 1975, these members or the United States alone could have argued that the proposed invitation was not adopted because two permanent members voted against it. Alternatively, the United States could have raised the preliminary question whether the proposed invitation was procedural. If, as suggested above, the motion had been separated into two parts, the preliminary question would relate only to the contested second part. The possibility of raising the preliminary question is explicitly laid down in the Four-Power Statement of June 7, 1945, with which France associated itself, on voting in the Security Council. The relevant part of it reads:

> 1. In the opinion of the Delegations of the Sponsoring Governments, the Draft Charter itself contains an indication of the application of the voting procedures to the various functions of the Council.

2. In this case, it will be unlikely that there will arise in the future any matters of great importance on which a decision will have to be made as to whether a procedural vote will apply. Should, however, such a matter arise, the decision regarding the preliminary question as to whether or not such a matter is procedural must be taken by a vote of seven members of the Security Council, including the concurring votes of the permanent members.[25]

As the charter contains no indication whatever by what vote the council could confer the rights of a member state on a nonstate entity, the preliminary question was in order. In view of the fact that the United Kingdom, a party to the statement, held the presidency in December 1975, it appears possible that the president would have called for a vote on the preliminary question and then for a vote on the question itself, and if the United States had not concurred in either vote, the president would have declared that the motion was not adopted in view of the negative vote of a permanent member. If the motion had been voted in parts, the same procedure could have been followed with respect to the second part of the motion and the results would have been the same with respect to that part.

A further point may be made. In the past there was controversy as to the binding force of the Four-Power Statement.[26] There is no need to review this controversy for the simple reason that the preliminary question and the resulting so-called double veto have their legal basis in Article 27, paragraphs 2 and 3. As the Soviet delegate, Mr. Gromyko, rightly it is believed, pointed out, the Four-Power Statement "is an interpretation of the provisions of the Charter."[27] Article 27 (2) applies only to procedural matters, whereas, according to paragraph 3 of Article 27, "decisions on all other matters," and this obviously includes the question whether a matter is procedural, "shall be made" by a qualified majority of seven—since the entry into force of the amendment to Article 27 on August 31, 1965, nine members including the concurring votes of the permanent members. The so-called double-veto procedure has a solid basis in the charter itself.[28] Still, whether and how it will be applied depends to a substantial degree on the president of the council. It might have been applied successfully in December 1975 for the reason stated above. In any event, those who were concerned about preventing the contamination of the Security Council by the majoritarianism of the assembly had the obligation, it is submitted, to use the available legal and constitutional procedure in order to forestall the adoption of an unconstitutional motion.

Alternatively, the president could have gone half-way, as did the president of the council in the question of Laos. The then president (Italy) called for a vote on the premilinary question proposed by the Soviet Union: "Should the vote on the draft resolution submitted in Doc. S/4214 be considered a procedural one?"[29] After the vote which was ten to one (USSR), the president, contrary to the Four-Power Statement and Article 27 (3), declared: "Therefore, the resolution should be considered procedural. It is the interpretation of the Chair, shared by the overwhelming majority of the members, that the draft resolution falls clearly under Article 29 of the Charter."[30] The Soviet delegate, correctly it is believed, observed:

> The President's interpretation of the vote is illegal. It is at variance with the Charter, it is at variance with the four-power declaration to which France subscribed, and it is at variance with the practice of the Security Council. For these reasons, it is null and void.[31]

. . .

Had this alternative procedure been followed, the United States, like the Soviet Union in 1959, would have had no effective remedy to challenge the president's ruling, but it could and should have made it quite clear that it stood for the application of the charter and that Article 27 (3) was not subject to parliamentary devices. No matter what the attitude of the United States may have been in and out of the United Nations during the cold war, there can be no doubt that it has an abiding interest in the observance of international law and the charter of the United Nations.[32] Law and the rule of law are basic values to free societies even, and especially so, in critical times, and it is a worthy effort to stand up for them. The United States was right in warning on September 12, 1975, against the "erosion of procedure."[33] It would have been even better and more to the point to warn against the "erosion of the charter" and use all the constitutional means available to it as a member of the council in defense of the charter. The scenarios outlined above indicate that the best chance for a successful defense was in connection with the proceedings of December 4, 1975. An attempt to resort to the preliminary-question procedure on January 12, 1976, would probably have been unsuccessful but it would have laid the basis for opposing sheer majoritarianism via rule 30 in the future.

The voting rules in Article 27 of the charter were and remain an essential condition for the creation and continued existence of the United Nations. More than that they were and remain an essential condition of United States and Soviet membership in the United Nations. If that condition is eroded, the continued membership of the United States, at any rate, may well become doubtful.

Notes

1. U.N. document S/PV.1856, November 30, 1975, p. 16.
2. Ibid., pp. 12-15. See also similar statements by Costa Rica, Japan, France, the United Kingdom, Italy, and Sweden, pp. 31, 33-35, 37, 41, 44-45, 56.
3. Ibid., pp. 64-65. The Soviet representative also referred to GA Resolution 3375 (XXX) as did the representative of Tanzania. Ibid., p. 58.
4. U.N. document S/PV.1856, November 30, 1975, p. 16.
5. See U.N. document S/11889, November 30, 1975.
6. Thus, Costa Rica, Italy, and the United States. U.N. document S/PV.1856, November 30, 1975, pp. 31, 46, 53.
7. Ibid., p. 37. Similarly the United Kingdom considered "that in accordance with the established procedures and rules of the Council the question of participation in any meetings of the Council is a matter which has to be decided at the time of those meetings themselves," p. 41.
8. U.N. document S/PV.1859, December 4, 1975, p. 3. Rule 37 reads:

Any Member of the United Nations which is not a member of the Security Council may be invited, as a result of the decision of the Security Council, to participate, without vote, in the discussion of any question brought before the Security Council when the Security Council considers that the interests of that Member are specially affected, or when a Member brings a matter to the attention of the Security Council in accordance with Article 35 (1) of the Charter.

Rule 39 reads:

The Security Council may invite members of the Secretariat or other persons, who it considers competent for the purpose, to supply it with information or to give other assistance in examining matters within its competence.

Since rule 38 lays down the rights of a member invited under rule 37, it may be useful to quote its text.

Any Member of the United Nations invited in accordance with the preceding rule or in application of Article 32 of the Charter to participate in the discussions of the Security Council may submit proposals and draft resolutions. These proposals and draft resolutions may be put to a vote only at the request of a representative on the Security Council.

9. U.N. document S/PV.1859, December 4, 1975, pp. 38, 39. (Editorial note: It should be noted that France, Italy, and Japan agreed that the PLO could be invited only under rule 39.)

10. Ibid., pp. 8-10.

11. Ibid., p. 41.

12. At the end of his speech, the representative of the PLO said to the absent U.S. representative that he wanted "to assure him that the so-called terrorists of today will be tomorrow the rulers, with their Jewish brothers of liberated Palestine—a Palestine for both Arabs and Jews, free of ethnic or religious discrimination, a Palestine free of racist Zionism." U.N. document S/PV.1859, December 4, 1975, p. 79.

13. E.g., the Soviet Union, U.N. document S/PV.1859, pp. 21, 22-25, 33-35.

14. Report of the secretary-general on "Questions of Invitations to Certain Regional Organizations Invited to Attend Previous Session of the Council (ECOSOC)," (E/2028), June 20, 1951, p. 3.

15. See resolutions 3375 (XXX), November 11, 1975, and 3237 (XXIX), November 22, 1974.

16. U.N. document S/PV.1856, November 30, 1975.

17. U.N. document S/PV.1870, January 12, 1976, p. 11.

18. U.N. document S/PV.1870, January 12, 1976, p. 21, (the representative of the USSR). The resolution was adopted 11 to 1 (United States) and 3 abstentions (France, Italy, and the United Kingdom), ibid., p. 57.

19. Ibid., pp. 13-15, 16.

20. Ibid., pp. 43, 44-45.

21. Ibid., pp. 59-60.

22. There is no question that the United States was fully aware of the gravity of the matter. Thus at one point its representative wondered whether the matter was one of procedure or of substance but while conceding that it was one of procedure considered it to be a case of "erosion of procedure" and "of fundamental concern to us." Ibid., pp. 51, 52. At another point he said: "What we may very well have to come to judge and are seeing here today is the commencement of an effort to subvert the open and public proceedings of the Security Council and replace them by the rule of an extra-legal, semi-secret *Apparat*, which is inaccessible to the membership of the United Nations and inaccessible to the processes of inquiry. There is a term for this: the term is 'totalitarianism.' " Ibid., p. 52. He also recalled that his "Secretary of State has spoken of the prospect that this institution will end as an empty shell." Ibid., pp. 53-55.

23. This was aptly characterized by the representative of the United Kingdom in the debate on the credentials of South Africa at the Twenty-Ninth Session of the General Assembly on November 12, 1974. Addressing himself to those who "suggested that the delegation of South Africa should be excluded from participating in our future proceedings," he stated: "Let me start by making the fundamental, if obvious, point that this Organization is governed by the Charter. It cannot, consistently with itself and with the role which it is designed to play in international affairs, disregard that Charter. We are either a law-abiding, law-respecting body or we are nothing, a mere talking shop. If we put aside the Charter whenever its provisions may seem to a majority of us— even, indeed, to a preponderant majority of us—inconvenient, then we lose all claim to authority and to credence. In short, the Charter is and must be the constitutional foundation for all that we do. Respect for the Charter must permeate all our decisions. That much, I trust, is common to all of us here today." U.N. document A/PV.2281, November 12, 1974, pp. 23-25.

24. Article 10 (2) of the statute provides the only exception to the voting rule in Article 27 (3) of the charter. On the subordination of the rules of procedure to the Charter, see Fitzmaurice, *The Law and Procedure of the International Court of Justice: Treaty Interpretation and Certain Other Treaty Points,* 28 Brit. Y.B.I.L. 1, (1951) p. 22; and P. C. Jessup, *Parliamentary Diplomacy,* 89 Hague Rec. des Cours 201, (1956-I), p. 204.

25. U.N. document 852, III/1/37 (i), 11 UNCIO documents 713 (1945).

26. See L. Gross, "The Double Veto and the Four-Power Statement on Voting in the Security Council," 67 *Harvard Law Review* 251, (1953) particularly pp. 256-262. With reference to the statement, Stone observed: "Insofar as it was an unrepudiated basis of the drafting of (Article 27), it is a proper, and indeed virtually authoritative, means of interpretation." J. Stone, *Legal Controls of International Conflict* 213 (1954). But see Fitzmaurice that "minutes, declarations, resolutions . . . having the character of an *agreed* interpretation should be regarded, if not as part of the treaty itself, then as ancillary thereto, and as part of the complex of instruments produced by the conference in connection with the treaty it drew up," note 69, pp. 12-13. Italics supplied. *Quere:* agreed by whom? See also S. D. Bailey, *Voting in the Security Council* 18 (1969); and B. V. Cohen, *The United Nations* 11 (1961).

27. 3 *SCOR,* no. 71 (1948), p. 42, quoted in Gross, *The Double Veto,* p. 266.

28. See Cohen, *The United Nations,* p. 12, who disagreed with the proposition in the text.

29. 14 *SCOR,* 848th meeting 12 (1959). The draft resolution sponsored by the United States, the United Kingdom, and France read:

> The Security Council decides to appoint a sub-committee . . . . and instructs the sub-committee to examine the statements made before the

Security Council concerning Laos, to receive further statements and documents and to conduct such inquiries as it may determine necessary and to report to the Security Council as soon as possible.

U.N. document S/4214, September 7, 1959. Text the same as adopted, see: 14 *SCOR*, supplement, July-September 1959; (S/1416), September 8, 1959. While setting up of a subcommittee was a procedural matter, the conduct of inquiries was, in the Soviet view, not a procedural matter and therefore the whole draft resolution was not procedural. See L. Gross, "The Question of Laos and the Double Veto in the Security Council," 54 *AJIL*, pp. 118, 122-124.

30. 14 *SCOR*, 848th meeting 13 (1959).

31. Ibid., pp. 13-14. Cited in Gross, "The Question of Laos," p. 118. For a defense of the procedure in the Laos case, see E. Kerley, "The Powers of Investigation by the United Nations Security Council," *AJIL* 892 (1961), p. 917, note 88. He distinguishes between investigation under Article 34 for the sole purpose of determining the council's competence which is subject to Article 27 (3) and the council's "general procedural capacity to receive information from persons willing to provide it as part of its consideration of a question," which is governed by Article 27 (2) of the charter. Ibid., p. 918. This "general procedural capacity" appears to be derived from the council's powers of discussion and consideration as well as from rule 39 of the council's rules of procedure. Ibid., pp. 905-907.

32. A change in the U.S. attitude on the Laotian question is implied in the text. It may be pointed out that the attitude of the United States is not unchangeable. Thus in connection with voting in the Security Council on the admission of the two Vietnams, the United States adopted a stand which at best is only linguistically different from the stand of the Soviet Union prior to 1955 on the simultaneous admission of Western- and Soviet-backed candidates for membership in the United Nations. The International Court of Justice ruled in 1948 that a member "is not juridically entitled to make its consent to the admission dependent on conditions not expressly provided by paragraph 1 of said Article" (Article 4 of the charter), (1948) ICJ Rep. 57, p. 65. Yet when the Security Council rejected the inclusion in its agenda of the application of the Republic of Korea, the United States vetoed the applications of the two Vietnams. Its representative stated that the United States "would have voted for the admission of the Republic of South Korea, the Democratic Republic of Viet-Nam, and the Provisional Revolutionary Government of South Viet-Nam but that it would "have nothing to do with selective universality, a principle which in practice admits only new members acceptable to the totalitarian States." U.N. document S/PV.1836, August 11, 1975, pp. 58-60; see also U.N. document S/PV.1834, August 6, 1975, p. 41 and U.N. document A/PV.2354, September 19, 1975, pp. 87-91. At a later meeting of the Security Council, the

U.S. representative recalled the court's ruling that "package deals" were not in order but applied it to the other side which linked the admission of the Republic of Korea "to the case of North Korea." He expressed the view that the Security Council is not "entitled, authorized or wise in linking these two matters in the face of the judgement of the Court and, indeed, of our recent well-established practice." U.N. document S/PV.1842, September 26, 1975, pp. 53-55. The United States then vetoed again the applications of the two Vietnams. U.N. document S/1868, September 30, 1975, p. 23.

33. See note 22 above.

THE U.S. ROLE IN THE U.N. SYSTEM

31. American Policies in the United Nations
Charles William Maynes

The power center of American foreign policy has seldom taken the United Nations very seriously. It has used the organization when convenient as an instrument for the pursuit of traditional foreign policy goals. Pursuing a global policy, U.S. officials may even have been surprised at the number of times they found a global body of use. Nevertheless, their resort to the United Nations was episodic, and they continued to regard it as marginal to the conduct of international relations.

That attitude is now changing. Slowly, a realization is spreading among U.S. policymakers that even a debating society—and the United Nations is more than that—can have a very significant impact on international relations depending on the subject debated and whether those speaking have influence on actions outside the forum of discussion. U.S. officials incrasingly realize that U.N. debates do have this imp^ct. As a result, whatever their private feelings or public statements, American officials are taking the United Nations much more seriously than in the past.

All of which poses a dilemma for the United States: we are taking the United Nations more seriously precisely at a time when our prestige there has never been lower. Thus, what we need to do is to develop a strategy for increasing U.S. influence in an organization that will continue to affect American foreign policy.

This chapter is reprinted with permission from *Foreign Affairs* (July 1976), pp. 804-819, as "A U.N. Policy for the Next Administration." Copyright 1976 by the Council on Foreign Relations, Inc.

To begin with, Washington must make an effort to understand an apparent contradiction in American attitudes toward the United Nations, a body we dismiss in one breath as powerless and denounce in the next as dangerous. An explanation for these conflicting attitudes can be found if we face up to the fact that on some subjects the United States now has no choice but to take the United Nations much more seriously whereas on other subjects it still has considerable discretion. The difference between disarmament issues on the one hand and economic issues on the other illustrates this point.

In the disarmament field, U.N. debates continue to have little impact outside the United Nations, principally because the superpowers maintain a virtually unchallenged monopoly of real power. It is a relatively futile exercise for the smaller powers to denounce the major powers, because the latter, if offended, will simply refuse to take the views of smaller states into account in their own bilateral negotiations. Everyone understands that U.N. debates have little leverage in the "real world" of disarmament talks. No one, therefore, gets terribly excited about "irresponsible" resolutions or debates in the General Assembly.

If we turn to economic issues, the United States is faced with a completely different reality. There, because of increased resource dependence, the rise of multinational corportions (now vulnerable to expropriation), and much greater interdependence in trade, the former economic hegemony enjoyed by Western countries like the United States has been significantly weakened (though not destroyed). The gap between U.N. rhetoric and the "real world" has significantly narrowed as a result. American policymakers are increasingly aware that U.N. debates can have a major impact on negotiations and foreign policy matters outside the world body. This awareness explains more than anything the recent U.S. willingness at the United Nations to enter into serious discussions with third world countries regarding economic subjects. The United Nations is probably the forum we prefer least for such discussions; and one has to be frank in admitting the grave disabilities of such organs as the General Assembly or the United Nations Conference on Trade and Development (UNCTAD) as negotiating forums. But we now understand that too negative a position in them gives rise to very negative repercussions elsewhere.

This altered relationship between U.N. rhetoric and outside reality, particularly on economic issues, helps to explain why American policymakers have become so disturbed by decisions which an allegedly unimportant organization is taking. Yet the United States is also on the defensive in the United Nations with respect to political issues, particularly in the last two years. To understand why U.N. decisions are suddenly having a much greater impact on the United States in the political field as well as the economic field, we need to go beyond the usual statement that the United Nations is now dominated by third world countries—that, after all, has been true since the early 1960s—and to introduce two important psychological considerations which help to explain our recent U.N. difficulties.

The first can be best explained by a phenomenon most of us—anxious to close the Vietnam chapter—prefer not to discuss: namely, that throughout the postwar period, it now seems clear, there was a rather large gap between American power as perceived by others and American power as actually projected by us in terms of raw military and economic resources. We never could really police the world, and our willingness to make important economic sacrifices through trade and aid for foreign objectives has been declining since the late 1950s. These realities notwithstanding, others continued to believe we had more power than we really did have; they structured their diplomacy accordingly, and Americans benefited from the much greater respect their views were accorded. This was true multilaterally and bilaterally, inside the United Nations and outside. Not the least of the destructive effects of our disastrous involvement in Indochina was to end a psychological advantage we were able to exploit for years within the United Nations and long after the "tyrannous majority" was in charge.

A remark once made by Lenin about the British underscores how others at certain periods in their history have benefited from a similar gap between perception and reality. To Lenin—and now to the British—it was ridiculous that England with a handful of troops could dominate a country as large as India, which had only to understand its true strength to drive the British out. But because the Indians thought the British had more power than they really did, they acted accordingly. (So did the Indonesians toward the Dutch; millions of Africans adopted a similar attitude toward the French.) When World War II exposed the extreme vulnerability of the British position in India, independence quickly followed. It is perhaps no accident that it took a war to close the gap between perception and reality for both Britain and the United States.

The second development that obviously has dealt a psychological blow to our political position inside the United Nations is Watergate. Today, American power is probably preceived by foreigners and ourselves to be significantly lower than it actually is. The public image of a weak former president altering his foreign policy on détente and the Panama Canal according to the latest speech of his main challenger, the cascade of domestic scandal, his administration's foolish decision (after years of neglecting Africa) to make Angola a test case of our ability to stand up to the Soviets, the cacophony of policy-level voices in that administration on defense and international economic questions, the spectacle of press reports quickly confirming that the former president took no moves in Congress to indicate support for his secretary of state's major shift in policy toward Rhodesia—all convince the world that America is a confused and troubled giant. It is no accident, in other words, that our worst period in the United Nations has coincided with our worst postwar domestic trauma.

All of which might make one despair since the trauma has been so far-reaching. Yet, it is an indication of the basic health of the country that already we see signs of a turn for the better. Those currently in contention for the presidency in 1976, for example, could hardly have been described as adherents of a weak foreign policy. (On the contrary, the danger lies in the other direction. As this country picks itself off the mat psychologically, it may overreact to Soviet power and lose some of the gains in Soviet-American relations carefully achieved over four presidencies.) Already, in other words, the 1976 elections which ended the crippling anomaly of an appointed president, placed the impact of Watergate on our international position behind us.

The election having taken place, we should now be able to avoid undue emphasis on the sorry record of recent years. Rather, we perceive that America in 1976 was much like France in 1957, on the eve of General de Gaulle's accession to office. Our current international position, like France's then, reflects certain long-run adverse trends; and these we must analyze and react against. But our position reflects what will surely turn out to be a temporary collapse of national will and leadership. With time, our pessimism will recede, our adversaries' confidence will decline. Like France's influence then, America's influence will be reestablished in the world because the real strength of the nation has not been lost. We have only to regain our composure and retrieve our common sense for this to happen.

Restored American confidence will provide a solid basis on which to reexamine American foreign policy in the United Nations. But even with that confidence restored, there is a new mood in the third world which we must comprehend if we are to place American policy in the United Nations in its proper framework.

II

Many post-1973 accounts of the U.N. confrontation between the third world and industrialized societies assume that the outstanding issues are essentially economic or financial in nature, since so many of our disagreements with the third world have centered around the so-called New International Economic Order (NIEO). Third world demands are seen as a collective ultimatum for higher levels of resource transfer from the developed world to the developing world. This view, however, is not an adequate picture of third world objectives, which remain more political than economic.

In fact, the current North-South confrontation is part of a continuing process in this century to widen the circle of international decisionmaking. As such, it represents the third major attempt to integrate dissatisfied powers into the central management of the international system. The first attempt involved Germany and Japan. Although the conflict with Germany and Japan obviously had several dimensions, a key element of their challenge to others was a demand that they no longer be treated as second-class members of the international system. It took fifty years of struggle and negotiation before their true integration into the management of that system (along with a curbing of their ambitions) was accomplished. The second attempt concerned the Communist states, particularly the Soviet Union and China. It has taken another lengthy period to arrive at a point where we can finally accord China her seat on the Security Council and can acknowledge that the Soviet Union has become a global power with legitimate interests which reach far beyond Eastern Europe. Today we are faced with the third effort of this century to enlarge the circle of those who have a determining voice in the conduct of international affairs.

Once we look at third world goals in this light, we begin to understand the ability of developing countries to maintain unity under very adverse economic circumstances. Unlike Germany and Japan or the Soviet Union, few countries of the third world have the national power base to compel acceptance or integration into the central management of the international system. Only through unity can they gain the role they seek. Consequently, unity persists for fundamental political reasons even when the economic costs of continuing the unity remain very high. Although, as Tom Farer has pointed out in this journal,[1] a common hatred of the colonial heritage is another cementing bond among many third world states, only recognition of this drive for international acceptance and for an assured voice at the critical negotiating table allows us to understand a phenomenon which can link colonial with noncolonial (Yugoslavia with Burundi); free market with socialist (Thailand with Algeria); significantly developed with barely touched (Argentina with Nepal); pro-American with anti-American (Brazil with Iraq).

Third world countries have experienced colonialism in different degrees and at different times. Since independence, however, they have all experienced in roughly equal measure a common feeling of marginality and irrelevance regarding their role in the international system. In this regard, developing countries, no less so than industrialized countries, recognize that with the collapse of the Bretton Woods system and the rise of new global challenges we have entered an era of international rule-drawing—in Secretary Kissinger's words the "most extensive series" of international economic negotiations in history. In such a period a place at the negotiating table tomorrow is becoming much more important than a lower price for oil today. The example of the Organization of Petroleum Exporting Countries (OPEC) is electrifying, in other words, not simply because the oil-producing countries have more money but because they now have a commanding voice in international affairs.

Viewing third world demands from this standpoint makes it possible to relate more coherently other features of the current U.N. confrontation between the United States and the third world. It is almost commonplace for anyone following U.N. affairs to observe that the United States is isolated in the world body primarily because of three issues: the Middle East, southern Africa, and the new international economic order. On all three, Washington has allowed a cross-regional, hostile alliance to develop which has alternately embarrassed and outraged the American government and its people.

At first glance, it would seem that the three issues have few real links (except those which Arab money and African poverty can establish). In fact, they are closely joined by one common element: all are viewed by the third world as symbols of its powerlessness in the international system. In all three cases, the industrialized world is seen as *interposing* itself either to prevent change or to control developments. Moreover, in the eyes of the third world, the *interposition* itself, almost more than the formal Western position, is highly objectionable.

Since October 1973, euphoria has developed in the third world precisely because developing countries have concluded that the West may no longer be able to interpose itself with its former effectiveness in any of these three central U.N. issues. In this perception, the oil weapon may have forced a new caution in the U.S. support of Israel; after Vietnam the unwillingness of the United States to become involved in civil conflicts abroad may have resulted in a new American reluctance to continue to encourage either a blocking or a slowing of the unfolding liberation of southern Africa; and third world unity, coupled with the needs of growing interdependence, may have compelled the West to take much more seriously than in the past the economic demands of the world's poor.

III

One stark formulation of the basic choices open to the United States in the face of a united third world appeared in the London *Financial Times:* "Do the Americans wish to split the third world, or negotiate with it or, conceivably, do both? From Dr. Kissinger's statements, it is impossible to tell." A central explanation for our weak position in the United Nations is that the past administration had no answer to this question. In his famous telegram to the Department of State, printed in *The New York Times,* former U.N. Ambassador Daniel Patrick Moynihan categorically asserted that it was a "basic foreign policy goal" to break up "the massive blocs of nations, mostly new nations, which for so long have been arrayed against us in diplomatic forums and in diplomatic encounters generally." Secretary Kissinger himself repeatedly denounced the "alignment of the nonaligned." Yet, as at UNCTAD IV in Nairobi in May 1976, he also called for cooperation, not confrontation, and in concrete situations he showed a willingness to work with a united third world.

It will be clear from the argument thus far that I think it is a mistake to attempt, certainly in self-defeating rhetoric but also in policy practice, to split the third world. The record since October 1973 suggests why. For much of that period Washington attempted both with words and actions to divide the third world, and the result was a spectacular diplomatic failure. Repeatedly Washington predicted what month after month failed to happen. Then, when we reversed course at the Seventh Special Session and attempted to encourage the emergence of moderate leadership within a united third world, we ended up with a significant diplomatic success. By coming forward at that session with a major policy statement which indicated that on basic principles America remained firm but that within the boundaries set by those principles we would honestly attempt to meet the legitimate grievances of the developing world, we sent an important signal to the developing countries: moderation can pay. The response of third world countries was instructive. There was no split. No one left the caucus. But the leadership role passed from the radicals to the moderates. Washington must continue to send this kind of signal—one of firmness on principles and of accomodation on problems consistent with those principles.

The alternative is the "union-busting" tactics endorsed by Ambassador Moynihan. These tactics, however, are likely to fail and may not even serve our interests. Can we expect some third world countries to side with us regarding economic issues on a regular and predictable basis against the majority of developing countries? In fact, it would be against their own national interests since their leverage with us derives precisely from that unity. Even State Department Counselor Helmut Sonnenfeldt has acknowledged in his secret address to U.S. ambassadors to European countries—in conformity with current practice subsequently published—that "dwarf states" can achieve real power internationally through unity.

But there is an additional consideration. We must begin asking ourselves more carefully whether such union-busting tactics, even if successful, would serve American interests. The world, after all, is entering a period of great economic uncertainty. With a total breakdown in the postwar economic framework, states are free to strike out independently, engaging in the international equivalent of wildcat strikes by arbitrary expropriations, sudden cutoffs of critical supplies, and refusal to honor earlier agreements. No state has a greater interest than the United States—a relatively satisfied and dominant power economically—in increasing the degree of collective pressure which can be brought to bear against states tempted to break the rules even as Washington negotiates a new set of them. Just as a sense of common interest in the European community recently led to group pressure on France to rescind the new tax suddenly imposed on Italian wine imports, so members of a third world bloc will have an interest in making certain that the actions of some temporarily dissatisfied state do not jeopardize future economic arrangements that benefit the vast majority. The American goal, therefore, should not be to break up the third world but to structure its diplomatic approach in such a manner as to encourage the rise of moderate leadership within a bloc that probably should not be split in any event.

The same approach is also relevant to the other two key issues in the United Nations which isolate America so totally. In the Middle East we cannot expect Egypt to abandon the Arab world; nor in southern Africa can we expect Zambia to separate itself from other African states. The United States can work for the creation of a negotiating atmosphere which permits Egypt and Zambia to argue persuasively with other Arab and African states that moderation pays. Like the moderate leadership in the American civil rights movement in the late 1960s, however, the moderate elements in the third world have gone years without victories and urgently require some to prove that a moderate course can produce results. Otherwise, we can expect the extremists of international politics to take over. But if America's general strategy should be to pursue a policy which enables leaders in the third world to outflank the radicals with the argument that moderation pays and extremism does not, what specific steps should be taken in the United Nations?

IV

Here, the United States must adopt a strategy of tough diplomacy on the one hand and practical accommodation on the other. Tough diplomacy is essential primarily to trace clearly those limits beyond which it would be unwise to push the United States because fundamental principles or vital national interests are involved. The Zionism resolution and Cuban-inspired actions on Puerto Rico are examples. On such issues, Ambassador Moynihan was right, and the United States must press its views on such subjects earlier, more vigorously, and at a much higher level than in the past.

At the same time, Washington must press for accommodation in those areas where changes in our policy are entirely consistent with our long-term interests. On these issues and others we have more influence than we often believe. For years the United States followed a narrow damage-limitation strategy in the United Nations, in part because America needed a low international profile as long as the Vietnam War continued. Yet the past two years—which have been the low point of U.S. influence in the United Nations—demonstrate that when the United States takes the initiative, it can, precisely because it remains so important and so powerful, have greater influence than perhaps any other U.N. member in determining the shape of the international agenda. The U.S. initiative on food in Secretary Kissinger's maiden speech to the General Assembly in 1973 and his major address to the Seventh Special Session in 1975 contained elements of concrete benefit to everyone (although they did not ensure follow-through); at the same time, they preempted initiatives which would have been much less to our taste. Washington should attempt to launch similar initiatives in the future. Indeed, the United States should begin to think of its objectives at the United Nations itself as much in terms of shaping the agenda for action there and elsewhere as in settling the problems themselves in the world body.

While the United States no longer has the potential in the United Nations to advance final formulations and expect blind acceptance by others, the alternative is not powerlessness. On any power continuum, the United States remains close to where it was. Rather than feeling sorry for ourselves because of the power we have lost, we should focus on the power we retain and determine to use it skillfully and with worthy purpose.

Opportunities to do this are various in the U.N. system, particularly in the technical fields. In the late 1970s, the United Nations will hold a major international conference on technology, a field both of American strength and of great political sensitivity to the third world, which is aware that the weakest section of the consensus resolution at the Seventh Special Session centered around this issue. The United States should begin now with a vigorous interagency effort designed to develop a stream of proposals specifying steps that can both improve the terms of current technology flows to the third world and assist these countries in developing new technology more suited to their own development requirements. Secretary Kissinger's Nairobi speech made an excellent beginning in this process which the present administration should accelerate. The U.N. Water Conference took place in 1977. In this field, unlike most, the American government, as opposed to private industry, plays a major role in the development of new technology. Washington had, therefore, a unique opportunity to make pledges of assistance which did not depend on subsequent compliance in the private sector. In short, in all major conferences, America's goal must be to place the United States at the cutting edge of international reform.

Consistent with the overall strategy of firmness and accommodation, the United States should take the following specific steps, both procedural and substantive. To begin with, if it is to maximize its influence within the United Nations, the United States must find ways to work with others in a regular caucus arrangement, accepting as a corollary that participation in a group entails willingness to compromise in an effort to arrive at a common position. In Geneva the United States operates as part of a developed-world caucus. In New York it does not. It should press for the creation of such a New York grouping. Though some of our allies might resist this (since at times it is politically expedient for them to set themselves apart from the United States), Washington should be able to overcome this opposition if it can honestly argue that its purpose is to unite with its allies in order to work out a realistic program of cooperation, not confrontation, with the third world. If our allies, in turn, are genuinely concerned about the U.N.'s future, they should agree to such a caucus since the alternative of U.S. isolation in New York is likely to lead to one of two results, each undesirable: renewed U.S. negativism or final U.S. disillusionment.

The executive branch must accept that with the increased prominence of international economic issues in the United Nations the role of the Congress in the formulation of our U.N. policy is totally changed. The problem is no longer simply stern congressional reactions to unpopular U.N. decisions. It is also congressional understanding of and agreeement to the kinds of specific commitments (usually involving follow-up legislation) that are essential to effective

American participation in international economic negotiations. With this in mind the administration should commit itself to executive-session presentation of our U.N. strategy to the relevant committees of Congress well before each session of the General Assembly.

A major effort should also be made in the General Assembly to correct the destructive effects of current voting practices there. Some have argued that one way to accomplish this would be to eliminate voting altogether. But to function, any parliamentary body needs to vote on some issues. Moreover, an isolated American decision to cease all voting would look like an act of pique, brought about only because we are no longer able to take advantage of our own former automatic majority.

There is, however, good reason for drawing sharp distinctions between General Assembly treatment of political issues and economic issues. In the case of political issues, voting is often an end in itself because it serves as a benchmark of diplomatic strength or of international feeling. In the case of economic issues, however, the obejctive should not be to win diplomatic victories but to reach consensus on concrete programs of action that governments will carry out long after the initial U.N. vote has been forgotten. Two courses of action therefore seem open to the United States. It could simply refuse to vote on all economic issues in the future. Alternatively, it could announce its intention to regard as invalid any General Assembly vote on an economic issue where a clear majority of key developed countries had indicated their opposition. In that event, Washington would refuse to cast a ballot. Either way, the United States would be emphasizing that U.N. General Assembly decisions in the economic area are not meaningful unless they enjoy the support of countries with the resources to put them into practice.

The United States should boycott U.N. technical meetings that are being twisted for political purposes. In December 1975, the United States and ten Western states pulled out of a minor U.N. Educational, Scientific, and Cultural Organization (UNESCO) committee meeting after Arab and Communist states voted to inject the General Assembly's "Zionism equals racism" resolution into proposed guidelines for mass media. Although the United States should not hesitate to act alone, its goal should be to develop blocs of states which will join with it in protecting the organization's integrity, as was the case at the UNESCO meeting. This can be done with a good conscience, because there is a difference between today's politicization of U.N. specialized agencies and yesterday's over the Chinese representation issue. Then the debate was over an up-or-down vote on admission. The United States did not attempt to twist the technical programs of the agencies in pursuit of a campaign against Communist China.

There exists the question of an appropriate American response to countries that take a consistently hostile attitude in the United Nations toward U.S. positions. It has been proposed that we strike back by means of the American aid program. No proposal is less likely to accomplish its objective. The Yugoslavs almost starved in 1949 rather than bow to Soviet economic pressure. The Cubans accepted enormous dislocation rather than accept American conditions for accommodation. Countries are not likely to change their general voting pattern in the United Nations for more foreign aid (particularly since we give so little). This is not to deny that the overall relationship between the United States and a particular country may deteriorate to the point where any aid relationship is unthinkable. Uganda is an example. Nevertheless, the best response to provocation in the United Nations is surely to reply in kind in the specific area of the confrontation.

If countries practice a double standard in the field of human rights, the United States and its allies should speak more forcefully of the human rights violations of those states that practice the double standard. If the Soviet Union assists in anti-American actions at the United Nations regarding Puerto Rico, which is in free association with the United States, Washington should make clear that it will raise the issue of the Baltic states, which are in forced association with the Soviet Union. If the United States is dissatisfied by economic positions taken by some countries in U.N. debates, then and only then should the United States make it clear that its *overall* economic relationship with those countries—on aid, Export-Import Bank credits, investment policy, trade promotion—will be that much more limited.

The foreign aid program itself should be used primarily affirmatively in the context of international economic negotiations both in the United Nations and elsewhere. Today, out of eighteen members on the Organization for Economic Cooperation and Development (OECD) Development Assistance Committee, the United States is one of four members—embarrassingly enough, the other three are Austria, Italy, and Switzerland—which have not accepted the target of 0.7 percent of gross national product for official development assistance. Even West Germany, our ally on virtually all international economic issues, has seen the negotiating advantages of accepting this target without a specific date of implementation. The U.S. administration should accept the 0.7 percent target (along with a determination to rebuild our aid program as an instrument of U.S. foreign policy), as part of a strategy to defuse extreme and destabilizing third world economic demands.

Finally, there remains the question of the highly sensitive and largely U.N.-created linkage between the issues of southern Africa and the Middle East. For both diplomatic and domestic reasons, decoupling these two issues should be a key foreign policy objective of the administration. Given the intractability of the Middle East problem, the only possible way for the United States to do this is to move to the forefront of Western powers pressing for racial justice in southern Africa.

Secretary Kissinger's April 1976 speech on Africa represented a welcome break from the past and marked the beginning of a sensible policy toward Rhodesia. But it did not go nearly far enough on the key U.N. issues of Namibia or South Africa itself; far more effective would be for the United States to join others in applying rapidly escalating economic and political pressure on South Africa to end its illegal occupation of Africa's last major colony. Regarding South Africa itself, the administration should declare that it will not recognize any partition of South Africa, as with the Transkei, unless a much more equitable distribution of land between blacks and whites is provided and until an impartial internationally monitored referendum of the native populations affected is carried out. The May 1976 success of black African states in blocking an Algerian-led effort to link Zionism with racism in two resolutions of the Economic and Social Council (ECOSOC) suggests rather eloquently that a strategy of tough diplomacy coupled with honest accommodation—e.g., Moynihan's earlier protests over the Zionism resolution, Kissinger's subsequent shift on our Rhodesian policy—does bring dividends and may enable us to break the explosive linkage between the Middle East and southern African problems.

V

There is a last and critical building block in a strategy for restoring U.S. influence in international organizations. Pressing hard for America's rightful role in U.N. bodies entails a need not only to accommodate legitimate policy interests of the third world but also to think repeatedly of new ways to address constructively its desire for a recognized and larger voice in the management of the international system. Here several possiblities are open outside the formal U.N. framework.

The ongoing twenty-seven nation Conference on International Economic Cooperation (CIEC) in Paris offers a unique opportunity for structured policy discussion between developed and developing countries on the future of the world economy. Yet, already signs are developing that the momentum of the Seventh Special Session is being lost. The third world countries have collectively and publicly complained of a lack of progress. Perhaps the thought of significant steps forward prior to the next election is too much to expect. It is important, however, to be ready to move quickly as soon as the electoral scene is clarified. The key point is to persuade the third world that the industrialized societies intend to work with them seriously.

In framing her economic proposals toward the third world, America must accord much greater recognition than she has to the belief among developing countries that their drive for acceptance as full partners in the international system requires industrialization. The American tendency to place almost exclusive stress on the agricultural sector or raw materials in third world development helps to persuade the Group of 77 that we are not in favor of their industrialization and thus of their full integration into the international system. There is no doubt that our current emphasis on agriculture and minerals is quite realistic in terms of the primary economic needs and opportunities of third world countries. But the point is precisely that third world goals reach beyond economics into the realm of politics. This is why the third world desire to industrialize is so intense, and U.S. economic proposals and statements must reflect that fact.

As to the problem of giving third world countries a greater share in international economic institutions, some further progress is needed. But there may be other means of giving the developing nations more of a feeling that they control their own fate. At the time of the Marshall Plan, the U.S. government delegated to the Organization for European Economic Cooperation (OEEC)—the agency set up by the West European aid recipients—much of the task of allocating American aid. The result was a system encouraging the Europeans to work together, developing among them a sense that American aid did not mean excessive American influence, bringing about a general feeling of regional responsibility and participation.

By analogy, a significant portion of Western aid to the third world might be directed away from bilateral programs or multilateral institutions to regional institutions under the control of states in the area which could then assume the responsibility for insisting on higher standards of performance. Donor states are bound to insist increasingly on such standards in allocating aid, yet the sensitive issue of outside interference or "neocolonialism" is at the same time raised. One way to solve this dilemma is to ask developing states, as we did the Europeans earlier, either to form special institutions like the OEEC or use existing institutions to shoulder the political burden of insisting on firm standards. Like the Europeans in the 1940s, one could hope they will press for enforcement of these standards because they would not like to see any one of their number waste precious aid resources that could be better used by someone else. The principle is important, and periodic audits could indicate whether the experiment should be encouraged.

In the same vein, the United States might withdraw from some organizations where its presence may be perceived as an effort at domination. Before joining the Ford administration, the under secretary of state for economic affairs and former assistant secretary for Latin American affairs publicly urged that we leave the Organization of American States (OAS). His successor should carry out this policy. Although Latin American states declare that they do not want the United States to leave the OAS, American officials involved with the subject concede that the statement is made without passion. The United States should also look at other regional organizations with a view to possible withdrawal; conversely, Washington could consider the admission of important third world states to, or their association with, key bodies such as the OECD, traditionally regarded as closed to all but the rich.

Finally, the administration should also recognize that one important source of third world discontent is the belief of its leaders that under the joint impact of détente and the highly personalized conduct of U.S. foreign policy since 1969 the United States increasingly treats small powers as marginal to the conduct of world affairs. This lack of attention at the top echelons of the U.S. government has extended even to the most important countries in the third world, and the disastrous results are apparent in the United Nations and elsewhere. The administration should quickly institutionalize formal contact with key third world countries bilaterally or in a regional or subregional context.

VI

The foregoing strategy clearly will not end our problems at the United Nations. The world organization took controversial decisions even when the United States enjoyed its automatic majority. Now that we do not have that majority, we must expect more such decisions. Yet the American future in the organization is far from hopeless. Quite the contrary; if the United States works aggressively both to defend its own interests and to understand and accommodate the interests of others, one very significant element of American influence in the world can again come into play. This is the perception of others that the United States has been and continues to be better at devising pragmatic, workable approaches to international problems than virtually any other state. Since the mid-1960s, the American government has mistakenly failed to exploit this potential source of influence. The administration must not make the same error. Then the United States can regain in the United Nations and in multilateral diplomacy generally the role which the strength and skills of this country suggest should be ours.

Notes

1. See Tom J. Farer, "The United States and the Third World: A Basis for Accomodation," *Foreign Affairs* (October 1975).

32. U.S. Policy Toward International Institutions
Seymour Maxwell Finger

In dealing with its major concerns, the United States should use a wide variety of international institutions. Emphasis in the security area should stress NATO with respect to any Soviet threat and the United Nations for preventing, stopping, or damping down conflicts in Asia, Africa, and Latin America, or at least insulating them from Soviet-U.S. confrontation. Accordingly, measures should be taken to strengthen the United Nation's capacity for peacekeeping and peacemaking. In arms control and disarmament, bilateral Soviet-U.S. relations will be crucial, but there is an important role for the Conference of the Committee on Disarmament and the United Nations General Assembly as fora for world opinion and for pressure on the two superpowers.

In the economic field this essay emphasizes the use of the World Bank group, the regional development banks, the International Monetary Fund (IMF), the Organization for Economic Cooperation and Development (OECD), and the General Agreement on Tariffs and Trade (GATT) for negotiations and operations in the areas of aid, trade, and monetary policy. This conclusion is based on the view that United States interests would be best protected in those institutions, that they include those governments responsible for the bulk of world production, and that they have a creditable operating record. In addition, there should be smaller core groups on specific problems and on the harmonization of economic policy among the major industrialized countries. On the other hand, there is a vital role for the United Nations General Assembly, the U.N. Conference on Trade and Development (UNCTAD), and the Economic and Social Council (ECOSOC) in the

This chapter is reprinted with permission from *International Organization* (spring 1976), pp. 347-360.

universal discussion of key issues. Experience has shown that over the years government attitudes and policies on major issues, though they cannot be imposed, can be educated and changed through this process. These changes in attitudes, in turn, make the international financial institutions more responsive to the needs of developing countries. Such responsiveness, which is crucial in a world of growing interdependence, would be further stimulatd by increasing the voting strength of the developing countries in the international financial institutions and their representation in the secretariats in these institutions. The existence of a large and growing new pool of capital in the Organization of Petroleum Exporting Countries (OPEC) countries may act as a significant prod in this direction. I have not emphasized the creation of new internationl machinery or the making of major changes in existing institutions because I believe that policies and attitudes are the crucial factors.

Peace and Security

Détente notwithstanding, it is clear that a major war threatening the existence of the United States can come only from the Soviet Union. Given the history of the past thirty years and the veto provisions of the United Nations Charter (Article 27), it is equally clear that the United Nations would be of little or no use to the United States in facing a direct Soviet threat. Consequently, primary reliance for American defense against such a threat must continue to rest in the forseeable future on U.S. military forces and the NATO alliance.[1]

The nuclear arsenal and potentials of the Soviet Union and the United States are obviously so far superior to those of any other nation that the "balance of terror" depends upon agreement between the USSR and the United States, as is now being attempted in Strategic Arms Limitation Talks (SALT) II. The equally serious *qualitative* nuclear race will also depend on Soviet-United States negotiations. However, pressure from the U.N. General Assembly may serve a useful purpose by prodding the two superpowers. Especially important in this context would be the conclusion of a treaty banning all nuclear tests, including those underground.

International institutions can also play a significant role in deterring nuclear proliferation. The Non-Proliferation Treaty, negotiated at the United Nations in 1967, has served a useful purpose, even though its effectiveness has been limited by the unwillingness of certain key countries to ratify it; e.g., China, France, India, and Brazil. As oil becomes more expensive, and the threat of oil reserve depletion looms, nuclear power becomes more important. Countries with nuclear potential will not forego nuclear development unless assured of nuclear fuels and technology for peaceful uses. Yet, the spread of nuclear potential for peaceful uses opens the door to military use and to terrorism. In the latter connection, strict control by the International Atomic Energy Agency (IAEA) is necessary. The inspection provisions included in the Non-Proliferation Treaty are a good beginning, but they must be substantially strengthened if the world is to be protected from nuclear threat as nuclear energy becomes more widely used. In particular, IAEA inspectors should have unrestricted access to all nonmilitary nuclear installations. Even if the Soviets block inspection on their territory, the United States should permit inspection of American nonmilitary nuclear sites as a means of inducing non-nuclear weapon states to do the same. Additionally, there must be agreements among the countries capable of exporting nuclear fuel and processing equipment on appropriate safeguards to include in sales agreements. One useful idea was the American proposal to the Non-Proliferation Treaty Review Conference last May in Geneva to limit the spread of nuclear enrichment and plutonium separation and processing plants by concentrating these potential weapons-making facilities in regional multinational centers.

The U.N. Role in Keeping the Peace

With adequate American defense strength and continued reliance on NATO for deterrence or defense against a possible Soviet threat, there would remain a substantial problem of conflicts in various parts of the third world. The latter, if not carefully handled, could draw in the Soviet Union and the United States. To deal with this threat, there should be a combination of what Bloomfield has called "spheres of abstention"[2] (where the United States and the Soviet Union could agree whether tacitly or formally to keep out) and strengthened U.N. and regional machinery for fact-finding, peacekeeping, and peaceful settlement. The role of the United Nations in preserving Zaire as a unified, nonaligned country, and in helping to stop the fighting in the Middle East is a matter of record. The United Nations has also helped to deter or prevent at least a dozen other conflicts. In October 1973, the Soviet threat to place its forces in Egypt, in order to prevent destruction of the Egyptian Third Army, could easily have led to a Soviet-American confrontation had there not been a U.N. Security Council and a nonaligned proposal to use a U.N. peacekeeping force instead.

The U.N. Emergency Force (UNEF) II is an excellent example of both the potential and the limitations of peacekeeping. It has the potential to dampen down conflicts which might otherwise draw in the Soviet Union and the United States in combatant roles. On the other hand, Soviet-American collaboration in bringing about a cease-fire, and Henry Kissinger's subsequent efforts in bringing abut two disengagement agreements between Egypt and Israel, demonstrate that U.N. peacekeeping is not a substitute for national efforts. Clearly, problems cannot simply be handed to the United Nations for solution with the thought that the United States can thereby avoid any involvement or responsibility. Rather, such action becomes a sharing of responsibility and involvement, with the bigger powers having a heavier responsibility.

The main immediate problems of U.N. peacekeeping involve agreement on ground rules, better preparation, and sounder financing.[3] UNEF II was launched on a relatively sound financial basis, with Soviet and American support and with all members who were assessed substantial contributions, except China, agreeing to pay for the operation. UNEF II may thus serve as a model for the establishment and conduct of future peacekeeping operations. Nonetheless, two substantial problems remain. First, there is still no provision for standby forces earmarked for peacekeeping duty, except by the Nordic countries, Canada, and the Netherlands, nor for the maintenance of a current roster of available forces; nor is there a provision for training. Strong efforts should be made in the U.N. Committee of 33 to reach agreement on these points. Second, financing is still inadequate. China has refused to pay for the operation, and late payments by member states continue to be a problem. States which have provided peacekeeping forces have gone unpaid for long periods, and forces from some low-income countries have had to be withdrawn entirely. It is tragic that an operation of this importance should be impaired due to the lack of relatively small sums of money. The U.N. Working Capital Fund, which might otherwise compensate for late payments, has been virtually depleted.

One answer might be the establishment of a new working capital fund specifically for peacekeeping. Such a fund would not be a substitute for assessments, but rather a reserve from which advances could be drawn, pending payments from governments. It would also meet shortfalls, such as the refusal of China to pay for UNEF II. It could be established either through an assessment on member states or through some autonomous source of income; for example, a tiny surcharge on international trade and/or communications or on licenses for mining the seabeds. Alternatively, states might be asked to pay one hundredth of 1 percent of their annual budgets for armaments in order to sustain this fund.

There is no question that the Security Council would be a preferred instrument of the United States for authorizing peacekeeping operations. The General Assembly has an overwhelming third world majority whose views are often contrary to American policy. The Assembly is also large and relatively unwieldy. In the entire history of the United Nations only one major peacekeeping operation has ever been initiated by the assembly, i.e., UNEF I. Thus, it is possible that a peacekeeping operation could be launched by the General Assembly if Security Council action were blocked by a veto. But such an operation would have to have the support, or at least the acceptance, of the two superpowers and a substantial majority of the assembly. It would be a rare situation indeed (though not inconceivable, in which this degree of support would not result in Security Council action.

As for coercive enforcement action, where participation by the members is binding, it is clear that only the Security Council is authorized by the charter (articles 25, 39, 41, and 42) to make such decisions. Enforcement action can be blocked by the negative vote of any of five permanent members of the Security Council, but this is the clear intent of the charter; it accords with practical realities; and it should reassure those who fear that U.S. security interests could be threatened by U.N. action.

The maintenance of peace might also be furthered by a more efficient worldwide communication system, as suggested by James Reston (*N.Y. Times*, May 21, 1975). Reston recalls the failure of communications between Cambodia and the United States during the Mayaguez incident of 1975 and the Greek-Turkish crisis over Cyprus and notes that there is no "hot line" network for countries as a whole, though the United States and the USSR have deemed it necessary to have their own. Yet communication with virtually every nation in the world could be available by satellite if the necessary earth stations, costing about $4 million each, were installed. Compared to the cost of conflict through misunderstanding, this would be a sound investment.

The General Assembly also has an important role in the airing of disputes. It can be argued, as Yeselson does, that General Assembly debates heat up the atmosphere and sometimes make solutions difficult. Nevertheless, to use Churchill's phrase, "Jaw, jaw is better than war, war." And Yeselson, while calling the United Nations "a dangerous weapon," still considers that the United States should use it for quiet diplomacy, mediation, and efforts to avert nuclear or environmental catastrophe.[4] Frequently, the General Assembly will provide the backdrop for such efforts.

In sum, from the U.S. standpoint, the United Nations and regional organizations should continue to be used for mitigation or resolution of conflict among smaller and medium-sized countries, particularly in Asia, Africa, and Latin America, in order to diminish the prospects of a Soviet-U.S. confrontation. To this end the United States should give these organizations encouragement and appropriate support, while relying on it own strength and NATO to deter or counter any direct Soviet thrust.

Management of the International Economy

The economies of the major industrialized countries have been intertwined to a point where there must be closer consultation on questions of money, trade, investment, inflation, and recession. This process has already started through informal agreements, through Committee III of the OECD, and through the IMF. With the reduction in tariffs on industrial goods to about a tenth of what they were before GATT and the spread of transnational corporations, the world is moving toward one market. The fine tuning of trade, monetary, and investment practices will require a harmonization of policies far beyond anything that has been experienced except in the European Economic Community.

Experts studying the field have concluded that there must be a core group working in very close cooperation among the major industrial countries, although its work must be related to global problems. Richard Cooper states: "Success or failure in the international monetary arena depends on agreement and cooperation among a dozen or so countries, in the important sense that other countries could violate agreements without undermining the regime." Cooper acknowledges the necessity for decisions that take account of the wider global arena, but believes that "in the monetary arena wide participation is desirable, but not so desirable as to allow it to hold up important cooperative steps between the key nations."[5] Philippe de Seynes also stresses the need for a central mechanism for coordinating monetary policies and controlling capital movements.[6] Miriam Camps, referring to earlier work by William Diebold, also argues that there must be far-reaching consulations among the various countries on monetary and trade policies "extending deep into the domestic sphere." However, she emphasizes that there must be a "process of fitting their new, more 'managed' interrelationships into a global framework."[7]

What type of framework would best meet these dual criteria? I am inclined to follow the suggestion made by Krause and Nye, which places major reliance on the International Monetary Fund, the Bank for International Settlements, and Committee III of the OECD.[8] It is doubtful that governments and treasuries of the major industrialized countries would permit a one-nation, one-vote General Assembly or

UNCTAD to make major decisions affecting their economies. The IMF provides a global context; its membership encompasses virtually all countries outside the Soviet group (CEMA) and China, and the latter do not presently constitute a major factor in international monetary relations. Furthermore, membership in the IMF is open to them if they want it and are prepared to abide by its articles. At the same time, the Fund has weighted voting, small committees which have the effect of weighted representation, and facilities which enable the monetary authorities of problem countries to consult frequently and closely. The twenty-member Executive Committee of the IMF, representing the entire membership, is an effective coordinating tool. Moreover, representatives of certain third world countries which take a demagogic stand at the U.N. General Assembly and UNCTAD tend to take a more professional position at the IMF.

What new steps should be taken by the IMF? Its Executive Committee has proposed the following elements as part of a new system:

1) stable but adjustable exchange rates; 2) a more symmetrical adjustment process that would require corrective action by both surplus and deficit countries; 3) SDR's taking over the roles of the dollar and gold; 4) a mechanism for transferring resources to developing countries as part of the new system of reserve-creation; 5) a Council of twenty, at the level of Treasury Minister or Central Bank Governor, to run the new system.[9]

Significant changes were made recently in IMF voting rules; more would be desirable. As the oil-producing countries gain a major share of world reserves and provide additional resources to the IMF, their added financial weight must be reflected in voting rights as a means of assuring their continued cooperation. Moreover, in order to encourage true negotiation rather than domination by a few highly industrialized countries, representation of the non-OPEC developing countries should also be increased.

The IMF has already made substantial use of committees in which voting is not weighted; e.g., the Group of Twenty.[10] Hopefully this practice will be developed further.

Trade

In the area of trade, it is much more difficult to sketch organizational arrangements. Ideally, an International Trade Organization (ITO), as envisaged in the 1947 Havana Agreement, would offer a vehicle for global trade coordination. However, opposition to this treaty in the

U.S. Senate in the years following Havana, and to a more modest proposal in 1960, may have made this an unpromising approach. There is no indication that the United States would accept anything like an ITO at this stage, and there is serious question as to whether other major trading nations would accept it either.

GATT has performed well in bringing about an unprecedented reduction in tariffs. According to Baldwin and Kay, the average American tariff has declined from 59 percent in 1932 to less than 10 percent today.[11] As they point out, the main obstacles to trade now are nontariff barriers, principally quantitative restrictions and export subsidies. These are being discussed in current GATT negotiations; i.e., the "Tokyo Round." Baldwin and Kay propose that GATT improve mechanisms for negotiation and means of settling disputes and develop new articles covering nontariff means of distorting trade and access to supplies. These goals would be furthered marginally by strengthening the GATT Secretariat as they suggest. Yet it is doubtful that the major trading countries would willingly give substantial autonomy to the Secretariat. As Cox and Jacobsen have noted, the more important the issues, the less likely governments are to surrender their control over decisions and allow organizational autonomy.[12]

Alongside the operating agencies mentioned above—the IMF, OECD, and GATT—there must be fora for uninhibited discussion of broad policy issues and principles that are vital to relations between the industrialized nations and the less developed countries (LDCs). This free interchange of ideas can bring about the basic teaching and learning of the fundamental concepts that will affect the economic relationships of the future. Richard Gardner has called attention to the role of the United Nations as a "catalyst for constructive change" by "influencing the political processes of states." He writes:

> In general, the agencies of the UN system have helped articulate the common interest of nations and helped conciliate the adversary interests. They have encouraged governments to take a more international approach and have strengthened the hands of outward-looking leaders in dealing with domestic political opposition. They have taken responsibility for compromises in situations where national leaders could not have taken responsibility alone. Thanks to them, nations have followed better economic policies than they otherwise might have done. In short, these institutions have certainly been instruments of a better world economic order.[13]

Krause and Nye also see GATT and UNCTAD "coexisting,"

with UNCTAD serving as a kind of "populist pressure group."[14]

Having represented the United States in the Economic Committee of the General Assembly from 1956 to 1963, and having watched closely since then, I have been impressed by the way prolonged discussion there can bring about major changes in attitudes on economic issues.[15] When the notion of soft loans was first advanced by the less developed countries in the form of "SUNFED," the concept was rejected by the United States and most other industrialized Western countries. Yet in 1959, the United States led the way to the establishment of the International Development Association (IDA) as a soft loan affiliate of the World Bank. Similarly, it took many years of discussion in the U.N. General Assembly and UNCTAD before industrial countries accepted the concept of nonreciprocal tariff concessions to the low income countries; now this doctrine is generally accepted and is being put into practice. The notion of compensatory financing to help developing countries which produce raw materials weather the vicissitudes of erratic markets was put forth in the 1950s but made little headway. In 1974, however, compensatory financing was incorporated in the Lomé Convention and in 1975 Kissinger proposed the establishment of a $10 billion facility in the IMF for this purpose.

These three examples illustrate a point which I believe is valid for the future, i.e., that concepts can be taught and learned in the General Assembly, but successful operating mechanisms for major programs are more likely to be located outside the United Nations itself. Can anyone believe that the United States and other major Western countries would have provided SUNFED, or any other organization based on a one-nation, one-vote principle, with the major resources that were required for IDA? Would it have been possible to negotiate detailed trade rules in the Second Committee or the General Assembly? Would the developed countries have even dreamed of putting a $10 billion compensatory financing fund at the disposal of the General Assembly?

Another point is crucial with regard to the General Assembly and UNCTAD—that the voting majority of the third world is most effective when used sparingly. Resolutions adopted over the strong objection of those whose cooperation is required for their implementation are meaningless. Their adoption in such circumstances does not change the minority position but may even tend to harden it and impede further negotiations. Far more effective has been the combination of pressure and patient negotiation, as in the establishment of the U.N. Special Fund in 1957[16] and in the agreement reached at the Seventh Special Session of the U.N. General Assembly in September 1975 on the principles of a "new international economic order." In this regard, the consultative procedures adopted by UNCTAD and those proposed by the Group of Experts in their report, "A New United Nations Structure for Global Economic Cooperation,"[17] are hopeful auguries for the effective use of U.N. institutions. The group's recommendations will now be studied by a committee of the General Assembly. My own experience at fifteen sessions of the General Assembly and numerous ECOSOC sessions leads me to conclude that government attitudes are the crucial factor, rather than procedural and administrative arrangements. However, even marginal assistance from such improvements would be most welcome.

International Cooperation for Economic Development

The Seventh Special Session of the General Assembly was noteworthy for the substantial degree of agreement between the industrialized countries and the third world on measures for assisting the developing countries. Agreement was reached on the following goals of the LDCs: (1) stabilizing their income from commodity exports; (2) obtaining preferential treatment in industrialized countries for their manufactured goods; (3) improving their access to capital and technology; (4) receiving a greater voice in the World Bank and the IMF.[18]

There were, however, significant differences as to how these goals should be approached. The developing countries' call for "indexation" of commodity prices to the prices of manufactured goods was rejected by most industrialized countries. The United States and other industrialized countries agreed that development assistance should be increased and the United States expressed its intention to do so; however, the U.S. representative specifically disavowed any firm commitment to a target of 0.7 percent of GNP in official development assistance set by the developing countries. While agreeing with the general objectives of placing special drawing rights (SDRs) in the center of the international monetary system, the United States expressed reservations about the setting of specific targets for the use of SDRs for development assistance until there is agreement on all of the interrelated components within a fully reformed international monetary system. Also, while agreeing that there should be an increased role for the developing countries in decision making in the international financial institutions, the United States argued that "participation in decision making must be equitable for all members and take due account of relative economic positions and contributions of members to the institution as well as the need for efficient international decision making."[19]

It is most significant that the developing countries accepted the central role of the World Bank group (along with bilateral assistance) in providing capital for development. The principal stress of the resolution is not on creating new institutions but on increasing capital flow from existing institutions and improving the terms. This is a major change from the 1950s and 1960s, when the developing countries strongly supported SUNFED and its successor idea, the United Nations Capital Development Fund (UNCDF), as the principal instruments for soft loans. (These would have placed control under the one-country, one-vote General Assembly.) The resolution adopted at the Seventh Special Session does urge developed countries, and developing countries in a position to do so, "to make adequate contributions to the United Nations Special Fund with the view of early implementation of a program of lending, preferably in 1976"; however, this appears to be little more than a pious hope. It seems to be generally realized that the parliamentary bodies in the major industrialized countries will not provide the massive sums required for development assistance to an international institution that does not have weighted voting. (In Fiscal Year 1975, the bank committed $5.9 billion, including $1.6 billion in IDA soft loans.)

The argument now turns on *how much* capital should be provided and whether or not there should be an *automatic* share of revenues, such as a given share of new SDRs income from exploitation of the seabeds, a tax on international communications, or a head tax. In favor of such automaticity is the fact that obtaining larger tax-levy appropriations for development assistance has become increasingly difficult. Moreover, levels of support are bound to fluctuate, often at the worst times from the standpoint of development. On the other hand, any release of funds accumulated automatically must raise the question of who would control their distribution. Some of the developments of the 29th and 30th Sessions of the General Assembly are hardly reassuring on this score. They provide little reason to believe that the standards of equity and fairness among those who have asserted leadership over the third world are superior to those of the United States and other industrialized countries. Perhaps a compromise could be reached on the automatic generation of funds which would be administered by the bank.

These considerations point to the conclusion that the World Bank group should remain the United States' principal outlet for development assistance, with bilateral assistance reserved for special cases. Increasing reliance should also be placed on the regional development banks in Asia, Africa, and Latin America. Certain reforms and changes in World Bank operations would, however, appear desirable: (1) There should be a redistribution of voting rights in favor of Japan, the OPEC countries, and developing countries generally. (Japan, with a much greater GNP than the United Kingdom, has only half as many votes.) The OPEC countries are becoming major providers of capital. They and the other devloping countries can rightfully demand a greater voice in bank policy making as quid pro quo for keeping the bank as the major international aid institution. (2) The ability of the United States to exercise a financial veto should be abolished through further diminution in the United States weight and necessary changes in the voting rules. The industrial countries as a whole would still have a majority of votes, but the United States would at least be required to convince them of its position; this would be a salutary restraint. (3) The bank should make more use of overall economic performance criteria rather than mere project evaluation in providing assistance and should be willing to participate in debt restructuring exercises.[20] (4) Because of its virtually monopolistic role among international institutions providing development capital, the bank has not been subjected to critical evaluation, or even much self-analysis. It should institute a periodic review of its activities by independent outside experts who could make suggestions for changes in its program and mode of operation. (5) More opportunity should be provided for personnel from developing countries in bank staff positions at all levels, in order to bring in diverse viewpoints. Care should be taken, however, to maintain the highest standards and to avoid undue politicization.[21] (6) There should be closer coordination between the bank's investment and preinvestment surveys carried out by the U.N. Development Program (UNDP). The latter is the world's largest program for technical and preinvestment assistance, currently running at almost half a billion dollars a year. These reforms are clearly desirable. In fact, the first three may be necessary conditions for continued recognition by the developing countries of the bank's central role.[22]

The recent establishment of a "Third Window" by the World Bank, designed to subsidize interest payments for LDCs borrowing from OPEC countries, is a welcome step. Unfortunately, contributions required to subsidize the interest rates have been coming in a mere trickle, and there is a dire need for an increase.

Remarks in the previous sections about the role of UNCTAD and the General Assembly as fora for the discussion of basic issues with respect to trade and payments certainly apply equally to the flow of capital and of science and technology to the developing countries, as well as to overall problems of economic development.

Another United Nations instrument of considerable potential significance is the recently established Commission on Transnational Corporations. Such corporations have become increasingly important for the transfer of both capital and technology, the totality of which cannot be provided by governmental and intergovernmental sources. But A. James Reichley has observed: "As a nation that has reaped great profits from the growth of the multi-nationals, we have a compelling interest in the elimination of abuses that, if they persist, are apt to stir first resentment and then resistance to an American commercial presence abroad. In particular, we should promote development of international agreements to make sure that the multi-nationals cannot juggle their books to avoid paying a fair share of taxes in foreign countries where they operate."[23]

In addition to active participation in the U.N. Commission on Transnational Corporations, the U.S. might discuss such agreements and codes of reciprocal obligations (host country/transnational corporations) in committees of the OECD and the World Bank. Also worthy of further development are management contracts and other arrangements whereby total or partial ownership of the enterprises is vested in the government or nationals of the host country—as is now being done in many OPEC countries and the socialist countries of Eastern Europe.

Because of space limitations and extensive coverage of the subject elsewhere, this essay will not deal with certain other major problems. The continuing Third U.N. Conference on the Law of the Sea will, of course, have substantial impact—positive or negative, depending on the degree of agreement that can be reach on supplies of energy, raw materials, and food, on pollution, and on the sharing of benefits between developed and developing countries. The degree to which governments follow up on recommendations of recent U.N. conferences on food, population, and environment will also have substantial impact.

Another conference of potential importance is the Conference on International Economic Cooperation. Because it is representative without being too large, this conference and its four special commissions (energy, raw materials, development, finances) might be a useful instrument for future consultations and negotiations. Undersecretary of State Charles Robinson has called these special commissions the "most important international institutional development since the United Nations."[24]

Conclusions

This essay has not emphasized the establishment of new institutions because I am convinced that it is less important to change the existing institutional framework than to change governmental attitudes and policies. For reasons set forth in the essay, I believe the United States should favor decision making on economic matters in institutions such as the World Bank, the IMF, OECD, and GATT, where there is a better correlation between influence on decisions and the ability to carry them out, rather than in the United Nations General Assembly or UNCTAD. There is, however, an important role for the latter two institutions as fora for the universal discussion of key issues, both for mutual learning and as a stimulant toward changes in governmental policies and attitudes.

While favoring American use of international institutions where our national interests are well protected, I believe the United States would be well advised to avoid policies that are narrowly nationalistic, short-sighted, or callous toward the developing countries. As Lincoln Bloomfield has put it: "The truly hard-nosed advice may well be that which recommends interpreting the national interest far more broadly—that is, by taking bold moves to pool authority and giving a new lead to cooperative rather than unilateral direction."[25]

Notes

1. For a fuller discussion of NATO and other alliances, see Ernst B. Haas, *Tangle of Hopes* (Englewood Cliffs, N.J.: Prentice-Hall, 1969).

2. Lincoln P. Bloomfield and Amelia C. Leiss, *Controlling Small Wars: A Strategy for the 1970's* (New York: Knopf, 1969), chapter 12.

3. S. M. Finger, "Breaking the Deadlock on United Nations Peacekeeping," *ORBIS* 17, no. 2 (summer 1973): 385.

4. See: Abraham Yeselson, Testimony before U.S. Senate Foreign Relations Committee, *Congressional Record* (May 15, 1975), S 8370; Abraham Yeselson and Anthony Gaglione, *A Dangerous Place: The United Nations as a Weapon in International Politics* (New York: Grossman, 1974); and also Hollis W. Barber, "The United States vs. the United Nations," *International Organization* (spring 1973): 139-164.

5. Richard N. Cooper, "Prolegomena to the Choice of a Monetary System," *International Organization* 29, no. 1 (winter 1975): 94. See also the Report of the Trilateral Commission Monetary Task Force, "Towards a Renovated World Monetary System," *The Triangle Papers*, no. 1 (New York, 1973). As Cooper notes, informal monetary arrangements are often superior to formal ones since they allow greater weight to the real powers. The meeting of the heads of government of France, the Federal Republic of Germany, Italy, Japan, the United Kingdom, and the United States in the fall of 1975, resulting from a French initiative, could lay the groundwork for better coordination of policies—on inflation, recession, monetary policy, exchange rates, energy, raw materials, and relations with the developing countries—among nations

which account for about two-thirds of world trade and production.

6. Philippe de Seynes, "Prospects for a Future Whole World," *International Organization* 26, no. 1 (winter 1972): 3.

7. Miriam Camps, *The Management of Interdependence* (New York: Council on Foreign Relations, 1974), p. 53.

8. Laurence B. Krause and Joseph S. Nye, "Reflections on the Economics and Politics of International Economic Organizations," *International Organization* 29, no. 1 (winter 1974): 323-342.

9. Richard N. Gardner in *New Structures for Economic Interdependence*, a report of a conference held in May 1975, under the auspices of the Institute on Man and Science, Rensselaerville, N.Y. See also comments by Robert Triffin on pp. 26-29 of the same volume.

10. Joseph Gold, "Weighted Voting Power: Some Limitations and Some Problems," *American Journal of International Law* 68, no. 4 (October 1974): 687-708.

11. Robert Baldwin and David Kay, "International Trade and International Relations," *International Organization* 29, no. 1 (winter 1975): 99-131.

12. Robert W. Cox and Harold R. Jacobsen, *The Anatomy of Influence: Decision Making in International Organization* (New Haven: Yale University, 1973).

13. Richard N. Gardner, "To Make the World Safe for Interdependence," *UN* 30 (New York: United Nations Association of the U.S.A., 1975), p. 15. See also Richard Falk "The UN: Various Systems of Operation" in Leon Gordenker, ed., *The United Nations in International Politics* (Princeton, N.J.: Princeton University Press, 1971), for his stress on the U.N. role in the formulation of a world public interest with respect to subject matter of a global dimension—nuclear weapons, oceans, environment, population, food.

14. Krause and Nye, "Reflections on the Economics and Politics of International Economic Organizations," p. 341.

15. The same phenomenon is recorded by Harlan Cleveland, not only with respect to economic issues but also anticolonial doctrine and some aspects of international law, "The Pace of Mutation," *UN* 30, p. 13.

16. See S. M. Finger, "The Third World Countries and the Arab-Israeli Question at the UN," *Middle East Review* (spring/summer 1975), p. 27, and "A New Approach to Colonial Problems at the United Nations," *International Organization* 26, no. 1 (winter 1972): 147-148. See also Arthur Lall, "Some Thoughts on the UN General Assembly as a Forum for Mediation and Negotiation," *Journal of International Affairs* 29, no. 2 (spring 1975): 63-69.

17. U.N. document E/AC.6219/29, May 29, 1975.

18. U.N. document A/Res/3362 (S-VII), September 16, 1975.

19 Statement by Ambassador Jacob Myerson, U.S. Representative in the Ad Hoc Committee of the Seventh Special Session of the U.N. General Assembly, September 16, 1975.

20. For supporting arguments see Charles Frank and Mary Baird, "Foreign Aid: Its Speckled Past and Future Prospects," *International Organization* 29, no. 1 (winter 1975): 133.

21. For an example of pitfalls to be avoided see S. M. Finger and John Mugno, "The Politics of Staffing the United Nations Secretariat," *ORBIS* 9, no. 1 (spring 1975): 117-145.

22. Kissinger proposed to expand the role and the capital of the International Finance Corporation, further attesting to the central role the United States envisages for the bank group. He did not specify, however, the locus of three other institutions he proposed: an International Investment Trust, an International Center for the Exchange of Technological Information, and an International Industrialization Institute.

23. A. James Reichley, "A Foreign Policy for the Era of Inter-Dependence," *Fortune* (April 1975), pp. 153-160. Also, an OECD working party has recently agreed on a draft code of conduct for transnational corporations which should be of some value, and at a minimum, should provide an interesting item for the agenda of the U.N. commission, *New York Times,* October 27, 1975, p. 41.

24. *New York Times,* October 17, 1975, p. 6.

25. Lincoln P. Bloomfield, *In Search of American Foreign Policy* (New York: Oxford University Press, 1974), p. 165.

33. U.S. Foreign Policy and the United Nations

Abraham Yeselson and Anthony Gaglione

One of the facets of American foreign policy is participation in the United Nations. The basic premise of this essay is that the role of the United Nations in world politics is improperly understood and that these misconceptions have contributed to confusion about relationships between the world body and American foreign policy. A good bit of mythology and wishful thinking have impaired a clear vision of the United Nations. Most observers tend to begin with the purposes and principles of the U.N. Charter, thereby obscuring national foreign policy objectives.[1] Others use majoritarian dicta in the United Nations in order to reject American policies.[2] Neither approach establishes the theoretical foundations for the development of those policy options which incorporate use of the United Nations.

We have developed such an approach.[3] Briefly, we contend that an organization based upon the sovereign equality of the members inevitably becomes an instrument for the promotion of the unique interests of each state. We begin with the question: *Who* brings *what* issues to the United Nations and *why*? Our research reveals four broad strategic categories, thereby clarifying the suitability of the United Nations as a diplomatic weapon. These strategies are: (1) the politics of embarrassment; (2) the politics of status; (3) the politics of legitimization; and (4) the politics of socialization.

Strategies

The *politics of embarrassment* reflects frustration and rage. It is an effort to inflict symbolic hurt when there is no possibility to take other action, e.g., Portugal bringing India to the Security Council as Indian troops were annexing Goa;[4] initiatives during and after the Soviet assault on Nagy's government in Hungary;[5] Soviet complaints about troops in the

Dominican Republic;[6] Argentina's protest in the Security Council following the kidnapping of Adolph Eichmann by Israeli agents.[7] Whether or not U.N. resolutions were adopted, there was no intent or possibility of changing the behavior of the defendant states. Analysts, describing these and similar cases as United Nations "failures," have simply ignored the objectives of initiating states.[8]

The *politics of status,* on the other hand, is directed toward more concrete objectives. Membership or presence in the United Nations is an important legitimizing symbol. Thus, during the cold war, the West forced Soviet vetoes while outvoting Communist-bloc choices.[9] Changing majorities have reversed the roles in recent years, but the most significant current use of the strategy is by the third world. Thus, the United Nations was used to inject the Palestine Liberation Organization into the negotiation of the Arab-Israeli conflict.[10] Anticolonial states have made the greatest use of this strategy. Simultaneously, the organization is used to deny status to undesirable governments, such as those in Transkei[11] or Rhodesia.

The *politics of legitimization* refers to use of the United Nations in order to add support for an ongoing foreign policy. There is no intention to substitute U.N. action for national policy, although that illusion may exist. The most successful use of this stratety was in Korea, where a United States decision to resist aggression was converted into an exercise in collective security. Another interesting example of the strategy was the Security Council debate durng the Cuban missile crisis.[12] At that time, Adlai Stevenson's oratory helped prepare millions of American television viewers for any sacrifice in support of the Cuban policy. Currently, anticolonialists and Arabs have used the United Nations to legitimize their attacks, including the use of force, against southern Africa and Israel.

Finally, the *politics of socialization* is an effort to use the United Nations in order to alter the balance of forces in favor of the initiating side. Naturally, it is the weaker party which is seeking external assistance. At times, the claim reflects desperation, e.g., Hyderabad's[13] and Hungary's[14] appeals for help during the military interventions of India and the Soviet Union. More often, the situation is less dramatic, e.g., Panama's 1973 Security Council effort to involve others in its negotiations with the United States over the Canal Zone.[15] Frequently, demands for condemnations of Israel by Arab states are directed against the United States as the major economic and military supporter of Israel. Users of the strategy hope that by isolating the United States in the United Nations they will influence American policymakers regarding Israel.

This description of conflict strategies at the United Nations is designed to facilitate a more rational analysis of options within the organization. We believe that the United Nations has limited utility as a means for pursuing national interest. This is true, even for those states capable of extracting maximum benefits from the organization. Some minority states, e.g., Israel and South Africa, can never hope to do more than defend themselves. On particular issues for other states, e.g., the civil war and Syrian invasion of Lebanon, the organization is similarly unavailable. The United States, long the dominant power in both the United Nations and world politics, must now adjust to minority status. This is rendered difficult by the assumption for some twenty years of a conjunction between U.N. principles and U.S. foreign policy. Many, therefore, interpret recent negative attitudes towards the United Nations as a rejection of the United Nations' ideals. Others, unimpressed by majoritarianism during the period of American domination of the organization, now insist that what is good for the world (majorities at the United Nations), is good for the United States.[16] Whether consciously or not, these positions reflect ideological preferences or basically flawed analyses of the uses made of the United Nations. They are not useful for preparation of meaningful guidelines for American policy in the world body.

Before suggesting appropriate guidelines, we must consider the United Nations as it is and will be in the predictable future. Since 1964 the United States has no longer controlled assembly majorities. In 1964, during the famous nonsession of the General Assembly, it became apparent that a majority opposed the United States effort to deny the Soviet Union its assembly vote because of failure to pay assessments for the Congo and Middle East peacekeeping operations. Increasingly, thereafter, majorities consisting of developing and Communist countries have determined the agenda, dominated debate, and defined the terms of resolutions. The effect of these developments is to deny the United States further opportunities to seize initiatives in the United Nations.

With regard to the politics of embarrassment strategy it appears to be of some value for minority states. Israelis, for example, refer constantly to Arab intransigence, acts of terror, hypocritical double standards, etc.; South Africans, when they are not silenced, do the same. In general, however, their remarks are ignored, ridiculed, and frequently greeted by massive withdrawals from the meeting rooms. As primary targets, these countries consider it vital to have their counterarguments made part of the public record.

The United States, although in the minority, must temper its anger because of global responsibilities. Normally, also, the United States is not subjected to direct assaults. Finally, given American strength and influence, resort to embarrassment politics tends to have little impact except to confirm the most hostile attitudes. When Ambassador Daniel Moynihan described President Amin as a "racist murderer,"[17] developing countries were outraged. Such an expansion of the use of *racism* was considered a distraction and dilution of their attack on white supremacy in southern Africa. Moynihan's statement was converted into further proof of American neocolonialism. Shortly afterwards, the "Zionism is racism" resolution was adopted in the General Assembly as an indirect rebuke to the United States.[18]

More concrete steps, such as raising in the Human Rights Commission the issues of imprisonment of Soviet dissidents or the murder of churchmen in Uganda, are doomed.[19] The Human Rights Commission, dominated by developing and Communist countries, concerns itself only with a handful of violators.[20] Anticolonialists define good and evil according to who commits crimes, rather than on the basis of the quality of the offense. Charges against majority members by the United States are, therefore, seen automatically as efforts to subvert the goals of the third world.

If anything, the United States is in an even poorer position in respect to the politics of status. Membership issues have always been the most prominent use of this strategy. Presently, however, the United States cannot hope to win support for its favorites. Instead, it must endure the endorsement of undesirable regimes such as the Cuban-aided Angolan government, or register opposition by use of the veto[21] (as in the case of Vietnam). This unhappy situation in the Security Council, the most congenial forum remaining to the United States, is exacerbated in the General Assembly. There, the most devastating example of American loss of influence was the invitation and treatment of Yasir Arafat and the PLO. As the Arafat invitation demonstrates, the United States has little recourse against this type of majoritarianism in the General Assembly. Majority manipulation of procedures, as in the refusal to accept the credentials of the South African delegation can be used to *delegitimize* a government. The tactic will be repeated and, perhaps, extended to other members. Even a retreat by the United States to legalistic arguments based on charter provisions provides no defense against the majority.

As a minority state, the United States is also excluded from using the strategy of legitimization. This strategy requires control of debate, votes, or both. During the cold war, the United States could tie its foreign policy to the United Nations, as was done during the Berlin blockade, the Korean War, and the Cuban missile crisis.[22] As became clear during the Vietnam War, attempts to stamp important foreign operations with the imprimatur of the world body will fail. The benefits of this strategy can be reaped only by those states having sufficient influence in the organization or the appropriate ideological credentials.

Socialization politics, or use of the United Nations to offset weakness, has never been important for the United States. Instead, as a global power the United States is a potential target. From 1945-1965, pro-Western majorities could blunt efforts by weaker opponents to use the United Nations to obtain external assistance. Thus, Guatemala in 1954[23] and Cuba during the Bay of Pigs invasion[24] in 1961 received short and unsympathetic hearings. That situation has changed. Should a dispute between the United States and a weaker country be brought into the organization today, support for the latter would be almost assured.

At best, therefore, the United Nations is, for the United States, an added dimension rather than the energizer of the foreign policy process. One must now analyze the impact of external initiatives in the United Nations on American foreign policy objectives. Winning or losing in the forum of the United Nations is not an end in itself. The basic dilemma for the United States is that the issues are defined and the resolutions are written by others. Thus, whenever the United States reacts negatively to particular actions which are inconsistent with policy objectives, it is forced to defend itself within a theoretical and moral paradigm designed to prevent exercise of such options. Having endorsed generalized statements against racism or colonialism, the United States is subjected to charges of hypocrisy and insincerity. Critics ignore the real tension between varied American interests and aims, on the one hand, and simplifications in the service of the goals of others at the United Nations, on the other.

An evaluation of American policy towards the Middle East, for example, reveals a complex mosaic of disparate interests. The strategic value and oil resources of the area underlie superpower rivalry. Arab-Israeli hatreds and wars overshadow other disputes involving radical and conservative Arab regimes, civil war in Lebanon, conflicting policies among oil producers and support, manipulation, and fear of Palestinians in Arab countries. Oil-dependent Western Europe and Japan pursue their own economic goals. Turbulence and instability intensify the danger that uncontrolled forces will incite unwanted confrontation between the United States and the Soviet Union.

Inevitably, foreign policy must deal with these realities and resulting contradictory tendencies in a manner calculated to serve American interests. Trade-offs must be made to preserve that dynamic equilibrium which will moderate Soviet influence, preserve key Arab friendships, continue the flow of oil to America and its allies, reduce tensions, assist Palestinian Arabs, and preserve the existence of the state of Israel. But all of these goals, as well as avoidance of hostilities with the Soviet Union are tied to preventing the outbreak of another Arab-Israeli war.

Use of the United Nations to sabotage negotiated solutions of the Arab-Israeli conflict endangers all the objectives of American policy. This is done by resolutions and other actions designed to impose selection of negotiators,[25] insult and infuriate the Israelis, and deny any legitimacy for the Jewish state.[26] America's complex interests, wealth, and influence permit this country to assume a mediating role. But a mediator must retain the confidence of all the parties, and those who sponsor extreme resolutions deliberately undermine that function by defining issues so that the United States emerges as an isolated champion of Israel. Not only are chances of war increased by such tactics at the United Nations, but the effectiveness of U.S. influence is simultaneously diminished.

Similar but different issues and problems confront the United States in southern Africa. Although the rhetoric emphasizes the key principles of self-determination, majority rule, and independence, the reality is somewhat different. An overall view of the anticolonialist position on the southern African problem clarifies the difficulties for American foreign policy within and outside of the United Nations. The white supremacist regime in South Africa is the ultimate target. Compromises satisfactory to Ian Smith in Rhodesia or to South Africa in Namibia are seen, correctly, as defenses for apartheid. Encouraged by the sweep southward of militant black African nationalism, the majority is unwilling to make any concessions.

The United States, especially disturbed by Cuban troop use in Angola and radical nationalism in Mozambique, is attempting to mediate among the parties. From the U.S. perspective, acceptance of the principle of majority rule in Rhodesia and of independence in Namibia are seen as valid bases for negotiated solutions. The intransigence of black Africans is based upon the relationship of these issues to apartheid. Since apartheid is nonnegotiable, they demand nothing less than surrender in the peripheral areas. In the final analysis American mediation efforts, necessarily assuming some legitimacy for the Rhodesian and South African authorities, are viewed as supportive of apartheid. Protestations that the United States opposes racism are swept aside, because this country continues to use its influence in favor of minimizing violence and strengthening moderation on all sides.

Détente

Finally, a word must be said about détente. Improvement of U.S.-Soviet relations rests primarily on the relationship between the leaders of the two countries. At the United Nations, evidence of Soviet commitment to détente will be their nonuse of an available majority on arms control and other directly negotiable questions. But others—Chinese, Arab, and black African leaders—can and do use the United Nations in order to force the superpowers to adopt mutually hostile positions. Each time the Russians must speak and vote for an outrageous resolution, the sincerity of their peaceful intentions towards the United States loses some credibility. The Chinese are particularly adept at inducing the Soviets to assert their anticolonialist "purity" by denying complicity in what the Chinese describe as "dual hegemony" with the United States.[27] By this tactic, the Chinese accomplish two purposes: (1) they undermine Soviet standing in the third world; and (2) strike a blow against Soviet-American détente.

The essential interrelatedness of *all* the great debates at the United Nations has become apparent. Thomas Farer writes:

> Three global issues shape what may be called the North-South confrontation. One is the question of how global income and wealth and decision-making authority with respect to international economic problems should be distributed. A second issue is the attitude of the United States toward the two white-supremacist regimes in Southern Africa. And the third is the United States role in the Arab-Israeli conflict. Although each issue represents a distinct axis of confrontation, they are linked by a single world view, a kind of ideology which imparts to them an intense emotional coherence.[28]

The evidence of these connections is overwhelming. Venezuela's Carlos Andre Perez greeted the delegates to the Third United Nations Conference on the Law of the Sea by warning against "present day colonialism of the seas."[29] National liberation movements selected by the Organization of African Unity and the Arab League were accorded observer status at later law of the sea conferences as well as other meetings on global issues.[30] Resolutions and statements by third world leaders never fail to link the political and functional.

The same pattern has held in a series of U.N. authorized conferences on the environment, population, women's rights, and living conditions. Western initiatives in the 1972 Stockholm conference on environmental dangers were treated as a "conspiracy of the haves to keep the have nots down and out."[31] The same attitudes greeted Western concerns over population problems in Bucharest two years later. The General Assembly then found that demographic issues were linked to "inequitable economic structures and relations of dependence and exploitation."[32] In 1976, a conference in Vancouver on human settlements ended its work with a statement of the rights of Palestinians and a denunciation of racism (including Zionism).[33]

The themes of guilt, atonement, and reparations were carried to their logical extreme at the Sixth Special Session, at which the assembly passed the Declaration on the Economic Rights and Duties of States. This document heralded the coming of a "new world economic order." As a whole it was a strident denunciation of Western economic philosophy and practice. Notice was served that economic relationships would henceforth reflect a new set of moral and legal norms.

Western leaders were clearly alarmed. Without accepting the principles of the Charter of Economic Rights and Duties of Nations, the Western states expressed their concern with the plight of the developing countries, promised greater assistance, and pledged cooperative consultations to resolve third world grievances.[34] As a result, a more moderate resolution, which nevertheless reaffirmed all previous resolutions, was adopted unanimously in the next General Assembly.[35]

Despite the appearance of relative harmony, developing countries had made no concessions, and the West denied that it had changed its interpretation of economic relations. Thus, the U.S. representative Jacob M. Meyerson emphasized that the United States rejected "any implication that the world had embarked on establishment of something called 'the new international economic order.'" He then proceeded to qualify American acceptance of virtually every principle embraced by the Group of 77.

During the Thirty-First Session, the General Assembly adopted a number of actions critical of the industrialized countries. A resolution "regretted" the failure of political will of developed countries to implement the new economic order and the U.N. resolutions.[36] On two other resolutions, the United States cast the lone dissenting votes. One recommended a target of 0.7 percent on GNP for "official development assistance"; the other urged the redeployment of industry to developing countries.[37] The bitterness and hostility of the third world was manifested in a resolution on southern Africa. After "strongly condemning" economic and financial support for Rhodesia, the resolution specifically cited the United States (along with Israel, France, West Germany, and the United Kingdom) for providing economic and other aid for the government of South Africa.[38] Any lingering thought that American initiatives during the Seventh Special Session had appeased the developing countries had become fantasy by the end of 1976.

This should not have been surprising. The West insists on development programs based on self-help, productivity, individual agreements, and the preservation of traditional economic, political, and legal norms. Third world leaders demand redistribution of wealth, technological and other transfers, acceptance of the entire anticolonialist world view, and the abandonment of the foundations of Western economic theory and practice. Westerners insist on the separation of economics and politics. To anticolonialists, they are fused.

The combination of misunderstanding and clashing interests has serious consequences. Real dialogue, which is a precondition for successful cooperation, is precluded. Majoritarianism replaces negotiation. The legal, economic, and political practices of the United States are under constant attack. At the United Nations, the United States is the defendant. Majorities define the issues, control the processes, and establish the conditions for American participation. Under these conditions, the United States, despite its enormous wealth and importance for the solution of global problems, has minimal influence on world order strategies.[39] Loss of control over a system which owes its birth and daily sustenance to the United States, and which this country dominated for decades, is a damaging blow to American prestige. Occasional, usually defensive victories are often magnified and incorrectly interpreted as signs of restored influence.[40]

Such superficial optimism ignores the degree to which third world victories in the United Nations reduce chances for American support for their objectives. Following the Sixth Special Session, the National Trades Council, an organization representing 600 leading transnational corporations, warned that adoption of the new economic order "would seriously deter, if not fully shackle foreign private investment."[41] Public criticism is reflected also in Congress. During recent hearings in both houses, supporters have had to contend with increasing anger and skepticism. This was obvious at a hearing of the Sub-Committee on International Organization in 1975. Representative Philip Crane observed:

> Unfortunately, recent events have demonstrated that a majority of [United Nations] members do not seem to care about such things as respectability, responsibility, or reasonable adherence to the United Nations Charter, to say nothing of the feelings of the nation that has been the organization's political and financial angel.[42]

Similarly, Representative Buchanan of Alabama, asked:

Do you believe that this is an instrument within which we can work to serve these purposes in the world and to reach those goals in the world that we believe to be right, an instrument that is more valuable to have than not to have?[43]

Representative Rosenthal noted further that the United Nations magnified and institutionalized hostile positions.[44] Clearly, such attitudes make it more difficult for Congress to support financial aid for U.N. projects and for assistance to developing countries.[45]

Executive sensitivity to the growing criticism and disillusionment in and outside of Congress was expressed on December 6, 1974, when Ambassador John Scali noted that the United Nations was being used for confrontation which "sows the seeds of new conflicts." Numerical majorities, he said, "brutally disregrded the sensitivity of the minority." This "pursuit of mathematical majorities" amounted to the "tyranny of the majority." Scali observed that the continuation of irresponsible conduct could cause the American people and the Congress to be less generous towards the United Nations in the future.[46]

This remarkable speech reflected a near complete reversal of U.S. attitudes. Nevertheless, it was not followed by fundamental policy revisions. Scali's successor, Ambassador Moynihan, was sharply and openly critical of majority postures, but his short tenure was marked by criticism of his "undiplomatic" style. William Scranton, more "polite" and low-key than Moynihan, revealed no particular policy differences. If the Scranton appointment was designed to soothe third world delegates, this tendency has been accelerated by the appointment of Andrew Young. Ambassador Young, a civil rights activist, indicated that the Carter administration would adjust policy at the United Nations to align American positions with those of the majority.[47] The attitude underlying this supposition is so dissimilar to our analyses that we must assume that the guidelines which follow will not be heeded for some time, if ever.

Guidelines

As a first step, the U.S. Mission to the United Nations should be strengthened. This may be opposed by those who are "disillusioned" with the organization and supported by others who "believe" in the United Nations. We are in neither camp. We contend that the United Nations is a useful and effective diplomatic weapon in the service of the global and local conflict goals of the third world, Arab, and Communist states. Complex political objectives, frequently in direct opposition to U.S. interests, are camouflaged by constant reference to human rights, charter principles, or international law.

At the mission, foreign policy analysts are required in the areas of Middle Eastern and African politics, and economic and social issues. They should be examining and reporting on the various initiatives in the United Nations from the perspective of motivation and impact on U.S. policy and interests. Knowledge of parliamentary procedures, precedents, and the language of the charter are necessary but minor skills. It is more important to relate the timing of a Security Council debate on the rights of the Palestinian Arabs to impending local elections on the West Bank, and the effect of a subsequent victory for hardliners on the prospects of a negotiated agreement. Extraordinary steps must be taken to avoid, where possible, being isolated in the vote when the intention of a resolution's sponsors is to weaken the U.S. role as mediator in southern Africa or the Middle East. Political skill is required to determine whether or how to participate in processes, e.g., generalized conferences on global issues, which will become forums for attitudes which are both hostile towards the United States and inimical to the realization of the purported objectives. The shift to minority status requires a more substantial diplomatic input than when the United States dominated the organization. It is comparatively easy to promote one's own policies, as during the first twenty years of the organization. It is much more difficult to calculate the intentions of others and draw the political consequences.

The dominant political voices at the United Nations are not likely to be supplanted in the foreseeable future. U.S. efforts to recapture former influence are doomed to failure; therefore, schemes to reform the organization are inappropriate. Majorities will not accept weighted voting formulas, minority vetoes in the General Assembly and other majoritarian organs and agencies, or other plans designed to redress the balance. If anything, the new majority will press for means to overcome minority obstructionism by enhancing the authority of forums which it controls (the West did precisely this in the Uniting for Peace Resolution in 1950), and by attacking the veto in the Security Council. Instead of initiating reform proposals, therefore, the United States should avoid such debates and stress whatever minority rights are written into the charter and rules of procedure.

This general attitude is required also in those areas where the United Nations has assumed the role of moral conscience of the world. Promotion of human rights is dysfunctional in the United Nations. The very concept of universal human rights is undermined by having them made the subject of ad hoc procedures. To the extent that an American administration is committed to supporting human rights, therefore it should take action outside the United Nations. Simultaneously, the reasons for following this course should be publicized in order to mobilize support for alternative means of achievement.

It is obvious that the United States has accepted responsibility for, and has an interest in contributing to, alleviation of hunger, sickness, poor housing, illiteracy, and other afflictions of developing peoples. No other country has contributed so much in these areas through Marshall Plan, Point Four, Alliance for Progress, other aid programs, the World Bank, and financial assistance to the U.N. agencies. The commitment is vast, and it has not been dependent on the articulation of needs by developing countries in the United Nations. Paradoxically, the United States is subjected to the most extreme attacks on these global issues, and is increasingly isolated in such forums as the specialized agencies, the U.N. Conference on Trade and Development, the United Nations Development Program, the Economic and Social Council, and, of course, special and regular sessions of the General Assembly.

This response to American policy on global matters stems from a world view which integrates anticolonial and anti-Israeli objectives with economic and social approaches to the redistribution of wealth. The majority demands endorsement of unacceptable economic principles and the abandonment of flexibility in dealing with complex political issues. From its defensive, minority posture the United States can do little more than protest against the "excesses" of the majority. Efforts to inject a more positive note, as in the Seventh Special Session, are co-opted and converted into majority successes.

Given the importance of global issues and the commitment of the United States to their solution, it becomes imperative to reappraise American involvement in United Nations processes. Repeated defeats in general conferences, which conclude with resolutions embracing the total anticolonialist ideology, diminish public and congressional support for administration policy. It follows, then, that, in the absence of assurances that the majority will adhere to conference objectives, the United States should not participate. It would then be easier to implement policies together with those states wishing to cooperate. In other situations, the United States should make clear that it will respond to unacceptable tactics by using other forums and means to carry out global policies. Through such actions, the United States may regain the stature and influence which is commensurate with the United States' importance and contribution to the solution of global problems.

Notes

1. See, for example, John G. Stoessinger, *The United Nations and the Superpowers* (New York: Random House, 1970).

2. See testimony of Richard Falk. Hearing, U.S. Senate, Committee on Foreign Relations, 94th Congress, 1st sess., pp. 153-161.

3. Abraham Yeselson and Anthony Gaglione, *A Dangerous Place* (New York: Viking Press, 1974).
4. Ibid., pp. 32-33.
5. Ibid., pp. 37-42.
6. Ibid., pp. 43-45.
7. Ibid., pp. 33-34.
8. See as one of many examples, Catherine G. Teng, *Synopses of U.N. Cases in the Field of Peace and Serenity, 1946-1967* (Carnegie Endowment for International Peace, 1968), *passim*.
9. More than 50 percent of Soviet vetoes were cast on membership issues.
10. Abraham Yeselson and Anthony Gaglione, "What Really Happened When Arafat Spoke at the U.N.," *Worldview* (March 1975), pp. 49-55.
11. General Assembly Resolution 31/6 (XXXI).
12. SCOR, Meeting 1022, October 23, 1962.
13. SCOR, Meeting 357, September 16, 1948.
14. Yeselson and Gaglione, *A Dangerous Place*, pp. 126-127.
15. Ibid., pp. 127-128.
16. Richard Falk, testimony, p. 154.
17. Speech to AFL-CIO convention, *The New York Times*, October 4, 1975, p. 1.
18. General Assembly Resolution 3379 (XXX).
19. For an account of the pressures which caused U.S. withdrawal of the complaint concerning Soviet dissidents, see *The New York Times*, March 8, 1977, p. 3.
20. Of the 32 members of the Commission, only seven (Austria, Canada, France, Italy, United Kingdom, United States, and West Germany) are likely to apply Western liberal standards to human rights questions. In its 1976 report, the commission cited specific violations in only Palestine, Chile, southern Africa, and Cyprus. U.N. document E/CN 4/1213, 1976.
21. See *U.N. Monthly Chronicle* 13, no. 11, p. 16.
22. Yeselson and Gaglione, *A Dangerous Place*, pp. 85-91, 95-99, 100-108.
23. Ibid., p. 43.
24. See General Assembly Resolution 1616 (XVI), April 1, 1961.
25. See Yeselson and Gaglione, *Worldview*, pp. 50-51.
26. An obvious example is the "Zionism is racism" resolution. See General Assembly Resolution 31/20 (XXXI) wherein the question of Palestine is considered without any reference to Israel or the rights of Israelis.
27. The Chinese Communists use this tactic whenever possible in debate. See, for example, the *United Nations Chronicle* 12, no. 9, p. 28.
28. Thomas J. Farer, "The United States and the Third World: A Basis for Accommodation," in Steven L. Spiegel, ed., *At Issue, Politics in the World Arena* (New York: St. Martins Press, 1977), pp. 111-112.
29. *U.N. Monthly Chronicle* 11, no. 7, p. 32.

30. For the Law of the Sea Conference, see *U.N. Monthly Chronicle* 11, no. 8 p. 111. At the 19th session of the 48-member Governing Council of the United Nations Development Program funds were voted for the "travel and other expenses of National Liberation Movements recognized by the O.A.U." Ibid. The report of the preparatory body for the United Nations Water Conference in March 1977 also included a provision for observer status to national liberation movements. See *U.N. Monthly Chronicle* 13, no. 3, p. 28.

31. See Daniel P. Moynihan, "The United States in Opposition," in Steven L. Spiegal, *At Issue, Politics in the World Arena,* p. 98.

32. *U.N. Monthly Chronicle* 11, no. 8, p. 97.

33. *The New York Times,* June 13, 1976, p. 20.

34. See Moynihan speech, *U.N. Chronicle* 12, no. 9.

35. General Assembly Resolution 3362 (S-VII).

36. General Assembly Resolution 31/178 (XXXI).

37. See *U.N. Chronicle* 13, no. 1, p. 51; and also General Assembly Resolution 31/63 (XXXI).

38. General Assembly Resolution 31/7 (XXXI).

39. This is less true, of course, in fora such as the IMF, IBRD, and the GATT.

40. A recent example of this occurred following two votes in the Executive Council of the International Labor Organization. The council voted not to investigate labor conditions in Palestine and establish a screening procedure to sift out issues which were not germane. American delegate Daniel I. Horowitz described these actions as "an important step toward the return to basic Principles." *The New York Times,* March 10, 1977.

41. *The New York Times,* December 13, 1974, p. 11.

42. Hearings, Sub-Committee on International Organizations, Committee on Foreign Affairs, February 4-5, 1975, p. 79.

43. Ibid., p. 31.

44. Ibid., p. 63.

45. One might note, in contrast, that Congress has *increased* aid to multilateral institutions.

46. *The New York Times,* December 7, 1964, p. 1.

47. Just before his appointment to the U.N. post, Mr. Young spoke about the United States in the United Nations: "Once we get on the right side of the moral issues in this world, then we can have an orderly approach to the problems of the Middle East and a genuine dialogue on the international economic order. . . . Up to now we've come down on the wrong side of too many issues." *The New York Times,* December 15, 1976, p. B13.

34. A New U.S. Policy Toward the United Nations
Ad Hoc Group on United States Policy Toward the United Nations

The members of the Ad Hoc Group on United States Policy toward the United Nations who cooperated in preparing this report are united by a conviction that we wish to record at the outset: that a central task of U.S. foreign policy in the crucial last quarter of the twentieth century is the building of effective world institutions to help solve critical world problems of vital importance to the American people and to all peoples and nations. These problems include the danger of the spread of local conflicts, the proliferation of nuclear and conventional weapons, the increasing financial burden of the arms race, the population explosion, the deterioration of the environment, food and energy shortages, underdevelopment, unemployment, and mass poverty.

Despite our country's differences with the developing nations, we believe that if the United States seeks sincerely to accommodate their genuine concerns, many will find it in their interest to cooperate with us in dealing constructively with these world problems through the U.N. system.

This chapter was prepared by an Ad Hoc Group on United States Policy Toward the United Nations, comprising scholars professionally concerned with international affairs, former U.S. delegates to the United Nations, and nongovernmental organization leaders. The ad hoc group met periodically during 1975-1976 and reached a consensus on the broad conclusions set forth in the report. While all the participants agreed on these conclusions, they did not necessarily concur in every specific recommendation. Members: Morris B. Abram, Thomas Buergenthal, John Carey, Norman Cousins, Seymour M. Finger, Thomas M. Franck, Richard N. Gardner, Bertram H. Gold, Rita Hauser, Philip E. Hoffman, Sidney Liskofsky, Charles William Maynes, John Norton Moore, Hans Morgenthau, Leo Nevas, Nathan Pelcovits, and Jerome Shestack.

We are deeply concerned that international performance in these areas is inadequate when measured against need. This is not the fault primarily of the United States. In the main, our country has played a role of constructive leadership in the history of the United Nations, and its overall record compares favorably to that of most other countries, many of which have used the United Nations for political warfare while demonstrating little concern for pressing global problems. Nevertheless, we find inescapable the conclusion that U.S. participation in the U.N. system has followed a declining path of effectiveness under both Republican and Democratic administrations during the last decade.

Rethinking the Problem

Recent disquieting events at the United Nations—the extremist rhetoric about economic issues, the campaign to delegitimize Israel by branding Zionism as racism and by calling on states to desist from economic aid to Israel, the failure to deal with international terrorism, the votes against Guam bases and for Puerto Rican independence, the use of the General Assembly as a forum for vilifying certain countries, including the United States (e.g., General Amin's speech), the tolerance by the membership of such practices, the failure to act on Lebanon and Angola—have intensified American disenchantment with the United Nations and its agencies. They have produced widespread doubts about its value and have led to a congressional call for a reassessment of our multilateral diplomacy.

Partly the problem is immediate and tactical—how to stem the tide of accelerating political abuse and misuse of the United Nations' deliberative bodies. This is not solely a task of ensuring due process and procedural fairness. To be sure, it remains necessary to protest against such acts as the twisting of the rules by the Security Council to seat the PLO with all the privileges of a member state. But procedural abuse is not the crux of the problem. Rather the problems in the assembly, and indeed throughout the U.N. system, have been caused by politicized behavior which has undermined the institutional capacity of the system to deal in an impartial and effective manner with questions of world concern. The question we face is whether it is possible to turn around political behavior so that the institution will become again an environment for useful dialogue and constructive action.

Beyond this, events have illuminated a basic and chronic impairment in the U.N. system: during the past decade, while the involvement of the United Nations in pressing global problems has increased, in many important respects it has become less responsive to the objective requirements of international cooperation. It has become less efficient in coping with world order problems such as: peacekeeping, economic development, promotion of human rights, protecting the environment, eradicating epidemic diseases, regulating the airways, and managing ocean resources—problems which are too global and too complex to be solved by one nation or even by all the Western nations together.

It has become increasingly difficult for the United States and other nations to conduct constructive multilateral diplomacy in the United Nations. Accelerated political abuse of U.N. bodies, the assertiveness of majorities that dictate not only the agenda but one-sided solutions, and their insensitivity to legitimate national interests, including those of the United States, have put strains on the effectiveness and credibility of multilateral institutions. Many Americans are so outraged by these developments that they have lost sight of the functional value to be found in U.N. agencies and U.N. activities. Congressional and popular support has been eroded to the point where any program that bears the U.N. label is suspect.

A Possible Approach

Whatever weight one attributes to the various causes of our predicament, clearly a corrective strategy is imperative. Its aim should be not punitive but remedial. The United States must act and be perceived as acting out of a genuine concern for the restoration of the United Nations as an effective institution for dealing with the world's vital interests. This means synchronizing *tough diplomacy*—speaking forthrightly to set the record straight, defending our interests vigorously and delineating the limits beyond which the United States will not be pushed—with a *readiness to accommodate* honest grievances and to bargain about the real economic and other interests of the devleoping world.

Some have criticized the policy of standing up to the majority as incompatible with accommodation, but this sets up false alternatives. A viable strategy recognizes that these are two sides of the same coin. Philosophically and in terms of practical politics, Congress and the American people will not make sacrifices or agree to favorable economic arrangements in an institutional context where America's legitimate concerns are ignored or brushed aside and the negotiating atmosphere is poisoned by venomous political debates. There can be no fundamental improvement in the United Nations or room for accommodation save by dealing with the third world—and the Communists for that matter—in a spirit of realism and candor. The developing nations must know that the United States cannot respond to their economic concerns if they are insensitive to vital political and economic interests about which the United States feels strongly.

This understood, our strategy should be to appeal to those elements in the developing world that are more interested in solving economic and political problems than in scoring ideological points. Accommodating such elements proved successful at the Seventh Special Session on economic issues in September 1975. Our purpose should be to identify and pursue interests we share with the moderates and pragmatists, to explore opportunities for working with leaders of developing nations who are ready to engage in collective bargaining. We must take into account the possibility of bargains in which we try to satisfy the priority concerns of the less developed countries (LDCs) in their economic development and in eliminating the remnants of colonialism in exchange for their cooperation in peacekeeping, enlarging respect for the entire range of human rights, and cooperating in solving world order problems. This strategy is credible only if the developing world is seen not as an ideological monolith but as an aggregation of nations with varying interests, many of which are in harmony with ours. Our approach should be positive, not only because there are limits to the power of negative thinking, but also because we can succeed in the long run only by enlisting allies and mobilizing the nondoctrinaire pro-U.N. constituency, including those in the third world.

Next Steps for U.S. Policy

Total withdrawal from the United Nations or total nonparticipation are not really sensible options, though it may be necessary to consider selective participation. The purpose is not to weaken the United Nations but to improve it. Nor is there profit in absenting ourselves totally from the assembly, which can often serve as a useful platform and negotiating forum. Even the most skeptical see value in U.N. peacekeeping operations and in the United Nations' public service activities. Even Israel, despite understandable frustrations, has chosen to stay in the United Nations which provides a certificate of legitimacy and an arena of communication in a cold diplomatic world.

We believe that the national interest in a stronger and more responsible United Nations would be best served by new U.S. policies in the following areas.

Making Multilateral Affairs Part of General Diplomacy

The key to successful action in the United Nations is to perceive and conduct multilateral diplomacy as an organic part of total diplomacy. Issues and interests do not divide neatly into bilateral and U.N. boxes. In recent years, the United States has come to perceive that a weak position in the United Nations can have a negative influence on its bilateral diplomacy. Just as poorly conceived bilateral diplomacy, particularly in the third world, undermines the U.S. influence in the United Nations, so do setbacks to the United States in the United Nations complicate U.S. bilateral objectives. We need to pay more attention to what goes on in U.N. and other multilateral forums, using American diplomatic leverage as needed to accomplish our purposes. Our concern about events at the 1975 General Assembly was twofold: that it impeded our foreign policy objectives, notably by making a Middle East settlement more difficult and that it impaired the integrity of the United Nations. Unless the threat to the integrity of the institutions of the United Nations is overcome or contained we may be compelled to fashion new international arrangements to cope with world order tasks.

We must, then, convey the message that we take very seriously policies and votes in the United Nations. A clear-cut measurement of "responsible" U.N. behavior is hard to define; but it is possible to discern consistent patterns of constructive as against destructive conduct in utterances and votes. The overall pattern of a country's U.N. behavior, and whether such behavior supports or undercuts our major foreign policy aims, should be taken into account in our overall relationship with them. U.N. behavior is an aspect of the national politics and diplomacy of each country and necessarily affects the bilateral relationship. The Department of State has recently recognized this fact by appointing an official in the Bureau of International Organization Affairs to monitor patterns of multilateral behavior, discern where vital American interests are at stake, and draw policy implications. The department is expected to alert foreign nations in advance about issues and votes the United States considers of major importance. This can be a constructive development provided that countries are not penalized for defending legitimate national interests (e.g., supporting a resolution on commodity agreements opposed by the United States), but rather for pursuing a consistent course of negative behavior that serves no genuine national interest and weakens international institutional structures. In implementing this diplomacy certain steps are indicated.

Diplomatic representations. Diplomatic approaches should be initiated with key nations (including missions by the regional assistant secretary of state) for a candid review of U.N. events and their implications. The purpose should be to define and register the American interest, and these nations should be informed that American cooperation on matters of interest to them cannot be unrelated to their behavior in U.N. forums and agencies on matters of interest to us. The United States must be concerned when countries with no active interest in such issues as the Middle East, Korea, Guam, Puerto Rico, and the Panama Canal, pursue certain policies and cast their votes for reasons of propaganda, bloc solidarity, or logrolling.

Such diplomatic approaches are especially imperative where nations have played an egregiously damaging role. On the diplomatic front, also, the United States should not leave the USSR in doubt about its displeasure over the major role played by Soviet representatives behind the scenes in launching the anti-Zionism offensive. This is a grave compromise of détente and calls into question Soviet cooperation in fostering a peaceful settlement of the Midddle East dispute.

In general, the most effective way to influence policies is for our ambassadors and their staffs to communicate more frequently and at a higher level with host governments on U.S. policies in multilateral institutions. This is particularly important since many of the 147 U.N. delegates act without instructions on the vast majority of U.N. agenda items. To be effective, our diplomacy must be consistent. Thus, courting a country whose behavior in international matters—e.g., early recognition of the Popular Movement for the Liberation of Angola (MPLA) in Angola, voting for the anti-Zionism resolution, unhelpful statements by the foreign minister—has been damaging is hardly effective diplomacy.

Diplomacy toward the Third World. The success of such a diplomatic approach toward the third world hinges on a specially designed effort to persuade moderate leaders that their true interests lie not in confrontationist demands of "have-nots" on the "haves," but in cooperating in seeking solutions to common world problems. On many real issues, such as providing help in capital formation and technology, aiding agricultural development and stabilizing export earnings, responsible leadership can be induced to seek negotiated solutions rather than confrontation. Moreover, we share with them real interests in promoting peaceful settlement of conflict, combating terrorism, and enlarging the area of respect for human rights. Approaches to the moderates need to be undertaken on a selective basis by analyzing the record. Many third world countries are likely to be receptive to such an approach and would join in cooperative and constructive efforts at the United Nations.

Aid and Trade. As a guideline in aid-trade policy a rule should be adopted that a consistent pattern of responsible or irresponsible behavior on important multilateral issues will be taken into account in bilateral aid and trade relationships. For example, granting access to

Eximbank credits and pricing arrangements on commodities involves hard choices in allocating limited resources which should take into consideration the entire spectrum of relationships, including the multilateral record. We believe Congress will properly want to consider the multilateral dimension of other nations' policies, even where the administration does not.

In aid-giving the principle needs to be established that responsible U.N. behavior is an important consideration in allocating development assistance. Under a new provision in the International Development and Food Assistance Act of 1975, assistance may be withheld from any country with a "consistent pattern of gross violations of internationally recognized human rights." A comparable approach should be taken by the United States where there is a consistent pattern of irresponsible behavior in multilateral bodies. This would not be an absolute criterion but a factor to be given due weight and balanced against other national interest considerations. (Humanitarian considerations should continue to be overriding, so that emergency relief in famine and other types of disaster would be dispensed on humanitarian grounds irrespective of the balance sheet of responsible behavior in U.N. forums.) To be effective, such a policy requires rebuilding our foreign aid program as a major tool of U.S. foreign policy, including a commitment to an increase in official development assistance and appropriation in full of our authorized contribution to the International Development Association (IDA). Otherwise our leverage is weak and it is unrealistic to speak of orchestrating aid policy according to a pattern of behavior in multilateral bodies.

UN context. It is more complicated to apply this approach to U.S. contributions to U.N. budgets without hurting institutions and programs we favor. (See Chart A.) Withholding money from assessed U.N. budgets as a sign of displeasure with certain programs presents difficulties. The financial management rules of the United Nations prevent the earmarking of contributions. Moreover, not paying dues to which we are committed by treaty (though the Soviets and others have occasionally followed this course) raises serious legal questions. If we delay payment it should be made clear that this is not a vindictive act but a principled move in line with the "Goldberg reservation" of 1965, which declared that we reserved the right to withhold funds from "certain" activities for "strong and compelling" reasons. Cutting off or reducing donations to voluntary programs presents no legal problems, but such programs generally support humanitarian and public service activities we favor, as the appended table makes clear. (See Chart B.) Besides, such broadside cuts could hurt responsible and friendly U.N.

CHART A

Assessed Contributions to International Organizations

[In Thousands of dollars; fiscal years]

		1976	1977 request
A.	United Nations and specialized agencies:		
	1. United Nations	$77,335	$87,185
	2. United Nations Educational, Scientific and Cultural Organization	....	....
	3. International Civil Aviation Organization	6,292	5,790
	4. World Health Organization	29,319	38,155
	5. Food and Agriculture Organization	13,570	20,798
	6. International Labor Organization	6,729	20,260
	7. International Telecommunication Union	1,308	1,470
	8. World Meteorological Organization	1,683	2,295
	9. Intergovernmental Maritime Consultative Organization	143	259
	10. Universal Postal Union	168	316
	11. World Intellectual Property Organization	105	136
	12. World Tourism Organization	....	....
	13. International Atomic Energy Agency	7,429	11,113
B.	Inter-American organizations:		
	1. Inter-American Indian Institute	62	88
	2. Inter-American Institute of Agricultural Sciences	4,405	4,758
	3. Pan American Institute of Geography and History	195	195
	4. Pan American Railway Congress Association	15	15
	5. Pan American Health Organization	15,862	19,009
	6. Organization of American States	25,001	27,005
C.	Regional organizations:		
	1. South Pacific Commission	457	713
	2. North Atlantic Treaty Organization	11,523	13,175
	3. North Atlantic Assembly	171	215
	4. Southeast Asia Treaty Organization	587	467
	5. Colombo Plan Council for Technical Cooperation	12	13
	6. Organization for Economic Cooperation and Development	11,237	15,850
D.	Other international organizations:		
	1. Interparliamentary Union	105	128
	2. International Bureau of the Permanent Court of Arbitration	2	3
	3. International Bureau for the Publication of Customs Tariffs	28	28
	4. International Bureau of Weights and Measures	165	209
	5. International Hydrographic Organization	25	25
	6. International Wheat Council	91	....
	7. International Coffee Organization	400	....
	8. International Institute for the Unification of Private Law	22	24
	9. Hague Conference on Private International Law	23	27
	10. Maintenance of Certain Lights in the Red Sea	6	6
	11. International Bureau of Exhibitions	11	17
	12. Customs Cooperation Council	796	896
	13. International Center for the Study of the Preservation and Restoration of Cultural Property	115	156
	14. International Organization for Legal Metrology	18	19
	15. International Agency for Research on Cancer	430	626
	16. General Agreement on Tariffs and Trade	1,969	2,186
	17. International Office of Epizootics	19	27
	Total	217,853	274,000

457

CHART B

VOLUNTARY CONTRIBUTIONS TO INTERNATIONAL ORGANIZATIONS AND PROGRAMS UNDER THE FOREIGN ASSISTANCE ACT

[In thousands of dollars]

	Fiscal year –			
	1975 actual	1976 proposed	Transition quarter proposed	1976 estimate (percent)
United Nations programs:				
U.N. Development Program	$77,897	$120,000	....	25.9
U.N. Children's Fund	17,000	15,000	....	19.4
International Atomic Energy Agency Operational Fund	2,500	3,500	....	27.6
World Meteorological Organization, Voluntary Assistance Program	1,500	1,500	....	24.0
U.N. Food and Agriculture Organization, World Food Program	1,500	1,500	....	29.7
U.N. Institute for Training and Research	400	400		26.7
International Secretariat for Voluntary Service	60	....		
U.N. Relief and Works Agency	23,200	26,700	13,400	21.0
U.N. Funds for Southern Africans	50	50	....	.04
World Heritage Fund	143	50	....	87.0
U.N. Disaster Relief Organization	[2]750	....		
Organization of American States[3]	....	20,800	5,800	66.0
Special multilateral fund for education, science and culture	....	7,590	2,080	66.0
Special multilateral fund, special projects	....	6,000	1,740	66.0
Special development assistance fund	....	6,410	1,760	66.0
Inter-American Export Promotion Center	....	800	220	66.0
Total, United Nations and OAS programs	125,000	189,500	19,200	....
U.N. Environment Program Fund[4]	5,000	7,500	....	31.0
Indus Basin:[5]				
Loans	200	10,000	....	28.0
Grants	9,000	22,500	4,500	78.0
Total, international organizations and programs	139,200	229,500	23,700	....
Other appropriations:				
Population planning and health:[6]				
U.N. Fund for Population Activities	20,000	21,000	4,600	28.0
Public Law 93-570 (UNRWA)	10,000	....		
Middle East Special Requirements Fund (UNRWA)	6,000	....		
International Narcotics Control[7]	4,000	4,000	....	[8]80.0
International Disaster Assistance	(2)	[2]200	....	[5]19.0
Security Supporting Assistance; U.N. Force in Cyprus	9,600	9,600	4,800	45.0
Grand Total	184,000	264,300	33,100	....

[1] Funds will not be used due to prohibitory language of Section 9 of Public Law 93-559.
[2] U.S. contribution of $750,000 to the U.N. Disaster Relief Office for fiscal year 1975 from international organizations account. For fiscal year 1976 $200,000 is proposed as a grant from the International Disaster Assistance Fund.
[3] Fiscal year 1974 and fiscal year 1975 funding from "Selected Countries and Organizations."
[4] Authorized by the U.N. Environment Program Participation Act of 1975.
[5] Program discussed in Near East South Asia volume.
[6] Program discussed in interregional volume.
[7] Funds requested and programs discussed in the Department of State presentation.
[8] Represents average pledges from all donors for calendar years 1975-77, excludes donations from other donors to UNDRO for specific disasters.

members as well as others.

We believe the following specific actions deserve consideration:

1. While continuing vigilant participation, the United States should continue its policy of delaying payment of dues to the U.N. Educational, Scientific, and Cultural Organization (UNESCO) and other agencies that persist in discriminatory or other improper actions.

2. The United States should disengage selectively from "tainted" programs, such as the action program in support of the decade to eliminate racism, which was redefined last November to include Zionism. This would implement the policy declared by the U.S. representative in the Fifth (Administrative and Financial) Committee, December 1975, that the United States could "no longer support this program."

The principle here is that any human rights or other meritorious program that is politically distorted ceases to be desirable. Credibility and principle now demand that we deduct from the U.S. contribution our share (25 percent) of the cost for any such program. Though the gesture would be mainly symbolic, it would help establish the principle. To drive home the point that we oppose not the commendable purposes of the program for the decade but its perversion, we should add an equivalent amount to voluntary U.N. programs we favor.

Selective Participation in UN Agencies and Programs

The United States should concentrate its energies on those agencies and programs where possibilities for constructive diplomacy are most promising. For political and security issues this means the Security Council. For despite the capacity of third world coalitions to exercise a passive veto, U.S. and allied interests can still be protected there and constructive peacekeeping action undertaken. On economic matters, action responsibility should be vested, to the largest extent possible, in the World Bank, the International Monetary Fund (IMF) and a reformed and strengthened General Agreement on Tariffs and Trade (GATT).

The United States should continue to participate actively and to assert leadership in the negotiations on the law of the sea, designed to produce agreement for the orderly use and management of the oceans and their resources—a major objective of U.S. foreign policy. Contrariwise, the United States should disengage from conferences and activities which reflect a perversion of technical agendas by "politicization" or discriminatory practices. Walkouts of U.S. and likeminded delegations—as occurred at the UNESCO world-media conference over its incorporation of the Zionism equals racism resolution in the official declaration—should be encouraged. Moreover, the United States should refuse to pay its share of the costs of such conferences and programs and, where it has reason to expect moves to politicize, announce this intention in advance.

Within the General Assembly the United States should focus efforts where consensus is possible and when practical matters are being advanced, such as food, law of the sea, drug abuse control, and protection of the environment. Though the assembly clearly has a useful role in launching such programs, every effort should be made to ensure that it does not interfere in operational functions. Selective involvement in assembly proceedings means participating where constructive discussion is possible; articulating a strongly held minority view where necessary on matters such as disarmament, satellite broadcasting, and rules governing expropriation of foreign porperty; supporting worthwhile programs such as peacekeeping, drug abuse control, and law of the sea; and explaining and protecting our policies and negotiating positions. We should, of course, retain a watching brief over all assembly-related activities, but on marginal issues or those designed strictly for propaganda, we should downgrade our participation. France and China have often followed a policy of the empty seat; the United States left the anticolonialism committee when it became a forum for vilifying America and one-sided espousal of national liberation movements. Our departure did not end the abuse but the committee lost its audience. We should make it clear that our absence is not simply a symbolic protest, but a judgment of where serious business is being conducted and where it is not.

The United States should vote less to affect the outcome than to make a point: to affirm convictions and underline the diplomatic as against the legislative uses of the assembly. There is nothing wrong with splendid isolation on a vote: it helps make the point. In general, the voting process as a way of making decisions should be devalued and we should work for increased use of consensus procedures in the assembly's decisionmaking process, especially on economic issues.

To improve its parliamentary position and enhance opportunities for positive action in U.N. bodies, the United States should concert with like-minded states. Consultation should be conducted in advance on all key issues, as well as through normal diplomatic exchanges during sessions. We should take the lead in forming an informal "world order coalition"—maintaining rapid communication among foreign ministries on crucial multilateral issues and engaging in advance planning. The core of the coalition would be our European allies, Japan, and likeminded developing nations. Diplomatic action of this nature should of course be complemented by maintaining diplomatic liaison with other sympathetic countries. We should make clear that such a coalition is not intended to split the third world.

Structural Reforms

We should work much harder at reforming and strengthening the work of U.N. agencies, even while recognizing that the prospects may not be too promising in the short run because of the overheated atmosphere at the United Nations and because only limited benefits can be expected from improved mechanisms unless they are accompanied by political will. Most promising is the approach of the Group of Experts on the Structure of the U.N. System, which designed a new structure for economic cooperation. The Group has proposed that contentious items before the General Assembly and the Economic and Social Council (ECOSOC) be referred to negotiating groups for consultation and conciliation. These groups would include countries "principally interested in the subject matter," who would function in private under a full-time chairman (who may travel to capitals to attempt to conciliate positions), and may take a year or two to reach agreement. Pending agreement the plenary body would normally refrain from pressing issues to a vote and give conciliation a chance to succeed.

Reassessing the Utility of U.N. Agencies

The United States should take a hard look at international institutions to which it belongs to determine whether they are still workable and still promote major American and world order interests. Where the machinery is no longer serving the purpose for which it was established, or is working inefficiently because of political taint or bureaucratic petrifaction, the United States should take the lead in organizing new and more manageable groupings which reflect our interests and are better able to deal with emerging world problems.

More controversial, but inescapable if the reassessment of U.S. policy toward the United Nations is to be comprehensive, is to take another look at our membership and extent of participation in U.N. specialized agencies. Some have become politicized and debased; some may no longer serve the national interest of the United States or even the broader world objectives of standard-setting, delivery of technical aid, and transnational communication for which they were created. The purpose of such an appraisal is not to kill the agency—others may find value in them—but to calculate whether we still have a net interest in belonging ourselves. The presumption should be for staying in, but U.S. policy should not exclude the option of renouncing membership in certain agencies when a careful appraisal indicates that our interest in a cooperative world order would be better served by getting out.

Pursuing Shared Interests with the Third World

Ultimately, effective multilateral diplomacy rests on the assumption that the West shares a common interest with much of the developing world in negotiated solutions to common economic and political problems. It is tied to a shared perception about the need to cooperate through international institutions and to fashion improved international arrangements to cope with world order problems. While the attitudes of the developing nations may differ from those of the West on many of these world order issues, we believe accommodations in the mutual interest are still possible.

Colonialism. A more positive American stance on southern African and human rights problems could help defuse the colonialist issue. In the United Nations, particularly because of the Byrd amendment, we are seen as lacking concern about colonialism and racism. Secretary of State Kissinger's African policy speech in Lusaka was a major step forward. Repeal of the Byrd amendment (which puts us in default of Security Council sanctions), joining the council on Namibia, a more accommodating stance on commissions of inquiry for southern Africa, and paying more attention to Africa in our diplomacy are other measures that will give the United States moral leverage.

Human Rights. Accommodation on colonialism should be linked to a more active posture on humanitarian and human rights considerations in foreign policy. A fitting bicentennial action would be U.S. adherence to the conventions on genocide, racial discrimination, forced labor, and the two covenants on human rights. (Of twenty-two treaties drafted by U.N. bodies the United States is a party to only three: the Supplementary Convention on Slavery, the Protocol Relating to the Status of Refugees, and the Convention on the Political Rights of Women.)

Even more important, we should call attention to human rights violations anywhere in the world on an objective basis and underscore our concern over the disturbing trend in the Human Rights Commission and other forums of deviation from their proper role as expert bodies examining issues on their merits. We should stress that we cannot accept the lack of balance in the human rights activities of these bodies—the disproportionate concentration of unsustained and exaggerated charges against one country as against the lack of interest in more serious violations elsewhere, the singling out of oppression in one country while turing a blind eye to political repression, torture, and mass murder in many other countries. And we should call attention to inhumane practices wherever they occur. We should intensify efforts to persuade Africans and Asians that our concern and theirs ought to extend not only to institutionalized racial/ethnic discrimination (Article 7 of the Universal Declaration to Human Rights) but also to mass murder (Article 3), torture (Article 5), arbitrary and unfair detention and trial (Articles 9, 10, 11), and denial of the right to emigration (Article 13).

We should seek common ground with countries which are beginning to share our perception about the importance of upgrading civil and political rights and combating the grosser forms of oppression. Specifically, an effort should be made to get their support for unblocking the implementation procedure under ECOSOC resolution 1503 and ending the selective morality applied in the operation of this and other implementation efforts of the Human Rights Commission and Sub-Commission on Prevention of Discrimination and Protection of Minorities.

A Just Economic Deal. The paramount issue for the developing countries is the economic relationship. The United States should regain the momentum of the initiative at the special session in September 1975 convened to foster a constructive dialogue on development and economic cooperation. The final document (Resolution 3363) incorporated much of the American plan, notably these recommendations: a facility to stabilize export earnings through the International Monetary Fund, replenishment of the International Development Association, increased capitalization of the International Finance Corporation (IFC), an international energy institute, a center for the exchange of technological information, a world grain reserve and an International Fund for Agricultural Development. While the United States had reservations about some aspects of the final document, a satisfactory accord was achieved on specific provisions and larger objectives. Now we should move in concert with Western allies and cooperative third world nations to implement the promises and build the institutions.

The special session showed that with good will in negotiation a very substantial measure of agreement on real concerns can be reached. The main message to the developing world is that more is to be gained from working with us than against us. A related message: since much of the program depends on congressional action or concurrence (e.g., participation in the tin, coffee, and other commodity agreements, increased capitalization of the IFC, replenishment of the International Development Association, enlargement of quotas in the International Monetary Fund), responsible behavior in the United Nations may become a practical prerequisite to success. America, in turn, must commit itself to the goals of the Second Development Decade, including the aid target, and pursue vigorous efforts to provide the developing world with access to our markets under conditions which protect American workers either through generous adjustment assistance or scheduled import entry. We must give clear and convincing evidence that we care about the issue of world poverty. Only then is there hope of success for the strategy of tough diplomacy and accommodation of the real concerns of the third world.[1]

Conclusion

The cardinal feature of American strategy, then, should not be a test of strength with the third world but a test of whether pragmatic interests will override ideological fixations. We should make a sustained effort to reestablish American influence through the synchronized diplomacy described above. This will enable us to determine whether present trends can be overcome by American leadership and honest bargaining or whether the trends are irreversible. If grievances are real and aspirations concrete, there is room for collective bargaining, provided political leaders on all sides substitute statesmanship for showmanship, focus on practical programs rather than abstract doctrines, and show a decent respect for one another's political and economic concerns. In such bargaining we can be sympathetic and friendly. If the response is nonetheless to debase the institutions, to rely on steamroller majorities, to avoid consensus, and to try to "legislate" rather than negotiate far-reaching changes in the world order, our recourse is clear—to downgrade politicized U.N. institutions, to participate selectively, and to fashion new institutions and new groupings around real interests.

Notes

1. (Editor's note.) It is interesting to see how many of the policies advocated in section 6 (Pursuing Shared Interests with the Third World) have been espoused by the Carter administration; e.g., a stronger stand for majority rule in Namibia and Zimbabwe (Rhodesia) and against apartheid in South Africa; repeal of the Byrd Amendment; emphasis on human rights everywhere; U.S. adherence to the conventions on genocide, racial discrimination, and forced labor and the two covenants on human rights; a more sympathetic attitude toward commodity agreements; replenishment of the IDA, enlargement of quotas in the International Monetary Fund; and increased development aid.

35. American Goals in a Changing United Nations
Philip M. Klutznick

In 1945 Beardsley Ruml observed that, "Everyone believes the U.N. is essential today; after five years people will believe that the U.N. is the greatest vision of man; after ten years, doubts will begin to creep in about the U.N. and its place in the world but all of you will still believe in it; after fifteen years, there will be general assumption that it cannot succeed; but after twenty years, everybody will revere and love it as the only alternative to the demolition of the world."[1] Events since then have, on the whole, supported his assessment. He projected accurately the progressive shifts that would mark future attitudes toward the United Nations even while he erred in the timing of each individual phase. Thus, we are today only where he thought we would be in 1960. We have not as yet overcome those doubts about the United Nations's chances for survival and success that Ruml realized would eventually supplant the euphoria of the early post-war period. At the same time, the alternatives before us today are indeed as stark and as inescapable as he claimed they would be thirty years ago.

One need only turn to the issues of nuclear energy and nuclear proliferation to accept his argument. We have witnessed in recent years a steep increase in the world-wide spread of nuclear technology, equipment, and materials. Pressures for greater utilization of nuclear power to meet ever-expanding energy needs are as persistent in the industrial nations as they are in the developing countries. The growing

---

This chapter is adapted from remarks delivered on June 17, 1976, at a Conference on U.S. Objectives in the U.N. System, sponsored by the Ralph Bunche Institute on the United Nations of the Graduate School and University Center, City University of New York.

trade in nuclear power plants, reactors, and fuel has created new dangers. Not the least of these are atmospheric pollution, nuclear accidents, and heightened risks of diversion, theft, or sabotage.

More importantly, these developments have undermined any hope that the spread of nuclear weaponry can be contained. The nuclear facilities that are already operating throughout the world, together with those scheduled for construction in the next decade, will provide a large number of countries with enough plutonium both to meet most of their energy needs and to create substantial arsenals of nuclear bombs. Nuclear proliferation has become an irreversible reality. In such a world the only alternative to international cooperation and a mutual respect for national differences, as Ruml suggested, is universal destruction in a nuclear war.

Nuclear proliferation, however, is by no means the only concern that forces us to choose between international cooperation and universal anarchy. An examination of the wide range of concerns currently managed by the U.N. family of agencies clearly reflects a growing appreciation of the benefits to be derived from joint efforts to solve common problems. It would be immodest to claim, nevertheless, that such endeavors are limited to the United Nations or that its efforts have invariably met with success. But it is vital to remember that the United Nations is something more than the sum of its political resolutions or of those all too frequent public expressions of ill will and frustration.

To mark the thirtieth birthday of the United Nations, the United Nations Association of the United States of America published a *New York Times* supplement evaluating its performance and achievements. This publication reminds us that the United Nations is:

1) Supplying life saving vaccines world-wide; 2) Providing nearly 500 young specialists from 46 nations; 3) Helping to eliminate small pox; 4) Helping to control the population explosion; 5) Bringing milk to the world's children; 6) Helping to protect consumers; 7) Developing more jobs in Third World countries; 8) Helping to battle the drug problem; 9) Helping refugees; 10) Helping to safeguard nuclear reactors; 11) Helping to wage war on cancer; 12) Wiping out malaria; 13) Helping to bridge the literacy gap; 14) Providing disaster assistance; 15) Helping to ensure clean water; 16) Establishing Earthwatch—the world's first global environmental monitoring system; 17) Functioning as the world's weatherman; 18) Assisting in world air safety; 19) Improving world postal service; 20) Assisting in the fight against famine; and 21) Helping locate new natural resources.[2]

Moreover, despite justified criticisms of the United Nations's failures in peacekeeping and of the miserably unbalanced resolutions of the General Assembly and even of the Security Council, it must not be forgotten that the United Nations has helped settle disputes in almost fifty countries, and that three United Nations agencies have won Nobel Peace Prizes.

When, therefore, serious people suggest that we need not tolerate the United Nations's moral flaws because its purposes can be realized equally well through other, less tainted means, they permit their justified pique over a reprehensible act to outweigh their practical sense as well as their understanding of the world in which we live.

In the aftermath of the General Assembly vote on Zionism, U.S. Ambassador Moynihan said: "The General Assembly today grants symbolic amnesty—and more—to the murderers of six million European Jews. Evil enough in itself, but more ominous by far, is the realization that now presses upon us—that if there were no General Assembly, this could never have happened."[3] Had there been no General Assembly, the feelings expressed in that resolution might indeed never have surfaced in such a malignant form. But it would have been there nonetheless, to fester as a sore in the body politic until its poison would be beyond a serum or a cure. The same General Assembly that committed this sin against a small people provided a platform for Ambassador Moynihan to warn the world and especially the Western world of the danger in our midst. As a Jew who has lived through the generation of the Holocaust and the glorious rebirth of the Jewish commonwealth, I remember too well the blinders that the free world and many of us wore when the horrible events were in the making. It is better to face such threats when there is time to cope with them than to have them suddenly emerge when it is too late.

The battle between good and evil is not a novel experience for the world. This is our world and those of us who believe in good triumphing over evil ought not to express a liking for evil hiding itself to perform its satanic deeds. As distasteful and discouraging as it may be we ought to recognize that a major function of the U.N. system is to expose such violations and transgressions. If we then do not prevent their occurrence or stop them when we see them, we must not blame the United Nations, but rather the forces of good who fail to act.

In the past the United States has often expressed ambivalence about specific acts of the United Nations. Yet even when we disagreed we usually responded in a statesman-like fashion. More recently, we have acted less like a great power and more like the carping objectors whom we disdained not too many years ago. A former high official of the

State Department, Herbert Prochnow, put it wisely: "The problem in this country has been whether to participate actively in the United Nations or just butt into the world's arguments from time to time."[4]

What has created this doubt and confusion? Some unfortunate facts and too many fictions. Clearly, the General Assembly resolution on Zionism and racism is a disgrace. Yet, in reality, the General Assembly cannot make Zionism racism by calling it that. Supreme Court Justice Cardoza, in a much cited opinion, stated that a legislative body has tremendous power, but the power does not extend to declaring black white and white black.[5] I am deeply hurt by the majority that from time to time gangs up on a little state in which I have a profound interest. Nevertheless, Israel has not withdrawn and other states that have been deeply offended by the U.N. process have not withdrawn.

The fact is that cooperation is far more difficult to attain and sustain than war. It demands greater compassion, understanding, and patience. One could illustrate this by analyzing other acts of the General Assembly or the activities of its subsidiary bodies and its family of specialized agencies. But this would not greatly add to our knowledge or understanding of the United Nations. What we ought to realize, however, is that in international cooperation, as in bilateral diplomacy, there are no permanent enemies or permanent friends. Already some of the alignments of months past are weakening and shifting. In the future there are likely to be further shifts and realignments.

To help correct current prejudices and misconceptions we must examine more thoroughly past myths and fabrications about the United Nations. These are that: (1) there is an automatic permanent majority arrayed against us; and (2) the U.N. system costs too much and the United States pays too much of the cost.

In my years of involvement with the United Nations the first charge has been made by many different nations. We seem to consider any group that frequently disagrees with our position as part of an automatic majority aligned against us. It is my contention, however, that one can distinguish between at least three distinct eras of so-called prevailing majorities in the thirty year history of the United Nations. Moreover, in two of these periods it was the Western powers and their supporters which comprised the majorities.

At the outset and until about 1956 to 1960, there was a clear-cut Western majority which prevailed on all important issues. This was the period when the Soviet Union used its veto frequently. During this time the United States prided itself on not using the veto. It was during this era that the famous Soviet walkout and the U.N. Korean effort occurred. It was also during this time that Khrushchev pounded his shoe and demanded a Troika Secretary-General.

The transition between the first and the second period of Western majorities in the United Nations is marked by the year 1957. It was my first experience as a member of the U.S. delegation to the General Assembly. It was the year of Ghana's entry into the United Nations and of "Little Rock"; it was the year of our tightrope walk in Algeria and Senator John F. Kennedy's famous challenge on that issue; and it was the year of the Soviet sputnik and the U.S. defensive posture in space. It may have marked the beginning of the Western decline in influence, although we could still muster a majority in the United Nations. We still abstained from the use of the veto, but the signs were growing ominous.

The civil war in the Congo plus the accelerated admission of African states marked the beginning of a new era. The West began to split. France no longer accepted our approach to collective responsibility for political decisions if it disagreed. The Soviet Union and its compatriots cooled on the Congo for a variety of reasons, not the least of which was the assassination of Lumumba. Nevertheless, under the leadership of the United States, Canada, most of Europe (especially the Scandinavian states), and many other nations, including those from Latin America, we maintained a majority for the principle of international cooperation and collective responsibility for the financial costs, despite disagreements by member states over certain political actions that the United Nations took in the Congo. U Thant affirmed his devotion to that principle. The United States won one vote after another. The West, except France, momentarily saved the United Nations from bankruptcy with the bond issue. We won the vote to take the question of collective fiscal responsibility to the World Court. We won on the proposition that article 19 applied to such undertakings.

During this second period, the West could still muster majorities but it met with greater difficulties and it required stronger efforts. This phase ended in 1964, when the issue of suspending the vote of the USSR for nonpayment arose. The U.S. then accepted some vague promise from Mr. Gromyko and the French that if we desisted they would voluntarily help out. In 1965, a committee of fourteen nations was established to resolve this conflict. It was my duty to represent the United States in this seven-month effort. Nothing happened. The day of a new majority had dawned. It was the birthday of U.S. vetoes and the beginning of a decline in American reliance on multilateral diplomacy. Our policy in the United Nations became less clear; our devotion to the principles which gave birth to the United Nations were frequently enunciated but not so frequently implemented.

Our concern for the future of Africa and Latin America also declined at that point. Finally, defeats in Asia on the diplomatic front with the emergence of the People's Republic of China and the shelving of Taiwan, coupled with the debacle in Vietnam, found the United States uncomfortable in what it had come to perceive as its natural habitat. We became a defensive minority and increasingly began to abandon multilateralism.

OPEC, the oil embargo, the PLO, and the Zionism-racism resolution resulted, in part, from Western neglect of the non-Western world and in part from the realization among African and Asian states that closer cooperation among themselves would strengthen their position vis-à-vis the West both in and outside the United Nations. The Soviet group naturally aided in this. Some of the United Nations's sturdy supporters in the United States were shaken by this development. They moved into the camp of those who opposed and even hated the U.N. system—not only the General Assembly, but even the life-saving agencies that provided the only hope for a better future among less fortunate peoples.

In a generation we have gone from the majestic heights of unquestioned leadership through the trials of challenged leadership to the ignoble role of dissidents. In desperation, the United States has even adopted financial pressures similar to the tactics and behavior we deplored, condemned, and excoriated when practiced by others.

The nation which most consistently fought for the principle of collective responsibility now picks carefully among a wide array those issues it chooses to support. It ignores its commitments to the United Nations unless others agree with what it wants done. Though I concur with the U.S. position on almost every act we condemn, I find it demeaning for this country to use the power of a relatively miniscule commitment to try to compel agreement. This does injustice to the spirit of America; it despoils the concept of international cooperation; and it weakens the substance of our righteous indignation against the abuses of the U.N. system.

If our case is strong enough, let us stand on it to the end; let us, if need be, solemnly declare our intention not to tolerate any longer such institutionalized banditry. But unless we feel that this country cannot in good conscience continue to support the U.N. Charter, let us not ignore the facts and realities and, just as those we have condemned in the past, enthrone lies in their stead. To end our commitment to the principles and activities of the United Nations might indeed be damaging to many countries that form the present majority in the United Nations. But it is unlikely that we would derive any benefits from thus destroying the hope of universal cooperation that the United Nations embodies.

Our anger is justified. But our answer must be to protect and to encourage the best talents and the creative programs of the United Nations and its agencies; we must seek to immunize the U.N. system and the peoples of the world against the destructive, self-seeking behavior of some of its members. This would do us honor. But, to use the power of a small purse to embarrass others and to disavow our commitments weakens and demeans our country.

It has been said that the U.N. system and its work costs too much and that the United States pays too much of the cost. No doubt much of the work of the United Nations and its agencies could be performed more efficiently and less expensively. This of course is a charge that is currently levelled against every international body as well as most national and subordinate political bodies.

When the United States "blinked" at the time of the showdown (over the financing of the United Nations in 1964), one of the prices was the hope of settling the payments from other nations who had been defaulting on their assessments. These countries then asked for the establishment of a committee of fourteen experts to consider the whole financial problem and organizational problem of the United Nations. This committee produced a unanimous report, which like most recommendations of experts, was observed in the breach more than in the performance.

As recently as May 20, 1975, a group of experts found that the United Nations's total expenditures in 1974 amounted to $1,500,000,000 (not including the expenditures of the World Bank and the International Monetary Fund). About four-fifths of this was devoted to economic and social programs; consequently only $300 million was available for administrative expenses. It is significant that in past years the total expenditures of the United Nations and all its agencies represented only 0.4 percent of the gross national product of all members. It is estimated that in 1974 the total expenditure was equal to that which its members spent on armaments in only 36 hours.

The United Nations does have its share of waste and inefficiency. Its operations could be improved and made more productive. However, when one considers the enormous waste of world-wide military expenditures, it becomes clear that the total paid toward the achievement of peace is modest at best.

The charge has often been made that the United States pays more than its share. This raises an important question: What is our fair share in light of our dominant industrial and economic position in the world?

In the early days of the United Nations, Senator Vandenburg insisted that the United States pay less than its proportionate share of the world's gross national product because no one nation should dominate the budget of the United Nations. Later that amount was reduced. It is true that from time to time we volunteer more than our proportionate share for certain programs. But we provide the additional support because we realize that these programs are in our national interest as well as in the interest of the United Nations.

In an excellent statement of the situation Samuel W. Lewis said:

> When we threaten sharply diminished American support for the United Nations, we need to weigh the consequences for the entire UN system—not merely for this or that piece. Our part of the annual bill for *all* aspects of the United Nations system totals about 450 million dollars. That is a lot of money—though I should point out by comparison that one modern aircraft carrier costs more than twice as much, about a billion dollars. And when we purchase but three B-1 bombers we will spend over 600 million. Unfortunately, many of the measures now being suggested for reducing our support would be extremely broad in their impact. For example, there are proposals now under consideration in various Congressional committees that would seriously cripple our participation, and might even end it. Recent bills would unilaterally reduce our financial support of the UN from the 25 percent we now pay to 15 percent or even to less than one percent of the total UN budget. And one pending bill would totally suspend United States participation in the General Assembly. Perhaps few people realize that under the present assessment rates the United States is treated specially—and favorably. If the "capacity to pay" formula used for calculating the dues of others, for example, the United Kingdom, France, the Soviet Union, were applied strictly to the United States, we would pay more than our present 25 percent.[6]

One final generalization current among critics of the United Nations is that it is in a mess. Yet, as Lord Gladwyn once said, "The United Nations mirrors the world. If you look into the mirror and see something ugly, don't blame the mirror." Clearly, the United Nations is not tranquil and peaceful, but neither is the world. Indeed were the United Nations to project an image of serenity and order, that image would be a fraud for it would not reflect the reality of the world. The easy problems rarely come its way. All it can do therefore is to work hard at solving the difficult and ugly crises that confront mankind. We must maintain the hope that through the process of applying the combined wisdom of the nations to the problems of the world we may yet be able to look in the mirror and find there the beauty of serenity and peace instead of ugliness.

The day may never come if in our bitterness over the evils around us, we forget to use our strength for good. One cannot expect that the international arena can be insulated from the age-old struggle between the forces of enlightenment and the forces of evil. Our choice therefore is to either leave the arena because we have lost our will to make the fight or to use it for those positive purposes to which we as a nation have always been committed.

Notes

1. Beardsley Ruml, from a speech delivered after the San Francisco Charter Sessions in 1945, unpublished.

2. "U.N. at 30," *New York Times* supplement on the United Nations, October 26, 1975.

3. Ambassador Patrick Moynihan, from his speech to the General Assembly on the passage by the General Assembly on the Zionism-racism resolution, 30th General Assembly.

4. Herbert Prochnow, former under secretary of state in the Eisenhower administration, from a speech delivered during his incumbency.

5. Justice Benjamin Cardoza, from an opinion in a tax case.

6. From a report made by a group of twenty-five experts on May 20, 1975, on the structure of the U.N. system.

Selected Bibliography

I. General

Barros, James, ed. *The United Nations: Past, Present, and Future.* New York: Free Press, 1972.

Boyd, Andrew. *United Nations. Piety, Myth, and Truth.* Baltimore, Md.: Penguin Books, 1962.

Claude, Inis L. Jr. *Power and International Relations.* New York: Random House, 1962.

———. *The Changing United Nations.* New York: Random House, 1967.

———. *Swords Into Plowshares: The Problems and Progress of International Organization.* 4th ed. New York: Random House, 1971.

Cox, Robert, ed. *The Politics of International Organization.* New York: Praeger, 1970.

Goodrich, Leland M. *The United Nations in a Changing World.* New York: Columbia University Press, 1974.

Goodrich, Leland M., and Kay, David A., eds. *International Organization: Politics and Process.* Madison: The University of Wisconsin Press, 1973.

Gordenker, Leon, ed. *The United Nations in International Politics.* Princeton, N.J.: Princeton University Press, 1971.

Jacob, Philip E., Atherton, A. L., and Wallenstein, Arthur M. *The Dynamics of International Organization.* Homewood, Ill.: The Dorsey Press, 1972.

Kay, David A., ed. *The United Nations Political System.* New York: Wiley, 1967.

Larus, Joel, ed. *From Collective Security to Preventive Diplomacy. Readings in International Organization and the Maintenance of Peace.* New York: Wiley, 1965.

Nicholas, H. G. *The United Nations as a Political System.* London: Oxford University Press, 1959.

Padelford, Norman J., and Goodrich, Leland M., eds. *The United Nations in the Balance.* New York: Praeger, 1965.

Plano, Jack, and Riggs, Robert E. *Forging World Order. The Politics of International*

Organization. New York: The MacMillan Co.; 1967.
Russell, Ruth B. *A History of the United Nations Charter.* Washington, D.C.: The Brookings Institution, 1958.
Stoessinger, John G. *The United Nations and the Superpowers: China, Russia and America.* 3rd ed. New York: Random House, 1973.
Waters, Maurice, ed. *The United Nations. International Organization and Admninistration.* New York: MacMillan, 1967.
Yeselson, Abraham, and Gaglione, Anthony. *A Dangerous Place: The United Nations as a Weapon in World Politics.* New York: Grossman Publishers, 1974.

II. Peacekeeping

Bloomfield, Lincoln P., et al. *International Military Forces: The Question of Peacekeeping in an Armed and Disarming World.* Boston: Little, Brown and Co., 1964.
Boyd, James M. *United Nations Peace Keeping Operations: A Military and Political Appraisal.* New York: Praeger, 1971.
Burns, Arthur Lee, and Heathcote, Nina. *Peace Keeping by UN Forces: From Suez to the Congo.* New York: Praeger, 1963.
Fabian, Larry L. "Toward a Peacekeeping Renaissance." *International Organization* 30, no. 1 (winter 1976): 153-161.
──────. *Soldiers Without Enemies: Preparing the United Nations for Peacekeeping.* Washington D.C.: The Brookings Institution, 1971.
Harbottle, Michael. *The Blue Berets.* Harrisburg, Pa.: Stackpole Books, 1972.
James, Alan. *The Politics of Peacekeeping.* New York: Praeger, 1969.
Miller, Linda B. *World Order and Local Disorder: The United Nations and Internal Conflict.* Princeton, N.J.: Princeton University Press, 1976.
Pelcovits, N. A. "UN Peacekeeping and the 1973 Arab-Israeli Conflict." *Orbis* 19, no. 1 (spring 1975): 146-165.
Rikhye, Indar J. *The Thin Blue Line: International Peacekeeping and its Future.* New Haven, Conn.: Yale University Press, 1974.
Rosner, Gabriella. *The United Nations Emergency Force.* New York: Columbia University Press, 1961.
Stegenga, James A. *The United Nations Force in Cyprus.* Columbus: Ohio State University Press, 1968.
Wainhouse, David W., et al. *International Peacekeeping at the Crossroads: National Support—Experience and Prospects.* Baltimore: The Johns Hopkins University Press, 1974.
────── and Associates. *International Peace Observation: A History and a Forecast.* Baltimore: The Johns Hopkins University Press, 1966.

III. Disarmament

Brennan, Donald G., ed. *Arms Control, Disarmament, and National Security.*

New York: Braziller, 1961.
Buchan, Alastair, ed. *A World of Nuclear Powers?* Englewood Cliffs, N.J.: Prentice-Hall, 1966.
Bull, Hedley. *The Control of the Arms Race.* 2nd ed. New York: Praeger, 1965.
Clemens, Walter C., Jr. *The Superpowers and Arms Control.* Lexington, Mass.: Lexington Books, 1973.
Dougherty, James E. *How to Think About Arms Control and Disarmament.* New York: Crane, Russak and Co., 1973.
Epstein, William. *Disarmament: Twenty Five Years of Effort.* Canadian Institute of International Affairs, 1971.
_____. *The Last Chance: Nuclear Proliferation and Arms Control.* New York: The Free Press, 1976.
Falk, Richard A., and Barnet, Richard J., eds. *Security in Disarmament.* Princeton, N.J.: Princeton University Press, 1965.
Falk, Richard A. and Mendlovitz, Saul H., eds. *Strategy for World Order.* Vol. IV. New York: World Law Fund, 1966.
Finkelstein, Lawrence S. "The United Nations and Organizations for the Control of Armaments." *International Organization* (winter 1962).
Fischer, Georges. *The Non-Proliferation of Nuclear Weapons.* New York: St. Martin's Press, 1971.
Guhin, Michael. *Nuclear Paradox: Security Risks of the Peaceful Atom.* Washington, D.C.: American Enterprise Institute for Public Policy Research, 1976.
Hopmann, P. Terence. "Bargaining in Arms Control Negotiations: The Seabeds Denuclearization Treaty." *International Organization* (summer 1974). pp. 312-343.
Kintner, William R., and Pfaltzgraff, Robert L., Jr., eds. *SALT: Implications for Arms Control in the 1970s.* Pittsburgh: University of Pittsburgh Press, 1973.
Lall, Arthur S. *Negotiating Disarmament. The Eighteen Nation Disarmament Conference: The First Two Years 1962-1964.* Ithaca, N.Y.: Cornell University Center for International Studies, 1964.
Marwah, Onkar, and Schultz, Ann, eds. *Nuclear Proliferation and the Near Nuclear Countries.* Cambridge, Mass.: Ballinger, 1975.
Melman, Seymour, ed. *Disarmament: Its Politics and Economics.* Boston: The American Academy of Arts and Sciences, 1962.
Newhouse, John. *Cold Dawn. The Story of SALT.* New York: Holt, Rinehart and Winston, 1973.
Pfaltzgraff, Robert L., ed. *Contrasting Approaches to Strategic Arms Control.* Lexington, Mass.: D.C. Heath, 1974.
Sanders, Benjamin. *Safeguards Against Nuclear Proliferation.* Cambridge: The MIT Press, 1975.
Singer, David J. *Deterrence, Arms Control and Disarmament.* Columbus, Ohio: Ohio State University Press, 1962.

Spanier, John W., and Nogee, Joseph L. *The Politics of Disarmament. A Study in Soviet-American Gamesmanship.* New York: Praeger, 1962.

Stockholm International Peace Research Institute. *World Armaments and Disarmament Yearbook 1976.* Cambridge, Mass.: The MIT Press, 1976.

———. *Arms Uncontrolled.* Cambridge, Mass.: Harvard University Press, 1975.

Sullivan, Jr., Michael J. "Conference at the Crossroads: Future Prospects of the Committee on Disarmament." *International Organization* (spring 1975), pp. 393-413.

United Nations. *The UN and Disarmament, 1945-1970.* New York: UN Publications, 1970.

Willrich, Mason, and Rhinelander, John B. *SALT: The Moscow Agreements and Beyond.* New York: The Free Press, 1974.

Young, Elisabeth. *A Farewell to Arms Control?* Baltimore: Penguin Books, 1972.

IV. The New International Economic Order

Albertson, Peter, and Barnett, Margery, eds. *Managing the Planet.* Englewood Cliffs, N.J.: Prentice-Hall, 1972.

Alpert, Paul. *Partnership or Confrontation? Poor Lands and Rich.* New York: The Free Press, 1973.

Angelopoulos, Angelos. *The Third World and the Rich Countries. Prospects for the Year 2000.* New York: Praeger, 1972.

Asher, Robert E. *Development Assistance in the Seventies.* Washington, D.C.: The Brookings Institution, 1970.

Bergsten, C. Fred. "The Threat From the Third World." *Foreign Policy* (summer 1973), pp. 102-124.

———, ed. *The Future of the International Economic Order: An Agenda for Research.* Lexington, Mass.: D.C. Heath, 1973.

Bhagwati, J. N., ed. *Economics and World Order: From the 1970s to the 1990s.* New York: MacMillan, 1972.

Bhattacharya, Anindya K. *Foreign Trade and International Development.* Lexington, Mass.: Lexington Books, 1976.

Chudson, Walter A. *The International Transfer of Commercial Technology to Developing Countries.* New York: UNITAR, 1971.

Cohen, Benjamin J. *The Quest of Imperialism: The Political Economy of Dominance and Dependence.* New York: Basic Books, 1973.

Cooper, Richard, ed. *A Reordered World.* Washington, D.C.: Potomac Associates, 1973.

Corbet, Hugh, and Jackson, Robert, eds. *In Search of a New World Economic Order.* New York: Halsted Press, 1974.

Dinwiddy, Bruce, ed. *Aid Performance and Development Policies of Western Countries: Studies in US, UK, EEC, and Dutch Programs.* New York: Praeger, 1973.

Erb, Guy F., and Kallab, Valeriana, eds. *Beyond Dependency: The Developing World Speaks Out.* New York: Praeger, 1975.

Gardner, Richard N. "The United Nations Conference on Trade and Development," *International Organization* (winter 1968), pp. 99-130.

Gardner, Richard N., and Millikan, Max, eds. *The Global Partnership. International Agencies and Economic Development.* New York: Praeger, 1968.

Gordenker, Leon. *International and National Decisions. A Field Study of Developmental Programs.* Princeton, N.J.: Princeton University Press, 1976.

Gosovic, Branislav. *UNCTAD. Conflict and Compromise. The Third World's Quest for an Equitable World Economic Order Through the United Nations.* Leiden: A. W. Sijthoff, 1972.

Gosovic, Branislav, and Ruggie, John G. "On the Creation of a New International Economic Order: Issue Linkage and the Seventh Special Session of the UN General Assembly." *International Organization* (spring 1976), pp. 309-345.

Hagras, Kamal M. *UN Conference on Trade and Development. A Case Study in UN Diplomacy.* New York: Praeger, 1965.

Hansen, Roger D. "The Political Economy of North-South Relations: How Much Change?" *International Organization* (autumn 1975), pp. 921-948.

Hansen, Roger D. et al. *The US and World Development. Agenda for Action 1976.* New York: Praeger, 1976.

Hirsch, Fred. "Is There a New International Economic Order?" *International Organization* (summer 1976), pp. 521-531.

Hutchinson, Joseph B. *The Challenge of the Third World.* Cambridge, Mass.: Cambridge University Press, 1975.

Jalée, Pierre. *The Pillage of the Third World.* New York: Monthly Review Press, 1968.

_____. *Imperialism in the Seventies.* New York: The Third Press, 1972.

Keohane, Robert O., and Nye, Joseph S. *Power and Interdependence: World Politics in Transition.* Boston: Little, Brown and Co., 1977.

Kimche, David. *The Afro-Asian Movement: Ideology and Foreign Policy of the Third World.* New York: Halsted Press, 1973.

Kotschnig, W. M. "The United Nations as an Instrument of Economic and Social Development." *International Organization* (winter 1968), pp. 16-43.

Legum, Colin, ed. *The First UN Development Decade and Its Lessons.* New York: Praeger, 1970.

Mates, Leo. *Non-Alignment: Theory and Current Policy.* Dobbs-Ferry, N.Y.: Oceana, 1972.

Meadows, Donella H. et al. *The Limits to Growth.* New York: Universe Books, 1972.

Meltzer, Ronald I. "The Politics of Policy Reversal: The US Response to Granting Trade Preferences to Developing Countries and Linkages

Between International Organizations and National Policy-Making." *International Organization* (autumn 1976), pp. 649-668.
Organization for Economic Cooperation and Development. *Flow of Resources to Developing Countries.* Paris: OECD, 1973.
Pearson, Lester B. *Partners in Development.* New York: Praeger, 1969.
Raichr, Satish, and Liske, Craig, eds. *The Politics of Aid, Trade and Investment.* New York: Halsted Press, 1976.
Richman, Barry M., and Copen, Melvyn. *International Management and Economic Development.* New York: McGraw-Hill, 1972.
Sauvant, Karl P., and Hasenpflug, Hajo, eds. *The New International Economic Order: Confrontation or Cooperation Between North and South?* Boulder, Colo.: Westview Press, 1977.
Sharma, D. N. *Afro-Asian Group in the UN.* Allahabad: Chaitanya Publishing House, 1969.
Smith, Tony. "Changing Configurations of Power in North-South Relations Since 1945." *International Organization* (winter 1977), pp. 1-27.
Sorensen, G. M. "UNCTAD III." *International Politics* (April-June 1972), pp. 147-159.
Spero, Joan E. *The Politics of International Economic Relations.* New York: St. Martin's Press, 1977.
Strange, Susan. *International Monetary Relations.* International Economic Relations of the Western World, 1959-1971, edited by Andrew Shonfield and Oliver Hermia, vol. 2. New York: Oxford University Press, 1976.
Symonds, Richard, ed. *International Targets for Develoment.* New York: Harper, 1970.
Trilateral Commission. *OPEC, The Trilateral World and the Developing Countries: New Arrangements for Cooperation 1976-1980.* The Triangle Papers, vol. 7 (1975).
United Nations Center for Economic and Social Information. *The Case for Development: Six Studies.* New York: Praeger, 1973.
United Nations Conference on Trade and Development. *Toward a New Trade Policy for Development.* New York: United Nations, 1964.
———. *Towards a Global Strategy of Development.* New York: United Nations, 1968.
———. *The Second United Nations Development Decade: Trends and Policies in the First Two Years.* New York: United Nations, 1974.
United Nations, Department of Economic and Social Affairs. *Implementation of the International Development Strategy.* New York: United Nations, 1973.
United Nations—Wassily Leontief et al. *The Future of the World Economy.* New York: Oxford University Press, 1977.
Wall, David. *The Charity of Nations: The Political Economy of Foreign Aid.* New York: Basic Books, 1973.
White, John. *The Politics of Foreign Aid.* New York: St. Martin's Press, 1974.

Wilcox, Clair. *A Charter for World Trade.* New York: Arno Press, 1972.
"World Politics and International Economics." *International Organization* (winter 1975) (Special Issue).
Worsley, Peter. *The Third World: A Vital New Force in International Affairs.* Chicago: The University of Chicago Press, 1973.
Yoder, A. "UNCTAD III - Insights into Development Policies," *ORBIS* (summer 1973), pp. 527-544.
Zartman, William I. *The Politics of Trade Negotiations Between Africa and the EEC.* Princeton, N.J.: Princeton University Press, 1971.

V. Monetary and Trade Policies

Bhattacharya, Anindya K. "The Influence of the International Secretariat: UNCTAD and Generalized Tariff Preferences." *International Organization* (winter 1976), pp. 75-90.
Brenner, Michael J. *The Politics of International Reform: The Exchange Crisis.* Cambridge, Mass.: Ballinger, 1976.
Calleo, David P., ed. *Money and the Coming World Order.* New York: New York University Press, 1976.
Calleo, David P. and Rowland, Benjamin M. *America and the World Political Economy: Atlantic Dreams and National Realities.* Bloomington: Indiana University Press, 1973.
Cox, Robert W., and Jacobson, Harold K., et al. *The Anatomy of Influence: Decision-Making in International Organization.* New Haven, Conn.: Yale University Press, 1973.
Dam, Kenneth W. *The GATT: Law and International Economic Organization.* Chicago: The University of Chicago Press, 1970.
Evans, Douglas. *The Politics of Trade: The Evolution of the Superbloc.* New York: Wiley, 1974.
Gruhn, I. V. "The Lomé Convention: Inching Towards Interdependence." *International Organization* (spring 1976), pp. 240-262.
Hodgman, Donald R. *National Monetary Policies and International Monetary Cooperation.* Boston: Little, Brown and Co., 1974.
Horsefield, J. K., ed. *The International Monetary Fund. 1945-1965: Twenty Years of International Monetary Cooperation.* Vol. I. Washington, D.C.: IMF, 1969.
Hudec, Robert E. *The GATT Legal System and World Trade Diplomacy.* New York: Praeger, 1975.
Johnson, H. G. *Trade Strategy for Rich and Poor Nations.* Toronto: University of Toronto Press, 1971.
Jordan, Robert, ed. *Multinational Cooperation.* New York: Oxford University Press, 1972.
Karasz, A. "The World Bank and the Third World." *Review of Politics* (October 1972), pp. 476-489.

Krasner, S. D. "The International Monetary Fund and the Third World." *International Organization* (summer 1968), pp. 670-688.

Mason, Edward S., and Ascher, Robert E. *The World Bank Since Bretton Woods.* Washington, D.C.: The Brookings Institution, 1973.

Meier, Gerald M. *Problems of a World Monetary Order.* New York: Oxford University Press, 1974.

Payer, Cheryl. *The Debt Trap: The International Monetary Fund and the Third World.* New York: Monthly Review Press, 1975.

Rowland, Benjamin M., ed. *Balance of Power of Hegemony: The Interwar Monetary System.* New York: New York University Press, 1976.

Schneider, William. *Food, Foreign Policy, and Raw Materials Cartels.* New York: Crane, Russak and Co., 1976.

Sklar, Richard L. *Corporate Power in an African State. The Political Impact of Multinational Mining Companies in Zambia.* Berkeley: University of California Press, 1975.

Smith, David N., and Wells, Louis T., Jr. *Negotiating Third World Mineral Agreements: Promises and Prologue.* Cambridge, Mass.: Ballinger, 1976.

Verbit, Gilbert P. *International Monetary Reform and the Developing Countries: The Rule of Law Problem.* New York: Columbia University Press, 1975.

Walters, Robert S. "International Organizations and Political Communication: The Use of UNCTAD by the Less Developed Countries." *International Organization* (autumn 1971), pp. 818-835.

VI. The Multinational Corporation

Barnet, Richard, and Muller, Ronald E. *Global Reach: The Power of the Multinational Corporation.* New York: Simon and Schuster, 1975.

Boarman, Patrick M., and Schollhammer, Hans, eds. *Multinational Corporations Governments: Business-Government Relations in an International Context.* New York: Praeger, 1975.

Cohen, Benjamin, *Multinational Firms and Asian Exports.* New Haven, Conn.: Yale University Press, 1975.

Fatemi, N. S. *Multinational Corporations.* 2nd ed. New York: Barnes, 1976.

Gilpin, Robert. *US Power and the Multinational Corporation: The Political Economy of Foreign Direct Investment.* New York: Basic Books, 1975.

Keohane, Robert O., and Nye, Joseph S., Jr. *Transnational Relations and World Politics.* Cambridge, Mass.: Harvard University Press, 1972.

Kindleberger, Charles P., ed. *The International Corporation.* Cambridge, Mass.: The MIT Press, 1971.

Moran, Theodore H. *Multinational Corporations and the Politics of Dependence: Copper in Chile.* Princeton, N.J.: Harvard University Center for International Affairs, 1975.

Organization for Economic Cooperation and Development. *International Invest-*

ment and Multinational Enterprise. Paris: OECD, 1976.

Sauvant, Karl P., and Lavipour, Farid G. *Controlling Multinational Enterprises: Problems, Strategies, Counter-Strategies.* Boulder, Colo.: Westview Press, 1976.

Stephenson, Hugh. *The Coming Clash: The Impact of Multinational Corporations on National States.* New York: Saturday Review Press, 1972.

Tharp, Paul A., Jr. "Transnational Enterprises and International Regulation: A Survey of Various Approaches in International Organizations." *International Organization* (winter 1976), pp. 47-73.

Turner, Louis. *Multinational Companies and the Third World.* New York: Hill and Wang, 1973.

United Nations. *Report of the Group of Eminent Persons to Study the Impact of Multinational Corporations on Development and on International Relations.* New York: United Nations, 1974.

United Nations Conference on Trade and Development. *Restrictive Business Practices: The Operations of Multinational Enterprises in Developing Countries. Their Role in Trade Development. A Study by Raymond Vernon.* New York: United Nations, 1972.

United Nations, Department of Social and Economic Affairs. *Multinational Corporations in World Development.* New York: Praeger, 1974.

United States Congress, Senate, Committee on Foreign Relations, Subcommittee on Multinational Corporations. *Multinational Petroleum Companies and Foreign Policy,* Hearings. 93rd Cong., 2nd sess. Washington, D.C.: U.S. Government Printing Office, 1975.

Vernon, Raymond. *The Economic and Political Consequences of Multinational Enterprise: An Anthology.* Cambridge, Mass.: Harvard University Press, 1972.

_____. *Sovereignty at Bay: The Multinational Spread of US Enterprises.* New York: Basic Books, 1971.

Wallace, Don, ed. *International Control of Investment: The Düsseldorf Conference on Multinational Corporations.* New York: Praeger, 1974.

Weinstein, Franklin B. "Multinational Corporations and the Third World: The Case of Japan and Southeast Asia." *International Organization* (summer 1976), pp. 373-404.

VII. Global Resource Issues

Bishop, A. S., and Munro, R. D. "The United Nations Regional Economic Commissions and Environmental Problems." *International Organization* (spring 1972), pp. 348-371.

Burt, John C. *Decision-Networks and the World Population Explosion: The UN and Institutional Innovation for Social Crises.* Beverly Hills, Calif.: Sage Publications, 1972.

Cheever, Daniel S. "The Role of International Organization in Ocean Development," *International Organization* (1968), pp. 629-648.

Christy, Francis T., Jr. , Clingan, Thomas A., Jr., Gable, John King, Jr., and Miles, Edward, eds. *Law of the Sea: Caracas and Beyond.* Cambridge, Mass.: Ballinger, 1975.

Eckholm, Erik P. *Losing Ground: Environmental Stress and World Food Prospects.* New York: Norton, 1976.

Engfeldt, L. G. "The United Nations and the Human Environment—Some Experiences," *International Organization* (summer 1973), pp. 393-412.

Gamble, J. K., Jr. *Emerging Regime of the Oceans.* Cambridge, Mass.: Ballinger, 1974.

Gardner, R. N. "The Role of the UN in Environmental Problems," *International Organization* (spring 1972), pp. 237-254.

Hollick, Ann L., and Osgood, Robert E. *New Era of Ocean Politics.* Baltimore, Md.: The Johns Hopkins Press, 1975.

Johnson, Brian. *The United Nations System and the Human Environment.* Brighton: Institute for the Study of International Organization, 1971.

Johnson, D. Gale. *World Food Problems and Prospects.* Washington, D.C.: American Enterprise Institute for Public Policy Research, 1975.

Johnston, Douglas M., ed. *Marine Policy and the Coastal Community: The Impact of the Law of the Sea.* New York: St. Martin's Press, 1976.

Kay, David A., and Skolnikoff, Eugene B. *World Eco-Crisis: International Organizations in Response.* Madison: The University of Wisconsin Press, 1972.

Kenneth, W. "The Stockholm Conference on the Human Environment," *International Affairs* (January 1972), pp. 33-45.

Kneese, Allen, Rolfe, Sidney E., and Harned, Joseph W., eds. *Managing the Environment: International Economic Cooperation for Pollution Control.* New York: Praeger, 1972.

Luard, Evan. *The Control of the Sea-Bed: A New International Issue.* Taplinger, 1974.

Rao, P. Sreenivasa. *The Public Order of Ocean Resources: A Critique of the Contemporary Law of the Sea.* Cambridge, Mass.: The MIT Press, 1975.

"Restructuring Ocean Regimes: Implications of the Third United Nations Conference on the Law of the Sea." *International Organization* (spring 1977).

Rowland, Wade. *The Plot to Save the World: The Life and Times of the Stockholm Conference on the Human Environment.* Toronto: Clarke Irwin, 1973.

Sewell, James P. *Functionalism and World Politics.* Princeton, N.J.: Princeton University Press, 1966.

Shinn, Robert A. *The International Politics of Marine Pollution Control.* New York: Praeger, 1974.

Strong, M. F. "One Year After Stockholm. An Ecological Approach to Management." *Foreign Affairs* (July 1973), pp. 690-707.

Symonds, Richard, and Carder, Michael. *The United Nations and the Population Quest 1945-1970.* New York: McGraw Hill, 1973.

Teclaff, L. A., and Utton, Albert E., eds. *International Environment*

Law. New York: Praeger, 1974.

The United Nations and Population: Major Resolutions and Instruments. Dobbs-Ferry, N.Y.: Oceana, 1974.

Weiss, Thomas G., and Jordan, Robert S. *The World Food Conference and Global Problem Solving.* New York: Praeger, 1976.

Winton, H. N. *Man and the Environment. A Bibliography of Selected Publications of the United Nations System, 1946-1971.* New York: Unipub, 1972.

World Bank. *Population Policies and Economic Development: A World Bank Staff Report.* Baltimore, Md.: The Johns Hopkins University Press, 1974.

Yates, George T., III, and Young, John H. *Limits to National Jurisdiction over the Sea.* Charlottesville: University Press of Virginia, 1975.

VIII. The U.S. Role in a Changing United Nations

Alker, Hayward R., and Russett, Bruce M. *World Politics in the General Assembly.* New Haven, Conn.: Yale University Press, 1968.

Bailey, Sidney D. *Voting in the Security Council.* Bloomington: Indiana University Press, 1969.

Barber, H. W. "The United States vs. The United Nations." *International Organization* (spring 1973), pp. 139-173.

Bloomfield, Lincoln P. *The United Nations and US Foreign Policy.* Boston: Little, Brown and Co., 1967.

Boyd, Andrew. *Fifteen Men on a Powder Keg.* New York: Stein and Day, 1971.

Cleveland, Harlan. *The Third Try at World Order. US Policy for an Interdependent World.* New York: Aspen Institute for Humanistic Studies, 1976.

Feld, Werner J. *Nongovernmental Forces and World Politics: A Study of Business, Labor, and Political Groups.* New York: Praeger, 1972.

Finkelstein, L. S. *The United States and International Organization.* Cambridge, Mass.: The MIT Press, 1969.

Gardner, Richard N. *The United States and the United Nations: Can We Do Better?* New York: Columbia University Press, 1972.

_____. *In Pursuit of World Order: US Foreign Policy and International Organizations.* New York: Praeger, 1966.

Hass, Ernst B. *Tangle of Hopes: American Commitments and World Order.* Englewood Cliffs, N.J.: Prentice-Hall, 1969.

_____. *The Web of Interdependence: The United States and International Organization.* Englewood Cliffs, N.J.: Prentice-Hall, 1970.

Hiscocks, Richard. *The Security Council: A Study in Adolescence.* New York: The Free Press, 1974.

Lall, Arthur. *The Security Council in a Universal United Nations.* New York: Carnegie Endowment, 1972.

Moskowitz, Moses. *International Concern with Human Rights.* Dobbs-Ferry, N.Y.: Oceana, 1975.

Riggs, Robert E. *US/UN: Foreign Policy and International organization.* New York: Appleton-Century Crofts, 1971

Rowe, Edward T. *Strengthening the United Nations: A Study of the Evolution of a Member State Commitment.* Berkeley, Calif.: Sage Publications, 1974.

Rubinstein, Alvin Z., and Ginsburgs, George, eds. *Soviet and American Policies in the United Nations. A Twenty Five Year Perspective.* New York: New York University Press, 1971.

Russel, Ruth B. *American Security Policy and the United Nations.* Washington, D.C.: The Brookings Institution, 1968.

———, with the assistance of Peter Clausen. *The General Assembly: Patterns, Problems and Prospects.* New York: Carnegie Endowment, 1970.

Sewell, James P. *UNESCO and World Politics. Engaging in International Relations.* Princeton, N.J.: Princeton University Press, 1975.

Sohn, Louis B., and Buergenthal, Thomas. *International Protection of Human Rights.* Indianapolis, Ind.: The Bobbs-Merrill Co., 1973.

Index

ABM Treaty, 48
Angola, 79, 80, 110, 406, 438, 440, 454
Apartheid, 79, 83, 88, 89, 96, 103, 104, 114, 322, 440
Arab-Israeli Conflict. *See* Middle East
Arafat, Yasir, 438
Argentina, 16, 21
Arms
  control of, 28-39, 40-55
  trade of, 10, 52, 55
Article 19 Crisis, 64, 72

Bantustan policy, 108, 111
Basic human needs, 251
Bophuhatswana, 98
Brazil, 16, 18, 36, 64, 169, 216, 217, 229, 364, 374, 421
Bretton Woods, 154, 212-215, 225
Byrd Amendment, 87, 105, 112, 461

Canada, 18, 21, 22, 61, 64, 169, 170, 171, 174, 177-178, 186, 262, 273, 283, 334, 374
Carter administration, 10, 28, 30, 32, 34, 37, 38, 98, 111, 444, 463
Charter of Economic Rights and Duties of Nations, 126, 131, 245, 313, 346, 442
Chile, 175-176
China, People's Republic of, 22, 26, 32, 53, 74, 75, 407, 413-414, 420, 422, 441; 459

Club of Rome, 195, 241, 247, 250, 291
Colombo, 131
Commission on Transnational Corporations. *See* UN Commission on Transnational Corporations
Committee on Peacekeeping. *See* UN Committee on Peacekeeping
Common heritage of mankind, 257, 258, 269, 273
Common Market. *See* European Economic Community
Conciliation, 321, 460
Conference of the Committee on Disarmament (CCD), 31, 34, 42
Conference on International Economic Cooperation (CIEC), 131, 147, 151, 152, 156, 161, 280, 330, 334, 415
Congo, 63, 74
Consensus, 315, 316, 339, 348, 352-254
Cuba, 63, 80, 414, 436, 438-440
Cyprus, 63, 64, 423. *See also* UN Force in Cyprus

Declaration on the Economic Rights and Duties of States, 442
Détente, 10, 30, 31, 32, 36, 309, 310, 441-442
Deutschemark, 221, 235, 236
Disarmament, 30-32, 40-55, 404
  UN Special Session on, 30, 38

East Germany (German Democratic

Republic), 22, 259, 283
ECOSOC. *See* UN Economic and Social Council
Egypt, 53, 410
Energy, 275-290
Energy and Conservation Act, 288-289
European Economic Community (EEC), 130, 147, 156-157, 171, 173, 191, 206, 225, 259, 301, 392
Exclusive economic zone (EEZ), 269-273
Export-Import Bank, 414

Federal Energy Administration (FEA), 278
Food and Agriculture Organization (FAO), 148
Ford, Gerald R., 228, 267, 268
France, 15, 16, 21, 22, 25, 26, 35, 51, 53, 66, 75, 79, 151, 170, 177, 219, 221, 341, 352, 383, 406, 420, 459

General Agreement on Tariffs and Trade (GATT), 131, 147, 149, 154, 190, 213, 214, 419, 424, 426, 432, 458
General Assembly. *See* UN General Assembly
Generalized System of Preferences (GSP), 126, 132, 161
Geneva Conference of Committee on Disarmament. *See* Conference of the Committee on Disarmament
Geneva Conventions 1958, 258, 261
Great Britain. *See* United Kingdom
Group of experts, 318, 319, 332, 460
Group of 77, 36, 131, 142, 162-164, 187, 225-263, 333

Hammarskjöld, Dag, 58, 382
Horn of Africa, 98, 99
Human rights, 82, 95, 96, 102, 111, 311, 340, 438, 445, 461, 462
Human Rights Commission, 317, 438, 461

Indexation, 126, 134
India, 16, 18, 21, 22, 25, 35, 52, 64, 405, 421, 435
Intergovernmental Maritime Consultative Organization (IMCO), 263
International Agricultural Development Fund, 329, 462
International Atomic Energy Agency (IAEA), 18-24, 28, 35, 36, 153, 154, 282, 283, 421
International Bank for Reconstruction and Development. *See* World Bank
International Chamber of Commerce (ICC), 162, 164, 165, 187
International Civil Service Commission, 328
International Court of Justice (ICJ), 348-350
International Development Association (IDA), 427, 455, 462
International Development Strategy, 246, 247, 250, 251
International Energy Agency (IEA), 147, 151, 279, 280, 282
International Finance Corporation, 462
International Labour Organization (ILO), 173, 250
International Monetary Fund (IMF), 123, 127, 128, 130-132, 134, 147, 149, 150, 155, 214, 224, 226-227, 229, 230, 233, 247, 334, 419, 424, 426, 432, 458, 470
International Resources Bank, 162
International Telephone and Telegraph Company, 175-176
International Trade Organization, 149, 425
Iran, 53, 76, 276
Israel, 16, 18, 52, 373, 436-440, 452
Italy, 233, 383

Jamaica Agreements (of IMF), 131, 211, 215, 224-237, 334
Japan, 22, 148, 150, 174, 212, 222, 234,

Index

235, 256, 259, 273, 279, 283, 301, 365, 407, 429, 430

Kissinger, Henry, 11, 59, 60, 74, 80, 81, 101, 110, 111, 162, 355, 408, 409, 411, 412, 415, 422, 461

Law of the sea, 130, 242, 255-263, 265-274, 319, 320, 431, 441
League of Nations, 58, 315-317
Lebanon, 57, 59, 63, 289, 437
Lima Declaration, 130
Lomé Convention, 130, 132, 133, 252, 253
London Suppliers Club, 21, 22, 24, 34, 37

Majoritarianism, 342-352, 355, 395, 413, 438, 443
Middle East, 11, 52, 57, 63, 65, 74, 152, 277, 283, 378, 382, 390, 410, 421, 436, 437, 440, 444, 445, 453, 454
Moynihan, Daniel P., 339, 356, 409, 411, 438, 444, 466
Multinational Corporations. *See* Transnational corporations
Mutual and Balanced Force Reduction, 31, 33, 34

Nairobi, 161-162, 165, 412
Namibia, 12, 80, 81, 85, 88, 89, 95, 97, 104, 440, 424
New International Economic Order (NIEO), 123-142, 246, 247, 250, 254, 263, 313, 333, 407
Nixon, Richard M., 231
Nongovernmental organizations (NGOs), 164
Non-Proliferation Treaty (NPT), 16-21, 23, 25-27, 34-36, 38, 420, 421
North Atlantic Treaty Organization (NATO), 33, 34, 53, 54, 57, 75, 151, 276, 316, 419, 421, 424
North-South relations, 35-37, 126, 158, 162, 220, 255-263, 272, 327, 333, 407, 441
Nuclear proliferation, 10, 15-27, 464, 465

Official Development Assistance (ODA), 127, 442
Organization for Economic Cooperation and Development (OECD), 4, 141, 147, 150, 154, 162, 173, 206, 215, 216, 219, 279, 355, 414, 416, 419, 424, 426, 431, 432
Organization for European Economic Cooperation, 416
Organization of African Unity (OAU), 98, 441
Organization of American States (OAS), 391, 417
Organization of Petroleum Exporting Countries (OPEC), 127, 134, 147, 149, 150-152, 157, 212, 251, 252, 277-284, 292-295, 297, 298, 408, 420, 429, 431, 469

Pakistan, 16-18, 52
Palestine Liberation Organization (PLO), 388-394, 436, 438, 450, 469
Paley Commission, 292-298
Paris Conference. *See* Conference on International Economic Cooperation
Peacekeeping. *See* United Nations, peacekeeping
Pollution control, 262, 263
Portugal, 79, 80, 104

Rambouillet, 151, 224, 228, 231, 334
Rapporteurs, 316, 317
Raw materials, 242, 243, 249, 250, 291-305
Regional development banks, 147
Rhodesia (Zimbabwe), 80, 81, 85-88, 95-97, 104, 112, 382, 440

Rome Conference. *See* World Food Conference (Rome)

Scali, John, 313, 444
Science and technology, 135
Security Council. *See* UN Security Council
Self-reliance, 139-142, 302
Smith, Ian, 81, 85-87, 104, 440
South Africa, 16, 18, 22, 25, 53, 79, 82-91, 94, 97, 98, 112, 169, 170, 341, 365, 373, 415, 437, 438, 440, 442
Southern Africa, 12, 79-92, 100-115, 408, 410, 415, 445, 461
Southwest African People's Organization (SWAPO), 88, 89, 97
Soviet Union. *See* Union of Soviet Socialist Republics
Special Drawing Rights (SDRs), 128, 131, 224, 225, 229, 428
Strategic Arms Limitation Talks (SALT), 17, 27, 28, 31, 33, 41, 43, 48, 49, 420
SUNFED, 427, 429

Technology transfer, 55, 128, 132, 135, 162, 163, 165
Third window, 131, 430
Third World. *See* Group of 77; North-South relations
Trade, 454, 455
Transkei, 97, 436
Transnational corporations (enterprises), 129, 135, 136, 138, 140, 167-173, 192, 195-202, 203-209, 430, 431
Treaty of Tlatelolco, 26
Truman Proclamation, 258, 268
Turnhalle Conference, 88, 89, 111

Uganda, 95, 414, 438
Underground Nuclear Weapons Treaty, 18
Unilateral Declaration of Independence (Rhodesia), 87, 104

Union of Soviet Socialist Republics (U.S.S.R.), 15, 22, 23, 26, 27, 29, 352, 406, 407, 414, 421, 435, 436, 454, 467
and arms control, 28-39, 40-55
and law of the sea, 256, 259, 270, 273
and peacekeeping, 11, 63-70, 72
United Kingdom, 22, 23, 51, 53, 79, 151, 169, 170, 177, 187, 196, 216, 221, 228, 233, 234, 236, 341, 383, 430
United Nations
Charter, 29, 62, 435
decision making, 314, 315, 330, 331
financing, 368, 369
membership, 62
peacekeeping, 11, 12, 57-69, 71-77, 392
UN Capital Development Fund, 429
UN Commission on Transnational Corporations, 204, 329, 430, 431
UN Committee on Peacekeeping, 65, 71, 422, 433
UN Conference on Trade and Development (UNCTAD), 131, 140, 149, 161-166, 206, 253, 319, 321, 329, 404, 419, 425-427, 430
UN Congo operation (ONUC), 11, 61, 64, 349
UN Development Programme (UNDP), 76, 430
UN Disengagement Observer Force (UNDOF), 61, 73, 74, 77, 388
UN Economic and Social Council (ECOSOC), 204-209, 313-315, 318, 415, 419, 428, 460, 462
UN Educational, Scientific, and Cultural Organization (UNESCO), 413, 458
UN Emergency Force (UNEF I and II), 61, 64, 71-74, 77, 349, 369, 423
UN Environment Programme (UNEP), 147, 153, 249
UN Force in Cyprus (UNFICYP), 65, 74, 75
UN General Assembly, 310, 311, 322, 339, 344, 348, 404, 423

Index 489

Sixth Special Session, 125, 126, 129, 130, 253, 442, 443
Seventh Special Session, 36, 161, 162, 253, 315, 328-330, 412, 428, 443, 452
UN Group of Eminent Persons, 155, 173, 187, 201, 205, 318
UN Industrial Development Organization (UNIDO), 130, 131
UN Institute for Training and Research, 288, 331, 353
UN Security Council, 60, 66-69, 72, 73, 310, 315-317, 341, 342, 351, 363-385, 388-397, 442, 438
UN Truce Supervisory Organization (UNTSO), 72
United States
  and Africa, 79-99, 100-115
  and arms control, 28-39, 40-55
  Congress, 33, 42-47, 80, 179, 259, 412
  and international institutions, 419-432
  and law of the sea, 255-259, 265-274
  and Middle East, 439
  and peacekeeping, 64-70
  and Third World, 35-37
  and United Nations, 403-418, 435-446, 449-464, 472

Vance, Cyrus R., 12
Veto, 395
Vietnam, 57, 63
Vladivostok Agreement, 27, 43
Vorster, John, 86-88

Waldheim, Kurt, 327
West Germany (Federal Republic), 15, 16, 18, 21, 22, 25, 35, 128, 151, 157 216, 283, 383, 407, 414
West Irian, 59
World Bank (IBRD), 127, 131, 132, 250, 428-431, 446, 458, 470
World Food Conference (Rome), 130, 248, 316
World Food Council, 147, 148

Young, Andrew, 98, 444
Yugoslavia, 407, 414

Zaire, 75, 98
Zimbabwe. *See Rhodesia*
"Zionism is racism" resolution, 100, 411, 413, 415, 438, 442, 450, 454, 458, 466, 477